W9-CBJ-322

The Craft
of
Public Administration

Ninth Edition

The Craft
of
Public Administration

George Berkley

University of Massachusetts

John Rouse

Ball State University

Boston   Burr Ridge, IL   Dubuque, IA   Madison, WI   New York   San Francisco   St. Louis
Bangkok   Bogotá   Caracas   Kuala Lumpur   Lisbon   London   Madrid   Mexico City
Milan   Montreal   New Delhi   Santiago   Seoul   Singapore   Sydney   Taipei   Toronto

Higher Education

THE CRAFT OF PUBLIC ADMINISTRATION, NINTH EDITION

Published by McGraw-Hill, a business unit of The McGraw-Hill Companies, Inc.,
1221 Avenue of the Americas, New York, NY 10020.
Copyright © 2004, 2000, 1997 by The McGraw-Hill Companies, Inc. All rights reserved. No part of this publication may be reproduced or distributed in any form or by any means, or stored in a database or retrieval system, without the prior written consent of The McGraw-Hill Companies, Inc., including, but not limited to, in any network or other electronic storage or transmission, or broadcast for distance learning.

Some ancillaries, including electronic and print components, may not be available to customers outside the United States.

This book is printed on acid-free paper.

4 5 6 7 8 9 0 DOC/DOC 0 9 8 7 6 5

ISBN 0-07-281740-2

Vice president and editor-in-chief: *Thalia Dorwick*
Publisher: *Lyn Uhl*
Sponsoring editor: *Monica Eckman*
Developmental editor: *Kate Scheinman*
Marketing manager: *Katherine Bates*
Project manager: *Richard H. Hecker*
Production supervisor: *Enboge Chong*
Senior media technology producer: *Sean Crowley*
Cover/interior designer: *George Kokkonas*
Cover image: *Image Stock*
Senior supplement producer: *David A. Welsh*
Compositor: *Shepherd-Imagineering Media Services Inc.*
Typeface: *10/12 Times Roman*
Printer: *R. R. Donnelley/Crawfordsville, IN*

Library of Congress Cataloging-in-Publication Data

Berkley, George E.
    The craft of public administration / George Berkley, John Rouse.—9th ed.
        p. cm.
    Includes bibliographical references and index.
    ISBN 0-07-281740-2 (alk. paper)
        1. Public administration. I. Rouse, John E. (John Edward), 1942- II. Title.

JF1351 .B47 2004
351—dc21

                                        2003043214

www.mhhe.com

Contents

Preface

Clash of Civilizations

In the post-September 11, 2001 world, it is ever more crucial to emphasize that no organization, including the United States of America, can be isolated from its cultural environment.[1] The 87,525 units of United States federal, state, and local governments function within a context. The context of the emerging *The Craft of Public Administration,* ninth edition, is the clash of civilizations.[2]

According to Samuel P. Huntington, Eaton Professor of the Science of Government and Director of the John M. Olin Institute for Strategic Studies at Harvard University, "A civilization is a cultural entity."[3] Huntington emphasizes that "differences among civilizations are not only real; they are basic. Civilizations are differentiated from each other by history, language, culture, tradition and, most important, religion."[4] Relations between God and man, the individual and group, citizen and state, parents and children, husband and wife vary according to civilization. The relative importance of rights and responsibilities, liberty and authority, or equality and hierarchy may differ significantly.

The clash of civilizations occurs because the world is becoming a smaller place. The fundamental conflicts are not primarily ideological or economic; the great divisions are cultural. Nation-states remain the world's most powerful actors. But the principal global conflicts occur between nations and groups of different civilizations.

Economic modernization and social change throughout the world separate people from longstanding local identities. The nation-state, as a source of identity, is weakened. Markets, crime, and terror penetrate national sovereignties. The civilization clash takes place at the micro and macro levels.

The micro-level struggle is over control of territory and each other. The macro-level struggle among competing civilizations is more comprehensive. Civilizations compete for relative military and economic power, fight for dominance

---

1. John M. Pfiffner and Frank P. Sherwood, *Administrative Organization* (Englewood Cliffs, N.J.: Prentice-Hall, 1960), p. 252.
2. Samuel P. Huntington, "The Clash of Civilizations," *Foreign Affairs,* Vol. 72, No. 3 (Summer 1993): 22–50. See "Clash of Civilizations," http://www.cc.colorado.edu/dept/PS/Findley/PS425/reading/Huntington1.html.
3. *Ibid.*
4. *Ibid.*

over international institutions and third parties, and promote particular political and religious values.[5]

"The world is afflicted with a daily, undiscriminating disease that must be halted by painful and at times dangerous treatment. The terrorists do not wage a political campaign by other means. They fight the very times in which they—and we—live," writes two-time Pulitzer Prize winner and *Washington Post* columnist Jim Hoagland. "Only a fool would now way that September 11, 2001, changed nothing—however much we want that to be true."[6]

In this global perspective, the responsiveness and competence of United States federal, state, and local government bureaucracies and public servants are vital aspects of understanding and fighting the causes of terror. "Technology continues to pull nations toward interdependence," concludes Hoagland.[7] The United Nations (UN) is a compromised, fragmented version of a disparate world political economy. The UN—and each of its units—depends on multilateral agreements for political consensus and action but needs unilateral leadership by many nations and leaders.

The internet and communications technology allow Americans to learn about the world—its prospects and its dangers. This opportunity requires U.S. governments, citizens, and leaders to utilize the skills, knowledge, and expertise associated with United States citizenship to meet increasing demands in more innovative ways.

The four pedagogical segments of this textbook—federalism, public personnel administration, budgets, and government regulations—succinctly organize the study of partisan, policy, and system politics—and government bureaucracies. Conflicting, diverse values challenge *The Craft of Public Administration* in ways not yet envisioned. Despite this clash of civilizations, all cultures must determine how public bureaucracy is to be responsive and act as an effective catalyst for serving people.

Four Pedagogical Segments

The Craft of Public Administration, ninth edition, is not just a textbook; it is a pedagogical gathering of pertinent yet limited literature, assembled to inform and interest college students in the dynamics of the public, or government, sector in the United States. The literature is limited because we choose not to write a book that is "everything one wants to know about public administration but is afraid to ask." Local, state, regional, and federal governments are too overwhelming and far-reaching to attempt a dictionary approach to the field. To comprehend projected federal government spending (state and local government spending not included), the literature of public administration is divided into four pedagogical segments:

- *federalism* (craft of public administration; relationships to economic development, political and bureaucratic culture; the structure of politics; partisan, policy, and systems politics; equality; efficiency; synergy; formal

---

5. *Ibid.*
6. Jim Hoagland, "War's Global Casualties," *The Washington Post,* October 17, 2002, p. A21.
7. *Ibid.*

organization; human relations). Chapters 1 through 4 focus upon the structure of American politics, or issues of U.S. federalism. Chapter 1 concerns "The Administrative Craft"; Chapter 2 deals with "The Ecology of the Administrative Craft"; Chapter 3 investigates "The Anatomy of Public Organizations"; Chapter 4 studies "The Physiology of Organizations."

- *public personnel administration* (people, patronage, merit, equal opportunity, affirmative action, job classifications, labor relations, leadership, charisma, communication, technology). Chapters 5 through 8 address matters of public personnel administration. Chapter 5 explores "People and Personnel"; Chapter 6 reviews "Public Sector Labor-Management Relations"; Chapter 7 develops the role of "Leadership"; Chapter 8 relates the importance of "Communication" in government bureaucracies.
- *budgets* (taxing, appropriations, spending, productivity, efficiency, effectiveness, motivation, privatization of government functions, planning, program evaluation). Chapters 9 and 10 examine priorities of taxing, budgeting, spending, productivity, and program evaluation. Chapter 9 addresses "Taxing, Budgeting, and Spending" and points out how partisan, policy, and systems politics impact the likelihood of higher taxes but fewer government programs and services. Chapter 10 probes "The Productivity Challenge" and outlines the pressures on government employees to do more with fewer resources.
- *regulations* (administrative law, administrative controls, administrative law judges, ethics, discretion, rules, procedures, administrative responsibility, administrative state, clientele relations). Chapters 11 and 12 explain administrative law, clientele relations, and government regulations. Chapter 11 outlines issues of "Administrative Law and Control" and describes the impact of administrative growth on democratic ideals, outlines traditional and contemporary cornerstones of American administrative law, notes the expanding role of administrative law judges, and probes how much law and control is enough. Chapter 12 develops the impacts of "Government Regulations and Regulatory Behaviors" and illustrates how economic, social, and subsidiary regulations are affected by administrative rules and rule making.

The narrative and case studies allow students to learn from analyzing the literature in conjunction with specific illustrations. Case studies force us to think about how the general (literature) affects the particular (case study) and how specific illustrations amend our perceptions of public administration literature. Examination of case study facts brings out the dynamic nature of the literature.

Public administration constitutes the "chemistry" of the United States. The two key principles that have come to embody the American ideal, equality and efficiency, are likewise the crucial determinants of how well the public, or government, sector functions in the United States. Democratic capitalism does not flourish if public infrastructures, such as schools, highways, institutions of public safety, and similar taxpayer-funded government operations are devalued and rendered ineffective.

Public sector functions, programs, and activities represent the "bottom line" expectations that society guarantees citizens. The domestic and military spending

Projected Budget Totals

	2002	2003	2004	2005	2006	2007
In billions of dollars:						
Outlays	2,052	2,128	2,189	2,277	2,369	2,468
Receipts	1,946	2,048	2,175	2,338	2,455	2,572
Deficit/surplus	−106	−80	−14	61	86	104
Debt held by the public	3,477	3,570	3,600	3,548	3,470	3,379
As a percent of GDP:						
Outlays		19.8	19.5	19.0	18.7	18.5	18.3
Receipts		18.8	18.8	18.9	19.2	19.2	19.1
Deficit/surplus		−1.0	−0.7	−0.1	0.5	0.7	0.8
Debt held by the public		33.6	32.7	31.2	29.2	27.1	25.1

Source: Office of Management and Budget, The Executive Office of the President, *Budget of the United States Government, Fiscal Year 2003,* Summary Tables, October 19, 2002, http://www.whitehouse.gov/omb/budget/fy2003/bud34.html.

priorities of the 1980s have forced public administration as a field to be more accountable, adjust to economic realities, and to evolve in unforeseen ways. The field is dynamic. The efficacy of *The Craft of Public Administration* depends upon people *effectively* relating to other people in the exchange of partisan, policy, and systems politics.

The actions and reactions of partisan, policy, and system politics bring to life the "chemistry" of equality and efficiency and of public and private relations in the United States. Professors Berkley and Rouse encourage feedback from professors and students on the effectiveness of *The Craft of Public Administration,* ninth edition. Your contributions will make future editions of this text reflect the dynamic "chemistry" of U.S. life as it is played out in everyday relations between the "equality" of government programs and services and the "efficiency" of private opportunities.

Conflicts of Values

The dynamics of public administration cannot be removed from the increasing diversity—and disparity—of American life and its many value systems. The development, implementation, and evaluation of public administration programs and services reflect not only a diversity of values but conflicts in values. As we study federalism, personnel, budgeting, and regulations, we do so realizing conflicts in values—and economic disparity—dominate our thinking of how government should function.

What conflicts in values should we keep in mind as we engage the dynamics of public administration?

- *Individualism versus Collectivism.* Individualism is represented by private initiative, personal choice, self-sufficiency, pursuit of materialism, and the private-enterprise economic system. The responsibility of the individual to him or herself contrasts with the responsibility of the individual to society. Collectivism is represented by government, the nation, states, government bureaucracies, public goods, and the "common good." Public administration consists of public goods, which are widely distributed to citizens. Governments implement public programs for the many, not the few.

- *Materialism versus Spiritualism.* Materialism, as a doctrine, espouses that comfort, pleasure, and wealth are the only or highest goals or values. Achievement of the "good life" is what many believe the American dream is about. The good life perhaps includes a home, yard, automobile, appliances, and the necessities that go with climbing ladders of economic success. Materialism incorporates the consumer society of shop and buy. American elections are contested primarily on economic or materialistic values, not on spiritual values. Spiritualism finds its origins in religious or moral thought. Materialism remains dominant in United States society, but spiritual values are not dismissed. Material well-being permits governments to offer programs to citizens for private use. Despite materialistic demands, moral authorities, or traditionalists, struggle against modernization and its manifestations.

- *Modernization versus Traditionalism.* Modernism sympathizes with modern ideas. Modern thinkers conform to present-day practices, standards, and tastes. Modernization designates certain contemporary tendencies. Traditionalism honors stories, beliefs, customs, conventions, and proverbs observed by generations throughout the ages. Conflicts over the functions of governments confront modernization and traditionalism. Modernization may mean "progressive" change. Modernization implies opposition to traditional values. Modernization has lead to industrialization and secularization. Traditionalism may be best defined as the desire to maintain values, customs, mores, and living patterns that have been established over time. Computer technology, feminist workforce values, video games, and government administrative systems may also reflect modernization. If governments emphasize modernization, they may be in conflict with traditional groups in their society. Modern public administration reflects modernization, but values espoused by Max Weber and other theorists are traditional, classic, and timeless.

- *Centralization versus Decentralization.* There are more than 87,525 units of public administration systems, or governments, in the United States. The most prevalent ones, of course, are the fifty American states. Counties, cities, townships, and special districts incorporate an administrative system that is fragmented and decentralized. The government in Washington may propose, but the people in the boonies dispose.

If authority is concentrated, advocates of centralization argue, more efficient decision making and policy implementation can be achieved. Decisions can be reached quickly. Policy can be implemented with fewer people at cross-purposes. Decentralization philosophy claims to be more democratic and responsive as it brings more people into the decision-making and policy-implementing processes. The possibility of a decision-making error is minimized.

- *Moral Value versus Opposed Moral Value.* In a country as large as the United States there are a wide range of values. Individualism and collectivism; materialism and spiritualism; modernization and traditionalism; and the legitimacy of opposed moral values impact public administration programs and units.[8]

The many dimensions of American public administration occur within these frameworks of philosophical thought.

- In a society that emphasizes individual freedoms, how does the "body politic" organize collective priorities for public services made available to individuals?
- How do material values effect the development of public programs?
- If public administration programs result in modernistic values, what role does traditionalism play?

Centralization and decentralization values are realized daily as more than 87,525 units of government collaborate in the craft of American public administration. Partisan, policy, and system politics are distinctive in programs and services of the national government, states, counties, cities, townships, and other special districts. And what happens when one moral value is opposed by another or other moral values?

- Should government/s be involved?
- What level of government should accomplish the tasks?
- How should the collective society pay for these programs and services?
- How strong is the private economy, which must be taxed to provide public programs and services?
- Consumerism is part of the materialistic culture. From the productivity of materialism comes taxation, or revenues for public programs and services. Should collective programs and services be implemented by private means or through government agencies?

The Craft of Public Administration, in its zillions of substantive and procedural facets, is manifest in such conflicts of values.

---

8. Daniel S. Papp, *Contemporary International Relations: Frameworks for Understanding,* 3d ed. (New York: Macmillan, 1991), pp. 578–593.

Acknowledgments

As principal author of the ninth edition of *The Craft of Public Administration,* I wish to express my thanks and appreciation to:

- George Berkley, author of the first four editions of this textbook, for the opportunity to coauthor the fifth, sixth, seventh, and eighth editions;
- Monica Eckman, Kate Scheinman, Rick Hecker, Anne Cody, Suzie Wright, and Terri Schiesl; McGraw-Hill Companies, for their encouragement and feedback on the development and evaluation of various stages of the writing and production;
- Joe Losco, chairman and professor, Department of Political Science, Ball State University, for his leadership in promoting a working environment conducive to integrating the tasks of teaching and research;
- faculty colleagues in the Department of Political Science, Ball State University, for creating an atmosphere where consensus is valued and productivity is recognized;
- The reviewers of this ninth edition: Lee Allen, Valdosta State University; Gerald Blasi, University of Missouri, St. Louis; Cynthia Bowling, Auburn University; Garry Frank, Drake University; John Hamman, Southern Illinois University, Carbondale; Lawrence Hubbell, University of Wyoming; Konrad Kressley, University of South Alabama; Nancy Lind, Illinois State University; Sheryl Lutjens, Northern Arizona University; John Portz, Northeastern University; John Robey, University of Texas, Brownsville; Winfield Rose, Murray State University; Bhim Sandhu, West Chester University; and Robert Schuhmann, University of Wyoming.
- employees of the more than 80,000 units of government in the United States, whose craft constitutes the challenges of federalism, personnel, budgets, and government regulations;
- thousands of Ball State University graduate and undergraduate students, past and present, who continually force me to think and rethink the dynamics of the public sector in the United States;
- the generous taxpayers of the State of Indiana, my employer, for access to a professional career that bridges the worlds of partisan, policy, and systems politics with the rich and varied literature of public administration; and
- Barbara Maves, my wife, and for many years, executive director of a government-funded, not-for-profit east central Indiana healthcare agency, which daily confronts the challenges of the craft of public administration.

These contributions in many ways enhanced my research and the writing of the ninth edition of *The Craft of Public Administration.*

John Rouse
jrouse@bsu.edu

The Administrative Craft

Chapter Highlights

The Heart of the Matter

Art, Science, or Craft?

Capital, Government, and Myths

Trust in Government and Politics

Partisan, Policy, and System Politics

Adversarial Legalism

Bureaucratic Legalism and Hidden Law

American Constitutional Principles

Summary

FDNY Personifies Public Administration

Why does New York City need a public sector, civic-based, government-run, taxpayer-funded fire department?

The Fire Department of New York (FDNY) is not a private company. It is a taxpayer-based, rule-bound, culture-driven local government assembly of committed, skilled public administrators. So why not privatize New York City (NYC) fire fighting—reducing the city's commitment levels to the lowest common denominator?

Consider the possibilities for privatization. First, fire protection could be negotiated among owners of individual skyscrapers. But who would be responsible to fight a fire that starts in building A and spreads to building B? A second idea might be to privatize the FDNY's function. The agency's costs might be reduced if its fire-fighting functions were outsourced to private companies. However, it would be difficult to make private companies obey strict rules on hiring, promoting, and firing fire fighters.[1]

Moreover, the city cannot write contracts to cover all eventualities, and privatized fire-fighter companies would have incentives to cut costs at the expense of public safety. Minimum-wage fire fighters might well offer ineffective, barebones services. The bottom line is this: When the stakes are high, citizens want dedicated civil servants to do whatever it takes to protect them and the greater good.

On September 11, 2001, New York City was turned upside down at 8:46:26 A.M. when a hijacked American Airlines Boeing 767 superjet was flown into the North Tower of the World Trade Center (WTC). The jet, loaded with 92 people and 15,000 gallons of jet fuel, crashed into the North Tower at 500 mph. The plane exploded into the 93rd to 98th floors with a force equal to 480,000 pounds of TNT. No one above the 92nd floor survived.[2]

At 9:02:54 A.M., the suicide-bent hijackers flew a United Airlines 767 jet into the South Tower with a similar payload of explosive jet fuel, striking the 78th through 84th floors. The South Tower collapsed first, at 9:59:04 A.M.; the North Tower fell at 10:28:31 A.M. Chalk clouds rose 30 stories high as steel, concrete, and people collapsed to Ground Zero.

The WTC twin towers symbolized America's financial might. At 110 stories each, they were engineering miracles. The buildings housed both private and public clients, from financial firms to government offices. Subway and commuter trains rolled by below. The WTC was larger than many cities. The concrete and steel infrastructures housed a multitude of restaurants, a tremendous shopping mall, and a world-class hotel.

The New York City financial manager, Comptroller William Thompson, later forecast that the economic impact of the WTC attack could reach $95 billion and cost 83,000 jobs. "While this devastating event can never be reduced to numbers, it is clear that New York City and the nation will continue to suffer its economic ramifications for years to come," stated Thompson.[3] Thirteen million square feet of private office space was destroyed, and another 30 million square feet of office space was damaged. Half of the city's $6 billion budget deficit is directly attributable to the terrorist attack.

The morning of the attack, fire engines and rescue vehicles rushed to the scene. Fire fighters, police officers, and emergency personnel rushed up stairwells in a heroic effort to rescue the occupants of the towers. "I remember coming down the steps, in the smoke, with water pouring in the dark," said Peter Genova, who worked in the North Tower. "And all I saw was dozens and dozens of firemen and cops going up those steps to try to help people. Twenty minutes later, the building was gone."[4] The instinctive efforts of fire fighters to save others cost many their own lives.

Skyscrapers can be constructed to withstand almost any stress, but their aesthetic appeal would be diminished and the costs would become prohibitive. The WTC towers initially withstood the impacts of the plane crashes. But they succumbed to the inferno of heat created by burning jet fuel. Temperatures of perhaps 1,000 to 2,000 degrees Fahrenheit likely weakened the buildings' steel supports. The external walls buckled, and the floors above fell straight down.[5]

The actual WTC death toll is 2,843, including 479 rescue workers and the 157 passengers and crew members on the two hijacked jets. Citizens from 67 countries perished in the attacks. Despite the huge loss of life, the evacuation was a success. Everyone who could get out did get out.[6]

Why were so many people able to escape from the two burning skyscrapers? The Port Authority of New York and New Jersey, owner of the WTC, had made crucial improvements after a bomb exploded in the basement of the North Tower in 1993, killing six people. Private and Public entities worked together to improve safety. In accordance with NYC building code standards, stairwells were well marked. The WTC towers had excellent stair systems, and building management took evacuations seriously. Each floor had assigned fire wardens. In addition, on September 11, 2001, the towers were half-empty when the planes hit. Officials project that between 5,000 and 7,000 persons were in danger in each tower—not the 10,000 to 25,000 per tower that might have been endangered had the towers been fully occupied; tourists were also few in number at 8:46 A.M. The observation deck on the 107th floor of the South Tower did not open until 9:30 A.M.

The sacrifices made by the FDNY and New York Police Department (NYPD) typify the selfless, lifelong commitments of many of New York's public safety workers. The NYPD lost 23 officers and the Port Authority of New York and New Jersey lost 37, but the New York Fire Department sacrificed 343 firefighters.

Entire FDNY companies were lost. The total dead was nearly thirty times the number the department had ever lost before in a single event. All five of the elite Rescue Companies and five of the highest ranking chiefs were killed. The ultimate sacrifice was paid by these city government employees. And the effects of the WTC disaster on the FDNY go beyond lives sacrificed. The fire department as an organization suffered severe losses of leadership and institutional memory.[7]

The FDNY—overwhelmingly white, Catholic, and male—is under political pressure to become more diverse, more representative of the city. In 2000, 94 percent of the 10,860 members of the FDNY were white, 3 percent black, and 3 percent Hispanic. This ethnic disparity is partially explained by the tendency to "pass down" the job from father to son, with the dinner table serving as a recruiting station. However, 22 percent of recent applications came from minority groups, compared to 7 percent in 2000.

The 343 FDNY public sector employees lost in the WTC attacks died trying to save their fellow citizens.

Then-Mayor Rudolph Giuliani had something to say to these civil servants at the New York City Fire Department promotion ceremony on September 17, 2001: "You're all my heroes."

Endnotes

1. Paul Krugman, "The Public Interest," *The New York Times,* October 10, 2001; http://www.nytimes.com/2001/10/10/opinion/10KRUG.html.
2. Jane Spencer and Mary Carmichael, "Deadly Miscues: In the First Moments after the World Trade Center Attack, Miscalculations by Heroic Rescuers Probably Cost Lives," *Newsweek,* http://www.msnbc.com/news/627959.asp?0sp=w12b2.
3. Timothy Williams, "Economic Impact of WTC Attack Climbs," *News.Yahoo.com,* September 5, 2002, http://news.yahoo.com.
4. Michael Powell, "New York: A City Turned Upside Down," *The Washington Post,* September 12, 2001, page A16; http://www.washingtonpost.com/ac2/wp-dyn/a14164-2001Sept11.
5. James Glantz and Eric Lipton, "Towers Withstood Impact, But Fell to Fire, Report Says," *The New York Times,* March 29, 2002, http://www.nytimes.com/2002/03/29/nyregion/29TOWE.html.
6. Dennis Cauchon, "For Many on Sept. 11, Survival Was No Accident," *USA Today,* December 20, 2001; http://www.usatoday.com/news/attack/2001/12/19/usatcov-wtcsurvival.htm.
7. David Schwartz and Christopher Stewart, "The Fire Department," *GothamGazette.com,* December 3, 2001; http://www.gothamgazette.com/iotw/firedepartment/.

Sources

E. J. Dionne, Jr., "No Time for Partisan Pleaders," *The Washington Post,* September 21, 2001, p. A37; http://www.washingtonpost.com/ac2/wp-dyn/A1148-2001Sep20; and Don Wyclif, "In Praise of Civil Servants," *The Chicago Tribune,* November 8, 2001; http://www.chicagotribune.com/news/columnist/chi-0111080042nov08.column.

Despite the heroic sacrifices of fire fighters, police officers, and numerous public service employees in New York City on September 11, 2001, the American citizenry views public administrators and government employees with very mixed emotions and perceptions. The heroes of September 11th caused more Americans to express confidence in the government, in political appointees, and in federal employees than had done so in many years.

The Princeton Survey Research Associates interviewed 1,033 randomly selected adults between September 27 and October 6 of 2001 to find out how they felt toward the federal government. Thirty-five percent of respondents (with a margin of error of plus or minus 3 percentage points) felt "very favorably" toward the federal government; a poll from July 2001 recorded that just 9 percent of the citizenry felt favorably toward Washington. Conversely, late September poll indicated that just 16 percent of the populace, as opposed to 45 percent the previous July, felt "somewhat or very unfavorably" towards Washington.

The poll also discovered that Americans trusted government more after September 11th, with the overall approval rating climbing from 29 percent to 57 percent. A separate *Washington Post* poll found that 64 percent of Americans now trusted Washington to "do what's right" nearly always or most of the time. The terror attacks on the WTC and Pentagon thus reshaped how Americans viewed their governments. In three decades of polling, the trust ratings had never been so high.

Confidence in rank-and-file federal employees also increased. But Americans still maintained that federal employees work for the government because of job security, pay, and benefits. Sixty-three percent of Americans believe that federal employees choose their life's work because they value a government paycheck rather than choosing a public service career because it is worthwhile employment.

The enhanced trust-in-government numbers, according to Paul C. Light, Director of Governmental Studies at the Brookings Institution, reflect the belief that government will serve the citizenry effectively in the future. The public opinion data offer no endorsement of larger versus smaller government or of particular changes in government priorities.[1] Instead, they simply demonstrate a renewed trust in public administration.

The words *public administration* express a concept that at first glance may seem abstract and nondescript. However, a closer look at the phrase helps relieve the ambiguity.

Public means the citizens of a given area—the people of a town, county, state, or country. If an issue is considered in the public domain, information and discourse about that issue are available to the people and can be known to all. The word *public* also refers to activities the state administers on behalf of the entire community.

Public administrators serve the people. Organized collectives of citizens constitute a variety of public communities in the United States. These publicly organized communities include national, state, and local governments. They include townships, state recreation areas, and public utilities. They include school, sanitary, and water districts. These communities administer public libraries, public parks, public defenders (police, fire, legal), public roadways, and public servants. In the event of war, citizens may be called upon to make the ultimate sacrifice to their national community—their lives. However, in peacetime, Americans are required only to pay taxes and obey the laws. When April 15 rolls around, citizens have a definitive economic opportunity to be patriotic by meeting their financial obligation to society. The one thing all public programs have in common is that they are financed by taxpayers, most of whom want a voice in how those dollars are spent.

U.S. taxpayers often pressure the government to reduce personnel and expenses for services. (There is correspondingly less demand to reduce services to citizens.) Since most services are delivered by local governments and their employees, the reduction of personnel and expenses must come first at the local level of operations, less so at the state level, and much less so at the centers of federal government operations.

As we study *public administration,* the abstract, nondescript, colorless images of public bureaucracies will fade away to be replaced by more concrete concerns about the development, evaluation, and implementation of programs that require our tax dollars. Such decisions are usually political in nature; a major function of politics is to allocate importance to numerous and often conflicting values in society. *Public administration* then, is the process of implementing those diverse values in our complex and ever-changing society. This process plays a vital role in the daily lives of all citizens.

One issue that affects public administration is the size and role of government. How big is government? According to Michael Hodges, federal spending consumes 24 percent of the economy; this works out to $6,909 per man, woman, and child. Federal expenditures constitute 34 percent of the economy if we count spending on regulatory compliance. In raw numbers, the federal government spends $1.9 trillion a year (2002). Social spending consumes 58 percent of this total. Individual income taxes account for 82 percent of all federal revenue, compared to 51 percent in 1950.[2]

Integrating economic, environmental, and social factors into the operations and management of governments challenges local, state, and federal executives—both elected and appointed. Sustaining, if not expanding, economic growth is but one priority of governments. Government spends about half what the nation "earns" each year. Is this amount excessive? The percentage of Gross Domestic Product (GDP) spent by the U.S. government is, in proportion to its economy, smaller than that of nearly any other industrialized nation.[3]

Government spending is more precisely evaluated in the context of population demographics, economic consumption, citizen production, and environmental consequences, all considered over time. To promote standards of a civil society, economic and political systems must proactively respond to population changes. The U.S. population increased from 151.3 million in 1950 to 281.4 million in 2000. Birth and immigration policies affect how the United States population grows, as well as affecting demands for limited resources, and pollution, deforestation, waste, and habitat choices. The more people, the more demand for government services—and the more government employees, bigger budgets, and higher taxes. Disparity in the tax burden may also increase, with some parts of the population shouldering more of the load.

While the U.S. has dramatically expanded, federal tax levels have remained relatively stable over the past forty-five years. The average tax level for the post-World War II period has been 18.5 percent of the GDP. Federal tax composition, however, has generally shifted away from corporate income taxes and excise taxes towards social insurance taxes, with the individual income tax continuing to produce the most revenue. State and local taxes, unlike federal taxes, have doubled—from 5.3 percent of the GDP in 1947 to 10.7 percent in 1998.

Approximately 87,525 units of government employ 19,155,000 wage and salary workers. Within this national distribution, local government units employ 53.2 percent, or 10,195,000 workers; they might be employed by cities, counties, courts, or special districts. State governments employ 5,677,000, or 29.6 percent of the total. They might receive their paychecks from the state police, motor vehicle bureaus, welfare departments, tax collections, natural resources, social services, lotteries, public schools or state universities. The federal government hires the smallest number of public sector employees. The feds employ 3,284,000, or 17.1 percent, of the total government employment force.[4] Let's begin to look at how these public sector workers interact to administer government functions. Just what is administration?

The Heart of the Matter

In a classic textbook, Herbert Simon, Donald Smithburg, and Victor Thompson define *administration* simply but graphically in this opening sentence: "When two men cooperate to roll a stone that neither could have moved alone, the rudiments of administration have appeared."[5] That illustrates much about what administration is and is not. The first and foremost ingredient of administration is *people*. A stone on a hill is not in itself involved in any form of administration. If that stone rolls down the hill by some act of nature, administration is not involved. People have to be present before administration can take place.

Defining Organization

Chester Barnard

A formal organization is a system of consciously coordinated activities or forces of two or more persons.

> —*Chester Barnard,* The Functions of the Executive *(Cambridge, MA: Harvard University Press, 1938), page 73.*

Daniel Katz and Robert L. Kahn

The first problem in understanding an organization or a social system is its location and identification. How do we know that we are dealing with an organization? What are its boundaries?

> —*Daniel Katz and Robert L. Kahn,* The Social Psychology of Organizations *(New York: John Wiley & Sons, 1966), page 14.*

Philip Selznick

. . . formal organization is the structural expression of rational action.

> —*Philip Selznick, "Foundations of the Theory of Organizations,"* American Sociology Review *Vol. 13, No. 1(1948), page 25.*

Dwight Waldo

. . . organization may be defined as the structure of authoritative and habitual personal interrelations in an administrative system.

> —*Dwight Waldo,* The Study of Public Administration *(New York: Random House, 1955), page 6.*

Source: Michael M. Harmon and Richard T. Mayer, *Organization Theory for Public Administration* (Boston: Little, Brown and Company, 1986). See "Defining Organization," page 17–21.

The second ingredient of administration is *action*. Two people looking at the stone are not, in that act alone, involved in administration. They must take some action regarding the stone before administration can enter the picture. There is no such thing as inactive administration (although many who have dealt with administrative agencies sometimes believe otherwise).

The third ingredient is *interaction*. If one person moves the stone, administration does not occur. At least two people must combine their efforts to move the stone for the activity to involve administration. The essence of administration is *people relating to people.*

People interacting with people to accomplish tasks—this is the essence of administration.

Art, Science, or Craft?

The title of this book clearly proposes that administration is a craft. Why this classification instead of another? Why not consider administration a science or an art?

Science is characterized by precision and predictability. A scientific rule is one that works all the time. In fact, rules in science are so rigid and final that they are not called rules at all, but laws. Two parts of hydrogen combined with one part of oxygen will *always* give us water, steam, or ice, depending on the temperature. While it is true that some sciences, particularly the social sciences, do not achieve such a 100 percent predictability level, it is also true that any scientific theory must stand up to rigorous, repeated tests to be considered valid. Administration uses scientific data, laws, and theories; for example, finance officers use mathematics and computers to keep a government agency's financial records. However, administration itself is not a science.

Although administrators use scientific laws, techniques, and data, they do so in ways that give individual imagination and temperament free rein. Usually a variety of successful solutions exist for dealing with a particular administrative problem, and a creative administrator may even devise a new solution on the spot. Administrative problems are rarely identical, and it is impossible to derive scientific equations that work the same way every time for such problems.

Administration shares traits with the arts as well as the sciences. Administrators often work in highly imaginative ways, employing a mix of methods, including intuition. Like painters and composers, administrators often find their own moods and personalities reflected in their work. There is, however, a vital difference that keeps administration from being characterized as an art: Artists create aesthetic works; administrators attempt to solve problems. The respective end products and the criteria for evaluating them differ.

Although public administration shares traits with both science and art, categorizing the field as one or the other obviously paints an incomplete picture. There is, however, a category more suitable—or at least more comfortable and workable— That category is *craft*.

There is never a precise formula that will invariably work best in all administrative situations. Not only do situations and people vary, but ideas for handling them are almost as infinite as the human mind. Still, we can establish an objective standard for most administrative situations: Did the solution result in more efficient completion of the desired task? This objective standard, lack of precise formula, changing situations, and problem solving are traits that best fall under the classification of craft. While science uses unvarying methods to achieve predicted results, and art uses diverse methods to achieve diverse, unpredictable results, a craft uses diverse methods to attain a desired result.

Public administration deals with the ongoing pressing problems of American society. Government administrators—executives, civil servants, and others—may well employ artistry and imagination in dealing with the demands of a variety of interests. However, they are not creating works of art. Similarly, administrators rely on hard evidence to resolve dilemmas of consequence to citizens. Yet the possibilities for resolution are virtually limitless—so administration is surely not a science.

Public administration, therefore, is neither art nor science, but can be described as a craft. Working in their craft, executives and civil servants seek to achieve objective goals and standards—with all the creativity, capability, and civility they can muster. In the always-evolving American administrative scene, the challenges of the craft of public administration are more demanding than ever before.

One of the toughest political challenges for any twenty-first-century president is shaping the modern welfare system. The term *welfare* originally referred to government as a "helper of the poor." The benefits the modern welfare state offers, however, reflect radical departures from the policy directives Franklin Roosevelt formulated in the 1930s. The current welfare state creates widespread dependency on government spending. Yet budget deficits and distrust of government accompany government programs, services, and spending.

According to *Newsweek* columnist Robert J. Samuelson, Americans are bereft of any consistent public philosophy by which to judge the effectiveness of their

First Encounters of the Bureaucratic Kind

The ability to adapt to a bureaucratic system is necessary to be able to function in the American society. *Most young people first experience bureaucracy as college freshmen.* Their views regarding
bureaucracy reveal the process of socialization that
leads to the acceptance of or resistance to a system
that can be inefficient or, at times, dysfunctional. Although the students experience frustration with the
long lines and waiting as well as with the impersonality of the administrative staff, they develop coping
mechanisms that enable them to accept the system
and conform in the long run.

Source: Glen J. Godwin and William T. Markham, "First Encounters of
the Bureaucratic Kind: Early Freshman Experiences with a Campus
Bureaucracy," *Journal of Higher Education* 67, no. 6
(November–December, 1996):660–692.

governments. In other words, no public philosophy spells out what governments
should and should not do. Budget deficits and federal debt trace their origins to an
inadequate taxing-and-spending philosophy. Though most taxpayers oppose tax
raises, they cannot agree on which programs should face revenue cuts. Little consensus exists on which government programs are necessary for the common good.

"Sooner or later," Samuelson argues, "we need to come to terms with the welfare
state. We need more rigorous standards for judging whose welfare is being advanced
and why."[6] The federal welfare state is too large for conservatives to abolish. It is too
expensive and unpopular for liberals to expand endlessly. The welfare state emerged in
the 1930s as an antidote to the insensitivities of free markets. More than 70 years later,
middle-class government welfare is a subject of increasing anxiety and contention.

Capital, Government, and Myths

Public administration is grounded in capital, bureaucracy, and democracy. Effective
government cannot exist without sufficient capital to finance buildings, programs,
equipment, skills, knowledge, and expertise.

The more poor the country, the more inefficient government programs, services, and operations will be. Richer countries can better afford effective government
bureaucracies. Legislatures tax the capital, profits, and wages that citizens earn. They
pass laws and commission government organizations to implement those laws. Government bureaucracies, then, make use of the dollars collected by democratically
elected legislatures. Government bureaucracies are created by taxing wealth.

Capital and bureaucracy depend on the political consensus created by democratic participation. In the 2000 presidential elections, when then-Vice President Al
Gore lost his petition to recount contested Florida votes by one vote in the U.S.
Supreme Court, the losers accepted the verdict. George W. Bush's victory rested on
the public's acceptance of democratic procedures in election politics.

Some call U.S. democracy a myth. Governments that create myths, sooner or
later, are apt to shed them. Myths set ideals and standards governments cannot
meet; self-government does not function effectively when citizens raise skepticism
and continuous contest over these fundamental assumptions. Citizens must believe
in the system, even when it is imperfect. They must agree to procedural rules for
the democracy to function effectively. And no democracy can protect the rights of
every individual when those rights conflict.

"The myths of our democracy are not delusions," says David K. Shipler. "They may be just part of the truth, or embellishment of an inner reality in our culture's creed. But coupled with our freedom to expose our flaws, the myths have power, because they celebrate the powerful ideas that government belongs to the people, that voting is a universal right, that all citizens are equal, that we are governed by the rule of law, that minority views are protected no matter how abhorrent to the majority."[7]

The myth of true democratic governance raises several difficulties. First, decreasing accountability of democratic institutions and processes fosters skepticism in the fairness and effectiveness of the system. Katherine Harris, Florida's Republican secretary of state during the 2000 election, appeared not to hold fast to the American myth of popular democracy when she denied Gore's request for a recount in certain Florida counties.

Second, the American middle class perceives itself as bearing more of the burden and receiving less of the benefits of government than it should. This perceived unfairness is important for public bureaucracy, because the bulk of the money collected to operate, finance, and expand government originates from the middle class. For a variety of reasons, many citizens insist that significant sectors of American society are increasingly excluded from democratic rule. This perceived "social apartheid" is creating serious economic disparities.

Third, the uniformity of intellectual thought on substantive policy questions closes out many economic and social options. The two political parties are often neither pragmatic nor flexible. They do not cope well with the ongoing, painful economic adjustment of the United States to its challenging role in the post-Cold War world.

Accountability, representation, and intellectual diversity challenge democratic rule. Public administrators are governed by laws, public bureaucracies are limited by the same, and freedom is manifest by a dynamic relationship between citizens and the state. If this relationship is not morally based, representative, and intellectually creative, government programs, services, and expertise suffer. The legitimacy of government functions becomes suspect.[8]

"For two generations, Government elites defined the great issues," writes Garry Wills. "Now, a tidal change in the culture is sweeping away traditional politics." In the title of an article in the *New York Times Magazine,* Wills asks: "Whatever Happened to Politics? Washington Is Not Where It's At."[9] What passes for politics, writes Wills, is Paula Jones's suit against former President Bill Clinton.

A stable structure for robust political debate is missing. Politics is no longer restricted to the political system; the electoral system no longer fosters sweeping, unprecedented change. In fact, the electoral system lags behind cultural change.

The controversial end of the 2000 presidential election and the trauma of September 11, 2001 raise even further questions about the viability of the American system of political economy. Prior to these events, the country often lacked the political machinery or public engagement to make progressive changes. The privileged, post-World War II elites could narrowly circumscribe what "politics" entailed.

However, politics cannot be separated from culture. Creative technologies, markets, and the courts relegate elections to johnny-come-lately arbitrators of political life. Consumerism and political rights emphasize individual prerogatives. Markets are driven by the purchases of consumer goods. Legal rights protect minorities—however they may be constituted—in the marketplace.

Wills argues that family and religion, as American institutions, promoted civic stability. Today, families are being redefined: Many children are born outside of marriage. Divorce is prevalent. These developments reflect definitive structural changes in family organization. Families are the first organized unit of of any society. Government programs are only as effective as the political consensus that arises when such social units agree on the common good; therefore, cultural changes effect political changes.

Public administrators respond and act in a cultural context. Whether fighting against terrorism or for more effective health care programs, politicians confront political—and cultural—wars. Television, radio, the internet, cell phones, and other technologies give citizens access to information for making personal decisions. The average American may feel she needs neither priest nor politician to tell her how to conduct her life.

Freedoms make it ever more difficult to mold political consensus. Public administration programs and policies—ideally, at least—are populist concepts built through ideas to which citizens adhere. U.S. citizens enjoy both political and economic privileges. They live in a society that stresses individual rights. They make demands on industries in the public and private sectors. They therefore demand responsiveness and expertise of government employees.

Before the 2000 election and the attacks on the World Trade Center and Pentagon, what used to be called "the Establishment" was already disappearing. The agenda-setting elite is gone. Wise men, or for that matter, wise women, do not exist in a society where sovereignty is less salient and where markets have more immediate impacts.

Marriage and family, as we have stated, are the fundamental institution of any society. In the United States, government and private industry likely come second and third; the media and religion are probably fourth and fifth. Why are the institutions of marriage, family, industry, religion, media, political parties, and governments under assault and constantly in flux?

Family structures and priorities changed once women became educated and realized a certain economic status. For two generations, as Wills notes, public policies encouraged citizens to make their own decisions—to not be bound by authorities in civic, religious, or private matters. The spread of egalitarianism has been slow but very persistent.

Despite these changes in culture, citizens still think in terms of public and private sectors. But these distinctions are being called into question. Dwight Waldo offers long-term insights into the notions of *public* and *private*:

> The concepts or *public* and *private* are very central in the conceptual and emotional structuring of the Western world. A great deal of our thought and action concerning government, law, morals, and social institutions relates one way or another to this distinction, a distinction which the modern experience has taught us to make. But we need to appreciate public and private are not categories of nature; they are categories of history and culture, of law and custom. They are contextual and subject to change and redefinition.[10]

As cultural notions about public and private rights and responsibilities change, pressure is brought to bear on political and governmental systems to change as well. The myth of government as omnipotent provider and protector is collapsing; however, trust in the public sector soared as our society agreed to tackle the threat of terrorism. How will we carve out a new sense of the role of government? The answer partly depends on whether we as a society maintain this new-found trust in our system of government and those who administer it.

Trust in Government and Politics

When hijacked airliners exploded into the World Trade Center and Pentagon on September 11, 2001, the United States suffered the largest single-day loss of life ever on American soil. Public trust in government surged in the wake of the September 11 attacks. What had government done to earn it?

Perhaps you have heard the old adage: "Trust is something that must be earned. You have to show me you're trustworthy." The post-September 11 confidence level approached that of 1966 when The "Great Society" Democratic Congress, elected on Lyndon Johnson's coattails in 1964, passed the Voting Rights Act, put Medicare on the books, enacted the first large federal education assistance law, and created a host of social and environmental measures designed to improve American lives.

After September 11, as we have mentioned, 64 percent of those polled in a *Washington Post* survey trusted government to "do what is right" most of the time or virtually always. In 1966, 65 percent approved grassroots citizen initiatives in one of the most productive periods of presidential-congressional cooperation in American history.

The 1966 approval ratings rewarded stewards of government for action taken. The 2001 citizen approval rating anticipated actions that were expected to come. According to *Post* columnist David Broder, government assumes two tasks. The first duty of government is to protect the people. The 2001 government-confidence surge reflected the belief that the U.S. government could employ its military-diplomatic-economic skills to confront political terrorism and economic recession.

The second task of modern government is to promote economic growth, providing for stable incomes and job security. The events of September 11 produced disastrous results for transportation, tourism, and the service sectors of the economy.

"Because this show of confidence in government rests on expectations of its future performance, it risks disillusionment," stated Broder. "Just as Johnson's dreams of a 'Great Society' were dashed on the rocks of Vietnam, inflation, and riots, these hopes of a successful war on terrorism and a return to prosperity could lead to disappointment."[11]

In the *Post* poll, among respondents earning $50,000 or more, the trust factor for government jumped from 31 to 69 percent. For those earning $30,000 to $50,000 the expressed trust soared from 28 to 67 percent.[12]

Post-September 11 support for government cut across ideological, racial, financial, and geographic lines. The terrorist attacks brought consensus to the U.S. political landscape—at least for the short duration. Expectations of victory are high. But the struggle to combat terrorism will no doubt be long, costly, and difficult.

Despite the high trust approval ratings in the federal government immediately after September 11, 2001, the country's good feelings for government to "do what is right" crested and is on the way back down to pre-attack levels. Public opinion experts imply that Americans "have returned to their more normal state of criticism and distrust of government."[13]

Partisan, Policy, and System Politics

American government employees exercise their skills, knowledge, and expertise within the framework of a fast-paced and ever-changing society. Three of the dynamic forces at work in our society are partisan politics, policy politics, and system politics. Partisan politics is concerned with which political party wins office. Policy politics deals with deciding which policies to adopt. System politics examines how administrative systems (decision structures) are set up.[14]

Public administration emphasizes two of the three forms of politics: policy and system politics. However, it originates from partisan politics. Partisan, policy, and system politics are not separate, exclusive applications of the craft in practice—they are highly intertwined. In a nutshell, citizens elect political partisans to public office; partisans establish public policies; and administrative systems implement the policies partisans have established. Consider an example: the administration of Central Park.

Central Park in New York City is a public park. Located in the middle of Manhattan, the park runs from 59th Street to 110th Street, from 5th Avenue to 8th Avenue. In the midst of some of the most expensive private real estate in the world, the park somehow survives the marketplace values of New York City. Central Park affords the citizens of New York a wide variety of playgrounds, bicycle paths, wooded areas, jogging paths, swimming pools, picturesque lakes, and other natural scenery. The facilities of Central Park are offered to the public on a first-come, first-served basis.

Who's in charge of Central Park? Are the politicians in charge? Are the police in charge? Are the bureaucrats from the parks department in charge? These types of questions demonstrate the subtleties of how politics shapes life in the public sector. Similar analogies may be made to federal lands, state parks, and municipal buildings. So who is really responsible for the upkeep of the facilities of Central Park? In a general sense, the people of New York are responsible. In a more direct way, the New York parks department, the police, and the mayor are responsible because they are the custodians of this public interest.

Whereas the concept of political responsibility is often abstract, administrative aspects such as hierarchy, chain of command, unity of command, span of control, due process, regulations, rules, and even bureaucratic ineptness are more definitive and recognizable. Politics, in its varied definitions, may be vague to many citizens; on the other hand, citizens have concrete experiences with bureaucracies.

How is the study of public bureaucracy different from the study of elections, executives, legislatures, or the courts? The study of bureaucracy focuses upon obeying authority; the study of elections, executives, legislatures, or the courts relates to the institutionalizing or democratic values. The study of public administration tells us what actually happens as bureaucracies carry out policies enacted by legislatures and approved by executives.

Decisions made by government officials, representing departments and agencies, reflect the policy and system politics that occur in public bureaucracies. Such decisions are monitored by political partisans within the framework of majority rule and minority rights.

Adversarial Legalism

Compared to other economically advanced democracies, the United States is uniquely prone to adversarial, legalistic modes of policy formulation and implementation, shaped by the prospect of judicial review. While adversarial legalism facilitates the expression of justice—allowing challenges to official dogma—its costs are often neglected or minimized.

A survey of existing research indicates the extent to which adversarial legalism causes (or threatens) enormous dispute-resolving costs and procedural delays, which in turn distort policy outcomes. Adversarial legalism, moreover, has increased in recent decades, as Americans have attempted to implement the ambitious, socially transformative policies of activist government through political structures, forms of legislation, and legal procedures that reflect deep suspicion of governmental authority.[15]

Public administrators rely on, and are vulnerable to, the law. Legalism in general, and laws in particular, tend to limit and influence the operation of a public institution much more than they do a private one. "This pervasive legal context is among the principal distinctions between public and private enterprise," note John M. Pfiffner and Robert Presthus. "In private management one is assured that he can do anything not specifically forbidden. In public administration, on the other hand, discretion is limited by a great number of laws, rules, and regulations."[16] To put it more succinctly, in private administration the law generally tells administrators only what they *cannot* do; in public administration, the law tells them what they *can* do.

The hiring and firing of employees, the purchase of equipment, and the adoption or even adjustment of a simple operational guideline have produced costly and frustrating litigation. To activist administrators, the law and its practitioners often seem to exist merely to tie their hands. Aggravating the problem for many public administrators is that their craft is becoming increasingly result-oriented. This contrasts sharply with the legalistic approach, which stresses the correctness of procedure. To the legal mind, justice is not a product but a process.[17]

The legal limitations placed on public agencies contribute to or create many of the other differences between them and private enterprise. Government organizations usually operate in a goldfish bowl, subject to scrutiny from politicians, the public, and the press. They must be ready to open their doors and their books to almost any outsider, even though the outsider's interest in the agency may be prompted by no more than idle curiosity.

The legal context within which the public sector functions also helps explain why its employees usually enjoy greater rights—and face greater obligations. Public agencies frequently possess less flexibility than private ones. The public organization must hold itself accountable. And new technologies have caused new legal dilemmas to sprout up.

The internet and terrorism threaten to alter public and private boundary delineations. The internet raises questions about applying laws to cyberspace communications; the legal principles surrounding this medium continue to evolve. In the

1960s, the U.S. Supreme Court cited the Fourth Amendment to the Constitution, which protects citizens against unlawful searches and seizures, as providing a "reasonable expectation of privacy" in telephone booths or street conversations. In the 1980s, the court reduced the scope of that protection.

In 1986, Congress passed the ECPA, or Electronic Communications Privacy Act. It outlawed nonconsensual interception and disclosure of electronic communications. Workplace privacy increasingly focuses on the internet and electronic communications.[18]

However, the terrorist attacks of September 11, 2001, or the impacts, results, implications thereof, now interfere with protections guaranteed by the ECPA. Attorney General John Ashcroft called for "sweeping authority" to investigate possible terrorists. Legislation, called the PATRIOT ACT, gives the attorney general flexibility to provide broad surveillance over the internet medium.[19]

Yes, the latter is in contradiction to the former. This is where the issue of "civil liberties" come to the fore. This is where partisan, policy, and system politics interact as debate continues.

Bureaucratic Legalism and Hidden Law

The establishment of law is one of the greatest achievements of human civilization. However, as Jonathan Rauch asks, what happens if law "starts getting off its leash?" Rauch portrays formal law as "bureaucratic legalism," with a focus on the legalistic bent of law in American society. Bureaucratic legalism posits that if citizens proceed through sufficient legal processes, the resulting outcomes will be procedurally correct and morally right. But does this always hold true when laws are applied to unique situations in American life?

What if the law is applied when an eight-year-old girl brings a nail clipper to school? Rauch points out that etiquette, norms, social codes, and customs exist to avert or resolve such conflicts. He says that these givens are "hidden laws." They are so deeply imbedded in our social structures that we forget they exist. Hidden law, says Rauch, entails everything from table manners to informalities by which neighbors settle land disputes.

Rauch believes that hidden law may be applied to issues such as adultery, pornography, assisted suicide, sexual harassment, and abortion, rather than relying on bureaucratic legalism. Bureaucratic legalism was in play when the Olympic athlete had to give back her gold medal because she took cold medication. It is also in force when a child is suspended or expelled for bringing a plastic squirt gun to school. The weapons policy did not include the word *plastic* when the city council outlawed guns.

When is hidden law relevant? Hidden law can be applied when we ask, "Is this offense worthy of notice? Maybe not. All right, we're going to pretend that it didn't happen." Bureaucratic legalism cannot make these distinctions. As Rauch explains regarding bureaucratic legalism:

> By its very nature, its standard of fairness is equal application, to absolutely everybody, all the time. It views Hidden Law as capricious and arbitrary and inequitable in that it makes distinctions between people based on very personal, local judgments. So, with Bureaucratic Legalism, it becomes virtually impossible to make exceptions.[20]

Bureaucratic legalism was manifest in the way the public responded to developments in the Monica Lewinsky-President Bill Clinton sexual affair. When a president or anyone else commits adultery, most folks do not particularly want to know. The Violence Against Women Act and the Independent Counsel law made certain that citizens had a right to know. It did not matter if they wanted to know or not.

As events turned out, much of the citizenry was more outraged with the law than with the personal conduct of former President Clinton. Clinton's personal behavior, many agreed, was odious. But they also found the application of the law and the behavior of the law's enforcers ridiculous and unrestrained. Conservatives applied a rigorous legal formalism to the Clinton-Lewinsky case, claiming that Clinton's answers in a legal case made him vulnerable to charges of perjury and subject to impeachment. Bureaucratic legalism won out over hidden law.

In the New Testament of the Bible, the hardline conservative religious party was known as the Pharisees. The Pharisees were a Jewish sect that observed the letter but not the spirit of religious laws. Denounced by Jesus as sanctimonious and self-righteous, the Pharisees viewed themselves as highly moral or virtuous based on their legalistic philosophy. The Pharisees not only rigidly observed the written law, but insisted on adherence to the oral, or traditional law, which grew out of popular usage.

Even in these days, law has religious origins. Laws may be applied with religious zeal, without exception, or not as precisely, upholding the spirit but not necessarily the letter of the law.

American Constitutional Principles

The craft of public administration is influenced by factors other than partisan, policy, and system politics and legalism. Our republican form of government, federalism, separation of powers, and constitutionalism—all of which will be discussed on the following pages—help put the craft into a larger perspective. Much is said pejoratively about public bureaucrats and their perceived power to operate without constraints in the American political system. However, a public administrator receives his or her authority for administrative decision making from certain constitutional principles. What are these principles?

C. Herman Pritchett cites four constitutional principles, embodied in the document signed September 17, 1787, that influence the lives of Americans every day.[21]

First, the Constitution established a *republican form* of government. Many Americans hold onto their grade-school conceptions of democracy in America, believing that we have a democratic form of government. We do have a democratic *philosophy* of government; however, the *structure* of our government is republican. What *is* a republican form of government? Simply stated, we send representatives—legislators and executives—to city hall, the general assembly, Congress, the governor's mansion, and the White House because it would be impractical for all citizens to vote and decide public policy on every issue. Although Article 4 of the Constitution guarantees "a republican form of government," the definition was left openended for future generations of Americans.

Second, the Constitution created a *federal system.* The original U.S. government set up in 1776 was a confederation, or a mere league, of states, in which each state retained its sovereign powers. Under the auspices of the 1787 Constitutional Convention in Philadelphia, the delegates formed a stronger central government that was to receive its authority from the people. Powers not transferred to the new national government were to be retained by the states. As the cornerstone of the U.S. governmental system, federalism encompassed a two-level structure of government that divided power between the central government and state governments, allocating independent authority to each level.

The condition of U.S. federalism has been altered by political conflicts and economic crises. The Civil War ended the political aspirations of those who wanted a confederate political system, and the economic collapse of the 1930s brought down a dual form of federalism in which states had been somewhat independent of the central government. Events culminating in the 1860s (Civil War) and 1930s (economic collapse) were stepping stones on the path to a more centralized American political economy in the twenty-first century. The Civil War was a crisis in federalism, as its effects encouraged greater centralization and caused the influence of the states to decline. The Great Depression of the 1930s was also a crisis in federalism, as the economic collapse caused the central government to intervene on behalf of the private economy. The Civil War and the economic depression thus had centralizing effects upon federalism. The federal government's influence expanded, as did the expertise, skills, and knowledge of public administrators. However, contrary to what the name implies, the United States are far from united on matters of politics and economics. Federalism, then, is the sometimes changing structure of federal and state politics in the United States.

Demographic federalism, a movement of the mid-1990s, redefined the relationship between the states and the federal government. Demographic federalism makes the federal government accountable for the health and financial security of the elderly and disabled. The states will be responsible for human capital and programs for workers, families, and children. These changes will have a significant impact on decision-making concerning economic and social policies.[22, 23] As sovereign communities, states promote their own economic interests, seeking political advantage over each other; this sometimes results in a state public sector being able to offer a better quality of life to its citizens.

The Constitution also advocates the *separation-of-powers principle*. Each branch of government is assigned a particular task: Congress makes the law, the executive branch administers the law, and the judicial system enforces and interprets the law. The separation-of-powers concept operates in tandem with the goal of limiting governmental powers. Separation-of-powers doctrine restrains one branch from usurping the powers of the others; the limitation of government powers inhibits the national government from overpowering the rights of the states and restricts the intrusion of government into private lives.

A system of checks and balances enables each branch to have some influence on the operation of the others. Congress regulates the kinds of cases the Supreme Court will hear, and the Senate ratifies treaties and approves executive appointments. The president appoints federal judges and vetoes laws, but the Senate must approve of his judicial appointments. The courts pass judgment on the validity of executive acts and interpret congressional statutes. With these checks and balances in place, abuse of power is less likely.

Finally, basic to the concepts of republicanism, federalism, and separation-of-powers is the idea of *constitutionalism.* Constitutionalism includes such ideas as rule of law, representative institutions, and guaranteed individual liberty. Two important elements of American constitutionalism are majority rule and minority rights. What happens when people disagree? The answer customarily given is "majority rule." It is here, however, that we must exercise caution. If 51 percent of the people voted to put the other 49 percent into concentration camps, we would hardly call this an exercise in democracy. When we think of constitutional democracy in American political culture, therefore, we must think not only of majority rule, but also of minority rights. This tenuous balance between the wishes of the majority and the rights of the few enormously complicates democracy, especially for public sector managers who must carry out the majority's mandate while simultaneously safeguarding minority interests. Public administration in a democratic society is a delicate and difficult task, requiring its practitioners to possess generous amounts of tolerance and tact. Those lacking such capacities may well do better in other fields.

Majority rule and minority rights even affect the workings of Congress. Because of the rules, the majority party can work its way more easily in the House of Representatives than in the Senate. In the Senate, regardless of which political party maintains a majority of U.S. senators, the leadership needs sixty senators to cut off debate. Until the magic number of sixty is reached, a minority can stall legislation. As the loyal opposition, the minority party has responsibilities to offer amendments to the suggested programs of the majority.

As previously emphasized, public administration uses art and science, but is essentially a craft. Considering public administration's grounding in constitutional principles incorporating majority rule and minority rights, the use of the term *craft* seems appropriate and realistic. With the limitations and diversity of constitutional guidelines, public administrators need to be "crafty" to fulfill their responsibilities.

In constitutional terms, then, public bureaucrats exercise power within the framework of a republican form of government, a federal system, the separation-of-powers principle, and constitutionalism. Federalism is the basis of the American constitutional system and American public administration.

William S. Livingston illustrates three ways in which the changing pattern of modern federalism has affected political bureaucracy.[24] First, he describes a cooperative federalism in which the *centralization of power* is accompanied by the *decentralization of governmental function.* The central government makes policy, then delegates the implementation of this policy to other levels of government. Since the New Deal era, the decentralization of governmental function has followed the centralization of governmental authority and power. State and national governments supplement each other and jointly perform a variety of functions. The federal food stamp program illustrates the centralization of power with the decentralization of administrative function.

Monies to finance the food stamp program are collected under the auspices of the federal purse and the sixteenth Amendment. Congress authorizes the Department of Agriculture to organize the food stamp program—to pen its varied regulations and to monitor its progress—but depends upon the county welfare offices in the fifty states for administration. So the national government, with its enlarged powers, supplements rather than supplants the tasks of the states and local jurisdictions.

State governors deal with issues ranging from education to energy to health care. Governors face tight budgets and rapidly rising costs for the joint federal-state Medicaid program. In regard to energy, President Bush's plan calls for the federal government to decide where electrical transmission lines are placed when state and local communities are stricken by the NIMBY ("not in my backyard") illness. According to Iowa Governor Tom Vilsack (D), "Governors want to maintain control of this."

A familiar question in the federal-state confrontations, at least for the nation's governors, is "How do we keep Washington from messing up our lives?" Governors often agree on education issues; that is, they agree until they must figure out how to pay for new government programs. Conflicts at the various levels of federalism transcend political parties or who occupies the White House. "Governors and mayors don't like to be told what to do," says Connecticut Governor John G. Rowland (R).[25]

Livingston's second illustration of how federalism affects bureaucracy considers the *highly decentralized* nature of the American political party system. Livingston concludes that the decentralization of power within the political parties enhances the decentralization of the political decision-making process and lends strength to federalism. The character of the parties supports federalism, and federalism, in turn, nourishes the decentralized character of the parties.

According to Livingston, American political parties are decentralized in three ways:

1. As discrete units, local parties exist to pursue control over state and local governments. Political parties are free associations of citizens who wish to influence the expenditure of taxpayers' dollars.
2. Because local parties are organized at the "grass roots," national parties exercise only periodic and ineffective control over local parties.
3. Local parties exercise considerable control over national parties. National political conventions are organized by collectives of state and local political parties. Forces of the religious right, for example, have captured many GOP local party organizations and insisted that certain social issues, such as abortion, pornography, homosexuality, and prayer in public schools become GOP priorities. The Republican National Committee (RNC) might think these concerns are divisive, but President Bush could not ignore the right wing's call for "family values."[26] These priorities originated at the grass roots of the GOP party structure. Political parties are private affairs; only public opinion constrains them.

The third, and final, feature that contributes to the increased vitality of modern day federalism is the *diversity of social values* in the United States. Livingston argues that the diverse people and values within a society determine the shape and character of political and governmental institutions. Federalism, as an arrangement of political power, responds to the changing values of society. What are the social values of American society?

Policies and values differ from state to state. Some states allow lotteries; others do not. Some states are restrictive in cigarette and alcohol sales; others are not. Some states maintain tough environmental standards; others do not. Some states have taken firm positions against racial and sexual discrimination; others back off. These illustrations indicate that public bureaucrats will have considerable difficulty enforcing laws mandated by the U.S. Congress if support for such policies does not emerge from the grass roots. From affirmative action to speed limits, public administrators have difficulty implementing laws that people do not support.

Public bureaucrats have been described as timid and ineffectual and at the same time as power-seeking and dangerous. In reality, their influence depends upon the consensus of political support for government laws and programs. Cooperative federalism, the grassroots nature of the political party system, and the diverse social values that Americans hold require public bureaucrats to share power and responsibility with federal, state, and local officials. Administrative federalism is the upshot of these political compromises.

People Without Organizations—Organizations Without People

No homogeneous conceptions of civil servants and public bureaucracies exist. These entities operate in the administrative worlds of behaviors, institutions, processes, and policies. These "worlds" significantly affect the lives of public administrators.

- The *behavioral world* entails an incredibly complex amalgam of personal needs, interpersonal relations, and small and large social groupings. The deportment, habits, and tendencies of individual men and women shape the context, structure, and functions of organizations.
- The *institutional world* reflects such institutions as the college environment in which students study, professors teach, and administrators implement academic programs. Institutions have histories. Policies and procedures are "institutionalized" into formats which develop over many years. Institutions are formally defined contexts in which administrators labor and in which clientele respond.

    Students achieve—or fail—within the contexts of formalized, institutionalized academic arrangements. The organizational context determines policies and procedures for selecting, monitoring, and promoting employees and delivering services. Police, firefighters, schools, libraries, and universities formalize— even make routine—employee behaviors.
- *Processes* are often formalized by print in local, state, and federal government functions. Communicating with employees and clientele, coordinating people and programs, motivating employees, and controlling reporting and budgeting procedures are all illustrations of the processes of public management.

    Students encounter processes as they seek a college degree. Penalties occur if you fail:

    to register for classes on time,
    to pay your tuition fees on time,
    to attend and arrive at class on time,
    to study effectively and consistently, and
    to meet prescribed—or even informal— academic deadlines.

    The college experience is a process for organizing your goals and objectives.

- *Policies* are developed, implemented, and evaluated by government administrators. Individuals may influence the policies and procedures of formal organizations. Students constitute an important clientele of any college or university. Campus bureaucrats and professors are employed by the institution, respond to the behaviors of clientele, develop and interact with collegiate processes, and formulate and amend institutional policies. Effective administration includes the development, implementation, and evaluation of public policies.

In summary, the individual and group behaviors of local, state, and federal government bureaucrats reflect *people without organizations*. Legal contexts, institutional arrangements, formal processes, and policy functions portray *organizations without people*.

Source: Robert T. Golembiewski, Frank Gibson, and Geoffrey Y. Cornog, *Public Administration: Readings in Institutions, Processes, Behavior, Policy* (Chicago: Rand McNally, 1976), pp. 1–10.

Summary

- The sacrificial and heroic performance of public servants in New York, Washington D.C., and Pennsylvania on September 11, 2001, caused more Americans to express confidence in government employees.
- The more people, the greater the demand for government services.
- Federal spending consumes 24 percent of the economy, or $6,909 per man, woman, and child; or 34 percent of the economy when counting regulatory compliance.
- Approximately 87,525 units of governments employ 19,155,000 wage and salary workers. Of this national distribution, local government units employ 53.2 percent, or 10,195,000. State governments employ 5,677,000, or 29.6 percent of the total. Federal government employs 3,284,000, or 17.1 percent, of the nationwide government workforce.
- Administration involves people, action, and interaction. People interacting with people to accomplish a task is what public administration is all about.
- Public administration involves artistry, but it is not an art. It makes use of science, but it is not a science. In these times of declining state, local, and federal budgets, government employees engage in a craft, seeking to achieve goals and meet standards with all the creativity, capability, and civility they can muster.
- Americans have no consensus on a public philosophy by which to judge the effectiveness of government-run, taxpayer-financed public sector programs.
- Compared to the growth of the United States economy, federal tax levels have remained relatively stable over the last forty-five years.
- A comparison of the percentage of Gross Domestic Product (GDP) spent by the U.S. government is, in proportion to the U.S. economy, smaller than that of nearly any other industrialized nation.
- Public administration is grounded in capital, bureaucracy, and democracy. In general, the poorer the country in capital, the less efficient its government programs, services, and operations.
- Politics cannot be separated from culture. Families are the first organizational unit of American life. Public administrators respond to and act in a cultural context.
- Delineations of *public* versus *private* are central to the conceptual and emotional structuring of the Western world.
- Trust must be earned.
- Partisan politics is concerned with which political party and personalities win office. Policy politics deals with deciding which policies to adopt. System politics examines how administrative systems (decision structures) are set up to implement policies.
- In private administration, laws generally tell administrators only what they cannot do. In public administration, laws tell them what they can do.
- The internet and terrorism threaten to alter the boundaries between the public and private sectors.
- The establishment of law, rooted in religious thought, is one of the greatest achievements of human civilization.
- The U.S. Constitution established a republican form of government and a federal system. It enacted the separation-of-powers principle and established the rule of law, representative institutions, and individual liberty. Public administration is grounded in constitutionalism.
- The centralization of power in U.S. federalism is not accompanied by the centralization of governmental function. Conflicts at various levels of federalism transcend political parties and who occupies the White House.
- Federalism is tempered by the diversity of social values in the United States.
- The worlds of behaviors, institutions, processes, and policies significantly affect the professional lives of public administrators.

In the next chapter, we will examine the environment in which public administrators practice their craft.

Case Study

*Public Administration as Chemistry**

The following case study illustrates how students encounter academic bureaucracies as they pursue educations on college or university campuses. Steady State University is located in College Corner, in the state of Commonwealth, USA.

Let us debate the issues and not the people.

—*Gregory A. Darrah, former SGA President*
Steady State University, College Corner,
Commonwealth, USA

Steady State University students were about to get an indoctrination into the whys and wherefores of United States government bureaucracy. The mix of public and private concerns helps determine the "chemistry" of the United States culture—how people relate to others and act or interact to reach a common goal. Students encounter cumbersome academic bureaucracies throughout their academic as well as extracurricular careers. Some of these bureaucracies are private colleges, but many are organized as government-funded and -regulated units.

A course in public administration is offered as part of the political science curriculum at Steady State University (SSU) in the town of College Corner, State of Commonwealth, USA. The college town is a uniquely American institution. The United States has a very institutionalized, economically developed, skilled population, within a society that strongly encourages individual initiative. To say that America is institutionalized is to emphasize that citizens soon find out their respective interests, then join groups or institutions to try to attain what they want for themselves and their families.

Postsecondary education in the United States is a study in decentralization. In 1800, there were 32 U.S. colleges, most of which had religious affiliations, none of which admitted blacks or women. Now there are 3,600 postsecondary institutions, including about 1,500 two-year colleges, 2,200 four-year colleges, and about 450 Ph.D.-granting institutions. In 1900, less than 3 percent of adult Americans aged 25 or older had a bachelor's degree; by 1970, that figure climbed to

10 percent, and by 1997, about 25 percent. Data show that 70 percent of women, 64 percent of men, 68 percent of whites, and 60 percent of blacks enrolled at a four-year college eventually graduate.[1]

One way to attain what one wants in life is to seek the opportunities afforded by a college education. That is why 16,500 students are enrolled at Steady State University—a Ph.D.-granting university. U.S. Census Bureau figures indicate that a household headed by a baccalaureate degree holder earns, on average, $40,000 more in yearly income than a household headed by someone with a high school diploma.

Consumerism is at the core of college marketing today. A "full-service college" responds to the full range of student expectations. Cable television in all dormitory rooms is part of the package. Vending and laundry machines activated by student charge cards are perks that might give a competitive recruiting edge.[2]

One the other hand, legalism is at the core of legislative endorsement of higher education. In 1862, Congress passed the Land Grant College Act, or the First Morrill Act, to provide funding for institutions of higher learning in each state. Officially known as the Serviceman's Readjustment Act of 1944, the GI Bill was signed by President Roosevelt to boost opportunities for World War II veterans. In 1954, in *Brown vs. Board of Education,* the U.S. Supreme Court declared the "separate but equal" approach to education as unconstitutional, opening opportunities for members of minority groups when school districts were ordered to run a single school system for all students, regardless of color.[3] The National Defense Education Act (NDEA) of 1958 and the Elementary and Secondary Education Act (ESEA) of 1965 set legal landmarks for promoting American colleges and universities. Government programs do not function without the enactment of laws.

The social values of College Corner are shaped by its relative lack of heavy industry, its abundance of young people and highly educated adults, and its plethora of cultural opportunities more characteristic of larger metropolitan areas. College towns are typically more politically liberal than towns without prominent colleges. They tend to be more tolerant of unusual behavior and eclectic ideas. The distinctive residential

*Chemistry is defined here as the composition, structure, properties, and reactions of a substance, and/or the elements of a complex entity and their dynamic interrelation. See *The American Heritage College Dictionary,* 3rd ed. (Boston: Houghton Mifflin, 2000).

landscapes of College Corner include the traditional faculty neighborhood, the fraternity district, and the off-campus student-rental area.[4]

Steady State student life administrators prefer to ignore a report from the Harvard School of Public Health that marijuana use among U.S. college students increased by 22 percent during the 1990s. The county prosecutor in which Steady State is located refuses to prosecute students for violating certain norms of the "hidden law."

The county jail already suffers from overcrowding. Law officials know that increased marijuana usage at Steady State reflects the group of high school drug users enrolling in college. Jailing college kids for breaking "hidden laws" further crowds—and taxes—the criminal justice system. Lawyers make a dime or two, but almost everyone else simply gets caught up in more paperwork.[5]

To PA students, the words inductive and deductive may be only esoteric reasoning methods. But all citizens interested in the pursuit of a college degree should pay close attention to five national trends. An inductive gathering of facts and figures point out the following deductive arguments.[6]

1. Increases in tuition make colleges and universities less affordable for most American families. However, in weak economies, enrollments grow faster.
2. Student federal and state financial assistance does not keep pace with tuition increases. Federal and state governments offer low-income undergraduate students financial assistance, as provided in the federal Pell Grant program, the nation's largest need-based support program for college students.
3. More students and families at all income levels borrow more than ever before to pay for college expenses. Borrowing, however, is a much greater burden on low-income students and parents.
4. Times of economic hardships—economic recessions—adversely impact state government services and personal finances. Decreases in tax revenues corresponds to lower funding of public services. Higher rates of unemployment may result in decreases of family income.
5. State government financial support for public higher education has increased. But tuition charges at state universities increased still more. From 1980 through 1998, state government appropriations rose 13 percent, but tuition revenues at state colleges and universities vaulted by 107 percent.

The challenges of SSU students occur in the portrait of political economy of attaining skills, knowl-edge, and expertise at taxpayer expense—and personal commitments. Human behaviors, policies, processes, and institutional arrangements take place and are organized in the mix of these trends.

Jacquette Glover is 19, an African-American political science major, pre-law student, and back bencher in deliberations of the Student Government Association (SGA) and Black Student Association (BSA). She is also a first-generation college student and a single mother. Glover has heard through the SGA and BSA grapevines that public administration is a tough course. "What's with all this focus on concepts?" Jacquette asks her public administration classmate, Maynard Wilkins.

"Well, first off, you've gotta attend class every day. Not just most of the time, but constantly," Maynard advises. "The professor says that half of life is just showing up. And, despite being an old guy, his logic makes some common sense; I got a D in my first public administration class." Now, Maynard is making a second trip down bureaucracy boulevard. "Concepts, writing, thinking, analysis, and arguments—but only based on facts," sighs Wilkins. "Professor Jachim says that everything is organized, even our class. Well, at least sometimes he's organized."

In class that day, the professor states that college students mostly relate to college bureaucracies. Are they responsive? Are they efficient? "This is the ATM generation, with TV and the internet," explains the professor. "Young kids don't comprehend the value of organization, laws, skills, and paperwork to help them be proactive against forces in sometimes very rigid organizations."[7]

Political Correctness as Intolerance

Political correctness, or an intolerance of criticism or debate, bothers both Glover and Wilkins. Jacquette's friends accuse Maynard of "antifeminist intellectual harassment." Professor Jachim, fully tenured, white, over fifty, jaded but not cynical, says, with some dismay, "Steady State could serve as a significant source of social criticism and an initiator of new modes and molders of attitudes. But our college president thinks it's more important to be true to our name."

Jacquette, revealing rare insight for her youth, blurts: "Almost no students value activity as citizens. They're passive in public, and hardly more idealistic in arranging their private lives. They settle for 'low success' and won't risk failure." Maynard chimes in: "SSU students don't give a damn about their apathy." Upon which Professor Jachim opines: "But apathy is not simply an attitude. It is a product of social institutions—namely, the structure and organization of Steady State itself."

SSU African-American students argue for more diversity in Steady State's social fabric. "The fallacy with this diversity stuff," says Jason Ashcraft, 23, a white, upper-middle class economics major, "is that it's reverse racism. Diversity does not mean fixed percentages of students by race, but diversity in curriculum offerings and student interests."

Jacquette, Maynard, and Jason all agreed that Steady State should fire incompetent professors. But Professor Jachim appears to stump the threesome, at least for the moment, as he advises: "You can fire the incompetents—after your parents, the faculty, the taxpayers, the state legislators, the alumni, and the SSU bureaucrats figure out a stationary definition of competence."

A centralized bureaucracy—the Commonwealth Commission on Higher Education (CCHE)—sets university tuition increases. CCHE has statutory responsibility for the statewide planning and coordination of higher education in Commonwealth, the administration of student aid programs, establishment of tuition increases, and performance of designated regulatory functions.

Statutory responsbilities of the CCHE include the approval of new academic programs at public two- and four-year institutions, an annual funding recommendation to the Governor of Commonwealth and the legislature on behalf of SSU and other public higher-education institutions, and the approval of off-campus offerings of public two- and four-year institutions. CCHE hires a professional staff, headed by a director, who orchestrate higher-education policies for all state colleges and universities. The commission is the midwife between the legislature and particular state institutions.

Administrative "worlds" encompass behaviors, institutions, processes, and policies. Jacquette and Maynard are about to encounter aspects of partisan, policy, and system politics. Partisan politics are neither recognized nor appreciated at SSU. State universities apparently grow in the middle of corn fields. Somehow they got placed there. Policy making refers to consuming alcohol at fraternity parties. System decision making focuses on drop-add dates for courses where grades are declining. Steady State College life combines diverse processes, procedures, and rules.

Jacquette and Maynard, as are most SSU students, are graduates of Commonwealth's high school system—

and its limitations. Unfunded mandates come with federal grants. The Commonwealth state legislature has no way to measure the effectiveness of its subsidy to Steady State students. Steady State's football is a deficit operation. Business, criminal justice, and communication majors are in demand. The humanities, liberal arts, and sciences are less popular. In the welfare state of SSU, students rely on the workings of the market as the "bottom line" decision maker.[8]

Steady State employs a very educated work force. Students at Steady State, however, live in the State of Commonwealth, which is known throughout the region for tolerating a mediocre secondary education system. Steady State is not the flagship university of Commonwealth. SSU is perceived as an opportunity institution where hard work and achievement are devalued. Many SSU students do not come from families with high expectations for themselves. There is a disconnect between professors and students. Professors think students could achieve more than they do. The behaviors of professors and students, as the two major institutional components, are frequently at cross purposes. Professors and students contribute to the SSU behavioral world.

Who Pays the Bills—Clients or Taxpayers?

The institutional world of Steady State is influenced primarily by the fact that SSU receives most of its financial support from the Commonwealth General Assembly. Students at Commonwealth pay only 37 percent of the costs of their education. Tuition last year went up a stunning 13.8 percent. If this trend continues, students will pay more out of their pockets for college expenses, while the state legislature and Commonwealth taxpayers pay less. "Public policy is clearly shifting," said Warren Madden, vice president for business and finance at Iowa State University, "from low tuition to expecting students to provide for a larger share." Public institutions enroll 83 percent of the nation's college students. Budget cuts and price increases directly impact these students and their families.[9]

Federalism is also part of the dynamics of Steady State; the centralization of power is not accompanied by the centralization of governmental function. The state legislature makes the laws and finances the institutional operations at Steady State, but the governmental functions are decentralized to each academic department. Federal government agencies also provide grants to be allocated, then implemented, by professors and students at Steady State. Again, the functions are delegated to the most local level of human interaction.[10]

SSU is essentially a unit of local government, located in College Corner, 113 miles from the state capital. But there is little distrust, if any, among alumni and citizens of the State of Commonwealth toward the integrity of SSU. Rarely do partisan politics affect what is taught, how the classes are delivered, or the ideologies of those teaching college courses. Policy and system politics emerge as professors express in the Faculty Senate that too much money is being spent on a football team that competes at a very low level. Of the 1,934 total employees at Steady State, only 637 are tenured professors. Steady State is a product of the middle-class government-funded welfare state; local business leaders and elected legislators look the other way when asked how tenured professors should be evaluated.

Steady State administrators, professors, and students are heavily invested in processes, procedures, and rules. Professors are protected by tenure. Their freedoms of speech are also protected by the first and fourteenth amendments. They can say pretty much what they want to in class. But professors are accountable as far as the processes by which they interact with students. Public administration consists of people, actions, and interactions, or people relating to people. Professors are bureaucrats who teach classes with certain knowledge, skills, and expertise. But procedures, rules, regulations and processes govern their interactions with students.

Administrators establish policies, and policy making affects both professors and students. The Steady State professors elect faculty representatives to the Faculty Senate, which forges curriculum policies. Steady State is governed by a complex arrangement of fragmented, yet egalitarian and somewhat democratic, committees of professors. The Faculty Senate decisions are advisory only. Faculty Senate decisions are not binding on Steady State's President or his administration. In essence, professors can have their say about university policy matters, but they possess no formal authority to change Steady State priorities.

Steady State affords personal choice and certain opportunities. Equality, diversity, and equity are immediate priorities, but personal achievements are recognized, respected, and rewarded.

Questions and Instructions

1. What "chemistry" is manifest in the instruction of your public administration class?
2. What impact does consumerism have on maintaining a clientele for Steady State University?
3. What force has legalism and law exerted in the history of American higher education?
4. Why is political correctness dishonest and unproductive? Is a commitment to diversity "reverse racism?"
5. What are the dynamics of federalism in the administration of Steady State University?
6. How do procedures and policies regulate the activities of Steady State students and professors?
7. Is public policy shifting at Steady State University?
8. How does culture affect the behavior of SSU students—and their professors?
9. How would you define teaching competence?
10. Why are U.S. colleges and universities admired throughout the world?

Insights-Issues/Public Administration as Chemistry

Clearly and briefly describe and illustrate the following concepts and issues. Interpret the word *role* in terms of impacts, applications, importance, effects, and/or illustrations of certain facts, concerns, or issues from the case study.

1. Role of consumerism and markets at Steady State University (private-sector decision making).
2. Role of partisan, policy, and system politics at Steady State University.
3. Role of legalism and laws for making activities at Steady State University "legitimate" and accepted by Commonwealth citizenry.
4. Role of federalism in the administration of higher education at Steady State University.
5. Role of procedures and policies at Steady State University.

Case Endnotes

1. Nick Gillespie, "The New College Try," *Reason,* December 1999, http://reason.com/9912/bk.ng.the.shtml.
2. Kristi L. Wiernicki, "Perspectives: Smorgasbord of Choices," NACUBO Business Officer, February 1998, http://www.nacubo.org/website/members/bomag/9802/perspectives.html.
3. "Looking Back on Education: Historical Events That Still Affect Us Today," http://npin.org/library/2000/n00484/lookingback.html; see also West Legal Directory, "Government Agencies and Programs: G. I. Bill," *West's Encyclopedia of American Law,* May 17, 2002, http://www.wld.com/conbus/weal/wgibill.htmg.
4. Blake Gumprecht, "The American College Town: A Research Prospectus," June 21, 2000, http://geography.ou.edu/collegetowns.html.
5. Robin Herman, "Survey Finds Increased Use of Marijuana and Other Illicit Drugs at U.S. Colleges in the 1990s," Harvard School of Public Health, PRESS RELEASES, October 27, 2000. http://www.hsph. harvard.edu/press/releases/press 10272000.html.
6. "CHAPTER 1: FIVE NATIONAL TRENDS," *Losing Ground: A National Status Report on the Affordability of American Higher Education,* May 2, 2002; http://www.highereducation.org/reports/losing_ground/ar2.shtml.
7. Wiernicki, *op.cit.*
8. Ryan C. Amacher and Roger E. Meiners, "Empowering Students by Increasing Competition Among Universities," *VERITAS: A Quarterly Journal of Public Policy in Texas,* Winter 2001. See also: James Engell and Anthony Dangerfield, "Forum: The Market-Model University: Humanities in the Age of Money," *The Harvard Magazine,* http://www.harvardmazine.com/issues/mj98/forum.html; and John Rouse, " 'Institution,' 'university' needs collide at Ball State," *The Muncie Star-Press,* May 5, 2000, p. 4a.
9. William Trombley, "Chapter 4: 2002 Update for the States: A Dire Situation," State Budget Shortfalls Trigger Escalating Tuition," *Losing Ground: A National Status Report on the Affordability of American Higher Education,* May 2, 2002; http://www.highereducation.org/reports/losing_ground/ar5.shtml.
10. Christen Baylis-Heerschop, "FEDERAL AID TO EDUCATION," http://www. nd.edu/~rbarger/www7/fedaid.html.

Case Sources

Ryan C. Amacher and Roger E. Meiners, "Empowering Students by Increasing Competition Among Universities," *VERITAS: A Quarterly Journal of Public Policy in Texas,* Winter 2001; Christen Baylis-Heerschop, "Federal Aid to Education," http://www.nd.edu/~rbarger/www7/ fedaid.html; James Engell and Anthony Dangerfield, "Forum: The Market-Model University: Humanities in the Age of Money," *The Harvard Magazine,* http://www.harvardmagazine.com/issues.mj98/forum.html; Nick Gillespie, "The New College Try," *Reason,* December 1999, http://reason.com/9912/bk.ng.the.shtml; Blake Gumprecht, "The American College Town: A Research Prospectus," June 21, 2000, http://geography.ou.edu/collegetowns.html; Robin Herman, "Survey Finds Increased Use of Marijuana and Other Illicit Drugs at U.S. Colleges in the 1990s," Harvard School of Public Health, Press Releases, October 27, 2000, http://www.hsph.harvard.edu/press/releases/press 10272000.html; "Looking Back on Education: Historical Events that Still Affect Us Today," http://ngpin.org/library/ 2000/n00484/lookingback.html; John Rouse, " 'Institution,' 'University' Needs Collide at Ball State," *The Muncie Star-Press,* May 5, 2000, page 4a; "The Students," http:porthurontokentstate.tripod.com/TheStudents/ The Students.htm; William Trombley, "Chapter 4: 2002 Update for the States: A Dire Situation, State Budget Shortfalls Trigger Escalating Tuition," http://www.highereducation.org/reports/losing_ground/ar5.shtml; "Truth or Consequences," HARDWICK, http://www.hardwickday.com/trends/ enroll/default.htm; West Legal Directory, "Government Agencies and Programs: G. I. Bill," *West's Encyclopedia of American Law,* May 17, 2002, http://www.wld.com/conbus/weal/wgibill.htm; Kristi L. Wiernicki, "Perspectives: Smorgasbord of Choices," NACUBO Business Officer, February 1998, http://www.nacubo.org/website/members/bomag/9802/perspectives.html.

Chapter Endnotes

1. Stephen Barr, "Survey Finds Americans Looking Favorably on Government and Its Workers," *The Washington Post,* October 11, 2001, p. B02.

2. Michael Hodges, "Grandfather Economic Reports: Federal Government Spending Report," March 2002, http://mwhodges.home.att.net/fed_budget.htm.

3. See William I. Buscemi, "Numbers? Borrrinnng!!!," *PS: Political Science & Politics* No. 4 (December 1997), 738–739.

4. David L. Brumbaugh, "The Level of Taxes in the United States, 1941–1998," April 13, 1999. See http://www.cyberhaven.com/taxlibrary/taxlevels.html. U.S. Bureau of Labor Statistics, Table 3: Union Affiliation of Employed Wage and Salary Workers by Occupation and Industry (Numbers in Thousands), 2001. http://stats.bls.gov/news.release/union2.t03.htm.

5. Herbert A. Simon, Donald W. Smithburg, and Victor A. Thompson, *Public Administration* (New York: Alfred A. Knopf, 1950), 3.

6. Robert J. Samuelson, "Clinton's Nemesis," *Newsweek,* February 1, 1993, p. 51; "Our Love-Hate Relationship with Government," *The Washington Post,* January 27, 1993, p. A19.

7. David K. Shipler, "The Myth of Democracy," *The Washington Post,* December 3, 2000, p. B7.

8. Jorge G. Castaneda, "Three Challenges to U.S. Democracy," *Kettering Review* (Summer 1997), 8–20.

9. Garry Wills, "Whatever Happened to Politics? Washington Is Not Where It's At," *The New York Times Magazine,* January 25, 1998, p. 27+.

10. Dwight Waldo, *The Enterprise of Public Administration* (Novato, CA: Chandler & Sharp Publishers, 1980), p. 164.

11. David S. Broder, "The Trust Factor," *The Washington Post,* October 3, 2001, p. A31.

12. Stephen Barr, "Trust in Government Surges During Crisis; Challenge Is to Keep It from Ebbing," *The Washington Post,* September 30, 2001, p. C2.

13. Francine Kiefer, "New surveys show a resurgence of public criticism of government after the 9/11 crest of support," *The Christian Science Monitor,* May 31, 2002; http://www.csmonitor.com/2002/0531/p02s02-uspo.hmt.

14. Aaron Wildavsky, *The Politics of the Budgetary Process* (Boston: Little, Brown, 1979), pp. 191–193.

15. Robert A. Kagan, "Adversarial Legalism and American Government," *Journal of Policy Analysis & Management,* Vol. 10, No. 3 (Summer 1991), 369–407.

16. John M. Pfiffner and Robert Presthus, *Public Administration,* 5th ed. (New York: Ronald Press, 1967). In regard to the subsequent sentence in the text, Donald S. Vaughn, former chair, Department of Political Science, University of Mississippi, points out that the law also tells the public administrator what he or she cannot do. Professor Vaughn cites the first eight amendments to the U.S. Constitution as a case in point.

17. See Alan M. Dershowitz in *The Best Defense* (New York: Random House, 1982). However, the same theme runs through many other legal statements and writings. Oliver Wendell Holmes, for example, once said that his job as Justice of the U.S. Supreme Court did not require him to "do" justice, but merely to see that the rules of the game were followed.

18. Daniel J. Appelman, "The Law and the Internet: Emerging Legal Issues," http://www.isoc.org/Iamp/paper/222/abst.html.

19. Carrie Davis, "Terrorist Attacks Spawn Greater Surveillance Powers," *The Internet Law Journal,* February 2, 2002.

20. Charlotte Hays, "TWQ Interview: Jonathan Rauch talks about the value of Hidden Law," *The Women's Quarterly,* Summer 2001.

21. C. Herman Pritchett, *The American Constitutional System* (New York: McGraw-Hill, 1981), pp. 7–8.

22. David Hosansky, "Reshaping The Federal-State Relationship," *Congressional Quarterly Weekly Report,* 54, no. 40 (5 October 1996), 2824–26.

23. Bert Waisanen, "Demographic Federalism: Defining the New Federal-State Relationship," *Spectrum: The Journal of State Government,* 69, no. 4 (Fall 1996), 53–58.

24. William S. Livingston, "Federalism in Other Countries: Canada, Australia, and the United States," in *Federalism: Infinite Variety in Theory and Practice* (Itasca, IL: F. E. Peacock Publishers, 1968), pp. 131–141.

25. David S. Broder and Dan Balz, "Bush Agenda Concerns Governors Over U.S. Role," *The Washington Post,* August 7, 2001, p. A02.

26. The term *right wing* is elusive. Almost without exception, "right wingers" are traditional thinkers on nearly every issue, value, and behavior confronting partisan, policy, and system politics. For example, they hold traditional views on abortion, religion, adultery, women in the workplace, sexual orientation, military spending, taxes, economic disparity, and foreign policy involvements. Therefore, a better description might be *traditionalists.*

The Ecology of the Administrative Craft

Chapter Highlights

Our Organized Society

Equality and Efficiency

Rights and Dollars

Ebbs and Flows of Government Expansions, Constraints,
  and Prospects

The Growth of Public Bureaucracy

Comparing Public and Private Administration Nuances

Interest Groups and the Greater Good

Washington's Power 25

Summary

Congestion and Transportation Ecology

If you are going to travel from one city to another in the United States, you are not likely to take a passenger train. Travel in the United States—for the most part—is by car or airplane. Local, state, and federal governments are committed to maintaining vast systems of taxpayer-supported highways and airports.

No public service challenges the ecology of our organized society as does the country's public transportation system. *Ecology* is the relationship between living organisms and their environment. Congestion fills a system to excess, whether we consider population or traffic. Reduced traffic congestion benefits the system—it improves air quality and conserves energy. If we apply the science of ecology to public transportation, we will gain an understanding of the relationships between transportation, people, and our environmental system.

Transportation is the lifeblood of American capitalism, the connector by which commerce takes place. Citizens venture into the marketplace by foot, bike, car, bus, subway, train, or plane. To sell

and realize profits, businesses must be accessible to consumers. Public transit provides that access, as well as promoting affordable mobility, congestion management, and support for neighborhoods.

Transportation in the United States comes in many forms. The trucking industry dominates America's interstate highways. Short-haul rail passenger service, though available in some cities, is not an option for most Americans. Car rentals provide flexibility but are costly. And the advent of wholesale terror makes airline travel ever more problematic and challenging.

All fifty states support taxpayer-funded and government-organized departments of transportation. State transit units supervise traffic patterns on the highways, for motorcoaches, for trains, and for airlines. Public transit systems help promote personal freedom and private commerce; ecology is the relationship between the private marketplace and the state's responsibilities for monitoring, supervising, and regulating personal freedoms and commercial activities related to transportation.

Transportation Organizations in the United States

Federal Transportation Organizations	*Transportation Interest Group Organizations*
U.S. Department of Transportation	American Concrete Pavement Association
Bureau of Transportation Studies	American Public Transportation Association
Federal Aviation Administration	American Trucking Associations Foundation
Federal Highway Administration	Association of American Railroads
Federal Motor Carrier Safety Administration	National Asphalt Pavement Association
Federal Railroad Administration	U.S. Army Corps of Engineers
Federal Transit Administration	U.S. Department of Energy
National Highway Traffic Safety Administration	
Research and Special Programs Administration	
U.S. Coast Guard	

The fifty states, District of Columbia, and Puerto Rico administer government-regulated transportation departments. Local public transit operators provide services in 319 urbanized areas with 50,000 or more residents each. Transit systems receive operating and capital funding from federal, state, and local governments—and even private sector sources. However, public transit remains essentially a public service provided and managed by local governments. Federal and state officials give way to local authorities, who set and adjudicate the boundaries of transit-related issues for their communities.

Sources: Paul Hawken, *The Ecology of Commerce: A Declaration of Sustainability* (New York: HarperBusiness, 1994); Hawken, Amory Lovins, and L. Hunter Lovins, *Natural Capitalism* (Boston: Little, Brown, 1999); Norman Y. Mineta, "Hearing on Congestion in the United States Transportation System," U.S. House of Representatives, Committee on Transportation and Infrastructure, April 4, 2001, p. 8; and Don Phillips, "Mounting Congestion Is Challenge to DOT," *The Washington Post,* May 15, 2001, p. A15.

The power of the federal Secretary of the Department of Transportation (DOT) is limited by constitutional guarantees to the states. Federal transit budgets are limited. A major share of the federal transportation budget "passes through" Washington, as major transportation-authorizing legislation must be renewed. The Secretary has a major role in policy decisions. However, the Secretary is limited as far as what he or she can do and spend.

Highway transit appropriations are continually reauthorized. The Federal Highway Administration (FHA) administers DOT's highway transportation programs as provided in legislation. The Administration is concerned with the operation and environment of highway systems, including highway and motor carrier safety. The Secretary must use federal, state, municipal, and private money to mold a coherent and efficient plan to permit people and freight to stay on the move.

Congestion is the toughest challenge facing the nation's transportation ecology, and it affects all modes of transportation. Our highway system is in heavy demand. Since the 1970s, highways have experienced a 143 percent increase in vehicle miles traveled. Over the same period, only a 5 percent expansion of roads has taken place. Mobility is declining in virtually every metropolitan area.

In addition to the FHA, the Federal Aviation Administration (FAA), Federal Transit Administration, Research and Special Projects Administration, and United States Coast Guard function under the authority of DOT. The FAA promotes—and regulates—the development and safety of air commerce. With a workforce of 49,000, including 15,000 air traffic controllers, the FAA has the most responsibility of any of DOT's units. As airline travel becomes increasingly common, air congestion contributes to the ecological challenges of travel in the twenty-first century.

Aviation traffic is expected to increase by almost 50 percent over the next several years, to more than one billion passengers by 2011. Since airline deregulation took place in 1978, air travel has become an essential form of transport. In the 1960s and 1970s, airline travel was a luxury. Now it is primarily a middle-class experience—connecting not just cities in this country, but throughout the entire world. Air travel has grown faster than any other mode of transportation. In 2000, 682 million passengers boarded commercial flights. This figure is twice the number of airline passengers counted in 1980.

Seven major airports—New York-LaGuardia, Newark, New York-Kennedy, Chicago-O'Hare, San Francisco, Philadelphia, and Los Angeles—are often congested with "significant passenger delays." Because proposed airport construction projects must be submitted to environmental scrutiny, new runways cannot be built quickly enough to allow capacity to catch up with demands.

Other agencies support and regulate transportation. The Federal Transit Administration (FTA) plans, develops, and finances the development of improved mass transportation facilities. Federal support for transit depends upon revenue from motor fuel taxes. The U.S. Coast Guard, a uniformed force, engages in law enforcement activities along the coasts. The American Public Transportation Association (APTA) is a leading participant in research and legislation regarding the transportation industry and issues relating to it. Transit demands are growing at record levels in cities around the country, especially in the near-gridlocked areas of the East and West Coasts. However, ecology concerns and regulations place legal contraints on the ability of state governments to issue permits to build new highways.

Highway congestion forces states and cities to turn increasingly to rail commuter and transit services. Rail commuter services transport suburbanites into central cities. Urban subways and light rail trolley services are other alternatives.

Freight and passenger rail systems help relieve the overcrowding on highways and at airports. Rail capacity is utilized most extensively in the Northeastern states. California, Washington, and Virginia are increasing their freight and passenger rail capacity. Whatever the mode of transportation, the federal and state governments face tremendous challenges in providing safe, environmentally responsible, and accessible public transit to both consumers and commerce.

Our Organized Society

Ecology is the study of the relationships between organisms and their environments, and public administrators not acutely aware of how environmental factors influence administration are doomed to failure. This chapter describes the relationship between public administrators and the environment in which they work.

Public administrators do not operate in a vacuum: Countless environmental factors buffet administrators, making their tasks remarkably complex. Public administration occurs within the framework of an organized society. The principle barriers to the effective implementation of public programs are the conflicts between the political principles of democracy and the economic principle of capitalism.

Public administration is also carried out within the political cultures of states and communities. Culture, tangible and intangible, affects the environment in which public administration takes place.

A drive down Main Street, U.S.A., will take you past banks, dry cleaning establishments, cafes, and retail stores. Keep driving and you'll pass churches, shopping malls, fast food outlets, factories, gas stations, and schools.

All are examples of organizations that affect our daily existence. Organizations must be managed or administered. We live in a complex society in which public organizations are needed if the smaller, private organizations are to thrive or operate at all. The alternative is anarchy.

Public organizations receive their lifeblood from legislative, executive, and judicial collectives in our organized society. Legislatures appropriate revenues to fund public programs. Presidents, governors, and mayors carry out the legislative will of the people. Courts adjudicate disputes between parties contesting, among other things, the delivery of government programs.

With its numerous organizations, modern America is the epitome of the organized society. The legislative, executive, and judicial branches of our national and state governments are the basic units of public organization. For example, the president and Congress enacted the Social Security program for the elderly; the Social Security Administration implements the policy; and judges decide disputed claims.[1]

Questions constantly arise concerning the fairness and efficiency of public organizations—questions that contribute to these organizations' administrative entanglements.

Why focus on equality versus efficiency, rights versus dollars, democratic capitalism versus political economy, and other trade-offs in the organized society? The answer is that public administration enjoys a very conceptual grounding in partisan, policy, and system politics. To comprehend the interplay of these definitive aspects of the field, students need to understand how government programs, agencies, and departments operate.

Thinking about the many applications of public administration requires reading, focusing, illustrating, applying, and comprehending concepts, terms, trends, facts, and principles of the field. Before departments and agencies implement goals, directives, and processes, administrators must develop an understanding of what the community wants from these units. Communities direct their public administrators to fight wars on many fronts—terror, poverty, ignorance, sickness, and even incompetence. Government cannot operate effectively if the community is not in agreement with its goals and policies.

Understanding public administration and its varied applications requires a mix of conceptual and analytical thinking, as well as deductive and inductive reasoning. A concept is a general notion or idea; conceptual thinking involves the formation of ideas, the recognition of patterns and relationships. Analytical thinking requires one to examine the constituents or parts of some larger concept, to find out their nature, proportion, function, and relationship to one another as one breaks a whole puzzle into separate parts. A deductive thinker reasons from a general, known principle to a specific, unknown conclusion, or from a premise to a logical conclusion. And an inductive thinker, by contrast, reasons from a particular fact or individual case to form a general conclusion.

Students learn to think by combining conceptual and analytical thought and deductive and inductive reasoning. This chapter and Chapter 1 are especially conceptual and inductive. In order to understand the principles (and principals) of public administration, students need to think conceptually and inductively, yet be analytical, and on occasion, deductive, as they think through the diverse challenges confronting public administrators.

Students cannot learn the dynamics of the organized society if they do not work to comprehend how, where, when, and why general concepts explain agency actions and how agency behaviors contribute to emerging conceptual definitions.

Equality and Efficiency

American society professes to provide equal opportunities for all citizens. This does not, however, guarantee that citizens will achieve equal results for their efforts. Your contribution in the competitive market depends on your skills, assets, and efforts and also on the supply of and demand for what you have to offer. As free speech does not guarantee an audience, free enterprise does not guarantee a demand for one's services. Effort does not guarantee excellence. Although a student studies long and hard for an exam, an "A" is not a foregone conclusion. It is easy to see that these factors, when applied to individuals in the marketplace, can result in unequal individual incomes.

Our organized society, therefore, exists in an environment of equal rights and unequal outcomes. But comes. Conflicts between these two phenomena result in tensions between the *political principles of democracy* and the *economic principles of capitalism.*

The United States is a democratic society with a capitalistic economic system. In keeping with our democratic political philosophy, we hold elections. In keeping with our economic philosophy, we let supply and demand decide who achieves financial success. Arthur Okun describes contemporary U.S. society as a "split-level institutional structure" because of the combination of democracy and capitalism.[2]

We have a "split-level institutional structure" because private institutions value efficiency, while public sector institutions favor equality. Efficiency gives the top-producers priority, and equality gives everyone priority.

So the services provided by public administrators reflect the concept of *equality.* The concept of *efficiency* comes from letting the marketplace decide what goods and services are produced and purchased. Services and programs produce that governments are available to all citizens. Police, fire, and sewers are usually provided by government. Electricity, water, gas, garbage, and telephone services, although regulated by government, may be provided for privately. Even though these utilities are produced privately, the government regulates their activities to assure "fairness" of delivery.

The rich and the poor have equal rights to travel on our network of interstate highways. The economic realities of the efficient marketplace may determine, however, that certain people lack any car to drive while others cruise along the turnpike in chauffeur-driven Mercedes. A public program is not maintained just for the very poor or the ultra rich, but for the masses of middle-class citizens.

In that respect, America's highway system serves as an example of an efficient economy—the more we drive, the more road and gasoline taxes we pay. "With the great quarrel between capitalism and socialism in mothballs," says

Suzanne Garment, "critics of the free market do not attack it by offering some grand, principled alternative. Instead, they march under the banner of prudence, calling for a pragmatic mixed economy that values markets but avoids the extremism preached by excessively principled free-market ideologues."[3]

The values of equality and efficiency are always in conflict. The pursuit of efficiency necessarily creates inequalities. Citizens make economic choices, such as buying a car or riding a bus. If we all choose to commute only by car, bus drivers will be out of work, the victims of our equal freedom of choice and the workings of our efficient economy. It is often the role of the public administrator to step in if one of these values begins to supersede the other. This is where the public administrator's regulatory powers come into play.

Through these powers, public administrators exercise great influence in determining the role of the marketplace. The public administrator does not, however, have unlimited regulatory power. As regulators of private interactions, public administrators are checked by limits on administrative power spelled out in laws such as the Administrative Procedure Act.[4]

In defending the state of affairs its equality versus efficiency, Okun says, "The market needs a place, and the market needs to be kept in its place."[5] The market is kept in its place by the limited regulatory powers of public administrators. So equality may be sacrificed for the sake of efficiency, and efficiency for the sake of equality. What provisions exist to protect the individual's equal rights in this market-driven economy? The issue of economic decision making in the late twentieth century focused on ensuring the right degree of mix between government and private sector participation. A purely government-led or a pure market-dictated economy will not only be ineffective in economic terms but also in social and political terms. The market is usually more efficient than the public sector, but the latter is needed to ensure that the allocation of resources is balanced.[6]

American society promotes equality by allocating social and political rights equally and distancing these rights from the marketplace of supply and demand. For example, due process is a constitutionally mandated guarantee. Governments in the United States must act with fairness, justice, equity, and reasonableness, irrespective of economic considerations. Accused criminals have the right to seek fairness in prosecution through due process. Equal opportunity is protected in a court of law by constitutionally mandated due process. Due process is the legal cornerstone of the craft of public administration.

There are two types of due process, *substantive* and *procedural*. *Substantive due process* refers to the content or subject of a law. *Procedural due process,* the more commonly litigated of the two, refers to the procedures used in implementing a law or administrative practice. Deciding whether a law is constitutional is part of procedural due process.

The concept of equality is also demonstrated in the open admissions policies of many state universities. These policies require a university to accept students from all ethnic groups and income levels. The taxpayers subsidize public education to guarantee fairness, justice, equity, and reasonableness in the admission of students. The state university must pay careful attention to due process. On the other hand, a private college is not required to follow due process as stringently as a public university. A private college may, with some restrictions, select only those students who meet certain criteria that may not be used at a state institution. Their adoption of standards of excellence embraces the value of efficiency.

The value of equality is embodied in guarantees grounded in basic citizen rights. The value of efficiency is embodied in market productivity. Public administrators operate in a complex environment in which these two fundamental values often collide. The challenge of public administration must be to maximize efficiency without sacrificing equality, and vice versa.

Rights and Dollars

Obviously, as we have already pointed out, a trade-off exists between our equal rights as individuals and the unequal distribution of wealth in our society. United States pursues an egalitarian political and social system. Yet, it generates gaping disparities in economic well-being.

We acquire and exercise our rights without any monetary charge; rights cannot be bought or sold in the marketplace. Thus, in a sense, rights infringe on economic efficiency, and the marketplace infringes on rights. The poor are disadvantaged in terms of buying and political power. Campaign financing and lobbying regulations favor persons with access to wealth. Yet the poorest person has the right to challenge the wealthiest business, or even our government, in our system.

The conflicting values of equality and efficiency are manifest in government organizations. Everyone has an equal right to apply for public sector employment, but certain people will be more efficient in fulfilling the tasks of a given position. On the one hand, we emphasize individualism—rights, self-interest, liberty, freedom, choices, and rewards. On the other hand, we value community—consensus, agreement, sacrifice, altruism, and commitment to the greater good.

This mixture of equality and efficiency is crucial to American economic development. If one does not have the right to enter the marketplace, one is not going to be productive, on an individual basis or for the greater good. Therefore, if women, minorities, or other persons are denied equal opportunities, they have no chance to benefit themselves or society, and our productiveness as a nation suffers. Most citizens support equal access to opportunities. However, many question whether we can or should guarantee equal outcomes.

Equality and rights are the groundings for community consensus. Individual citizens agree on what elements constitute a satisfactory community for all. Markets value efficiency. Communities tax market profits and commit them to public administration programs—schools, streets, transit systems, parks, libraries, and other public services. Capitalistic markets depend upon community consensus, or democracy, and on the efficient use of community resources.

Table 2.1 contrasts equality and efficiency. The terms listed in the table are neither all-inclusive nor mutually exclusive as applied to American politics, governments, parties, or leaders; they are simply meant to provoke thinking, discussion, questions, and commentary.

TABLE 2.1

Contrasting Equality and Efficiency

Equality	Efficiency
fairness	advantage
socialism	capitalism
public	private
community	individualism
government	business
inductive	deductive
democracy	bureaucracy
mediocrity	excellence
employees	executives
rights	responsibilities
chaos	order
collective bargaining	merit
access	restricted
common	elite
equal opportunity	affirmative action
republicanism	fascism
elections	courts
horizontal	vertical
egalitarianism	authoritarianism
tolerant	judgmental
incompetence	expertise
open	closed
level	hierarchy
modernization	traditionalism
decentralization	centralization
average	superior
diversity	homogeneity
Christianity	religion
April 15th	July 4th
Democrats	Republicans
female	male
bottom-up	top-down

Note: These terms are neither all inclusive nor mutually exclusive as applied to American governments and politics. They are offered as discussion points in the ecology of American public administration. The mix of these concepts is witnessed in the development, implementation, and evaluation of government programs and functions.

Equality as Investment?

Nations forge trade-offs between income equality and economic efficiency. Scholars and policy-makers argue that greater equality reduces investment and dampens the incentive to work. Lane Kenworthy, however, argues that a more eqalitarian distribution of income encourages consumer demand—as a greater number of workers become able to purchase consumer goods. If this premise is correct, egalitarian governmental policies would benefit efficiency, not dilute it.

Kenworthy offers evidence based on cross-sectional data from seventeen advanced industrialized economies over the period 1974–90. He finds no adverse impact of greater equality on investment or work effort. According to his research, higher levels of equality associate with stronger productivity, growth, and trade performance. A national emphasis on equality does not adversely affect productivity, trade balances, inflation, or unemployment.

Source: Lane Kenworthy, "Equality and Efficiency: The Illusory Trade-off," *European Journal of Political Research,* Vol. 27, No. 2, 1995, pp. 225–54.

Two crucial questions for our democratic and capitalistic society are where and how the organized modern society establishes boundaries between the *domain of rights* (equality) and the *domain of the capitalistic marketplace* (efficiency). Conflicts between these domains are inevitable and pose dilemmas for our split-level, political economy.

Our democratic, capitalist society searches continuously for better ways to establish clear boundaries between the domains. The marketplace needs equality to put some *humanity* into *efficiency;* our democracy needs efficiency to put some *rationality* into *equality.* Capitalistic and bureaucratic systems will be more effective if they are more humane. Equality will be more acceptable to those who value efficiency, and hence, less chaotic, if consistent standards are applied to the diverse applications of the democratic principle.[7]

Democracy is characterized by equality, due process, fairness, participation, suffrage, and electoral politics. Capitalism implies efficiency, productivity, hierarchy, competition, and entrepreneurship. Public administration finds its origins in democracy but owes much to the fundamental principles of capitalism.

The modern organized society can also be described as a *political economy.* Our society is *political* in that citizens have the opportunity to organize and set priorities about what is important to them. The *economy* comprises the collective productivity of goods and services our society generates. The split-level structure of the political and economic systems affects public policy and administration. Communities cannot expect to have public services without providing an ample supply of *revenues,* raised by taxing citizens and businesses. Our organized society, therefore, depends upon the political system and the structure of the economic sector. The maintenance of the relationship between political power and economic structure is vital to the future of American democracy. Public administrators depend upon capitalism to generate economic growth to pay their salaries and to finance the delivery of their services to the American people.[8]

The thrust of democratic capitalism comes from the opposing values of political power and economic structure. Middle-class citizens who do not possess the means of economic production agree to the private ownership of capital stock; meanwhile, wealthy citizens, who own the instruments of economic production, ac-

With the New Deal, government became a legitimate means for attempting to solve matters once considered private in American society. Government entered banking, stocks, pensions, housing, employment, public works development, management of the economy, and deficit spending. Although its enemies described the New Deal as socialistic, FDR's central purpose was to preserve the capitalist system by bringing about recovery. Government assumed the societal responsibilities that private corporations could not.

The New Deal, in expanding the role of public administration, saw the establishment of numerous government agencies commissioned to revitalize the private sector. The Federal Deposit Insurance Corporation, established in 1933, guaranteed bank deposits and fostered renewed confidence in the national banking system. The Securities and Exchange Commission (1935) regulated stock exchanges, hoping to prevent a repetition of the events of 1929.

The postwar years saw an unprecedented growth in the size and scope of the federal government. Although the Roosevelt-era New Deal gave birth to the concept of big government, it was really World War II that provided the impetus to expand government spending and bureaucracy until it became much larger and more powerful than ever before.[15]

The Social Security Administration (1935), which provides unemployment insurance, is an early illustration of intergovernmental attempts to share political, fiscal, and administrative responsibilities. The federal government collected the money; the states administered the legislation; and the private sector financed the program by payroll deduction. The public sector's expanded role allowed it to experiment with new plans for merging the talents of the public and private sectors to alleviate problems in society. One of the provisions authorizing payment of pensions to workers past the age of sixty-five applied to about half of the working population. In 1934 Congress created the Federal Housing Administration, now part of the Department of Housing and Urban Development, to administer an amortized home mortgage program that resulted in the suburbanization of America. After obtaining low-interest loans for repayment over twenty-to twenty-five-year periods, many Americans achieved home ownership. The National Labor Relations Board was established in 1935 to supervise the right of workers to join unions and bargain collectively. By providing protection to farmers and wage earners, the New Deal fostered the buildup of big agriculture and big labor as a check on big business. In establishing these agencies, the federal government also assumed much larger responsibilities for regulating the movements of the economy, providing security, and protecting underprivileged groups.

Public investment became a permanent policy. Although revenues were appropriated in ways that enhanced the national wealth (low-cost housing, schools, hospitals, post offices, and highways), budget deficits and a steady increase in the federal debt were viewed as a necessary evil.

As the economy grew and revenues increased, the need for public administrators also expanded. The public sector had achieved parity, in some respects, with the private sphere. Public works projects generated an incalculable contribution to the quality of American life through the construction of roads, streets, schools, parks, swimming pools, and playgrounds. The charisma of FDR promoted the myth of an activist president that proved impossible for later presidents to measure up to.

The concept of a president with a vision for the United States—one that is larger than life—traces its orgins to FDR. Much of this emphasis is due not only to FDR, but to the economic and political circumstances that existed during his twelve-year tenure.[16] The administrative state of the twenty-first century owes its origins to the government initiatives and reforms of the 1930s.[17] Leaders are often defined by their problems, challenges, and enemies, and by how they respond to all of them.

1965: Great Society

Lyndon Johnson (LBJ) (1963–1969) was a protégé of FDR. First elected to Congress in 1937, Johnson saw firsthand the positive role government could play in American life. He believed, as FDR had, that government could do good things for people. The most significant achievement of Lyndon Johnson's presidency was the sweeping social change he established through legislation. However, Johnson's success belies the enormous challenges he faced to fulfill his far-reaching agenda. His initiatives, especially those dealing with civil rights, were opposed not only by Republican lawmakers but by southern Democrats as well.[18]

Among the key measures LBJ successfully championed were voting rights for southern blacks, termination of racial discrimination in public accommodations, establishment of federal aid to education, and origination of the Medicare system to help America's hard-pressed senior citizens. Johnson's administration saw the establishment of the Office of Economic Opportunity (1964), Department of Housing and Urban Development (1965), Model Cities Program (1966), and Department of Transportation (1966). At the same time, millions of acres of new park land and wilderness were preserved. Johnson's celebrated "War on Poverty" focused national attention on the stubborn problem of hunger and want in the midst of plenty. Johnson, recalling the potentialities of government action he had witnessed in the New Deal era, called for a Great Society.

Under this umbrella, he advocated government support of equal employment, voting rights, air pollution control, highway safety, public broadcasting, food stamps, labor training, fair housing, Social Security increases, and civil service pay raises. Federal deficits under Johnson ranged from $1.6 billion in 1965 to $25.1 billion in 1968. However, LBJ's last budget request provided a $3.2 billion surplus in 1969. Although Johnson is remembered for committing the country's resources to the unpopular Vietnam War, he was mostly a pragmatic president who responded to the needs of America's middle class.[19]

How did the philosophy of the Great Society influence the conduct of public administration? Although sincere in undertaking such efforts as eliminating poverty and racism, caring for the sick, and educating the masses, Johnson became caught up in a "credibility gap" of what government—domestically and internationally— could accomplish. Opponents charged that corruption and inefficiency were rampant among a laundry list of new federal government programs. As World War I had ended the Progressive Era and the New Freedom, and as World War II had concluded the New Deal, the Vietnam War proved to be the most disastrous and divisive armed conflict since the Civil War and a calamity for the Great Society.

Political tragedy occurred not only in foreign policy. Despite the Great Society's efforts to attend to the needs of the poor and downtrodden—especially blacks—the destructive ghetto riots of the middle and late 1960s led to widespread perceptions that government assistance was not working. Public bureaucracy and public administrators were despised and disparaged. The tendency to downgrade and malign institutions of public administration, regardless of their tasks, limits, and records, is a theme that Ronald Reagan, the antithesis of Wilson, FDR, and LBJ, capitalized on.

1985: Reagan Revolution

The "body politic" of the United States is more pragmatic than ideological. Rarely have the citizens of this nation strayed from the middle of the political road. Wilson was pragmatic in responding to the causes of the Progressive Era, FDR was pragmatic in responding to the causes of the depression, and LBJ was pragmatic in responding to the human and environmental concerns of the 1960s. Then, in 1980, the public elected a president who championed the ideology of the conservative wing of the minority party. Reagan's logic was simple: Why should the national government tax the people and then send the money back to the states? Why not let the states do the taxing and administer the programs?[20]

The Reagan administration (1981–1989) began by rejecting the moderate to liberal consensus that had come to dominate both Democratic and Republican administrations since the election of FDR in 1932. Reagan envisioned a better America based on less government and more individual enterprise. Not since FDR had there been such a massive redirection of public goals. The essence of the "revolution" was Reagan's belief that our problems were caused by high government spending and by government intervention in the private marketplace.

On defense issues, the conservatives got their rapid defense buildup, but failed to sustain it. The overall trend in the second Reagan term was a resumption of regulatory growth. On trade issues, Reagan talked a hard line. But William A. Niskanen, Jr. writes that "for the first time since World War II, the United States added more trade restraints than it removed." Neither Reagan nor Bush scaled back on affirmative action programs or clean air regulations. Abortion remained legal. Organized prayer is still not permitted in the schools.

Budget deficits did not dilute the influence of big government. Conservatives failed to discredit the notion that solving problems is government's responsibility. Reagan will be remembered as a better communicator than persuader; his accomplishments did not constitute a lasting conservative revolution in policy. No one knows yet the philosophical impact of George W. Bush's War on Terrorism. Conservatives may yet achieve a revolution, but Reagan in the 1980s and Gingrich in the 1990s had to realize their failure to make converts and not just conquests.

The perspective of presidents during the 1960s and 1970s had been that if something was wrong, government had a responsibility to attempt to correct it. In contrast, Reagan planned a full-scale retreat from the march toward a welfare state for the masses. Although Reagan's rhetoric was *revolutionary in purpose,* his actions were *evolutionary in practice.*[21] Reagan talked tough, sometimes in revolutionary tones, but governed pragmatically, or in evolutionary ways.

Reagan the person was a "throwback" to simpler times. LBJ tried to be all things to all people. He governed in the charismatic shadows of FDR and John F. Kennedy. FDR, JFK, and Reagan had at least one thing in common: They used rhetoric effectively to raise support for their agendas. Under Reagan, tax cuts and the buildup of defense took precedence over balancing the budget.

The budget deficits emerging from the Reagan administration made "fiscal conservatives" out of politicians from all jurisdictions and political stripes during the 1990s. Reagan budget deficits ranged from a low of $127.9 billion in 1982 to a high of $220.7 billion in 1987. The implication for later domestic or foreign programs was a trend toward leaner budgets at all government levels. Public administrators will continue to attempt to do more with less, and taxpayers will continue to demand the same level of service delivery without increasing costs.

Early in the 1980s, Reagan gave the fight against inflation precedence over the previous administration's attempts to moderate the recession. Congress passed Reagan's tax cuts, but did not make corresponding domestic spending cuts. Despite the reduction in tax revenues, defense spending increased, and the deficit grew larger while the recession worsened.

Reagan's income tax cuts dramatically reduced revenues for domestic benefits and services. The recession reduced the business profits that were usually taxed for public programs. Public administrators were affected by deep cuts in grants to state and local governments and in programs serving the poor. However, the chief sources of federal budget growth since the 1950s—Social Security, Medicare, government employee pensions, and other middle-class programs—were too politically sensitive for the Reagan administration to cut.

Another priority for the Reagan administration was economic growth without a commitment to economic fairness. Tax rates were framed to provide the greatest benefits to high-income families. Reagan focused on reducing the marginal tax rates that would enhance savings, investment, and the work ethic, espousing the idea that the economic benefits would "trickle down" to the poorest segments of society.

The Reagan administration's policy toward regulation valued productivity over health, safety, civil rights, and the environment. The growth of productivity in the 1970s had slowed, in part due to environmental regulations. During the Reagan years, natural resource policy focused upon the development of energy resources rather than conservation. Even public lands and wilderness areas were no longer sacred.

Ironically, deficits later became a means of advancing the Reagan Revolution. President Clinton was pressured to curb federal spending and to restrain the growth of major federal entitlement programs. An increasing portion of the taxpayer's dollar was devoted to paying for interest on the federal debt. Benefits and services were curtailed. As federal programs were reduced, state and local jurisdictions were forced to search for new ways to finance and implement services that Washington no longer paid for.

The shift of political power away from Washington and toward state and local governments reflects Republican political philosophies. The middle class continues its revolt against taxes, and local services are therefore reduced or kept to a minimum. Due to their lack of political clout in the economic system, the poor feel the effects more than the middle class and, certainly, more than the upper class.

Wilson, FDR, and LBJ advocated government intervention to provide a measure of equal opportunity in our democratic, capitalistic system. Reagan, rather than overthrowing cardinal elements of the New Freedom, New Deal, and Great Society, sought to redirect government's role in society toward efficiency and productivity. Federal spending certainly did not decrease under Reagan.

Reagan, however, changed the agenda from *proportionally more* spending to *proportionally less* spending. The power of the federal government had been further enhanced by two World Wars and conflicts in Korea and Vietnam; wars enhance federal budgets and tend to centralize federal power. During World War I, World War II, Korea, and Vietnam, national defense expenditures increased considerably and enhanced the dominance of the federal government.

The benchmarks—1915, 1935, 1965, and 1985—illustrate the ebb and flow of government response to the demands of citizens. The political, social, and economic environment of the day has tremendous influence on public administrators. We can see that presidents, in leading and marshalling support from public bureaucracies, respond pragmatically to the dynamics of their times.

Believing that in the 1990s, as in the 1930s, conditions were imposing new requirements on government, President Clinton set out to transform the remnants of the New Deal party into a diverse and durable coalition capable of dominating American politics and advancing the progressive tradition into the twenty-first century.[22]

The concept of a rhetorical presidency, as discussed by Woodrow Wilson in his study, "Constitutional Government in the United States," reflects doubts on executive power. The executive office of the president is hemmed in by a rigid and formal Constitution and the informal historical development of the American party system. In a rhetorical presidency, the president sheds his traditional role of executive officer, exchanging one type of power for another. Such a president provides strong opinion leadership rather than governing by executive power. Wilson, FDR, LBJ, and Reagan used rhetoric effectively.[23]

Bill Clinton represented the theses of Wilson, FDR, and LBJ, while Newt Gingrich carried Reagan's banner. Clinton and Gingrich confronted each other's perspectives on politics in an emerging set of American politics that E. J. Dionne, Jr. called "the new radicalism." Clinton and Gingrich espoused fundamentally different approaches to economic turbulence, moral uncertainty, and international disorder. The new conservatives wanted to resolve the country's political crisis by shrinking government. They denied any link between economic developments and the country's moral condition. Family, church, neighborhood, workplace organizations—traditional institutions—should forge a solution to the moral crisis.[24]

The theses of Wilson, FDR, and LBJ—that a free market economy could not function properly in the absence of rules, workers' rights, government spending on public goods, and continuing public investments to enhance the skills and opportunities of the work force—was the political argument Clinton advocated. He did not seek absolute equality or anything like it, but he warned that rising inequality was dangerous for American democracy.

The adversaries of Gingrich argued that the new conservatism reached back not to Reagan, but to the Gilded Age of the 1890s. If only economic change goes on unfettered, the new conservatism argued, everyone will be better off. The language of the new conservatives was that of joyful anarchism. They were reluctant to acknowledge that "a capitalist society depends on noncapitalist values in order to hold together and prosper."[25]

The purpose of progressivism is not to use government to destroy the free market; instead, progressives believe, government should strengthen the institutions of civil society. But progressives abdicated the definition of liberty to their conservative adversaries. Progressives failed to confront the politics of liberty and community and assure citizens that government would not weaken the bonds of civil society.

Clinton campaigned for president in 1992 and 1996 as a "New Democrat." As the new conservatives ventured toward the extremes of political traditionalism, the New Democrats supported states' rights and a less activist national government that provides citizens with mechanisms to help themselves (through programs such as job training) rather than a varied assembly of expensive social services.[26] The Clinton political model stressed pragmatism and moderation.

According to *National Journal* columnist William Schneider, the Reagan political successes of the 1980s were not without costs. "Reagan's success in the 1980s had the effect of ideologizing the GOP: Stick to the right, and you can be another Reagan. Clinton's success in the 1990s has deideologized the Democrats: Stick to the mainstream, and you can be another Clinton."[27]

However, the presidency of George W. Bush took a completely contrasting approach to leading and governing. Bush called for faith-based government funding, tax cuts, and unilateral foreign policy making. The United Nations and allies were consulted—but in an after-the-fact fashion. Clinton, the personality, is destested by the younger Bush. But so is Iraq's Saddam Hussein. The fallout from the human trauma of September 11, 2001, replaced partisan, policy, and system politics focusing on pragmatism, moderation, and the evolution of mainstream policy making.

The events of September 11 redefined definitions of liberal and conservative. Now that post-Cold War boundaries are passing, the challenges for American leaders and government institutions will be to embrace new ideas and policies emerging from reconstructed political centers of domestic and world politics.

The successes of any president's agenda are determined largely by whether he can govern from the political center, recognizing that government is not the solution to all problems, nor the cause, but must be a tool, a conduit, a mechanism, a catalyst to provide opportunities to those willing to accept responsibility. According to Leon Panetta, at one time President Clinton's chief of staff, this government largesse—and limitation—are the essence of the "vital center" from which most Americans want the president and Congress to govern.[28]

The Growth of Public Bureaucracy

The organization of federal, state, and local jurisdictions is evidence of the fragmented nature of public administration in the United States. The concept of federalism, or the structure of politics in the United States, implies a system of authority apportioned constitutionally between the national and state governments.

Frederick S. Lane points out the three principal dimensions of federalism: *political, fiscal,* and *administrative.* The political dimension accounts for the ways in which local, state, and national jurisdictions participate in decision-making processes. The fiscal dimension indicates which jurisdictions pay what amount for services. The administrative dimension tells us which level will supervise the administration of various services. Lane concludes: "Federalism is a contradiction: it tries to marry diversity and central direction."[29]

According to the United States Bureau of the Census, federal, state and local governments number 87,900. They provide transportation, public safety, health care, education, public utilities, and an array of court systems. State and local governments employ about 7.5 million workers. Local governments—such as counties, cities, special districts, and towns—employ almost two-thirds of these workers. In many states, citizens are served by more than one local government unit.

There are 87,525 units of local government. Of these, 38,971 are general-purpose local governments.

- Counties (3,034) may contain cities or towns and often include unincorporated rural areas. There are 35,937 subcounty governments (townships and municipalities).
- Townships (16,504) often encompass suburban or rural areas and may or may not contain municipalities. Townships do not exist in some states. In 2002, township governments decreased by 696—or 4 percent since 1952.
- Municipalities (19,429) are self-governing bodies or any formally created subnational government. Municipalities enact ordinances or local laws. Municipal courts have exclusive jurisdiction over violations of municipal ordinances. In 2002, there were 2,624 more municipal governments than in 1952—a 16 percent increase.
- School districts (13,506) include elementary, middle, secondary, and postsecondary government institutions. Postsecondary special districts provide academic or technical courses or both in colleges, universities, professional schools, community or junior colleges, and technical institutes. The educational services industry also includes libraries, vocational schools, and specialized training institutes. Over the past half-century, the number of school districts has decreased by 80 percent—from 67,355 in 1952 to 13,522 in 2002.
- Special districts (35,052) are independent, limited-purpose governmental units (see table 2.2). They usually operate a single function or activity. Large percentages of special districts administer natural resource usage; examples include drainage, flood control, irrigation, soil, and water conservation

TABLE 2.2
Special District Governments by Function, 2002

Function	Number	Percent
Total	*35,356*	*100.0*
Single-Function Districts		
Total single-function districts	32,157	91.0
Natural resources	7,026	19.9
Fire protection	5,743	16.2
Water supply	3,423	9.7
Housing and community development	3,413	9.7
Sewage	2,020	5.7
Cemetaries	1,670	4.7
Libraries	1,582	4.5
Parks and recreation	1,314	3.7
Highways	767	2.2
Health	743	2.1
Hospitals	735	2.1
Education*	530	1.5
Airports	512	1.4
Utilities other than water supply**	485	1.4
Other	2,194	6.2
Multiple-Function Districts	*3,199*	*9.0*

*Primarily school building authorities.

**Includes electric power, gas supply, and public transit.

services. Special districts have increased by 265 percent—from 13,340 in 1952 to 35,356 in 2002.[30]

Demands for government services have multiplied with an expanding population. (The population of the United States in 1950 was 157,813,000. In 2000, the population had increased to 283,230,000.) The federal government has devolved or decentralized, turning many services over to state and local governments; devolution is the practice whereby the federal government delegates to state and local governments the development, implementation, and management of government programs. The practice of welfare reform illustrates federal government devolution. The 1996 Welfare Reform Act provided block grants that gave state governments the prerogative to devise programs that meet their needs. The nature of government services, as provided by state and local governments, will continue to change as relationships between federal, states, and local jurisdictions shift and the United States enters the political economy of the twenty-first century.

Comparing Public and Private Administration Nuances

Public and private administration differ in important ways. These differences can be compared in two areas: as they pertain to *substantive* and *procedural* issues.

Substantive issues of public and private administration include questions concerning politics versus profits, the measurement of objectives, and management versus administration. These are all areas of potential conflict.

Procedural issues address management as a universal process. Issues for procedural deliberation include open versus closed systems, methods of evaluation, criteria for decision making, personnel systems, planning and efficiency.[31]

Substantive issues refer to conceptual or abstract concerns such as goals, objectives, means, ends, values, results, and priorities. Nobel Prize-winning author Herbert Simon argues that the means and ends of public administration differ significantly from those of private administration.[32] He maintains that the importance of an end or value should not be ignored and that the process, or means, of management is a value in itself and cannot be separated from other values.

The purpose of a college education, for example, is to seek learning, training, and knowledge about the significant values of life. The *end* is learning, training, and knowledge. Education is the *substance* and the institution is the *procedure*. The institution provides the procedural means for attaining the specific substantive ends. The *means* are provided by the curricula of the respective disciplines. In other words, the *means* for achieving the learning, training, and knowledge you seek are to meet the requirements of your discipline's prescribed curricula by attending classes and successfully completing exams.

Justice and the implementation of justice can also illustrate *ends* and *means.* Justice, in the philosophical realm, is an *end* in itself, a commonly held value. Justice can only be found in the United States by a *means*—due process of law. Justice is an example of a substantive issue; the matters of the judicial process constitute processes, authorities, and institutions that enforce procedural concerns. By unpacking the distinctions between substantive and procedural issues in public administration, we can clarify the differences between administration in the private and the public sectors.

Substantive Issues

1. **Politics versus Profits**—Decision making in public bureaucracies is achieved by meeting the objectives of compromise, consensus, and democratic participation. These objectives are different from the private sector's emphasis on the concepts of efficiency, rationality, and profit. Although the goals of public administration and private administration both respond to outside clientele pressures, their concepts of bottom-line accountability differ: one's god is a consensus of citizens concerned about the issues confronting an entire community, and the other's god is profit.

2. **Measurement of Objectives**—The private sector ultimately makes rational decisions based upon clear, concise, and quantifiable statements found in the

sales ledger. The public sector deals with social intangibles such as health, welfare, and common defense.

3. **Management versus Administration**—In the private sector, the term "management" commonly refers to those persons in line *positions,* whereas in the public sector, the term "administration" refers to those in line *functions.* Line personnel command, have authority, and are generalists; staff personnel possess knowledge and skills, give advice, and are specialists. The term *management* is characterized by decision making in the private sector corporate model of hierarchy.

Procedural Issues

1. **Open versus Closed Systems**—Procedural concerns, such as accountability, reflect the *dilemma* of the open versus closed system, or the goldfish bowl of public administration versus the closed board room of private administration.

2. **Methods of Evaluation**—Community leaders seek consensus, agree to compromise, and advocate citizen participation to find support for policies. In contrast, efficiency, rationality, and concern for profit cause private sector entrepreneurs to view corporate evaluation differently. The public sector focuses on social good; the private sector emphasizes fiscal control. The two may, in some cases, be incompatible.

3. **Public versus Private Decision-Making Criteria**—Although the formal steps in decision making may be similar in both public and private administration, the criteria managers use to make decisions are not. The definition of the goal or problem, the desired consumer response, and the allocation of resources may apply similarly to both sectors: the logic, or mode of thinking, behind decision making differs.

    The public sector university's bookstore is, for example, under very different constraints from a privately run bookstore across the street. The public sector bookstore demands a higher standard in procedural process (the manner in which a function is carried out) and maintains certain expectations and guarantees in hiring, firing, promotions, and general conduct of bookstore business. The private sector bookstore can sell items based upon the supply and demand of the marketplace; the public sector bookstore must respond to every course, no matter how esoteric or obscure, and to every program offered by the state university.

4. **Personnel Systems**—Several differences exist in personnel systems. Unlike an applicant in the private sector, an applicant for a full-time civil service position governed by a merit system will go through a fixed process, monitored by law. Public sector employees also enjoy the privileges of administrative due process because laws prescribe guidelines for the recruitment, selection, promotion, and retention of employees. Merit plans that evaluate skills, knowledge, and expertise are a hiring tool, but they may differ greatly from agency to agency. Private enterprise employees have no guarantees of due process.

5. **Long-Term and Short-Term Planning**—Planning may be considered part of the process of decision making. The private sector manager does not need to seek consensus among employees before acting; the manager alone makes decisions, and the company's profit or loss ledger reflects success or failure.

For the public sector employee, planning becomes hazardous if leadership is continuously changing after elections.

Public officials need program continuity and political stability to carry out their responsibilities consistently. In the private sector, planning is easier because there are no automatic demands of due process or legally prescribed guarantees concerning hiring, firing, and promotion.

6. **Efficiency**—Hierarchical control, coordination, planning, meritorious performance, and lines of authority are emphasized in both the public and private sectors. However, the bottom line, or profit concern, of the private sector allows managers to realize success or failure immediately; in the public sector, with its less precise methods of evaluation, it may take longer to evaluate the efficiency and success of a public service.

Blurring or Bifurcation?

On the substantive issues we have discussed (politics versus profits, measurement of objectives, and management versus administration), a comparison of the public and private sectors reveals more blurring than bifurcation. A comparison of procedural issues (open versus closed systems, methods of evaluation, public versus private decision-making criteria, personnel systems, planning, and efficiency) reveals distinctions in regard to the accountability factor, but similarities in developing participative personnel systems to evaluate the expertise, knowledge, and skills of employees.

The public sector is grounded in *political equality* with consideration for everyone's opinion, seeking consensus, compromise, and democratic participation. The private sector is based upon *economic efficiency,* seeking definitive results, rationality in decision making, and the maximization of profit. In practice, the realities of political equality and economic efficiency blend into what many call the "American System." To a larger degree than most people realize, Alexander Hamilton's "American System" still plays a critical role in American economic development. The government uses investment and trade policies to promote American industry and create jobs. President Dwight D. Eisenhower's Interstate Highway System was a 1950s version of Hamilton's system of canals. Charlene Barshefsky, U.S. Trade Representative, followed Hamilton's lead when she signed agreements making certain U.S. companies were able to access world telecommunications markets. Profits for the rich may mean jobs for the rest of us. If so, perhaps special interests and national interests are joined.[33]

Public administration, then, differs in significant ways from private administration. These differences hinge largely on the greater legal accountability of the former and the greater flexibility of the latter. Determining which sector is the most efficient remains a complex question, subject not only to differences in products and procedures but also to differences in purposes and processes.

Interest Groups and the Greater Good

The corps of Washington lobbyists has grown steadily since the New Deal, but especially since the early 1970s. This growth parallels the growth in federal spending and the expansion of federal authority into new areas. Voters may appear to demand political reform, but government is unlikely to change except in composition.

The unwieldly size and contradictory complexity of modern governments has developed due to the cumulative inertia of entrenched lobbyists and special-interest groups. Reforms continue, but they come only gradually. Substantive change can come from the presidency or the electorate, but not unless individuals are willing to make personal sacrifices for widespread social welfare.[34]

Lobbyists compete vigorously to safeguard traditional spending in their areas of interest. Industries, labor unions, ethnic groups, religious groups, professional organizations, citizen groups, and even foreign business interests all periodically—and some continuously—seek to exert pressure on national and state legislatures to attain legislative goals. *Pressure by interest groups usually has a selfish aim: Their members wish to assert rights, win privileges, or benefit financially.* A group's power to influence legislation is often based less on its arguments than on the size of its membership, its financial resources, and the astuteness of its lobbyists. If there were any doubt about the increasing presence of special interests in American politics, within the Capital Beltway—the interstate highway that circles Washington, D.C.—there are 2,200 trade groups that employ more Washingtonians than any other organization except government or travel and tourism.

Expert articulation of particular citizen interests drives public bureaucracies in the United States. Legislatures write vague laws. Public administrators interpret those statutes with specificity in the *Federal Register.* The statutes are then codified in the *Code of Federal Regulations.* The public philosophy of the United States in the twenty-first century is no longer capitalism, but instead *interest group liberalism,* a concept developed by Theodore J. Lowi. Lowi claims that capitalism has declined as an ideology and is dead as a public philosophy. Capitalism, the old public philosophy, has become outmoded since World War II because the elite, such as lobbyists, no longer agree on whether government should play a role in making policies for private citizens or for private sector businesses. Republicans and Democrats, as participants in interest group liberalism, fully agree that government should be a player in monitoring, if not directing, the relations among private citizens.[35] Interest groups reflect partisan bearings. Labor unions lean toward Democratic Party candidates, while many, but not all, business groups flock toward Republicans.

As the Great Depression ended and World War II began, U.S. capitalism came to be called "conservatism," but Lowi argues that this description is a misnomer. He states that capitalism never became conservative, but declined because it became irrelevant and erroneous. Capitalist ideology, according to Lowi, did not endure as the public philosophy because it could accept only one legitimate type of modern social control—competition. Lowi concludes that the old dialogue between liberalism and conservatism "passed into the graveyard of consensus," spelling the "decline of meaningful adversary political proceedings in favor of administrative, technical and logrolling politics. In a nutshell, politics became a question of equity rather than a question of morality. Adjustment comes first, rules of law come last, if at all."[36] As interest groups clash, the priority becomes equal opportunity for any group to put forth its unique version of how life should be conducted. The values of any particular organization are secondary.

In interest group liberalism, diverse groups check the values, or perspectives, of opposing interests by arguing for their own set of values in the great American marketplace of ideas. Milk producers, tobacco growers, billboard advertisers, movie makers, bankers, physicians, broadcasters, cable TV operators, farmers, entrepreneurs, and energy interests are represented by a few of the more than two thousand lobbyists who insist that their concerns should be written into law. Whether liberal or conservative, the elite want to use the power and funding of government for their personal ends.

According to Lowi, the most significant difference between liberals and conservatives, Democrats and Republicans, can be found in the interest groups with which they identify. The values of organized interest groups guide Congress members in casting their votes, presidents in shaping their programs, and bureaucrats in exercising their administrative discretion. The only necessary guidelines for framing laws depend upon the validity or legitimacy of interest group demands.[37]

The philosophy of interest group liberalism is pragmatic, with government playing the role of broker, and is optimistic about government's role; that which is good for government is also good for society. The liberal process of private interaction with public officials is accessible to all organized interests and offers no value judgments concerning any particular claim or set of claims. Interest group liberalism defines the public interest as the amalgamation of claims of various interests. The principle of representation extends into public bureaucracy as administrators provide due process and a voice to all citizens.

To represent such diverse political, economic, and cultural interests, legislatures make open-ended, vague laws and issue broad delegations to public administrators to regulate interests in society. Says Lowi: "It (interest group liberalism) impairs legitimacy by converting government from a moralistic to a mechanistic institution. It impairs the potential of positive law to correct itself by allowing the law to become anything that eventually bargains itself out as acceptable to the bargainer. . . . Interest group liberalism seeks pluralistic government in which there is no formal specification of means or of ends. In a pluralistic government there is, therefore, no substance. Neither is there procedure. There is only process."[38] In other words, procedures and processes become vital, and substance and values are at the mercy of the strongest interests.

In recent years, private interests have contributed ever increasing amounts of money to participants fighting to either the status quo of the political system or to change it, subsequently purchasing privilege, power, and profit. It would not be an exaggeration to assert that the American government—president, executive branch, and Congress—has been bought and sold. The Madisonian faction is firmly in the saddle and rides the nation.[39]

Quid pro quo (one thing in return for another) is a pragmatic approach to America's version of democratic capitalism. Access to capital dominates democracy. Do rich people and interest groups give large sums of money to politicians to promote good and just causes? Lee Hamilton, a Congressman from Indiana for more than a generation, reveals that "money, money, money, and the money chase" dominates political talk on Capitol Hill. As columnist Robert Higgs states, "the root of the problem lies not in the takers, who will always find a way to take, but in the givers. Foxes do not voluntarily evacuate the henhouse," Higgs speculates. "The hydra-headed government now dominating this country is inherently corrupt."[40]

In an era when politics seems, increasingly, to be the pursuit of self-interest under the banner of some high-sounding principle, one can be excused for doubting whether the opponents of campaign finance reform are really so passionately devoted to the protection of the First Amendment. Nonetheless, the free speech argument is important enough to address on its merits.[41]

Washington's Power 25

Pressure groups manipulate the laws by which we live. A generation ago, lobbyists were portrayed as fat, cigar-smoking men who lined the pockets of lawmakers with $100 bills. This stereotypical description no longer applies, but the connotation of corruption persists. Rallying constituents through "grass roots" telemarketing has become as suspect as the old images of back-room bribery. The onslaught of a thousand identical post cards is discounted as a lobbying trick, and a hundred calls originating from a telephone bank arriving in the office on the same day are recognized for what they are. The new lobbying is much more subtle.

Researchers, rather than high-priced lobbyists, now inhabit the offices of Washington's most powerful interest groups. The clout of these groups depends on the sincerity of support they receive from actual voters back home. The ability to "buy" politicians or manipulate a groundswell of last-minute phone calls has less relevance than it used to. The "iceberg" principle of legislative success posits that the powerhouses of interest group persuasion are not very visible at the Washington "waterline" of influence. But these interest "icebergs" are very big and very menacing, and they "run" in deep political waters.

FORTUNE Magazine surveys political clout in the nation's capital. According to *FORTUNE,* Washington's Power 25 is "an authoritative, impartial, empirical survey of the trade associations, labor unions, and other pressure groups that wield the greatest influence on the nation's legislative system." Polltakers Mark Mellman and Bill McInturff asked nearly 2,200 Washington insiders to rank the most powerful lobbying groups. These insiders included members of Congress, their staffs, and senior White House officials.

The Power 25 is a highly eclectic collection of political pressure group players (see table 2.3). The Mellman and McInturff survey rebuts the premise that campaign contributions buy power in Washington. Just three of the top ten organizations—the Association of Trial Lawyers of America, the American Israel Public Affairs Committee, and the American Medical Association—owe their high rankings to their substantial campaign contributions.

According to *FORTUNE* reporter Jeffrey H. Birnbaum, interest groups are valued more for the votes they can deliver on behalf of certain candidates than for direct monetary contributions. Memberships of most of the Power 25 are geographically dispersed and politically active, and members focus their activities on a narrow range of issues. They are true believers in the organization's cause, and they turn out in droves on election day. The low voter turnout of recent years means that committed voters may spell the difference between victory and defeat for partisans. And reelection is high on the priority agenda of partisans.

TABLE 2.3
The Power 25: Top Lobbying Groups

After winning the presidency in 2000, the Grand Old Party undoubtedly developed a new Washington establishment under George W. Bush. The Power 25 survey—*FORTUNE* magazine's list of Washington's most powerful lobbying groups—reflects the change. For the first time in four years, the Power 25 has a new number 1: the heavily Republican National Rifle Association.

Rank	Association	Previous Rank
1	National Rifle Association of America	2
2	AARP	1
3	National Federation of Independent Business	2
4	American Israel Public Affairs Committee	4
5	Association of Trial Lawyers of America	6
6	AFL-CIO	5
7	Chamber of Commerce of the United States of America	7
8	National Beer Wholesalers Association	19
9	National Association of Realtors	15
10	National Association of Manufacturers	14
11	National Association of Home Builders of the United States	16
12	American Medical Association	13
13	American Hospital Association	31
14	National Education Association of the United States	9
15	American Farm Bureau Federation	21
16	Motion Picture Association of America	17
17	National Association of Broadcasters	20
18	National Right to Life Committee	8
19	Health Insurance Association of America	25
20	National Restaurant Association	10
21	National Governors' Association	12
22	Recording Industry Association of America	40
23	American Bankers Association	11
24	Pharmaceutical Research & Manufacturers of America	28
25	International Brotherhood of Teamsters	23

Source: "The Washington's Power 25" by Jeffery H. Birnbaum, *Fortune,* May 28, 2001. Reprinted by permission of *Fortune.*

Fully half of the top ten organizations polled by the *FORTUNE* polltakers base their politics in long-established grassroots networks. Members of the American Association of Retired Persons (AARP), National Federation of Independent Business (a small-business lobby), National Rifle Association (NRA), Christian Coalition, National Right to Life Committee, and AFL-CIO are known to dominate town hall meetings.

"Populism is not the same as liberalism," emphasizes Birnbaum. "The survey shows how narrowly the political spectrum is concentrated at the moderate center and right. Only four of the Power 25 are labor unions. What's more, ideologically conservative interest groups outrank their left-leaning counterparts."[42] For example, the pro-gun NRA is ranked number 1, while Handgun Control, Inc. has a power index of 68. The National Right to Life Committee is ranked at 18, whereas the pro-choice National Abortion and Reproductive Rights Action League (NARAL) lands at 43. The environmental lobby, the Sierra Club, is number 37. Other environmental interest groups are ranked even lower. "Good government" groups post similarly low power rankings.

The low rankings of liberal interest groups call into question ***who*** lobbies best and ***what*** works most effectively. Birnbaum lists some perhaps obvious conclusions about who and what works best. They include:

- lobbyists with access in Washington
- grassroots lobbyists at home
- publicists for free media
- advertisers for paid commercials
- scholars that shape arguments

"No one disputes that money buys influence in Washington," Birnbaum points out. "The only question is what kind of spending buys the most."[43] Another *FORTUNE* survey points out the importance of lobbying expenditures—the oldest, most straightforward, nonglamourous, and inoffensive type of influence peddling. The more money a group allocated to traditional lobbying efforts in Washington, the more influence the group exercised. "We couldn't find any direct relationship between campaign donations and clout," concludes Mellman. "The only place we could find a modest correlation with influence was in spending on lobbying."[44]

Summary

- Ecology is the relationship between private economic developments, or the marketplace, and the state's responsibility for monitoring, supervising, and regulating personal freedoms and commercial activities. Government employees do not operate in a vacuum, but in a complex environment.
- Modern America is the epitome of the organized society. The organized society exists in an environment of equal rights and unequal outcomes. Conflicts result between the political principles of democracy and the economic principles of capitalism.

- Students learn to think by a combination of conceptual and analytical thought and deductive and inductive reasoning.
- Congestion is the toughest challenge in the nation's transportation ecology.
- The craft of public administration is changing as the economy shifts from manufacturing towards services—in both outputs and employment.
- The political economy of the United States is one of democratic capitalism. The thrust of this ideology comes from the opposing values of political power and economic structure.

- Democracy is characterized by equality, due process, fairness, participation, suffrage, and electoral politics. Capitalism rests on efficiency, productivity, hierarchy, competition, and entrepreneurship.
- Rights are acquired and exercised without any monetary charge. Rights cannot be bought or sold in the marketplace, but they may infringe on economic efficiency.
- Public administration finds its origins in democracy but owes much to the fundamental principles of capitalism.
- The "body politic" of the United States is more pragmatic than ideological.
- Woodrow Wilson, Franklin D. Roosevelt, and Lyndon B. Johnson shared the theses that free market economy could not function properly in the absence of rules, workers' rights, government spending on public goods, and continuing public investments to enhance the skills and opportunities of the workforce.
- The ebb and flow of government expansion and constraints may be understood by examining four critical periods in the twentieth century: the eras around 1915, 1935, 1965, and 1985.
- In 1992, for the first time in American history, federal, state, and local service jobs outnumbered manufacturing jobs.
- Federal, state, and local governments now number 87,900, with 87,849 of them local. Within this allocation, counties number 3,034, townships 16,506, municipalities 19,431, school districts 13,522, and special districts 35,356.
- Demands for government services have multiplied with an expanding population. In 2000, the United States population was 283,230,000.
- The dimensions of U.S. federalism are political, fiscal, and administrative.
- As demands for government services multiply with an expanding population, the federal government has devolved, or turned over many services to state and local governments.
- Americans opt for market justice over political justice. Benefits are allocated by the economic marketplace—not by government programs and policies.
- The U.S. cultural emphasis is on individualism—not political participation. Citizens separate their personal lives and interests from matters of national life. America is a country of individualism par excellence.
- Substantive issues of public and private administration raise questions concerning politics versus profits, measurement of objectives, and management versus administration. Procedural issues concern open versus closed systems, methods of evaluation, decision-making criteria, personnel systems, planning, and efficiency.
- Pressure groups manipulate the laws by which we live. The clout each of these groups yields depends on the sincerity and depth of support from actual voters back home.
- Quid pro quo (one thing in return for another) is the pragmatic approach that defines America's version of democratic capitalism. Access to capital dominates democracy.
- The public philosophy of the United States is interest group liberalism. Whether liberal or conservative, elites utilize the power and purse of government for personal ends.
- The philosophy of interest group liberalism is pragmatic—with government exercising its role as broker. In a pluralistic government, procedure and process may be as importance as substance.
- The effectiveness of interest groups among elected officials, consumers, and government bureaucrats depends, in large part, upon the group's number of members, the size of its budget, and the expertise of its staff in Washington and/or any one of fifty state capitals.

Now that we have explored the ecology of the craft of public administration, we are ready to move to another important subject that public administrators must be aware of—the anatomy, or structure, of government organizations.

Case Study

Public Impacts of Private Interests

The following case study illustrates the public impacts of private interests. It portrays how state and local government priorities are misdirected in favor of welfare for the rich. The ecology is evident in the minds of many. In this scenario, the rich get richer at the expense of the middle and lower classes.

> It comes to why the ballparks matter to us—because exactly comparable people played a comparable game in this ballpark for generation after generation.
>
> —*George Will*
> The Washington Post

> What is more Boston than Fenway Park?
>
> —*Peter Gammons*
> *Boston native and ESPN-TV commentator*

Almost a hundred years ago, when distinctions between the public and private sectors in the United States were far less complex, a baseball park was built in Boston. On April 20, 1912, Fenway Park officially opened for professional competition.[1]

After two rainouts, the Red Sox defeated the New York Highlanders (now parading around as the New York Yankees) 7–6 in 11 innings in the first professional baseball game played at Fenway Park. Baseball was pastoral in its origins, but the sport was an urban game.

Woodrow Wilson had not yet been elected by the smallest of margins over Bob Taft and Teddy Roosevelt. The Progressive Era had not yet begun. The Federal Trade Commission was not around to monitor unsavory business practices. Children were exploited in the labor force. World War I was yet to be played out on the hillsides of Europe, the federal income tax did not exist, and the Federal Reserve Board had not been created to regulate the American monetary system.

Except for Fenway and Wrigley Field in Chicago, the old parks of the golden age of American baseball are gone—victims of people's discomfort and inconvenience, their own obsolescence, and wrecking balls. They include Ebbets Field, Brooklyn; Polo Grounds, Manhattan; Braves Field, Boston; old Comiskey Park, Chicago; Sportsman Park, St. Louis; Briggs Stadium, Detroit; Forbes Field, Pittsburgh; Crosley Field, Cincinatti; Shibe Park, Philadelphia; and Griffith Stadium, Washington.

The interiors of these fields of dreams were covered with advertising. No provisions were made for sanitation, the handicapped, or overcrowded seatings. Nothing was standardized. Conformity was not a concern.

Students do not have to be baseball fans to realize that this industry is permitted to operate as an economic cartel—better known as a monopoly. Organized baseball is an association of industrialists—and the industry is professional baseball.[2]

Major League Baseball (MLB) enjoys a complete monopoly of the sport. Franchise owners threaten to relocate their teams unless they receive large tax subsidies and related perks from their home cities. Institutional, ideological, and political factors prevent the repeal of baseball's antitrust exemption.

Next to the old North Church, Bunker Hill Monument, the U.S.S. Constitution, and Freedom Trail, the Red Sox—a baseball team that has not won a World Series since the year World War I ended, 1918—confuse public and private concerns about as much as any culture permits. The Red Sox are Boston's "800-pound gorilla." The Boston American League baseball club does—and gets—what it wants.[3]

The Red Sox are a beloved New England institution. But the team is part of a larger legalized, formalized, routinized, controlled, wealthy monopoly of American professional baseball teams Major league baseball commissioner Bud Selig, also owner of the Milwaukee Brewers, strongly supported efforts to secure public monies for the private interests of Boston's American League baseball club.

Welfare for the Rich?

Red Sox management lobbied state and local government officials to soak the Boston and Massachusetts taxpayers to the tune of $352 million for a new ballpark. The team's plan relied heavily on ticket surcharges and game-day parking fees to repay the city's investment in the project. The team was to cover any cost overruns on the purchase of adjacent properties and pay for the cleanup for the $665 million project.[4]

But the power in Boston and Massachusetts is dispersed. The governor, mayor, state senate president, and state house speaker supported the appropriation of 352 million taxpayer dollars to destroy the old park—and building a new stadium next door. The new stadium project needed the approval of the Boston City Council. The land would not come cheaply.[5]

The city was required to exercise eminent domain for compensating land owners adjacent to the 1912 structure. Not only did Boston's public sector elites lobby for large taxpayer spending for a new stadium, but the city's private sector elites called for "welfare spending" for the community's 800-pound gorilla—amounting to public welfare for the very rich. Prominent leaders from the Boston business community played behind-the-scenes roles in efforts to craft spending compromises.

Proponents for new sports facilities argue that infrastructure spending improves local economies in a number of respects:

- Building the new arena or stadium creates construction jobs.
- Fans and team employees generate new spending in the community—expanding local employment.
- The team brings in tourists and company personnel to the host city—also enhancing local spending and employment.
- A "multiplier effect" operates to increase local income—causing still more new spending and job creation.[6]

"Economic growth takes place when a community's resources—people, capital investments, and natural resources like land—become more productive," write Roger G. Noll and Andrew Zimbalist.[7] Most spending emerging from new stadium construction is a substitute for other local recreational spending, for example, at movie theaters and restaurants. Stadium construction is a consumption expense rather than an investment that produces more long-term jobs and local businesses.

Professional sports are popular with the American public. New stadium technology intensifies the tendency of sports teams to seek new homes. Approximately 115 professional teams aspire to move into new arenas or stadiums. The construction boom for housing these teams is heavily subsidized by federal and local taxpayers, and the tax bills will not stop until all payments are made. Taxpayer subsidies to pro sports are difficult to curb because the pro teams are so popular.[8]

Red Sox ownership wanted to demolish Fenway and replace it with a $665 million replica across Yawkey Way. The new place would include ten thousand more seats, more luxury boxes, more concessions, more merchandise-sales areas, in-stadium team offices, better clubhouse facilities, and a parking garage—all of the amenities found at modern-day ballparks.[9]

Enter Dan Wilson and Save Fenway Park (SFP)—an interest group with approximately 500 contributors. SFP, as a community, citizen-based group, sought a compromise that would meet the needs of the team, fans, and taxpayers. The interest group posed a question both pragmatic and sentimental: Why not just renovate Fenway Park?[10]

Age may be on the side of the old ballpark. Fenway is a national treasure; it is a historic landmark, the oldest baseball park in the major leagues. The park preceded Babe Ruth. Ted Williams swung his bat in the batter's box. Carlton Fisk homered off the foul pole. Bucky Dent homered over the Wall. This baseball diamond is a living baseball museum and the number one tourist attraction in Massachusetts.

The Boston Globe commissioned a public opinion poll to gauge how citizens felt about investing their tax dollars into a private venture. Only 34 percent of those polled supported the ballclub's financing plan—despite the team's promise to repay the public's $352 million investment. "The bottom line is Bostonians don't want public money used for this project," concluded Gerry Chervinsky, the CEO who conducted the survey.[11]

The SFP organization and Fenway Community Development Corporation (CDC) released a detailed plan to renovate the park as an alternative to the club's desire to build a new, nearly $1 billion stadium. The SFP renovation plan proposed building three decks, replacing nearly all the seating, and constructing parking garages and other related facilities on adjacent lots. The plan would preserve the Green Monster (the left-field wall) and the brick facade of the 1912 structure along Yawkey Way.

"This process has demonstrated that a public planning process can lead to something that satisfies everyone's needs," stated Fenway CDC president Lisa Soli. "It's in stark contrast to the backroom deals that surrounded the Red Sox plan." Boston is the cradle of American democracy. But Boston politics feature concentrations of political power and rigid economic structures. Fighting both city hall and the city's 800-pound

Red Sox Attendance by Decade

Decade	Total Attendance for Decade (in millions)	Average Annual Attendance
1912–19	3.6	450,823
1920–29	3.3	326,899
1930–39	4.8	482,117
1940–49	9.6	963,382
1950–59	11.3	1,131,197
1960–69	11.5	1,150,469
1970–79	18.2	1,815,588
1980–89	19.6	1,955,117
1990–99	23.3	2,325,372
2000–2002	2.6	2,620,740

Source: From www.espn.com website. Courtesy ESPN.com.

gorilla is difficult! SFP and CDC have proven that participatory politics takes energy, commitment, time, and windows of opportunity. The SFP-CDC plan received favorable reviews from city council members and community groups.[12]

The Red Sox drew 2,650,862 fans in 2002, the best year in club history. The team is a very good market draw despite having the highest average ticket prices in all of major league baseball, a team that failed to make the playoffs, and the smallest ballpark in the major leagues—just 33,871 seats. The small park is regularly sold out, even though every home game is televised throughout New England. During the 2002 season, Red Sox fans filled Fenway Park to 97.4 percent capacity. In baseball's smallest arena, the Red Sox were 11th in total MLB attendance—averaging 32,726 fans.

What perspectives can this Fenway Park case offer students of public administration?

A review of history helps place current dilemmas into an expanded understanding. Baseball still is America's first sport, its national pastime. For many, after a day at the office, toiling for the boss and the all-American dollar, family and baseball come next.[13] The season is a daily process extending from February to almost November. Baseball is a democratic game, as even smaller athletes can play second base. The game has been exported to Cuba, the Carribean, and Asia.

The golden era of baseball was a product of the Progressive Era, when President Wilson traveled through Europe trying to make "the world safe for democracy."

Fenway Park opened the same day the Titanic sank, when a ship's safety in a sea full of icebergs depended mostly on the captain's experience—not on technology. Television and the internet were not yet around to blend notions of public and private.

Baseball and Ecology

How does the industry of organized baseball relate to its environment? Baseball and the ecology of American society share many common features. Equality is promoted if one can swing a bat and pitch a ball. Efficiency is ingrained in the baseball fabric, too: If you can really swing a bat and throw a ball with speed, a market may exist for your skills. At this juncture, supply and demand enter the picture. Professional baseball players average $2 million each season. Civil services may get a piece of this economic windfall as federal, state, and local governments tax baseball's titanic-like salaries.

The decision to tear down Fenway Park or—to renovate it—points out public and private differences. In terms of politics versus profits, the governor, mayor, state legislature, and city council must balance economic interests with their own political goals. The baseball team, as a private sector endeavor, is mostly focused on the bottom line—profits. How do Boston citizens measure team versus city objectives? Is the trade-off World Series wins versus good garbage pickups? Citizens may hear different points of view from "Red Sox management" and the "city administration."

When taxpayer dollars are spent, decision-making procedures must be open to everyone. "Last time I checked, this was a democracy," stated Rob Sargent of the Massachusetts Public Research Interest Group. "This is precisely the kind of thing that should be debated in public."[14] The Red Sox management, state and city administrations, well-connected media from *The Boston Globe* and *The Boston Herald,* corporate executives, and big labor engaged in convoluted attempts to secure $352 million to permit Boston's 800-pound gorilla to sit where it wanted. In the minds of many, subsidizing the Sox meant the "rich getting richer" at the expense of the middle class.

Boston is historic, wealthy, Irish, European, and sometimes sophisticated. The town's major industry is higher education. The state of Massachusetts is frequently referred to as "Taxsachusetts." State and local governments prosper in these environs. As Tip O'Neill, late Speaker of the United States House of Representatives, famously pointed out, "All politics are local."

The Green Monster is part of a private domain—but also part of a very public park. The Big Dig is a $14-billion-dollar public-sector effort to bury Boston's expressways underground and make the city "richer in green"—not only in commerce and in federal dollars, but in trees, parks, and clean air. The people of Massachusetts are pragmatic, seeking compromises between the extremes of equality and market forces. Pragmatic Bostonians insist that the market needs a place, but also needs to be kept in its place.

The law of supply and demand is short-term, and sports is show business. The secret of Fenway's appeal may be based on the ecology of this confined field of dreams. If Fenway's 33,871 seats were not so scarce, perhaps not so many folks would make the effort to fill them. The long queues along Yawkey Way to buy tickets at $60 each are egalitarian: The line forms at the rear—regardless of one's race, sex, color, or creed.

Some things do not change. Teddy Roosevelt was the original Progressive thinker and actor. Industries—and markets—come and go. New concentrations of skills, expertise, and wealth emerge. A better method of community decision making in response to MLB's economic power might be to invoke antitrust laws to break up the cartel—forcing the American and National leagues to compete against each other.

Professional baseball salaries and school teachers' salaries are not even in similar ballparks. However, the prospects for reducing taxpayer subsidies to sports teams are not good. Karl Marx was wrong. Religion is not the opiate of the people; baseball is.

Principle and Principal Coincide?

The new Red Sox management determined that the old baseball park, after all, had both principle, or moral worth, and principal, or monetary value. Engineering designs to rebuild the 1912 structure deemed not feasible by the former owners are now more than probable. The near century old park's capacity would be increased to almost 44,000. Renovations will be accomplished over a three-year span. Two new decks will be added.[15]

The principle of this case study is that the Boston baseball club is saving a sporting shrine of historical value. The new Red Sox management estimates the cost of building a new stadium at approximately $300 million. A rough estimate of renovation costs is about 60 percent of that amount. The principal is the money the Red Sox and Massachusetts save by keeping Fenway adjacent to the Fens. Scarce taxpayer dollars may be directed to pay for public projects more directly benefitting citizens and the common good.

Questions and Instructions

1. How might deductive and inductive thinking affect citizen decision making for and against industry monopolies?
2. "Rights are acquired and exercised without any monetary charge." What does this statement mean?
3. Explain the term *political principles of democracy* and *economic principles of capitalism* as they relate to the choices citizens confront in society.
4. In what circumstances should government employees apply principles of equality and efficiency?
5. "America is the country of individualism par excellence." What does this statement mean?
6. Public- and private-sector prerogatives differ on substantive and procedural issues. Explain why this is so.
7. In interest group liberalism, diverse groups check the values, or perspectives, of opposing interests by arguing for their own set of values in the marketplace of ideas. Explain and illustrate.
8. Is Major League Baseball a monopoly? If so, why? Explain and illustrate.
9. Baseball is pastoral in its origins, but the sport matured as an urban game. How did the ecology of the times affect baseball and the larger American culture? Explain with specific examples.
10. "Karl Marx was wrong: Religion is not the opiate of the people, baseball is." Explain this statement.

Insights-Issues/Public Impacts of Private Interests

Clearly and briefly describe and illustrate the following concepts and issues. Interpret the word *role* in terms of impacts, applications, importance, effects, and/or illustrations of certain facts, concerns, or issues from the case study.

1. Roles of equality and efficiency in making short- and long-term decisions for or against a new baseball park.
2. Roles of rights and dollars in affording all citizens procedural guarantees in regard to the effects of new construction plans.

3. Role of progressive thinking for opposing, reforming, or accepting baseball industry monopolies.
4. Role of substantive and procedural issues for determining public-private decision-making alternatives if historic Fenway Park should be taken down.
5. Role of special interest groups for promoting—and questioning—construction of a new baseball stadium in Boston.

Case Endnotes

1. Robert F. Bluthardt, "Fenway Park and the Golden Age of the Baseball Park, 1909–1915," *Journal of Popular Culture,* Vol. 21, No. 1 (Summer 1987), 43–51.
2. Jerold J. Duquette, *Regulating the National Pastime: Baseball and Antitrust* (Westport, CT: Prager Publishers, 1999); see also John Rouse, "Corporate Welfare, Taxpayer Subsidies, and Home Field Advantages, *Public Administration Review,* Vol. 61, No. 5 (September/October 2001), 630–635;
3. Tom Farrey, "Historic Fenway Faces Uncertain Future," November 8, 2000. http://espn.go.com/mlb/s/2000/1031/849361.html.
4. Meg Vaillancourt, "Lawmakers, Red Sox reach tentative agreement," *The Boston Globe,* July 26, 2000.
5. Kathleen O'Toole, "Luxury stadiums point up problems with pro sports monopolies, economist says," *Stanford [Online] Report.* http://www.stanford.edu/dept/news/report/news/january7/stadiums.html;
6. Roger G. Noll and Andrew Zimbalist, "Sports, Jobs, & Taxes," *The Brookings Review,* Vol. 15, No. 3 (Summer 1997), 35–39. http://www.brook.edu/pub/review/summer97/noll.htm.
7. *Ibid.*
8. Michael Gee, "Baseball's fields of bad dreams: New stadiums not a big draw, *The Boston Herald,* May 7, 2001; O'Toole, *op.cit.*
9. Darren Rovell, "Fenway: Classic or Clunker? Part II," *ESPN.com,* November 3, 2000. http://espn.go.com/mlb/s/2000/1103/854882.html.

10. Kimberly Anne Konrad, "Fenway Park's Green Monster," *CRM Online,* Vol. 23, No. 10 (2000), pp. 13–15; CRM:Cultural Resource Management. http://crm.cr.nps.gov/issue.cfm?volume=23&Number=10.
11. Meg Vaillancourt, "Red Sox Plan Loses in City Poll; Public Funding for a New Ballpark Strikes Out," *The Boston Globe,* July 10, 2000, p. A01. http://www.boston.com/dailyglobe2/192/metro/Red_Sox_plan_loses_in_city_poll%2b.shtm. See also Rouse, "SOX PLAN STRIKES OUT . . . Ten reasons/arguments for saving Fenway Park," *The Boston Phoenix,* April 6–13, 2000. http://www.bostonphoenix.com/archive/features/LETTERS.htm.
12. Meg Vaillancourt, "Opponents Offer Alternative Fenway Plans," *The Boston Globe,* August 23, 2000. http://www.boston.com/news/packages/fenway/0813_alternative.htm.
13. See Rouse, "Fenway and Family Values," *The Harvard Crimson,* April 20, 2000. http://www.thecrimson.com/opinion.
14. Steve LeBlac, "Ballpark Opponents Critical of Closed-Door Meeting," *The Associated Press,* May 9, 2000.
15. Gorden Edes, "Red Sox Explore Adding 10,000 Seats to Fenway," *The Boston Globe,* October 11, 2002, p. A1.

Case Sources

Jim Caple, http://espn.go.com/mlb/columns/caple_jim/865956.html; Peter Gammons, http://espn.go.com/gammons/s/fenway_plan.html; Seth Gitell, "Talking Politics:Fenway Follies," *The Boston Phoenix,* June 14–22, 2000. http://www.bostonphoenix.com; Vaillancourt, "Red Sox Adviser Shifts on Rebuilding Fenway," *The Boston Globe,* September 25, 2001; Scott Van Voorhis, "Polls Blast Sox Renovation Flip," *The Boston Herald,* September 27, 2001;

"Welfare for the Wealthy: The Fight to Save Fenway Park, *Designer/Builder: A Journal of the Human Environment* (November 1999), copyright McGraw-Hill Companies, 2002.

Chapter Endnotes

1. Emmette S. Redford, *Democracy in the Administrative State* (New York: Oxford University Press, 1969), p. 3.

2. Arthur M. Okun, *Equality and Efficiency: The Big Tradeoff* (Washington, D.C.: The Brookings Institution, 1975), p. 4.

3. Suzanne Garment, "Making A Case for Regulation," *The Washington Post,* February 2, 1997, p. A8.

4. Henry T. Abraham, *Freedom and the Court: Civil Rights and Liberties in the United States* (New York: Oxford University Press, 1977), pp. 110–129.

5. Okun, *Equality and Efficiency,* p. 119.

6. Ralph D. Christy, "Markets or Government? Balancing Imperfect and Complementary Alernatives," *American Journal of Agricultural Economics* 78, no. 5 (December 1996): 1145–1157.

7. *Ibid.*

8. Lester M. Salamon and John J. Siegfried, "Economic Power and Political Influence: The Impact of Industry Structure on Public Policy," *American Political Science Review* 71, no. 4 (December 1977): 1026–1043.

9. Adam Przeworski and Michael Wallerstein, "Democratic Capitalism at the Crossroads," *Democracy* 2, no. 3 (July 1982): 52–68.

10. John Pollacco, "Old Economy vs. New Economy," *Business Times,* January 31– February 6, 2001, http://www. businesstimes.com.mt/2001/01/31/focus.html.

11. Robert E. Lane, "Market Justice, Political Justice," *American Political Science Review* 80, no. 2 (June 1986), 383–402. See also Jennifer Nedelsky, *Private Property and the Limits of American Constitutionalism* (New York: Oxford University Press, 1990).

12. Harry Holloway with John George, *Public Opinion,* 2d ed. (New York: St. Martin's Press, 1986), p. 157.

13. William Watts and Lloyd A. Free, eds., *The State of the Nation* (New York: University Books, Potomac Associates, 1967), p. 97.

14. John D. Hicks, George E. Mowry, and Robert E. Burke, *A History of American Democracy* (Boston: Houghton Mifflin Co., 1966), pp. 552–558; and Henry Bamford Parkes, *The United States of America: A History* (New York: Alfred A. Knopf, 1968), pp. 560–564.

15. Larry D. Gerber, "World War II and the Expansion of Government in America," *National Forum* 75, no. 4 (Fall 1995): 30–34.

16. Robert J. Samuelson, "Roosevelt Romanticized: FDR Made the Modern Presidency—Dooming His Successors to Failure and Unpopularity" *Newsweek* 28, no. 17 (October 21, 1996): 52.

17. Hicks, Mowry, and Burke, *A History of American Democracy,* pp. 670–691; and Parkes, *The United States of America,* pp. 628–645.

18. Stephen Gettinger, "Fulfilling the Great Society," *Congressional Quarterly Weekly Report* 53, no. 23 (10 June 1995): 1615–1618.

19. See Doris Kerns, *Lyndon Johnson and the American Dream* (New York: Harper & Row, 1976), pp. 210–250; Lyndon Baines Johnson, *The Vantage Point: Perspective of the Presidency, 1963–1969* (New York: Holt, Rinehart, and Winston, 1971); John E. Schwarz, *America's Hidden Success: A Reassessment of Public Policy from Kennedy to Reagan* (New York: W.W. Norton & Co., 1988).

20. Larry Berman and Bruce Allen Murphy, *Approaching Democracy* (Upper Saddle River, N.J.: Prentice Hall, 1996), p. 125.

21. Jonathan Rauch, "What Revolution?," *National Journal,* (January 21, 1989): 158. See also John L. Palmer and Isabel V. Sawhill, eds., *The Reagan Record* (Washington, D.C.: The Ballinger Press, 1984); "The Reagan Record," *The Urban Institute Policy and Research Report* 14, no. 1 (August 1984): 1–17; "Perspectives on the Reagan Years: Popular vs. Political Leadership," 17, no. 1 (April 1987): 1–3.

22. All from, "Budget Deal Is the New Deal for Democrats," *Los Angeles Times,* 12 May 1997, p. B5.

23. Robert Eden, "The Rhetorical Presidency and the Eclipse of Executive Power: Woodrow Wilson's 'Constitutional Government in the United States,' " *Polity* 28, no. 3 (Spring 1996): 357–379.

24. E. J. Dionne Jr. "The Era of 'Big' Government: Why You'd Miss It if It Went," *Kettering Review* (Summer 1997): 32–39.

25. *Ibid.,* 36.

26. Larry Berman and Bruce Allen Murphy, *Approaching Democracy* (Upper Saddle River, N.J.: Prentice Hall, 1996), p. 128.

27. William Schneider, "What Democrats Have Learned," *National Journal,* 30, no. 13 (28 March 1998): 726.

28. Leon E. Panetta, "The True Balance of Power," *The New York Times,* February 2, 1997, vol. 146, no. 50691, p. 15.

29. Frederick S. Lane, *Current Issues in Public Administration* (New York: St. Martin's Press, 1982), p. 156.

30. U.S. Census Bureau, Federal, State, and Local Governments, 2002 Census of Governments, Preliminary Report No. 1 The 2002 Census of Governments, GC02-1 (P), issued July 2002. See Ellis Katz, "Local Self-Government in the United States," *Issues of Democracy: An Electronic Journal of the U.S. Information agency,* Vol. 4, No. 1 (April 1999). http://usinfo.state.gov/journals/itdhr/0499/ijde/ijde0499.htm.

31. Michael A. Murray, "Comparing Public and Private Management: An Exploratory Essay," *Public Administration Review* 35, no. 4 (July/August 1975): 364–371.

32. Herbert A. Simon, Administrative Behavior (New York: Macmillan, 1957).

33. Walter Russell Mead, "To Tether Big Business to the National Interest, Read Hamilton," *Los Angeles Times,* 23 February 1997, pp. M2, 6.

34. Jonathan Rauch, "The End of Government," *National Journal* 28, no. 36 (7 September 1996): 1890–1896.

35. Theodore J. Lowi, *The End of Liberalism: The Second Republic of the United States* (New York: W. W. Norton & Co., 1969).

36. *Ibid.,* 43.

37. *Ibid.,* 51.

38. *Ibid.,* 63.

39. Richard N. Goodwin, "Perspective in Politics," *Los Angeles Times,* 30 January 1997, p. A9.

40. Robert Higgs, "The Futility of Campaign Finance Reform," The Independent Institute, 1997. http://www.independent.org/tii/content/op_ed/ahiggsscam.html.

41. Andrew Bard Schmookler, "When Money Talks, Is It Free Speech? PACs Give Big Bucks to Buy Access and Influence," *The Christian Science Monitor,* 10 November 1997, 15.

42. Jeffrey H. Birnbaum, "Washington's Power 25," *FORTUNE,* December 8, 1997. Power 25 ranking updated to May 28, 2001; http://www.cnn.com/ALLPOLITICS/1997/11/18/fortune.25/index1.html.

43. Jeffrey H. Birnbaum, "How to Buy Clout in the Capital," *FORTUNE,* December 6, 1999; http://www.transnationale.org.

44. *Ibid.*

The Anatomy of Public Organizations

Chapter Highlights

The Basis of Organization

Points about Pyramids

Line and Staff

Centralization and Decentralization

The HHS Organizational Framework

The Craft and Political Culture

Summary

The Authority Never Changed—How We Managed Did

The following statement was made by Raymond W. Kelly, Police Commissioner, New York Police Department (NYPD), before the United States Senate Judiciary Committee, July 18, 2001. Kelly spoke regarding the management of the Federal Bureau of Investigation (FBI). He had served in twenty-five different commands for the NYPD.

From 1996–1998, Kelly, as Under Secretary for Enforcement at the U.S. Treasury Department, supervised the Department's enforcement bureaus— including the U.S. Customs Service; U.S. Secret Service; Bureau of Alcohol, Tobacco, and Firearms; Federal Law Enforcement Training Center; Financial Crimes Enforcement Network; and Office of Foreign Assets Control. As U.S. Customs Service Commissioner, Kelly directed over 19,000 employees responsible for enforcing laws and protecting American citizens.

I came to Federal law enforcement after a thirty-year career in the New York City Police Department. I also served in the United States Marine Corps. The one thing both organizations have in common is that they are very hierarchical. While

both encourage initiative on the part of their front-line troops, the fact remains that both organizations insist on adherence to a strict chain of command.

They also maintain tight spans of control. For example, the span of control in the New York City Police Department begins with a sergeant and five police officers, lieutenants reporting to captains and so on through to the very top ranks of the organization. . . .

When I came to federal law enforcement, first as Under Secretary of the Treasury for Enforcement and later as Commissioner of U.S. Customs, I was struck by the relatively loose span of control and the horizontal structure of enforcement agencies.

Where my municipal and Marine Corps experience was very hierarchical, federal law enforcement tended to be more lateral. For example, when I first arrived at Customs, there were 20 Special Agents in Charge scattered across the United States, 100 Resident Agents in Charge offices, and 55 more attachés in twenty-four foreign countries—all reporting to one assistant commissioner in Washington.

The ratio of that span of control was more than surprising. It was unmanageable—certainly on a day-to-day basis. The result was that the investigative arm of the Customs Service was balkanized under the various Special Agents in Charge. Routine, centralized management in Washington was often weak and uninformed.

To correct the situation, we divided the country into three administrative regions: East, Central, and West. The Special Agents in Charge in each region had to report to a new director for each of the regions. Those three directors, in turn, reported to the assistant commissioner. Our attachés abroad were directed to report to a new deputy in the existing office of Foreign Relations. The result was a much more managable span of control.

The assistant commissioner in Washington could get a quick picture of what was happening nationally and internationally by talking to three people who reported to him, instead of forty. Similarly, with three deputies, the assistant commissioner could execute and follow up on policy, making certain his orders were not only transmitted, but also complied with. In addition, inspections on a much more frequent basis could be conducted.

With big, widely dispersed organizations, it is not enough for headquarters to send teams to the field to conduct periodic inspections every few years. There should be daily oversight. And a rational span of control allows that to happen.

The balkanization . . . was not limited to the Customs Office of Investigation. It affected the Office of Field Operations as well, where Customs personnel were assigned to 301 ports of entry located across the country. For a time, individual port directors tended to set their own policy. That led to "port shopping" by brokers and others who found that the rigor in which Customs regulations were being enforced varied from port to port.

The policy of "power to the ports" was encouraged for a time as managers tried to apply to the federal government the devolution of power that was becoming popular in American business. The problem is federal law enforcement is *not* a business enterprise. Its employees are responsible for enforcing the law, not making sales quotas.

They are armed and have authority to conduct personal searches, make arrests, and use deadly force.

This kind of authority demands tight spans of control, close supervision, rigorous chain of command and oversight. . . . Internally, the lack of consistently executed policy led to complaints of unevenness and favoritism in disciplinary procedures and promotions. Discipline for the same transgression, for example, might be dispensed differently depending on the region of the country or whom an employee knew within the Service. We changed that by establishing an agencywide Disciplinary Review Board with rotating membership.

One of the problems Customs experienced with the public was inconsistency in the way in which passengers arriving at various international airports were subjected to searches. Customs had broad authority to detain and search travelers, and did so. What was missing was a coherent policy that was closely supervised and uniformly adhered to. Once that policy was in place and closely supervised, the number of searches of law-abiding travelers plummeted, and the number of seizures of narcotics and other contraband increased.

The authority never changed. What changed was how we managed it. . . . Where none of the forty thousand police officers in the New York City Police Department is normally more than an hour or so away from headquarters, federal law enforcement has thousands of agents scattered across multiple time zones and even continents. . . .

The head of the agency must be persistent in demanding to know what is happening in the field and in making certain national policy is carried out there. Otherwise, power will devolve in a vacuum of leadership to the entrenched careerists in the field, where policy may be applied unevenly, if at all. . . .

[E]very law enforcement agency needs a robust internal affairs function within its ranks. While inspector generals and other outside entities can play an oversight role, nothing is more effective in preventing and pursuing corruption within law enforcement than a credible Internal Affairs

Unit. It takes a good insider to catch a bad one. . . . [I]nternal affairs needs to be staffed by the best and brightest investigators. . . .

An organization is only as good as the people who are recruited and trained to work for it. Federal law enforcement, and the FBI in particular, has a reputation for attracting highly skilled and highly motivated individuals. . . . The challenge is not who to manage, but how to manage them; how to manage a large, far-flung workforce with a broad and complex law enforcement mission. That's a heavy lift for anyone.

To lighten the load and manage effectively, I would recommend focusing on four essentials . . .

- Impose a strict managerial hierarchy.
- Maintain a tight span of control.
- Inspect regularly to make certain policy is being implemented in the field.
- Insure integrity through a robust internal affairs program within the agency.

Source

http://www.fas.org/irp/congress/2001_hr/071801_ kelly.html.

Every public administrator works within an organizational framework. Effective administrators have a solid understanding of general organizational principles and the structure of their particular organization. This chapter examines key organizational principles that have a major impact on public administration.

The *anatomy* of U.S. public bureaucracy—its organizational framework or administrative structure—owes much of its development to the 1933–1945 era of the Depression, World War II, and Franklin D. Roosevelt's leadership skills during the New Deal. In the 1990s, Republicans argued that the welfare state FDR created and nurtured had gotten out of control. Much of what FDR accomplished is thus now under attack. Many agencies in the federal bureaucracy that were created during the FDR era face privatization, consolidation, or elimination.

For Roosevelt, change was policy. "It is common sense to take a method and try it. If it fails, admit it frankly and try another. But above all try something," FDR said. Through the New Deal, Roosevelt built dams and brought electricity to millions, created farm subsidies and unemployment insurance, regulated a stock market gone out of control, set up a Social Security program for the elderly, and gave unions the right to organize. While many agencies no longer exist as they were created, other federal agencies and departments absorbed many functions in a greatly expanded welfare state.

The Basis of Organization

The structures of most public organizations are rather complex. These complexities can, however, be simplified by taking a look at the fundamental principles of organization outlined by Luther Gulick, who classified organizations into four categories. These categories are based on an organization's *raison d'être*—the reason it was established. The categories are *purpose, process, place, and clientele.*[1]

Purpose

Organizations established on the basis of *purpose* are oriented toward the accomplishment of specific tasks. Examples of organizations developed on this basis are school systems, fire departments, and the branches of the military. These organizations engage in purpose-specific activities and seldom extend beyond their purpose.

Process

A *process* organization is oriented not so much toward accomplishing specific goals but toward performing certain functions. From our understanding of the law as process, we might guess that a good example of such an agency is a city legal department. Process organizations concern themselves almost completely with the procedural aspects of administration.

Place

Organizations under this heading serve particular locales. These agencies provide a variety of services to the people in a particular neighborhood, city, county, or other region.

Clientele

Closely linked to *place* organizations, *clientele* organizations are a less common feature of our administrative landscape. These agencies serve particular groups of people, such as seniors, children, or people of a particular ethnic background.

Obviously these categories overlap, and many organizations fall into more than one. Fire departments are not only established for the purpose of putting out fires, but are also organized to serve particular geographic areas; yet purpose, not place, is the main reason for establishing a fire department. Most organizations are established not on the basis of just one of Gulick's categories, but through a combination of purpose, process, place, and clientele, regardless of which factor dominates.

Of the three branches of government, the executive, legislative, and judicial, the executive has the widest range of responsibilities. Through the power vested by the U.S. Constitution in the office of the President, the executive branch includes the Office of Management and Budget (OMB), National Security Council (NSC), and Council of Economic Advisers (CEA). OMB oversees administration of the federal budget. NSC advises the President on matters of national defense. CEA offers economic policy recommendations.

As of 2000, the executive branch employed about 97 percent of all federal civilian employees, excluding postal workers.[2] It is composed of the Executive Office of the President (EOP), fourteen executive cabinet departments, and nearly ninety independent agencies, each of which has clearly defined duties. Each of the fourteen executive cabinet departments administers programs that oversee an element of American life. The highest departmental official of each cabinet department, the Secretary, is a member of the President's cabinet. Each department is described here, and table 3.1 lists the number of employees in each.

- **Defense (DOD):** Manages the military forces that protect the country and its interests, including the Departments of the Army, Navy, Air Force, and a number of smaller agencies. The civilian workforce employed by the

TABLE 3.1

**Federal Government Executive Branch Civilian Employment,
Except U.S. Postal Service, September 2000
(employment in thousands)**

	United States	Washington, DC area
Total	1,700	272
Executive Departments		
Defense, total	623	64
Army	207	19
Navy	177	25
Air Force	148	5
Other	91	14
Veterans Affairs	216	7
Treasury	142	23
Justice	123	22
Agriculture	103	11
Interior	73	8
Transportation	63	10
Health and Human Services	62	28
Commerce	47	21
Energy	16	5
Labor	16	5
State	11	9
Housing and Urban Development	10	3
Education	5	3
Independent Agencies		
Social Security Administration	64	2
National Aeronautics and Space Administration	19	4
Environmental Protection Agency	18	6
General Services Administration	14	5
Tennessee Valley Authority	13	0
Federal Deposit Insurance Corporation	7	3

Source: U.S. Office of Personnel Management.

Department of Defense performs various support activities, such as payroll and public relations.

- **Veterans Affairs (VA):** Administers programs to aid U.S. veterans and their families, runs the veterans' hospital system, and operates our national cemeteries.
- **Treasury:** Regulates banks and other financial institutions, administers the public debt, prints currency, collects federal income taxes, and carries out law enforcement in a wide range of areas, including counterfeiting, tax, and customs violations.

- **Justice (DOJ):** Enforces federal laws, prosecutes cases in federal courts, and runs federal prisons.
- **Agriculture (USDA):** Promotes U.S. agriculture domestically and internationally and sets standards governing quality, quantity, and labeling of food sold in the United States.
- **Interior:** Manages federal lands, including the national parks and forests; runs hydroelectric power systems; and promotes conservation of natural resources.
- **Transportation (DOT):** Sets national transportation policy; operates the Coast Guard (USCG) except in time of war; plans and funds the construction of highways and mass transit systems; and regulates railroad, aviation, and maritime operations.
- **Health and Human Services (HHS):** Sponsors medical research, approves use of new drugs and medical devices, runs the Public Health Service, and administers Medicare.
- **Commerce:** Forecasts the weather, charts the oceans, regulates patents and trademarks, conducts the census, compiles statistics, and promotes U.S. economic growth by encouraging international trade.
- **Energy (DOE):** Coordinates the national use and provision of energy, oversee the production and disposal of nuclear weapons, and plans for future energy needs.
- **Labor (DOL):** Enforces laws guaranteeing fair pay, workplace safety, and equal job opportunity; administers unemployment insurance; regulates pension funds; and collects and analyzes economic data at the Bureau of Labor Statistics.
- **State:** Oversees the nation's embassies and consulates, issues passports, monitors U.S. interests abroad, and represents the United States before international organizations.
- **Housing and Urban Development (HUD):** Funds public housing projects, enforces equal housing laws, and insures and finances mortgages.
- **Education:** Provides scholarships, student loans, and aid to schools.

Numerous independent agencies perform tasks that do not originate within the jurisdictions of executive departments or that are more efficiently executed by an autonomous agency. Some smaller but well-known independent agencies include the Peace Corps, Securities and Exchange Commission (SEC), and Federal Communications Commission (FCC). The majority of these agencies employ fewer than one thousand workers, and many count fewer than one hundred.

The largest independent agencies are:

- **Social Security Administration (SSA):** Operates various retirement and disability programs and Medicaid.
- **National Aeronautics and Space Administration (NASA):** Oversees aviation research and conducts exploration and research beyond the Earth's atmosphere.
- **Environmental Protection Agency (EPA):** Administers programs to control and reduce pollution of the nation's water, air, and land.

- **General Services Administrations (GSA):** Manages and protects federal government property and records.
- **Tennessee Valley Authority (TVA):** Operates the hydroelectric power system in the Tennessee River valley.
- **Federal Deposit Insurance Corporation (FDIC):** Maintains the stability of and public confidence in the nation's financial system by insuring deposits and promoting sound banking practices.

Local Government as Plural, Not Singular, Noun

The concept, local government, incorporates more than cities. The term may include a county, a city, a school district and community college district—plus numerous specialized and politically independent entities whose purposes entail regional mass transit, wastewater treatment, firefighting, mosquito abatement, and flood control. Los Angeles County, for example, includes 88 cities.

Policymakers, periodically, get alarmed by the proliferation and complexity of local government. County-level commissions monitor annexations and formations of new cities and special districts. The effects of highly decentralized land-use powers on growth patterns concern policymakers. Community leaders debate regional reorganizations. Government fragmentation questions the responsiveness of coordinated government action. Cries of "wasteful duplication" and "local control" fail to probe the structure of local governance.

Partisan, policy, and system politics produces political fragmentation—or the geographic and functional division of power among local governments. Political fragmentation effects government services and land use regulation. Proliferation of local governments frustrates policy coordination of transportation, housing, and environmental protection initiatives. Government structures may separate fiscal needs from resources. Citizens become confused and dissensus emerges.

Four distinct roles suggest differences in local government structure.

1. *Service provision.* Local government is the primary provider of routine public services. Trash collection, fire protection, and public education are illustrations. Competitive economic theories function in tandem with political fragmentation. Fragmentation sorts citizens into "communities of interest." Similar tastes for services and tax levels result.

2. *Land use and economic development.* The so-called "police power" affords cities and counties the power to create zoning ordinances, rules for subdividing land, and building regulations. Partisan politics decide land-use patterns for constructing growth-supportive infrastructures, such as sewer lines. Localities often regulate land use in their narrow self-interests, yet they may slight area-wide concerns.

3. *Equity.* Political fragmentation may separate fiscal resources from social needs. Equity distributes and redistributes life's chances. Separate taxing-and-spending jurisdictions may lead to service disparities. Unequal service distributions may reflect government fragmentation per se. Or different "tastes" for services may emerge from inequality. Redistributive policies attempt to rectify disparities among local governments.

4. *Representation.* Government fragmentation emphasizes effective political representation and accountability. Decision making closer to home builds faith in government services. However, general purpose governments focus on more global budgeting. Overall taxing and spending levels are set. Tradeoffs are made between competing services. Community service demands competition between services shared by larger populations in a interconnected region.

Source: "The Controversy over Local Government Structure," http://www.ppic.org/publications/ PPIC112/ppic112.chap1.html.

Points about Pyramids

The organizational structure of most institutions is best thought of as a pyramid. The organization must delegate its work to a number of employees. To make sure that these employees do the work and to see that their efforts are coordinated, the organization appoints supervisors. These supervisors may be numerous enough that they, in turn, require supervisors. As a result, one or more levels of hierarchy tend to emerge in any sizeable organization, with the number of persons at each level dwindling until the tip of a pyramid is reached. The pyramid model brings with it the concepts of *unity of command, chain of command,* and *span of control.*

Unity of command describes the exclusive relationship between those who follow orders and those who give them orders. No one can serve two masters. This maxim has held true for work organizations, particularly those operating under the bureaucratic norms of delegation, specialization, and accountability, and accounts for much of their success.

Requiring an individual or a group to respond to the orders of two or more superiors may produce conflict, confusion, and even chaos. If unity of command does not exist, conflict and confusion will not only characterize those being commanded but those doing the commanding. In other words, multiple superiors will not only confuse their subordinates but also each other.

The unity of command principle may conflict with the methods of some boards and commissions. Such multiple-headed bodies are considered suitable only for semijudicial organizations (such as regulatory commissions) or for certain policymaking or advisory functions. If an organization is administering a program, if it is *doing* things, then the reins of its authority should converge eventually into one pair of hands. Responsibility can then be pinpointed, and conflicting orders, internecine warfare, and a host of other organizational ills can be avoided.

Unity of command usually requires a *chain of command,* the second concept in the pyramid model. In any large organization, the person at the top cannot oversee all that is going on below; he or she needs others to help do this. Frequently, these helpers cannot supervise all those beneath them. As a result, several echelons of command may emerge, theoretically allowing commands to proceed downward in a neat, orderly flow. Unity of command means that the captain of A Company does not give orders to the soldiers of B Company. Within a chain of command, the battalion major does not give direct orders to soldiers from either company, but works instead through their company commanders.

Even less structured organizations observe, to some degree, the same principle. The college dean, if he or she has reason to be disturbed by the behavior of a particular professor, will usually first contact the professor's department chairperson before taking any direct action against the faculty member. In this way the chain of command at the university streamlines the administrative process.

A third concept linked to a pyramidal structure is *span of control.* Span of control refers to the number of units, whether individuals or groups, that any supervising unit must oversee. Unlike unity of command and chain of command, span of control does not constitute a principle of organization; instead, it serves as a frame of reference. Put another way, span of control is not something that organizations *ought* to have, but something they *do* have. Usually, a government organization develops guidelines for span of control based on an organization's mission. A challenge exists in making sure that the number of subunits to be supervised is neither too many nor too few—to make sure that the supervisor's span of control is neither too great nor too small. Unfortunately, public administration provides no hard-and-fast criteria for determining such things. As with so many other questions concerning this capricious craft, the only intelligent answer is the highly unsatisfactory, "It all depends."

Public administrators in America have functioned with relatively narrow spans of control. It is rare to find a manager overseeing more than twelve subordinates or subunits, and it is not rare to find a manager overseeing as few as three. The tighter the span of control, the more intervening levels between top and bottom, increasing paperwork and procrastination. A tight span of control also leads to decisions made and policies formulated too far from the scene of action. It can lead to difficulties in acquiring and retaining the services of top-notch people in vitally important, but no longer top-rated, positions.

As with so much in public administration, span of control becomes a question of finding a proper balance for each situation. In finding this balance, we must assess the specific circumstances involved, keeping in mind that a gain achieved by moving in one direction may be offset by some losses. These losses do not, however, necessarily cancel the gain. If an executive has 100 agencies under his or her tutelage, some consolidation is almost always needed, even at the expense of creating more administrative levels. However, every consolidation carries a price tag that we must be willing to pay if we wish to reap the benefits.

Figures 3.1 and 3.2 illustrate how the principles of unity command, chain of command, and span of control need to be grounded in political compromise, consensus, and democratic participation.

President George W. Bush is not the first chief executive to call for a slimmer federal government. In 1983, President Reagan offered his five-year "bulge project." Facts and figures regarding span of control, chain of command, and unity of command were tabulated in the effort to shrink government. A decade later, President Clinton commissioned Vice President Al Gore to reinvent government. The actual number of government middle managers declined by 40,000 between 1993 and 1998, but most job descriptions were merely reclassified into nonmanagerial jobs. Position titles such as Management Support Specialist and Team Leader contained *de facto* management duties.

Paul C. Light points out flaws in the slimmer-government campaign the second Bush administration has launched. First, political layers of government hierarchy are ignored. The Bush order to flatten the federal span of control overlooks about a third of the bureaucractic bloat. Political appointees account for a small fraction of the total federal workforce, but they occupy between 25 and 40 percent of the layers in federal agencies.

Second, the Office of Management and Budget (OMB) and Office of Personnel Management (OPM) do not have the capacity to monitor the implementation of real reductions. Stymied by their own hierarchies, OMB and OPM have no way to monitor how federal agencies create or dismantle their bureaucracies.

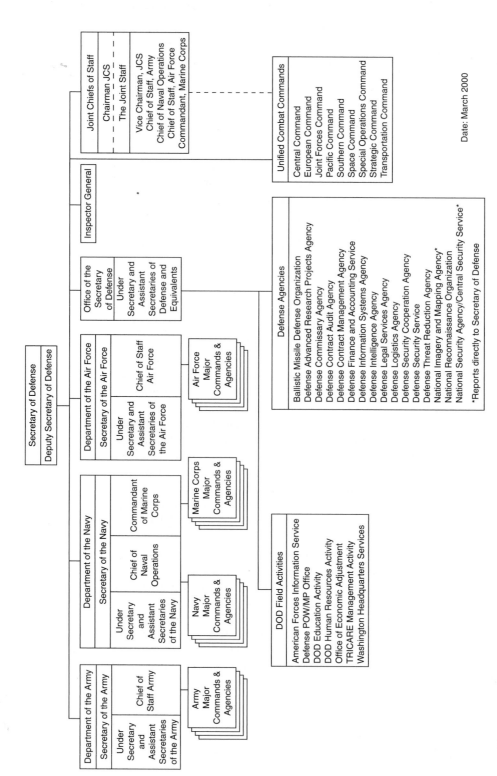

Secretary of Defense
Deputy Secretary of Defense

Department of the Army
Secretary of the Army
Under Secretary and Assistant Secretaries of the Army
Chief of Staff Army
Army Major Commands & Agencies

Department of the Navy
Secretary of the Navy
Under Secretary and Assistant Secretaries of the Navy
Chief of Naval Operations
Commandant of Marine Corps
Navy Major Commands & Agencies
Marine Corps Major Commands & Agencies

Department of the Air Force
Secretary of the Air Force
Under Secretary and Assistant Secretaries of the Air Force
Chief of Staff Air Force
Air Force Major Commands & Agencies

Office of the Secretary of Defense
Under Secretary and Assistant Secretaries of Defense and Equivalents

Inspector General

Joint Chiefs of Staff
Chairman JCS
The Joint Staff
Vice Chairman, JCS
Chief of Staff, Army
Chief of Naval Operations
Chief of Staff, Air Force
Commandant, Marine Corps

Unified Combat Commands
Central Command
European Command
Joint Forces Command
Pacific Command
Southern Command
Space Command
Special Operations Command
Strategic Command
Transportation Command

DOD Field Activities
American Forces Information Service
Defense POW/MP Office
DOD Education Activity
DOD Human Resources Activity
Office of Economic Adjustment
TRICARE Management Activity
Washington Headquarters Services

Defense Agencies
Ballistic Missile Defense Organization
Defense Advanced Research Projects Agency
Defense Commissary Agency
Defense Contract Audit Agency
Defense Contract Management Agency
Defense Finance and Accounting Service
Defense Information Systems Agency
Defense Intelligence Agency
Defense Legal Services Agency
Defense Logistics Agency
Defense Security Cooperation Agency
Defense Security Service
Defense Threat Reduction Agency
National Imagery and Mapping Agency*
National Reconnaissance Organization
National Security Agency/Central Security Service*

*Reports directly to Secretary of Defense

Date: March 2000

FIGURE 3.1 Department of Defense.

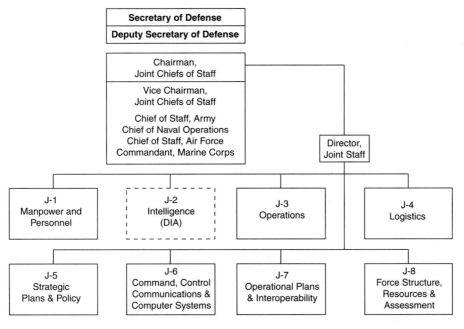

FIGURE 3.2 Joint Chiefs of Staff.

Third, the Bush appointees promoted an overly detailed workforce plan. President Bush promised to eliminate 40,000 mid-level management positions. According to Light, Bush should concentrate on removing whole *layers* not numbers of individual workers. Light believes federal management layers should be reduced to no more than ten. Most federal agencies do not hire the human capital needed to do human resource planning. Gore's reinventing government campaign pruned human capital from federal government agencies to the extent that human capital planning is no longer viable.

Light succinctly analyzes the federal bureaucracy's chain of command and span of control options. No administration can ignore the political hierarchy at federal agencies. The "way to flatten government is to redline the layers and start cutting," states Light. "Then [the administration] should ask every person who stands between those front-line employees and the President to justify his or her job. Flattening is really that simple."[3]

Line and Staff

The individuals working in the pyramid examples discussed earlier—U.S. Army companies and large state universities—are called *line personnel.* Another group of people to be considered are *staff personnel.*

While line personnel are primarily concerned with implementing policy, staff personnel are the working members of an organization who do not implement policy.

Line agencies and employees are directly responsible for furthering an organization's goals. Staff employees are primarily concerned with assisting senior administrators in the determination of policy and the effective operation of the agency.

Line people are generalists who occupy positions of authority in the organization and command implementation of the organization's operations. The Departments of Agriculture, Commerce, Defense, Education, Energy, Health and Human Services, Housing and Urban Development, Interior, Justice, Labor, State, Transportation, Treasury, and Veterans Affairs constitute the major line agencies of the federal government. These organizations administer clientele programs and deal directly with the public.

The primary line officers are members of the President's cabinet. These line and staff departments and agencies were established in the following order:

1789: State, War, Treasury, Attorney General
1798: Navy
1829: Postmaster General
1849: Interior
1870: Justice
1889: Agriculture
1903: Commerce and Labor
1913: Commerce, Labor (split)
1939: Office of Management and Budget
1947: Defense (replaced Navy and War)
1953: Health, Education, and Welfare
1965: Housing and Urban Development
1966: Transportation
1971: Postmaster General removed from cabinet
1974: Office of the U.S. Trade Representative
1977: Energy
1979: Health and Human Services, Education (HEW split into HHS and Education)
1989: Veterans' Affairs
1993: Environmental Protection Agency, United Nations Ambassador

Note: The Office of Management and Budget and the Office of U.S. Trade Representative are part of the Executive Office of the President and are not executive departments.

Source: Barbara J. Saffir, "Evolution of Cabinet," *Washington Post,* February 9, 1993, p. A15.

The expansion of the President's cabinet has occurred over time. The U.S. Constitution does not provide specifically for a cabinet, but Article II, Section 2 stipulates that a President may seek advice from heads of the executive departments. Cabinet status puts an agency on stronger footing when dealing with the Office of Management and Budget on fiscal and policy matters. In 1993, President Clinton proposed that the Environmental Protection Agency receive cabinet status. He also elevated the position of Ambassador to the United Nations to cabinet level.

Staff people are specialists who provide skills, knowledge, and expertise to line personnel. For example, staff personnel draw up job classifications, program computers, or provide legal services. These are the employees who are most accurately referred to as the "staff." Staff agencies aid the chief executive and line personnel in developing, evaluating, and implementing public policies. Within the

The Department Head versus Your P.A. Professor— Line versus Staff

A student of political science need go no further than his or her university bureaucracy to note the tensions inherent between staff and line personnel. Faculty members in the Department of Political Science are selected, retained, and promoted based upon their skills, knowledge, and expertise in a subfield or subfields of political science. Political science faculty are hired to teach a certain specialty, such as political theory, political parties, legislative studies, the presidency, constitutional law and jurisprudence, law and courts, federalism and intergovernmental relations, state politics, public policy, urban politics, comparative politics, foreign policy, or public administration.

As experts in particular aspects of political science, faculty are "staff" advisors in your college or university to the chairperson of the Department of Political Science, a "line" official. Line officials are in command; they have authority as specified in the university's administrative guidelines. In the political science department the chairperson is a generalist in the discipline of political science. The dean, provost, and president of your college or university are also line officials.

A certain amount of tension between the political science department chair and a certain faculty member who teaches a specialty in political science is almost a given. An individual political science professor might consider courses in public policy and administration to be most important in the department's academic curriculum. The department chair must evaluate and balance this and other recommendations of the political science professors under his or her supervision as he or she makes decisions as to what courses to offer students.

The faculty member, as specialist, promotes student interest in a certain subfield or subfields of political science. The department chair, as generalist and the administrative authority in command of the political science administrative unit, has the responsibility to see that all subfields of political science receive appropriate emphasis in course offerings. Department heads, implementing line functions, and faculty, carrying out staff teaching assignments, have different program priorities. It is not difficult to imagine that they, as line and staff employees of your college or university, would often come into conflict as each person seeks to do his or her job as responsibly and as ably as possible.

Executive Office of the President of the United States, for example, the main staff agencies are the White House Office, Office of Management and Budget, Council of Economic Advisors, National Security Council, Office of Policy Development, Office of the U.S. Trade Representative, Council on Environmental Quality, and Office of Science and Technology Policy.

The essence of staff work is thought, fact-finding, and planning.[4] Staff units are usually formed on the basis of process. An organization's computer center, for example, is typically comprised of people engaged in a process while serving a variety of purposes, places, and clientele within the larger organization.

In a school system, the computer center prepares attendance figures for principals, correlates statistics on children with learning disabilities for the director of special education, and pinpoints certain cost trends for the budgeting department. The latter function illustrates that staff agencies may serve not only line departments, but also other staff units.

The bureaucratic pyramid, in its pure form, makes no provision for staff units and their personnel. Traditionally, staff units have played only a small and shadowy role in the structure of work organizations. The place they occupied was usually at the hands or feet of the organization's leader, providing advice and assistance.

However, staff services and personnel have increased tremendously. They now occupy a greater place in an organization's structure, play a greater role in its activities, and consume a greater portion of its budget. In so doing, they provide the organization with new benefits and new problems.

Problems stem from the model pyramid's lack of provision for staff units. It is difficult, at times almost impossible, to establish the correct niche for staff within an organization's hierarchy. Staff people tend to be specialists whose expertise does not lend itself to a graded ranking except, possibly, within their own ranks. The authority of a line unit is fairly definite. Its personnel know which units are above them and which ones are below. The authority of a staff unit is, by contrast, much more nebulous and elusive. Such authority is determined by whatever need the line units have for the staff group at a particular time, the proficiency the staff can demonstrate in meeting this need, the administrative and political skills the staff demonstrates in its relationships with other units within the organization, and a variety of other factors.

Specialization tends to destroy hierarchy. The more the members of an organization are differentiated from each other in terms of separate, specific skills, the more difficult it becomes to position them on a hierarchical scale. Knowledge, in and of itself, knows no hierarchy. There is no "higher" or "lower" knowledge. Thus, the increasing presence of staff personnel is disrupting many bureaucratic organizations as specialists begin to dominate generalists in making agency policies. Staff people are undermining the cherished bureaucratic principles of unity of command, chain of command, and span of control.

Unity of command requires one channel of authority, but specialization creates several channels. The specialists, in one way or another, start giving orders relating to their areas of expertise. That these orders are not labeled as such and stem not from rank but from expertise does not fundamentally alter the situation. If the organization intends to use the energies and abilities of specialists, it must respond to what they say. To the extent that the specialists' capabilities are used, the authority of line personnel, particularly those in a supervisory capacity, is undermined.

The contrasting assignments of line (generalist) and staff (specialist) personnel generate a good deal of conflict and tension in organizations. At times, line people will complain that staff people are not sharing enough responsibility. More often, however, line personnel resent the intrusions of staff people. To line employees, the activities of staff personnel frequently seem more subversive than supportive.

To reduce the rivalry and rancor that may creep into line-staff relationships, organizations try to integrate the two as much as possible. They may make staff people spend time familiarizing themselves with line functions and line personnel, sometimes requiring staff personnel to perform some line functions for a time. They may recruit their staff people from the ranks of the line personnel, giving them special training for their new positions.

There is no "correct" organizational arrangement of *unity of command, chain of command, span of control,* and *line and staff.* Therefore, these organizational principles vary from organization to organization and are based upon the most satisfactory way to serve the needs of clientele.

Centralization and Decentralization

One issue that has bewildered public managers since the beginning of public organization is *centralization.* Arguments have been raised on the devolution affecting the balance between nation and state as states have undertaken policy reforms that work to their individual advantage at the expense of national interest. *Devolution* is perceived to be an attempt to simplify incentives for common interests. However, reforms should balance multiple interests within the framework of the larger government.[5] In early times, concern focused largely on how to achieve this, for even the simplest communication between headquarters and the field often took weeks, months, or, in a few instances, years. Egyptian pharaohs, Roman emperors, and Chinese mandarins spent a good deal of time wondering how to control and use the energies of subordinates in distant subunits.

The emphasis has shifted. Now the number one concern often centers on how much centralization should be achieved. Centralization is no longer viewed as an unmixed blessing. Its opposite, decentralization, has become the watchword, if not the battle cry, of many theorists and practitioners involved in the administrative craft. Several movements throughout U.S. history have tried to downsize and decentralize government. Assaults on big government began with Thomas Jefferson and continued with the Jacksonian Democrats, the states' rights movement, and the antistatism movements of the twentieth century.[6]

The "citizen legislator" is a quaint vestige of early American democracy that continues to dominate state government. Forty-one states have legislatures that meet part time—some for as little as thirty days a year—and their members spend the rest of the time practicing law, tilling fields, or staffing shops as ordinary citizens. However, the federal government's desire to send power to the states is increasing these legislators' workload and making it tough for them to keep up.[7] Only months after Congress turned control of welfare over to the states, legislatures around the country began considering whether to hand off responsibility for the poor once again, this time to county and local governments.[8]

We have seen how decentralization has characterized our country's *political* system since its inception. While such political decentralization may facilitate and foster *administrative* decentralization, it does not necessarily ensure it—at least not in all instances.

Political decentralization calls for policies to be developed as much as possible at the lower levels (the "grass roots"). *Administrative decentralization* requires that the organizations charged with carrying out these policies allow their subunits a great deal of autonomy in interpreting and applying them. When a city institutes its own health program, political decentralization is at work. If at the same time the health department refuses to set up neighborhood centers or insists that even the centers' most minor decisions must be made at headquarters, the program is not administratively decentralized.

Centralization and *decentralization* are relative terms. Nearly every organization of any size and scope must, to some extent, decentralize, for once it sets up subunits, it must grant them some discretion in carrying out their functions. The

Who Controls Welfare?

Neither the president nor governors have as much control over welfare as they would have us believe. Welfare recipients are affected more by cyclical economic forces than by government regulations. Perhaps more important, welfare is ultimately a local matter. Lawmakers in Washington or the state capitals may pass grandiose reforms, but low-level officials have a lot of discretion in carrying them out.

Source: Bradley R. Schiller, "All Welfare Is Local," *The New York Times,* January 28, 1997, p. A21.

question, therefore, becomes a matter of deciding how far this independent discretion should go. Many argue that it should be pushed to the maximum limits.

Decentralization, or its lack, is no abstract concept in public organizations. An organization's *tasks, values,* and *organizational structures* are related to unique political, administrative, and economic characteristics. And the structural arrangements of an organization are never value-neutral. The locations of decisions affect an administrator's objectives and values. The perspectives of federal employees located in Washington are different from the perspectives of those implementing services in Peoria. As Miles's Law states, "Where you stand depends upon where you sit."

States respond to increased marginal expenditure costs and reduced federal aid. States may also have to overcome spending limits and short-term policy perspectives. State finance research should focus on state spending determinants, interactions with local governments, federal aid changes, discretionary tax changes, and whether budgets are structurally balanced.[9] It is believed that state governments will gain control of many social programs presently run by the federal government. Legislators and other state officials will finally have the flexibility to choose which programs will work best for their situation. Experts believe that no single pattern of welfare and Medicaid reform will emerge. They also believe that reforms will evolve over time as states learn from their experience and that of other states.[10]

The structure of an organization affects the delivery of services to its clientele. Public organizations must mobilize resources to perpetuate themselves and their values. Decisions cannot be imposed from the top down if people in the subunits do not subscribe to the values and methods of implementing particular services. Administrators sometimes entertain *reorganization* plans to gain more control over the structure of the organization's policies and programs. Since any reorganization is implemented by the permanent bureaucracy, or the employees in the field accomplishing the everyday tasks of the organization, any decisions to decentralize or recentralize are of great consequence to the organization. These decisions should be made with sensitivity to the skills, knowledge, and expertise of field employees who must carry out the organization's values and purposes.[11]

The Reagan Administration saw centralization as the best way to put its values into action and to achieve its goals. For most of the 1980s, the administration "devised a strategy for centralizing unprecedented decision-making power in the White House."[12] The Reagan Administration centralized the budgetary process, the federal appointments process, decision making in the executive branch, and control of federal regulation.[13] A future president may take the opposite approach and opt for decentralization as a way of expressing a different set of values and achieving different goals. As we have mentioned, two types of decentralization exist: *political* and *administrative.*[14]

Political Decentralization

Political decentralization describes the allocation of powers among territories, which in this context refers to states, provinces, counties, municipalities, and other local governments. According to this approach to governing, general-purpose government officers residing in a specific territory coordinate public sector activities, because they are in closer contact with citizens and may alter programs according to particular territorial priorities. Political decentralization advances few real restrictions for guidelines and control, keeping them at a minimum to allow for local discretion. The territories, or subunits, possess considerable power, coordinating and reshaping resources coming into their geographic areas to meet local needs. Manifestly parochial and unable to formulate and act on national goals, politically decentralized systems experience difficulty "vertically" integrating a diverse set of governmental activities. The transfer of political power from nation to state to community constitutes a vertical pass-through of influence at each level. How is this vertical pass-through frustrated in a decentralized system?

Issues such as equal opportunity, the environment, and occupational safety illustrate the barriers to vertical pass-through that the parochialism of local jurisdictions poses. Congress may, for example, impose affirmative action criteria for implementing equal opportunity goals for every state in the union. If local groups of citizens are opposed to civil rights, however, equal opportunity policies may be frustrated.

Likewise, when administrative specialists in the Environmental Protection Agency (EPA) interpret U.S. environmental statutes to mean that private industry must control its waste emissions, EPA field officials may be frustrated in their efforts to enforce these laws if a community values the economic status of that industry more than clean air or water. If occupational safety is a concern of federal officers but not of local government, industry, and labor leaders, then Congress and the Occupational Safety and Health Administration may be wasting their time attempting to convince local residents otherwise. Groups of citizens in every political jurisdiction must be committed to the goals of the organization, at least in some fashion, for procedures and processes to be effective in implementing these goals.

Administrative Decentralization

Administrative decentralization occurs when a public organization delegates powers to subordinate levels within the same department or agency. The delegating authority may revise or retract such delegations at will. The central office of a bureaucracy in Washington may transfer federal government functions to regional or state offices, for example.

Where political decentralization pertains to powers allocated among geographic areas, administrative decentralization emphasizes functions, or specialties, and lines of authority for implementing agency functions. Functional and professional specialties of the central office bureaus and agencies are held in high regard in the field offices.

Politically decentralized jurisdictions grapple with "vertical" integration of governmental activities; *administratively decentralized* systems experience difficulties with "horizontal" integration of governmental activities. While a city might relate to a vertical hierarchy of state and federal governments for policy determination in political decentralization, federal administrators might horizontally coordinate the activities of several agencies within the same geographic area in an example of administrative decentralization. In such operations, problems are often addressed in a fragmented manner with specialists (staff) dominating the narrowly focused programs, and generalists (line) concerned for the whole project and guidelines emanating from the central office.

For example, the issue of civil rights concerns several federal departments and agencies; specific policies need horizontal coordination for implementation at the grassroots level. Those departments challenged to coordinate civil rights regulations based upon the administrative discretion of bureaucrats include the Departments of Commerce; Education; Health and Human Services; Housing and Urban Development; Justice; Labor; and Transportation. Independent agencies also involved include the Commission on Civil Rights, the Equal Employment Opportunity Commission, and the Small Business Administration. The line officials of these departments and agencies could be in agreement on general purposes, desiring to implement civil rights statutes; however, the more narrowly focused specialists within each bureaucracy may disagree on the specifics.

Administrative decentralization is played out at the Department of Health and Human Services. Centralization occurs within the office of the HHS Secretary. Decentralization occurs within the program operating components.

HHS faces a number of external and internal forces. External forces include:

- *The diversity and size of operating programs.* A very diverse array of objectives, cultures, and approaches are located under the HHS departmental umbrella.
- *Vague, difficult goals.* Goals are often contradictory, vague, not unified, and difficult to measure.
- *Fragmented accountability structures.* HHS programs mirror the fragmented American policymaking system.
- *Fragmented program authority.* Program responsibilities reach across the federal government. Congress fragments program authority. Some HHS programs have common areas of authority with other departments or agencies.
- *Different program responsibilities.* HHS offers a wide range of administrative and policy mechanisms. Some programs are produced by HHS. Others are funded by HHS and administered by state and local communities. Block grants, funded by HHS, are given to local governments for program implementation.
- *Controversial issues.* HHS is affected by some of the most controversial domestic policy issues in our society, including abortion, welfare reform, and payment for health services. Forces external to the department often prevent HHS from articulating a clear position on these issues. For example, HHS does not distribute contraceptives. However, HHS funds programs that Planned Parenthood, a health care not-for-profit agency, implements instead.
- *Diverse constituencies.* Constituency or interest groups call for very different approaches to specific sets of programs. Multiple perspectives dominate a program area. HHS deals with a considerable amount of ambiguity.

Internal forces that put pressure on HHS include:

- *Multiple policy perspectives.* HHS internal politics often reflect diverse external policy and political agendas. The HHS Secretary, Deputy Secretary, or an Assistant Secretary may argue for different perspectives and agency approaches. The Deputy Secretary may have articulated a staff concern, while an Assistant Secretary focused on a line, or program, approach. If this dynamic occurs, agreement on policy direction and loyalty to a single agenda as defined by the Secretary became problematic.
- *Conflicting policy approaches.* Diverse program components may spell different approaches to similar policy problems. Health research agencies may develop effective treatment forms, but the treatments may not be reimbursed by the agencies charged with financing these services. Unit leaders conflict over solutions.
- *Staff-line competition.* The Deputy Secretary represents staff functions, and the Office of the HHS Secretary focuses on the skills, knowledge, and expertise of employees. Meanwhile, program units implement line, or program, functions. At HHS, staff gurus in the Secretary's office came to second-guess the decisions of the program-operating components. They eventually overturned program decisions. The Office of the Secretary increased its personnel over the years, and the increased staff numbers in the Secretary's Office permitted them to monitor program, or line, decisions more closely. They were then able to substitute their judgments for those of the operating unit staffs.
- *Gaming filtering units.* The HHS budget for fiscal year 1999 was $450 billion. The Department employs about 59,000 persons. HHS is the largest grant-making agency in the federal government—providing 60,000 grants each year. With 800 million claims, HHS is also the nation's largest insurer. The Department's programs are administered by eleven operating divisions which emanate from headquarters in the Washington area and ten regional offices.

  In order to filter information and package decision memos before they reached the Secretary's office, filtering units were established. However, the creation of these units did not guarantee more effective decision making. The filtering units did not represent varying perspectives within HHS, so program units found ways to bypass filtering units. Line, or program, operations (generalists, positions of HHS authority, and command implementation) conflicted with staff (skills, knowledge, and expertise) perspectives. Line and staff functions generated different priorities and communication techniques. The need for filtering units illustrates the complexity of HHS demands and differences.

The HHS Organizational Framework

Former HHS Secretary Donna Shalala (1993–2001) applied several principles to the Department as an organization. Traditional roles of the Office of the Secretary include providing services to the Secretary and Department, giving advice on policy direction, coordinating program and policy coordination, and handling external affairs. Shalala added:

- An emphasis on the *program units* as the heart of HHS. The program units, called Operation Divisions or OpDivs, are the focal points of HHS *raison d'être*. These units perform the workload of the Department. They are responsible to their own constituencies and also to Congressional committees and subcommittees. Functions once located in the Office of the Secretary, such as personnel and procurement, were delegated to the OpDivs under Shalala.
- An assumption that *staff units* do not control or second-guess program units. Strong personalities led most of the staff units, called Staff Divisions or StaffDivs. Tensions between program units and staff divisions decreased substantially when this principle was applied. Some program-operating responsibilities once assigned to staff operations were repositioned under line delegations.

  Secretary Shalala designated staff units as running operations that are "value added" to the department. In this revised HHS staff-line functioning, staff units are to advise the Secretary on issues which should be on her decision plate and to serve as resources for the operation divisions whenever needed.
- An *organization structure* that seeks to minimize hierarchy and reduce layers of accountability. HHS adopted a more consensus-based, flat organization structure—or a collegial, "board of directors" decision-making approach. The flatter arrangement replaces a tall, hiearchical chain of command with layered administrative structure. As organizations become more knowledge-based, technological, and educated, the trend is likely to continue towards consensus-grounded administrative systems.

  The new HHS organization structure reflects the preeminence of operating units (see figure 3.3). The goal is to empower line officials—making them structurally responsible for operating programs under their jurisdictions.[15]

Governmental Structure and American Values

Decentralization has its proponents in every political camp. Suspicion of the dangers inherent in a strong, centralized government dates back beyond the American Revolution. Participation, access, and responsiveness are characteristics of decentralized systems that in principle promote flexibility and democracy within federal organizations at the grass roots. By allowing flexibility within federal guidelines, political decentralization helps state and city officials to meet the needs of their constituents. Rigid functional categories of administratively decentralized systems restrict the options of leaders representing general-purpose governments.

Students of political decentralization argue that governors and mayors are more able than nonelected bureaucrats to effectively allocate available resources according to local priorities. But cogent arguments exist *against* political decentralization as well. Local jurisdictions may be fragmented and ineffective; states some-

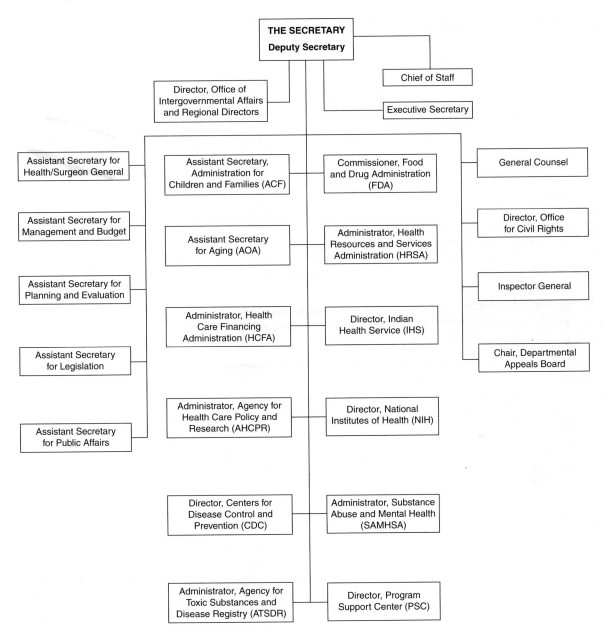

FIGURE 3.3 HHS organization chart.

times refuse to grant sufficient resources for local bureaucracies to implement functions in a professional and effective manner. Accusations of unprofessional behavior and political graft undermine citizens' confidence in the legitimacy of local governments. Regional and national concerns may be overlooked, ignored by smaller jurisdictions or may be unmanageable for them.

Will "Uncentralization" End Pyramid Dominance?

" The image of the 'good organization' was a pyramid," states Harland Cleveland, a former president of the American Society for Public Administration. Throughout history, organized government stood aligned with organized religion and an organized military. Hierarchy was regarded as functional: Employees did pretty much what they were told.

However, as Cleveland points out, "Pyramid building was always, and still is, essentially un-American. The real American tradition calls for the invention of systems in which nobody is in general charge—and, in consequence, each citizen is partly in charge." Cleveland goes on to discuss alternatives to centralization as an organizing concept. Decentralization, at the opposite spectrum, still preserves hierarchy; decentralization simply extends the authority of the hierarchy. The real opposite of centralization, emphasizes Cleveland, is "uncentralization."

Employees favor flexible systems. Flexibility promotes personal initiative, voluntary cooperation, joint ventures, committee work, and networking. Un-centralization requires widespread agreements on common norms and standards, as well as clarity of purpose. Therefore, uncentralized system function effectively with continuous consensus building. "Most of what each of us does from day to day does not happen because someone told us to do it," Cleveland asserts. Consensus, however, does not mean unanimous consent.

Widespread availability of relevant information enables mutual adjustment—or common understanding of moral rules, norms, conventions, and mores. "The key to a genuinely uncentralized system," concludes Cleveland, "is mutually agreed standards on whether is central to the system and thus cannot be left to individual choices or market outcomes."

Cleveland poses a pertinent question for "nobody-in-charge" systems. How does everybody get in on the act—and still get some action?

Source: Harlan Cleveland, "The Future is Uncentralized," Donald C. Stone Lecture, National Conference of the American Society for Public Administration, San Diego, April 4, 2000.

Conflicts between political and administrative decentralization models pit the values and priorities of geographic area (Peoria) against administrative function (Washington). Local partisans champion the political will of the former; national leaders insist upon the dominance of the latter. A balance between the extremes usually results. The vertical and horizontal mixing of political and administrative decentralization illustrates that values, tasks, and organizational structure interrelate in an effective organization.

Structural arrangements selected for implementing a task directly affect the success administrators enjoy in achieving their objectives and values. Decentralization moves government closer to citizens, offering elected officials and voters opportunities to more closely witness the programmatic and fiscal consequences of their decisions. Decentralization also gives decision makers the flexibility to meet local conditions.

However, centralization of functions at the state level may promote more uniform policies, resulting in certain economies of scale, and may eliminate the impacts of local fiscal disparities on the quality and costs of services. The ebb and flow of centralizing and decentralizing decisions in individual states is constant.

Decisions to centralize or decentralize public organizations cannot, therefore, be divorced from values, tasks, and organizational structure. An appropriate organizational design facilitates an administrator's values and objectives; an inappropriate organizational structure frustrates his or her purposes.

A variety of political, administrative, and economic characteristics typify public program functions. As new values and technologies emerge, organizational objectives change; new technologies affect community values. Issues affecting governmental centralization and decentralization include political, administrative, economic, and technological factors that may point the agency in conflicting directions while attempting to integrate its values, tasks, and organizational structure into an effective organization.

In a dynamic society espousing democracy and capitalism, we may ask: an effective organization for whom, what, when, where, and how?

The Craft and Political Culture

Many are claiming that the United States is in the midst of a culture war over moral values and life-styles.[16] Therefore, an understanding of culture is of great value to public administrators. To recognize the expectations and guidelines for professional behavior in one's culture is to promote understanding of the organization.

The culture of an organization provides guidelines for member behavior and performance. For example, class size is one feature of academic culture. The number of students in class influences the type and number of assignments professors may require. If the number of students in your class reaches into the hundreds, you may assume that your professor will emphasize short-answer examinations instead of essays. However, the culture of small classes allows your professor to be more personable in his or her approach to teaching and gives the professor more flexibility for evaluating your writing skills and critical thinking abilities. An understanding of classroom culture can help you steer toward classes where you are likely to perform best.

For our purposes, *culture* is defined as "that complex whole which includes knowledge, belief, art, morals, law, custom, and any other capabilities and habits acquired by man as a member of society."[17] An awareness of culture is crucial for understanding the development, implementation, and evaluation of public administration.

Culture, or ways of life common to a society, government organization, or interest group, includes the *ideal* and the *real*. Ideal cultural patterns focus on what citizens do or say if they adhere completely to recognized cultural standards. Real behavioral patterns refer to actual citizen observations and behaviors. Various aspects of culture, such as religious rituals, work habits, beliefs and ideologies, and marriage relationships, relate to and affect one another.

Culture may be divided according to:

- *Technology,* or the ways in which people create and use tools and other material artifacts;
- *Economics,* or the patterns of behaving relative to the production, distribution, and consumption of goods and services;
- *Social organization,* or characteristic relations among individuals within a society, including the division of labor, the social and political organization, and the relationship between a society and other societies;
- *Religion,* or ways of life relative to the human concern for the unknown;
- *Symbolism,* or systems of symbols (such as language, art, music, and literature) used to acquire, order, and transfer knowledge.[18]

The nature of our organized society and developments in the history of public administration underscore the importance of political and bureaucratic culture in the public administration environment. Partisan, policy, and system politics operate within a larger framework of political culture. *Political culture,* according to Daniel Elazár, is "the particular pattern of orientation to political action in which each political system is embedded."[19]

Culture puts limits on individuals in organizational settings. An organization is a subculture. For example, your public administration class is a subculture of the Department of Political Science, which is a subculture of a larger academic unit—usually a college of humanities, a subculture of the university or college. An understanding of the concept of culture is vital because we must recognize that an organization's members or employees are not free agents in any society.

Any organization is part of a larger social system. At least indirectly, its employees are thus subject to a larger set of values. Certain cultural patterns of conduct and belief can be found in any organization. The culture of an organization reflects a consensus of the particular values of that organization, but no organization can be isolated from its cultural environment.[20]

An understanding of culture can provide an advance indication of how people will act in a situation. A keenly developed sensitivity to culture can also be a substitute for experience. If you expect to climb the ladder of managerial success, pay close attention to your organization's culture. Traditions, customs, and patterned modes of behavior run through organizations. If you understand such structuring influences, you may even be able to facilitate changes in the organization.

According to J. Steven Ott, there are three levels of organizational culture and their interaction (figure 3.4).[21] Level 1A includes artifacts, technology, and art. Level 1B entails patterns of behavior, familiar management tasks, visible and audible behavior, and norms. Level 2 focuses on values, testable in the physical environment and only by social consensus. Level 3 concludes with basic assumptions and their relationship to the environment; the nature of reality, time, and space; the essence of of human nature; the nature of human activity; and the nature of human relationships.

On your college or university campus, illustrations of artifacts, technology, and art (Level 1A) are abundant. The administration building, main library, health center, basketball arena, football stadium, or parking garage qualify. The technology of the shuttle bus that circulates to and from the dorms and classroom buildings or the artwork of plant life maintained by the grounds keepers illustrate organizational culture Level 1A.

Certain norms of deportment are expected of students and faculty. Visible and audible expected behavior patterns include arriving at class on time. Familiar management tasks comprise daily routines for college classroom productivity and performance. These types of behaviors illustrate Level 1B.

Level 2 includes values that are testable in the physical environment and by social consensus, providing greater levels of awareness about organizational culture. The classroom limits or promotes effective exchanges between students and professor. The heating or cooling systems may malfunction, the lighting may be poor, the acoustics may be weird, the chairs may have splinters in them, or the roof may leak. The physical environment of the classroom contributes to the culture of the academic exercise. The social consensus may well be that the class should adjourn

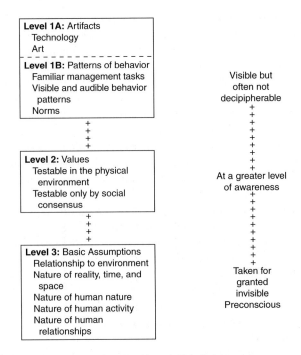

Level 1A: Artifacts
Technology
Art
- - - - - - - - - - - - - - -
Level 1B: Patterns of behavior
Familiar management tasks
Visible and audible behavior
    patterns
Norms

+
+
+
+

Level 2: Values
Testable in the physical
    environment
Testable only by social
    consensus

+
+
+
+

Level 3: Basic Assumptions
Relationship to environment
Nature of reality, time, and
    space
Nature of human nature
Nature of human activity
Nature of human
    relationships

Visible but
often not
decipipherable
+
+
+
+
+
+
+
+
+
At a greater level
of awareness
+
+
+
+
+
+
+
+
+
Taken for
granted
invisible
Preconscious

FIGURE 3.4 Levels of organizational culture and their interaction

Source: J. Steven Ott, From *The Organizational Culture Perspective,* 1989. Reprinted with permission of the author.

pronto, but that's not Professor Jones's decision; in fact, the professor insists that hot or cold air, lighting, acoustics, splinters, or rain should *not* interfere with the exciting revelations of public administration! The physical environment is now suspect, therefore the social consensus for continuing the class tests the culture, dictated to the students by the professor.

After students sit in a cold (or hot) classroom; follow the professor's lecture in near darkness; listen to the professor's voice as it bounces off the ceiling, to the radiator, to the concrete floor, back up to the ceiling, and finally into their brains; pull splinters from their hands and other extremities from a forty-year-old chair; and see a $50 public administration textbook ruined by rain pouring through a hole in the roof, students question basic assumptions about the nature of reality, time, and space concerning the culture, or ways of life, common to a college classroom. The questioning of these basic assumptions, at Level 3, examines the relationships of students to their cultural environment. The components of culture are *material* and *nonmaterial*. As figure 3.4 shows, the basic assumptions of Level 3 are often invisible and outside of consciousness.

Physical layout and organizational techniques are illustrations of material culture. Both contribute to the environment of public administration by focusing upon the interaction between habitat and culture and by emphasizing how and why certain actions occur. As students attend different classes, they move from one classroom culture to another. In chemistry, a chart showing the elements is part of the material culture. In biology, a skeleton hangs for the professor's demonstration to students. In architecture, drawing boards are a common feature of material culture.

Technology plays a key role in influencing material culture. Equipment and techniques affect the character of an organization. Personal computers are likely to be more helpful to you than typewriters when you are conducting research or writing a paper. The use of a videocassette recorder or DVD player in college classrooms expands teaching methods. If technology becomes increasingly complicated, an organization may have more difficulty in entering a new field of endeavor.

Not all culture is observable in the same way as material culture. Nonmaterial culture includes beliefs, systems of communications, and modes of conduct. Rituals, taboos, and jargon are modes of conduct that influence important aspects of nonmaterial culture. All organizations follow these prescribed formulas when employees act in ritualistic unison, observe a system of taboos, or speak in a peculiar jargon. One of the rituals of college classes is to arrive on time; cheating on examinations is taboo. Public administrators communicate in an "alphabet soup" jargon of acronyms for departments, agencies, and programs.

Material and nonmaterial culture may conflict if organization members confuse patterns of conduct with changes occurring in the world outside the organization. In other words, your nonmaterial value system, or beliefs, may not line up with the realities of the material world, which can result in *cultural lag.* Our organized society is constantly changing. Our values and preferences, however, tend to remain the same. The challenge is to respond appropriately to the changes in society without altering core values.

Material and nonmaterial bureaucratic cultures reflect a larger political culture. Political culture, as Elazár notes, includes perceptions held by the general public and politicians concerning the nature of politics and the perceived role of government in society. A statewide political culture gives citizens a framework for what to expect from government and for how they perceive office holders, bureaucrats, and campaign workers. Political culture outlines the boundaries and practices of citizens, politicians, and public officials. Elazár carves out three types of political culture in the United States and describes the relation of bureaucracy to each type. The three types of political culture are *individualistic, moralistic,* and *traditionalistic.*

Individualistic—In this type of political culture, politics is viewed as dirty. Only professionals participate in politics, and parties dole out favors and responsibilities among them. Party cohesiveness is strong; competition arises between parties, not over issues. New programs are not to be initiated unless public opinion demands them. Political competition focuses on winning office to reap tangible rewards. Government is viewed as a marketplace and economic development is favored. The appropriate spheres of activity are largely economic. Bureaucracy is viewed ambivalently. A loosely implemented type of merit system is favored. Indiana, Nevada, New Jersey, and Pennsylvania are states that reflect the individualistic political culture.

Moralistic—In a moralistic political culture, the practice of politics is viewed as healthy and as every citizen's responsibility. Everyone can participate. Political parties are vehicles to attain goals believed to be in the public interest. Party cohesiveness is subordinate to principles and issues. Competition is over issues, not parties. Political orientation focuses upon winning office to implement policies.

The Culture of Corruption

It has not just been Ulysses S. Grant, Warren G. Harding, and Richard M. Nixon—our most famously scandal-burdened presidents—who wrestled with accusations of corruption. John Adams and John Quincy Adams, two of the most incorruptible men in U.S. political history, were also harried throughout their presidencies by accusations of corruption and abuses of power. Rutherford B. Hayes, a paragon of propriety, was known during his unhappy administration as "His Fraudulency" for having allegedly stolen the 1876 election from Samuel J. Tilden.

Harry S. Truman, a folk hero today for what Americans like to remember as his plain-speaking honesty, was buffeted by charges of "cronyism" and "corruption"—for creating what Nixon and many others in 1952 liked to call the "mess in Washington." Even Dwight D. Eisenhower, famously genial, enormously popular, legendarily honest, suffered from embarrassing revelations about his chief of staff, Sherman L. Adams, and other improprieties. What happened in the late 1990s to Bill Clinton is in many respects part of the ordinary pattern of U.S. political life.

In an era when charges are made—in the media and in courtrooms—against government officials on a rather frequent basis, the terms *corruption* and *scandal* virtually become synonymous in the minds of many Americans. But they have different implications. While both signify moral unsoundness, corruption denotes legal violations, or the breaking of laws, whereas scandal simply offends someone's moral values.

So, as the Monica Lewinsky scandal offended notions of sexual morality (personal lies) to millions, incidences of abortions, poverty, racism, economic disparity, lowering of education standards, and social welfare policies (institutional lies) are scandals to others. Officials in the Clinton administration offended the moral feelings of many citizens, creating scandal, but not necessarily resulting in corruption, or the breaking of laws.

Source: Alan Brinkley, "The Culture of Corruption," *Los Angeles Times*, November 2, 1997, p. M1.

Government in a moralistic system is viewed as a commonwealth, answering directly for the general welfare and common good of the people. Appropriate spheres of activity include any area that will enhance the community through nongovernmental action. New programs are initiated without public pressure if they are believed to be in the public interest. Bureaucracy is viewed positively, bringing desirable political neutrality. A strong merit system is favored. Colorado, Michigan, Minnesota, North Dakota, Oregon, Utah, Vermont, and Wisconsin reflect the moralistic political culture.

Traditionalistic—Politics is viewed as a privilege in which only those with legitimate claim to office should participate. Participation in politics is limited to the appropriate elite. Political parties serve as vehicles to recruit people for public offices not desired by established power holders. Party cohesiveness depends upon family and social ties and is highly personal. Competition is between the elite-dominated factions within a dominant party. The orientation to politics depends upon the political values of the elite.

Government is viewed as a means of maintaining the existing order. Appropriate spheres of activity are those that maintain traditional patterns. New programs are initiated if the program serves in the interest of the governing elite. Bureaucracy is viewed negatively, as it depersonalizes government. Merit should be controlled by the political elite, so no merit system is favored. Mississippi, South Carolina, Tennessee, and Virginia are states reflecting the traditionalistic political culture.

Some states fall into more than one type of political culture. Those states that are mainly moralistic political cultures yet also have individualistic traits are California, Iowa, Kansas, Montana, New Hampshire, South Dakota, and Washington.

States that are mainly individualistic but have moralistic traits as well are Connecticut, Illinois, Massachusetts, Nebraska, New York, Ohio, and Rhode Island.

States that are individualistic yet traditional are Delaware, Hawaii, Maryland, and Missouri. Those that are traditionalistic, yet individualistic are Alabama, Arkansas, Florida, Georgia, Kentucky, Louisiana, New Mexico, Oklahoma, Texas, and West Virginia. States that are traditionalistic, yet moralistic are Arizona and North Carolina.[22]

Political culture, then, can be said to encompass a state's orientation to political action. Culture includes knowledge, belief, art, morals, law, customs, capabilities, and habits institutionalized within an organization's environment. Material culture is observable, focuses upon relationships of people distributed in space, and includes tools and techniques for fulfilling organizational purposes. Nonmaterial culture is not so obvious because it incorporates belief systems and patterns of conduct. No organization can be isolated from its cultural environment. This means the bureaucratic culture of the government organizations in a particular state cannot be divorced from that state's political culture.

When one examines the various aspects of public or government organization, one must look beyond mere facts and seek out factors that define reality or the culture of government, including:

1. the history of government, or how it developed;
2. the role of government as perceived by members of society;
3. the structures and processes considered proper to government; and
4. the values, mores, and habits of the primary people, especially the elected and appointed officials and the bureaucrats working beneath those officials.[23]

Culture impacts the everyday operations of a government organization. Culture resides in the ideas, values, norms, rituals, and beliefs of *socially constructed realities,* or organizations. Patterns of belief or shared meaning cause organizations to adopt their own ways of perceiving problems and resolving them.[24] The dynamics of culture incorporate traditions, perceptions, attitudes, assumptions, perspectives, values, and behaviors.

Summary

- The *anatomy* of public bureaucracy is its organizational framework or administrative structure.
- *Purpose, process, place,* and *clientele* explain why an organization was established.
- Of the three branches of government, the executive, legislative, and judicial, the executive has the widest range of responsibilities. As of 2000, the executive branch employs about 97 percent of all federal civilian employees, excluding the postal service.
- Principles for building a new agency are to keep it flat, focus on performance, and prepare for quasi-government status.

- *Unity of command* shows the relationship between those who order and those who follow orders. Unity of command usually requires a *chain of command,* because in any large bureaucracy, the person at the top cannot oversee all that is going on below. *Span of control* refers to the number of units—individuals or groups—that any supervising unit must oversee.
- *Staff personnel* are specialists who provide skills, knowledge, and expertise to line personnel. Staff functions to provide planning, fact finding, and support for line executives.
- Staff units in the Executive Office of the President include the White House Office, Council of Economic Advisers, Office of the U.S. Trade Representative, Office of Management and Budget, National Security Council, Council on Environmental Quality, Office of Policy Development, and Office of Science and Technology Policy.
- *Line personnel* are primarily concerned with developing, implementing, and evaluating policy. Line administrators are generalists. They legitimize authority and are in command. Line employees are directly responsible for furthering an organization's goals. Staff and line employees sometimes come into conflict. This should come as no surprise because their goals and functions are inherently different.
- Line departments in the federal government include Agriculture, Commerce, Defense, Education, Energy, Health and Human Services, Housing and Urban Development, Interior, Justice, Labor, State, Transportation, Treasury, and Veterans' Affairs.
- *Decentralization* occurs when an organization delegates powers to subordinate levels within the same department or agency. Political decentralization allocates power among states, counties, cities, and other local governments. Decisions to centralize or decentralize cannot be divorced from the values, tasks, and structure of an organization. Americans seem to agree that governmental power should be shifted to the states. However, a 10 percent increase in efficiency as a result of state control would reduce government costs by less than 0.5 percent.[25]
- *Political culture* consists of the pattern of political action within a political system. Any organization is part of a larger social system. Indirectly, an organization's employees are therefore subject to a larger social system. Its employees are also subject, indirectly, to a larger set of values. No organization can be isolated from its cultural environment.
- Throughout history, organized government stood in tandem with organized religion and an organized military. Hierarchy was regarded as functional.
- An organization's purpose needs clarity and comprehensive understanding. Uncentralized systems function effectively with continuous consensus building. Consensus, however, does not mean unanimous consent.
- Physical layout, organizational techniques, and technology illustrate material culture. Beliefs, systems of communication, and modes of conduct illustrate nonmaterial culture. Our nonmaterial values or beliefs may not line up with the realities of the material world, which can result in cultural lag.
- Corruption and scandal signify moral unsoundness. Corruption denotes legal violations, or the breaking of laws. Scandal simply offends moral values. Scandal surrounding sexual immorality may be emblematic of personal lies. Poverty, racism, economic disparity, lowering of education standards, and social welfare policies may be symbolic of institutional lies.
- Culture may be divided according to technology, economics, social organization, religion, and symbolism.

The next step in understanding the craft of public administration is to examine some key theories about organizations. That is the focus of the next chapter.

Case Study

Bobby Knight and Hoosier Culture

This case study illustrates potential conflicts in chain of command, unity of command, and span of control; line and staff and administrative decentralization; real and ideal cultures; material and nonmaterial cultures; traditionalism and individualism; and cultural identity. How could Indiana University President Myles Brand have "played" basketball coach Bobby Knight at a one-to-ten scenario—not a zero-sum outcome?

> What makes a university better is what you get out of it. The essence to getting an education is creating advantages for yourself.
>
> —*Bobby Knight*
> *Texas Tech basketball coach*

As men's basketball coach at Indiana University (IU) from 1971 to September 2000, Bobby Knight led the Hoosiers to three NCAA titles (1976, 1981, and 1987) and eleven Big Ten championships. He also coached U.S. teams to gold medals in the 1984 Olympics and 1987 Pan American Games. Knight's teams won 763 games over the duration, and not once was the Indiana basketball program on NCAA probation.

At IU and Texas Tech, Knight is a state government employee; his salary is paid by the taxpayers of Texas. As head of the Department of Men's Intercollegiate Basketball at Texas Tech University, Knight is regulated by provisions of state and federal laws. With certain skills, knowledge, and expertise, Knight is a government bureaucrat—and a basketball coach par excellence.

Born October 25, 1940, in Massillon, Ohio, Robert Montgomery Knight grew up in nearby Orrville, where he played basketball, football, and baseball for the Orrville Red Raiders. He played college basketball for three seasons (1960–1962) at Ohio State University. (Freshmen did not play varsity sports.) He started only two games. As a bench player, Knight was the "sixth man" on OSU's national championship team.

Knight coached high school basketball in Cuyahoga Falls, Ohio. He subsequently joined the Army to coach the U.S. Military Academy team at West Point. He arrived at Indiana University on April Fools day, 1971. He taught a class on basketball fundamentals while he was coach at Indiana. He is known to some as a jerk, bully, and abuser. Al Neuharth, founder of *USA*

Today, says that Knight often reminds him of the great World War II Army general, George S. Patton, Jr. Neuharth points out that Knight

- teaches discipline, as well as winning;
- develops team players, not just run-and-gun hotshots; and
- makes sure most players graduate from college.[1]

Knight never apologizes. "If my kids left and weren't successful, if they were on the bread line or selling drugs or in jail for one thing or another, then I would have a lot of questions about what my methods were leading to," Knight insists. "But when I have kids come back and talk about their experience here, what it's meant to them and I see what they're doing, then I'm just not sure what there is that I'm supposed to apologize for."[2]

Others disagree. Knight's quick temper and agressive behavior toward players and others finally cost the legendary coach his job. On September 10, 2000, IU President Myles Brand fired Knight for a continuing pattern of "defiant and hostile" behavior. Paragraph 9 of Knight's contract read: "If the university at any time desires, Coach Knight shall cease to serve as head basketball coach when so advised in writing."[3]

Brand stated: "He is a legendary coach who has won three national championships, had graduation rates among the highest in the country, run a crystal-clean program with no NCAA violations, and been a great philanthropist. But he has failed to live within the guidelines by which he promised to abide."[4]

Why Did Myles Brand Fire Bobby Knight?

As IU President, Brand is a generalist, occupying a position of authority and commanding the organization's operations. As men's basketball coach, Knight was a specialist who provided coaching skills, knowledge, and expertise to line personnel director President Brand in IU's chain of command. Why did President Brand fire Coach Knight?

President Brand fired Coach Knight because:

- Knight refused to work within the "normal" IU chain of command in the athletics department.

- The coach made angry remarks about university officials and trustees.
- Knight refused to participate in previously scheduled events for IU alumni.
- He did not abide by sanctions as catalogued in IU's "zero tolerance policy" (ZTP).[5]
- Finally, of course, Knight confronted freshman IU student, Kent Harvey, 19, regarding proper manners and civility.

Harvey claimed Knight grabbed and intimidated him. (Knight is known for his intimidating presence.) Harvey is the stepson of Mark Shaw, a former Bloomington radio talk-show host and a critic of Knight. Harvey spoke to the coach, referring to him as "Knight." Knight reportedly said to young Harvey: "Son, my name is not 'Knight' to you. It's 'Coach Knight' or it's 'Mr. Knight.' I don't call people by their last name, and neither should you."[6]

Knight's run-in with Harvey resulted in "inappropriate physical contact," which violated IU's zero tolerance policy and was cause for immediate termination. IU's ZTP did not include due process guidelines. Brand insisted that a half-dozen accusations against Knight were on record, and that no single offense reached the level for firing Knight. Taken together, all the offenses resulted in a pattern of conduct outside the boundaries of the zero tolerance policy guidelines.

As head of IU's chain of command, Brand asked Knight to resign. The coach refused, violating Brand's unity-of-command order. Brand then fired Knight. As the word filtered out to IU students, two thousand people—mostly students—marched on the athletic complex, Showalter Fountain, and at the President's home. During campus unrest, Harvey and Brand were hanged in effigy. The next day Knight bade farewell to the students at a talk in Dunn Meadow; crowd estimates ranged from six to ten thousand. Brand called Knight's talk "gracious."

Culture is defined as "that complex whole which includes knowledge, belief, art, morals, law, custom, and any other capabilities and habits acquired by man as a member of society."[7] Cultural awareness is crucial for understanding the development, implementation, and evaluation of any government program, including that of the men's basketball program at IU, funded by the Indiana taxpayers. Culture—or ways of life common to a society, government organization, or interest group—includes the ideal and the real.

Ideal cultural patterns focus on what citizens do or say if they adhere completely to the recognized standards of the culture. Real behavioral patterns refer to people's actual observations and behaviors.[8] In 2000, 52 percent of white college basketball players graduated from college; 35 percent of black players graduated, yet the graduation rate for IU men's basketball players was 79 percent during the 1990s. What happens if one of Knight's players cuts class? "I'm too scared to find out," a smiling 7-foot, 285-pound Texas Tech center, Mickey Michalec, told ESPN. In the Knight-IU academic world, the real culture approximated the ideal.[9]

Culture places limits on individuals in organizational settings. An organization is a subculture within a larger culture. An understanding of the larger culture is vital because we must recognize than an organization's members or employees are not free agents in any society—including that of Indiana University.

One-to-Ten and Zero-Sum Games

College basketball is no one-to-ten game. Players do not get credit in the media for playing hard. Instead, NCAA college hoops is a zero-sum game: One team wins, the other loses. Stamina, conditioning, physical abuse, hard work, long hours, mental toughness, and competition make the difference—this is the culture of college basketball. In Knight's career at IU, the Hoosiers had no NCAA violations for recruiting or academics. They made it into the NCAA tournament for fifteen straight years. IU won more basketball games in the 1970s, 1980s, and 1990s than any team in the Big Ten conference.

Any organization, whatever its limits or prospects, is part of a larger social system. At least indirectly, its employees are subject to a larger set of values. Certain cultural patterns of conduct and belief are found in any organization. Culture reflects a consensus of the values of that organization.

In an era when charges are made—in the media—against controversial public figures on a daily basis, the terms *corruption* and *scandal* become virtually synonymous in the minds of many Americans. How many times has a TV clip, portrayed Knight throwing chairs? Perhaps hundreds. How many times did Knight throw a chair? Once. How many times did Knight intimidate players or others? Many. Has Knight been convicted of assaulting anyone? No. Has he been charged in a court of law? No. Knight's behavior may be a scandal, but so far, none of it has ever proved illegal. Knight is certainly no criminal.

Bobby Knight and Bill Clinton

Bobby Knight and Bill Clinton have one thing in common. The left wing—grounded mostly in government-funded colleges and universities—abhors physical violence. The right wing—originating in private wealth and status and in small-town America—abhors sexual misdeeds. The left accuses Knight of physical abuse. The right accused Clinton of sexual misbehavior. Both extremes employ the media to make their cases known.

But no organization can be isolated from its cultural environment.[10] Understanding culture gives one an advance indication of how people may act in a given situation. Traditions, customs, and patterned modes of behavior are common to all organizations. Knight is a bright, hard-working, high-achieving, and charismatic college basketball coach. Clinton is a bright, hard-working, high-achieving, and charismatic former president. But going beyond what tradition, customs, and modes of conduct permit is sometimes a matter of smart people doing dumb things.

Physical layout and organization techniques are examples of material culture. Technology plays a key role in influencing material culture; equipment and techniques affect the character of an organization. College basketball is played between two teams of five players each, with players trying to throw the ball through an elevated basket precisely ten feet from the floor on the opponent's side of the rectangular court. Lighting technology for every arena varies. The size of the court is standard—54 × 90. The three-point goal line is 19.9 feet from the end of the court. The free throw circle is a radius of 6 feet. These dimensions reflect college basketball's material culture.

Nonmaterial culture includes beliefs, systems of communications, and modes of conduct. All organizations follow prescribed formulas. Employees may act in ritualistic unison, observe a system of taboos, or speak in peculiar jargon. If our nonmaterial value system is not in sync with the realities of the material world, the result is **cultural lag**.[11]

Society is constantly changing, but many human values and preferences remain much the same. The challenge is to respond appropriately to changes in society without altering core values. Knight is a talented coach because he has developed techniques to defeat teams with varying skills. Yet his players learned and graduated.

Indiana culture is primarily traditionalistic south of U.S. highway 40 and especially individualistic north of that demarcation. Except for the region near Chicago,

nowhere in Indiana is the culture moralistic. Participation is limited to the appropriate elite in traditional politics. Party cohesiveness depends upon family and social ties and is highly personal. Government is viewed as a means of maintaining the existing social order.[12]

Traditionalism versus Individualism?

Traditionalism conflicts with individualism in the Knight–IU case. Traditionalism implies that IU should have terminated the controversial coach a long time ago. An upright, conservative, and successful foul-mouthed megalomaniacal boor is still a foul-mouthed megalomaniacal boor. No assault or battery should be accepted in sport. Knight personifies a person of means who feels he is above the law and norms of society.

Individualism gives Knight a lot more rope. The ends, at least in part, justify the means. Bad language and screaming obscenities are contextual; record and performance are the bottom line. The players get educated. They win, they don't cheat, and they do well in life. You know where he stands. Knight is honest, productive, and loyal to IU. Politics is viewed as dirty in individualistic politics. Only professionals participate. Parties dole out favors and responsibility, government is a marketplace.

In the 1960s *College Edition: Webster's New World Dictionary of the American Language* (predating current definitions of *political correctness*) the word *Hoosier* is defined as a "mountaineer, dirty person, or tramp; a native or inhabitant of Indiana."[13]

Terms such as mountaineer, dirty person, tramp, or vagrant bring to mind the phrase "white trash." The United States, historically, is a "white trash country." Immigrants fled here from other countries to find opportunities in capitalism, democracy, and personal flexibility.

Bobby Knight became head basketball coach at Indiana University in 1971. Knight arrived in Bloomington approximately a decade after Webster published its interpretations of the word *Hoosier*. Knight assumed leadership of a college basketball program in a state called the "Appalachia of the midwest." Indiana enjoys more in common, democraphically, with Kentucky that it does with Ohio, Michigan, Wisconsin, Iowa, and parts of Illinois.

While Knight coached IU, Indianapolis discarded its image as Indiana-no-place. The Lilly Corporation emerged as the world's most prominent drug company. Late-night-talk-show host Dave Letterman invented "stupid pet tricks." Two Republicans (Otis Bowen and Bob Orr) and two Democrats (Evan Bayh and Frank

O'Bannon) were elected governor of Indiana during Knight's twenty-nine years as IU's coach. None affected the culture as much as Knight.

Knight gave Indiana University and the state of Indiana a new cultural identity. He redefined the word *Hoosier*—as a determined, focused, well-trained, skilled, hard-working, respectful, all-for-the-team, loyal, overachieving college student—who also happened to be a basketball player. Knight taught hard work and 100 percent effort, and he inspired confidence and loyalty that allowed IU teams to excel beyond their natural abilities.

Culture resides in the ideas, values, norms, rituals, and beliefs of socially constructed realities, or organizations. Belief patterns or shared meanings cause organizations to adopt certain ways of perceiving and resolving problems. Culture includes traditions, perceptions, attitudes, assumptions, perspectives, values, and behaviors.

Moralistic politics is viewed as healthy and as every citizen's responsibility. Political parties are vehicles to attain goals believed to be in the public interest. Competition takes place over issues, not parties. Indiana, as a state government, does not practice moralistic politics. In traditionalism and individualism, the bottom line is authority (line) and power (Brand) versus specialist (staff) and talent (Knight).

Could a moralistic ideology have ushered in compromise and consensus between Brand and Knight?

- Indiana culture pays attention to traditionalism and individualism. The moralistic idea of the greater good, if active in Indiana, is imported in from elsewhere.
- President Brand defended his power and position. Brand and the IU Trustees fired the intimidating Coach Knight.
- Just because Knight was not paranoid does not mean that they were not after him. No bureaucrat, however talented, can ignore the culture outside his or her immediate organization.

Questions and Instructions

1. Define *culture.* Apply the definition in this case.
2. Name some ideal cultural patterns in this case.
3. Name some real cultural patterns in this case.
4. Culture places limits on individuals. What limits did it place in this case?
5. An organization is a subculture within a larger culture. How do staff and line come into play in this case? Explain.
6. Physical layout and organization techniques illustrate material culture. How is this true in this case?
7. Nonmaterial culture includes beliefs, systems of communication, and modes of conduct. How did these elements play out in Knight's case? Explain.
8. How might moralistic precepts at IU have brought the traditionalism of Brand (authority/line) and the individualism of Knight ("I did it my way"/staff) into compromise and an escape from the zero-tolerance, zero-sum game? Explain.
9. How did the cultural identity of Indiana change during Knight's twenty-nine-year tenure as IU's basketball coach? Explain.
10. Why did Knight have more influence on the culture of Indiana than Otis Bowen, Bob Orr, Evan Bayh, and Frank O'Bannon—all governors of the Hoosier state?

Insights-Issues/Bobby Knight and Hoosier Culture

Clearly and briefly describe and illustrate the following concepts and issues. Interpret the word *role* in terms of impacts, applications, importance, effects, and/or illustrations of certain facts, concerns, or issues from the case study.

1. Role of culture in the firing of Knight.
2. Role of chain of command, unity of command, and span of control in the firing of Knight.
3. Role of traditionalism and individualism in arguments for and against firing Knight.
4. Role of staff-line conflicts in arguments for and against firing Knight.
5. Role of Knight in developing a new cultural identity for the state of Indiana.

Case Endnotes

1. Al Neuharth, "Would you want your son on Knight's team?" USA Today, November 1, 2000, http://www.usatoday.com/news/comment/columnists/neuharth/neu044.htm.

2. "Knight Defends Record After Choking Accusation," http://espn.go.com/ncb/news/2000/0317/430679.html.

3. Indiana University, "IU Announces Removal of Basketball Coach Bob Knight," September 10, 2000, http://www.iuinfo.indiana.edu/ocm/releases/knight0910.htm.

4. *Ibid.*

5. Zero tolerance did not begin with Miles Brand and Bobby Knight. In the 1980s, the state and federal governments fought illegal drugs. By 1994, the Safe and Drug-Free Schools and Communities Act required schools that received federal funds to expel students who brought weapons to school. Brand and the IU Board of Trustees adopted their zero tolerance policy to encourage Knight to temper his "pattern of inappropriate behavior" with fans, student athletes, and basketball officials. Knight, in part, was fired because he lectured a student on the proper way to address an adult.

6. Rex W. Huppke, "Indiana Investigating Knight again, "*The Associated Press,* September 8, 2000, http://sports.yahoo.com/ncaab/news/ap/20000908/ap-knight-student.html.

7. John M. Pfiffner and Frank P. Sherwood, *Administrative Organization* (Englewood Cliffs, NJ: Prentice-Hall, 1960), pp. 249–272. See Rhys H. Williams, "Is America in a Culture War? Yes—No—Sort of," *The Christian Century,* Vol. 114, No. 32 (November 12, 1997), pages 1038–1043. Quotes from Tylor's Primitive Culture in Leslie A. White, "The Concept of Culture," *American Anthropologist,* Vol. 61, No. 227 (April 1959). White reports that there is great divergence of view among anthropologists as to a definition of culture.

8. Thomas R. Dye, *Power & Society: An Introduction to the Social Sciences* (Monterey, CA: Brooks/Cole, 1987), p. 39.

9. Don Williams, "Grad Rates Focus of TV Special," *The Lubbock Avalance-Journal,* March 1, 2002, http://www.redraiders.com/stories/030102/mbb_030102104.shtml.

10. Pfiffner and Sherwood, *op.cit,* 252.

11. *Ibid.,* p. 264.

12. Daniel J. Elazár, *American Federalism: A View from the States* (New York: Harper & Row, Publishers, 1984), p. 109.

13. *Webster's New World Dictionary of the American Language, College Edition* (Cleveland and New York: The World Publishing Company, copyright 1960), p. 699.

Case Sources

"Bob Knight—former Indiana University Basketball Coach," *The Indianapolis Star,* September 15, 2000, http://www.starnews.com/library/factfiles/ people/k/knight_bob/knight.html; "Knight Offers Life Lessons, Dodges Controversy in Appearance at Ball State," *The Associated Press,* April 20, 2001; Myles Brand, "Academics First: Reforming Intercollegiate Athletics," January 23, 2001, http://www.indiana.edu/~pres/speeches/press_club.html; Ibid., "Open Letter to the Media," February 2, 1998; Graham Couch, "Keeping Knight Keeps IU from Becoming a Basketball Factory," *Columbia Chronicle Online,* Vol. 33, No. 27 (May 22, 2000), http://www.ccchronicle.com/back/00may22/sports2.html; Jonathan Grossberg, "The Ironic End to a Great Era in Indiana," *The Brown Daily Herald,* September 19, 2000, http://www.browndailyherald.com; Bobby Knight with Bob Hammel, *Knight: My Story* (New York: St. Martin's Press), 2002; John Laskowski, "Playing for the General," *Indiana Alumni Magazine* (November–December 2000), http://www.indiana.edu/~alumni.magtalk/nov.dec00/thegeneral.html; Mike Leonard, "Professor May Help Redefine 'Hoosier,' " *The Bloomington Herald-Times,* January 28, 2001; Rhonda Chriss Lokeman, "Indiana U. Should Hit Knight Where It Hurts," *The Kansas City Star,* May 21, 2000, http://www.positivecoach.org/news/20000521_lokeman.html; Gareth Morgan, *Images of Organization* (Beverly Hills, CA: Sage, 1986); John Rouse, "Knight Not the Insidious Element at IU by Far," *Evansville Courier & Press,* September 21, 2000, http://www.courierpress.com; Chris Suellentrop, "Assessment: Bob Knight," March 15, 2002, http://slate.msn.com; "Suit Contends Indiana Broke Law in Firing Knight," *Sports Illustrated,* October 3, 2000, http://sportsillustrated.cnn.com/basketball/college/news/2000/10/03/knight_lawsuit_ap/;Steve Wilstein, "Knight May Be Asked to Quit," *The Associated Press,* May 12, 2000, http://www.onlineathens.com/stories/051200/dog_0512000045. shtml; Mike Wright, "A Knight to Remember," *Indiana Alumni Magazine* (November–December, 2000),. http://www.indiana.edu/~alumni/megtalk/nov-dec00/knightremember.html.

Chapter Endnotes

1. Luther Gulick and L. Urwick, *Papers on the Science of Administration* (New York: Institute of Public Administration, 1937), p. 15.

2. U.S. Department of Labor, Bureau of Labor Statistics, "Career Guide to Industries: Federal Government, Excluding the Postal Service," http://www.bls.gov/oco/cg/cgs041.htm.

3. Paul C. Light, "From Pentagons to Pyramids: Whacking at Bloat," *Government Executive,* July 1, 2001, http://www.govexec.com; "It's the Layers, Not the Numbers, That Count," *Government Executive,* March 1, 2001, http://www.brook.edu/views/Op-ed/Light/20010301.htm.

4. John M. Pfiffner and Frank P. Sherwood, *Administrative Organization* (Englewood Cliffs, N.J.: Prentice-Hall, 1960), pp. 170–188.

5. John D. Donahue, "The Devil in Devolution," *The American Prospect* no. 32 (May–June 1997): 42–48.

6. Mary O. Furner, "Downsizing Government: A Historical Perspective," *USA Today* 126, no. 2630 (November 1997): 56–58.

7. Dana Milbank, *Wall Street Journal,* 8 January 1997, p. A1.

8. Judith Havemann, "After Getting Responsibility for Welfare, States May Pass It Down," *The Washington Post,* January 28, 1997, p. A1.

9. Steven D. Gold, "Issues Raised by the New Federalism," *National Tax Journal* 49, no. 2 (June 1996): 273–287.

10. Hal Hovey, "The Challenges of Flexibility," *State Legislatures* 22, no. 1 (January 1996): 14–19.

11. David O. Porter and Eugene A. Olsen, "Some Critical Issues in Government Centralization and Decentralization," *Public Administration Review* 36, no. 1 (January/February 1976): 72–84.

12. Harold Seidman and Robert Gilmour, *Politics, Position, and Power: From the Positive to the Regulatory State,* 4th ed. (New York: Oxford University Press, 1986), p. 127.

13. *Ibid.*

14. Herbert Kaufman, "Administrative Decentralization and Political Power," *Public Administration Review* 29 (January/February 1969): 3–15.

15. Beryl A. Radin, *Managing Decentralized Departments: The Case of the U.S. Department of Health and Human Services* (Arlington, VA: The PriceWaterhouseCoopers Endowment for the Business of Government, 1999), p. 24

16. See Rhys H. Williams, "Is America in a Culture War? Yes—No—Sort of," *The Christian Century* 114, no. 32 (November 12, 1997): 1038–1043. Quotes from Tylor's Primitive Culture in Leslie A. White, "The Concept of Culture," *American Anthropologist* 61, no. 227 (April 1959). White reports that there is great divergence of view among anthropologists as to a definition of culture.

17. Thomas R. Dye, *Power & Society: An Introduction to the Social Sciences,* 4th ed. (Monterey, Calif.: Brooks/Cole, 1987), p. 39.

18. *Ibid.,* p. 40.

19. Daniel J. Elazár, *American Federalism: A View from the States* (New York: Harper & Row, 1984), p. 109.

20. John M. Pfiffner and Frank P. Sherwood, *Administrative Organization* (Englewood Cliffs, N.J.: Prentice-Hall, Inc., 1960), pp. 249–272.

21. J. Steven Ott, *The Organization Culture Perspective* (Chicago: The Dorsey Press, 1989), p. 62.

22. Elazár, *American Federalism,* 136.

23. Harold F. Gortner, Julianne Mahler, and Jeanne Bell Nicholson, *Organization Theory: A Public Perspective* (Fort Worth, Tex.: Harcourt Brace, 1997), p. 71.

24. Gareth Morgan, *Images of Organization* (Beverly Hills, Calif. Sage, 1986).

25. John D. Donahue, "The Disunited States: 'Devolution'—Shifting Power from Washington to the Fifty States—Is No Cure for What Ails American Government," *The Atlantic Monthly* 279, no. 5 (May 1997): 18–21.

The Physiology of Public Organizations

Chapter Highlights

Democracy in Bureaucracy

Baseline Originals in Organizational Life

Neoclassical Theories

Human Relations Theories

Women, Men, and Management Styles

Gender Gap in Government

Summary

Public Service as Organization Theory

Individualism is a priority in American life. Consumerism and the market follow close behind, with notions of "the greater good" and community bringing up the rear among citizen expectations and concerns. From the vantage point of organization theory, public service derives its support from community commitments—not selfish notions of individualism.

What is a public service career? Public servants today often have exciting careers. College professors, firefighters, police officers, air traffic controllers, grammar school teachers, diplomats, sanitation inspectors, elected representatives, moon walkers (of the NASA variety), soldiers, sailors, jet fighter pilots, peace corps volunteers, economic development specialists, mayors, governors, and presidents are engaged in public service careers. They represent and are employees of the community.

Dedication, work, tolerance, and love forge the depth, width, and psychological boundaries of community. "The United States is by definition a place on the map, but is not intrinsically a community," writes former Colorado governor, Richard D. Lamm. "A community is not geography—it is not who lives in an area—it is the web of human

relationships of the people who live in a particular place. Every house is not a home, and every spot on the map is not a community."

Public servants earn academic degrees in many disciplines, including aerospace technology, geology, environmental science, business, law, criminal justice, sociology, social work, computer science, finance, journalism, telecommunications, military science, political science, public administration, accounting, natural resources, history, economics, law enforcement, and civil engineering. Workplaces include local, state, and federal governments, along with nonprofit organizations. Bureaucrats, as government employees are often called, do not always have boring jobs. They shape urban designs, school curricula, immigration procedures, environmental regulations, air safety, railroad crossings, and Middle East peace accords. The marketplace fails to effectively function without the trust and safety instilled by public servants.

In terms of organization theory, working for the Children's Defense Fund, Habitat for Humanity, or the statewide Transportation Planning region requires a different set of values than working for Enron, accounting firms, banking, real estate, or other forms of corporate profiteering. Lobbying for the rights of children, ensuring that families have homes, and organizing citizen input before building new interstate highways are all examples in which public servants work for the long-term interests of community, region, state, and nation.

Satisfying short-term, private consumer wants does not make the list of organizational priorities for public servants. Answering the needs of people and community does.

Source

Richard D. Lamm, "The Elusive Concept of Community," *Kettering Review,* 28–36.

Physiology is the study of life processes, activities, and functions. As a medical student must study physiology to understand how the human body works, students of public administration must be familiar with *organizational theories* so they will be prepared to confront the realities of bureaucracy. This chapter provides a look at the most influential and helpful organizational theories and theorists.

Democracy in Bureaucracy

Bureaucracy and *democracy* are the central pillars of the public and private organizations of our society. Bureaucratic hierarchy and democratic equality influence the vital processes and functions of all organizations. Despite the apparent paradox, bureaucracy and democracy are both antithetical and complementary.

In partisan politics, we periodically elect presidents, governors, and mayors. In such electoral processes, we take advantage of the fundamental principle of democracy. While in office, however, presidents, governors, and mayors depend upon principles of bureaucracy, which apply formalism, strict rule adherence, impersonality, unity of command, chain of command, span of control, and similar values to the exercise of authority. Authority in a bureaucracy is checked by democratic voting procedures, but only on a periodic basis. As we consider the functions and processes of organizations, therefore, an understanding of the philosophical differences between bureaucracy and democracy is crucial.

The development of our organized society underscores the need for democracy in the administrative state. We, the voting public, come into contact with numerous public and private organizations each day. Government constantly exercises its influence on the public. Legislatures allocate public functions to administrative structures. What input should employees and clientele have in internal decision making within public organizations? Can there be democracy in bureaucracy? How democratic should life in organizations be?

If you are not already employed, in a matter of years, even months, you will probably enter the American workforce. You may be employed by a business, labor, social, or public organization. You may be full of ideas and energy to tackle your employer's challenges and problems, and you will want to be heard. How much democracy will exist in your bureaucratic workplace? The *authoritarian tenets of bureaucracy* and the *egalitarian tenets of democracy* are major forces shaping life and the pursuit of happiness in the twenty-first century. These concepts

Bureaucracy and Democracy Are Not Esoteric

Bureaucracy and democracy—concepts, terms, ways of working life—may seem esoteric, even to government employees. They are key aspects of government-operated, taxpayer-financed, public sector organizations. Capital is a necessity if public bureaucracy is to function well and if democracy is to realize a diversity of expression.

The respective definitions of capital, bureaucracy, and democracy, are economic wealth, employee skills and responsiveness, and the relatively free articulation of opinions. Capital does not necessarily mean money, but it often does. Money is wealth, or economic access to what one wants in life. And, simply stated, wealth is power.

Wealth also implies having good health and access to good health systems, educational and economic opportunities, high expectations for youth, transportation options, viable communities, strong family structures, respect for the aged, and meaningful religious beliefs.

Wealth is very different, of course, from income. Most government workers have incomes. We support ourselves and our families through our incomes. We also contribute to health insurance and retirement plans, as do our taxpayer-based employers. But most government employees—public safety officials, teachers, military personnel, transit workers, and not-for-profit employees, among others—maintain incomes, yet have very limited access to wealth.

Of the three concepts—capital, bureaucracy, and democracy—democracy is the most challenged or threatened, even pleading for its very existence. Most government workers are not likely to speak out or exercise their due process rights if they suspect that their salaries, may be affected—even indirectly.

Bureaucracy, according to Max Weber's theories, is structured by hierarchy, chain of command, specialization of task, a specified sphere of competence, established norms of conduct, and records, paperwork, or similar documentation. Government employees are expected to be responsive to citizen-clients. A certain level of competence is demanded.

Any citizen can file to compete for elective office. That's the democratic way. But how many political candidates have access to skilled campaign officials and large bank accounts (wealth) to make their candidacies competitive?

Definitions of *public* and *private* regulate the relationships between capital, bureaucracy and democracy. As Dwight Waldo wrote in *The Enterprise of Public Administration* (1980), "Concepts of public and private are very central in the conceptual and emotional structuring of the Western world. . . . A great deal of our thought and action concerning government, law, morals and social institutions relates one way or another to this distinction. . . . But we need to appreciate public and private are not categories of nature; they are categories of history and culture, of law and custom. They are contextual and subject to change and redefinition." (p. 164)

Professor Waldo suggests redefinition, reevaluation, and restatement of the nature, culture, and context of capital, bureaucracy, and democracy as they are played out on the public and private stages of American governments and politics. Do partisan political leaders advocate space shields or provide a Patients' Bills of Rights? The Departments of Health and Human Services, and Defense, are governed and administered according to laws. Nurses, medical doctors, and other caregivers are private sector entrepreneurs or employees of not-for-profits. The U.S. government provides soldiers and strategy for military missions. Private sector groups produce tanks, airplanes, missiles, ships, guns, uniforms, and boots. In both health and defense administration (HHS and DOD), the government produces little or nothing. In wars on disease, in military conquest and economic advantage, citizens make sacrifices for the common good.

On matters of life (health) and death (military power), priorities of capital, bureaucracy and democracy are vigorously debated. In efforts to redefine, reevaluate, and restate the parameters of public and private life, citizens determine what they owe the state (society), and what the state owes them. In determining such boundaries, democracy is a prevalent—and as effective—as citizen access to incomes and wealth.

Source: "Bureaucracy and Democracy Are Not Esoteric" by John Rouse, as appeared on ASPA Online Columns, website www.aspanet.org, July 17, 2001. Reprinted by permission of the author.

interact with other organizational philosophies, such as capitalism, nationalism, industrialism, and socialism, all historical antecedents to democracy and bureaucracy.

Defining democracy is not easy. We live in a democracy. In the classical sense, though, our system of *political economy,* or politics and economics, is not a democracy, but a republic. We have a democratic *type* of government; however, we have a republican *form* of government: In our republic, elected officials represent us in our state and national legislatures. Other tenets of democracy call for "rule by the people." However, who are "the people"? How, and by what means, do they "rule"?

Democracy is not an economic, social, or ethical concept, but a political one. It emphasizes the values of liberty, equality, human worth, human dignity, and freedom by guaranteeing the right to secret voting. With these values come free expression of ideas, free association of persons, representation, legislatures, due process of law, and the privilege of assuming our soap box and speaking our minds about virtually anything.[1]

While democracy has a leveling, or *horizontal,* feature about its application, bureaucracy is *vertical.* Democracy implies equality and equal opportunity; bureaucracy also denotes hierarchy. Every four years American citizens vote for or against a presidential candidate because of the candidate's support of political principles as expressed in the party's platform. The party platform serves as a voters' guide to how its leaders should address the nation's challenges during the next term. Voting, which espouses equality, is a political right in a democratic society.

However, once a candidate becomes president, the direct democratic powers of voters are diluted. Voters may encourage members of Congress to oppose the president's new programs, for example, but the rights of suffrage in our electoral democracy come up only periodically. Except for those periodic elections, the premises of bureaucracy, or hierarchy, assume preeminence in our system. Public institutions—ranging from health to defense—develop, evaluate, and implement public policies.

The oft-used term *bureaucracy* has two meanings. In its most popular sense, the concept refers to any substantial public organization or group of organizations, as in "federal bureaucracy" or in "welfare bureaucracy." The other meaning is more specialized; it refers to a particular method or manner of administration. A bureaucracy in this sense is an organization or group of organizations that operates in a particular way.

What constitutes the bureaucratic way of doing things? The German sociologist Max Weber (1864–1920) was the first to define it. He saw bureaucracy as an impersonal system operating on the basis of "calculable rules" and staffed by full-time and professional (as opposed to political) employees. Bureaucracy presupposes hierarchy, but this hierarchy is based on organizational rank, not on social status or other considerations.

The chief characteristic of a bureaucracy in Weber's sense of the word was its uniform, nonarbitrary, and nonpersonal method of administering public affairs. "Bureaucracy," wrote Weber, "is like a modern judge who is a vending machine into which the pleadings are inserted along with the fee. The machine then disgorges the judgment based on reasons mechanically derived from the code."[2]

In Weber's view, bureaucracy is a bloodless mechanism devoid of the capriciousness and color we associate with human activity. Yet the positive features of

Protestant Ethic and Capitalism

Max Weber wrote *The Prostestant Ethic and the Spirit of Capitalism* in 1904–1905, with the intention of showing why a total revolution in the organization of society, or the rationalization of life, occurred only in the West and not in other parts of the world. However, Weber's intention has been obscured by much philosophizing and myth making about the so-called "Protestant Ethic."

Source: Daniel Bell, "The Protestant Ethic," *World Policy Journal* 13, no. 3 (Fall 1996): 35–38.

such an administrative approach, characterized by impersonality and professionalism, must not be overlooked. Impersonality implies impartiality, and professionalism opens the possibility for an employee selection system based less on social status and more on personal skill.

This bureaucratic ideal has made headway in Europe, especially in Germany. As such, it has brought more uniformity, predictability, and equality to public administration.

Because bureaucratic systems rest upon a highly systematized administrative arrangement, they often show resistance to change. The devotion to calculable rules often causes rule-conscious bureaucrats to "go by the book," regardless of the situation. Such routinized organizational behavior may, however, prove advantageous. France, with its long history of unrest and upheaval, has often been held together by its plodding but enduring bureaucracy.

Although the bureaucratic style has conquered the public sector in Western Europe, it has scored somewhat less decisively in this country. The dynamics of U.S. political bureaucracies, especially in state and local jurisdictions, are highly personal. It is often *who* one knows rather than *what* one knows that affects the administrative system. Just as personalities often count for more than parties or principles in policy making, so personalities often outweigh "calculable rules" in policy execution. This is not always true, but it happens often enough to differentiate U.S. administration from that of other economically developed democracies such as England, France, or West Germany.

Lessened concern for abiding by the rules provides many rewards. Although U.S. administration has often been accused of stodginess, and rightly so, it is perhaps less than its Western European counterparts. It is much easier to bend, if not break, the rules in the United States than elsewhere in the world of modern democratic capitalism. The U.S. administrative setup, reflecting vast differences in bureaucratic cultures, can more easily accommodate individual idiosyncrasies and initiatives.

Before breaking out into cheers, the antibureaucratic enthusiast should note some of the benefits that we thereby forego. A system more open to the influence of individual personality is open to caprice and whim. As calculable rules become more easily manipulated, the system is also more vulnerable to corruption. If change can sometimes come more quickly, then such change may spring not only from public demand but from personal desire as well.

The distinctiveness of U.S. administration should not be overstated: The bureaucratic way of doing things is scarcely a stranger to our shores. And the systems of other countries are certainly not incapable of capriciousness or change. Yet for both good and ill, bureaucracy in Weber's sense characterizes the U.S. public sector less than it does that of many other modern developed nations.

Normative Vectors

The norms or values of public administration are grouped into three general areas, or normative vectors.

- *Concerns about efficiency and effectiveness.* These areas of concern focus primarily on the workings of government and the way its goods and services are distributed and delivered. A public dollar should be expended with as much care and deliberation as feasible. This attitude toward government values the ability to mobilize, organize, and direct resources.
- *Concerns about rights and the adequacy of governmental process.* These themes scrutinize a government's relationship with its citizens. Individual liberties provide a sense of equity; each citizen should be treated as an individual, according to his or her circumstances. As concerns arose about the manner in which governments treat people, the notion of due process emerged. Rights, due process, and equity focus on measuring the quality of interaction between an agency and its clientele. This focus is rooted in democratic theory. It reaches as far back as Aristotle.
- *Concerns about representation and the exercise of discretion.* These themes point toward controls the citizenry has over the workings of government and its agents. Accountability implies external standards of correct action and is thus institutionalized. Legal, political, and bureaucratic sanctions induce competent and conscientious administrative performance. Administrators must act in accordance with moral obligation. Accountability, responsibility, and responsiveness put representation into operation.

Source: Michael M. Harmon and Richard T. Mayer, *Organization Theory for Public Administration* (Boston: Little, Brown, 1986). See Chapter 3, "The Normative Context of Public Administration," pages 34–53.

Interpretations of Bureaucracy

According to Dwight Waldo, the term "bureaucracy" has two interpretations. The *popular-pejorative* interpretation is widely recognized in society: Bureaucracy is bad because bureaucrats are timid, ineffectual, power-seeking, and dangerous.

A second interpretation of bureaucracy is *descriptive* and *analytical.* This interpretation says that bureaucracy fosters advanced legal and economic systems and, therefore, advances civilization. Descriptive and analytical terms related to this interpretation include *form of government, formalism, rules, impersonality, hierarchy, expertise, records, large-scale, complex, efficiency,* and *effectiveness.*

In reality, the concept of bureaucracy is neither good nor bad. Bureaucracy simply is; it exists. The concept of bureaucracy encompasses procedures for organizing people within a certain culture in order to achieve a particular set of goals and objectives. *Bureaucracy exists for accomplishing tasks.* The tasks range from fighting dictators to fighting poverty.

How, then, are the societal values of democracy and bureaucracy antithetical, yet complementary?

According to Waldo, there are two problems in reconciling democracy and bureaucracy. One concern focuses upon the definition of the *administrative unit.* Any organization able to respond to clientele is a unit. The function of a unit of bureaucracy may be defined by the manner in which the organization responds to its clientele. Academic departments, as administrative units at a college or university, are organized depending upon college and student demands for certain skills, knowledge, and expertise.

For example, English and math may be the largest departments on campus because most colleges mandate that students take courses in these subjects. Meanwhile, the departments of philosophy, anthropology, and foreign language may be smaller because the demand for courses taught by those departments is lower.

Waldo's concern is the status and weight accorded to *nondemocratic values.* Liberty and equality are democratic values; nondemocratic values include national security, personal safety, productivity, and efficiency. If the chairperson of an academic department is elected by members of that unit, the values of democracy have predominated. However, if the department head is selected by the dean of the college, then the values of bureaucracy—efficiency and productivity—have taken precedence.

Baseline Originals in Organizational Life

Max Weber, Frederick Winslow Taylor, Elton Mayo, and Chester Barnard form an intellectual baseline of early classical thinkers concerned with the anatomy and physiology of private and public organizations. Thinking of the organization as a "rational machine" provides a useful metaphor in understanding this approach to organizational behaviors.[3]

Max Weber

Weber's work on the nature of bureaucracy is considered by many the most important of its kind. Weber was trained in law, history, and economics. He viewed action as both individual and social. Weber postulates the *ideal-type* of bureaucracy, not referring to "goodness" or "badness," but suggesting a standard or model for organizational environment. Characteristics of the ideal-type may be found in any organization.

In the following list, John M. Pfiffner and Frank P. Sherwood summarize components of Weber's ideal-type. These components contribute to our understanding of the functions and vital processes of organizations.

- *Emphasis on form.* Bureaucracy's first, most cited, and most general feature, according to Weber, is its emphasis on form of organization. In a sense, the rest of the components are examples of this.
- *The concept of hierarchy.* The organization follows the principle of hierarchy, with each lower office under the control and supervision of a higher one.
- *Specialization of task.* Incumbents are chosen on the basis of merit and ability to perform specialized aspects within a total operation.
- *A specified sphere of competence.* This flows from specialization of task. It suggests that the relationships between various specializations should be clearly known and observed in practice. In a sense, the job descriptions used in many American organizations are a practical application of this requirement.
- *Established norms of conduct.* There should be as little unpredictability as possible in the organization. Policies should be clearly enunciated, and the

Shame versus Official Censorship

Moral censorship is a strong weapon of the culture-war propaganda that can intrude upon a person's privacy in ways unmatched by any kind of bureaucracy. Some observers believe that conservatives try to use shame as an alternative to official censorship and as a means to instill a sense of fear and self-loathing among free-thinking individuals. The true meaning of shameful behavior is somewhat obliterated. Moral censorship applies more to nonconformity and nonacceptance of prevalent trends than to immorality. Real shame and repentance come from within, and not from outside pressures.

Source: Carl F. Horowitz, "The Shaming Sham," *The American Prospect,* no. 31 (March–April 1997): pp. 70–76.

individuals within the organization should see that these policies are implemented.
- *Records.* Administrative acts, decisions, and rules should be recorded to insure predictability of performance within the bureaucracy.[4]

Weber emphasized the universality of bureaucracy by emphasizing its rationality. His observations on bureaucracy coincided with the industrial revolution in Germany at the turn of the century. In seeking rationality in human behavior, Weber concluded that the ideal-type is the best means for achieving rationality at the institutional level.

Weber also assumed freedom for bureaucrats. Far from promoting a master-slave relationship, he emphasized that people were free agents, even within nineteenth-century economic bureaucracies.

Finally, Weber forecast a general separation of policymaking and administration. The ideal-type organization is grounded in predictable decision-making processes and is staffed by professionals; therefore its bureaucracies should not be subverted by nonprofessionals, according to Weber. In this view, professionals organize and implement expertise. Nonprofessionals, armed only with opinions about expertise and goals, do not fit into Weber's game plan. Neither the monarch ruling by divine right nor the elected American president would be part of Weber's ideal-type framework.[5]

Frederick Winslow Taylor

Mass production suffered a long and fitful birth when it appeared in America in the eighteenth century and slow development afterwards. Oliver Evans, Linus Yale, Lillian and Frank Gilbreth, and Henry Ford later made huge contributions to its development. But it was Frederick Winslow Taylor who developed the underlying theory of scientific management that gave mass production its enduring form. Scientific management captivated the American consciousness and catapulted Taylor's ideas onto center stage, where they have remained. Yet until the publication of Wellford Wilms' "The One Best Way," little was known about the man who revolutionized the workplace.[6]

Frederick Taylor (1856–1915) is often called the father of scientific management. He recognized the importance of technology, work, and organization to the functions and vital processes of bureaucracies. In the opening of his classic, *The Principles of Scientific Management,* Taylor wrote:

> The principal object of management should be to secure the maximum prosperity for the employer, coupled with the maximum prosperity for the employee.
>
> The words *maximum prosperity* are used, in their broad sense, to mean not only large dividends for the company or owner, but the development of every branch of business to its highest state of excellence, so that prosperity may be permanent.[7]

According to Taylor, scientific management is both liberating and economically rational. Employees and employers are assumed to be rational. Through rationality in the work process, labor and management determine the proper way to complete a task.

Taylor, like Weber, assumed the importance of the individual and foresaw the shift of power from both the *bourgeoisie* (economic elites) and the *proletariat* (masses) to the *expert* (possessor of skills and knowledge).

Taylor emphasized cooperation in the workplace and spoke of making life better for each employee. He represented a pre-World War II line of thought that there are principles and laws that order our knowledge of the world. By seeking to use the scientific method, organizations become impersonal but rational.

Elton Mayo

In 1932, Harvard Business School professor Elton Mayo (1880–1949) and a team of researchers completed a five-year study outside Chicago, Illinois, at the Hawthorne plant of the Western Electric Company. Later published as *The Human Problems of an Industrial Civilization,* Mayo's research found that many problems in worker/management relations are caused not by insufficient task specialization or inadequate wages, but by social and psychological forces. The Hawthorne Experiments, as they were subsequently known, were the first systematic research to expose the *human factor* in work situations. The study marked a major turning point in the history of administrative theory and practice.[8] The Hawthorne Experiments encouraged management to conceptualize organizations as a *social institutions.*

According to Pfiffner and Sherwood, Mayo's Hawthorne findings contributed to the ideological revolution in organization and management in two ways: by challenging the physical or engineering approach to motivation, and by becoming the first real assault on the purely structural, hierarchical approach to organization. In other words, Mayo felt there was no scientific or best way to motivate employees to be productive. The "father knows best" authoritarian way of running an organization was seen as only one of several approaches available. The whims of scientific management were no longer accepted as gospel; the human relations movement was underway.[9]

Elton Mayo concluded from studying the Hawthorne Experiments that informal organization is more important in determining worker cooperation than formal organization; that output is set by social norms, not individual abilities; and that the group heavily influences the behavior of individual workers. Mayo's experiment showed how a group of young, female employees at Western Electric

Company reacted positively to every change made in their working conditions while they were working in the test room. However, another experiment conducted along the same lines produced quite different results.

Mayo and his colleagues persuaded the management of the company to put a group of men engaged in making parts of telephone switches on a piece-rate incentive system. This new system would allow the men to increase their earnings without undue physical strain, and these were depression times when most workers seemed desperate to earn more money; therefore, the researchers and the company expected a great jump in productivity. Their expectations came to naught. Output remained the same.

The research group then began to investigate why the workers responded or, rather, failed to respond. Unlike the young, female relay assemblers, most of whom expected to get married and leave their jobs before too long, the male workers had developed a work culture of their own. They had become a cohesive and compact group with their own codes, rules, and norms. Among these rules were prohibitions against doing too much or too little work. So solidly entrenched were these understandings among the male employees that they remained impervious to any enticements from management. The men rationalized that the incentive plan was an attempt to eventually cut out some jobs or to reduce wage rates. The company assured them that this was not the case and pointed to its record, which indicated no instance of its ever having acted in such a manner. The men remained unconvinced, so productivity went on at the same level.[10]

Mayo and his associates had come up against the informal organization, grounded in large part on informal communications. This phenomenon has interested and intrigued organizational theorists ever since, and their research shows far-reaching ramifications.

Chester Barnard

Chester Barnard (1886–1961) is the final member of the baseline foursome. Intrigued by the experiments at the Hawthorne plant, Barnard formulated a theory of organizational life that focuses on *the organization as a system, formal and informal organizations, and the role of the executive.* In *Functions of the Executive,* Barnard distinguishes between *organizational purpose* and *individual motive.* He postulates that each person in the organization reflects a dual personality, one organizational and the other individual. As an individual leaves home and enters the workplace, he or she becomes "the organization man or woman."

An organization is a collection of actions focused toward a purpose; an equilibrium is necessary for an organization to sustain itself. A successful equilibrium must exist between the organization and its employees. The organization receives energies and productive capacities from employees, and employees receive compensation, benefits, and meaning from their work.[11]

Although the distinction between formal and informal organization is now commonplace, Barnard introduced these concepts in the late 1930s as new analytic tools for examining organizational life. According to Barnard, *formal organization* is comprised of the consciously coordinated activities of people, while *informal organization* entails the unconscious group feelings, passions, and activities of the same individuals. Informal organization is essential to the maintenance of formal structures and relationships. The formal organization cannot exist without its informal counterpart. Not all activity can be structured by a chain of command because of the reality of informal organization.

Finally, Barnard addresses *executive functions* of organizations. These functions are:

- maintaining organization communication,
- securing essential services from individuals, and
- formulating the purpose and objectives of the organization.

Barnard writes that the functions of the executive are "those of the nervous system, including the brain, in relation to the rest of the body. It exists to maintain the bodily system by directing those actions which are necessary more effectively to adjust to the environment. But it can hardly be said to manage the body, a large part of whose functions are independent of it and upon which it in turn depends."[12]

The writings of Weber, Taylor, Mayo, and Barnard form an axis around which the theory and practice of public organizations revolve. Focusing upon three early organizational themes—system, hierarchy, and structure—writers who follow these classical thinkers assume that understanding human rationality is central to theorizing about organizational physiology.

Neoclassical Theories

The neoclassical perspective toward organizational theory is represented by the works of Luther Gulick and Herbert Simon. "Decision-set" organizational theory is characterized by several important themes, including decision making as the heart and soul of administration; administrative capacity as measured by efficiency; an emphasis on organizational roles, not individual roles, as they relate to decision making; and instrumental rationality as the center of operation.

Luther Gulick

In 1937, Luther Gulick and Lyndall Urwick edited the *Papers on the Science of Administration,* a collection of eleven papers reflecting the predominant thinking concerning organizations in Europe and the United States prior to World War II. Divided into two groups, the papers examined structural aspects and social and environmental aspects of organization.[13]

Gulick's "Notes on the Theory of Organization," in which he introduced the acronym POSDCORB, has influenced teaching and thinking about public administration for over sixty years. Gulick's POSDCORB (Planning, Organizing, Staffing, Directing, Coordinating, Reporting and Budgeting) helped shape the Wilsonian separation of politics from administration, the need for a division of work to reach organizational objectives, and the efficiency criterion for judging governmental activities. In POSDCORB, Gulick outlines the work of the chief executive:

- *Planning* is working out in broad outline the tasks that need to be done and the methods for doing them to accomplish the purpose set for the enterprise.

- *Organizing* is the establishment of the formal structure of authority through which work subdivisions are arranged, defined, and coordinated for the defined objective.
- *Staffing* is bringing in and training the staff and maintaining favorable work conditions.
- *Directing* is the continuous task of making decisions and embodying them in specific and general instructions as well as serving as the leader of the enterprise.
- *Coordinating* is the important duty of interrelating the various parts of the work.
- *Reporting* is keeping the top executive informed as to what is going on, and keeping subordinates informed through records, research, and inspection.
- *Budgeting* includes fiscal planning, accounting, and control.[14]

Herbert Simon

After World War II, in 1947, Simon illustrated the decision-set perspective in "The Proverbs of Administration," incorporated later into his classic, *Administrative Behavior.* Simon viewed the decision as the central act of organization and instrumental rationality as the basis for decision making. By *instrumental rationality,* Simon meant that the individual is rational and responsible only within the environment of a particular organization. The organizational environment encompasses the purposes of rational behavior; autonomous individuals behave only within the confines of those organizational purposes.

In emphasizing the decision as the basis for administrative theory, Simon distinguished between *value* premises and *factual* premises of public administrators. He wrote, "The process of validating a factual proposition is quite distinct from the process of validating a value judgment. The former is validated by its agreement with the facts, the latter by human fiat."[15] In other words, the facts of any circumstance are validated by the given set of values in which those facts, or actions, occur.

Simon focuses upon the *means-end* sense of rationality as most significant. Administrators weigh the means, ends, and consequences of acting; therefore, Simon suggests, decisions may prove objectively rational, subjectively rational, deliberately rational, organizationally rational, or personally rational. Regardless of adverb, to be rational means to consider *only* those choices present within a prescribed system of values. Government employees are not autonomous individuals. The organizational environment of the department or agency articulates the values that determine rational behavior. In other words, an employee is rational and responsible only within the environment of a particular department or agency. A government employee acts rationally only within the framework of the department's preestablished goals and purposes.

Values, on the other hand, are arbitrary, regardless of their origins. Human decree, sanction, or authority validates a certain set of organizational values. Executives, legislatures, and judges decide by fiat that a set of values, encompassed in laws and implemented by bureaucrats, are of importance to organizations and to society. Citizens of public organizations then respond to the rules and regulations and the boundaries these values impose upon them.

Miles's Law

Rufus E. Miles, Jr. proudly claims to have parented Miles's Law. The law states that, "Where you stand depends on where you sit." Miles says he discovered the law while serving as a division director of the former Bureau of the Budget. He noted that a budget examiner might be a constant critic of an agency whose budget he oversaw, yet if the examiner were to be later hired away by the agency, he would promptly do a 180° turn and become one of the agency's most adamant advocates. The position a bureaucrat takes thus depends on what position he is in, or "Where you stand depends on where you sit."

Miles points out in illustration how John Gardner, as chairman of President Johnson's Task Force on Education, authored a report strongly favoring the removal of Education from the Department of Health, Education, and Welfare. Shortly thereafter, Gardner was appointed secretary of HEW. When asked whether he now planned to push for Education's removal from HEW, he firmly and flatly rejected any such nonsensical idea.

All decisions in organizations only satisfy and suffice, that is, they *satisfice.* Our focus on choices and decision making and our acceptance of organizational premises brings us to the limit of administrative rationality. This final Simon theme, that of *satisficing,* recognizes that rationality, or human reasoning, is bounded by administrative settings. After analyzing the problem and considering the complexities of the situation, administrators "satisfice," surveying their options and selecting the first one they find at least minimally satisfactory.

With respect to employee "satisficing," Simon concludes that rationality is bounded. In describing *bounded rationality,* he concludes that an administrator's reasoning options are limited by unconscious habits and skills, values and conceptions of purpose, and degree of information and knowledge.[16]

Human Relations Theories

As we have seen in the previous passages, Max Weber speaks in *bureaucratic* terms; Frederick Taylor writes in *productivity* terms; Chester Barnard thinks in *organizational* terms; and Herbert Simon stresses *decisional* terms. Writing histories of the increasing bureaucratization of society, each of these authors emphasizes *efficiency* in some form as a potent force in any organization, but also concludes that organizations embody not just task but social purposes. In other words, they believe that if conflict exists within the organization, individuals must subordinate their interests to those of the organization.

For example, if students are not learning in a classroom, the onus usually is placed upon the students to change their behavior or study habits to respond to the professor's demands. Likewise, if the college's basketball team is losing, the assumption is that the players are not responding to their coach's leadership. Student athletes must subordinate their actions to the coach's instructions for the benefit of the team.

Human relations theories question such assumptions, placing responsibility on the professor to change his or her teaching methods and on the coach to change his or her leadership style and set up a new strategy for winning games. This shift in responsibility makes for several new ways of envisioning organizational structure and function.

Mary Parker Follett

An early prophet of human relations thinking was Mary Parker Follett (1868–1933). While the classical and neoclassical writers were attempting to construct a field of public administration along systematic and somewhat mechanical lines, Follett was marching to the beat of a different drummer.

She had become impressed with the psychological factors she had seen at work in her active life as an organizer of evening schools, recreation agencies, and employment bureaus and as a member of statutory wage boards. Already the author of two books on political science, *The New State* and *Creative Experience,* she embarked on a series of speculations in the 1920s concerning the functions and vital processes of organizations. Her work signaled the advent of a new era in administrative theory.[17]

In various papers and articles, Follett depicted administration as essentially involved with reconciling the agendas of both individuals and social groups. An organization's principal problems, in her view, were not only determining what it wanted its employees to do, but guiding and controlling the employees' conduct in such a way as to get them to do it. This, she indicated, was a much more complex task than previous writers had suggested.

Follett not only anticipated what was to become the human relations school of administration, she also foreshadowed the humanistic school that was to grow out of it. She urged organizations to stop trying to suppress the differences that may arise within their boundaries and to seek instead to integrate those differences, allowing them to contribute to the organization's growth and development. She advocated replacing the "law of authority" with the "law of the situation," admonishing organizations to exercise "power *with*" rather than "power *over*" their members.

A philosophical analysis of Mary Parker Follett's writings on democratic and organizational theories reveals similarities with the feminist theory of the time. These similarities include the notion that human relations supersede individual rights, the theory that knowledge is context specific, her sensitivity to the role of power as an obstacle in the development of knowledge claims, and her method of conflict resolution through the integration of opposing interests. Her writings provide important insights into modern organization and management principles.[18]

While Follett's writings did not go unnoticed, they failed to score the impact that similar ideas would later achieve. This was perhaps due partly to the fact that she was a woman writing in a society not yet willing to take women thinkers seriously. A more serious obstacle, however, may have been that she was an iconoclast, challenging the sacred credos of her time. She died during the same year Elton Mayo wrote on the Hawthorne Experiments. Mayo's work was the first systematic research to expose the "human factor" in work situations. Mayo's study, as we have seen, marked a major turning point in the history of administrative theory and practice.

Maslow, McGregor, and Likert

Like Follett, organizational psychologists Abraham Maslow, Douglas McGregor, and Rensis Likert wrote from a progressive, humanistic viewpoint. They have profoundly influenced the teaching and practice of public administration concerning the role of democracy in bureaucracy, advocating an expanded scope and encouragement of individual initiative by allowing employees to make many of their own decisions on the job. These authors call for *less hierarchy and more humanity in organizational life* and emphasize *the integration of individuals in organization.*

Writing in *Motivation and Personality* (1954), Maslow identifies a hierarchy of personal needs that the organization must contend with to successfully integrate the individual. He writes that food and shelter are the first needs humans seek to meet. Once these needs are met, people seek freedom from physical harm and deprivation. Next, the desire for affectionate and supportive relationships with family, friends, and associates becomes a priority. Then people seek to gain the recognition of worth from their peers. Finally, when all these needs have been met, humans can seek to actualize their inner potential, to release their creative abilities, to achieve everything they hope for in life.[19]

Like Maslow, McGregor's thinking is essentially optimistic concerning individuals' capacity for self-actualization. McGregor examines the possibilities for merging individual and organizational demands in ways that would prove satisfactory to both. In *The Human Side of Enterprise* (1960), McGregor outlines management's conventional view of harnessing human energy to meet organizational requirements. McGregor calls this Theory X, and then boldly steps forward with a new theory of administration he calls Theory Y.

Theory X is based on these assumptions:

- The average person is by nature lazy. He or she will work as little as possible. Such an individual lacks ambition, dislikes responsibility, and prefers to be led.
- By nature resistant to change, such a person is gullible, not very bright, and the ready dupe of the charlatan and the demagogue. This person is furthermore inherently self-centered and indifferent to organizational needs.

Theory Y, or McGregor's new way of merging individual and organizational demands, takes a more humanistic approach:

- People are not naturally passive, lazy, and dumb. They are, on the contrary, eager for opportunities to show initiative and to bear responsibility.
- Work is a natural activity and people by nature want to perform it.
- People work best in an environment that treats them with respect and encourages them to develop and use their abilities.
- There is no inherent and intrinsic conflict between the goals of the organization and the goals of the individual member. Meeting the goals of the individual will only result in a more productive organization.[20]

Rensis Likert, writing in *The Human Organization* (1967), develops four systems that positively or negatively influence the integration of individuals into organizations:

- System 1 is *punitive authoritarian* and closely resembles McGregor's Theory X. System 1 administrative leaders have no confidence or trust in their subordinates.
- System 2 is *benevolent authoritarian* and is more generous and humanitarian toward the employee. While System 1 takes everything from the individual

and gives little in return, System 2 rewards employee behavior only as prescribed directives are followed. If the employee does his or her tasks as prescribed, he or she is dutifully rewarded. System 2 leaders are condescending in bestowing their confidence and trust, engaging in something resembling a master/servant relationship with subordinates.

- System 3 is *consultative* and allows still more participation by employees. Administrative leaders in such an organization may be democratic, allowing free discussion regarding policymaking, but still assume final responsibility for all decisions. System 3 illustrates substantial but not complete confidence and trust in subordinates.
- System 4 is a *participative group model* and closely resembles McGregor's Theory Y. Senior bureaucrats promote complete confidence and trust in employees in all matters. Employees provide guidance and participate in coordinated problem solving. Employees are not treated punitively.

According to Likert, administrative leaders adopting the participative style achieve from 10 to 40 percent greater productivity, experience much higher levels of employee satisfaction and much better employee health, enjoy better labor relations, suffer less absence and less turnover, obtain better product quality, and, finally, record better customer satisfaction as a result of better products and services than managers operating with System 1, 2, or 3 styles.[21]

Women, Men, and Management Styles

The increasing number of women working for local, state, and federal governments raises questions about the role of femininity in psychological, social, and cultural contexts. How do gender differences—in language, leadership theories, and communication styles—affect public sector employees?

The terms *Sex* and *gender* are often used interchangeably. *Sex role theory* examines the concepts of masculinity and feminity. A form of social determinism categorizes individuals into gender stereotypes; femininity, in particular, is produced by socialization into the female role. Domination, ambition, cynicism, and rebelliousness characterize masculinity. Consideration, tact, dependence, and emotion characterize femininity.

Sex indicates a biological difference. *Gender* notes psychological, social, and cultural differences. Gender emerges from social patterns not determined by genes or hormones. Social structure is not unchangeable; femininity and masculinity are historically mutable. Gender applies at three levels:

1. As a dimension of personal identity
2. As an element of social order
3. As a cultural symbol

Gender and language. The male conversation style stresses dominance, while females stress socialization and cultural factors. Men and women belong to different subcultures. Language is literally "manmade"; men determined the meanings of words. Feminine language forms are thus often pejorative, reflecting the traditionally inferior position of women in society and in the family. In public discourse, men are sometimes more at ease than women. Male and female speech differs in explicitness and directness. In women's culture, task performance is requested, not demanded; hedges and disclaimers occur frequently, directness is rude, conflict and aggressive actions are skirted. The context and institutionalization of language perpetuates assumptions of group homogeneity.

Women are said to bring values of intuition, communication, and social aptitude to organizations. Women rate high in people-oriented leadership skills, while men rate higher on business-oriented leadership skills. The business world now questions the military hierarchy structure it adopted after World War II. Women are energetic and enthusiastic, they keep people informed, they let others know how they perform, and they set high standards. Men are more likely to build on knowledge gained through experience, to innovate, to be open to new ideas, and to take risks. They also gauge the larger view of things, control their emotions, delegate, share objectives, and are accountable; they are good team players, and they are persuasive (table 4.1).

Women and men express diverse communication styles. Women focus on relationships, not just content. They differ from men in communication aims, modes, and strategies. Women perceive information as contextual and arising from circumstances, while men portray information as fixed and abstract. Women exude compassion, empathy, and the capacity for moral vision. Men are identified with hierarchical management. Women integrate the private and public part of their lives, and collaboration results.[22]

"Organizations are gendered," write Joyce Fletcher and Deborah Merrill-Sands. They argue that systems, practices, structures, and norms of modern organizations reflect masculine values and life situations. "Organizational change efforts that take account of deeply rooted masculinity," say Fletcher and Merrill-Sands, "focus on systemic issues."[23]

Change efforts focus on two premises. First, our commonsense "knowledge" about organizational life is narrow and limited in scope. A gendered set of norms about effectiveness and success creates idealized images of work, workers, and success that indirectly maintain gender segregation and gender inequity in the workplace.

Second, the "ideal" worker is derived from a masculine social context. Traditional masculine norms are reinforced within the organization. These deeply rooted norms are accepted *fait accompli*. Workers who do not fit masculine norms are less likely to be promoted or considered valuable. These mental models manifest themselves, concretely, in work practices, structures, processes, and everyday routines.

Identifying and analyzing mental models helps us to examine gender equity in organizations. Behavior, systems, and processes—both formal and informal—give us fertile ground for an examination of gender implications. When mental models are made explicit, the status quo is disrupted. Men and women find new ways to look at their organization and to discuss issues and values.

TABLE 4.1

Sex Differences in Managerial Styles

Male Managers	Female Managers
The executives worked at an unrelenting pace, and took no breaks in activity during the day.	The executives worked at a steady pace, but with small breaks scheduled throughout the day.
They described their days as characterized by interruption, discontinuity, and fragmentation.	They did not view unscheduled tasks and encounters as interruptions.
They spared little time for activities not directly related to their work.	They made time for activities not directly related to their work.
They exhibited a preference for live encounters.	They preferred live encounters but scheduled time to attend to mail.
They maintained a complex network of relationships with people outside their organizations.	They maintained a complex network of relationships with people outside their organizations.
Immersed in the day-to-day need to keep the organization going, they lacked time for reflection.	They focused on the ecology of leadership.
They identified with their jobs.	They saw their own identities as complex and multifaceted.
They had difficulty sharing information.	They scheduled time for sharing information.

Source: From *The Female Advantage: Women's Ways of Leadership* by Sally Helgesen, copyright © 1990 by Sally Helgesen. Used by permission of Doubleday, a division of Random House, Inc.

Gender Gap in Government

The United States has never had a woman President or Vice President. No woman had been nominated for either office by a major party until July 12, 1984, when Democratic Party Presidential Nominee Walter Mondale chose Geraldine Ferraro as his running mate. The first woman to serve in the Cabinet was Frances Perkins; she was appointed by Franklin Roosevelt as Secretary of Labor in 1933. The President's Cabinet was established in 1789. A total of 498 Cabinet members have served since then, of which 29, or 5.8 percent, were female. Madeleine Albright became the highest-ranking woman ever to serve in the United States government when she was named Secretary of State by President Clinton in 1996. Sandra Day O'Connor became the first woman ever appointed a Supreme Court Justice in 1981. Ruth Bader Ginsberg joined the court in 1993.

Women make up 52 percent of the adult population, 28.5 percent of President Bush's Cabinet, 13 percent of the United States Senate, 13.8 percent of the United States House of Representatives, 22 percent of the United States Supreme Court, 20.6 percent of federal judges, 10 percent of state governors, 19.9 percent of state senators, 23.3 percent of state representatives, 9 percent of state judges, and 20.8 percent of big city mayors.

At the time of this writing, five of the nation's 50 governors are women. Only 19 women have ever served as the governor of a state since Nellie Taylor Ross was elected Governor of Wyoming in 1925. Currently 17 women serve as Lieutenant Governor, 13 as Secretary of State, 8 as Attorney General, 11 as State Treasurer, 6 as State Auditor, and 4 as State Comptroller. Ten states have a woman as their chief education officer.

Systems Theory Characteristics

Systems theory was built on the previous commentary of Max Weber, Chester Barnard, and Herbert Simon. Michael M. Harmon and Richard T. Mayer constructed systems theory—probing organizations as purposive entities. Closed systems experience little or no vulnerability from external forces. Open systems emerge as social and technological changes bring uncertainty and interdependence.

According to Harmon and Mayer, five characteristics form the basis of systems theory:

1. Each part of an organization can only be understood in terms of its relation to the other parts.
2. The parts of the organization, including their interrelatedness, are important insofar as they contribute to the overall functioning of the organization.
3. Organizations, conceived as wholes, may be thought of metaphorically as biological organisms, replete with needs and goals that are superordinate to and conceptually separate from the conscious needs, purposes, and goals of individuals parts or members.
4. The needs and goals of organizations may be conceived either statically (in terms of survival or maintenance of order) or dynamically (in terms of purposive change).
5. Organizational activity is understandable only in the context of the external environment, which provides the resources and conditions the organization depends on for its survival and the realization of its purposes.

Systems theory originates from structural/functional sociology and promotes understanding of the social system or organization as a whole.

Source: Michael M. Harmon and Richard T. Mayer, *Organization Theory for Public Administration* (Boston: Little, Brown, 1986), p. 158.

Airport Security as American Community

Community is defined as ownership or participation in common. People live together and share work and social interests within a community. The events of September 11 put a large dent into the excesses of American individualism and brought to light the generosity of our national community that had previously been taken for granted and even abused.

Post-September 11 American flag waving may be a superficial gesture, but it nevertheless indicates that new community paradigms are emerging. These new forms must be nourished and continuously examined. Airport security may be an important catalyst for developing this new consciousness of country and community.

This journey is not linear. The Afghanistan war, terrorism, and travel safety prove once again that necessity is the mother of invention. If everything were rational in this politically right-of-center nation, the question of federalizing baggage screening at 142 major airports would be a no-brainer. Airport and plane safety should be the responsibility of federal public administrators—of federal bureaucrats, if you will!

There is nothing wrong with equipping public servants with the appropriate skills, knowledge and expertise to protect the citizenry from insidious attack. This task, however, should not be handled by local or state government employees. Like the Central Intelligence Agency (CIA), the Drug Enforcement Agency (DEA), the Federal Aviation Agency (FAA), the Federal Bureau of Investigation (FBI), the Internal Revenue Service (IRS) and the Secret Service, airport inspectors should be federalized. Possible reforms include a new Justice Department workforce of 28,000 federal employees to screen passengers and to inspect luggage and carry-on bags at airports. A $3.00 surcharge on each ticket would cover the costs of security reforms.

The late Aaron Wildavsky distinguished between policy politics, or which policy should be adopted; partisan politics, or which political personality will win office; and system politics, or how decision structures will be set up. National security is a system and policy concern. Federalizing airport security should not be partisan. Yet partisans vehemently oppose efforts to move from privatization to federal employees.

Yeshiva University Professor of Law John McGinnis offers insights to the advantages of federalization. Federalization creates a marketplace for governments. Government decisions are improved as they are pushed closer to the people they affect, and federalization increases civic responsibility.

A variety of interest groups, including government and flight attendant associations, have offered policy inputs on this issue. *The Washington Post* reported that 93 percent of respondents from a Business Travel Coalition survey—including 216 executives—say that airport security personnel should be federal employees.

Senators Fritz Hollings (D-S.C.) and John McCain (R-Ariz.) are leading the reform efforts on Capitol Hill. "Overwhelming majorities of the American people believe that [screening passengers] is now a law enforcement function, and law enforcement functions, like the Border Patrol and other functions to ensure security, are federal responsibilities," said McCain on a *Fox News Sunday* program.

Critics of these efforts may not realize that federalized airport security personnel could be fired or suspended by the Department of Justice. Regardless of Civil Service laws, they would not be permitted to strike.

Certain conservatives fear employee federalization would benefit organized labor and work against the House Republican majority. The way to improve airport security, they say, is to threaten to fire inefficient low-wage workers.

Before September 11, 2001, the American public distinguished their personal lives from events of national life. The citizenry chose *market justice* over *political justice*. Personal benefits are gained primarily through the economic marketplace. In the establishment of community, political justice and government policies are important.

The threat of terrorism upset the American cultural myopia of *individualism par excellence* as never before. Airport and plane safety serves the greater good as well as the individual citizen. The effective exercise of capitalism depends on the safety—and opportunities—of the entire community. The terror watch is a civic responsibility—by government jurisdictions, public sector employees, and airport consumers. System and policy politics must dominate as terrorism explodes. Short-term partisan politics come in a distant third to policy priorities and system concerns.

Believers in effective government should promote the skills, knowledge and expertise of public sector employees. Selecting public employees for airport security—with career proficiencies not unlike those of the CIA, FBI or Secret Service—is the most effective way to protect citizens, enhance commerce, and rebuild community.

Source: "Airport Security as American Community" by John Rouse, as appeared on ASPA Online Columns, website www.aspanet.org, November 15, 2001. Reprinted by permission of the author.

Conflicts and Organization Character

Organization character is not divorced from an organization's ideological orientation. Labor-management differences may make ideologies more prominent. Conflicts over organization change often reflect ideological struggles.

Roger Harrison identifies competing organization ideologies, which in turn specify goals and values. What should employees expect of the organization? What should the organization expect of its employees? Who is valued, who is vilified, who is rewarded, and who is punished?

Harrison's four ideologies are:

1. *Power orientation.* Power-oriented government employees seek to dominate the organization, maintain absolute control over subordinates, compete for territory, expand control at the expense of others, bargain to their own advantage, justify abrogating agreements, and value growth for its own sake.
2. *Role orientation.* Role-oriented public sector employees are preoccupied with legality, legitimacy, and responsibility. They aspire to be as rational and orderly as feasible. Agreements, rules, and procedures replace or regulate competition and conflicts. These employees carefully adhere to defined rights and privileges.
3. *Task orientation.* Task-oriented government employees value goals, programs, and policies—and their accomplishment—as supreme. The aspiration need not be economic. Authority is legitimized if it is grounded in appropriate knowledge and competence. If power is based solely on power or position, it is not legitimate.
4. *Person orientation.* Person-orientation public sector employees serve the needs of their members. The unit exists to meet needs that members cannot meet by themselves. Individuals influence others through example, helpfulness, and caring. Person-oriented employees prefer consensus methods of decision-making.

The interests, values, and structural qualities of people are often juxtaposed against the interests, values, and structural qualities of organizations. Ideological tension and struggle are manifest in people and organizations.

Source: Roger Harrison. Reprinted by permission of *Harvard Business Review.* From "Understanding Your Organization's Character," by Roger Harrison, *Harvard Business Review,* May/June 1972. Copyright © 1972 by Harvard Business School Publishing Corporation; all rights reserved.

Summary

- Individualism is a priority in American life, with consumerism and the market following close behind. Satisfying short-term, private consumer wants is not a priority for public organizations. Meeting the needs of people and the community is.
- In efforts to redefine, reevaluate, and restate the parameters of public and private life, citizens determine what they owe the state (society)—and what the state owes them.
- Bureaucracy and democracy are not esoteric. They are at the center of what occurs in the public and private organizations of American society.
- *Physiology* is the study of life processes, activities, and functions.
- In a classical sense, our system of political economy, or politics and economics, is not a

  democracy, but a republic. We have a democratic *type* of government, but a republican *form* of government.
- Democracy implies equality, while bureaucracy implies hierarchy. Bureaucracy exists to accomplish tasks ranging from fighting dictators to fighting poverty.
- While democracy has a leveling, or horizontal, quality in its application, bureaucracy is vertical.
- The popular view of bureaucracy tends to be pejorative. The descriptive-analytical approach promotes our understanding of behavior, policies, processes, and institutions. Bureaucracy is neither good nor bad; it exists for accomplishing tasks.
- The norms or values of public administration entail concerns about efficiency and

effectiveness, the adequacy of governmental processes, and representation and the exercise of discretion.

- Max Weber's *ideal-type* of bureaucratic organization emphasizes form, hierarchy, specialization of tasks, specified spheres of competence, established norms of conduct, and record keeping.
- The advent of large-scale bureaucracy has seen the shift of power from both the bourgeoisie, or economic elite, and the proletariat, or the masses, to the experts, those who possess valued skills and knowledge.
- The Hawthorne Experiments of the 1930s encourage managers to conceptualize organizations as social institutions.
- The functions of the executive are to maintain organizational communication, secure essential services from individuals, and formulate the purposes and objectives of the organization.
- The acronym POSDCORB outlines the work of the chief executive in terms of planning, organizing, staffing, directing, coordinating, reporting, and budgeting.
- Formal organization is only part of the study of bureaucracy. Every organization has its informal counterpart—the unconscious group feelings, passions, and activities that exist in any group of people. Informal organization is essential to the maintenance of formal structures and relationships.

- *Sex* indicates biological differences. *Gender* denotes psychological, social, and cultural differences. Gender emerges from rearing patterns, and social practices rather than from genes or hormones.
- Systems theory originates from structural/functional sociology and promotes an understanding of the social system as a whole. Closed systems experience little or no vulnerability from external forces. Open systems emerge as social and technological changes bring uncertainty and interdependence.
- Weber stresses bureaucratic terms, Taylor productivity terms, Barnard organizational terms, and Simon decisional terms. Weber, Taylor, Barnard, and Simon all emphasize efficiency.
- Human relations thinkers—Follett, Maslow, McGregor, and Likert—emphasize principles of equality. They call for less hierarchy and more humanity in organizational life.
- *Community* is defined as ownership or participation in common. People live together and share work and social interests in a community. National security is a system and policy concern. Federalizing airport security is not partisan.
- Organization ideologies relate to power, role, task, or people.

Case Study

Transportation Infrastructures as Organization Theory

The United States interstate highway system organizes roadway commerce. The legend of the U.S. highway network explains how Americans travel from one state to another. Even-numbered interstates go east and west; odd-numbered interstates go north and south. These highways are formalized by maps depicting public organizations—easily recognized as the fifty American states. Highways provide access to forty-four

major airports throughout the country. Systems theory promotes an understanding of the social system as a whole. In this case study, how do organization theories promote or demote the development of commerce?

Commerce is really as interesting as nature.

—*Henry David Thoreau (1817–1862)*
U.S. philosopher, author, and naturalist

Transportation modes reflect theories of organization. The organization values of a national transportation system, by necessity, are every citizen's values.

Terrorism and security threats have caused Americans to probe how we conduct our domestic commerce, commute to our jobs, react to social organization and institutions, mobilize amidst crisis, and shape our culture and politics in conflict and cooperation.

"The country would be better off if citizens flew flags of sacrifice, discipline, and tolerance in memory of those who perished on September 11," argues Tony Foster, two-term mayor of Big Burb. "Big Burbians must reduce our energy dependence on countries where no religious reformation, no industrial revolution, and no guarantee of individual rights typify values of everyday life."

Responding to pressures for responsiveness and efficiency, Americans invest billions of dollars in interstate highways, private railroads, state-of-the-art airports, and a technology-senstitive airline industry. Cars, trucks, trains, and airplanes move goods and people. The economics of airlines, trucking, and rail lines reflect incredible investments of human skill, infrastructure, and commerce.

Formal organization theory stresses the formal, structural arrangements within public organizations. The globalization of work environments, demands of the corporate world, and diversity of family life make the soul searching of post–September 11, 2001, ever more meaningful.

Physiology is the study of life processes, activities, and functions. Similarly, the physiology of an organization is the study of its vital structures and functions. Bureaucracy and democracy are central pillars of both private and public organizations. Our system of political economy, or politics and economics, is not a democracy, but a republic. All of these structural arrangements affect the workings of American organizations.

The more modes of transportation available to the citizenry, the more the potential for freedom. Transportation policy promotes the participative group model of decision making. If freedom of movement is a value, safe modes of transport are essential. The means of commerce are primarily highways and planes, but not trains. The ends are determined by the means.

Normative vectors—efficiency and effectiveness, rights and the adequacy of governmental process, and representation and the exercise of discretion—are challenges that face Big Burb and the state of Commonwealth. Efficiency and effectiveness are planning issues. Citizen participation and stronger partnerships require a focus on rights and the adequacy of the governmental process. Big Burb or central city priorities depend on representation and the exercise of discretion.

"Local governments can help reduce air pollution, fuel consumption, and traffic congestion," Mayor Foster points out. "Most traffic congestion is the result of work-related commuting: too many people driving too many cars within the same area at the same time."

The Intermodal Surface Transportation Efficiency Act of 1991 (ISTEA) requires the coordination of state transportation decisions with state goals for land use, energy conservation, environmental protection, and community vitality. ISTEA, reflecting a federal point of view, mandates a new state planning process and stronger partnerships with local officials to achieve this coordination.

In Commonwealth's largest metropolitan city, Big Burb, auto-dependent urban growth threatens environmental quality, requires an expensive infrastructure, and promotes the worst features of democracy—namely, fragmentation—and of bureaucracy—namely, unresponsiveness and excessive routinization. ISTEA legislates "flexible use" transit alternatives—including commuter rail, light rail, and subway developments.

Systems theory suggests that governments function like biological organisms. Inputs from the environment are crucial to effective decision making. Open systems theory examines relationships, questions structures, and promotes interdependence. Open systems interact with their environments—promoting constant feedback.

Planning Inclusive Decision Making

The State of Commonwealth Department of Transportation (COMDOT) employs two separate but parallel processes to bring citizens and local officials into transportation decision making. The Strategic Management Strategy attempts to involve the public in bringing a fresh perspective to the agency's operations. Reflecting systems theory, COMDOT created an internal department, the Office of Strategic Initiatives, and a Strategic Management Committee comprised of COMDOT senior management to oversee the strategic process, guide its implementation, and evaluate its results.

"Our approach was that everyone is an expert," said Barbara Tompkins, Director of COMDOT's Office of Strategic Initiatives. "We wanted to assure that all participants were able to contribute equally, and that we looked at transportation from a broad range of perspectives."[1] In the philosophy of Frederick Taylor,

COMDOT elicited expertise, but the agency defined the term rather broadly. In the state of Commonwealth, citizens are the experts.

Participants identified the forces affecting transportation, including trends in education, the economy, health care needs, demographics, the environment, technology, globalization, resource availability, cultural values, and government. Citizens were asked to discuss future transportation needs in the context of this larger picture. They were discouraged from focusing on specific transportation projects.

After World War II, railroads connected the political economy of the United States. Today, interstate highways and airports orchestrate the flow of social and economic commerce. These infrastructures were organized on Max Weber-Luther Gulick theories: form, hierarchy, task specialization, competence, norms of conduct, records, planning, organizing, staffing, directing, coordinating, reporting, and budgeting.

Soon after ISTEA was enacted, about three hundred people gathered at the state capital to discuss how to implement the act. The Process for Transportation Investment Decisions (PTID) is a method for making state transportation project decisions based on long-range planning and regional cooperation. The PTID process places priority on:

- preserving existing transportation facilities and improving operations;
- promoting shared authority and responsibility for decisions between state and local agencies; and
- broadening the decision-making process and increasing public involvement in the process.[2]

Urban and rural areas compete for scarce dollars. Two-thirds of the state's population resides in the heavily populated areas near the capital city of Big Burb. Big Burb must confront urban congestion, air quality violations, increased single-occupancy vehicle use, and aging physical infrastructures.

"Transportation is key to the productivity, and therefore the success, of virtually every business in America," emphasizes Norman Mineta, U.S. Secretary of Transportation. "Congestion and delay not only waste our time as individuals, they also burden our businesses and our entire economy with inefficiency and higher costs." Transportation, as an industry, accounts for 11 percent of the U.S. economy. (Health care accounts for 15 percent.) In 1999, transportation-related goods and services produced between $980 billion and $9.3 trillion for the U.S. gross domestic product.[3]

In Commonwealth, the railroad industry contributes to the development of state and local transportation plans. New regulations permit railroads to be members of Metropolitan Planning Organizations (MPOs). Railroads have significant roles in setting local transportation policies. ISTEA mandates the development of state and metropolitan transportation plans that consider freight movement and shape transportation decisions through a planning process.

Short-line railroads are making extensive infrastructure improvements. They operate approximately 50,000 miles of track. Unlike highays, they control right-of-way and the timing of traffic, making them more efficient for freight movement. "Replacing rails and ties and rebuilding equipment is an ongoing process for railroads," says Frank Turner, president of the American Short-Line and Regional Railroad Association (ASLRRA). "It's just a matter of money."[4]

Intermodal Management Planning Coordination

Commonwealth Governor Mike Rush and the General Assembly adopted a twenty-year transportation plan as required for each urbanized area of over 50,000 people throughout the United States. Railroad interests influenced strategies and projects in the Big Burb metro area. The Intermodal Management System (IMS) and Safety Management System (SMS), reflecting systems theory, promote passenger and freight system connections.

President Dwight Eisenhower is credited with the origination of the interstate highway system in the mid-1950s. The interstate highway plan includes 42,000 miles of limited-access, modern highways. The Federal Aid Highway Act (FAHA) of 1956 commenced what is known today as the interstate system. FAHA provided for federal funding of 90 percent of the cost of the interstates. States contributed the remaining 10 percent.[5]

Standards were highly regulated—lanes 12 feet wide, shoulders 10 feet wide, 14-foot minimum bridge clearance, grades 3 percent or less, and travel speeds designed for 70 miles per hour. The first stretch of interstate—eight miles—opened in Topeka, Kansas, on November 14, 1956. The last link was completed in Los Angeles in 1993. In 1957, the red, white, and blue shield symbol for Interstate numbering began. Highways running north-south are odd-numbered, while highways running east-west are even-numbered. Three-digit interstate highway numbers designate beltways or loops.

The number of airline passengers in the United States, according to the Federal Aviation Administration (FAA), is expected to rise by 39 percent between 2000 and 2012—from almost 26 million to 36 million. "The system is close to a saturation point," said Daniel D'Agostino, president of the Newark, New Jersey, Tower local of the National Air Traffic Controllers Association (NATCA). "There are plenty of routes up in the air. The unfortunate thing is these planes have to come down to the ground." Even by 2001, approximately 25 percent of flights were delayed or canceled.[6]

In response to the systems theory-based 1998 revisions of ISTEA, Mayor Foster and the Big Burb City Council enacted a three-year program to reduce the number of cars on city streets (promoting ride sharing and preferential parking for high-occupancy vehicles). The Big Burb City Council and state of Commonwealth General Assembly found consensus to finance construction of a twelve-mile light rail system (LRT) on an abandoned rail line. By reducing automobile volume, LRT is expected to provide cleaner air, reduce traffic congestion, and increase efficiency.

Estimated costs of the project are $625 million. Half of the costs are to be paid by the taxpayers of Big Burb and the state of Commonwealth. The remaining portion will be financed with federal grants. LRT is to extend from the Big Burb International Airport to the Big Burb branch of Steady State University to Citizen Park, home of the Big Burb Braves, a major league baseball team.

Systems theory promotes resource planning—stressing delineations of efficiency and effectiveness. Citizen inputs to the intermodal approach to transportation reflect the salience of rights and the adequacy of the governmental process. Equity, discretion, and representation are reflected in the planning process and its commitment to fairness for Big Burb and its surrounding bedroom communities.

The United States is an organization of immense political economy, affected by capital, human and material wealth, public and private sector bureaucracies, and the fragile play of democracy and opportunities; all organized in appropriate philosophical fashion. The challenges of Big Burb and the state of Commonwealth typify citizen choices in other states. Freedom of movement is grounded in commerce and ease of transportation.

Physiology includes life processes, activities, and functions. Democratic capitalism, as an organizing theory in the United States, promotes citizen decision making. Air, rail, highway, and water infrastructures operate within the rules of democracy, but they also respond to laws of supply and demand. Freedom is based on access, capital, technology, and human skills. Applications of systems theory can either promote or restrict the human side of enterprise.

Questions and Instructions

1. Describe theories of public and private organization emerging from reforms of transportation infrastructures. Illustrate your ideas.
2. How are the writings of Max Weber and Luther Gulick realized from the Intermodal Surface Transportation Efficiency Act of 1991 (ISTEA)?
3. Frederick Taylor saw the shift of power from the bourgeoisie (economic elite) and the proletariat (masses) to the experts (possessors of skills and knowledge). How do the facts of the Big Burb case illustrate this shift?
4. The Process for Transportation Investment Decisions (PTID) calls for promoting shared authority and responsibility and broadening the decision-making process. The writings of which organization theory authors likely influenced the organizations in this case study to develop the PTID?
5. Systems theory originates from structural/functional sociology and promotes an understanding of the social system as a whole. Explain the salience of systems theory for light rail alternatives in Big Burb and the State of Commonwealth.
6. How do normative vectors play out in this case study? Explain.
7. How is freedom of movement grounded in commerce and ease of transportation? Explain.
8. If effective rail modes do not emerge as transportation alternatives, what are the prospects for airplane and airport saturation of personnel, equipment, and costs? Explain and illustrate.
9. How do highway, rail, and air infrastructures contribute to redefinitions of the United States political economy? Explain.
10. Elton Mayo encouraged the perception of organization as a social institution. How would the development of intercity passenger rail systems contribute to new ways of organizing the political economies of Big Burb and the State of Commonwealth? Explain and illustrate.

Insights-Issues/Transportation Infrastructures as Organization Theory

Clearly and briefly describe and illustrate the following concepts and issues. Interpret the word *role* in terms of impacts, applications, importance, effects, and/or illustrations of certain facts, concerns, or issues from the case study.

1. Roles of bureaucracy and democracy as central pillars of private and public organizations in developing intermodal management planning coordination for Big Burb and State of Commonwealth transportation infrastructures.
2. Roles of facts versus values, ends versus means, satisficing, and bounded rationality for developing Big Burb and State of Commonwealth transportation infrastructures.

3. Role of systems theory for understanding the development of intermodal management planning for Big Burb and State of Commonwealth transportation infrastructures.
4. Roles of bourgeoisie (economic elite), proletariat (masses), and experts (possessors of skills and knowledge) for developing and coordinating intermodal management planning for Big Burb and State of Commonwealth transportation infrastructures.
5. Roles of the writings of Max Weber, Luther Gulick, and Elton Mayo for developing intermodal management planning coordination for Big Burb and State of Commonwealth transportation infrastructures.

Case Endnotes

1. See National Transportation Library, *Surface Transportation Resource Guides: Case Studies;* Jenny Wilson, "Minnesota DOT's Strategic Management Process: Reorienting Daily Decisions," pp. 5–7, http://ntl.bts.gov/DOCS/ TID.html.
2. *Ibid.,* p. 2.
3. Lee Bruno, "Transportation: The Future of Commuting," *Redherring,* February 8, 2002, http://www.redherring.com/insider/2002/0208/1713.html.

4. See FleetOwner, Online Exclusive, *PRIMEDIA* Business Magazines & Media, October 8, 2001.
5. "Interstate Highways," May 24, 1999; http://geography.about.com/library/weekly/aa052499.htm.
6. "No Relief in Sight for Travelers, More Flights, Passengers to Tax Overburdened Airports, *The Associated Press,* March 13, 2001, http://abcnews.go.com/sections/us/DailyNews/airlines010313.html.

Case Sources

See U.S. Department of Energy, National Renewable Energy Laboratory, "Beating the Traffic with Commuting Alternatives," DOE/GO-10095-171, May 1995, http://www.eren.doe.gov/cities_countries.beattra.html; Jolene M. Molitories, Rodney E. Slater, and Gordon J. Linton, Bureau of Transportation Statistics, National Transportation Library, "ISTEA Regulations and Railroads," http://ntl.bts.gov/DOCS/395ISTEA.html; Jolene M. Molitoris, Rodney E. Slater, and Gordon J. Linton. "Surface Transportation Policy Project Resource Guide: Case Studies," http://ntl.bts.gov/DOCS/TID.html; *The Columbia Dictionary of Quotations* (New York: Columbia University Press, 1995); Lawrence Dwyer,

"Intermodialism and ISTEA: The Challenges and the Changes," *Public Roads On-Line,* (Autumn 1994), http://www.tfhrc.gov/pubrds/fall94/p94au1.htm; Erik Ledbetter, "Railroad Preservation and ISTEA: Are You on Board?" April 10, 2001, http://www.rypn.org/Editorials/010410ISTEA/; Martin Ringle and Daniel Updegrove, "Is Strategic Planning for Technology an Oxymoron?" *CAUSE/EFFECT,* Vol. 21, No. 1 (1998), 18–23; Jochen Schneider, "Public-Private Partnerships for Urban Rail Transit," September 1, 1999, http://faculty.washington.edu/~jbs/itrans/todsch1.htm.

Chapter Endnotes

1. Dwight Waldo, *The Enterprise of Public Administration* (Novato, Calif.: Chandler & Sharp, 1980), pp. 33–47.
2. H. H. Gerth and C. Wright Mills, eds. *From Max Weber: Essays in Sociology* (New York: Oxford University Press, 1946), p. 197.

3. Michael M. Harmon and Richard T. Mayer outline the most important contributions to conceptual theories of public organizations. They describe six perspectives that bridge the theoretical with actual practice in public organizations. These perspectives, as analyzed

by various authors, focus upon three organizational themes—system, hierarchy, and structure. See Harmon and Mayer, *Organization Theory for Public Administration* (Boston: Little, Brown, 1986).

4. John M. Pfiffner and Frank P. Sherwood, *Administrative Organization* (Englewood Cliffs, N.J.: Prentice-Hall, 1960), pp. 56–57.

5. *Ibid.,* p. 217.

6. Wellford W. Wilms, "Father Time, The One Best Way," *The Los Angeles Times,* June 1, 1997, p. 6.

7. Frederick Winslow Taylor, *The Principles of Scientific Management* (New York: W. W. Norton, 1947), p. 9.

8. Elton Mayo, *The Human Problems of an Industrial Civilization* (New York: Macmillan, 1933). Also see F. J. Roethsberger and William J. Dickson, *Management and the Worker* (Cambridge, Mass.: Harvard University Press, 1946).

9. F. J. Roethsberger and William J. Dickson, *Management and Worker* (Cambridge, Mass.: Harvard University Press, 1946), p. 552.

10. Pfiffner and Sherwood, *Administrative Organization,* p. 102.

11. Chester Barnard, *Functions of the Executive* (Cambridge, Mass.: Harvard University Press, 1968).

12. *Ibid.,* p. 217.

13. Luther Gulick and Lyndall Urwick, eds., *Papers on the Science of Administration* (New York: Institute of Public Administration, 1937).

14. Gulick, "Notes on the Theory of Organization," in Gulick and Urwick, *Science of Administration,* p. 13.

15. Herbert A. Simon, "The Proverbs of Administration," *Public Administration Review* 6 (Winter 1946): 53–67.

16. Herbert A. Simon, *Administrative Behavior: A Study of Decision-Making Processes in Administrative Organization,* 3rd ed. (New York: The Free Press, 1976).

17. Mary Parker Follett, *The New State: Group Organization—The Solution to Popular Government* (New York: Longmans, Green, 1918); *Creative Experience* (New York: Longmans, Green, 1924); and *Dynamic Administration,* Henry C. Metcalf and L. Urwick, eds.

18. Noel O'R. Morton and Stefanie A. Lindquist, "Revealing the Feminist in Mary Parker Follett," *Administration & Society* 29, no. 3 (July 1997): 348–372.

19. Abraham Maslow, *Motivation and Personality* (New York: Harper and Brothers, 1954).

20. Douglas McGregor, *The Human Side of Enterprise* (New York: McGraw-Hill, 1960).

21. Rensis Likert, *The Human Organization: Its Management and Value* (New York: McGraw-Hill, 1967).

22. Thomas Walken, "Women Managers: The Myth of Male Leadership," *Business Leader,* May 1999, http://www.businessleader. com/bl/women.html; Marie-Therese Glaes, "Women, Men, and Management Styles," *International Labour Review,* Vol. 138, No. 4 (1999), 431–446.

23. Joyce Fletcher and Deborah Merrill-Sands, "Looking Below the Surface: The Gendered Nature of Organizations," *CG Gender,* Vol. 3, No. 1 (April 1998), http://www.simmons.edu/ gsm/gsm/cgo/looking.html.

People and Personnel

Chapter Highlights

Conflicting Doctrines in American Public Administration

Procedures and Policies

Employee Recruitment

Merit-Based Recruitment Arrangements

Does Federal Hiring Need a Fix?

The Postrecruitment Phase

Promotion

The Challenges of Public Personnel Administration

The Changing Demographics of the Federal Workforce

The True Size of Government

Equal Opportunity and Affirmative Action

Performance Ratings

Individual Performance Measurement

Position Classifications

Summary

We Are Not Welcome the Way Whites Are

New York City, by far the largest municipal government in the United States, has a population of approximately 7.5 million and 411,651 full-time-equivalent government employees. Of those local government employees, the New York Police Department (NYPD) employs 465 captains—a group of senior officers whose ranks include the most prominent and powerful commanders.

Of the 465 police captains, only 9 are black males. Why, in a city where the 2000 census reports 25 percent of the population is African-American, are so few police captains of African descent?

The answer lies not only in the numbers and percentages of whites and blacks, but in history, culture, aptitude, and motivation.

In 1990, 7.7 percent of NYPD's sergeants were black. By the end of the decade, the percentage

NYPD Demographics of Black Males in Elite Commands

	Total	Black Males
Emergency Service	501	37
Mounted Unit	124	3
Major Case detectives	43	3
Harbor Unit	159	2
Aviation Unit	59	1
Totals	886	46

of front-line black supervisors decreased to 5.7 percent. Black men are likewise absent in the elite commands. Major case detectives, Emergency Service, Mounted, Aviation, and Harbor units—almost all white—constitute the elite commands (see table on the previous page).

Data indicate that the percentages of uniformed black males increased from 7.7 percent (1974) to 9.2 percent (2000). Uniformed females at the NYPD have enhanced their numbers sixfold since 1974. Black women made significant advances within the NYPD ranks, too. Black women at the NYPD have increased from near statistical insignificance in 1974 to almost 5 percent in 2000. Black female supervisors have increased likewise, and Hispanic representation jumped by nearly 500 percent.

Why, then, has the proportion of black male officers been in decline since 1990?

A brief history lesson provides some context. Upon being rebuffed by the Anglo-Saxon culture, New Yorkers of certain ethnicities formed other organizations, which contested the dominance of white Protestants. Many Irish men, speaking English but not part of the dominant Protestant culture, became cops. Some Italians formed the Mafia. Therefore, the Irish long ago began a public service employment pattern that continues to this day. They have a long-standing tradition of becoming NYC police officers. It's all in the family—fathers, brothers, uncles, and now, perhaps, mothers and daughters have joined the NYPD.

The oldest organization in the history of humanity is the family. Government is likely second. While Irish-Americans were encouraged to join the ranks of the NYPD, African-Americans did not enjoy either the family prodding or the access their Irish neighbors had. But is it the fault of the organization, namely the NYPD, that black men have not become NYPD officers—at least not in proportions reflecting the city's demographics? After three decades of trying, the NYPD—in pursuit of a fully representative workforce—has failed to attract and advance black men.

This disparity between black and white exists despite the election of a black mayor, David N. Dinkins; the appointments of a black police com-

missioner, Lee P. Brown, and chief of patrol, Wilbur Chapman; and an affirmative action program advocated by both Democratic and Republican mayors. The City leadership explicitly promoted the belief that more black NYPD officers would improve the force's effectiveness. Even with black political and administrative leadership supporting that goal, the number of black males barely increased.

Geography is also a factor with NYPD officers. New York lacks a residency requirement for its officers, so white men from the suburbs dominate each police academy class. Without a fully representative force, tensions between the NYPD and residents persist. Are black officers better prepared than white officers to negotiate the behavior of lower-economic-class African-Americans and immigrants? Are the tensions and confrontations racial—or economic?

The NYPD hierarchy believes in diversity, and in fact champions it, perhaps exaggerating its successes, while the NYPD white rank-and-file officers resist demographic changes in the force. Diversity is a community value. But the NYPD function, in itself, is not grounded in diverse representation. Its structural-functional operations are anchored in the skills, knowledge, and expertise of officers.

As we have discussed, American society reflects a tension between the values of equality and efficiency. The struggle for more black male NYPD officers is more of a challenge to efficiency than equality. The right to apply for a NYPD position reflects a commitment to equality; the city relies on civil service rules, which reflect efficiency, to gauge the qualifications of officers. After the Civil War, reforms designated that such rules replace a system of political spoils with objective hiring measures. However, controversy surrounds the civil service tests.

The civil service exam controversy surrounds their value as predictive tests. The primary arbiter of promotion to sergeant, lieutenant, and captain are multiple-choice exams. These tests focus on police-related knowledge, including NYPD rules, regulations, tactics, and criminal law. Top scorers are ranked on an eligibility list.

C. J. Chivers, a *New York Times* reporter, asks: Do these tests actually measure police aptitude? Do the exams predict supervisory skills? The value of the tests is questioned by many officers and police officials. Leadership—courage, judgment, and integrity—is crucial at the station houses and on the police beats. Civil service rules, over which the NYPD has limited control, reflect merit-based standards for public service at the NYPD. Civil service rules, or standards, have stymied the promotions of a large proportion of potential black officers.

In any bureaucracy, "who one knows" may be as important as "what one knows." At the NYPD, connections within the police hierarchy are critical. Friends in high places whom officers rely on to get what they want are called "hooks." Police officers insist that hooks are directly related to choice assignments, and maintaining a good set of hooks is essential to a successful career. Even in equality, some are "more equal" than others.

"We are not welcome the way whites are," says a NYPD black police recruiter. "We do not have the same opportunities."

What the recruiter may be saying is this: The overt racism of yesteryear is gone. However, young black male professionals likely do not have the same

- background (family encouragement),
- education (reminders of merit requirements),
- motivation (personal drive to become a police officer),
- culture (police station as mini-city hall), and
- hooks (friends in all the right places) as their white counterparts.

Equality, as such, provides no guarantees—it only provides access. Affirmative action—without paths to achievement—is limited. The NYPD, reflecting efficiency, is a government-regulated opportunity structure for all races. The NYPD promotes merit. Merit affords mechanisms for achievement. As achievements increase, manifestations of race and sex discrimination decrease.

Source

C. J. Chivers, "For Black Officers, Diversity Has Its Limits," *The New York Times,* April 2, 2001.

"Let me control personnel," George Kennan has said, "and I will ultimately control policy. For the part of the machine that recruits and hires and fires and promotes people can soon control the entire shape of the institution."[1]

Few administrative theorists or practitioners would dispute this statement, and in the course of history, few able administrators have thought or acted otherwise. Their attitudes and approaches to the subject, however, have often differed.

Thomas Jefferson, for example, believed that civil servants should be provided with "drudgery and subsistence only" so that they would not want to stay too long in office.[2] This would enable the country to escape the establishment and growth of an administrative class, a development that Jefferson greatly feared. Other public administrators have taken a different tack, working toward strengthening the competency and professionalism of civil servants.

Conflicting Doctrines in American Public Administration

Herbert Kaufman provided a foundation for describing conflicts in the doctrines of public administration—a foundation that remains solid in the twenty-first century. He notes that different values are reflected in different periods in American history.

The quests for representativeness, for neutral competence, and for executive leadership reflect succeeding norms of public personnel administration.[3]

The quest for *representativeness* has its roots in the colonial period. In our republican system, government bureaucrats are accountable to policies initiated by representatives of the voters. The quest for *neutral competence* originated in the 1880s with abuses of legislative supremacy, the long ballot, and the spoils system. The goal of this quest was "taking administration out of politics."

The quest for *executive leadership* was an effort to deal with such governmental issues as budgeting, reorganization, fragmentation, and the size of the bureaucracy. The personnel function is an essential part of these issues.

In addition to these "quests," it is helpful to examine Donald E. Klingner's and John Nalbandian's description of factors affecting public personnel practices that may contribute to the conflicting values in public administration. These factors are:

- *Value influences.* These considerations especially concern the rights of the individual, administrative efficiency, responsiveness, and social equity.
- *Mediating activities.* These interventions include affirmative action, human resource planning, productivity, and labor relations.
- *Core functions.* These essentials focus on the procurement, allocation, development, and sanction of human resources.[4]

Procedures and Policies

Public organizations in this country use essentially one of two different methods of establishing and operating personnel systems. One method stresses *political appointment and election,* while the other emphasizes an *objective determination of merit.*

Units of the Revolutionary army frequently elected their own officers and once the hostilities ended, states and their communities elected most of the administrators they would need. This practice has continued in many places. Many cities and towns, particularly older ones, follow the same practice. Some New England communities elect as many as fifty officials. Newer areas of the country, such as the Far West, disdain such practices, but even they maintain county organizations with many elective posts. No other major country in the world elects so many of its administrators as does the United States. Most state governments elect some officials whose tasks would be regarded in Europe or Canada as purely administrative.

The selection of civil servants by merit and by political patronage are not mutually exclusive, argues James E. Leidlein. Fears that any relaxation of a merit-based system will lead to the returned dominance of political patronage are not warranted.[5]

Although election, dating back to the foundations of U.S. government, is supposed to give the people a deciding voice in determining who will administer their government, it can lead to abuses such as misleading promises and a reliance on campaign funding from special interests. Most of the electorate finds it impossible to know all the candidates for whom they must vote.

Political appointment also has a long history in the United States, dating back to colonial times. Even John Adams, who considered himself something of a paragon of political propriety, felt constrained to provide his ne'er-do-well son-in-law with a government job. Such practices gained increased favor with the arrival of Andrew Jackson at the White House. Jackson strongly adhered to Jefferson's views on rotating public servants in office. At the same time, Jackson did not believe that this would entail any loss of public confidence. As he put it, "The duties of all public servants are, or at least admit of being made, so plain and simple that men of intelligence may readily qualify themselves for their performance."[6] Old Hickory's espousal of this philosophy was fortified in that he had a virtual army of job seekers at his back clamoring loudly for the plums of patronage.

From Jackson's time on, U.S. presidents frequently found themselves besieged by persons seeking positions on the public payroll. One aggressive appointment seeker jumped into Abraham Lincoln's carriage to ask for a job while the president was riding through Washington. Lincoln started to listen to him but then drove him away, saying, more in despair than in anger, "No I will not do business in the street."

When a disappointed job seeker assassinated President James Garfield in 1881, the nation's appetite for such administrative practices began to dampen. Political appointment continues to play a prominent role in U.S. administrative life, however. Our presidents, for example, fill nearly one hundred times more appointments than do British prime ministers.

The assassination of President Garfield did have its effect: It gave rise to an alternative method of recruitment, namely the *merit system.* Two years after the president's violent death, Congress passed the Pendleton Act, setting up a systematized procedure for hiring and employing vast numbers of federal civil servants in nearly every category. The merit system principle has continued to grow. It not only encompasses over 90 percent of positions in the federal government, but includes increasing numbers of employees in state and local governments. About two-thirds of our states have comprehensive merit systems that cover the vast majority of their job holders. Even those states without comprehensive merit systems make some provisions for merit-style appointments. The federal government has helped prod states and municipalities to move in this direction, for federal grants-in-aid frequently require the recipient agency to operate a merit system of some sort.

The Pendleton Act, passed in 1883, provided the substance of modern merit principles:

- *First,* administrative reform focused upon *nonpolitical appointments* in attempting to neutralize the civil service. Such nonpartisanship in selecting, promoting, and regulating public bureaucrats was a reaction against the evils of the spoils system.
- *Second,* the Pendleton Act embraced *egalitarianism,* the most important legacy of Jacksonian democracy. Congress, in adopting civil service reform, refused to pattern the U.S. career system after the British. The American merit system would be open to all applicants of appropriate aptitude and skills. Theoretically, at least, all classes of citizens may contest for government employment.
- *Third, competence,* as determined by competitive examinations, was instituted in the Pendleton Act's provisions. The requirement was that exams be practical, related to the duties to be performed, and not grounded in theoretical or scholarly essays based on academic achievement.[7]

The Plum Book and the Prune Book

College students may aspire to become Washington policymakers. Two books that provide guidelines, facts, and positions for postgraduate students seeking jobs in the upper ranks of the federal government are the "Plum Book" and the "Prune Book."

The Plum Book, released every four years alternately by the Senate Committee on Governmental Affairs or the House Committee on Government Reform, carries the formal title of *United States Government Policy and Supporting Positions.*

The Prune Book, published by the Council for Excellence in Government, profiles fifty-six of the most important U.S. Senate-confirmed government positions. It details five senior management jobs common to most agencies—chief operating officer, chief information officer, chief financial officer, general counsel, and inspector general.

The Plum Book catalogs more than seven thousand jobs at the prerogative of the President. They usually are appointed positions—including agency heads, immediate subordinates, policy executives, and advisors. The Prune Book examines issues relating to staffing the upper echelons of the executive branch and probes the challenges that face presidential appointees.

The Plum Book and the Prune Book are designed to facilitate presidential transitions every four years. They combine interests of partisan, policy, and system politics.

Source: Katy Saldarini, "2000 Plum Book Lists Sought-After Jobs in Next Administration," *Government Executive,* November 10, 2000.

More recently, the Civic Service Reform Act of 1978 established the merit system principles that the government employs today (Table 5.1). The Act states, in addition to many other merit principles, that:

> Recruitment should be from qualified individuals from appropriate sources in an endeavor to achieve a workforce from all segments of society, and selection and advancement should be determined solely on the basis of relative ability, knowledge, and skills, after fair and open competition which assures that all receive equal opportunity.

Another key part of the 1978 law states:

> Employees should be retained on the basis of the adequacy of their performance, inadequate performance should be corrected, and employees should be separated who cannot or will not improve their performance to meet required standards.

To summarize, key *merit system principles* are: recruiting, selecting, and advancing employees on the basis of their abilities, knowledge, and skills; providing equitable and adequate compensation; training employees to assure high-quality performance; guaranteeing fairness for applicants and employees; and protecting against coercion for political purposes.

Despite the law, the merit system has its detractors, who say that such a system eventually leads to a triumph of mediocrity, with initiative and enterprise sacrificed to the pressures of security and the forces of stagnation. Even when a merit system encourages merit, the argument continues, it may lead only to a *meritocracy* that shuts out otherwise capable people who cannot pass the tests or meet formal and sometimes fatuous requirements of the system.

Although the merit system may have lost some of its luster, it retains a good deal of support from both theorists and practitioners. Even if it leads to a "meritocracy," they say, it is still likely to be more egalitarian and democratic than a system built on political contacts and allegiances. When operated properly, it attracts better people and encourages them to stay and develop their capabilities.

TABLE 5.1

Expansion of Merit System and Public Service During Presidential Terms

President	Term	Events
Chester Arthur	1881–1885	Through the Pendleton Act of 1883, created U.S. Civil Service Commission and the merit system.
Grover Cleveland	1885–1889	Extended the competitive civil service in 1888 by 5,320 positions through blanketing in the Railway Mail Service. Congress created the Interstate Commerce Commission, the first federal regulatory commission. Woodrow Wilson's "The Study of Administration" was published in *Political Science Quarterly*.
Benjamin Harrison	1889–1893	Extended the competitive civil service by blanketing in the Indian Service, Fish Commission, and Weather Bureau.
Grover Cleveland	1893–1897	Increased the size of the competitive civil service by 32,000 positions with one order in 1896.
William McKinley	1897–1902	Revised the civil service rules in 1899, which excepted over 5,000 positions from the competitive civil service. In 1901, Galveston, Texas, became the first city to install a commission form of government, and Oregon became the first state to adopt initiative and referendum.
Theodore Roosevelt	1902–1909	Showed strong support for the civil service reform movement after serving as Civil Service Commissioner from 1889 to 1895. In 1906, Bureau of Municipal Research founded in New York City to further the management movement in government. In 1908, Staunton, Virginia, appointed the first city manager.
William Taft	1909–1913	Extended the competitive civil service by 39,000 positions by blanketing in fourth-class postmasterships and assistant postmasters and clerks. Frederick W. Taylor published *The Principles of Scientific Management.* In 1912, Taft Commission called for a national executive budget, position classification first adopted at the municipal level in the city of Chicago. Sumter, South Carolina, became the first city to install a council-manager form of city government, and Congress approved an eight-hour day for federal employees.
Woodrow Wilson	1913–1921	Almost doubled the federal workforce to a total of nearly 1,000,000 during World War I. In 1913, the sixteenth Amendment to the Constitution created the first permanent federal income tax, the Federal Reserve Act created a central bank responsible for monetary policy. In 1914, Dayton, Ohio, became the first major city to have a city manager. In 1920, the Retirement Act created the first federal civil service pension system, and the Nineteenth Amendment gave women the right to vote.
Warren Harding	1921–1923	Saw the comprehensive civil service hold, during the postwar reductions, the ground it had previously gained. In 1921, the Budget and Accounting Act established (1) the Bureau of the Budget in the Department of the Treasury and (2) the General Accounting Office as an agency of Congress. In 1923, the Classification Act brought position classification to Washington-based federal employees and established the principle of equal pay for equal work.

continued

TABLE 5.1

Expansion of Merit System and Public Service During Presidential Terms, *continued*

President	Term	Events
Calvin Coolidge	1923–1929	Extended the competitive civil service in 1927 by blanketing in the Bureau of Prohibition. In 1926, Leonard D. White's *Introduction to the Study of Public Administration* was the first text on public administration.
Herbert Hoover	1929–1933	Placed 13,000 previously excepted positions in the competitive civil service.
Franklin Roosevelt	1933–1945	Established new temporary emergency agencies, with the majority excepted from the competitive civil service during the Great Depression; saw the Ramspeck Act of 1940 extend the competitive civil service to more than 182,000 permanent positions; increased the number of federal employees during World War II to 3,816,300 in 1945. In 1933, New Deal began, Tennessee Valley Authority (TVA) established by Congress as independent public corporation. In 1935, Social Security program created. In 1937, the Brownlow Committee's report stated that the "President needs help" and called for the reorganization of the executive branch. In 1939, the Hatch Act passed to inhibit political activities by federal employees, the federal government first required states to have merit systems for employees in programs aided by federal funds.
Harry Truman	1945–1953	Alternately expanded and contracted the federal workforce, which challenged personnel management. In 1945, the Manhattan Project marked the federal government's first major involvement with science in a policymaking role. In 1946, the Employment Act created the Council of Economic Advisors and asserted that the policy of the federal government was to maintain full employment. In 1949, the National Security Act created the Department of Defense.
Dwight Eisenhower	1953–1961	Through an executive order in 1953, a Schedule C class of positions were excepted from the competitive civil service. In 1955, the Second Hoover Commission recommended the curtailment and abolition of federal government activities that competed with private enterprise; the Department of Health, Education and Welfare (HEW) was created. In 1958, the National Aeronautics and Space Administration(NASA) was created. In 1959, New York City became the first major city to allow collective bargaining with its employees, Wisconsin became the first state to enact a comprehensive law governing public sector labor relations, and the Advisory Commission on Intergovernmental Relations (ACIR) was established.
John Kennedy	1961–1963	Signed Executive Order (EO) 10925 requiring "affirmative action" be used in employment, EO 10988 encouraging the unionization of federal workers.
Lyndon Johnson	1963–1969	In 1965, the Department of Housing and Urban Development (HUD) was established, Medicare was created through amendments to the Social Security Act. In 1966, the Freedom of Information Act allowed greater access to federal agency files. In 1967, Age Discrimination in Employment Act was passed.

continued

TABLE 5.1

Expansion of Merit System and Public Service During Presidential Terms, *continued*

President	Term	Events
Richard Nixon	1969–1974	In 1969, Executive Order 11491 granted federal employees rights to join or not to join labor organizations, created the Federal Labor Relations Council (FLRC) to supervise the creation of bargaining units and elections. In 1970, the Bureau of the Budget (BOB) was given more responsibility for managerial oversight and renamed the Office of Management and Budget (OMB); the Postal Reorganization Act created the U.S. Postal Service as a public corporation; Hawaii became the first state to allow state and local government employees to strike; the Environmental Protection Agency (EPA) was established. In 1974, the Congressional Budget and Impoundment Control Act revised the congressional budget process and created the Congressional Budget Office (CBO).
Jimmy Carter	1977–1981	Guidelines prohibiting sexual harassment by Title VII of the Civil Rights Act (1964) were posted. Zero-based budgeting required of federal agencies. The Presidential Management Intern Program was established. In 1977, the Department of Energy was created. In 1978, the Civil Service Reform Act abolished the U.S. Civil Service Commission and replaced it with (1) the Office of Personnel Management (OPM), (2) the Merit Systems Protection Board (MSPB), and (3) the Federal Labor Relations Authority (FLRA).
Ronald Reagan	1981–1989	The "Reagan revolution" attacked the quality and size of government. It reflected widespread citizen dissatisfactions—real and perceived—with government programs. Reagan said government was "not the solution to the problem. Government *is* the problem." The Civil Service Reform Act was not used to rebuild a merit system in serious disrepair. The roles of government bureaucratic authority and power in a democratic system were questioned. Without funding and leadership, career civil servants, regardless of their acclaimed merit, were caught in a Catch-22.
George H.W. Bush	1989–1993	Urged government officials to uphold the highest ethical standards and called government service an opportunity for public service, not private gain. In 1989, the National Commission on Public Service, the Volcker Commission, called for a revitalization of the public service.
Bill Clinton	1993–2001	Emphasized reinventing-government theme, performance review, and a revitalized bureaucracy. In 1993, Executive Order 12871 created the National Partnership Council calling for a new framework in labor-management relations. Reforms in position classification, pay and promotion opportunities advocated. Downsizing of the federal government initiated.
George W. Bush	2001–	Revoked National Partnership Council requiring federal agencies to form labor-management partnerships; promoted open competition on federal and federally funded or assisted construction projects; and in order to secure the United States from terrorist threats or attacks, established the Office of Homeland Security.

Sources: Data from U.S. Civil Service Commission, *Biography of an Ideal: The Diamond Anniversary History of the Federal Civil Service* (Washington, D.C.: U.S. Government Printing Office, 1958); Patricia Wallace Ingraham, *The Foundation of Merit: Public Service in American Democracy* (Baltimore: The Johns Hopkins Press, 1995); Jay M. Shafritz and E. W. Russell, *Introducing Public Administration* (New York: Addison Wesley Longman, 1997), adapted from Jay M. Shafritz and Albert C. Hyde, *Classics of Public Administration,* 4th ed. (Fort Worth, Tex.: Harcourt Brace, 1997).

In a 1990 decision, the United States Supreme Court ruled that the U.S. Constitution prohibits partisan political considerations for hiring, promoting, or transferring most public employees. The ruling clearly prevents a mayor or local chief executive from reserving nonpolicymaking jobs such as road equipment operations, prison security, highway repair, or parks department positions for the party faithful. Although the practical impacts of the ruling are difficult to assess, the Supreme Court dealt a sharp blow to political patronage at all levels.

In conclusion, the federal government labor force is now enlisted mostly on the basis of merit, though in the early twentieth century employees were hired on the basis of patronage. While enlistment on the basis of merit forbids involvement in politics, patronage enlistment actively encouraged political involvement. According to Ronald N. Johnson and Gary D. Libecap, the inherent corruption and inefficiency in the patronage system led to its demise. The adoption of the merit system of recruitment imposes effective controls over the performance and actions of the labor force.[8]

Employee Recruitment

If the merit principle has become the most widely accepted basis for personnel operation in U.S. administration, it nevertheless continues to arouse controversy and pose problems. In terms of recruitment, there is first the task of making sure that the system truly rewards merit. Most civil service systems make extensive use of comparative examinations to bring this about. While such exams may weigh the merits of the various candidates more impartially than a system built on favoritism would, they offer difficulties of their own.

For one thing, the exams must be *predictive*. In other words, high scores on the examinations should correlate with high performance on the job and vice versa. This is not necessarily the case. The issue of validity (whether test results are accurate or appropriate) and other recruitment criteria have come to the fore, thanks to the increased effort to recruit members of minority groups into government service. Civil rights supporters claim that many of these criteria serve to exclude blacks, Puerto Ricans, Chicanos, and others. Specifically they charge that these tests fail to determine the true capability of a job applicant. A study in Chicago found that a black police recruit would perform as well on the job as white recruit who scored 10 percent higher on the entrance exam.[9] In other words, the entrance test failed to measure the true ability black applicants have for police work.

The federal government encourages test validation as a means of ensuring and expanding equal opportunity. The move to include more members of minority groups in public administration is part of a larger movement aimed at making government agencies more representative of the public they serve. This brings us to another issue in administration. Government agencies have at times become "captive" to one or more sector of society. The *captive agency,* a term used by public administration scholar Brian Chapman, tends to recruit heavily from one particular ethnic, religious, social, or geographical group.

If the federal government is to effectively manage the tasks and programs assigned to it through legislation, it must have a sufficient and qualified workforce. One important element that departments and agencies must consider in their workforce

---

Government Jobs for Students

The website *www.studentjobs.gov* provides a wealth of data on federal job openings and information on the federal government's hiring processes, programs, and employment benefits. The website posts an e-mail notification system every twenty-four hours for newly posted vacancies. The openings are designed to match a student's personal job-search profile. *www.studentjobs. gov* offers links to student employment pages for more than fifty agencies and to article describing student job opportunities.

The Office of Personnel Management (OPM) and Department of Education created *www.studentjobs. gov*, which is designed for high school and college students seeking temporary employment with the federal government. Applicants for *www.studentjobs.gov* must be at least sixteen years old. About half of government employees are ages between forty-five and sixty. Only 5 percent are twenty-nine years or younger.

The full URL for the website is *http://www. studentjobs.gov.*

Source: Stephen Barr, "Website Encourages Young People to Think About Working for Uncle Sam," *The Washington Post,* July 13, 2001, p. B02. "Government Jobs for Students: New Website Helps Find Summer and Temporary Jobs," http://usgovinfo.about.com/library/weekly/aa071301a.htm

---

planning is the number and kinds of employees who will retire from 2003 to 2006. A substantial portion of the federal workforce is eligible to retire during that period.

The General Accounting Office (GAO) estimates that by 2006, about 31 percent of employees at the twenty-four major federal agencies—or 493,000 people—will be eligible to retire, and about half of those eligible will opt for retirement. Agencies must ensure that they will have an adequate workforce to carry out their missions. The Office of Personnel Management (OPM) stresses the importance of integrating strategic human capital management into agency planning. OPM is focusing more attention on developing workforce-planning tools to help agencies respond effectively.[10]

Limitations to Merit

A pure merit system for all public service appointments would be grounded in competition based on merit rules. However, no administration functions on a pure merit system. Exceptions always exist, including:

- *Elected officials.* Some officials are elected, not appointed. No civil service gauge is employed in an election.
- *Political appointments.* Elected officials may choose friends, neighbors, or college roommates as political advisers. No civil service gauge is employed for these appointments.
- *Affirmative action.* To hasten the advancement of members of a disadvantaged group such as women or certain ethnic minorities, that group receives hiring preference. No civil service gauge is employed for such hirings.
- *Internal appointments and transfers.* Sometimes promotion is restricted to existing staff. The search is conducted inside the organization, not externally, to minimize transaction costs. In such cases, opportunities are provided for insider career development.[11]

Merit-Based Recruitment Arrangements

Merit-based recruitment arrangements include these elements:

- A job analysis leading to a written statement describing duties, or a job description, and the knowledge and skills required of the job holder (the person specification).
- An advertisement disseminated to affected groups—including a summary of the job analysis.
- A standard application form.
- A scoring scheme based on the person specification.
- A short-listing procedure to reduce applications, if pertinent, to a manageable number.
- A final selection procedure based on the person specification. A panel interview is included in the process.
- An appointment procedure based on the scoring scheme.
- Notification of results to selected and rejected candidates.[12]

Does Federal Hiring Need a Fix?

The September 11, 2001 terrorist attacks on the World Trade Center and the Pentagon brought to the fore a concern about government hiring: the federal hiring process apparently needs a fix. Job applicants think that hiring at federal departments and agencies takes too long, and complaints about federal hiring are longstanding. Within the next several years, large numbers of federal employees will retire. A new set of federal recruitment demands is likely to emerge.

Is anything being done to speed up federal government hiring? Applicants must realize that government hiring processes are procedural, regulated by law, and are grounded in pursuit of the common good. The kinds of education and experience that the government needs are rapidly changing, and suitable applicants are difficult to recruit.

The hot skills the Federal Bureau of Investigation (FBI) needs are in the fields of science, computer science, and foreign language. Fewer than half the jobs are filled by applicants with law enforcement experience. According to FBI Assistant Director Sheri A. Farrar, 20 percent of the new agents have backgrounds in computer science and technology, about 10 percent have experience in physical and natural sciences, and another 10 percent possess engineering backgrounds. Another 20 percent are proficient in certain foreign languages—Arabic, Farsi, Pashto, Urdu, Chinese, Japanese, Korean, Russian, Spanish, and Vietnamese.

In fiscal year 2000, only 13 percent of the 60,000 federal job openings at the midcareer level (GS–12 to GS–15) were filled from outside the government. Not all agencies are ready to go outside the government to fill jobs. This internal priority for filling federal jobs underscores another need for changes in the hiring system.

The inside vs. outside dilemma is not new. Discouraging outsiders from seeking federal jobs gives advantages to insiders, who already have government experience. Government personnel directors may even write narrow job qualifications to favor persons who already work for them. Talented and highly qualified persons may be emliminated because of this preference for inside recruitment.

Another hiring problem relates to modern technology. Both agencies and applicants may have become too dependent upon the internet and online applications to the exclusion of personal interviews. According to Kay Coles James, OPM director, agency officials must "take the time to meet finalists for federal jobs and conduct structured interviews in which each applicant is asked the same set of questions by experts."

Federal government personnel departments are positioned between the proverbial rock and hard place. Taxpayers lobbied for downsizing in the 1990s. In the process of steam lining and reinventing government, personnel offices lost experienced employees to retirement. Agencies now realize that the internet should not be their only recruitment mechanism. They need to return to colleges and universities for effective recruiting.

The war against terrorism makes federal hiring improvements more pressing, challenging agencies and their personnel. Recruitment reformers insist that federal employment personnel be more citizen-focused. Post-September 11th governments must attract the highest-caliber applicants to meet their pressing needs.[13]

More than 15.1 million full-time-equivalent workers were employed in state and local governments in 2000—a 2.2 percent increase over 1999, according to the Commerce Department's Census Bureau (table 5.2). Of that total, local governments reported 11 million full-time-equivalent (FTE) employees. State governments reported 4.1 million.

Full-time equivalents are the number of full-time employees who could have been employed if the hours worked by part-time employees had been combined into full-time positions. For example, two people working half days would be considered one full-time equivalent. The 2000 Annual Survey of State and Local Government Employment and Payroll indicates that most full-time-equivalent employees worked in education (7.8 million), hospitals (929,000), or police protection (867,000). Other FTE groupings occur in corrections, streets and highways, public welfare, health, judicial and legal positions, financial administration, and fire protection (table 5.3).

The Postrecruitment Phase

After a recruit qualifies for and receives an employment appointment, he or she still has obstacles to overcome before claiming full-fledged membership in the agency or organization. During the *probationary period,* employees measure the skills, knowledge, expertise, and responsiveness of every employee. During this time, the recruit can be dismissed without the safeguards that protect those who have successfully completed such a phase. Probationary periods vary in length from six to twelve months to as long as seven years. The shorter terms are common in state and local governments, while the federal government and some other subnational jurisdictions require longer probations. The time frames may also vary depending upon

TABLE 5.2
Total Civilian Employment of the Federal Government by Branch, Agency, and Area (April–May 2001)

Agency	Total, All Areas			United States			Washington, DC-MD-VA-WV Metropolitan Statistical Area		
	May 2001*	April 2001	Change	May 2001*	April 2001	Change	May 2001*	April 2001	Change
Department of the Treasury	159,274	164,723	-5,449	157,898	163,356	-5,458	22,538	22,560	-22
Department of Defense	670,568	668,723	1,845	616,772	614,957	1,815	63,119	62,975	144
Defense, Military Function Total	645,849	644,929	920	592,127	591,239	888	62,398	62,258	140
Defense, Civil Function Total	24,719	23,794	925	24,645	23,718	927	721	717	4
Department of the Army	227,870	227,956	-86	205,062	205,118	-56	19,003	19,095	-92
Department of the Army, Military Function Total	203,152	204,163	-1,011	180,418	181,401	-983	18,282	18,378	-96
Department of the Army, Civil Function Total	24,718	23,793	925	24,644	23,717	927	721	717	4
Corp of Engineers	24,699	23,774	925	24,625	23,698	927	702	698	4
Cemeterial Expenses	19	19	. . .	19	19	. . .	19	19	. . .
Department of the Navy	182,557	182,286	271	174,527	174,135	392	24,660	24,564	96
Department of the Air Force	154,438	152,613	1,825	147,651	146,021	1,630	5,123	5,059	64
Defense Logistics Agency	23,680	23,680	. . .	22,942	22,942	. . .	2,007	2,007	. . .
Other Defense Activities (Excluding Defense Logistics Agency)	82,023	82,188	-165	66,590	66,741	-151	12,326	12,250	76
Department of Justice	126,711	126,595	116	124,162	124,034	128	21,831	21,887	-56
Department of the Interior	72,982	69,538	3,444	72,601	69,162	3,439	7,936	7,846	90
Department of Agriculture	100,084	95,895	4,189	98,797	94,616	4,181	11,213	11,151	62
Department of Commerce***	39,151	40,090**	-939	38,381	39,320**	-939	20,074	20,167**	-93
Department of Labor	16,016	15,977	39	15,973	15,935	38	5,364	5,358	6
Department of Health and Human Services	63,323	63,111	212	63,064	62,853	211	28,227	28,157	70
Department of Housing and Urban Development	10,154	10,170	-16	10,067	10,083	-16	3,059	3,051	8
Department of Transportation	64,131	63,901	230	63,629	63,405	224	10,487	10,419	68
Department of Energy	15,689	15,627	62	15,681	15,619	62	5,230	5,222	8
Department of Education	4,581	4,617	-36	4,576	4,612	-36	3,195	3,231	-36
Department of Veterans Affairs	223,137	222,669	468	219,864	219,388	476	6,658	6,640	18

	Total, All Areas			United States			Washington, DC-MD-VA-WV Metropolitan Statistical Area		
	May 2001*	April 2001	Change	May 2001*	April 2001	Change	May 2001*	April 2001	Change
Independent Agencies	1,045,438*	1,046,704**	−1,266	1,038,237*	1,039,556**	−1,319	71,842*	71,788**	54
Advisory Council on Historic Preservation	36	38	−2	36	38	−2	28	28	...
African Development Foundation	27	27	...	27	27	...	27	27	...
American Battle Monuments Commission	367	368	−1	15	15	...	15	15	...
Appalachian Regional Commission	10	10	...	10	10	...	10	10	...
Architectural and Transportation Barriers Compliance Board	43	43	...	43	43	...	43	43	...
Armed Forces Retirement Home	757	750	7	757	750	7	600	597	3
Naval Home	156	152	4	156	152	4	...	...	...
U.S. Soldiers' and Airmen's Home	601	598	3	601	598	3	600	597	3
Arctic Research Commission	9*	9*	...	9*	9*	...	3*	3*	...
Barry Goldwater Scholarship and Excellence in Education Foundation	2*	2*	...	2*	2*	...	2*	2*	...
Federal Reserve Board of Governors	1,650	1,645	5	1,650	1,645	5	1,650	1,645	5
Chemical Safety and Hazard Investigation Board	34	34	...	34	34	...	34	34	...
Christopher Columbus Fellowship Foundation	1*	1*	...	1*	1*	...	1*	1*	...
Commission of Fine Arts	7	7	...	7	7	...	7	7	...
Commission on Civil Rights	76	78	−2	76	78	−2	51	53	−2
Committee for Purchase from People Who Are Blind or Severely Disabled	21*	21*	...	21*	21*	...	21*	21*	...
Commodity Futures Trading Commission	553	552	1	553	552	1	345	341	4
Consumer Product Safety Commission	473	473**	...	473	473**	...	350	351**	−1

continued

139

TABLE 5.2
Total Civilian Employment of the Federal Government by Branch, Agency, and Area (April–May 2001), *continued*

	Total, All Areas			United States			Washington, DC-MD-VA-WV Metropolitan Statistical Area		
	May 2001*	April 2001	Change	May 2001*	April 2001	Change	May 2001*	April 2001	Change
Corporation for National and Community Service	585	591	–6	583	589	–6	294	299	–5
Court Services and Offender Supervision Agency for the District of Columbia	830	820	10	830	820	10	830	820	10
Defense Nuclear Facilities Safety Board	95	93*	2	95	93*	2	84	82*	2
Environmental Protection Agency	17,968	18,008	–40	17,919	17,960	–41	6,019	6,018	1
Equal Employment Opportunity Commission	2,746	2,722	24	2,746	2,722	24	655	656	–1
Export-Import Bank of the United States	412	418	–6	412	418	–6	388	393	–5
Farm Credit Administration	276	275	1	276	275	1	180	178	2
Farm Credit System Insurance Corporation	9	9	. . .	9	9	. . .	9	9	. . .
Federal Communications Commission	1,946	1,951	–5	1,944	1,949	–5	1,620	1,623	–3
Federal Deposit Insurance Corporation	6,532	6,465	67	6,524	6,457	67	2,442	2,433	9
Federal Election Commission	344	338	6	334	338	6	344	338	6
Federal Emergency Management Agency	4,826	4,881	–55	4,763	4,824	–61	2,150	2,139	11
Federal Financial Institutions Examination Council	7*	7*	. . .	7*	7*	. . .	7*	7*	. . .
Federal Housing Finance Board	104	106	–2	104	106	–2	104	106	–2
Federal Labor Relations Authority	208	208	. . .	208	208	. . .	120	120	. . .
Federal Maritime Commission	123	122	1	123	122	1	118	117	1
Federal Mediation and Conciliation Service	279	279	. . .	279	279	. . .	62	65	–3
Federal Mine Safety and Health Review Commission	44	44	. . .	44	44	. . .	40	40	. . .
Federal Retirement Thrift Investment Board	103*	103*	. . .	103*	103*	. . .	103*	103*	. . .
Federal Trade Commission	1,008	996	12	1,008	996	12	856	847	9

	Total, All Areas			United States			Washington, DC-MD-VA-WV Metropolitan Statistical Area		
	May 2001*	April 2001	Change	May 2001*	April 2001	Change	May 2001*	April 2001	Change
General Services Administration	13,921	13,899	22	13,836	13,814	22	4,734	4,752	–18
Harry S. Truman Scholarship Foundation	3	3	...	3	3	...	3	3	...
U.S. Holocaust Memorial Museum	227	231	–4	227	231	–4	225	229	–4
Inter-American Foundation	36	39	–3	36	39	–3	36	39	–3
International Boundary and Water Commission: United States and Mexico	268	272	–4	268	272	–4	1	1	...
International Boundary Commission: United States and Canada	10	4	6	10	4	6	2	2	...
International Joint Commission: United States and Canada	23	23	...	15	15	...	12	12	...
U.S. International Trade Commission	370	373	–3	370	373	–3	370	373	–3
James Madison Memorial Fellowship Foundation	6	6	...	6	6	...	6	6	...
Japan-United States Friendship Commission	4*	4*	...	4*	4*	...	4*	4*	...
Marine Mammal Commission	13*	13*	...	13*	13*	...	10*	10*	...
Merit Systems Protection Board	222	221*	1	222	221*	1	125	128*	–3
Morris K. Udall Scholarship and Excellence in National Environmental Policy Foundation	20*	20*	...	20*	20*	...	1*	1*	...
National Archives and Records Administration	2,836	2,859	–23	2,836	2,859	–23	1,218	1,224	–6
National Aeronautics and Space Administration	18,850	18,867	–17	18,829	18,846	–17	3,984	3,990	–6

*Preliminary or previous month's employment totals (or portions thereof) were used for current month, as report for current month was not received by input cutoff date.

**Revised.

***Includes census enumerators for the 2000 Decennial census.

Source: "Employment and Trends," http://www.opm.gov/feddata/etmay01.pdf.

T A B L E   5 . 3

Employment of Federal Wage and Salary Workers, Excluding the Postal Service (Employment in thousands)

Occupation	Employment, 2000		Projected % Change, 2000–10
	Number	Percent	
All Occupations	1,917	100.0	−7.6
Management, Business, and Financial Occupations	513	26.7	−5.9
Engineering managers	18	0.9	−22.3
Purchasing agents, except wholesale, retail, and farm products	30	1.6	−5.0
Compliance officers, except agriculture, construction, health and safety, and transportation	36	1.9	−5.0
Management analysts	45	2.3	12.0
All other business operations specialists	127	6.6	−5.0
Accountants and auditors	38	2.0	−24.0
Tax examiners, collectors, and revenue agents	39	2.1	4.5
Professional and Related Occupations	589	30.7	−3.2
Computer scientists and systems analysts	15	0.8	10.0
Computer software engineers	14	0.7	−6.9
Electronics engineers, except computer	22	1.1	−16.0
Engineering technicians, except drafters	23	1.2	−11.7
Biological scientists	18	0.9	−5.0
Physical scientists	32	1.6	−4.3
Lawyers	25	1.3	14.0
Physicians and surgeons	23	1.2	4.5
Registered nurses	49	2.6	4.5
Service Occupations	145	7.6	2.8
Healthcare support occupations	25	1.3	−4.8
Correctional officers and jailers	14	0.7	13.3
Detectives and criminal investigators	22	1.2	28.3
Police and sheriffs patrol officers	16	0.8	28.3
Food-preparation- and serving-related occupations	16	0.8	−23.6
Office and Administrative Support Occupations	398	20.8	−18.7
First-line supervisors/managers of office and administrative support workers	24	1.3	−5.0
Procurement clerks	19	1.0	−25.5
Word processors and typists	20	1.0	−38.2
Secretaries, except legal, medical, and executive	48	2.5	−24.0
Construction and Extraction Occupations	43	2.2	−10.0
Construction trades and related workers	36	1.9	−10.8

continued

TABLE 5.3

Employment of Federal Wage and Salary Workers, Excluding the Postal Service (Employment in thousands), *continued*

Occupation	Employment, 2000		Projected % Change, 2000–10
	Number	**Percent**	
Installation, Maintenance, and Repair Occupations	101	5.3	−10.5
Electrical and electronic equipment mechanics, installers, and repairers	19	1.0	−18.5
Aircraft mechanics and service technicians	19	1.0	−14.5
Production Occupations	49	2.6	−13.5
Inspectors, testers, sorters, samplers, and weighers	15	0.8	−24.0
Transportation and Material Moving Occupations	64	3.4	−4.8
Air traffic controllers	24	1.2	4.5

Note: May not add to totals due to omission of occupations with low employment.

Source: U.S. Office of Personnel Management, http://www.bls.gov/oco/cg/cgs041.htm.

the nature of the position. While a fledgling sanitation person may acquire permanent status in six months, an officer of the police force may have to wait the entire year. A teacher, on the other hand, may not be awarded tenure until three years have passed. The longest probation periods are usually found at colleges and universities where new faculty members may be scrutinized for seven years before achieving tenure. Some positions, such as political appointments to high-level posts, confer no privileges or permanency.

Training is also an aspect of the postrecruitment phase. Some agencies do nearly all their own recruit training; these include police departments, fire departments, and the like. Other public bodies, such as school systems and public health agencies, expect the newcomer to have the needed basic skills. Usually, the higher the professional level of the position, the more likely it is that the recruit will have obtained the essential training prior to appointment.

Training of all types is receiving increasing attention in public administration. A fast-moving and fast-changing society exhibits a strong need for, and must place increasing emphasis on, wide-ranging and high-level skills. Not so long ago, a police officer's training consisted of some on-the-job supervision. Today an officer is likely to receive many weeks or months of schooling at a police academy. The same holds true for many other public positions. Street cleaners are now apt to operate fairly complicated equipment where previously they may have pushed brooms, and so they, too, must receive a certain level of instruction to cope with once-simple tasks.

A survey by the Public Agenda Foundation conducted among eight focus groups nationwide and a national, random telephone survey of 1,000 American adults on welfare reform indicated that 77 percent of the respondents—black, white, and welfare recipients—believed that enrollment in job training and education programs is absolutely essential. Only a minority of the respondents (19 percent) believed that reducing the benefits of most welfare recipients would be effective welfare reform.[14]

The fastest growing area of attention in recent years may be *in-service training*. The upsurge of interest in this training method arises from the growing realization that in a modern society scarcely anyone is ever fully trained for the rest of his or her career. Not only must skills be continually upgraded, but new skills must be acquired if the employee and the organization are to meet changing demands and work patterns. Administrators are progressively accepting the notion that education is a lifelong process and that the organizations they manage must provide training on a nearly nonstop basis throughout an employee's career.

Promotion

Once an employee achieves tenure as a member of the organization, promotion possibilities may emerge. Advancement may come in the form of a pay increase; an increase in grade at the present level; or a move up to a new level, usually with at least some new duties and responsibilities.

Merit systems customarily provide two basic criteria for promotion: *seniority* and *merit*. In the majority of instances, both factors enter into consideration. The question in evaluating this system is, "Which of these, seniority or merit, is the most conducive to effective administration?"

The answer at first seems obvious: Merit is usually deemed the most effective method for determining who shall rise. But *who determines what is meritorious?* Seniority presents obvious drawbacks. It rewards the incompetent along with the competent. James E. Brennan argues that it is far better to raise the salaries of low-paid employees who have proved worthy to competitive averages while decelerating salary increases among the more highly paid. Once inequities are resolved, Brennan emphasizes, merit increases should be based on job values rather than human values.[15]

According to the Merit Systems Protection Board (MSPB), one of every 8.8 employees is promoted over a three-year period. In any given year, 11.4 percent of the federal workforce receive promotions. About 1 in 8 employees assigned to professional or administrative jobs is promoted from a GS-11 to a GS-12 position each year. At GS-13, the rate is 1 in 20, and at GS-14, about one in 25. Compensation for a GS-12 is about $72,400 in the Washington area. (See tables 5.4 and 5.5 for salary examples.)

Once a person reaches the middle grades of most federal occupations, it is normal to spend 10 to 15 years at a given grade level. These promotion rates mean that many of the persons working in professional and administrative jobs will never advance—over the entirety of their career—beyond the GS-12 level. Employees working in Washington have a better chance for promotion than employees assigned to field offices, where the offices are smaller.[16]

TABLE 5.4

Average Annual Salaries in the Federal Government in Selected Occupations, March 2001

Occupation	Salary
All Occupations	*$51,565*
Patent administrator	102,392
Astronomer	89,734
Attorney	86,673
Financial manager	79,840
Computer scientist	75,351
Economist	74,089
Podiatrist	73,172
Chemist	70,435
Electrical engineer	69,560
Statistician	68,901
Architect	68,872
Microbiologist	67,835
Accountant	64,767
Personnel manager	64,411
Librarian	63,651
Chaplain	63,366
Ecologist	61,936
Intelligence agent	61,424
Budget analyst	56,706
Physical therapist	55,213
Social worker	54,129
Botanist	53,131
Nurse	51,019
Engineering technician	50,850
Law clerk	46,533
Border Patrol agent	43,917
Fire protection and prevention worker	33,915
Secretary	33,354
Police officer	32,934
Medical technician	30,183
Dental assistant	27,387
Nursing assistant	26,992
Mail and file clerk	26,038

Source: U.S. Office of Personnel Management, http://www.bls.gov/oco/cg/cgs041.htm.

TABLE 5.5

Base Rate Table for General Federal Pay Schedule (2002)

GS Grade	Step 1	2	3	4	5	6	7	8	9	10
1	14757	15249	15740	16228	16720	17009	17492	17981	18001	18456
2	16592	16985	17535	18001	18201	18736	19271	19806	20341	20876
3	18103	18706	19309	19912	20515	21118	21721	22324	22927	23530
4	20322	20999	21676	22353	23030	23707	24384	25061	25738	26415
5	22737	23495	24253	25011	25769	26527	27285	28043	28801	29559
6	25344	26189	27034	27879	28724	29569	30414	31259	32104	32949
7	28164	29103	30042	30981	31920	32859	33798	34737	35676	36615
8	31191	32231	33271	34311	35351	36391	37431	38471	39511	40551
9	34451	35599	36747	37895	39043	40191	41339	42487	43635	44783
10	37939	39204	40469	41734	42999	44264	45529	46794	48059	49324
11	41684	43073	44462	45851	47240	48629	50018	51407	52796	54185
12	49959	51624	53289	54954	56619	58284	59949	61614	63279	64944
13	59409	61389	63369	65349	67329	69309	71289	73269	75249	77229
14	70205	72545	74885	77225	79565	81905	84245	86585	88925	91265
15	82580	85333	88086	90839	93592	96345	99098	101851	104604	107357

Note: There are 32 regional pay areas. All 32 of the pay areas adjust the base chart salary from 8.64% to as high as 16.98% above the base rate.

Source: http://federaljobs.net/99gsf.htm.

A *promotion* is a change to

1. a position at a higher grade level within the same job classification system and pay schedule, or
2. a position with a higher rate of pay in a different job classification system and pay schedule.

A promotion is always a change to a higher grade and should not be confused with periodic within-grade increases, quality step increases, or merit salary increases, which provide salary increases within the scheduled step rates of a particular grade.

Promotions may occur through several processes. Employees compete for promotion when they apply for higher-graded positions. All applicants are evaluated and ranked for the position on the basis of their experience, education, skills, and performance record. Selections from among the best qualified applicants are based upon management's needs and the overall objectives of the organization. This type of promotion is characterized as a promotion through competitive procedures. A promotion may result from position reclassification to a higher grade due to a gradual accretion of responsibilities. The position to which an employee is promoted is clearly either an outgrowth of his/her present position or a successor to their present position.

The Rationale for Job Tenure

Remuneration for government employment is based on position rather than performance. Good performance originates from an employees's sense of duty, not from incentive pay. A tenure system can be wholesale or piecemeal: Tenure may be provided for all existing civil servants who have held a particular position for a certain number of years, or awarded to any public employee who holds a position for a certain amount of time.

Government employees enjoy greater protection from dismissal than do private sector employees. Tenured employment in the civil services is grounded in three elements:

- *Civil servants serve the state.* They must be responsive to the government, but they have longer-term concerns than elected government officials.
- *Long-term career paths encourage discipline within work.* The risk of losing secure future employment is a serious threat.
- *Long-term career paths publicly associate a civil servant with his or her job.* This job identity make civil servants want to safeguard their reputations. More generally, long-term career paths encourage discipline and good community.[17]

The Challenges of Public Personnel Administration

Federal, state, and local governments employ 19,155,000 wage and salary workers. Of this national distribution, local government units employ 53.2 percent, or 10,195,000, workers. State governments employ 5,677,000, or 29.6 percent. The federal government hires 3,284,000, or 17.1 percent, of America's government employees. Almost all government employees are paid with tax dollars. Given the costs, the public has a real interest in keeping governments efficient, effective, and economical. To serve that interest, local, state, and federal governments must:

- attract high-quality job applicants;
- hire a reasonable share of the high-quality applicants;
- train and develop employees;
- motivate employees to perform at their best; and
- retain good performers and remove poor ones.

Any employing organization's ability to achieve these goals is closely linked to its personnel policies, systems, and procedures. For the federal civil service, those policies, systems, and procedures are inextricably bound to the concept of merit as defined through various laws and regulations. Today the U.S. civil service is experiencing a "quiet crisis" in its inability to meet government goals. Evidence suggests that "the government is not perceived as an 'employer of choice' by many graduates of the country's most highly rated academic institutions."[18] Ironically, "since the federal government employs relatively more managers, professionals, and technicians than other U.S. employers, the skills required of federal workers are greater, on average, than those employees in the nation as a whole."[19] This negative attitude toward federal employment is therefore damaging. Results of one survey said that less than half of senior-level federal managers and executives would work for the government again if they had a choice.[20]

The Changing Demographics of the Federal Workforce

Federal civilian employment reached a peak of nearly 3.4 million persons during World War II, receded to 2.0 million in 1947, and subsequently rose to 2.5 million in 1951. After nearly fifteen years of only minor fluctuation, federal government civilian employment reached almost 3.0 million in 1967 and fluctuated in the range of 2.8 to 3.0 million between 1968 and 1984. Beginning in 1985, federal government civilian employment again exceeded 3.0 million and increased to 3.1 million by 1987. A downward trend began in 1990 and continued through 1995.

The demographic composition of the labor force has changed and will continue to change. The Office of Personnel Management and U.S. Bureau of Labor Statistics data indicate that many workforce changes and conditions are more prevalent in the federal workforce than in the nonfederal sector of government employment. The nonfederal workforce includes private sector employees and state and local government employees.

Total federal employment declined by 2.7 percent, or 48,902 workers, from 1,804,591 as of September 30, 1998, to 1,755,689, as of September 30, 2000. Reductions occurred at the Departments of Defense, Veterans' Affairs, Agriculture, and Energy. The five largest increases occurred at the Departments of Health and Human Services, Commerce, State, Justice, and Treasury. The shift to a predominantly professional and administrative workforce is continuing to improve the representation of women in these jobs. The percentage of women holding administrative and professional jobs rose from 40.9 percent in 1998 to 42.6 percent in 2000.

Adjustment to changes in the number of women, minorities, and older workers in the federal government can be accomplished through a variety of human resource policies and programs such as providing child care, flexible work schedules, diversity training, and reemployment incentives. Demographic differences in the federal workforce indicate that different policies and programs may be needed in different agencies and regions. Workforce planners should consider specific needs of the workforce and the organization.[21]

In addition to the differences between the federal and nonfederal workforces in terms of gender, minority, and age characteristics, there were also differences in these characteristics within the federal government by agency and geographic region.

The average age of federal civilian nonpostal employees is 46.3 years; length of service is 17.1 years; 41 percent have bachelor or higher degrees; 55 percent are men; 45 percent are women; 30.4 percent are minorities; and 7 percent are disabled. Within the workforce, 17.1 percent are black, 6.6 percent Hispanic, 4.5 percent Asian-Pacific Islander, and 2.2 percent American Indian-Alaskan natives.

The True Size of Government

Former President Bill Clinton declared in his 1996 State of the Union address that "the era of big government is over." However, the employee headcount in the federal civil service clouds the true size of government. The count of all the people who deliver goods and services for Washington reaches far beyond the civil service payroll.

A more realistic headcount, according to Paul C. Light, includes the following tabulations:

- 1.9 million full-time permanent civilian federal workers
- 1.5 million uniformed military personnel
- 850,000 U.S. Postal Service workers
- Federal contractors and grant recipients working under mandates imposed on state and local governments ($200 billion in federal contracts; $55 billion in grants)
- 4.7 million jobs in state, county, and municipal governments implementing federal mandates in air, water, health, and safety regulations
- 4.25 million civilian, military, and postal jobs

Using these numbers, the standard federal employee headcount of 1.9 million expands to nearly 17 million. And this figure does not even include full-time equivalents for part-time or temporary workers for Uncle Sam. The U.S. military reserves alone number 884,000.

Light, the Douglas Dillon Senior Fellow and Founding Director of the Center for Public Service at the Brookings Institution, calls these estimates of the true size of government the "shadow of government." He writes:

> The shadow government casts through its vast inventory of private, nonprofit, and state and local partners is a blend of intent and accident. On the one hand, it reflects decades of perfectly appropriate contracting for impeccably commercial activities and non-inherently governmental functions. On the other hand, the shadow also reflects decades of personnel ceilings, hiring limits and unrelenting pressure to do more with less. Under pressure to create a government that looks smaller and delivers at least as much of everything the public wants, federal departments and agencies did what came naturally: They pushed jobs outward and downward into a vast shadow that is mostly outside the public's consciousness.[22]

The shadow of government raises doubts about what constitutes "public service." The federal government relies on a sizable shadow to do its job, and this shadow is not numbered in the civil service headcount. Presidents claim that the era of big government is over. But federal personnel ceilings and freezes have policy impacts: They brought about the shadow government—a large corps of contract, grant, and mandate employees—which produce federal goods and services.[23]

Private contractors provide public services for a price. Civil servants labor for a wage. Drawing lines between public and private in these situations may be especially difficult. Contractors and civil servants do similar jobs—perhaps even occupying the same office at the same time. Good reasons exist for using contract, grant, or mandate employees. Civil servants and shadow workers may share a common sense of service. At the very least, shadow workers have public obligations.

But the downside of maintaining a shadow government cannot be ignored. The President and Congress must ask tough questions about who works in the shadow government and under what circumstances. Federal workers are regulated by a rule-bound merit system. A very different system is allowed for private contractors. The Boeing Company and the National Aeronautics and Space Administration (NASA) employees work on U.S. space shuttles. But when it comes to chains of command, personal accountability, and organization responsibility, the budgets of each are figured with contrasting "bottom lines" in mind.[24]

Equal Opportunity and Affirmative Action

Equal employment opportunity refers to the idea that "no person should be denied the opportunity for employment because of discrimination based on race, color, religion, sex, national origin, or physical disability.[25] While *equal opportunity* is essentially a passive concept, *affirmative action* is an active one. *Affirmative action implements equal opportunity for minorities and women.*

In some ways, equal employment opportunity redefines the merit system to emphasize that the merit philosophy not only recruits, selects, and advances employees on the basis of their relative abilities, but also calls for a workforce representative of all people. Equal opportunity is principal among the ideas that fuel the American way of life. Honest people often agree on the lofty goals of equal opportunity but disagree on the manner in which such a sometimes vague philosophy is carried out.

As a passive strategy, equal opportunity implies nondiscrimination. Equal opportunity and nondiscrimination are passive instruments of public policy because they rely on families, schools, and pertinent forces in U.S. society to abolish stereotypes and prejudices that prohibit the creation of a balanced workforce. Affirmative action is an active strategy, intended to ensure equal opportunity.

With the possible exception of trade unionism, which we shall examine in a subsequent chapter, no issue in the post-World War II era has engaged public personnel administration as has the quest for equal opportunity. Public administration is an integral part of modern society and, as such, is not impervious to society's pressures and concerns. As the campaigns for the rights of women and minorities emerged and accumulated legitimacy and recognition, they shook and buffeted public personnel administration along with the rest of American life. There is no question that personnel administration needed the shake-up. The federal government has a somewhat questionable record in equal opportunity.

The controversy over affirmative action arises from the noble aspiration of providing equal employment opportunity for all Americans. As noted earlier, in private administration the law tells administrators only what they *cannot do,* and in public administration the law tells administrators what they *can do.* The implementation of equal employment opportunity and affirmative action is, therefore, grounded upon a host of federal, state, and local laws.

Certain pieces of legislation have been crucial in the attempt to achieve *social equity* through proportional representation in the nation's workforce: the Civil Rights Act of 1964, Executive Order 11246 of 1965, and the 1972 Equal Employment Opportunity Act.

The development of the affirmative action concept began in the mid-1960s with the passage of the most far-reaching civil rights law since Reconstruction following the Civil War. The Civil Rights Act of 1964 prohibits job discrimination on the basis of race, sex, religion, national origin, age, or physical disability, and the Equal Employment Opportunity Commission was simultaneously created for the purpose of administering the law. The law gives operational meaning to the 1954

Americans with Disabilities Act

The purpose of the Americans with Disabilities Act (ADA) is to provide a clear and comprehensive national mandate for the elimination of discrimination against individuals with disabilities. The ADA gives people with disabilities access to employment, housing, public accommodations, education, transportation, communication, recreation, institutionalization, health services, voting, and public services. This affects more than 43 million Americans with one or more physical or mental disabilities. The ADA defines "qualified individual with a disability" as a person with a disability who, with or without reasonable accommodation, can perform the essential functions of the job that such individual holds or desires.

The ADA prohibits discrimination on the basis of disability in employment, public services, and public accommodations. The Equal Employment Opportunity Commission (EEOC) issues regulations to carry out the requirements of the Act. New buses and trains must be accessible to the disabled. If not handicapped accessible, existing transportation facilities must be altered and rendered accessible. This regulation includes access to rapid and light rail systems. Telecommunications companies now operate relay systems that allow hearing- and speech-impaired Americans to use telephone service.

Employers with 15 or more employees are prohibited from discriminating against qualified individuals with a disability in job application procedures; hiring, advancement, or discharge of employees; employee compensation; job training; and conditions or privileges of employment. Absence of persons with disabilities in the decision making process impairs tenets of democratic values and deprives society of talents that contribute to economic and social developments. The United States Census Bureau reports that nearly 20 percent or about one in every five Americans experience some level of disability.

Both de jure and de factor discrimination against the disabled occurs. Social and cultural norms, institutionalized by laws, may be a catalyst to discriminatory practices against persons with disabilities. Legislation is recognized as a mechanism for social change. Although costly and entangled in government regulations, the ADA enjoys support from partisan, policy, and system politics.

Sources: United States Office of Personnel Management, *Federal Civilian Workforce Statistic: Demographic Profile of the Federal Workforce as of September 30, 1996* (Washington, DC: U.S. Government Printing Office, 1997), 6. "Census: 1 in 5 Americans Has Disability: 53 million reported some level of disability in 1997, Census reports," March 17, 2001, http://usgovinfo.about.com/library/weekly/aa031701a. htmn3032901i; "Understanding The Americans with Disabilities Act," "The Consumer Law Page," http://consumerlawpage.com/ article/disact.shtml.

Supreme Court desegregation case of *Brown v. Board of Education*, which holds that the previous doctrine of "separate but equal" facilities for the races will no longer satisfy Constitutional requirements and specifically that blacks everywhere are permitted to attend the same public schools as whites.

President Lyndon Johnson signed Executive Order 11246 in 1965. It repeated nondiscrimination and affirmative action language used earlier, requiring government contracts to prohibit discrimination by the contractor and to use affirmative action to ensure that workers are employed without regard to race, creed, or color. The 1972 legislation also requires state and local governments to develop affirmative action plans.

Other pieces of legislation with an impact on affirmative action include the Equal Pay Act of 1963; amendments to the Fair Labor Standards Act of 1938; the Age Discrimination in Employment Act of 1967, amended in 1978; Title VI of the Vocational Rehabilitation Act of 1973; and the Vietnam Veteran's Readjustment Assistance Act of 1974.[26]

In the government workplace of the twenty-first century, the modernist feminist agenda squarely confronts conservative traditionalism. Tradition calls for women to focus and commit their energies to "kitchen, children, and school," expecting women to find satisfaction in feeding their families, comforting their husbands, raising children, praying and obeying, and teaching youngsters about God and country. This traditional view runs against the new and increasingly important presence of women in the marketplace.

The 1990s brought the Clarence Thomas/Anita Hill sexual harassment hearings before the U.S. Senate Judiciary Committee and the Paula Jones and Monica Lewinsky charges against President Clinton out of the closet and placed them on the political agenda—thrusting them into the *marketplace of ideas.* The broader issues raised include a woman's evolution and/or liberation from the more restrictive roles of children, church, and schools. A woman's right to choose abortion and economic opportunities and protections in the workforce (including freedom from sexual harassment and other forms of discrimination) constitute the *new moral values.* The sexual harassment controversies featuring Thomas, Hill, Jones, and Clinton are symbolic of greater, more significant economic changes in U.S. society. Women exert more power than ever before in America's political economy.

Social conservatives call for government to put the "father knows best" genie back into the bottle of traditional values. But attempts by either the right or left to "legislate morality" confront a pragmatic political culture and economic realities. Economically and politically, women—as their power in society grows—will cast aside the arbitrary nature of male authority. The issues of sexual harassment and affirmative action plans in the workplace divide males and females of all races. Women do not want to be exposed, patronized, fondled, or harassed. They seek respect for their professionalism, and, indeed, demand it. The sexual harassment arguments of Hill and Jones reverberated throughout American politics and government workplaces.

Reverse Discrimination

The problem of reverse discrimination emerged in the Supreme Court cases of *Regents of the University of California v. Allan Bakke* (1978) and *Weber v. Kaiser Aluminum and Steel Corporation and United Steelworkers Union* (1979). *The Bakke case was a public sector concern. The Weber case was a private sector matter.* The distinction is crucial, because legalism in general and laws in particular circumscribe and influence the operation of a public institution more than a private one.

Bakke was a white male suing the medical school of the University of California at Davis for admission, claiming that the medical school rejected his application in favor of less qualified minority students. In a voluntary attempt to correct years of minority discrimination, the medical school established a quota for minority students for each entering class. The Supreme Court's ruling agreed that Bakke had been unfairly denied admission, but the scope of the decision was carefully narrowed.

First, the medical school is a public institution, supported by taxpayers. Second, the case was one of admission to a public university, not a public sector employment matter. Third, although the court outlawed the quota system, it played a different kind of judicial politics. If public sector bureaucracies avoided an inflexible quota system, affirmative action programs would remain constitutional. In this way, the court allowed public organizations to consider racial and sexual differences in accepting students. In other words, quotas were made illegal for the public sector; but race and sex remain acceptable for consideration in entrance requirements. The Bakke decision confused employers, bureaucrats, lawyers, and court watchers.

If the Bakke case left the constitutionality of affirmative action in doubt, the Weber Supreme Court decision made at least some headway in settling the issue. Because the Kaiser/Weber case was a private concern, no public sector monies were involved. As free agents in a democratic society, the Kaiser Aluminum Company and United Steelworkers Union cooperated in establishing an affirmative action program for minority employees.

Brian Weber, a white lab technician with more seniority than two black applicants, filed suit, claiming reverse discrimination against the company and the union. By placing minorities in 50 percent of the openings in a training program, and thereby establishing a quota system, management and labor created a voluntary program that gave special preference to blacks. The Louisiana plant was located in a region where 39 percent of the local workforce was black. Fifteen percent of the employees of the plant were black, but only 2 percent of the skilled craft workers were black. Therefore, the Weber case raised not only the issue of equal employment opportunity, but also concerns about a representative workforce.

The Supreme Court decided in favor of the affirmative action program sponsored jointly by management and labor, concluding that Title VII of the Civil Rights Act of 1964 was passed for the particular purpose of improving the economic plight of black Americans. In other words, private sector employers could voluntarily establish a hiring and promotion program grounded upon improving the employment skills of blacks. To repeat an earlier distinction, the law tells the manager only what he cannot do in the private sector, such as the Kaiser case; however, the law tells the administrator what he can do in the public sector.

Technically, courts address only the particular set of facts of any case brought before them. To a large degree, the courts in the United States are passive units of fragmented and decentralized federal and state judicial bureaucracies. Courts consider only cases that merit jurisdiction before particular tribunals. Plaintiffs must take their particular set of grievances into court. To do so, plaintiffs need the skills of talented lawyers, money to finance such actions, and the patience and ego strength to see things through, win or lose.

Affirmative action issues concern *quotas, layoffs, work environments,* and *compensation.* The most controversial issue affirmative action raises is whether an employer can establish quotas for making employment decisions. Quotas, of course, specify that a precise percentage of appointments have to be minorities, women, and/or handicapped persons.

The Declining Importance of Affirmative Action

David H. Rosenbloom maintains that the importance of affirmative action began declining in the 1980s for at least three reasons:

1. There is *no strong consensus* favoring affirmative action, which reduces the organizational coherence and political integrity of affirmative action programs.
2. There is a *continuing constitutional stalemate* concerning affirmative action, as shown by the nonlinear direction of various Supreme Court cases.
3. There are *priority internal demands* such as executive leadership, retrenchment, and productivity that affect the commitment to affirmative action.[27]

The Origins of Affirmative Action

Affirmative action, the set of public policies and initiatives designed to help eliminate past and present discrimination based on race, color, religion, sex, or national origin, is under attack.

- Originally, civil rights programs were enacted to help African-Americans become full citizens of the United States. The *Thirteenth Amendment* to the Constitution made slavery illegal; the *Fourteenth Amendment* guarantees equal protection under the law; the *Fifteenth Amendment* forbids racial discrimination in access to voting. The 1866 Civil Rights Act guarantees every citizen "the same right to make and enforce contracts . . . as is enjoyed by white citizens. . . . "
- In 1896, the Supreme Court's decision in *Plessy v. Ferguson* upheld a "separate, but equal" doctrine that proved to be anything but equal for African-Americans. The decision marked the end of the post-Civil War Reconstruction era as Jim Crow laws spread across the South.
- In 1941, President Franklin D. Roosevelt signed Executive Order 8802, which outlawed segregationist hiring policies by defense-related industries which held federal contracts. Roosevelt's signing of this order was a direct result of the efforts of black trade union leader A. Philip Randolph.
- During 1953, President Harry S. Truman's Committee on Government Contract Compliance urged the Bureau of Employment Security "to act positively and affirmatively to implement the policy of nondiscrimination . . . ."
- The 1954 Supreme Court decision in *Brown v. Board of Education* overturned *Plessy v. Ferguson.*

- The actual phrase *affirmative action* was first used in President Lyndon Johnson's 1965 Executive Order 11246, which requires federal contractors to "take affirmative action to ensure that applicants are employed, and that employees are treated during employment, without regard to their race, creed, color, or national origin."
- In 1967, Johnson expanded the Executive Order to include affirmative action requirements to benefit women.
- Other equal protection laws passed to make discrimination illegal were the 1964 Civil Rights Act, Titles II and VII of which forbid racial discrimination in "public accommodations" and racial and sex discrimination in employment, respectively; and the 1965 Voting Rights Act adopted after Congress found "that racial discrimination in voting was an insidious and pervasive evil which had been perpetuated in certain parts of the country through unremitting and ingenious defiance of the Constitution."

Much of the opposition to affirmative action is framed on the grounds of so-called "reverse discrimination and unwarranted preferences." In fact, fewer than 2 percent of the 91,000 employment discrimination cases pending before the Equal Employment Opportunities Commission are reverse discrimination cases. Under the law as written in Executive Orders and interpreted by the courts, anyone benefiting from affirmative action must have relevant and valid job or educational qualifications.

Source: "The Origins of Affirmative Action" by Marquita Sykes, as appeared on the website, www.now.org, 4/2/02. Reprinted by permission of the National Organization for Women, Inc.

What is the significance of affirmative action in our society? Affirmative action challenges public sector managers and some employees, but it also promotes representativeness in government bureaucracies. Affirmative action raises issues of potential and real discrimination that confront women, minorities, and disabled employees. The visibility of affirmative action issues heightens our awareness of discrimination in the workplace.

Perceptions about affirmative action produce a great deal of political and administrative rhetoric. However, the impact, in terms of concrete results, for the purported beneficiaries is questionable. Until the affected groups attain more education and experience, changes will come slowly and progress will likely be incremental. To its credit, however, affirmative action forces government departments and agencies to broaden and intensify their recruiting efforts, to examine the validity of their examinations, and to question the value of recruitment and promotion criteria. It stimulates innovation and makes governmental organizations more open. The administrative branch becomes, as a result, more representative of the population it serves.

Affirmative action, referred to as *equal opportunity* under the Civil Rights Act of 1964, means to many Americans in the twenty-first century the use of practices such as setting quotas and giving preferential treatment. Many argue that affirmative action should be based on criteria of *class* instead of considerations of *race or sex*.[28] To others, affirmative action is a policy aimed at eliminating discrimination in employment based on race, color, religion, sex, or national origin. It does not encourage the hiring or promotion of unqualified people just because they are minorities or women, nor does it impose quotas. It is not reverse discrimination, because it promotes equal opportunity.[29]

Bill Clinton argued that affirmative action must be reformed rather than eliminated. Despite its flaws, affirmative action has been effective in providing equal opportunity to women and minorities. It must be eliminated only when discrimination is finally abolished.[30] Critics of affirmative action are often silent about the veterans' preference program, which benefits mostly males. Since 1944, federal agencies have provided preferential hiring consideration to veterans as a means of rewarding them for service to their country. Many argue that women are especially disadvantaged by veterans' preference.[31] Opponents of affirmative action may have an easier time removing affirmative action from government offices and institutions than from American culture. In the following instance, even conservatives accepted the merits of an affirmative action candidate:

> The curtailment of affirmative action may mean less than is generally expected. . . .
> Affirmative action is now a firmly established institutional practice, indeed
> virtually a reflex of many university, corporate, and political decision makers. (As
> Mr. George Herbert Walker Bush's appointment of Clarence Thomas illustrates,
> even conservatives need the legitimacy of multiracial representation.) Just as
> discrimination did not end with formal rulings against it, neither will affirmative
> action end with formal rulings.[32]

The bottom line is that affirmative action has contributed to the process of public administration, if not to its substantive content. Affirmative action forces governments to hire, promote, and fire employees under the auspices of legal procedures and administrative due process.

Efforts to Remake the Federal Personnel System

The Clinton administration, according to *Washington Post* writer Stephen Barr, inaugurated plans to reorganize the way the bureaucracy recruits, hires, classifies, promotes, and fires federal workers as part of its "reinventing government" initiative.[33] After twelve years of Republican indifference to the federal personnel system, the Clinton administration described the system as broken. "Hiring is complex and rule-bound; managers can't explain to applicants how to get federal jobs. The

The U.S. Senior Executive Service and Diversity

A diverse Senior Executive Service (SES) corps may be an organizational strength that contributes to achieving results. Diversity brings a wider variety of perspectives and approaches to influence policy development and implementation, strategic planning, problem solving, and decision making.

The Senior Executive Service was established by the Civil Service Reform Act of 1978. The Act states that the policy of the federal government is to ensure equal employment opportunity in the workforce. Agency heads may set salaries of SES members at any one of six rates. In 2000, SES basic salaries ranged from $106,200 (ES-1) to $122,400 (ES-6), not including locality payments. In 2000, the locality payments ranged from 6.78 percent to 15.01 percent.

From fiscal years 1990 through 1999, the career SES varied in size from a high of 7,583 in 1992 to a low of 6,183 in 1998. During the 1990s, the number of career SES employees overall decreased, while the representation of women and minorities in the career Senior Executive Service steadily increased.

The proportion of women in the SES went from about 10 percent in 1990 to about 22 percent in 1999. Similarly, the percentage of minority members in the SES grew from about 7 percent to about 13 percent over the decade. The amount of growth minorities experienced as a group was more modest than that of women. From 1990 through 1999, about 25 percent (1,298) of the 5,294 career SES appointments were women, and 14.4 percent (793) were minorities.

Overall, the proportion of minority employees in the federal workforce increased slightly in 2000. Black employees represented 17.6 percent, Hispanics 6.6 percent, Asian/Pacific Islanders 4.3 percent, and Native Americans 2 percent. Minorities in GS-13 through GS-15 grades numbered 19.2 percent in 2000. Women in those grades reached 30.7 percent.

The Office of Personnel Management (OPM) provides Congress with an annual report on employment of minorities and women in the federal government.

Sources: Stephen Barr, "Minorities Are Holding Their Own in a Shrinking Workforce," *The Washington Post,* June 6, 2001, p. B02. *Senior Executive Service: Diversity Increased in the Past Decade* (Washington, D.C.: U.S. General Accounting Office, 2001), p. 111.

[job] classification and pay system are inflexible." The report was written by Vice President Al Gore's National Performance Review.

Once hired by the government, most employees are placed in one of 450 job categories and ranked on the General Schedule, which outlines fifteen pay ranges that correspond with fifteen work grades (see table 5.5). The report, "Reinventing Human Resources Management," called for improvements in the awards and bonus system, employee training, the Senior Executive Service (see box above), and labor-management relations.

The report also proposed extending probationary periods from one to a maximum of three years and eliminating "time-in-grade" requirements, which propel people through the personnel ranks. The report ignored what has been a problem for the bureaucracy: the role of political appointees, their increasingly short tenures in the executive branch, and how they relate to senior career managers.

Gore's efforts aimed to eliminate federal programs, shift them to the states, or offer them to the private sector. However, according to Barr, some officials inside the Clinton administration become concerned that the themes of the first round of reinvention—customer service, performance measurement, and improved labor-management relations—were deemphasized by political appointees as they focused on ways to save money through privatization, program elimination, or devolution to the states.[34]

Performance Ratings

If an organization is going to use merit rather than seniority as a standard for promotion or demotion, how does one determine job performance? The most common method used is for a superior to give a subordinate a *performance rating*. The system seems simple, but in practice it generates complications and controversies.

The essence of the performance rating problem lies in the absence of objective data and procedures for making these systems work effectively. Even when a supervisor attempts to be fair and impartial, neutral criteria are often scarce. Administrative decision makers too often give into personal whims and capricious actions. However difficult these ratings systems are to administer, they are universally part of the government workplace and culture.

Workforce morale and *government performance* are closely related. The ability of a government to function effectively and efficiently is related directly to the quality, competency, and motivation of its workforce. Despite positive attitudes toward their jobs and the work they do, only about half of the respondents in a survey of federal workers would recommend the federal government as an employer, while over one-fourth say they definitely would not. Several factors traditionally viewed as reasons to remain in federal employment lost strength as retention factors in one three-year period according to surveys conducted for the Merit Systems Protection Board. These included the intrinsic value of the work; salary; current health insurance benefits; and the opportunity to have an impact on public affairs.

Many employees argue that the federal government's performance management program does not create an atmosphere that strongly encourages quality performance. Large percentages of employees believe their work units can increase the quantity and quality of the work they perform with the same people.[35]

Individual Performance Measurement

All public organizations find it necessary to measure employee performance. As the demands of governments have changed, the meaning of the term *performance management* has changed as well. Rating employees once involved using a trait-based form. Factors such as neatness, punctuality, politeness, and sociability were important indicators of performance satisfaction. Public sector managers were less focused on work outputs. The evaluation process, even in the public sector, was often secretive. The employee did not participate. In some cases, he or she never knew the rating received.

This format is no longer considered good practice for the organization, the employees, or the citizen-consumers of public service. Instead, public sector performance management should be:

- *Task-oriented.* The evaluation must be grounded in results—and not in personal traits. Results are measured against predefined goals and targets.
- *Participative.* The employee is involved in the evaluation alone with his or her supervisor. Both engage in setting goals at the start of the rating period. Employee and supervisor appraise results together at the end.
- *Developmental.* Evaluation processes do more than rate employees; they help employees to improve performance, identifying resources for training and support required to achieve this end.

Performance appraisals may define expectations, make clear when job performance is successful, specify when improvement is needed, and be used to set future goals. Taking responsibility for performance appraisals in local governments, developing performance standards, evaluating the appraisal system, distributing bonuses and cash awards, and implementing incentive plans all make significant differences in creating productive governments.

Employee performance must be linked to promotion; the best people must rise to management levels. Managers are paid more to make difficult personnel and policy decisions. Do service-wide performance schemes deliver worthwhile improvements in employee performance? The evidence is inconclusive. Budgetary constraints often limit the amounts of performance pay enhancements. A large lag-time occurs between the appraisal period and the payment of rewards.

Performance-pay schemes permit managers to make variable payments. However, most employees receive similar ratings; managers are often unwilling to make hard-and-fast distinctions regarding subordinate skills. Finally, employees often perceive their pay as inadequate. Small performance-pay bonuses are thus unlikely to motivate employees, especially since more employees are left out than included in pay enhancements and the majority may resent any process that gives the minority more compensation. Finally, management's performance-pay decision making methods may be skewed. Overall, employee morale may suffer under such programs.

Position Classifications

Public sector personnel organizations have systems of *position classification.* The federal government, for example, allocates positions by fifteen basic grade levels, ranging from GS (General Schedule) 1 to GS 15. Each level receives more pay, and, ostensibly, requires more in terms of ability and output than the level below it. Within each grade level there are ten steps, each paying more than the preceding one. The higher steps of any grade pay more than the lower steps of the grade just above it. Consequently, an employee working at the tenth step of grade 12 will be earning more than an employee at the first step of grade 13 (see table 5.5). Advancement from one step to another takes place chiefly on the basis of seniority.

Personnel Bureaucracies

The Civil Service Reform Act of 1978 (CSRA) constitutes a major restructuring of federal civil service in the United States, and the Civil Service Commission (CSC), in particular. The functions once administered by the CSC (1883) are now allocated to three separate personnel bureaucracies. The Office of Personnel Management (OPM), as the central personnel agency directly answerable to the president, aids the president in establishing rules for administering civilian employment; advises the president on employment matters; executes, administers, and enforces civil service laws, rules, and regulations; coordinates research to enhance public personnel administration; and maintains and upgrades existing personnel practices such as examinations, executive development, and performance evaluations.

OPM has no authority over employee appeals. The appellate and quasi-judicial responsibilities previ-ously implemented by the CSC are now vested in the Merit Systems Protection Board (MSPB). The MSPB decides most appeals and complaints, issues regulations regarding the nature and scope of its review, establishes time limits in which appeals must be settled, and orders corrective and disciplinary action against employees, departments, agencies if appropriate. As an independent federal agency, the MSPB is constituted as a bipartisan organization, consisting of three board members appointed by the president and confirmed by the Senate.

The CSRA's final structural change created the Federal Labor Relations Authority (FLRA). The FLRA determines appropriate units of representation, supervises labor organization elections, decides unfair labor practice cases, rules on negotiability issues, rules on exceptions to arbitration awards, mediates disputes, settles impasses, and prosecutes unfair labor practices.[36]

Advancement from one grade to another is based in theory on merit, although in practice seniority enjoys consideration too. *The premise for adopting classification schemes is that different positions require varying degrees of ability and amounts of responsibility.* The adoption of a classification plan has long been considered essential for the effective operation of a merit system, for it places the emphasis on *what* rather than *who* a person knows. An effective position classification program provides a basis for a fair and workable personnel operation that may reward good performance and penalize poor performance without fear or favor. In principle, such a position classification framework is open and objective.

One crucial question is, "How many classifications should there be?" Should the various jobs be distributed throughout a large number of separate grades and levels, or should they be compressed into a comparatively few broad categories? If the federal government's personnel system features fifteen grades with ten steps each, is this too many, too few, or about right?

The problem has no precise answer. There are no specific criteria defining narrow and broad classifications. To some, the federal government's fifteen grade levels may seem too numerous. To others, they may seem too few. We do know, however, that moving in either direction will yield both advantages and disadvantages.

A personnel system employing numerous narrow classifications organizes its job structures more precisely at each level. If there are two classifications for typists rather than one, better typists can be placed in the upper class and less capable typists can be put in the lower one. In principle, if typist A does better work than typist B, then A can be given a higher rating than B. It is further assumed that A will be given not only more money and more status, but also more difficult and more responsible assignments. In this sense, using many relatively narrow categories can be fairer to all concerned. Narrower categories also permit more extensive use of promotion as an incentive. More levels mean more possibilities for promotion, and at the same time, such promotional opportunities can be used as a sanction against those who fail to perform adequately.

Many public organizations have relatively few classification levels, particularly in the lower range of jobs. Postal workers, police officers, fire fighters, and others can usually move up only to a position of command. There are relatively few such positions in most organizations, so opportunities for promotion are limited.

Narrow and numerous job classifications also present distinct difficulties, however. The more classifications there are, the more personnel work the organization must do. Each classification must be carefully described and demarcated, and each job must be carefully plugged into the right classification. This results in a system that is not only costly but that can be cumbersome and complicated.

Use of numerous and narrow classifications may alleviate problems because those performing somewhat more demanding tasks can more easily receive recognition. This pattern can, for the same reasons, create tensions and prompt questions such as: "Why should he be classified higher than I am when my job requires as much or more responsibility as his?" Arguments frequently emerge over whether a position should be put into one class or another. For example, in a regional office of one federal agency, a personnel officer balked at classifying a job at grade level 14, despite pleas and exhortations from the agency's other top officials that he do so. The personnel officer himself held only a grade 13 position, and he could not bring himself to categorize the new post at a higher level than his own.

The application of state and federal position classification plans is documented in the appropriate codes of laws. For example, in Texas, the position classification plan, the salary rates, and provisions in the General Appropriations Act apply to hourly, part-time, temporary, and full-time salaried employments in the state departments, agencies, or judicial entities specified. The articles of the General Appropriations Act appropriate money to

- general government agencies
- health and human service agencies
- the judiciary, except for judges, district attorneys, and assistant district attorneys
- public safety and criminal justice agencies
- natural resources agencies
- business and economic development agencies
- regulatory agencies
- agencies of public education

The position classification plan, as specified by Texas law, does not apply to

- a constitutional officer or official
- an elected officer or official

- an officer appointed by the governor
- the chief executive of a state agency
- a teacher in a public school, special school of the state, or state institution of higher education
- personnel in state institutions of higher education
- a professional compensated for services on a fee basis
- an employment excluded from the plan by executive order of the governor or at the direction of the legislature

The Texas position classification plan includes specifications for experience, training, education, knowledge, skills, abilities, and physical conditions as "wanted by employing officers of the state," though these specifications "do not have the force of law." (See http://www.capitol.state.tx.us/statutes/go/go065400.html.) The Texas classification plan is found in Chapter 654 of the government code.

The position classification system in the federal government is based on two fundamental principles:

- There should be substantially equal pay for substantially equal work.
- Variations in pay should be proportionate to substantial differences in the difficulty, responsibility of the job and in the qualifications required.

Under the General Schedule (GS) classification system, individual positions are classified to an occupational group, a series representing a specific occupation within that group, and an appropriate grade, which has a salary range provided by law. The same applies to the Federal Wage System (FWS) classification system, except that salary ranges are based on prevailing rates, or rates paid by private employers for similar work in the wage area. The rates are established through geographic wage surveys. The classification of a civilian position consists of the position title, pay plan, series, and grade.

Classification decisions, whether made by managers or by Human Resources Specialists, are based on the

- nature and variety of the work
- difficulty of the work
- authority and responsibility exercised
- extent of supervisory controls over the work
- qualifications required to do the work

The position description is a record of duties assigned to an individual position in a class (see box on next page). It compared positions to ensure uniformity of classification and serves as a basis for other human resources decisions. It includes a description of assigned duties and responsibilities—including pertinent information concerning the position. It catalogs specific duties and responsibilities assigned to a position by the appropriate authority, time to be devoted to each duty, and essential and marginal functions. A new position description is promptly filed with the Human Resources Department (HRD) if an employee vacates a position. The HRD then reconfigures the proper classification of the position based on the assigned duties and responsibilities of the position.

Assistant Professor Faculty Position

The University of Texas School of Social Work

The School of Social Work at the University of Texas at Arlington invites nominations and applications for a tenure-track faculty position for annual year (AY) 2004–2005. Applications from persons from underrepresented groups are especially encouraged.

Qualifications: A Doctorate in Social Work or related field and an MSW (Master in Social Work) with at least two years post-MSW full-time practice experience is required. ABDs (all but doctorates) may be considered. In addition, applicants for the faculty position must also have an identified area of scholarship and a strong commitment to funded research and publication.

Teaching Areas for Faculty Position: The ability to teach across the BSW, MSSW, and PhD levels is highly desirable, and the ability to teach in at least two areas of the curriculum is required. Emphasis will be placed on teaching Human Behavior and the Social Environment and/or Research.

The University of Texas at Arlington is a 100-year-old Institution with approximately 20,000 students. It has Carnegie classification of Doctoral/Research University—Extensive. The second largest of fifteen institutions in the University of Texas System, it is located on a 388-acre campus in the heart of the Dallas/Fort Worth Metroplex. The School of Social Work enrolls approximately 204 students in the BSW program, 490 in its MSSW program, and 51 in its PhD program. In addition, the School houses the Community Services Clinic; The Center for Child Welfare; The Center for Research and Technology; The Community Services Development Center; and the Legislative Internship Program. The School also has a Dual Degree PhD Program in Comparative Social Policy with the Universidad Autonoma de Nuevo Leon in Monterrey, Mexico and a distance education MSSW program with West Texas A&M University in Canyon, Texas.

Review of applications will begin immediately and continue until the position is filled. E-mail or mail a letter of interest, curriculum vita, and names and full contact information for three references to:

Tom Smith
Ph.D. Professor and Search Committee Chair
The School of Social Work, The University of Texas at Arlington
Box 19129, Arlington, Texas 76019-0129
Telephone: 817-272-3964; Fax: 817-272-5227; E-mail: tsmith@uta.edu (See website: http://www2.uta.edu/ssw/ad.htm.)

Sources: "Assistant Professor Faculty Position" ad from the University of Texas at Arlington, School of Social Work website, www.uta.edu/ssw/ad. Reprinted by permission of the University of Texas at Arlington, School of Social Work.

Summary

- The quests for *representativeness, neutral competence,* and *executive leadership* are norms of public personnel administration. Value, mediation, and core functions are factors affecting public personnel practices.
- Public organizations in the United States use two methods of establishing and operating personnel systems: (1) *political appointment* and *election* and (2) an objective determination of *merit.*
- The Pendleton Act of 1883 questioned the practice of *nonpolitical appointments,* embraced *egalitarianism,* and recognized *competence,* as determined by competitive examinations related to duties performed.
- The expansion of the merit system and development of public service are closely associated with the passage of legislation and presidential leadership.
- Key *merit system principles* are: recruiting, selecting, and advancing employees on the basis of their abilities, knowledge, and skills; providing equitable and adequate compensation; training employees to assure high-quality performance; guaranteeing fairness for applicants and employees; and protecting against coercion for political purposes.

- Equality provides no guarantees; it only provides access. Affirmative action—without ways to achieve—is limited.
- The Plum Book and the Prune Book are designed to facilitate presidential transitions every four years. They combine the interests of partisan, policy, and system politics.
- *Test validity* for predicting on-the-job performance and other selection criteria pose problems for public agencies grounded in merit principles.
- A pure merit system for all public service appointments would be grounded in competition based on merit rules. However, no administration functions on a pure merit system.
- Two basic criteria for promotion are *seniority* and *merit.*
- Training is receiving increasing attention. A fast-moving and fast-changing society exhibits a high need for wide-ranging and high-level skills.
- Federal, state, and local governments employ 19,155,000 wage and salary workers. Of this national distribution, local government units employ 53.2 percent, or 10,195,000, workers. State governments employ 5,677,000, or 29.6 percent. The federal, or national, government hires 3,284,000, or 17.1 percent, of America's government employees.
- A promotion is the change of an employee to a position of a higher grade level within the same job classification system and pay schedule, or a position with a higher rate of basic pay in a different job classification system and pay schedule.
- Remuneration for government employment is based on position rather than performance. Good performance originates from an employee's sense of duty, not from pay.
- The employee headcount in the federal civil service obscures the true size of government. The people who deliver goods and services for Washington reach far beyond the civil service payroll.
- Private contractors provide public services for a price. Civil servants labor for a wage. Drawing lines between public and private may be especially difficult in such cases.

- Representative bureaucracy is a basic policy goal that public personnel managers pursue. A separate but related policy choice is whether to pursue that goal *passively* or *actively.* A passive strategy is *equal opportunity.* An active strategy is *affirmative action.*
- The *importance* of affirmative action is *declining* because: (1) no strong consensus exists favoring affirmative action; (2) U.S. Supreme Court decisions regarding affirmative action are nonlinear; and (3) executive leadership, retrenchment, and productivity take priority over affirmative action programs in government agencies.
- Public sector performance management must be task-oriented, participative, and developmental.
- The demographics of the federal, state, and local workforces are changing.
- The average age of federal civilian nonpostal employees is 46.3 years; the average length of service is 17.1 years. About 41 percent of civilian employees have bachelor or higher degrees; 55 percent are men; 45 percent are women; 30.4 percent are minorities; and 7 percent are disabled. Within the overall workforce, 17.1 percent are black, 6.6 percent Hispanic, 4.5 percent Asian-Pacific Islander, and 2.2 percent American Indian-Alaskan natives.
- The premise underlying *position classification* schemes is that different positions require varying degrees of ability and impose varying amounts of responsibility.
- The position description is a record of duties assigned to an individual position in a class. It compares positions to ensure uniformity of classification and describes assigned duties and responsibilities.
- Public personnel administration, more than anything else, is a process encompassing *procedures, rules,* and *regulations.*
- The recruitment, selection, and promotion phases are grounded in *legislation* and *law,* reflecting the values of accountability and responsiveness to the public.

Case Study

Is Equality for Women at VMI Real?

The military is a classic example of government bureaucracy—it includes hierarchy, a pyramidal form, task specialization, spheres of competence, norms of conduct, and paperwork. West Point, Annapolis, and Colorado Springs assimilated women into their corps decades ago. VMI, or Virginia Military Academy, did not. U.S. Supreme Court Justice Ruth Bader Ginsburg, was "skeptical" about this and VMI was under "scrutiny."

> The history of American freedom is, in no small measure, the history of procedure.
>
> *—Felix Frankfurter*
> *late U.S. Supreme Court Justice*

Seven members of the U.S. Supreme Court, in *United States v. Virginia* (1996), "struck a blow" for equal opportunity for women at single-sex, government-funded military colleges. The all-male Virginia Military Institute (VMI), the nation's oldest military college, was declared open to female applicants. "Save the Males" was the plea of VMI leaders and alumni who wanted keep VMI segregated by sex.

Regardless of sex, race, or disability, every citizen has the right to apply to a public college. The ideology of equal opportunity is as American as apple pie; affirmative action plans and programs implement equal opportunity. The tenets of diversity, representativeness, competence, and a merit system are matters of consequence in this regard.

The military is a classic example of a government bureaucracy. Hierarchy, a pyramidal form, task specialization, spheres of competence, norms of conduct, and paperwork all characterize military organizations. West Point and Annapolis integrated women into their corps decades ago. When would it happen at VMI?

Justice Ruth Bader Ginsburg Writes the Decision

Writing the 7-1 decision (one Justice recused himself), Justice Ginsburg concluded: "There is no reason to believe that the admission of women . . . would destroy" VMI.[1] The Court affirmed that VMI had vio-

lated the Equal Protection Clause. Justice Clarence Thomas did not participate in the decision because his son, Jamal, attended VMI at the time. Justice Antonin Scalia was the lone dissenter. The High Court opined that the state-supported VMI's all-male policy violated women's constitutional right to equal protection.

The Virginia Military Institute (VMI) was established in 1816 as one of three Virginia state military posts. During that era, VMI was known as the Lexington Arsenal. VMI, the emerging military bureaucracy of the nineteenth century, stored arms for Western Virginia. Two decades later, the arsenal emerged as a military college.

George C. Marshall, VMI class of 1901, five-star General of the Army, author of the Marshall Plan, winner of the 1953 Nobel Prize for Peace, was a VMI citizen-soldier.

In 1839, VMI was established as the nation's first state-supported military college. Union troops shelled and burned the Institute in 1864. VMI men fought in World War I, World War II, Korea, Vietnam, Grenada, Panama, and Operation Desert Storm. VMI remained all-male from its founding.

As the late Justice Felix Frankfurter state, "The history of American freedom is, in no small measure, the history of procedure." In 1990, a complaint was filed with the United States Attorney General, and the United States then sued the Commonwealth of Virginia and VMI. The allegation was that VMI's all-male admissions policy violated the Equal Protection Clause of the Fourteenth Amendment.

The federal courts demanded that the state of Virginia remedy the equal protection violation. A six-day trial ended when the court ruled that VMI could: (1) admit women to the corps of cadets, (2) abandon state support and continue its admissions policy as a private institution, or (3) establish parallel institutions or programs. The Commonwealth created the Virginia Womens' Institute for Leadership (VWIL) at nearby Mary Baldwin College as a parallel program for women. VWIL was designed to achieve the same end results as VMI—but by different means. VMI uses the adversative model of education, while VWIL used the cooperative model. The VWIL program did not adhere to the grueling rat line and spartan barracks life typified by the VMI culture.

VWIL then proposed a Cooperative Confidence Building Program. The Mary Baldwin program included an ad hoc physical training program and a non-military VWIL House. But the intangibles were also important. VMI had a $131 million endowment, and over 150 years of tradition, history, and alumni support. Mary Baldwin College had a less illustrious history and a $19 million endowment. Six years after the VMI litigation commenced, the U.S. Supreme Court decided the merits of VMI-VWIL merits. The VWIL program at Mary Baldwin College did not remedy the violation; in fact, Ginsburg wrote, the VWIL program was "significantly unequal" and a "pale shadow" of VMI.

Levels of Scrutiny

The Equal Protection Clause exists to prohibit invidious discrimination—arbitrary, capricious, and unjust behavior against a protected group. Equal protection brings on debates about reverse discrimination, hate crimes, and gay rights. The courts employ a variety of judicial tests called levels of scrutiny to evaluate equal protection cases. The levels of scrutiny are rational basis, intermediate scrutiny, and strict scrutiny.

Rational basis analysis is the most lenient level of scrutiny. For example, the streets are made for automobile traffic—not as sleeping grounds for homeless people—so a court would not be likely to find that a homeless person was discriminated against when forced to sleep elsewhere. Intermediate scrutiny comes into play when the government discriminates on the basis of certain suspect classifications such as gender or illegitimate birth; the court would scrutinize such an action carefully. Strict scrutiny comes into play when the government discriminates against certain suspect classifications such as race or national origin. The government would have to have a very compelling reason to overcome strict scrutiny.

Justice Ginsburg announced a new standard of equal protection review of gender classification—skeptical scrutiny. Skeptical scrutiny is distinguished from strict scrutiny, the equal protection standard applied to race classifications. Skeptical scrutiny favors the female sex only. It affords women (as a class) a degree of legal protection not available to any other group in American society.[2]

Under skeptical scrutiny, no qualified individual can be denied an opportunity on the basis of his or her sex. Ginsburg utilized the standard of intermediate scrutiny—concluding that Virginia provided no evidence of a substantial interest in diversity or equal opportunity for women historically.

In response to the Supreme Court decision against VMI, Janet Gallagher, director of the American Civil Liberties Union's (ACLU's) Women's Rights Project, said, "The decision is a historic blow to government-sanctioned discrimination against women." Eleanor Smeal, President of the Feminist Majority Foundations, stated, "At last, 'separate but equal' for women and girls in military academies goes to the dustbin of history—where it belongs."[3] The National Organization for Women (NOW) National Secretary, Karen Johnson, a retired U.S. Air Force lieutenant colonel, stated, "Finally, we have an affirmation that the qualities important for military leaders—integrity, tenacity and bravery—have nothing to do with a person's sex."[4]

Theodore Olsen argued the case before the Supreme Court on behalf of VMI. According to Olsen, the VMI style of education benefits certain young males who cannot do as well in a coeducational environment. The bootcamp, uniquely adversarial-style education builds confidence in these males. If even a few women are admitted, the benefits—the uniqueness—of VMI would largely be destroyed. Accommodating women would force VMI cadets to respect personal privacy. Abuse and harrassment by upperclassmen toward underclassmen, considered valuable to the VMI experience, might be viewed as sexual harassment if applied to female cadets.

Not all women agreed with Ginsburg's opinion. Phyllis Schlafly, President of Eagle Forum, a conservative group, opined: "Feminists want to gender-neutralize society so they can intimidate and control men. The feminists' long-time, self-proclaimed goal is an androgynous society. Repudiating constitutional intent, history, tradition, and human nature, they seek to forbid us, in public or private life, to recognize the differences between men and women."[5] Anita K. Blair, General Counsel of the Independent Women's Forum and a member of the VMI Board of Directors, stated, "If women as a class had disapproved of VMI's all-male status, they could easily have caused the state legislature to change it or even stop funding VMI."[6]

VMI Considers Privatizing

VMI leaders and alumni considered going private to preserve the school's 157-year all-male tradition. The Court decision directed VMI to admit women or forfeit state funding; a private institution can, of course, be all-male or all-female. VMI spent $14 million defending its all-male policy. "Why must a school with a 157-year-old tradition of leadership and excellence in the education of young men be sacrificed on another altar of gender rights and political correctness?" asked Michael Brook, a VMI board member.[7]

Josiah Bunting, VMI Superintendent, stated that he could make ten phone calls to wealthy alumni and raise millions to convert VMI to private status. However, privatizing VMI was not a very good option. The state of Virginia owns the VMI campus and its buildings. The property value was $137 million in 1995. VMI would have to increase its endownment to $180 million just to go private.

The annual revenue provided by the state of Virginia—$10 million—would also have to be accounted for from private sources. The Virginia General Assembly would need to approve any VMI privatization, and VMI would have acquired the real estate and buildings at full-market value. "If the state just handed VMI over to a private foundation, the state would be participating in the discrimination (against women) by directly supporting it," according to Allen Ides, a Washington and Lee University law professor.[8]

On September 21, 1996, VMI announced that, in a 9-8 vote, the Board of Visitors had decided that VMI should admit women. VMI formed the Coeducation Group—divided into seven subcommittees studying the challenges associated with coeducation. VMI alumni, faculty, staff, cadets, and Board of Visitors members were subcommittee members. They visited other coeducational colleges in order to learn about the mistakes that had been made in their transitions to co-education.

Some of the gender challenges at VMI were unique:

- Barracks are the center of corps activities and crucial to the VMI experience. All cadets are required to live in barracks during their years at VMI. Barracks life, however, is characterized by a total lack of privacy.
- Physical training and stress are commonplace at VMI. Cadets must complete a one-and-one-half-mile run in 12 minutes, 60 sit-ups in two minutes, and five pull-ups. All cadets undergo identical physical training and performance evaluations.
- The adversative system of education, described as both doubting and confrontational, permeates VMI's education. Freshmen "Rats" regularly endure workouts, sweat parties, flaming, and Rat-challenge activities. Upperclass cadets have a free hand in initiating Rats to life at VMI.

Rats are treated like the lowest creatures on earth. The purpose of this treatment is to build the individual Rat into a citizen-soldier. More than 20 percent of freshman drop out.

However, some women did well at VMI. "Female VMI cadets measure up and excel," reported a 2000 story in the Associated Press. Women constituted less than 5 percent of the student body—53 females among the 1,200 cadets at VMI. In the fall of 2000, all of VMI's classes were coeducational for the first time. Erin Claunch broke a gender barrier by becoming the first woman to rise to battalion commander—the second-highest military post. "I just wanted to blend in and be a good cadet," said Claunch, who led half of the 1,200-member cadet corps during her senior year.[9]

The 5-foot-4, 125-pound Claunch outperformed men on VMI's stringent physical fitness requirements. "Not a day goes by that you don't read something about how there should be changes in certain standards for men and women," Superintendent Bunting noted. "But this young woman and the others in her class said, 'Judge us as cadets and recognize us if we achieve in your system.' And she has."[10]

According to Claunch, she did not experience sexual harassment or discrimination. Rumors of harassment, she admitted, made her nervous. In 1999, VMI's top cadet was dismissed for allegedly demanding sex from female cadets.

Matters of Consequence

Diversity, equality, representativeness, competence, affirmative action, and merit system tenets are matters of consequence in the case *United States v. Virginia*. A culture that has not been diverse at any time in its 157-year history is unlikely to become so on its own volition. Women account for more than half of the United States population and half of U.S. college students. Once women were permitted to attend, they mastered the merit system skills at VMI.

Equal opportunity is essentially a passive concept. As a passive strategy, equal opportunity simply implies nondiscrimination. Equal opportunity and nondiscrimination are passive factors in policy making. They rely on families, schools, and the forces of good will in society to abolish stereotypes and prejudices. The courts are a catalyst, too.

Affirmative action is an active strategy. It is intended to ensure—even implement—guarantees of equal opportunity. At VMI, once equal opportunity was accepted, women benefited from affirmative action procedures. The history of American freedom is, in no small measure, the history of procedure.

Questions and Instructions

1. Feminists, according to conservatives, want to redistribute power from the "dominant" class (the male patriarchal system) to the "subordinate" class (nominally women, but actually only the feminists). What data support this division—that men are the "dominant" class, women the "subordinate" class?
2. According to conservatives, feminists call for adherence to the "unreasonable woman" rule, allowing the victim rather than the law to define the offense. Explain.
3. Skeptical scrutiny provides an unprecedented degree of legal protection to individuals—without regard to the needs of society or civilizations itself. Explain this assertion in reference to the VMI case.
4. Theodore Olsen, representing VMI before the Supreme Court, argued that the VMI style of education (adversarial boot-camp methods) benefits certain males who do not compete as well in coed college settings. What do you think this statement means?
5. VMI's adversarial system of education is described as both "doubting" and "confrontational." How can this be so? Explain.

6. Intermediate scrutiny recognizes interference or discrimination on the basis of suspect classifications—sex or illegitimate birth, for example. Government action in such a case must be no more extensive than necessary. Explain how this statement applies in the VMI case study.
7. Equality provides no guarantees; it only provides access. Affirmative action—without pathways to achievement—is limited. Even when denials to access based on sex no longer exist, achievement may remain a challenge. Explain this from the perspective of women attending VMI.
8. The U.S. Supreme Court has a nonlinear record regarding affirmative action-related cases. No strong consensus exists, and the constitutional stalemate is continuing. How did the internal demands of VMI prompt new breakthroughs—if there were any? Explain.
9. Should admittance to VMI be based on the criteria of class—but not sex or race? How do class—and/or sex—discriminations matter? Explain.
10. Justice Felix Frankfurter said, "The history of American freedom is, in no small measure, the history of procedure." Explain and illustrate.

Insights-Issues/Is Equality for Women at VMI Real?

Clearly and briefly describe and illustrate the following concepts and issues. Interpret the word *role* as meaning impacts, applications, importance, effects and/or illustrations of certain facts, concerns, or issues from the case study.

1. Role of skeptical scrutiny for providing legal remedies to VMI female applicants.
2. Role of the quests for representativeness and neutral competence for admitting women to VMI.
3. Role of equal opportunity and/or affirmative action for admitting women to VMI.
4. Roles of the "dominant class" (males) and the "subordinate class" (females) in regard to equality at VMI.
5. Roles of Justice Ruth Bader Ginsburg, single-sex colleges, and gender classifications in the VMI case.

Case Endnotes

1. "VMI Must Admit Women, Supreme Court Rules; Decision Also Likely to Affect Citadel," June 26, 1996, http://www.cnn.com/US/9606/26/scotus.vmi.update/.
2. Anita K. Blair, "*United States v Virginia:* The New and Improved Equal Protection Clause," Spring 1997, The Federalist Society, 2001, http://www.fed-soc-org/Publications/practicegroupnewsletters/ civilrights/cr010203.htm.
3. "U.S. Supreme Court Overturns VMI's All-Male Policy: ACLU Says Ruling Ends Chapter in Sex Discrimination," June 26, 1996; http://www.aclu.org/news/n062696a.html.
4. "NOW Leaders call Supreme Court Decision on VMI a 'Mixed Bag' Victory," June 26, 1996, http://www.now.org/press/06-96/06-26-96.html.
5. "Feminist Assault on Reasonableness," *The Phyllis Schafly Report,* Vol. 30, No. 4 (December 1996).
6. Blair, *op.cit.*
7. "The VMI Decision: VMI Considering Going Private," *The Charleston News & Courier,* June 28, 1996, http://www.charleston.net/news/citadel/vmi28.html.
8. *Ibid.*
9. Kia Shant'e Breaux, "Female VMI Cadets Measure Up and Excel," *The Detroit News,* April 16, 2000. http://detnews.com/2000/nation/0004/16/all-37533.htm.
10. *Ibid.*

Case Sources

"Equal Protection of Law and Other Concepts Related to Equality, Justice and Fairness," February 12, 2001, http://faculty.ncwc.edu/toconnor/325/325lect03.htm; "Exclusionary Policies," January 17, 1996 transcript, http://www.pbs.org/newshour/bb/law/vmi_1-17b. html; Colleen M. McFeely, "Letters to the Editor," *The Washington & Lee University Law News,* Vol. 24, No. 3 (September 3, 1996, pp. 3–4), http://www.wlu.edu/~lawnews/vol24no3-page3.html; "One More Male Bastion Bites the Dust, Women Must be Admitted to All-Male Virginia Military Institute," The Feminist Majority Foundation and New Media Publishing, Vol. 8, No. 2(1996), http://www.feminist.org/research/report/82_eleven.html; Tracy "Archie" Taylor, "VMI Decision '96," *The Washington & Lee University Law News,* Vol. 24, No. 4(October 22, 1996), 4–7; http://www.wlu.edu/lawnews/vol24no4-page4.html; "VMI Must Give Up State Funds to Stay All-Male," June 27, 1996, http://centralohio thesource.net/Files3/9606279.html; "Top VMI Cadet Dismissed For Allegedly Demanding Sex", *The Joplin Globe* (online edition), June 27, 1999, http://www.joplinglobe.com/archives/1999/990627/natnwrld/story1.html.

Chapter Endnotes

1. Quoted in John Franklin Campbell, *The Foreign Affairs Fudge Factory* (New York: Basic Books, 1971), pp. 139–140.
2. *Ibid.,* p. 47.
3. Herbert Kaufman, "Emerging Conflicts in the Doctrines of Public Administration," *The American Political Science Review* 50 (December 1956): 1057–1073.
4. Donald E. Klingner and John Nalbandian, *Public Personnel Management: Contexts and Strategies* (Englewood Cliffs, N.J.: Prentice-Hall, 1985).
5. James E. Leidlein, "In Search of Merit, A Practitioner's Comments on 'The Staffing Function in Illinois State Government after Rutan' and 'Curbing Patronage Without

Paperasserie,' " *Public Administration Review* 53, no. 4 (July–August 1993), 391–392.

6. *Quoted in Paul Van Riper, History of the United States Civil Service (New York: Harper &* Row, 1958), p. 36.

7. Steven W. Hays and T. Zane Reeves, *Personnel Management in the Public Sector* (Boston: Allyn and Bacon, 1984), p. 16.

8. Ronald N. Johnson and Gary D. Libecap, "Patronage to Merit and Control of the Federal Government Labor Force," *Explorations in Economic History* 31, no. 1 (January 1994): 91–120.

9. Cited in Patrick V. Murphy, *The Criminal Justice System in Crisis* (Syracuse, N.Y.: Maxwell School of Citizenship and Affairs, 1972).

10. *Federal Employee Retirements: Expected Increase Over the Next Five Years Illustrates Need for Workforce Planning* (Washington, D.C.: U.S. General Accounting Office, 2001).

11. The World Bank Group, "Administrative & Civil Service Reform," http://www1.worldbank.org/publicsector/civilservice/recruitment.htm.

12. *Ibid.*

13. Stephen Barr, "In Push to Improve Government Hiring, OPM Issues Guidelines— Again," *The Washington Post,* April 7, 2002, p. C03.

14. "The Values We Live By: What Americans Want from Welfare Reform," *Spectrum: The Journal of State Government* 70, no. 3 (Summer 1997): 5–6.

15. James E. Brennan, "Merit Pay: Balance the Old Rich and the New Poor," *Personnel Journal* 64, no. 5 (May 1985): 82–85.

16. Stephen Barr, "Expectations of Promotion Are Not So Great, Study Finds," *The Washington Post,* February 21, 2002, p. B02.

17. The World Bank Group, "Administrative & Civil Service Reform," http://www1. worldbank.org/publicsector/civilservice/recruitment.htm

18. U.S. Merit Systems Protection Board, *Attracting Quality Graduates to the Federal Government: A View of College Recruiting* (June 1988), p. vii.

19. The Hudson Institute, *Civil Service 2000, A Report Prepared for the U.S. Office of Personnel Management* (June 1988), p. 10.

20. *The Washington Times,* May 25, 1989, p. B5.

21. *The Changing Workforce: Demographic Issues Facing the Federal Government* (Washington, D.C : U.S. General Accounting Office, 1992), p. 3.

22. Paul C. Light, "The True Size of Government," *Government Executive,* January 2, 1999, http://govexec.com/news/index.cfm.

23. Paul C. Light, *The True Size of Government* (Washington, D.C.: Brookings Institution, 1999).

24. "The Changing Shape of Government," Policy Brief no. 45, February 1999, http://www.brook.edu/dybdocroot/comm/policybriefs/pb045/pb45.htm.

25. Ralph C. Chandler and Jack C. Plano, *The Public Administration Dictionary* (New York: John Wiley & Sons, 1982), p. 246.

26. Klingner and Nalbandian, *Public Personnel Management,* pp. 62–69.

27. David H. Rosenbloom, "The Declining Salience of Affirmative Action in Federal Personnel Management," *Review of Public Personnel Administration* 4 (Summer 1984): 202–205, 248–249.

28. Raymond W. Mack, "Whose Affirmative Action?" *Society* 33, no. 3 (March–April 1996): 41–44.

29. Nancy Stein, "Questions and Answers about Affirmative Action," *Social Justice* 22, no. 3 (Fall 1995), 45–53.

30. "The Future of Affirmative Action: President Clinton's Remarks," *Congressional Digest* 75, nos. 6–7 (June–July 1996): 166–169.

31. Ann Crittenden, "Quotas for Good Old Boys," *The Wall Street Journal,* June 14, 1995, p. A18.
32. Paul Starr, "Civil Reconstruction: What to Do Without Affirmative Action," *The American Prospect,* no. 8 (Winter 1992), 7–14.
33. Stephen Barr, "Administration Drafts Plan to Remake Personnel System," *The Washington Post,* December 16, 1993, p. A23.
34. Stephen Barr, "Shaving the Fat, Sparing the Meat: Agencies Grapple with Reinvention's Phase II, *The Washington Post,* January 30, 1995, p. A13.
35. *Working for America: A Federal Employee Survey* (Washington, D.C.: U.S. Merit Systems Protection Board, 1990).
36. Joseph R. Grima, Permanent Secretary, Office of Prime Minister, Malta, "Administrative & Civil Service Reform," The World Bank Group, http://www1.worldbank.org/publicsector/civil service/individual.htm.

Public Sector Labor-Management Relations

Chapter Highlights

A Social-Work Model of Unionism

Decline, Transformation, or Reformation?

Union Members in 2001

State and Local Government Labor Issues

Alternatives for Avoiding a Work Stoppage

Collective Bargaining for Federal Employees

Conflicts in State Civil Service and Collective
  Bargaining Systems

Zero-Sum versus One-Ten Power Games?

Radical Individualism and Labor Unions

Public Sector Labor Law Impacts

Reasons for Union Prominence

Summary

The Collective Bargaining Hodgepodge

American unions may have the best songs, but for decades, management has held the best cards. Labor rights of Americans lag behind those of other nations. The legal bottom line varies widely in local, state, and federal government labor relations and collective bargaining.

Support for unions is growing, according to a poll commissioned by the Associated Press. The poll showed that 51 percent of women under age 65, 48 percent of men, under age 65, and 59 percent of adults aged 18 to 34 were more pro-union than adults over 65 (38 percent). The importance of protecting workplace rights is increasingly recognized.

A hodgepodge of statutes, ordinances, attorney general's opinions, executive orders, and court decisions govern worker rights in the public sector. Not even federal government employees are regulated by a single policy governing labor management relations.

Until 1967, public sector workers were denied the right to form and join unions. The power of a government to implement the terms and conditions of employment for government workers was absolute. However, federal courts in 1967 gave the First Amendment freedom of association clause priority over government sovereignty claims. The courts protected the constitutional right of public employees to organize and join unions, discarding the sovereignty doctrine in the process.

The great majority of federal employees were granted unionization and collective bargaining rights under the Civil Service Reform Act and Postal Reorganization Act. State and local labor relations laws reflect the diversity of the fifty states. The mid-1970s witnessed debates on national labor legislation for state and local government employees. However, agreements to standardize labor relations in the states never materialized. More than

110 separate state statutes govern public sector labor relations. Numerous local ordinances, court decisions, attorney general's opinions, and executive orders augment the statutes.

Unionization in government usually occurs along professional lines. Public education is the largest public employer by far in state and local governments; college and university professors initiated collective bargaining in 1967. Major faculty unions include the National Education Association (NEA), American Federation of Teachers (AFT), and American Association of University Professors (AAUP). Firefighters are the most highly organized of municipal employees. The large majority belong to the International Association of Firefighters (IAFF). Healthcare, transit workers, and prison workers offer prospects for future government union growth.

State labor legislation ranges from a single comprehensive statute providing coverage to all public employees (Iowa) to coverage for firefighters only (Wyoming) to the complete outlawing of collective bargaining (North Carolina). Wisconsin was the first state (1959) to establish collective bargaining rights for local government employees. Legislation or related policies mandate bargaining, meeting, or conferring with at least one group of public workers in forty-two states. State legislatures enacted most of the bargaining laws from the mid-1960s through the mid-1970s.

The District of Columbia and 29 states provide bargaining coverage by statute for all major employee groups. This coverage may be realized through a single comprehensive public employee relations policy or through separate policies for different functions. "Bargaining laws are the single most important factor in determining the tone and character of public employer-employee relationships in state and local government," write Richard C. Kearney and David G. Carnevale. States sponsoring comprehensive bargaining laws are industrialized, urbanized, and relatively affluent jurisdictions.

Arizona, Arkansas, Colorado, Louisiana, Mississippi, North Carolina, South Carolina, and Virginia permit no formal collective bargaining. In these states, firefighters and teachers benefit from some form of bilateral relations for one or more employee groups. On the other end of the spectrum, California, Connecticut, Delaware, Florida, Hawaii, Illinois, Massachusetts, Michigan, New Mexico, New York, Ohio, and Rhode Island, have comprehensive collective bargaining laws. Since the 1970s, only Illinois, Ohio, and New Mexico have passed major collective bargaining laws.

The comprehensive-bargaining states catalog the following provisions in labor-management relations legislation:

1. Employee rights
2. Employer rights
3. Administrative agency (or machinery for administering public sector labor relations)
4. Unit determination
5. Recognition procedures
6. Scope of bargaining
7. Impasse resolution procedures (as strikes are prohibited or severely restricted)
8. Union security (or options for securing a union as the exclusive representative of a bargaining unit). Closed shop, union shop, agency shop, fair share, dues checkoff, and maintenance of membership are alternatives for securing union security.
9. Unfair labor practices (ULPs) of both employers and unions.

The table in this section outlines labor-management essentials of bargaining laws in the states. The table lists whether each state has bargaining legislation in place for state public employees, local government workers, police officers, firefighters, and K–12 public school teachers.

Sources

Richard C. Kearney with David G. Carnevale, *Labor Relations in the Public Sector,* 3rd ed. (New York: Marcel Dekker, 2001), see chapter 3, "The Legal Environment of Public Sector Labor Relations," pp. 45–80; "Support for Unions Growing While a Majority of Workers Want More Protection of Workplace Rights, According to Labor Day Polls (September 1, 2001)," *Labor Research Association (LRA) Online,* September 1, 2001, http://www.laborresearch.org/polls/ unions_good.html.

State Bargaining Legislation as of 1999
(X = Collective bargaining
Y = Meet and confer provisions)

State	State	Local	Police	Firefighters	K–12 Teachers
Alabama		Y		Y	Y
Alaska	X	X	X	X	X
Arizona					
Arkansas					
California	Y	Y[1]	Y[1]	Y[1]	X
Colorado					
Connecticut	X	X	X	X	X
Delaware	X	X[1]	X	X	X
Florida	X	X[1]	X	X	X
Georgia				X	
Hawaii	X	X	X	X	X
Idaho				X	X
Illinois	X	X	X	X	X
Indiana	X				X
Iowa	X	X	X	X	X
Kansas	Y	Y[1]	Y[1]	Y[1]	X
Kentucky			X	X	
Louisiana					
Maine	X	X	X	X	X
Maryland	X	X[2]			X
Massachusetts	X	X	X	X	X
Michigan	X	X	X	X	X
Minnesota	X	X	X	X	X
Mississippi					
Missouri	Y	Y		Y	
Montana	X	X	X	X	X
Nebraska	X	X	X	X	Y
Nevada		X	X	X	X
New Hampshire	X	X	X	X	X
New Jersey	X	X	X	X	X
New Mexico	X	X	X	X	X
New York	X	X	X	X	X
North Carolina					
North Dakota	Y[2]	X[2]	Y[2]	Y[2]	X
Ohio	X	X	X	X	X
Oklahoma		X	X	X	X
Oregon	X	X	X	X	X
Pennsylvania	X	X	X	X	X
Rhode Island	X	X	X	X	X
South Carolina					
South Dakota	X	X	X	X	X
Tennessee					X

continued

State Bargaining Legislation as of 1999, *continued*

State	State	Local	Police	Firefighters	K–12 Teachers
Texas			X[1]	X[1]	
Utah					X
Vermont	X	X	X	X	X
Virginia					
Washington	X	X	X	X	X
West Virginia	Y[2]	Y[2]	Y[2]	Y[2]	Y[2]
Wisconsin	X	X	X	X	X
Wyoming				X	

[1]Local option permitted.
[2]Meet and confer established by attorney general's opinion.

Source: Richard C. Kearney, *Labor Relations in the Public Sector.* (New York: Marcel Dekker, Inc., 1992, 2e) Reprinted by permission of Marcel Dekker, Inc., New York, NY.

A Social-Work Model of Unionism

U.S. organized labor has never opposed American capitalism. In that, at least, labor leaders maintain an anti-ideological orientation. Labor leaders view themselves as a powerful interest group in a pluralistic U.S. society; in their view, unions serve the interests of dues-paying members. They rarely form alliances with social movements where rights and freedoms extend beyond their legal dimension.

The year 1973, considered a crossroads, signified the end of thirty-five years of U.S. economic dominance, during which Americans enjoyed the highest living standards in the world. After this time, union bargainers could depend no longer on the growth and stability of the nation's economy to justify their wage and benefits demands. A new global megastate replaced, in part, the nation-state. The new reliance on transnational capital and the development of networks outside the frameworks of nation-states forged close-knit, autonomous economic entities.

"At stake in labor's decline," writes Stanley Aronowitz, "is, in addition to its economic character, nothing less than the political and social climate of American society. That we have growing inequality in America—income differences are greater than in any advanced industrial society—may be ascribed mainly to the erosion of trade union power rather than to some mysterious market mechanism."[1] The old social compact was no longer in force—a compact that promoted close wage and price regulation along with high levels of mass personal and social consumption. A kind of social-work model of unionism replaced the more militant labor versions. The demise of labor unions as democratic institutions is a crucial factor, too. The absence of a genuine sovereignty for rank-and-file members contradicts the basic rationale for unions.

The viability of public sector unions depends on this historical context. Organized labor, in the past, carried out mass strikes and elections to gain recognition. Unions advanced race and gender demands, and union leadership included blacks and women. Unions engaged in solidarity struggles with other workers. They were committed to civil rights. However, union membership and power in the private sector declined as the corporate offensive accelerated. The organization of public employees in the 1960s and early 1970s was the exception to the ineffectiveness of private sector union activities.

Public sector union leaders and employees are challenged as never before. They must convince taxpayers of the justice of their position and their economic worth. The larger electorate is inundated with high taxes and antiwelfare propaganda. But public sector labor executives rarely educate the citizenry with broader understandings of the economy and portraits of the country's future. Picket lines can educate taxpayers and consumers. Individualism within the movement and worldwide economic dynamics waylay effective union responses. Organized labor movements often appear "disarmed, outflanked, and bewildered" by the challenges of these times.

Unionization is greater in the public sector, worldwide, than in the private sector. The United States fits that pattern—and increasingly so. Differences in collective bargaining coverage between the public and private sectors are more evident in the United States than in other advanced countries. The demographic and occupational composition of workers in both sectors explains why this is so. Though public sector union members outnumber their private sector counterparts, public sector workers, in fact, are more likely *not* to be union members. They are more likely to be women, nonwhite, older, more educated, white collar, or professional.

Federal laws govern the workplaces of federal government employees, while state and local laws govern the domains of state and local government employees. State laws vary across states and across occupations. According to Richard B. Freeman, U.S. public employee union members do not outnumber private sector union members because of a more favorable legal framework. Legal differences governing unionization and collective bargaining between the two sectors do not explain the mobilization of public sector unions. Instead, different management responses to similar laws provide an explanation. Public sector employees desire influence on workplace decisions. More so than in the private sector, government workers seek decision-making prerogatives on how to

- do and organize work,
- promote training access,
- decide on pay raises for work group personnel,
- set goals for the work group, and
- establish safety standards and practices.

In other words, public sector employees promote an employee organization that is more independent of management than do private sector workers.[2]

Unionization rates in the public sector outnumber those in the private sector by about four to one. Members of private sector unions number about 9 percent of the workforce. Of the 19,155,000 government workers in the United States, a number that includes local, state, and federal workers, 41.8 percent are represented by labor unions. At the federal level, 36.6 percent of the 3,284,000 employees (17.1 percent of the total U.S. government labor force) are represented by labor unions. Labor unions represent 47.5 percent of local government employees—10,195,000 workers, accounting for 53.2 percent of the total workforce.

State government workers—numbering 5,677,000, or 19.6 percent of the total workforce—register a 34.5 percent labor union membership. Teachers, firefighters, and police officers are heavily unionized.[3]

Enhanced power for public employees is grounded in politics. Public sector employees possess power outside the collective bargaining process because government workers may attain power through the political process. As voters and through unions, government employees are a force in electing public sector leaders. In the private sector, employees are rarely stockholders who vote and select management. As budgets of school board members, fire departments, or police departments are increased, all parties—management, labor, and clientele—benefit.

Public sector employees are constrained by civil service regulations. Government activities cannot be easily moved from state to state. However, the privatization of certain government functions may be changing this prospect. Military bases sometimes close; as demographics change, public schools may close, too. Differing economic environments and differences in labor-management interactions between the sectors cause public sector management to be less resistant to unionization.

Union organizing is increasing in the service sector, which includes hotels, motels, and nursing homes, and in government. In contrast, union activities are sluggish in most of the private sector. This is partially due to fears that companies may close, if employees try to unionize, and move their operations to another town, state, or even country.

Leo Gerard, a steelworkers' union president, concludes that the difference in union membership is due more to this factor than to the intense antiunion campaigns orchestrated by private employers. Why is it easier to organize workers in government offices, hospitals, and hotels than in factories? "You can't threaten to move the public sector out of Ohio," Gerard pointed out. "You can't threaten to move a hospital or nursing home to Mexico or China."[4]

Economic recovery stalls, falling tax revenues, and privatization efforts confront public sector workers and their labor unions. Declining corporate profits, a lousy stock market, nervous consumers, and tax reductions undercut state government budgets. Soaring healthcare costs and public demands for improved schools also drain public coffers. In a country based on individualism and personal rights, antigovernment rhetoric is frequently at a high pitch.

Challenges facing public sector labor include:

- Using current positive government balance sheets to secure gains for the future during collective bargaining
- Gearing up to fight against privatization, which means utilizing enhanced research, mobilization, legal, and public relations or communications capacities
- Expanding political power—promoting increased voter registration, increased political action fundraising, and enhanced grass roots mobilization
- Working with private sector labor organizations to build a labor movement consensus on the importance of public services
- Expanding efforts to organize the unorganized in collective bargaining states and focusing energies to win bargaining rights in key nonbargaining states.[5]

Decline, Transformation, or Reformation?

The decline, transformation, or perhaps reformation of public sector unionism occurs within the context of our changing political culture. With the decline of the middle classes, lack of real wage increases, and growing numbers of high-income families and families below the poverty line, the U.S. political economy is increasingly becoming more segregated into the wealthy and the poor. The decline of trade unions, the greater numbers of women in the workforce, the loss of manufacturing jobs to overseas workers, and growing immigration are often blamed for our country's woes. Higher wages, lower taxes, job training, barriers to foreign trade, and business recruitment of the poor are suggested to end the trend toward economic disparity.[6]

Unions in the United States originally arose to combat the terrible work and wage conditions of the early Industrial Revolution. After the Great Depression of the 1930s, organized labor, which then existed only in the private sector, was thriving and calling for macroeconomic policies advocating high employment and high wages. Since then, membership in public sector unions such as teachers' and firefighters' unions has grown, while unionism in general is declining.

Public opinion surveys that span fifty years show a major transformation in labor union membership demographics and politics. The Bureau of Labor Statistics reports that membership in labor unions increased to 16.6 million in 1993 from 16.4 million in 1992. This increase in union membership followed fourteen consecutive years of decline. The increase matched the overall increase in the labor force, and labor union share remained steady at almost 16 percent.

Public sector unionism is a product of the Great Society of the 1960s and has changed the overall labor movement emphasis from high employment and high wages to an emphasis on the redistribution of society's economic resources. Today, public sector unions represent a larger percentage of the U.S. labor movement than ever before. See table 6.1 for union membership and density by metropolitan areas in 2000.

Private union membership has ebbed as public unions experienced meteoric membership increases. The enhanced importance of public sector unionism as a component of the overall U.S. labor movement is leading to increased demands for more government intervention in the economic arena.

Leo Troy, in describing the rise and fall of American trade unions, argues that organized labor has changed its philosophy of "more" for its clients to a philosophy of "more government intervention" in America's political economy.[7] Troy claims a philosophical division between America's private sector and public sector unions concerning the definition and implementation of "more government intervention" in our economy and society. Private sector unions wish to enhance their clients' incomes. Public sector unions, says Troy, argue for raising taxes so that client salaries may be increased.

Troy claims that public sector unions and private sector unions are on a collision course. "On one hand, private sector unions want government to vigorously apply macroeconomic policies to stimulate economic growth and avoid depression; on the other hand, public sector unions want a redistribution of the national income from the private to the public sector in the form of social services and transfer payments."[8]

TABLE 6.1

Union Membership and Density by Metro Area in 2000 (numbers in thousands)

Metro	Employed	Members	Percent Union	Percent Private	Percent Public
Buffalo	497.8	154.8	31.1%	21.1%	73.1%
New York	8,756.6	2,042.8	23.3	14.6	70.1
Sacramento	774.7	173.3	22.4	11.6	58.2
Detroit	2,629.4	571.5	21.7	16.7	57.6
Milwaukee	909	188.3	20.7	13.9	68.2
Las Vegas	620.8	123.4	19.9	16.8	43.7
Pittsburgh	935.5	178.9	19.1	14.3	55.1
Seattle	1,641.5	310	18.9	13.4	46.8
Chicago	4,096.3	750.7	18.3	13.8	50.2
Minneapolis	1,421.4	253.3	17.8	12.4	58.2
St. Louis	1,267.9	224.1	17.7	15.4	36.1
Philadelphia	2,703.9	471.1	17.4	11.7	55.1
Grand Rapids	579.8	97.3	16.8	11.7	58.5
San Francisco	3,359.3	552.7	16.5	10.8	53.7
Portland	1,072.6	172.8	16.1	9.6	58.3
Cleveland	1,419.8	223.8	15.8	10.1	54.7
Hartford	516	81.2	15.7	9.3	50.8
Los Angeles	6,621.1	989	14.9	8.9	51.6
Louisville	508.9	74.2	14.6	12.2	31.7
San Diego	1,199.7	165.7	13.8	8.3	44.1
Columbus	779.3	106	13.6	7.2	50.4
Boston	2,555	332.8	13	7.3	52.3
Cincinnati	887.2	107	12.1	8.5	34.7
Washington	3,533	415.2	11.8	6.3	29
Indianapolis	704.7	78.6	11.2	9	26.4
Kansas	891.2	97.7	11	9	23.5
Jacksonville	502.7	47.8	9.5	4.3	40.2
Denver	1,231.2	109.8	8.9	5.8	27.6
New Orleans	590.5	51.9	8.8	6.3	20.8
Miami	1,635.9	143	8.7	4.3	39.7
Nashville	567.8	45.9	8.1	6	22.6
Salt Lake City	655.9	52.7	8	5.2	22.8
Phoenix	1,370.4	90.9	6.6	4.6	20.9
Orlando	810.7	53.8	6.6	4.8	25.8
Houston	2,002.4	122.7	6.1	4	21
Atlanta	2,122	124.3	5.9	4.4	17.2
Norfolk	610.1	34.3	5.6	4.2	10.7
Tampa	1,010.1	52.1	5.2	2.7	23.6
Charlotte	6,610.2	34	5.1	4	13.7
Dallas	2,669	134.5	5	3.4	18.2
Greensboro	604.9	26.7	4.4	3.2	13.3
San Antonio	710.1	25.6	3.6	1.6	11.7
Austin	522.5	15.8	3	1.3	10.2
Raleigh	581.4	14.1	2.4	1.2	6.3

Source: From "Unions Have the Resources for Growth in Major Metropolitan Areas, Sept. 9, 2001," as appeared on the website www.lraonline.org. Reprinted by permission of the Labor Research Association.

Is Work Less Economic and More Social?

Jobs should not just improve our incomes, we think. Like candy and cars, they should also enhance psychic well-being. They should be gratifying and stimulating . . . the boundaries between work and leisure are blurring . . . work has become less manual and more mental, less regimented and more collaborative and—as an activity—less economic and more social.

> —*Robert Samuelson, "Work Ethic vs. Fun Ethic,"*
> The Washington Post, *September 3, 2001, p. A21.*

Despite being larger than private sector unionism, public sector unionism is most likely in transformation. The rise of public sector organized labor activities in the 1960s and 1970s was followed by a leveling, or maturation, through the 1980s and 1990s, and into the twenty-first century.

With the growth of unionism in the 1970s, the challenges began to overshadow the benefits. Public employee organizations began to arouse increasing anxiety and alarm. The power of public sector unionism proved most powerful at the state and local levels. The growing number of collective bargaining rights did not occur simply because of political pressures. Union leaders had become more proficient in using bargaining strategies.

Union Members in 2001

In 2001, 13.5 percent of wage and salary workers were union members, unchanged from 2000, according to the U.S. Department of Labor's Bureau of Labor Statistics. The union membership rate declined from a high of 20.1 percent in 1983, the first year for which comparable union data are available. Some highlights from the 2001 data are:

- In both 2001 and 2000, about 16.3 million wage and salary workers were union workers.
- Nearly 4 in 10 government workers were union members in 2001, compared with less than 1 in 10 private and salary workers.
- Protective service workers, a group that includes police officers and firefighters, had the highest unionization rate among all occupations, at 38 percent.[9]

Membership by Industry and Occupation

In 2001, workers in the public sector continued to have unionization rates about four times higher than their counterparts in private industry. The unionization rate of government workers was 37.4 percent, compared to 9 percent among private sector employees. Union membership rates among government employees have held steady since 1983, while those of private nonagricultural employees have declined. Local government, which includes many workers in the heavily unionized occupations of teachers, firefighters, and police officers, had the highest unionization rate, at 43.1 percent.

The power of public sector labor unions is tenuous; government labor unions retain their membership levels, but their power is suspect. The best organized government employees are teachers; teachers have the right to strike in eleven states. Teacher strikes are illegal in twenty-four other states, but local governments are permitted to bargain with school boards. In the other fifteen states, school boards do not have to bargain with teacher unions. Local governments position teacher bargaining rights midway between powerful industrial unions such as the United Auto Workers (UAW) and groups such as farm laborers, domestics, supervisors, managers, and independent contractors not protected by labor regulations at all.

The labor rights of Americans lag behind those of other nations. Employers enjoy a virtually unlimited right to enforce their perspectives in the workplace. Union organizers are prevented from articulating their point of view on workplace production. U.S. labor-management standards do not meet the criteria established by the International Labor Organization (ILO). The ILO, an arm of the United Nations, affirms workers' right to organize, bargain collectively, promote the speedy resolution of grievances and, with limitations, strike and conduct sympathy strikes. The ILO opposes the hiring of permanent replacement workers during strikes. U.S. labor laws permit employers to replace workers permanently if they strike for higher wages.[10]

According to Richard D. Kahlenberg, the decline of labor promotes U.S. economic inequality. Organized labor declined as a percentage of the nonagricultural workforce from 35 percent in 1954 to 13.5 percent in 2000. "The United States," Kahlenberg writes, "has about three times more inequality than European countries and Japan when measuring the wage gap between the top 10 percent of workers and the bottom 10 percent."[11] The decline of organized labor strength leads to rising economic inequality. In addition, as the U.S. population grows, more stress is placed on the political and economic systems to meet citizen expectations.

Union bargaining gives employees higher wages and benefits, slicing them a larger portion of the economic pie. Unions, representing a great array of employees, articulate different points of view on workplace issues. They engage business in battle over political and economic policies. They contest management's stand on the minimum wage, the Earned Tax Credit, healthcare, and Social Security. Weak labor laws contribute to the decline in labor and progressive politics, argue the anti-neocapitalists. Social change cannot take place without a strong labor movement.

How do private sector labor relations and macroeconomics impact public sector labor relations? To paraphrase Dwight Waldo again, the distinctions between public and private center on the structure, or organization, of U.S. society. Our constructions of public and private find their origins in the First and Fourteenth Amendments to the U.S. Constitution and in the opportunities provided by American capitalism. Americans are taught to think in terms of public and private differences. But, as Waldo says, applications of public and private are not categories of nature. They are constructs of history and culture, of law and custom. They fit into the context of U.S. and international macroeconomics and are, as Waldo writes, subject to continual change and redefinition.[12]

Public and private unions may be in some decline and not as strong as they once were, but neither shows signs of extinction. The United States is not unique in the decline of private sector unionism. Contrary to some assertions, unionism in the

---

Public Sector Unions

Teachers Unions

American Federation of Teachers/National
    Education Association
American Association of University Professors
    (AAUP)

Protective Services Unions

International Association of Firefighters
    (IAFF)
Fraternal Order of Police (FOP)
Police Benevolent Association
Service Employees International Union (SEIU)

Local Transit Employee Unions

Amalgamated Transit Union (ATU)
Transport Workers Union (TWU)
United Transportation Union (UTU)

State and Local Government Employee Unions

American Federation of State, County, and
    Municipal Employees (AFSCME)
Assembly of Government Employees (AGE)

Source: Michael Ballot, with contributions from Laurie Lichter-Heath, Thomas Kail, and Ruth Wang, *Labor-Management Relations in a Changing Environment,* 2d ed. (New York: John Wiley & Sons, pp. 474–478, 1996).

---

private sectors of Canada and Western Europe has also declined, and for the same reason—because of structural changes in the labor market.[13]

David Lewin cites key factors for the rise in public unionism during the decline of overall unionism.[14] Among those factors at work from 1960 to 1975 were the passing of state laws permitting collective bargaining by state employees and the rapid growth in public employment.

During the late 1970s and throughout the 1980s, however, political and economic factors changed. From a political and economic environment that promoted employee unionism and collective bargaining rights, the situation shifted to current attitude, which emphasizes imposing penalties for illegal strikes by public employees.

Troy, Distinguished Professor of Economics at Rutgers University, Newark, calls private sector unionism the "*Old Unionism*" and public, or government, sector unionism the "*New Unionism.*" The Old Unionism shares about 7 percent of the nonfarm labor market, the percentage it had at the start of the twentieth century. While the Old Unionism is in decline, the New Unionism continues to expand. In the first year of the Clinton presidency, New Unionism rose nearly 5.5 percent, or 370,000, to more than 7 million members. The New Unionism is more widely distributed across the country than the Old Unionism ever was.

According to Troy, public, or government, sector unionism constitutes attempts to "organize the organized." The most organized of full-time public employees are firefighters, teachers, police officers, and sanitation workers. Why is Old Unionism in a permanent state of decline? Markets produce structural changes in labor arrangements. The shift from a goods-dominated to a service-dominated labor market assists the transformation. Increasing substitution of "high tech" for traditional manufacturing accompanies the decline of Old Unionism.

Competition abhors monopoly. State and local governments account for the bulk of public employees. As these governments extend their encouragement of unionization and bargaining, the disparities in the strength of the New and Old Unionism will grow. Troy states that a great potential exists for the unionization of state and local government employees.

The permanent decline of Old Unionism (the private sector model) is attributed to market competition, fundamental structural changes, and market "repeal" of the National Labor Relations Act. The NLRA states and defines the rights of employees to organize and to bargain collectively with their employers through representatives of their choosing. Union leadership and its supporters were late in recognizing the new environment confronting the Old Unionism.[15] The reform of labor relations and the steady increase in the number of labor unions show that Old Unionism is in a continuous decline and that New Unionism is rapidly taking over. Aside from profound changes in the structure of the labor market, New (public sector) Unionism will also increase the strength of organized labor.[16]

State and Local Government Labor Issues

Collective bargaining has been used by state and local government employees since the 1960s. Arguments questioning collective bargaining for government employees include the following:

- *Sovereign power and public accountability.* Many believe that public sector collective bargaining infringes on the sovereign power of the state. Unions directly affect the sovereign power of the state to determine service levels of different programs (police, fire, library, and sanitation, for example) and rules and regulations (production, benefits, and vacation days, for example).

    The government unions, as private interest groups, would unduly influence public, or communitywide, decisions. The union seeks to increase the pay and benefits its members receive. Unionized municipal departments are likely to have higher expenditures (budgets) than nonunionized departments. Also, private interest groups, in this case government unions, are not accountable to the public or community. Elected officials are accountable to the electorate or the populace that elects them. The electorate may vote the government officials out of office, but not government workers.

- *Fiscal responsibility and public budgeting.* Public sector unions soon encountered fiscal realities. In the 1960s and 1970s, union demands caused state, county, and municipal budgets to inflate, raising taxes, especially property taxes. States began to impose tax and/or spending limits. Elected officials operated with fixed budgets and small reserves. Union monetary demands were curtailed. These fiscal constraints slowed the growth of public sector unionism. Funds were reallocated, employment was cut, and citizens faced lower levels of public services.

- *Public goods and monopoly.* Government as a monopoly supplier is of concern to the citizenry. Government is the only supplier of certain public goods (police and fire protection, for example). In elementary and secondary education, public schools significantly outnumber private schools and maintain "near-monopoly" powers.

    Obviously, a strike or work stoppage would completely interrupt the provision of these services to customer citizens. However, citizens are not without redress. They may flee the city, county, or state if they are not pleased with the level of government services provided and/or the taxes charged to support that level of services. This flight reduces the community's tax base, causing reductions in the level of services government provides.

- *The right to strike.* If government is monopolist and, therefore, the only supplier of essential services, strikes by government employees may endanger the health and safety of the population. The tasks of police, fire, and sanitation workers are perhaps more paramount than the functions of school teachers and transit workers. In the public sector, the costs are primarily on the users of the service. However, with government employees, the users, or citizens, are also the employers.

   Strikes are legal for some government workers in twelve states: Alaska, California, Hawaii, Idaho, Illinois, Minnesota, Montana, Ohio, Oregon, Pennsylvania, Vermont, and Wisconsin. In 24 states, strikes are either not covered by public sector labor relations laws or are prohibited. But no sanctions or penalties are specified for striking in violation of antistrike laws. Fifteen states penalize striking workers severely, including their employee association or union.[17]

Near-monopolies, however, occur in the private sector as well. If employees of private airline companies went on strike, their actions would not only inconvenience millions of travelers but could cost the U.S. economy billions of dollars. When UPS (United Parcel Service) employees walked out, the USPS (United States Postal Service) could not adequately handle the overflow of packages. If employees of private sector utilities agreed on a work stoppage, telephone, gas, electricity, and cable television services might come to a sudden halt.

Alternatives for Avoiding a Work Stoppage

In those cases where a stalemate is reached and the bargaining process breaks down, alternatives are available for avoiding a work stoppage or strike.

A device sometimes used when labor-management negotiations flounder is *mediation.* The mediator, or in some cases mediators, help carry out negotiations between the disputing parties. They may group both sides around a table and try to find ways to open previously entrenched positions or to point out possibilities for conciliation. When conflicts among the parties push disputes beyond negotiation, the mediator may even put the two sides in separate rooms and run from room to room in a continuing effort to break the deadlock. Some jurisdictions authorize fact-finders to shift to mediation when their recommendations have failed to dissolve the differences separating the parties.

Mediation is an art. According to one experienced practitioner, a good mediator should

- have a good sense of timing, knowing when to advise each side on when to make each move;
- avoid relieving the parties themselves of responsibility to solve the dispute;
- be able to distinguish the power contest between the negotiating parties from internal power struggles (such as union leaders fearful of losing face with their members); and
- avoid passing judgment on the merits of the respective positions.[18]

Another alternative to a work stoppage is *fact-finding*. Under this process, an individual or, more frequently, a mutually acceptable panel is set up to review the disputed issues and make recommendations. These recommendations are not binding, but if the fact-finding machinery has been properly constituted, and if its analysis of the facts is accurate, both sides will be under a good deal of pressure to accept its suggestions.

Neither mediation nor fact-finding assures a peaceful settlement to a labor dispute. For that type of guarantee we must turn to a third alternative, *interest arbitration.* This device differs from the other two in one crucial respect: it produces a definite decision that is usually binding on both sides. When binding arbitration has been agreed upon, the arbitrator's word is final and there is no further appeal.

If arbitration is not accepted by either party at the outset, it does not guarantee a peaceful resolution, but it is rarely used without such prior agreement. One typical way of setting up arbitration is for each side to choose a representative and for the two representatives to choose a third member of what then becomes an arbitration panel.

Administrators tend to view third-party proceedings such as fact-finding, mediation, and arbitration with some suspicion. While they recognize that such devices help considerably to avoid strikes, they often feel that they result in decisions injurious from a management perspective. Third parties have nothing at stake except their own future arbitration or mediation business. They show a tendency, it is felt, to split the issue down the middle, with perhaps some leaning toward the labor side. Some administrators question not only the learning toward labor but also whether most disputes should automatically be split down the middle. They feel many issues do not lend themselves to that type of decision. In any case, management loses control in such proceedings, and decisions are made by those who cannot be fully aware of all their implications and who do not have to live with them.

Unionists have tended to look more favorably on third-party intervention. They have particularly favored arbitration. As a firefighters' union official once expressed it, without compulsory arbitration in the background, collective bargaining for employees becomes collective begging.[19]

Collective Bargaining for Federal Employees

The Federal Service Labor-Management Relations Statute, Title VII of the Civil Service Reform Act of 1978, allows nonpostal federal employees to bargain collectively through labor organizations of their choice and thereby participate with agency management in the development of personnel policies and practices and other decisions that affect their working lives.[20] The 1970s through 1990s saw the federal labor-management relations program evolve from a simple executive order that provided for consultation between agency management and employee organizations to a formal collective bargaining program established by law.

The program is enforced by an independent administrative agency, the Federal Labor Relations Authority (FLRA), as well as by the federal courts. The latest available data from the Office of Personnel Management (OPM) shows that about 1.3 million federal employees, or 60 percent of the total nonpostal federal workforce, were represented by unions. They were represented by 101 labor organizations in 2,266 bargaining units.

The Lloyd-LaFollette Act of 1912 established the right of federal employees to belong to labor organizations as long as the organizations did not impose a duty on employees to engage in or assist in a strike against the government. But it was not until 1962, when President Kennedy issued *Executive Order 10988,* that a federal labor-management relations program was officially established.

The order was the result of a presidential task force study that found that 33 percent of federal employees, mostly in the postal service and among blue-collar workers, belong to employee organizations. Since they lacked guidance, the various agencies of the government had proceeded on widely varying courses in dealing with these organizations. Some, such as the Tennessee Valley Authority and various units of the Department of Interior, had engaged in close to full-scale collective bargaining with the trade unions that represented their employees, but most had done little or nothing.

Among other provisions, Executive Order 10988 recognized the right of federal employees to join, or refrain from joining, employee organizations and established procedures for granting recognition to federal employee organizations. These organizations were given the right to consult or negotiate with agencies on matters that concerned working conditions and personnel policies within the limits of applicable federal laws and regulations.

Certain other matters, including the agency's mission, its budget, its organization and assignment of personnel, and the technology needed to perform its work, were deemed "management's rights" and, therefore, nonnegotiable. The order also allowed individual agencies to establish procedures to deal with grievances, appeals, and negotiation impasses, but it specifically precluded strikes or binding arbitration as means of resolving such disputes. Arbitration hearings by private arbitrators were permitted for employee grievances so long as the arbitrators' decisions were advisory and not binding.

Executive Order 10988 provided for a variety of union recognition policies. The percentage of employees supporting the union in the bargaining unit determined the type of recognition.

- *Exclusive recognition.* A union had to show that it represented at least 10 percent of the employees in the unit. The union then had to be chosen by a majority of the employees of the unit to be their representative.
- *Formal recognition.* A union had to show it represented 10 to 50 percent of the unit employees. If the union could show that 10 to 50 percent of the unit employees belonged to the union, the employer-agency had to consult the union on personnel matters.
- *Informal recognition.* This status was granted if less than 10 percent of the unit employees were members of the union. However, the employer-agency had no obligation to meet, consult, or negotiate with the union.[21]

In 1969, a review of the program by an interagency study committee indicated that the policies of Executive Order 10988 had brought about more democratic management of the workforce and better employee-management cooperation, and that negotiation and consultation had produced improvement in a number of personnel policies and working conditions. The review also found that union representation of employees in exclusive bargaining units had expanded greatly to include 52 percent of the total federal workforce subject to the order.

As a result of the study committee's recommendations, *Executive Order 11491* was issued on October 29, 1969. The new order retained the basic principles and objectives underlying Executive Order 10988 and added a number of fundamental changes in the overall labor-management relations structure. A Federal Labor Relations Council (FLRC), composed of the chairman of the Civil Service Commission, the director of the Office of Management and Budget, and the secretary of Labor, was established as a central body to administer the program, make final decisions on policy questions, and adjudicate three types of labor-management disputes:

1. Negotiability appeals.
2. Exceptions to arbitration awards.
3. Appeals of decisions by the Assistant Secretary of Labor for Labor-Management Relations on unfair labor practice and representation cases. Although the Federal Service Labor Management Relations Statute was modeled after the National Labor Relations Act applied to the private sector, it also carried over many policies and approaches from the executive order program. As a result, federal labor relations bargaining is different from labor-management relations programs in the private sector in several ways:

   - *"Bread and butter" issues* that are the focus of private sector bargaining, including issues such as wages, fringe benefits, and many others relating to hiring, firing, promoting, and retaining employees, usually cannot be negotiated in federal contracts. Since the first executive order, federal sector bargaining has been limited to the way personnel policies, practices, and procedures are implemented.
   - *Traditional bargaining incentives* (i.e., strikes and lockouts) are prohibited.
   - *"Agency shop"* or *"fair share" representation fees* are prohibited. Under the federal program, employees are entitled to select a union to represent them, but they cannot be compelled to join or pay a fee for the representation that the union is required to provide.

Working Conditions

Working conditions vary by occupation and, in some instances, by size and location of the state or local government. For example, chief executives in very small jurisdictions may work fewer than 20 hours a week; in larger jurisdictions, they often work more than 40. Chief executives in large jurisdictions work full-time year round, as do most county and city managers. Most state legislators work full-time only when in session, usually for a few months a year, and work part-time the rest of the year. Local elected officials in some small jurisdictions work part-time.

Most professional, financial operations, and office and administrative support occupations in state and local government work a standard 40-hour week in an office environment. However, workers in some of the most visible local government jobs have very different working conditions and schedules. Firefighters' hours are longer and vary more widely than those of most workers. Many professional firefighters are on duty for several days in a row, working over 50 hours a week, because some must be on duty at all times to respond to emergencies. They often eat and sleep at the fire station. Following this long shift, they are then off for several days in a row or for the entire next week. In addition to irregular hours, firefighting involves the risk of death or injury. Some local fire districts also use the services of volunteer firefighters, who tend to work shorter, regularly scheduled shifts.

Law enforcement work also is potentially dangerous. The injury and fatality rates among law officers are higher than in many occupations, reflecting the risks in apprehending suspected criminals and responding to various emergency situations such as traffic accidents. Most police and detectives work 40 hours a week, with paid overtime when they testify in court or work on an investigation. Because police protection must be provided around the clock, some officers work weekends, holidays, and nights. Many are subject to call anytime their services are needed and are expected to intervene whenever they observe a crime, even if they are off duty.

Most driver/operator jobs in public transit systems are stressful and fatiguing because they involve dealing with passengers, tight schedules, and heavy traffic. Subway operators and bus drivers with regular routes generally have consistent weekly work schedules. Those who do not have regular schedules may be on-call and must be prepared to report for work on short notice. To accommodate commuters, many operators work "split shifts," for example, 6 A.M. to 10 A.M. and 3 P.M. to 7 P.M., with time off in between.

A number of other state and local government jobs also require weekend or night work. Because electricity, gas, and water are produced and used continuously, for example, split, weekend, and night shifts are common for utility workers.

Earnings

Earnings, like working conditions, vary by occupation, size of the state or locality, and region of the country. As in most industries, professionals and managers earn more than other workers. Table 6.2 lists earnings in the occupations having the largest employment in state and local government.

The International City/County Management Association (ICMA) reported the 2000 median annual salaries of selected executive and managerial occupations in local government, shown in table 6.3.

Employer-provided benefits—including health and life insurance and retirement benefits—are more common among state and local government employees than among workers in the private sector.

No federal program illustrates the merger of partisan, policy, and system politics better than "reinventing government," espoused in *Executive Order 12871,* enforced by former President Bill Clinton, and monitored by former Vice President Al Gore. President Clinton introduced the Executive Order on October 1, 1993. The order created the National Partnership Council (NPC) which, in turn, established a framework for a new era in labor-management relations.

Under Gore's leadership, the federal government changed its thirty-year history of tense, sometimes bitter, labor-management relations by treating unions as its partners. The NPC stressed joint problem-solving approaches for managers, supervisors, and union officials.

NPC espoused four key principles: cutting red tape, putting customers first, empowering employees to get results, and cutting back to basics. These principles steered the federal bureaucracy in efforts to reinvent government. Reinventing government intersected partisan, policy, and system politics. Clinton and Gore were politically involved with the reinventing process. They hammered home

TABLE 6.2

Median Hourly Earnings of the Largest Occupations in State and Local Government, 2000

Occupation	State Government	Local Government	All Industries
First-line supervisors/managers of police and detectives	$25.94	$27.42	$27.50
Bus drivers, transit and intercity	23.54	14.68	12.36
Police and sheriff's patrol officers	21.35	19.09	19.13
Registered nurses	20.51	22.67	21.56
Firefighters	16.28	16.71	16.43
Child, family, and school social workers	15.80	17.20	15.13
Correctional officers and jailers	15.32	14.06	14.99
Recreation workers	14.47	8.40	8.24
Eligibility interviewers, government programs	14.27	13.57	13.65
Highway maintenance workers	13.80	12.54	12.82

Source: "Career Guide to Industries: State and Local Government, Excluding Education and Hospitals," 2002–03 Edition. http://www.bls.gov/oco/cg/cgs042.htm.

downsizing, reengineering, and continuous improvements of local, state, and federal governments. Policymaking and execution, or governance, was emphasized too. Policy and system politics—á la reinvention—stressed top-down accountability, customer service, competition, and performance measurement.

NPC asked: What do we expect government to do? How may bureaucratic powers be held accountable to elected officials and then, to the people?

The role of unions in the federal workplace got more emphasis. Employees had more of a voice in how work was performed. They had input into performance expectations for their jobs. Workers participated in shaping bonus and award programs. Management offered nonmonetary awards, such as a day off.

The Council proposals made significant changes in how jobs were classified. They influenced pay patterns and the promotion opportunities afforded workers. On occasion, employees moved up and transferred jobs at a faster rate. The system for hiring employees was changed. Greater control was placed in the agencies' hands rather than in the Office of Personnel Management.

Executive Order 12871, labor-management partnership, government reinvention, and Gore—politically—did not survive the 2000 presidential election, which was eventually decided by the U.S. Supreme Court by one vote. On February 17, 2001, President George W. Bush revoked *EO 12871.* NPC no longer existed.

The Bush revocation directed agency heads to rescind any rules, regulations, or policies which carried out the Clinton order. Organized labor forces were prepared to modify the existing Clinton order. However, the mixture of partisan, policy, and system politics convinced the Bush administration to cancel formal partnership relations between organized labor employees and federal managers. Conservative forces, such as the Heritage Foundation, encouraged Bush to cancel the agreements.[22]

TABLE 6.3

Median Annual Salary for Selected Executive and Managerial Occupations in Local Government, 2000

Occupation	Salary
City manager	$75,000
Engineer	64,596
Information services director	61,657
Assistant chief administrative officer	60,427
Chief administrative officer	59,664
Chief financial officer	60,882
Economic development/planning director	58,220
Fire chief	57,000
Chief law enforcement official	55,862
Human resources director	54,440
Public works director	54,309
Health officer	52,125
Human services director	50,396
Parks and recreation director	50,086
Chief librarian	42,940
Purchasing director	47,467
Clerk	39,811
Treasurer	38,508
Chief elected officials	5,400

Source: "Career Guide to Industries: State and Local Government, Excluding Education and Hospitals," 2002–03 Edition. http://www.bls.gov/oco/cg/cgs042.htm.

Conflicts in State Civil Service and Collective Bargaining Systems

Joel Douglas, professor of public administration at City University of New York and arbitrator of government-employee relations, explores the impacts of the emergence of public sector labor relation systems on the legal structure and the design of state civil service systems. According to Douglas, many jurisdictions have developed "dual personnel systems," with civil service and collective bargaining provisions existing side by side.

Collective bargaining and state civil service merit systems often contradict each other. As of 2000, twenty-nine states had enacted public sector collective bargaining legislation covering state employees.

In the public sector, collective bargaining is multilateral—not bilateral, as in the private sector. Managerial authority is widely shared in the public sector. Multilateral bargaining includes more than two distict parties; thus, in multilateral bargaining, no clear dichotomy divides union and management. Public sector collective bargaining is highly decentralized. Almost all bargaining is carried out on a single-government-unit basis. Union bargaining agreements exist among 90 unions with 2,218 bargaining units. These agreements cover more than one million federal employees.[23]

University of Maryland Baltimore Glossary of Labor Relations Terms

Agreement, Collective Bargaining (another term for Memorandum of Understanding/MOU)

A written agreement or contract that is the result of negotiations between an employer and a union. It sets out the conditions of employment (wages, hours, benefits, etc.) and ways to settle disputes arising during the term of the contract. Collective bargaining agreements usually run for a definite period—one, two, or three years.

Arbitration

Where it is available, a method of setting a labor-management dispute by having an impartial third party hold a formal hearing, take testimony, and render a decision. The decision is usually binding upon the parties (i.e., the University, the union, and the employees).

Bargaining Agent

A labor organization which is the exclusive representative of all employees in a bargaining unit, both union and nonunion members.

Bargaining Units

Defined by the Maryland higher education collective bargaining law as three on each UM campus consisting of regular exempt, nonexempt, and sworn police employees.

Checkoff

A provision, which is many times found in the collective bargaining agreement or MOU, that allows union dues, assessments, and initiation fees to be deducted from the pay of union members who decide to use the check off. The employer then transfers the payments to the union on a scheduled basis.

Collective Bargaining

A method of mutually determining wages, hours, and terms and conditions of employment through negotiations between representatives of the employer and the union. The results of the bargaining are set forth in a collective bargaining agreement. Collective bargaining determines the conditions of employment for all employees holding jobs in a bargaining unit.

Exclusive Representative

An employee organization that has the right to solely represent the bargaining unit for purposes of collective bargaining.

Fair Share

A fee (usually called an agency fee) paid to the union by members of a bargaining unit who have not joined that union. The fee pays for services and benefits which the union has negotiated for all members of the bargaining unit.

Free Riders

A term used by unions to designate nonmembers within the bargaining unit who obtain, without cost, the benefits of a contract/MOU gained through the efforts of the dues-paying members.

Grievance

A formal complaint usually lodged by an employee or the union alleging a misinterpretation or improper application of one or more terms in a collective bargaining contract/MOU. The method for dealing with grievances is through a grievance procedure negotiated in the union contract/MOU. If a grievance cannot be settled at the supervisory level, it can be appealed to higher levels of management.

Grievance Arbitration

The appeal of grievances to an impartial arbitrator for final and binding determination, sometimes called arbitration of "rights." The arbitrator determines the meaning of the contract/MOU and clarifies and interprets its terms. Arbitration, where it is available, is usually the last step in the grievance procedure.

Grievance Procedure

The steps established in a collective bargaining contract/ MOU for the handling of grievances made by or on behalf of employees.

Impasse

A deadlock in negotiations. After bargaining in good faith, the parties have failed to reach an agreement on one or more issues.

Labor Board

Defined by the Maryland higher education collective bargaining law as the State Higher Education Labor Relations Board (SHELRB), an independent state unit. The SHELRB is a five-member panel appointed by the governor after July 1, 2001 and approved by the Senate. The SHELRB is responsible for establishing procedures for and overseeing elections for exclusive representatives, as well as investigating and taking action regarding unfair labor practices.

Labor Organizer

A person usually employed by a union, (usually the regional or international union) whose function is to enlist the employees of a particular employer to join the union.

Management's Rights

Certain rights that management maintains as fundamental to the ability to manage and operate the organization. They are not required, negotiable subjects of collective bargaining. These rights are often expressly reserved to management in the management's rights clause of the bargaining agreement. They include the right to hire, promote, suspend, or discharge employees; to direct the work of employees; and to establish operating policies.

Memorandum of Understanding (MOU)/Labor Contract

The resulting agreement reached by the parties during the negotiations/bargaining process. Also known as a collective bargaining agreement or contract.

Public Employee

A person who is employed by a municipal, county, state, or federal agency or state college or university.

Representation Election

Secret balloting by employees in a bargaining unit for the purpose of selecting a bargaining agent or no representation.

Shop Steward/Steward

A union representative of a group of fellow employees who carries out duties of the union within the workplace. Example: Handling grievances, collecting dues, recruiting new members and monitoring compliance with the contract. The steward usually is either elected by other union members or appointed by higher union officials. The steward usually remains an employee while handling union business. Some release time (with or without pay) may be available to stewards under specific language in many collective bargaining contracts.

Supervisor

An individual (regardless of his/her job description or title) having authority, in the interest of the employer, to hire, transfer, suspend, lay off, recall, promote, discharge, assign, reward or discipline other employees of the employer. A supervisory employee is also one who has responsibility for directing employees, answering their grievances, or recommending disciplinary action, if authority is not merely clerical but requires independent judgment.

Unfair Labor Practice

An act or omission on the part of either the union or management which violates the regulations set forth by the State Higher Education Labor Relations Board.

Source: Abridgment from "Collective Bargaining at UMB: Glossary of Labor Relations Terms" on the University of Maryland, Baltimore website www.umaryland.edu. © 2001 University of Maryland, Baltimore. Reprinted by permission.

As has been mentioned, nearly four in ten government workers were union members in 2001, compared with less than one in ten private wage and salary workers. Protective service workers, a group that includes police officers and firefighters, had the highest unionization rate among all occupations, at 38 percent. The unionization rate of government workers was 37.4 percent, compared with 9.0 percent among private sector employees.

Union membership rates of government workers have held steady since 1983, while those of private nonagricultural employees have declined. Local government, which includes many workers in the heavily unionized occupations of teachers, firefighters, and police officers, had the highest unionization rate, at 43.1 percent.

Labor relations systems supersede but do not replace existing civil service merit systems. State legislatures often fail to terminate procedures for civil service merit systems, yet they have not successfully integrated labor relations systems with civil service merit systems, resulting in numerous problems. Dual personnel systems develop in many jurisdictions. Douglas reveals that dual personnel systems are commonplace, but they are not recommended. Collective bargaining and civil service merit systems do not blend well. Civil service merit systems flourish where there is a statutory commitment to merit, subjects have been removed from bargaining and reserved to merit systems, and management rights are designated and are not subject to bargaining.[24]

The structure of civil service and labor relations legislation is consistent, in as far as civil service statutes predate collective bargaining laws in every state. The legislatures' silence enlarges the scope of negotiations and allows issues to be litigated. Confusion exists, however, over primary and concurrent jurisdiction, the scope of bargaining, and election of forum as bilateralism replaces unilateralism in public sector workplace decision making.

Zero-Sum versus One-Ten Power Games?

Traditional labor-management relations are a zero-sum game (one side wins, the other loses). Traditional bargaining focuses on pay and benefits. The end result is to secure more pay to buy a new automobile as increased compensation for a dull, dead-end job. Workers have changed and now demand more of their employment arrangements. "Workers not only want enough pay to enjoy their time off the job, they wants satisfaction on the job," according to Robert M. Tobias, president of the National Treasury Employees Union (NTEU) from 1983 to 1999.

IRS employee surveys indicate that employees appreciate challenging work and are most satisfied when their knowledge, skills, and abilities are utilized effectively. Annual reports of the National Partnership Council show that job satisfaction and productivity increase if employees are included in improving work processes and procedures. U.S. Department of Labor studies of state and local governments reveal that including employees in productivity designs results in continuous improvement and employee satisfaction.

A hostile labor-management environment leads to the traditional union focus on processing the grievances of a small number of employees. Employee involvement in creating new work processes, determining organizational strategies, and solving workplace problems abandons a zero-sum game in favor of a game of one-to-ten. Personally secure managers recognize that they do not have all the solutions to workplace problems. Nor do managers have all the knowledge, skills, and abilities to enhance agency productivity and public satisfaction. More personally secure managers thus share authority with adequately trained employees who then exercise discretion and become much more productive.

The politics of a sum zero "game" results in one side "winning" and the other "losing." One side goes home "empty handed." No political compromises occur. All or nothing labor management "game" bet the state legislature and government or public sector workers.

Meanwhile, a one to ten "game" would spell that if the government workers could not attain a "ten," perhaps they could reach a "four, five, or six." For example, Teachers could bargain for higher wages, but not permitted to strike. Or bargaining is permitted, but negotiations on health insurance are not allowed. The situation is not "either-or." Alternatives and flexibility exist. Most government employees do not respond well to an "either-or" (sum-zero) arrangement.

Union leaders and managers are no longer playing a zero-sum game where one side wins and the other goes home empty-handed. Replacing this either-or approach is the one-to-ten game, in which everyone gains something from workplace disagreements. Union leaders are no longer there to protect employees from the vices of management. Manager-union processes now promote improving employee satisfaction; developing up, down, and lateral communications throughout the organizational structure; and focusing on the political and leadership skills required to make significant changes.

Employee protection, therefore, is no longer the only union role. "Unions need to expand their role to include improving employee satisfaction," Tobias stresses. "Doing so will create shared experiences that strengthen the labor community. And a union that focuses on the 95 percent of workers who've never dealt with a formal grievance will increase membership rates and become a vital organization."[25]

Abandonment of the zero-sum adversarial relationship lowers costs. Fewer grievances, arbitrations, unfair labor practices, and lawsuits occur. With the one-to-ten employee enhancement style of management-labor relations, greater human and monetary savings occur. The result is increased productivity and improved employee and consumer-customer-citizen satisfaction.

Radical Individualism and Labor Unions

Public sector labor agreements take place within the cultural context of America's fundamentally egalitarian ideology. Our culture emphasizes individual self-reliance. Citizen status, even personal identity, is derived from individual association to the economy and from what one does for a living. Civic membership, as in belonging to a labor union, intersects personal identity with social identity. Social capital may be measured in terms of associational membership and public trust.

Social capital is often said to be on the decline. Expressions of individualism may undermine civic commitment. The decline of political participation follows a very linear trail to the demise of social capital. Welfare-state liberalism, as illustrated by government-funded and -supported public universities, is juxtaposed against neocapitalism. Big business and big government create problems—and often not solutions. More than in comparable countries, Americans think markets are more fair than the mechanisms of local, state, and federal governments.

Corporate formalism, public and private, is accompanied by legalistic notions of the common good. On matters of sex and race, American policy incorporates pharisaic definitions of how governments are to adjudicate "the good life." History shows that labor union membership contributed significantly to the relative affluence and attendant independence of middle-class Americans. (College professors realize the benefits of tenure, a routinized, egalitarian labor guarantee. Many benefit from the sacrifice of the few. Individuals receive benefits and goods even when they do not contribute to the group's efforts.)

Despite renditions of past labor achievements, membership is what facilitates comprehensive labor agreements for government workers. The National Air Traffic Controllers Association (NATCA) succeeded where the defunct Professional Air Traffic Controllers Organization (PATCO) failed. NATCA, confronting the radical individualism spawned by terrorism, became the first nonpostal employee union to bargain with management over wages. NATCA bargained over money for the 14,300 air traffic controllers it represents and negotiated supervisory staffing levels. The Federal Aviation Administration (FAA), as management, represented the public trust.

NATCA and the FAA—labor and management—met at the critical intersection between personal identity and social indentity. Personal identity focuses on what air traffic controllers do for a living, or their skills, knowledge, and expertise. Social identity promotes the safety of U.S. airline travel. Citizens may disagree if the United States faces a civic identity crisis. September 11 called into question what constitutes civic identity. Airline safety has become not just a social crisis for the greater good, but a personal crisis for anyone who flies airplanes regulated by the FAA.[26]

In first class or coach, salaries and benefits of air traffic controllers, articulated by associational membership in the NATCA, a public sector labor union, are of vital concern to all passengers on spaceship earth.[27,28]

Public Sector Labor Law Impacts

Richard B. Freeman and Casey Ichniowski offer five broad conclusions about the role of labor law in the rise of collective bargaining in the public sector.[29]

1. *The legal environment is critical in determining whether public sector employees bargain collectively with their workers.* The probability that a municipal department is governed by a collective contract is enhanced by favorable state public sector labor laws.
2. *Economic benefits and costs do not readily explain the timing of public sector labor laws.* Public sector labor laws call for legalization of union activities, requiring managers to "meet and confer" with unions, requiring managers to bargain with unions, and mandating arbitration or certain final closure

mechanisms to provide a contract.[30] A review of comparative state literature does not explain why certain states enact laws earlier rather than later.[31]

3. *Public sector laws favorable to collective bargaining raise wages in nonunion as well as union departments.* Laws enhance the bargaining power of unions and affect economic outcomes and alter management decision making in both union and nonunion departments. Public sector union members in states favoring collective bargaining receive 6 percent higher salaries, on average than municipal workers in states with unfavorable laws.[32]

4. *Among states that obligate employers to bargain, wages are no higher with compulsory arbitration than with other dispute resolution mechanisms. Wages are noticeably higher with strike-permitted laws.* Potential arbitration creates an environment in which municipalities accept high negotiated settlements as public sector officials fear arbitration processes will result in even higher wages.

   Evidence indicates that arbitration laws reduce strike rates. Although compulsory arbitration states do not differ noticeably from duty-to-bargain states, states that permit strikes pay between 2 and 9 percent higher salaries than states prohibiting strikes. In other words, strike-permitted states' laws raise pay; arbitration-permitted states' laws have effectively no impact on pay.[33]

5. *Arbitrators do not favor one side or the other nor respond greatly to the facts of a case when labor and management make "reasonable" proposals; rather, they tend to "split the difference."* Arbitration occurs in a wide range of settings. Most involve a third-party arbitrator or panel of arbitrators hearing and deciding how a dispute is to be resolved. Arbitrators weigh facts but do so differently. Because offers and facts are often unrelated, arbitrators "split the difference" when employers and employees propose alternatives that reflect diverse sets of facts.[34]

The secret to handling all or most of the labor troubles that occur in the public sector is good management. Nearly all sides consider this the sine qua non of good labor relations, and mediocre management probably causes more labor trouble than militant union leadership. Many management people agree with this statement. Union excesses, say some, spring perhaps most often from managerial misdeeds and mistakes. The real key to achieving peace on the public labor front may lie in developing better policies and better administrators.

Reasons for Union Prominence

The reasons for union prominence in the public sector include: (1) changes in the legal environment, (2) changes in public attitudes, and (3) changes in economic conditions. Recent changes in each of these areas will certainly affect the future of public sector unionism, as they have affected their course for the last thirty years.

The changes in the legal environment brought about the striking expansion in public sector union participation between 1960 and 1976. From 1976 through 1986, there was little or no growth in union expansion in the public sector. The proportion of government workers affiliated with unions or unionlike organizations hovers unchanged at around 36 percent.

Changes in public attitudes toward unions paralleled the expansion of public sector unions between 1960 and 1976. By allowing public employees to bargain collectively, legislatures recognized that the sovereignty of state government was not threatened by union activities. The 1976 to 1986 period witnessed a consolidation of public unions. Public attitudes toward public sector unions became less favorable during this period.

Unlike private unions, public sector unions have political power that affects demand for government services, budgets, and outcomes of local elections. Growth in number of government employees and in budgets results directly from citizen demands for increases in government services.

Changes in economic conditions affect growth in the number of public sector employees, programs, and budgets. When the economy slows, the demand for public services naturally slows as well.

The future of public sector unionism rests on these same three factors. Changes in the legal environment, changes in public attitudes, and changes in economic conditions will shape the future of public sector unionism. Legislation and executive rulings will again be crucial. Union supporters advocate a uniform national law permitting government employees to join unions and requiring public sector employees to bargain collectively, but public support for unions has not grown. Women and part-time workers change the composition of the workforce. Demographic trends may again influence the demand for public services, leading to more schools, teachers, and related public services. An increase in the number of school teachers will enhance the leverage of government workers. An increase in the number of elderly will increase the demand for government services. The demand for public services may be met through more privatization of government functions, but not all public services are suitable for private sector implementation.[35]

In summary, the argument is made that unions are still needed to protect the worker. Evidence shows that as unions decline, the gap between executive and worker pay is growing. Instead of freeing the worker, automation has made it possible for management to expect even more from employees. Employee participation in management is still controlled by management or administration.[36]

Student Employees Win Bargaining Rights

Student employees at the University of Washington (UW) now carry union cards. The Washington state legislature granted collective bargaining rights to the approximately 3,700 Academic Student Employees at UW who work, typically, between five to ten years as Teaching, Research, or Staff Assistants. Teaching assistants, readers, graders, and tutors at UW account for approximately 50 percent of UW instructional hours.

"We welcome the passage of this law that extends the many benefits represented by collective bargaining rights to UW's Academic Student Workers," said Kristin Intemann, UW Teaching Assistant in Philosophy. The Public Employment Relations Commission certified the Graduate Student Employee Action Coalition/UAW (GSEAC/UAW). A framework has now been provided for GSEAC/UAW and UW to bargain over wages, benefits, hours, and working conditions.

Collective bargaining for Academic Student Employees is finding a market at universities in California, Massachusetts, and New York.

Source: UAW News, "GSEAC/UAW Welcomes New Collective Bargaining Law, Files for Union Certification," March 14, 2002.

Summary

- Transportation is a catalyst for personal and collective sets of economic improvements.
- A kind of social-work model of unionism replaced the more militant labor versions of petition.
- Unionization is greater in the public sector than in the private sector. The unionization rate in the public sector outnumbers that of the private sector by about 4 to 1.
- Public sector unionism is a product of the Great Society of the 1960s and changed the overall labor movement emphasis from high employment and high wages to redistribution of society's economic resources.
- The decline, transformation, or perhaps reformation of public sector unionism occurs within the context of our changing political culture. Despite being larger than private sector unionism, public unionism is in *transition.* About 37 percent of government workers engage in collective bargaining. Future government unionization depends upon organized labor's ability to organize the unorganized.
- Unions (on the positive side) usually prevent strikes or shorten those that do occur. Union leaders much prefer to resolve disputes by negotiation. Public employee unions bring public sector problems before the public.
- Trade unionism, according to its detractors, erodes the concept of government work as a public service. Unions perpetuate some of the worst features of personnel systems. They diffuse responsibility and make accountability more difficult to pinpoint. Unionization greatly increases the political involvement of public employees.
- In 2001, 13.5 percent of wage and salary workers were union members; this translates to about 16.3 million wage and salary workers.
- The power of public sector labor unions is tenuous. The best organized government employees are teachers. The labor rights of Americans lag behind those of people of other nations.
- In both the public and private sectors, the fundamental role of labor unions is not merely to secure economic benefits, but to take collective action in order to avoid unfair or fraudulent controls by management.
- Major issues in state and local government labor relations focus on the sovereign power of the state and public accountability of government-based unions, perceived pressures of public sector unions on fiscal and budgeting issues, government as the monopoly supplier of certain public goods, and the right of public sector employees to strike.
- When collective bargaining fails, alternatives for avoiding strikes include *mediation, fact-finding,* and *arbitration.*
- The increasing financial strain experienced by all levels of government in the 1980s brought on a reaction against growing union influence.
- "Bread and butter" issues usually cannot be negotiated in federal government contracts. Strikes, lockouts, and "agency shop" practices are prohibited in the public sector.
- Civil service statutes predate collective bargaining laws in every state. To determine the relationship between the potentially conflicting merit and collective bargaining systems, states have enacted statutes to specify the role of collective bargaining.
- Public sector collective bargaining includes: (1) mandatory subjects that must be negotiated, (2) prohibited subjects that may not be bargained, and (3) permissive subjects that may be bargained.
- The percentage of organized full-time employees varies by type of government. Of all public sector employees, 37 percent are part of labor organizations.
- The District of Columbia and twenty-nine states provide bargaining coverage by statute for all major employee groups. This coverage is realized through a single comprehensive public employee relations policy or separate policies for different functions.

- Nearly four in ten government workers were union members in 2001, compared with less than one in ten private wage and salary workers. Protective service workers, a group that includes police officers and firefighters, had the highest unionization rate among all occupations, at 38 percent.
- The decline of labor has accompanied U.S. economic inequality.
- Traditional labor-management relations are a zero-sum game.
- Corporate formalism, public and private, is accompanied by legalistic notions of the common good. History shows that labor union membership contributed significantly to the relative affluence and attendant independence of middle-class Americans.
- The legal environment, economic benefits and costs, favorable collective bargaining laws, compulsory arbitration, strike-permitted laws, and labor-management arbitrators account for many developments in the emergence of collective bargaining in the public sector.
- Explanations for union growth in the public sector include: (1) changes in the legal environment, (2) changes in public attitudes, and (3) changes in economic conditions.
- The absolute prerequisite for good labor relations is good management.

Case Study

The FAA, PATCO, and NATCA—and Civil Aviation

The following case study illustrates how economics, job stress, management, government employees, and air safety get caught up in a zero-sum game of partisan, policy, and system politics. The Air Traffic Controllers (ATCs)—exhausted, frustrated, and underpaid, considering their life-and-death responsibilities; positioned with malfunctioning equipment; burdened by insensitive and ineffective managers—became their own victims.

> They are in violation of the law, and if they do not report for work within forty-eight hours, they have forfeited their jobs and will be terminated.
>
> —*Ronald Reagan, August 3, 1981*
> *PATCO employee ultimatum*

The Federal Aviation Administration (FAA), Professional Air Traffic Controllers Association (PATCO), and National Air Traffic Controllers Association (NATCA) are—or were—regulators and orchestrators of U.S. civil aviation. They fight—or fought—over who controls the federal workplace. Air traffic controllers guide pilots to, around, and from airports throughout the country.

PATCO confronted former President Ronald Reagan and lost. On August 3, 1981, PATCO and almost 13,000 air traffic controllers (ATCs) went on strike after negotiating for months with the federal government.[1] PATCO demanded across-the-board raises at $10,000 for each member, reduction of the work week from 40 to 32 hours, and improved retirement benefits. The media and politicians emphasized PATCO's pay demands. PATCO leaders attempted to focus on hours worked, working conditions, and job pressures.

Two days after the walkout, Reagan fired 11,359 ATCs, about 70 percent of the workforce.[2] Labor law in the United States more often than not supports private property rights. President Reagan had the legal right to fire the PATCO strikers. He declared a lifetime ban on the rehiring of the strikers by the FAA. The turbulent history of FAA-PATCO indicates that both sides took opposing and uncompromising positions. Deep-rooted problems existed.

However, PATCO expected cooperation, if not support, from the Reagan White House regarding the union's call for shorter working hours and higher pay, although PATCO strikers were already the best paid of all AFL-CIO union members. Reagan had sent the union a sympathetic letter when campaigning for the presidency in 1980.

On October 20, 1980, Reagan wrote to PATCO President Robert Poli: "You can rest assured that if I am elected President, I will take whatever steps are necessary to provide our air traffic controllers with the most modern equipment available and to adjust staff levels and work days so that they are commensurate with achieving a maximum degree of public safety."[3] PATCO adherents—along with the Air Line Pilots Association—endorsed Reagan during the 1980 election. Reagan pledged to do whatever was necessary to meet PATCO's needs—and ensure the public's safety. Deregulation—in play since 1978—had worsened already stressful ATC job conditions.

August 3, 1981, was the first day of the strike. The FAA—relying on scabs—was able to keep air traffic at 70 percent of prestrike levels. The FAA's contingency plan functioned smoothly, and the strike's effects were minimized. Approximately 3,000 supervisors, 2,000 nonstriking controllers, and 900 military controllers manned airport towers. The FAA ordered airlines at major airports to reduce scheduled flights. Flights during peak hours were reduced by 50 percent, and nearly 60 percent of small airport towers were shut down indefinitely. Safety was the first priority.

The public—flying or not—sided with the FAA and the federal government. PATCO strikers did not generate much citizen support; for one thing PATCO members earned already above the national salary average. The unionized ATCs did not anticipate public fallout over perceived union disregard for public safety. Union militants were arrested, jailed, and fined. Some PATCO members jeopardized their home mortgages and economic livelihoods when they decided to strike.

How did the strike effect the U.S. political economy? The airlines employed 340,000 people. Daily commercial flights numbered 14,000. Planes carried 800,000 passengers—60 percent of them business travelers. Air transportation was a $30-billion-per-year business. Air cargo planes moved 10,000 tons daily. Fresh fruit, flower, and fish markets were in jeopardy. Healthcare priorities depended on access to blood supplies.

The politics of this conflict had a touch of irony. Reagan emerged from the conflict perceived as a strong president, an effective and decisive leader. This view was in direct contrast to the public's view of his predecessor, Jimmy Carter. Reagan pointed out that he was the first president to be a lifetime member of the AFL-CIO. In firing the strikers, Reagan was accused of "brutal overkill." But pilots and machinists crossed PATCO picket lines. Poli was criticized for damaging labor's image, for calling an ill-advised strike.

The 1981 demise of PATCO was not very pretty. "We're not on strike over money. Not 10 or 20 percent of these people would have walked out over money. People are tired of being dumped on, and they want to make it to retirement," said striker Robert Devery.[4] ATC job grievances began during the Carter administration. Reagan decertified the union. He called in military air controllers. He gave the 11,000 strikers an ultimatum: Return to work, or you are fired. Most strikers did not return.

Markets, economic development, and technology highlight the necessity that ATCs enjoy access to a participative model of collective bargaining where work rules, grievance systems, and wage standards may be discussed with higher levels of human civility. An atmosphere of unity and good feeling is essential in this industry. Adaptation to new technologies is omnipresent.

Reagan's PATCO policy—designed to break the strike—began a downward slide to economic conditions that resulted in a less effective labor movement. A weaker labor movement led to a dramatic rise of U.S. income inequality. In 1973, the family income of the richest 5 percent of Americans was 11.3 times the income of the poorest 20 percent. In 1999, the richest made 19.1 times what the poorest earned. Studies indicate that declining unionization caused about one-fifth of this increased inequality.[5]

Twenty years after President Reagan fired the air controllers, NATCA President John Carr stated: "The PATCO strike was a watershed event in labor history. From those ashes, we have built a relationship with the FAA based on trust, honor, and integrity, and we are doing our best within the limitations of collective bargaining in the federal sector to co-manage the National Airspace System."[6] With twenty years as a job limit for air controllers, retirements could bring a 50 percent job turnover.

George W. Bush, like his father and Reagan, is anything but public-sector-union-friendly. After taking office in 2001, he ordered an end to all labor-management partnerships in the federal government.

The FAA as Civil Aviation History

The Air Commerce Act of May 20, 1926, was the cornerstone of the federal government's regulation of civil aviation. This landmark legislation was passed at the urging of the aviation industry. Industry leaders believed the airplane could not reach its full commercial potential without federal action to improve and maintain safety standards. The Act charged the Secretary of Commerce with fostering air commerce, issuing and enforcing air traffic rules, licensing pilots, certifying aircraft, establishing runways, and operating and maintaining aids to air navigation.

- *Labor Law:* A contractual or statutory right or responsibility given to various parties (for example, labor or management) and protected by law.
- *Labor Relations:* How the parties (labor or management) apply and accommodate each other's rights and responsibilities.

In 1938, the Civil Aeronautics Act transferred federal civil aviation responsibilities from the Commerce Department to a new independent agency, the Civil Aeronautics Authority. In 1940, President Franklin Roosevelt created two agencies—the Civil Aeronautics Administration (CAA) and the Civil Aeronautics Board (CAB). The CAA monitored ATCs, airman and aircraft certification, safety enforcement, and airway development. The CAB monitored safety rule making, accident investigations, and economic regulation of the airlines.

The Federal Aviation Act of 1958 created the Federal Aviation Agency (FAA) as an independent agency. Safety rule making was taken from the CAB and given to the FAA. In 1967, the Department of Transportation (DOT) commenced operations. With a new name, the Federal Aviation Administration (FAA) emerged under the auspices of DOT. The CAB's accident investigation function was transferred to the new National Transportation Board (NTSB). The Airline Deregulation Act of 1978 enhanced the industry's competitive environment.[7]

The FAA is the U.S. government bureaucracy with primary responsibility for the safety of civil aviation. The FAA is headed by an Administrator, who is assisted by a Deputy Administrator. Reporting to the Administrator are five Associate Administrators who implement the agency's principal functions. The field organization includes nine geographical regions and two major centers. The FAA's major functions include

- regulating civil aviation to promote safety and fulfill the requirements of national defense;
- encouraging and developing civil aeronautics, including new aviation technology;
- developing and operating a common system of air traffic control and navigation for both civil and military aircraft;
- research and development with respect to the National Airspace System and civil aeronautics;
- developing and implementing programs to control aircraft noise and other environmental effects of civil aviation; and
- regulating U.S. commercial space transportation.[8]

Nearly 90 percent of the eligible FAA workforce are represented by various unions (see table). Labor organizations representing FAA employees include:

AFGE—American Federation of Government Employees
AFSCME—American Federation of State, County, and Municipal Employees
LIUNA—Laborer's International Union of North America
NAATS—National Association of Air Traffic Specialists
NAGE—National Association of Government Employees
NATCA—National Air Traffic Controllers Association
NFFE—National Federation of Federal Employees
NUDAI—National Union of Drug Abatement Inspectors
PAACE—Professional Association of Aeronautical Center Employees
PASS—Professional Airways Systems Specialists

Union dues are 1.5 percent of step 1 of an employee's federal government grade level. Dues withholding per pay period for 1998 were as follows:[9]

Grade	Dues (per pay period)
FG–9	$19.09
FG–11	23.10
FG–12	27.70
FG–13	32.93
FG–14	38.93

Labor Organizations Representing FAA Employees

Union	Bargaining Units	Labor Agreements	Employees Represented
AFGE	14	5	1,300
AFSCME	5	0	2,200
LIUNA	1	1	150
NAATS	1	1	2,400
NAGE	3	1	400
NATCA (AT)	3	1	15,700
NATCA (AF)	5	1	1,350
NATCA (ABA)	1	0	100
NATCA (AIR)	1	0	530
NATCA (ARC)	1	0	500
NATCA (AFS)	1	0	13
NATCA (AAM)	1	0	42
NATCA (ARP)	1	0	286
NFFE	2	2	1,000
NUDAI	1	0	25
PAACE	3	2	400
PASS (AF/AEA)	1	1	7,500
PASS (AVN)	1	1	250
PASS (AFS)	2	1	3,500
PASS (AIR)	1	0	150
PASS (AOP)	1	0	18
Total	**50**	**17**	**37,814**

Source: FAA Center for Management Development, Palm Coast, FL. "Basic Labor Relations,"
Overview. Historical Perspective, Stand-Alone Modules (SAMs), 2001;
http://www.cmd.faa.gov/LR-SAMs/M-032/Chap-1/032-1-05.htm.

Contract negotiations may begin when

- the union requests its first meeting with management to discuss a written contract, or submits its contract proposals;
- management requests a meeting with the exclusive representative to discuss a written contract, or submits its contract proposals;
- either party notifies the other of its intent to renew, extend, or renegotiate the existing contract—within the time frame specified in the existing collective bargaining agreement.[10]

In 1998, NATCA members negotiated a collective $200 million raise over three years. For the first time, a nonpostal employee union bargained with management over wages. Federal managers, policymakers, and politicians managed to keep pay off the negotiating table for the forty-year history of modern federal labor relations.

Salaries of controllers in high-traffic centers were increased by as much as $10,000. Reductions in supervisory ranks—decreasing the ratio of managers to front-line personnel from 1-to-7 to 1-to-10—financed the controller salary increases. The NATCA bargained not only over money for the 15,700 air traffic controllers it represented at the time, but also over supervisory staffing levels.[11]

One-to-Ten versus Zero-Sum Labor Decisions

Economics, job stress, and management were the most publicized aspects of the PATCO strike. Except for certain military ATCs, the FAA enjoys a monopoly for hiring and training air traffic controllers. The sensitivity of the culture implies that the economics of air control are a one-to-ten game of labor-management relations—not an absolute zero-sum game, as practiced by President Reagan in 1981.

Aviation employees focus on these factors:

- *New sources of safety data.* Improving air safety depends on collecting and analyzing safety data, developing safer systems, and taking corrective action before accidents occur.
- *Incentives to report safety issues.* Aviation employees are encouraged to report safety problems. Employees who report safety problems are protected. The Justice Department prosecutes potential criminal activities.
- *Reducing accidents and tracking problems.* Accident reduction is a priority. Human performance errors need examination. Pilots and mechanics demand improved training programs. User-friendly technology—in the cockpit and control towers—enhances skills, knowledge, and expertise.[12]

What power government employees enjoy is grounded in politics. Yet the dominant power of the marketplace is obvious. Labor rights in the United States lag behind those in other developed nations. The legal environment is critical. PATCO members violated the law. They decided to strike against the policies of their employer—the FAA. President Reagan acted within the confines of law.

The ATCs—exhausted, frustrated, and underpaid considering their life-and-death responsibilities; positioned with malfunctioning equipment; burdened by insensitive and ineffective managers—became their own victims. President Reagan spoke for the community of the collective welfare, national interests, and the greater good.

Questions and Instructions

1. How do issues such as individualism and community impact the FAA, PATCO, NATCA, and civil aviation challenges? Explain.
2. PATCO and NATCA illustrate the dynamics of "New Unionism." How is "New Unionism" different from "Old Unionism"? Explain.
3. Why is the PATCO strike considered the "watershed event" in "New Unionism" labor history? Explain.
4. Why is an atmosphere of unity and good feeling essential in the civil aviation industry? Explain.
5. Nearly 90 percent of eligible FAA workers are represented by unions. Why is this so? Explain.
6. In the public sector, collective bargaining is multilateral—and not bilateral, as in the private sector. Using the FAA, PATCO, NATCA, and civil aviation as your illustration, explain why this is so.
7. Union leaders and managers are no longer playing a zero-sum game. How does the zero-sum adversarial relationship lower costs? Using the FAA, PATCO, NATCA, and civil aviation as your illustration, explain why this is so.
8. Social capital may be on the decline. Individualism may undermine civic commitments. Using the FAA, PATCO, NATCA, and civil aviation as your illustration, explain why this is so.
9. The legal environment is critical in determining whether public sector employees bargain collectively with their workers. Using the FAA, PATCO, NATCA, and civil aviation as your illustration, explain why this is so.
10. The ATCs (Air Traffic Controllers) are public sector employees. Aside from obvious safety demands, how are their job assignments crucial to the economy? Explain.

Insights-Issues/The FAA, PATCO, and NATCA—and Civil Aviation

Clearly and briefly describe and illustrate the following concepts or issues. Interpret the word *role* as meaning impacts, applications, importance, effects and/or illustrations of certain facts, concerns, or issues from the case study.

1. Role of individualism and community as impacting the FAA, PATCO, NATCA, and civil aviation.
2. Role of markets, economic development, and technology as impacting the FAA, PATCO, and NATCA—and civil aviation.

3. Role of "New Unionism" and "Old Unionism" as impacting the FAA, PATCO, and NATCA—and civil aviation.
4. Role of federal laws as impacting the FAA, PATCO, and NATCA—and civil aviation.
5. Role of corporate formalism—public and private—as legalistic notions of the common good as impacting the FAA, PATCO, and NATCA—and civil aviation.

Case Endnotes

1. Jason Manning, "The Air Traffic Controllers' Strike," 2000, http://wolfstories2.tripod.com/id33.htm.
2. History Channel, "Speeches: Ronald Reagan, Fortieth U.S. President, on the Striking Air-Traffic Controllers," http://www.historychannel.com/speeches/archive/speech_227.htm.
3. Manning, *op.cit.*
4. "When Air Traffic Controllers Took on Ronald Reagan: Lessons of PATCO," *Socialist Worker Online,* August 3, 2001, http://www.socialistworker.org/2001/374/374_10_PATCO.shtml.
5. David Moberg, "The Consequences of the Air Traffic Controllers' Strike, 20 Years Later," *The Progressive Magazine Media Project,* http://www.progressive.org/pmp0701/pmpmj2601.html.
6. "NATCA Marks 20th Anniversary of PATCO Strike," National Air Traffic Controllers Association, AFL-CIO Media Center, August 8, 2001, http://www.natca.org.

7. "A Brief History of the Federal Aviation Administration and Its Predecessor Agencies," http://www.faa.gov/apa/history/briefhistory.htm.
8. "An Overview of the Federal Aviation Administration," http://www.faa.gov/apa/history/overvue.htm.
9. NATCA: Frequently Asked Questions: "How Much Are Dues?" http://eea.natca.net/faq.htm
10. "FAA Bargaining Unit Contracts, Collective Bargaining Agreements," http://fedlabor.org/Contracts/.
11. Jonathan Walters, "The Power of Pay," *Government Executive,* January 1, 1999, http://www.govexec.com/news/index.cfm.
12. The White House, Office of the Press Secretary, "New Public-Private Partnerships to Increase Aviation Safety," January 14, 2000; http://clinton4.nara.gov/WH/New/html/20000114.html.

Case Sources

FAA Office of Public Affairs, "Historic Labor Agreement for New Partnership," June 15, 1998, http://www.faa.gov/apa/pr/jun/dot11598.html; Owen F. Lipsett, "Should Reagan Fly Off Into The Sunset?" *The Phoenix Online,* February 20, 1998; http://www.sccs.swartmore.edu/org/phoenix/1998/1998-02-20/7.html; Joseph A.

McCartin, "Marking a Tragic Anniversary," *History News Service,* August 3, 2001; http://www2.h-net.msu.edu/~hns/articles/archives/2001/080301a.html; Brian Trumbore, "Educate Yourself: In Honor of Ronald Reagan," http://www.buyandhold.com/bb/en/education/history/2001/ronaldreagan.html.

Chapter Endnotes

1. Stanley Aronowitz, *From the Ashes of the Old: American Labor and America's Future* (New York: Houghton Mifflin Company, 2002).

2. Richard B. Freeman, "Through Pubic Sector Eyes: Employee Attitudes Toward Public Sector Labor Relations in the U.S.," in *Public Sector Employment in a Time of Transition,* edited by Dale Belman, Morley Gunderson, and Douglas Hyatt, pp. 59–84.

3. U.S. Bureau of Labor Statistics, "Table 3: Union Affiliation of Employed Wage and Salary Workers by Occupation and Income 2001, http://stats.bls.gov/news.release/union2.t03.htm; "Union Members Summary: Union Members in 2001," *News,* January 17, 2002, http//stats.bls.gov/news.release/union2.nrO.htm. State union membership rates continue to show a clear geographic pattern. All states in the East North Central, Middle Atlantic, and Pacific regions had union membership rates above the national average of 13.5 percent, while all states in the East South Central and West South Central regions had below average rates.

4. Steven Greenhouse, "Labor Leader Sounds Do-or-Die Warning," *The New York Times,* February 19, 2001. According to a survey tabulated at the Cornell University School of Labor Relations, managers at 70 percent of factories where organizing drives are ongoing threaten to close if workers unionize. Survey data indicate workers often say threats to close discourage them from voting to join labor unions.

5. Greg Tarpinian, "Public Sector Workers and Unions Today," *LABORRESEARCH Online,* May 16, 2001; see http://www.laborresearch.org/dis.shtmlpubsec.txt.

6. Richard B. Freeman, Robert B. Reich, Josh S. Weston, John Sweeney, William J. McDonough, and John Mueller, "Toward a Apartheid Economy?" *Harvard Business Review* 74, no. 5 (September–October 1996): 114–127.

7. Leo Troy, "The Rise and Fall of American Trade Unions: The Labor Movement from FDR to RR," in *Unions in Transition: Entering the Second Century,* ed. Seymour Martin Lipset (San Francisco: ICS Press, Institute for Contemporary Studies, 1986), pp. 75–109. See also: Troy, "Is Unionism in Permanent Decline?," *The Chicago Tribune,* September 1, 1986, section 1, p. 11.

8. *Troy,* "The Rise and Fall," p. 106.

9. U.S. Bureau of Labor Statistics, "Union Members Summary," January 17, 2002, http://www.bls.gov/news.release/union2.nr0.htm.

10. Rodger Doyle, "U.S. Workers and the Law: Labor Rights of Americans Lag Behind Those of Other Nations," *Scientific American,* (August 2001).

11. Richard D. Kahlenberg, "Labor Organizing as a Civil Right," *The Century Foundation New Ideas for a New Century,* Idea Brief No. 15, August 2000, www.tcf.org; Richard B. Freeman and Joel Rogers, *What Workers Want* (New York and Ithaca, N.Y.: Russell Sage/Cornell University Press, 1999), p. 1.

12. Dwight Waldo, *The Enterprise of Public Administration: A Summary View* (Novato, Calif.: Chandler & Sharp, 1980), p. 164.

13. Troy, "Is the U.S. Unique in the Decline of Private Sector Unionism?" *Journal of Labor Research* 11, no. 1 (spring 1990): 111–114.

14. David Lewin, "Public Employee Unionism in the 1980s: An Analysis of Transformation," in *Unions in Transition: Entering the Second Century,* ed. Seymour Martin Lipset (San Francisco: Institute for Contemporary Studies, 1986), pp. 241–264; see also: Chimezie A. B. Osigweh, "Collective Bargaining and Public Sector Union Power," *Public Personnel Management* 14 (Spring 1985): 75–84; Douglas M. McCabe, "Labor Relations, Collective Bargaining, and Performance Appraisal in the Federal Government Under

the Civil Service Reform Act of 1978," *Public Personnel Management,* 13 (Summer 1984): 133–146; and R. Douglas Collins, "Agency Shop in Public Employment," *Public Personnel Management* 15 (Summer 1986): 171–179.

15 Troy, *The End of Unionism: A Reappraisal* (St. Louis, Mo.: Center for the Study of American Business, 1994); *The New Unionism in the New Society: Public Sector Unions in the Redistributive State* (Fairfax, Va.: George Mason University Press, 1994).

16. Troy, "The End of Unionism: A Reappraisal," *Current,* no. 373 (June 1995): 26–33.

17. Michael Ballot, with contributions from Laurie Lichter-Heath, Thomas Kail, and Ruth Wang, *Labor-Management Relations in a Changing Environment,* 2d ed. (New York: John Wiley & Sons, 1996), pp. 478–482.

18. George Bennet, "Tools to Resolve Labor Disputes in the Public Sector," *Personnel* 50, no. 2 (March–April 1973).

19. *Boston Herald-American,* March 28, 1973.

20 *Federal Labor Relations: A Program in Need of Reform* (Washington, D.C.: U.S. General Accounting Office, 1991). GAO Publication GAO/GGD–91–101.

21. Ballot, *Labor-Management Relations,* p. 429.

22. Donald F. Kettl, *Reinventing Government? Appraising the National Performance Review* (Washington, D.C.: Brookings Institution, 1994).

23. Stephan Barr, "A Labor-Management Thicket Awaits Bush Administration," *The Washington Post,* January 12, 2001, p. B02.

24. Joel M. Douglas, "State Civil Service and Collective Bargaining Systems in Conflict," *Public Administration Review* 52, no. 1 (January/February 1992): 162–172.

25. Robert M. Tobias, "Giving Up the Good Fight," *Government Executive,* March 28, 2000, http://www/govexec.com.

26. Robert Bellah, et al. "Individualism and the Crisis of Civic Membership,"

http://www.religion-online.org/cgi-bin/relsearchd.dll/showarticleitem_id=224.

27. Robert D. Putnam, *Bowling Alone: The Collapse and Revival of American Community* (New York: Touchstone Books, 2000).

28. Jay Walters, "The Power of Pay," *Government Executive,* January 1, 1999, http://www/govexec.com.

29. Richard B. Freeman and Casey Ichniowski, "Introduction: The Public Sector Look of American Unionism," in *When Public Sector Workers Unionize,* ed. Richard B. Freeman and Casey Ichniowski (Chicago: University of Chicago Press, 1988), pp. 1–15.

30. Richard B. Freeman and Robert G. Valletta, "The Effects of Public Sector Labor Laws on Labor Market Institutions and Outcomes," in *When Public Sector Workers Unionize,* eds. Richard B. Freeman and Casey Ichniowski (Chicago: University of Chicago Press, 1988) pp. 81–103.

31. Henry S. Farber, "The Evolution of Public Sector Bargaining Laws," in *When Public Sector Workers Unionize,* eds. Freeman and Ichniowski (Chicago: University of Chicago Press, 1988), pp. 129–166.

32. Freeman and Valletta, "The Effects of Public Sector Labor Laws."

33. Freeman and Valletta, "The Effects of Public Sector Labor Laws," pp. 97–99.

34. David E. Bloom, "Arbitrator Behavior in Public Sector Wage Disputes," in *When Public Sector Workers Unionize,* eds. Freeman and Ichniowski (Chicago: University of Chicago Press, 1988), p. 122.

35. Linda N. Edwards, "The Future of Public Sector Unions: Stagnation or Growth?" *AEA Papers and Proceedings* 79, no. 2 (May 1989): 161–165.

36. John Buell, "The Future of Unions," *The Humanist* 57, no. 5 (September–October 1997): 41–42.

Leadership

Chapter Highlights

Leadership and Needs of the Situation

Leadership Qualities

Competence and Decision-Making

Leaders, Followers, and Charisma

Max Weber and Charisma Power Centers

Charismatic Leader Behaviors

Historical Conditions Favoring Charisma

Institutionalizing the American Presidency

The Limits of Leadership

Summary

Bubba Bill Clinton and Charisma

Bill Clinton got the nickname "Bubba" because he is an Arkansas "good ole boy," the son of a single mother (his father died in a car accident before he was born) who was reared in near poverty, and called a very poor southern state home. Clinton was said to be the "first black president" because of his friendly relations with African-Americans. He was a 12-year governor of his home state, and U.S. president—a man with great strengths and outsized flaws—for eight years.

Was Bill Clinton a President of Charisma?

An examination of charisma has three elements we must consider: (1) the laws and traditional taboos of American culture and society; (2) the individual leadership, largely emotional, called charisma, or the cult of personality; and (3) the mass of administrators, or American people, citizens, or voters, who responded to Clinton's leadership and personality. Fear, anxiety, and human dysfunctions lead to

"charisma-hungry" circumstances. Meaning and a greater sense of community emerge from the trauma.

Charisma requires emotional arousal among followers. The global character of the leader's power is crucial. Adherents and opponents react emotionally to charismatic personalities. Citizens put their trust in their leader, who they believe will somehow take care of things. The psychological distance between leader and follower prevents constant objective feedback and evaluation. Charisma is not the followers' objective assessment of the leader's ability to meet their specific needs.

Clinton's Republican enemies certainly insisted that Clinton practiced urchin, even depraved, values, if indeed Clinton was not an urchin himself. In contrast to his successor, George W. Bush, Clinton was a man with no dad, virtually no money, and suspect family values. His strengths and failures were on constant display: his successful stewardship of the economy; his easy mastery of the details of federal programs and policy; his contagious optimism about the future; his highly personalized and *ad hoc* approach to foreign policy; his aggressive pursuit of wealthy activists and their controversial big-money political contributions; and his sloppy and dishonest personal traits that jeopardized it all.

Clinton was a talking, thinking, feeling, engaging, tenacious, boot-straping, poker-faced, political personality up from the pits of lower-economic-class, white southern America. (Some might say he came from "white trash.") In one generation, Bubba Bill made it from the outback of American life to its pinnacle—the White House. He governed with flair, substance, style, determination—and ease. Why do smart people do dumb things? Go figure.

Clinton gave the appearance of caring about the everyday problems of Americans. He addressed these challenges sensitively and fluently. He moved the Democratic Party from the left of the U.S. political spectrum to the center, and he kept the party united behind him.

"Yes, he's an SOB," Democrats were known to conclude, "but he's *our* SOB." Clinton exuded a larger-than-life persona that came to dominate America's political culture in the last years of the twentieth century. As President, Clinton was a smart, articulate, and charming chief executive—an activist in office on matters big, small, and middling.

Questions about his personal (not his policy or job-related) character, his duplicitous personal dealings, and his inveterate womanizing become ingrained in the American culture. He was called "boorish," "irresponsible," and "reprehensible"—by friends and foes. Historian Arthur Schlesinger, Jr. forecast that Clinton would be politically weakened for the remainder of his second term. That prediction never materialized.

Achievements and Sins

How did Clinton—a President virtually alone with his achievements and sins, but with a popularity poll rating of 65 percent—survive the heat, the hatred, and his culturally conservative opponents? Why was the articulate and savvy former Rhodes Scholar dumb enough to seduce (or to be seduced by) a young intern in the Oval Office? Wouldn't a one-time constitutional law professor know that there would be hell to pay if his sexual affair with Monica Lewinsky found its way before a federal grand jury?

The prospect that "Slick Willie," as Clinton was known by his adversaries, would emerge from his tribulations was not very likely. Clinton's skills, knowledge, and expertise for the job were overshadowed by his base sexual instincts. How did Clinton escape what Hillary Clinton called "a right-wing conspiracy?" No President had ever been impeached on charges related to personal transgressions.

In middle-class America, no county prosecutor would spend a dime to prosecute a husband for experiencing what columnist Gene Lyons calls, "an oral endearment" with an over age young woman. Yet the Republican Pharisees in Congress were determined to have their way. You play, and you pay. According to Pharisaic doctrine, the "letter" of the law counts more than the "spirit" of the law.

The Clinton years witnessed economic boom, balanced federal budgets, and world respect. America is a right-wing country centered on individual prerogatives. Since World War II, our identity as a right-wing country—promoting personal rights at the expenses of the common good—has been institutionalized, or made virtually routine. Americans worship at the altar of the marketplace. The listing of rights goes on and on: economic demands, religious mores, lower taxes, military spending, sexual exploits, school vouchers, racism, guns, energy waste, environmental excesses, drug abuse, bankruptcy guarantees, and abortion.

The United States is a rights-focused country. Citizens often exercise their God-given rights at the expense of the greater good. By falling prey to the whims of human sexuality, Clinton—along with his detractors, the legalistic Pharisees—willingly engaged in the "rights" culture. The media cooperated—willing to probe, record, and comment on, even lie about, the dangers of Bubba's rising libido.

First, the laws and traditional taboos of American society are clear. A President does not have a sexual affair with a twenty-four-year-old female intern. That deed is not traditional. (Well, perhaps it is in France, but Washington is not Paris.) If either party lied about the "oral endearment," the law might be violated. Ergo, the phrase "lying about sex" became part of the American political vernacular.

However, Ken Starr, the independent prosecutor, was by no means independent or fair-minded. Neither were the investigating committees on Capitol Hill. In his zeal to prosecute Clinton, the prosecutor was never definitive about what type of "sexual relations" took place. Did the former President have a coitus relationship with the young intern? Or was Bubba's affair with Monica something less than that consummation?

Second, millions of Americans identified with urchin-poor Bubba from Arkansas making good in his life. Besides, Clinton was smart, articulate, and charming, and his personal skills included knowledge and expertise. He seemed to care about the everyday problems of Americans. He suffered not just a partisan or policy attack, but a personal one.

"We are concerned about *public* policy," one prominent Democrat said. "They are concerned about *pubic* policy." For the first time in American history, the opposing party was going after a President's persona—not his wayward policies and programs. The "independent" prosecutor and Capitol Hill Pharisees sought to destroy the President's person—not his legislative policies.

Finally, the American people, citizens, and voters are not extremists in their religious, political, and economic views. The Clintons always argued that the right-wing hatred against them was political, not personal, in origin. They knew Americans were generally satisfied with the economic and social policies promoted by the Clinton White House. Clinton won respect for his job commitment. On the Larry King television program on December 22, 1999, Clinton said: "I love this job." Clinton's political gifts and sheer tenacity won the admiration of the masses.

The American right wing made attempts to throw Clinton out of office because he lied, under oath, about a sexual affair, which in and of itself is a lie. The taxpayers paid upwards of $70 million in the effort to remove Clinton from the White House. Laws are the bottom-line expectations of human behavior (or morality) in U.S. society.

No County Prosecutor Would Do So

Most Americans do not want to make acts of oral sex criminal. They deemed Starr's actions to criminalize sexual infidelity as unreasonable, even unfair. Acting as a modern-day Pharisee, Starr chose to attempt to criminalize Bubba Bill's statements concerning the "oral endearment"—a legal measure which no county prosecutor would touch. (And that's no pun.)

Citizens concentrate on how government policies impact their lives. Most Americans do not concern themselves with partisan political battles. They certainly do not involve themselves in monitoring neighbors' sex lives, or lack thereof.

Clinton was not vindictive. Neither was his wife, Hillary Rodham Clinton, who won a U.S. Senate seat in New York State in 2000. Clinton the policy-maker was damaged by the stupidity of his personal actions. But Clinton maintained his verve, was tough-minded, did not demonize his opponents, and continued to lead the country when his future looked bleak, even hopeless.

Was Clinton Charismatic?

Did the greater good survive myopia? Yes. With his adversaries and the media's abuse of his persona, Clinton refused to give in to the short-term pressure to resign. No doubt some of what was said about Clinton was true. What was not true—or even real—was the hysteria that developed in the country at the behest of the Pharisees, partisans, and media wags.

Adultery is a personal sin—not a government policymaking transgression. Starr and his band of Pharisees assumed that the American masses did not know the difference. Clinton appeared unfazed by the gross overstatement of the personal charges, and continued to govern effectively, showing the public that he knew his own morality, even if others were not so sure.

Fairness is a common human quality. The Pharisees, partisans, and media were unfair and unreasonable with Clinton and his personal sins—regardless of what the law said. Violation of the fairness ideology is what caused the masses to side with Clinton and not his adversaries.

Clinton stood up to an unreasonable implementation of the law. For that personal fortitude, he became charismatic.

Sources

Carl M. Cannon, "Judging Clinton," *The National Journal,* January 1, 2000, 14–25 (Sydney J. Freedberg, Jr. contributed to this report); Joe Conason and Gene Lyons, *The Hunting of the President: The Ten-Year Campaign to Destroy Bill and Hillary Clinton* (New York: St. Martin's Press, 2000); and Jeffrey Toobin, *A Vast Conspiracy: The Real Story of the Sex Scandal that Nearly Brought Down A President* (New York: Touchtone, 1999).

Leadership and Needs of the Situation

Anyone who hopes to spell out the qualities of a leader is engaged in a perilous and problematic mission. One helpful observation, however, can be made at the outset. *Leadership is, to a great extent, determined by the needs of the situation.* "It is more fruitful to consider leadership as a relationship between the leader and the situation than as a universal pattern of characteristics possessed by certain people," Douglas McGregor notes.[1] In a similar vein, William J. Reddin, after surveying the research on management style, concludes that "no single style is naturally more effective than others. Effectiveness depends on a style's appropriateness to the situation in which it is used."[2] There is, in short, no ideal leadership style and most probably no ideal leader.

Leaders can be endangered by limiting their analysis of a situation in terms of previous successes, by failing to integrate new data, and by losing their sense of humility. The most effective leaders view their positions as opportunities to constantly learn, accept each situation on its own terms, and remain open to new ideas. According to Karlene Kerfoot, a humble attitude will lead to the greatest learning.[3]

If some leaders can lead only when no one is above them, others can only lead successfully when the reverse is true. There are people who would do well in the second highest position of a large organization but who would flounder if placed in overall command of a small one. In other words, they are natural seconds-in-command. Arthur Schlesinger puts Dean Rusk, who served as Secretary of State during the Kennedy and Johnson administrations, into this category. Writes Schlesinger of Rusk:

> He was a superb technician: this was his power and his problem. He had trained himself all his life to be the ideal chief of staff, the perfect number-two man. The inscrutability which made him a good aide and a gifted negotiator made him also a baffling leader. When Assistant Secretaries brought him problems, he listened courteously, thanked them, and let them go; they would depart little wiser than they came. Since his subordinates did not know what he thought, they could not do what he wanted. In consequence, he failed to imbue the Department with positive direction and purpose. He had authority but not command.[4]

Optimism, Conviction, Civility, Humor, and Nostalgia

As president, Ronald Reagan projected optimism, conviction, and nostalgia for a simpler time in America. His memory poignantly beckons Americans once again to recall a political past when Presidential leadership seemed more simple and open than it is today. President Reagan opposed Communism and spoke of "the magic of the marketplace," as he unselfconsciously put it, that stood for irreducible verities in American government and politics. Conservative scholars ridicule mainstream academics who conclude Reagan was a mediocre leader. They praise his unwavering devotion to conservatism, his strong leadership, his civility, and his humor.

Sources: The New York Times, February 24, 1998, page 20A; see also Stephen Goode, "The Reagan Legacy," *Insight on the News* 13, no. 39 (27 October 1997): 10–14.

Situational differences requiring different leadership styles are not based only on matters of hierarchical position. Different types of organizations may also demand different types of leaders. Many a successful business executive has failed miserably after attempting to transfer with all his or her administrative prowess to the public sector. Few public sector executives test their leadership skills directing a business firm. If so, they would probably frequently fail. Furthermore, an organization may need different leaders at different stages of its existence.

The relationship of leadership ability to the particular situation that calls the leader into being makes the task of defining and detailing a list of general leadership qualities elusive and difficult. Certain qualities do, however, seem to characterize most leaders in most situations. Although this list does not constitute a formula, since one could possess all the qualities on the list and still be unable to lead, it does provide a basis from which the student may gain a perspective on one of the most intriguing and enigmatic aspects of the administrative craft.

Leadership Qualities

Probably no quality is more pertinent and pervasive among successful leaders than the quality of *optimism*. To lead successfully, one must believe that his or her leadership will make a difference. No matter how dismal a journey, the leader must be able to see positive results.

Harlan Cleveland stresses this quality of leadership. "Prophecies of doom," he reminds us, "do not in fact move people in action."[5] Indeed, they are more likely to have the reverse effect. To be happy, one must believe in the possibility of happiness, the great Russian writer Tolstoy once suggested. The same holds true for leadership. To exercise leadership, one must believe in its possibilities.

That *energy* and *enterprise* must accompany such optimism should be reasonably obvious. This does not mean that every luminary in the ranks of leadership has been a whirlwind of activity, but one cannot hope to meet leadership's obligations without some deliberate and diligent application of one's talents. Leaders often do not seem to be working hard at their jobs, but such appearances can be deceptive. A leader may be relaxed and easygoing, but laziness and indolence will usually lead to failure.

What about *intelligence?* Certainly, it is rare to find a leader who is both dumb and successful, and some have been extraordinarily brilliant. Take Napoleon and William Pitt, those young titans who confronted each other across the English Channel at the beginning of the nineteenth century. Each was at home in a variety of disciplines, including mathematics, languages, and the law. In this country, and during the same period, a President (Thomas Jefferson) had come to power who was accomplished in architecture, science, agriculture, law, political theory, and many other fields of study. Nevertheless, when it comes to correlating intellectual ability with leadership, some qualities seem more crucial than others.

According to Albert C. Yates, good leaders must be virtuous people who can be trusted to make the right choices to restore optimism and spirit to the society. Intelligent leaders without virtue can lead society toward selfishness and cynicism. *Virtue* embodies all that is good and right in human life and is a combination of values such as commitment, integrity, compassion, truth, and competence. A dynamic relationship between leadership and values sustains a good democratic society.[6]

One vital intellectual skill is *verbal ability.* Communication skills usually accompany leadership ability, no matter what the situation. A ditch digger who becomes the foreman of the work gang will probably be able to communicate better than all, or at least most, of the other members of the gang.

An interesting study on this point was done years ago. Researchers tested the vocabularies of people from various occupations. They used a multiple-choice test that presented the subjects with numerous words, ranging from the commonplace to the obscure. Each word was followed by four others, one of which was a synonym, and the object was to pick the synonym. The group that placed highest on the test consisted of business executives who outscored all the professional groups, including college professors. The test was given at a time when relatively few businesspeople had a college education. Yet, as a group, they demonstrated the greatest facility at word recognition.

An ability to communicate was crucial in Dean Rusk's rise to administrative prominence. Although sharing Arthur Schlesinger's view that Rusk was more suited for a number-two than a number-one position, journalist David Halberstam writes, "A brilliant expositor, he had a genius for putting down brief, cogent, and forceful prose on paper—a rare and much-needed quality in government."[7] It was this ability, reflected in the cables that he sent back while serving with the army in India during World War II, that led to Rusk being "discovered" by his superior and being slotted for the wider opportunities that came his way when the war ended.

Much more complex is the question of *creativity* and *judgment.* The problem is that these two qualities are not always compatible. Good idea people, as Daniel Katz and Robert L. Kahn point out, tend to be enthusiastic and somewhat impulsive and may fail to subject their ideas to searching criticism. They frequently have a hard time translating ideas into action, and when they do, they may fail to follow through because they soon sprout another idea that they want to work on.

Katz and Kahn maintain that leadership puts more of a priority on reasoned judgment than creativity, and if a leader can have only one of these qualities, he or she is better off with the former. One can always make up for lack of creativity by surrounding oneself with people who are creative.[8]

Lincoln's Greatness Is Forgotten by Too Many

February 12 was once a day of national celebration and remembrance. No more. In fact, most schoolchildren today, and most adults, might not be able to identify the date as the birthday of one of the country's most revered figures, Abraham Lincoln.

What a shame. Public awareness of Lincoln and his achievements has reached low ebb.

What special qualities helped the hayseed lawyer win the 1860 presidential election, preserve the Union, and end slavery?

One of Lincoln's most endearing attributes was his unpretentious humanity. Born in 1809 in a Kentucky log cabin, and raised on the Indiana and Illinois frontier, the "great commoner" was a self-made man driven by restless ambition. Tall and lanky, homely and gawky, he worked as a rail splitter, farmhand, carpenter, butcher, ferryman, storekeeper, postmaster and surveyor before becoming a self-educated attorney.

Elected to the Illinois legislature in 1834, he served four terms, distinguishing himself by his honesty and courage. Early on, Lincoln displayed a rare ability to deflect criticism and generate sympathy through his folksy storytelling and self-deprecating humor.

Lincoln also developed an effective blend of moral idealism and political realism. During the 1850s, he denounced "the monstrous injustice" of slavery and earnestly opposed its extension into the new territories of Kansas and Nebraska. But his keen awareness of the practical limits of public opinion and constitutional law kept him from advocating immediate abolition in the Southern states.

Before 1862, he never questioned the right of people to own slaves in those states where it was legal.

Such principled pragmatism infuriated militant abolitionists, then and since, but Lincoln believed that a democratic republic requires balancing ideals with realities.

Still another distinctive attribute of Lincoln as leader was his humility and flexibility. He was not afraid to admit a mistake or to change his mind. When the Civil War erupted, for instance, he confessed that he was poorly prepared to lead the nation into such a massive conflict. Yet he was eager to surround himself with talented, outspoken lieutenants whose often contrary views helped educate and mature the inexperienced president.

Likewise, the profound challenges and harrowing traumas of the "terrible war" transformed and elevated Lincoln. He grew into greatness. His law partner, William Herndon, said that Lincoln "grandly rose up" to meet the stern demands of a nation in peril. As commander-in-chief, Lincoln displayed a courageous decisiveness.

He was willing to do whatever necessary to "subdue the enemy" and preserve the Union: making compromises to keep the Republican Party from fragmenting and the border states from seceding, instituting an unpopular military draft and martial law, limiting free speech and *habeas corpus,* liberating slaves under Confederate control, and enlisting blacks in the Union military.

Finally, Lincoln was a master of political rhetoric. He knew full well the power of carefully chosen words to inspire courage and sacrifice.

Even though he had little formal schooling, he sustained a lifelong passion for reading. He especially loved Shakespeare, the Bible, and the Declaration of Independence. Such sources taught him the virtues of taut, simple, direct prose. He strove to keep his speeches short and pithy so as to invest each phrase with exceptional force and clarity.

The result was a distinctive style of expression that embodied both Lincoln's own democratic ideals and those of the fractured nation. The final sentence of his second Inaugural Address retains a potent immediacy that reminds us of his peculiar greatness and of American ideals not yet fully achieved:

> With malice toward none, with charity for all, with firmness in the right, as God gives us to see the right, let us strive on to finish the work that we are in, to bind up the nation's wounds, to care for him who shall have borne the battle, and for his widow and orphan, to do all which may achieve a just and lasting peace among ourselves, and with all nations.

Source: David Shi, "Lincoln's Greatness Is Forgotten by Too Many," as appeared in *The Indianapolis Star,* February 12, 2001. Reprinted by permission of David E. Shi, President, Furman University.

Good leaders rarely lose their heads or give in to their emotions. Instead, they deal with situations and the people involved in a disinterested manner best designed to achieve the results they have in mind. This observation is confirmed by research. Burleigh Gardner cites one study of several hundred executives, which showed that they maintained a detached, objective view of their subordinates. Other studies, says Gardner, tend to corroborate this finding.[9] This does not mean that a good leader should be a cool and clammy individual, lacking warmth and empathy. Rather, it indicates that he or she should be able to keep personal feelings in check and to objectively appraise the needs of the situation.

The Swiss psychologist Jean Piaget, well-known for his pioneering work with children, offers an observation that may aid in summing up this rather illusive leadership quality. Piaget points out that when a child stands in front of another person, the child will tend to identify the other person's left arm as the right and vice versa. This is because the left arm of the person the child is facing is on the right side of the child's body. The child is unable to put himself or herself in the other person's shoes.

As people grow older, they usually manage to make this change, at least to the point of distinguishing between the right and left sides of a person they are facing. But everyone still retains some degree of difficulty in seeing situations from the other person's position, particularly when more than physical position is concerned. The good leader will be able to do this better than most. By objectively assessing situations from various points of view and acting accordingly, he or she exercises the influence that leadership betokens.

Competence and Decision-Making

The preceding list of leadership qualities is admittedly a short one and may seem more notable for what it omits than for what it includes. Left out are at least three characteristics that are usually associated with leadership—technical competency, decisiveness, and charisma. Let us examine the first two qualities, then take an in-depth look at charisma.

Technical Competency. Government in the United States has traditionally placed a great emphasis on technical competency in selecting leaders for its various administrative agencies. Americans usually insist that school superintendents be educators, public health commissioners be doctors, and public works commissioners be engineers, or at least persons with some engineering background. Appointing technically trained people to administrative positions is often equated with progressive government and is considered a repudiation of administration by political hacks. A city-manager-run city will more likely appoint a professional law enforcement specialist as its police commissioner than will a city dominated by political bosses, although the latter also seems to be bending to this trend.

Many European countries, however, view the matter differently. They stress administrative skills and background rather than demonstrated technical expertise. When France consolidated its two major police forces in 1968, the government appointed as its new policy head a man who had previously been the chief of staff in Ministry of Education. He was neither an educator nor a police officer, but a professional administrator.

Which is the correct approach? Certainly technical expertise has much to recommend it. People who understand the work of their subordinates will possess tangible advantages when it comes to directing them. At a minimum, a supervisor who is technically expert can gain the respect of his or her subordinates in a way that a nontechnician would be unable to do.

Administrative theorists even in this country have long looked askance at the "specialist syndrome," however. The leader of an organization or an organizational unit must be able to relate the unit to its external environment. This, so the claim goes, is best done by a professional administrator. He or she is much more likely to possess the expanded frame of reference that the leader needs to manage the organization in a productive manner. Failure to assess the external environment can be, and often has been, disastrous to many organizations.

The technically trained and experienced leader has assembled a network of prior associations and preferences as well. The leader's background makes him or her more prone to favor some activities over others and to listen to some people more than others. He or she may lack the overall and objective perspective that the generalist administrator can provide.

These considerations take on heightened importance the more one engages the organizational hierarchy. As many writers have pointed out, the higher the administrative level, the more time the administrator spends on "external" in contrast to "internal" matters. As Katz and Kahn note, the larger and more complex an organization becomes, "the greater will be the commonality of their management substructures."[10] This indicates that because organizations are becoming larger and more complex, their administrative positions are becoming more alike and are therefore demanding fewer specialist skills.

Other factors also lend support to the oft-heard administrative adage that "the technician should be on tap and not on top." As David E. Lilienthal has said, the technician's work usually has a terminal point: the bridge is built, the vaccine has been discovered, the patient has been cured and discharged. The administrator has to think in different terms. His or her task is never done, because in administration there is never any real completion.[11]

Some of these problems were evident in the administration of the Vietnam War. According to former Undersecretary of the Air Force Townsend Hoopes, the military leaders could think only in terms of winning the war. They avoided the question of whether some means of achieving victory might produce more problems than they solved or whether it would even be in the United States' interest to win the war. Theirs was a "can do" policy, which, while productive and useful in some situations, can prove disastrous in others.[12] Instead of questioning the usefulness of air power to begin with, for example, military officials during the Vietnam War devoted their efforts to trying to make it more efficient. The failure to evaluate the means used to achieve limited goals had devastating results.

One thing is certain—the abilities that make a person a proficient specialist in his or her field do not automatically equip him or her for administrative leadership in that field. The first-rate teacher too often turns into the third-rate principal. In writing about scientists and administration, C. P. Snow observed that "to be any good, in his youth at least, a scientist has to think of one thing, deeply and obsessively, for a long time. An administrator has to think of a great many things widely, in their interconnections, for a short time."[13] There are exceptions—Snow himself, for example—but more often than not, the qualities that make for excellence in a specialty do not coincide and frequently conflict with the qualities that make for excellence in administering organizations devoted to that specialty. We may posit, then, that technical competence in the field is an advantage to an administrator, presuming that everything else is equal. The problem is that everything else is usually not equal. While such competence may be useful, particularly at the first level of supervision, it tends to pose increasing disadvantages as one moves to the higher reaches of organizational life. It is, consequently, omitted here as a necessary quality for administrative success.

Decisiveness. A quality that is often imputed to successful administrators is the ability to make quick decisions. To be sure, decision making is what administration is about. George C. Marshall maintained that the capacity to make decisions was the rarest gift that the gods could give a person. When one scrutinizes the record of many notable government executives, however, one frequently finds not a chronicle of speedy decision making, but almost its opposite. Historians have constantly commented on Franklin Roosevelt's penchant for procrastination. Some claim it was his most characteristic trait. Winston Churchill was also not keen on making decisions that demanded immediate action. Unless it was imperative to make a major decision at once, Churchill would approach an issue by calling a meeting and asking for various views. Then he would request memoranda on the subject and hold another meeting. John F. Kennedy is another example. While he sought to present himself as a firm and decisive leader, his favorite book was a biography of a British prime minister named Melbourne. Lord Melbourne was a leader who ardently espoused and acted on the belief that one should "when in doubt what should be done, do nothing."[14]

Successful leaders prefer peace and quiet over agenda raisers and program controversy. Decisions often interrupt the peace and quiet of office politics. The complexities and implications of decision making may cause changes in agency programs, budgets, and careers. When decision makers make decisions, they must take sides. Careers of administrators and employees may be affected. In governments, there are many interests—personnel related and programatic—with which to contend. A decision by a governmental administrator may cause reverberations throughout the staff, other governmental agencies, the legislative branches, clientele groups, the press, and the public—all of which must be taken into account. A good decision maker must be like a good billiard player: Every time he or she goes to hit the ball, the decision maker must figure out what will happen when that ball hits another ball, which in turn will hit another. Any decision of consequence is likely to set off a chain of events where the ultimate impact may prove difficult to anticipate.

For reasons such as these, speedy decision making does not always make for good decision making, and good decision makers have usually taken cognizance of this fact. While there is little dispute that any administrator has to be able to make decisions before time runs out, many of the best executives have persistently preferred to stretch the time limit to the near maximum. As society and the apparatus

---

Personality and Charisma Do Make a Difference

In an age of complexity, change, large enterprises, and nation-states, leaders are more important than ever. A leader's effectiveness depends on his or her personality and charisma and not solely on his or her control over bureaucratic structures. In a model of leader effectiveness, the age of U.S. presidents accounts for approximately 20 percent of the change in presidential needs for power, achievement, and affiliation. Needs of the president and leader self-restraint in using power, the president's age, and crises account for 24 percent of diversity of presidential charisma. A combination of the president's age, crises, needs, and charisma predict from 25 percent to 66 percent of changes in presidential performance.

Source: Robert J. House, William D. Spranger, and James Woycke, "Personality and Charisma in the U.S. Presidency: A Psychological Theory of Leader Effectiveness," *Administrative Science Quarterly* 36, no. 3 (September 1991): 364–397.

---

that governs it become increasingly complicated, we may find that quick decision making, although it occasionally will be necessary, will become less and less characteristic of success in administration.

Charisma. The capacity to be colorful and heroic, to stir the emotions of people and capture their hearts and minds, has long been regarded as a powerful leadership tool. Many of those we regard as outstanding leaders have possessed these traits. They include not only political leaders such as Franklin Roosevelt, Winston Churchill, John F. Kennedy, and Ronald Reagan, but also some more purely administrative leaders such as Robert Moses, New York City's famous builder of bridges, highways, and parks, and Harry Hopkins, FDR's dynamic aide. While a charismatic leader has the ability to inspire and convince followers, reliance on charisma alone is certainly problematic, perhaps dangerous.

Leaders, Followers, and Charisma

The relationship between leadership and charisma is also important in understanding charisma. Katz and Kahn argue that charisma originates from people's needs and from dramatic events in association with leadership. Most persons are in no position to evaluate suggestions for organizational change; therefore, charismatic leadership is most appropriate for formulating policies and altering organizational structures. Since followers are often not knowledgeable concerning specific programs for attaining organizational goals, subordinates allow leaders much flexibility for such decisions.

However, as Katz and Kahn emphasize

> . . . charisma is not the objective assessment by followers of the leader's ability to meet their specific needs. It is a means by which people abdicate responsibility for any consistent, tough-minded evaluation of the outcome of specific policies. They put their trust in their leader, who will somehow take care of things. Charisma requires some psychological distance between leader and follower. Immediate superiors exist in the work-a-day world of constant objective feedback and evaluation. They are very human and very fallible, and immediate subordinates cannot build an aura of magic about them. Day-to-day intimacy destroys illusion. But the leader in the top echelons of an organization is sufficiently distant from the membership to make a simplified and magical image possible.[15]

To put charisma into operation, Katz and Kahn emphasize the use of two particular measures. The degree of emotional arousal among followers and the global character of the leader's power as perceived by followers are crucial for charismatic success. Both adherents and opponents react emotionally to charismatic personalities; the leader's portrait is global and not discriminating. Specific weaknesses are overlooked in the great leader.

Katz delineates three types of interpersonal relations between charismatic personalities and followers:

- One type of charismatic leader may symbolize the followers' *wishful solutions to internal conflicts.* Instead of searching for deeper meanings and motives, followers seek release from their internal conflicts. They project their fears, aggression, and aspirations upon social measures that facilitate symbolic solution. In his or her personality and program, the charismatic leader offers symbolic solution.
- A second type of charismatic leader entails an *aggressor,* or father figure, who possesses overwhelming power; the follower is unable to escape the exercise of such power. In this type of interpersonal relation between leader and followers, there is no new ideology; but the followers identify with the aggressor, or father figure.
- A third type of charismatic leader maintains an *interpersonal relationship void of internal conflict* with followers. In assuming that their charismatic leader may advance their interests, followers magnify the power of their leader.[16]

The concepts of power and leadership enjoy common properties; however, they are not the same. Leaders exercise power. A leadership act involves choosing power instruments. Leadership is the point at which power is activated. Leadership entails attempts on the part of a leader, or influencer, to affect, or influence, the behavior of a follower or followers.

When the Iran-Contra scandal stymied the Reagan administration in the later years of his presidency, many blamed the charismatic President's "distant" leadership style for the fiasco. George Bush, the prototype "organization man," was unable to escape more immediate implications in the scandal. Reagan positioned himself as victim, while Bush's role appeared to be more complicated in efforts to cover up the scheme.

A charismatic leader may fail to fully develop the abilities of subordinates, as they become overly dependent upon the leader. When the leader is absent, the organization will tend to flounder, and when he or she departs for good, it may fall to pieces.

Charismatic leadership also may inhibit communication. Subordinates become reluctant to give the leader unpleasant information or advise against policies that may be unwise. Often they lose the ability to discriminate between wise and unwise policies, for they have surrendered much of their capacity for independent judgment. This can be crucial, because a charismatic leader may not only be forceful but also foolish.

History provides numerous examples of charismatic leaders who vigorously led their nations down the road to ruin. Adolf Hitler and Benito Mussolini are two examples, but we do not have to turn to such extreme examples to see how charismatic leadership can malfunction. Robert Moses may have built more bridges, tunnels, and highways than any man in recent history, but many New Yorkers today are questioning the wisdom of his activity. His final masterpiece, the New York City World's Fair of 1965, turned out to be a startling economic disaster.

The case of University of California physicist Ernest Lawrence offers another illustration of how charisma can lead to catastrophe. Lawrence, a charismatic leader, became head of an important laboratory at the University and persuaded many younger scientists to work with him in building two highly expensive devices, both of which turned out to be unworkable. Physicists elsewhere had branded both projects silly and impractical from the start, but the charismatic Lawrence wrangled sufficient funds, and his star-struck subordinates gave him enthusiastic support.

While charisma is positive in many ways, its main danger in public administration is the possibility that a charismatic leader's personality may negate important advice and challenges from subordinates and citizens.

Max Weber and Charisma Power Centers

Max Weber's three "pure types" of authority are: *rational; traditional;* and *charismatic* grounds. In his rational emphasis, Weber believed in the "legality" of patterns of normative rules. He insisted upon the right of those elevated to authority under these rules to issue commands. This focus constituted legal or *rational* authority. In his traditional emphasis, Weber believed in the sanctity of immemorial traditions. He recognized the legitimacy of the status of those exercising authority under such traditions. This focus constituted *traditional* authority. In Weber's charismatic emphasis, the German scholar espoused devotion to the specific and exceptional sanctity, heroism, or exemplary character of an individual person. This focus constituted *charismatic* authority.[17]

In the Bible, the word *charisma* is translated "gifts." In Romans 12, the New English Bible translation, Paul contrasts the "enthusiastic" display of charisma with its institutional dynamics: "The gifts we possess differ as they are allotted to us by God's grace, and must be exercised accordingly: the gift of administration, in administration."[18]

Verses 6, 7, and 8 specifically refer to administration and point out how *charisma* in this application could become the focus of ecclesiastical organization and offices.[19]

In 1 Corinthians 12, there is a long passage about "gifts of the spirit." Verse 4 of this chapter refers to such "gifts" as wisdom, knowledge, faith, healing, miracles, prophecy, delineation of true and false spirits, and ecstatic utterances and interpretation of ecstatic utterances.[20] These gifts or charisma set apart particular individuals who have and use them.

Weber focused on the function and exercise of power in society. He concluded that there are three major points of influence for examining charismatic leaders and their impacts. They are:

1. *The law and the traditional taboos* of the particular culture or society. These might include laws, rules, regulations, customs, mores, taboos, routines, and

Major Concepts in Leadership

A *leader* is a person who has the authority to decide, direct, and represent the objectives and functions of an organization.

A *manager* is a person who has the authority to direct specific organizational resources in order to accomplish objectives.

Authority is the license an organization grants that gives an individual the right to use its powers and resources.

Credibility is the recognition by an organization that one is competent to use its powers.

Source: Robert A. Portnoy, *Leadership: What Every Leader Should Know About People,* 1986. Reprinted by permission of the author.

certain ascribed standards. These properties are thought to be rational, grounded in prescribed ways of acting and behaving.

2. *Individual leadership,* largely emotional, which Weber labeled *charisma.* This is also referred to as the *cult of personality.* These personalities might include the president, governor, mayor, coach, pastor, priest, rabbi, or other community leaders. This property is thought to often be irrational, as it goes against the grain of how issues confronting the organization have been handled, dealt with, brokered, and accepted.

3. *The mass of administrators* who carry out the laws and policies of the organization, or government; in short, the bureaucracy, also referred to as the followers. In a governmental office, it's the employees. In U.S. society, it's the citizens. In a religious organization, it's the parishioners. On the state university's athletic teams, it's the players. These properties emphasize a rational response, grounded in prescribed ways of responding to the dictates of leaders, manager, and other authorities.

Charisma, then, is not merely the appearance of a dynamic, excited, motivated, committed, passion-filled person. Charismatic persons persuade followers to change their old ways of responding to the organization's challenges and problems and act in creative, determined, and new ways to accomplish the tasks assigned to the government bureaucracy. In the history of organizations, there are occasions when a great man or woman arrives on the scene or comes from the ranks of the organization. The immense personal magnetism of the charismatic leader causes followers to rid themselves of their old, dysfunctional ways and become more productive than ever for the new leader and the organization. The charismatic leader dominates decision making regardless of the logic of his or her positions. The followers abandon rational thinking and follow the new leader, perhaps a Pied Piper, into the unknown future of the organization. Charismatic leaders encounter challenges in democratic societies. Their followers are often educated and not easily seduced, for long periods of time, by leaders turned Pied Pipers.[21]

The One-Minute Leader

Back when a book called *The One-Minute Manager* hit the bestseller lists, I tried to compress in a similar compass what I had learned, from experience and from study, about leadership. My tongue was only half in cheek. There had to be a market niche for a learning tool that leaders, who are usually in a hurry, could absorb on the run.

For the generalist leader, I reasoned, the steepest part of the learning curve is not skills but attitudes. Those of us who presume to take the lead in a democracy, where nobody is even supposed to be in charge, seem to need an arsenal of eight attitudes (reading time: one minute) indispensable to the management of complexity:

First, a lively intellectual curiosity, an interest in everything—because everything really is related to everything else, and therefore to what you're doing, whatever it is.

Second, a genuine interest in what other people think, and why they think that way—which means you have to be at peace with yourself for a start.

Third, a feeling of special responsibility for envisioning a future that's different from a straight-line projection of the present. Trends are not destiny.

Fourth, a hunch that most risks are there not to be avoided but to be taken.

Fifth, a mindset that crises are normal, tensions can be promising, and complexity is fun.

Sixth, a realization that paranoia and self-pity are reserved for people who *don't* want to be leaders.

Seventh, a sense of *personal* responsibility for the *general* outcome of your efforts.

Eighth, a quality I call "unwarranted optimism"—the conviction that there must be some more upbeat outcome than would result from adding up all the available expert advice.

Source: Harlan Cleveland, "The One-Minute Leader." Reprinted by permission of the author.

Charismatic Leader Behaviors

Perspectives on charismatic leadership in times of cultural and technological change are pertinent to understanding the dynamics of charisma. What common behaviors do charismatic leaders activate?

Robert J. House offers six categories of charismatic leader behaviors:

1. *Role modeling.* The role model espouses a set of values and beliefs in which followers should believe. The model's emotional responses to rewards or punishments elicit similar emotional reactions from followers.
2. *Image building.* In the cult of personality, charismatic leaders portray an image or images to followers. In the institutionalization of charisma, perceptions are as important as realities. Therefore, the creation and maintenance of an image or images are crucial considerations.
3. *Goal articulation.* In organizational leadership, the development of an institutional mission and goals is an ongoing process. The creation and maintenance of an institutional mission and goals requires leadership skills whereby the leader merges his personality characteristics with the organization's social structure. The leader provides the organization with a special identity. In pointing out organizational goals, the leader articulates goals that transcend the movement or cause. Such goals are ideological rather than pragmatic. Moral overtones abound.
4. *Exhibiting high expectations and showing confidence.* Charismatic leaders communicate high performance expectations for followers. Such leadership

enhances subordinates' self-esteem and affects the goals followers accept for themselves. As the charismatic leader spells out to his followers that they are competent and personally responsible, subordinates perceive themselves as competent. Leaders seek to enhance motivation, performance, and satisfaction in followers.

5. *Effect on followers' goals.* Followers may evaluate their performance according to standards the leader has articulated in specific and high expectations. The leader's expectations allow followers to derive feedback on their personal behaviors.

6. *Motive arousal leader behavior.* The degree of emotional arousal among followers entails House's final category of charismatic leader behaviors. Adherents and opponents react emotionally to charismatic leaders. The enthusiasm of one group's responses is matched by the mistrust of the other group. The organizational maintenance of emotional arousal is pertinent to the long-term success of the charismatic leader.[22]

House describes four personal characteristics of charismatic leaders. Charismatic leaders exercise *dominance,* personify *self-confidence,* exhibit *influence,* and maintain *strong convictions* in the moral righteousness of their beliefs.[23]

Why does charismatic leadership emerge in the environment of movements for change? What historical circumstances explain such emotional arousals among followers? Weber indicates that charisma and personality blend most readily "in times of psychic, physical, economic, ethical, religious, political distress."[24]

Historical Conditions Favoring Charisma

Erik H. Erikson suggests that large numbers of people become "charisma hungry" under historical conditions in which religion wanes. Charismatic leaders minister well during three kinds of distress:

- One distress condition is *fear.*
- A second, and related, condition is *anxiety.* The condition of people not knowing who they are creates an "identity vacuum" and "anxiety."
- A third historical condition, in Erikson's terms, is *existential dread.* In this type of distress, people experience circumstances in which the rituals of their human existence become dysfunctional. The leader, under such conditions, may offer meaning and provide followers with a greater sense of community, emerging as a charismatic leader. In offering salvation from fear, anxiety, and existential dread, the charismatic leader creates new forms of safety, identity, or rituals.[25]

Crisis, therefore, is important to the emergence of charismatic leadership. Crises foster the emergence of charismatic leaders judged as more effective than the group leaders who emerge in noncrisis situations.[26]

Therefore, charismatic movements develop and multiply during times of widespread distress in society. The charismatic leader, by virtue of unusual personal qualities, promises the hope of salvation. Perceived by followers as specifically salvationist or messianic in nature, the charismatic leader offers himself or herself to those persons in distress as peculiarly qualified to lead them from their distressful predicament.

Institutionalizing the American Presidency

The institutionalization of the American presidency and the charismatic leaders who have held the office over the past two centuries point out the historical maturing of one U.S. public sector—government organization. Some charismatic presidents might include Washington, Jefferson, Jackson, Lincoln, Teddy Roosevelt, Wilson, Franklin Roosevelt, Truman, Eisenhower, Kennedy, Lyndon Johnson, Reagan, and perhaps even Clinton. The test of these charismatic personalities is not whether they had individual dynamism, but whether they influenced the American masses to change their old dysfunctional, perhaps destructive, ways and implement bold changes.

According to Lyn Ragsdale and John J. Thesis, III, the presidency becomes institutionalized when it attains high levels of:[27]

- *Autonomy* (the independence of the presidency from other units). The growth of the organization's budget is an indicator of autonomy. The $1.7 trillion budget shapes the stability and value of the U.S. government. As the presidency becomes more institutionalized, administrations offer policy proposals independent of Congress. Since the Great Society of the 1960s, autonomous presidents have acted contrary to the wishes of Congress because of executive access to budgets.
- *Adaptability* (the longevity of units in the presidency). Flexibility permits presidents to create, modify, and eliminate administrative units. Adaptability is the safety valve of an organization's institutionalization. Units may be added to the Executive Office of the President (EOP) by executive order, public law, and presidential reorganization plans.
- *Complexity* (the differentation of subunits and staff in the office). Complexity is an internal aspect of institutionalization. It points out the division of labor and specialization. The unit's differentiation improves its stability and makes it more difficult to dismantle. Complexity also promotes the unit's intricate internal identity. An indicator of complexity is the organization's total number of units, compartments, divisions, and the like.
- *Coherence* (the managable volume of work). Coherence addresses the abilities of the organization to manage its work load. If tasks are erratic or excessive, coherence is low. Work load follows more predicatable patterns as criteria are developed. Clearance procedures for budgets, legislation, and executive orders enhance coherence. The strongest determinants of changing levels of institutionalization are measures of national government activities. Commitments to social security, medical care, unemployment, and education, for example, are illustrated by an ever-expanding social welfare budget. Challenges, problems, and enemies define presidents: Teddy Roosevelt fought the special interests. Wilson fought World War I and child labor. Franklin Roosevelt fought the Great Depression, World War II, and the wealthy. Truman dropped the bomb. Kennedy adapted to television and confronted the Soviets in Cuba. Reagan, confident yet simplistic in a complex era, cut the federal budget. And Clinton, despite the foibles of his personal

life, withstood criticisms of his presidency from a zealous prosecutor and an out-of-control media.

Ragsdale and Thesis explore institution and institutionalization. According to these researchers, institutionalization occurs as an organization acquires value and stability as an end itself. Ragsdale and Thesis write:

> As an organization achieves stability and value, it becomes an institution. Stability denotes that the organization is no longer a mechanistic entity, easily altered or eliminated. Instead, as an organization institutionalizes, it survives various internal and environmental challenges and achieves self-maintenance—it exists in the future because it has existed in the past. . . . As an organization institutionalizes, it acquires a distinctive identity, a way of acting, and tasks it acts upon, which are all deemed to be important in and of themselves.[28]

In processes of organizational institutionalization, stability and values merge. The longer the organization exists, the greater the prospects for developing distinguishing structures, capabilities, and liabilities. Personal interests within the organization and the dynamics of the outside environment interact to result in institutionalization.

Themes of instutionalization are illustrated in both public and private organizations. Leaders, or managers, differ. In all organizations, personalities, leaders, and decision-making methods vary. The features of autonomy, adaptability, complexity, and coherence indicate how your college or university has continued through the years and achieved importance despite changes in individual or outside environmental constraints.

The Functions of Institutional Leadership

The relationship between leadership and organizational character is more transparent when examined in the context of the leader's key tasks.

1. *The definition of institutional mission and role.* The setting of goals is a creative task that entails self-assessment and discovery of the true commitments of the organization as determined by effective internal and external demands. The failure to set aims in the light of these commitments is a major source of irresponsibility in leadership.

2. *The institutional embodiment of purpose.* The task of leadership is not only to make policy but to build policy decisions into the organization's social structure. This too is a creative task. It means shaping the "character" of the organization, sensitizing the organization to the complex dynamic of thinking and responding, so that the execution and elaboration of policies,

according to their spirit as well as their letter, will be achieved more reliably.

3. *The defense of institutional integrity.* The leadership of any policy fails when it concentrates on sheer survival; institutional survival, properly understood, is a matter of maintaining values and distinctive identity.

4. *The ordering of internal conflict.* Internal interest groups form naturally in large-scale organizations because the total enterprise is, in one sense, a polity composed of a number of suborganizations. The struggle between competing interests always has a high claim on the attention of leadership. This is so because the direction of the enterprise as a whole may be seriously influenced by changes in the internal balance of power.

Source: Phillip Selznick, *Leadership in Administration* (University of California Press, 1984), pp. 61–63.

The Limits of Leadership

One real, yet often overlooked, or at least underestimated, aspect of leadership is that its diverse literature applies to as many situations as there are government organizations.

"In a bureaucracy that contains people with brains and consciences," wrote Charles Frankel following his tour of duty in Washington, "an unspoken bargain binds the man at the top to his subordinates. If they are to be the instruments of his will, he must, to some extent, be an instrument of theirs."[29] Most writers on administration agree. "A manager is often described as someone who gets things done through other people," notes British organizational theorist Rosemary Stewart. "We tend to forget that this means he is dependent upon them."[30]

In a complex bureaucracy the problem intensifies. Tsar Nicholas II was one of the few truly autocratic rulers of his time. Yet he experienced constant frustration in getting his smallest orders carried out. "I do not rule Russia," the weary monarch once sighed. "Ten thousand clerks do."[31]

Why Smart People Can Be So Stupid

The behavior of smart people—from presidents to prosecutors to college professors—is sometimes so incredibly stupid as to appear inexplicable. Why do intelligent persons act so dumb—when their lives and livelihoods might be in danger?

Why can smart people be so stupid?

You are in college now. You realize that the attainment of skills, knowledge, and expertise are valuable personal goals. You are learning how to think smart, act smarter than most your peers, work harder than they, and keep from repeating crucial mistakes in your personal life. Yet no one is immune from doing dumb things.

Bill Clinton engages Monica Lewinsky in sexual hanky-panky in the Oval Office. Richard Nixon covers up the truth about the Watergate break-in. Bobby Knight, a basketball genius, insults friend and foe alike. Teddy Kennedy drinks too much, then drives—and a young woman dies.

According to Robert J. Sternberg, stupidness and smartness are not opposites. Highly intelligent people, says Sternberg, commit singularly idiotic acts. Stupidity is the opposite not of smartness but of wisdom, says Sternberg. In college life, many suffer from an imbalance of foolishness—or in brief, stupidity.

Sternberg emphasizs four main tendencies leading to personal stupidity:

- *The egocentrism fallacy.* We foolishly think we are so incredibly smart. We assume the world should revolve around us and our egocentric personalities.
- *The omniscience fallacy.* As egocentric personalities, we foolishly insist the reason the world revolves around us is because we know much more than others do, or even all we need to know.
- *The omnipotence fallacy.* We believe that the special knowledge we glean in college makes us omnipotent, or all-knowing. We can do whatever we want and get away with stupid actions.
- *The invulnerability fallacy.* We believe we can get away with repeated stupidities because we possess superior intelligence. Therefore, we foolishly feel invulnerable to attack or even perhaps to criticisms.

People are not reliable judges of their own stupidity. Smart persons may be unwise. Students would be wise to consider how egocentrism, omniscience, omnipotence, and invulnerability invade their study habits and personal lives.

Sources: Gregory Mott, "Stupidity for Dummies," *The Washington Post,* May 7, 2002, p. HE01; Robert J. Sternberg, ed., *Why Smart People Can Be So Stupid* (New Haven, Conn.: Yale University Press, 2002).

American presidents have consistently discovered their office to provide far less power than they expected. Franklin Roosevelt depicted Lincoln as "a sad man because he couldn't get it all at once, and nobody can." Roosevelt's own battles with his bureaucracy are almost legendary. He once wearily described his efforts to balance the special interests of diverse government agencies as akin to boxing a featherbed.

Truman and Eisenhower suffered from the same problem. John F. Kennedy took office with the idea of changing Washington bureaucracy. But he found that when he wanted a simple sign taken down, it did not come down, even after he had given the order for its removal three times.

To many students, the president of the university may appear out-of-touch with the immediate concerns of the students. College presidents confront the external and internal demands—more conflicting than not—of legislators, trustees, faculty, service staff, and community leaders.

David Lilienthal, who held such posts as the chairmanships of the Tennessee Valley Authority and the Atomic Energy Commission, once defined leadership as a humanistic art. It requires, he said, "a humanistic outlook on life rather than mere mastery of technique. It is based on the capacity for understanding of individuals and their motivations, their fears, their hopes, what they love and what they hate, the ugly and the good side of human nature. It is an ability to move these individuals, to help them define their wants, to help them discover, step by step, how to achieve them."[32]

The challenge of leadership is thus the challenge of humanism. Its successful exercise lies less and less in giving orders and more and more in developing the innate capacities of human beings. But to this must be joined a sense of mission, bolstered and buttressed by some degree of vision. The story is sometimes told of three stonecutters asked what they were doing. The first replied, "I am making a living." The second, busily at work, answered, "I am doing the best job of stonecutting in the whole country." The third, looking up with a gleam in his eye, said, "I am building a cathedral."[33]

The conclusion is obvious. Only the third person can become an effective manager, or better yet, leader.

Summary

- Anyone who hopes to spell out the qualities of a leader is engaged in a perilous and problematic mission. One helpful observation can be made at the outset: *Leadership is, to a great extent, determined by the needs of the situation.*
- *Leadership qualities* include optimism, conviction, humor, civility, energy, enterprise, virtue, intelligence, verbal ability, creativity, and judgment.
- Technical proficiency, decisiveness, and charisma pose special challenges for leaders, employees, and clientele in public organizations.
- A leader strives towards blending moral idealism with political realism.
- *Leadership and management are not the same.* Leadership incorporates the functions of management, that is, directing the organization's resources to accomplish objectives.
- In an age of complexity, change, large enterprises, and nation-states, leaders are more important than ever. *Personality and charisma do make a difference.*
- Max Weber's "pure types" of authority are *rational, traditional,* and *charismatic.* Weber believed in the "legality" or rationality of patterns of normative rules. He believed in the sanctity of immemorial traditions. Weber espoused devotion to the specific and

exceptional sanctity, heroism, or exemplary character of an individual person, or charisma.

• Weber focused on the function and exercise of power in society. He develops three major points of influence for examining charismatic leaders and their impacts. They are: (1) The *law and the traditional taboos* of the particular culture or society. (2) *Individual leadership,* largely emotional, which Weber labeled *charisma.* (3) The *bureaucrats,* or *mass of administrators,* who carry out the laws and policies of the organization or government.

• For the generalist, the steepest part of the learning curve is not skills, but attitudes.

• Erik Erikson suggests that large numbers of people become "*charisma hungry*" under historical conditions in which religion wanes. Particular conditions of distress, namely fear, anxiety, and existential dread, bring on the dynamics of charismatic leaders.

• Charisma is not the *objective assessment* of a leader's ability to meet followers' specific needs. It is a means by which people abdicate responsibility for any consistent, tough-minded evaluation of the outcome of specific policies. They trust their leader, who will somehow take care of things.

• The concepts of power and leadership enjoy common properties, but are not the same. Leaders exercise power. A leadership act is a choice of power instruments. *Leadership is the point at which power is activated.* Leadership entails attempts on the part of a leader, or influencer, to affect, or influence, the behavior of a follower or followers.

• A *leader* is a person who has the authority to decide, direct, and represent the objectives and functions of an organization.

• A *manager* is a person who has the authority to direct specific organizational resources to accomplish objectives.

• *Authority* is the license an organization grants to give an individual the right to use its powers and resources.

• *Credibility* is the recognition by an organization that one is competent to use its powers.

• The presidency becomes institutionalized when it attains high levels of four features: *autonomy, adaptability, complexity,* and *coherence.*

• As an organization achieves stability and value, it becomes an institution. In processes of organizational institutionalization, *stability and values merge.* The longer the organization exists, the greater the prospects for developing distinguishing structures, capabilities, and liabilities.

• The *functions* of institutional leadership are (1) definition of the institutional mission and role, (2) institutional embodiment of purpose, (3) the defense of institutional integrity, and (4) the ordering of internal conflict.

• The behavior of smart people is sometimes so incredibly stupid as to appear inexplicable.

 ## Case Study

The Supreme Allied Commander

Leadership, to a great extent, is determined by the needs of the situation. Situations create leaders, to be sure, but leaders also create their situations. Such was the case with Dwight D. Eisenhower. The Eisenhower case study describes primarily policy and system politics—or the administrative politics of World War II's ultimate challenges: mayhem, destruction, strengths, weaknesses, deaths, and evil.

Leaderhip: the art of getting someone else to do something you want done because he wants to do it.

—*Dwight D. Eisenhower*
World War II Commander and U.S. President

Dwight (Ike) David Eisenhower, leader of the posse comitatus to rid the world of Hitler's evils and post-World

War II American President, was not charismatic, creative, assertive, or even very politically partisan. According to historian Stephen Ambrose, he exuded the qualities of love, honesty, faithfulness, responsibility, modesty, generosity, duty, and leadership—and a hatred for war.

British Field Marshall Bernard Montgomery was not especially impressed with Ike's soldiering abilities, but recognized "his real strength lies in his human qualities. He has the power of drawing the hearts of men toward him as a magnet attracts the bit of metal. He merely has to smile at you, and you trust him at once."[1]

The *New York Times* polled a group of historians in 1961, asking how they would rank America's presidents. Eisenhower scored a rating of 22. This ranking placed him in the low-average category, rated even below Herbert Hoover. But Eisenhower's contribution to humankind rests not only on his years at 1600 Pennsylvania Avenue.

In some respects, Ike's first fifty years were spent in almost total obscurity. World War II afforded him the chance to move from a lieutenant colonel in 1941 to a five-star general in 1945. He commanded an integrated, multinational alliance of ground, sea, and air forces. As Supreme Allied Commander of the Allied Expeditionary Force, he led the most powerful military force—navy, air force, and army—ever assembled. He was the principal architect of the successful Allied invasion of Europe during World War II—and the subsequent defeat of Hitler and Nazi Germany. Ike's conduct of this command illustrates his administrative leadership skills.

George C. Marshall, Chief of Staff, was the one who chose Eisenhower for this difficult assignment. The difficulties confronting Eisenhower were not so much from the military as from the political situation. Leadership, to a great extent, is determined by the needs of the situation. All kinds of people, parties, and pressures had to be skillfully managed or led. They included the British armed forces and their various leaders, British public opinion, British political leaders, conflicting French interests, other Allied forces and their governments, exile governments in London, and Ike's own troops, their commanders, his military and political superiors in Washington, and the American press and public opinion.

Ike as an Institutional Leader

Eisenhower frequently evaluated the Allied institutional mission and role. He assessed commitments of the Allied force that by December 1944 numbered

4,500,000. The Americans, British, French, Canadians, and others constituted the Allied social structure, forming the "character" of the Allied organization. These nationalities embodied the purpose of Allied existence. Ike relied on U.S. President Franklin D. Roosevelt (FDR), British Prime Minister Winston Churchill, and Marshall as Allied forces defended the institutional integrity of the Allied operations.

Behind Ike's modest geniality lay a great singleness of purpose. Eisenhower realized that the alliance would falter and flounder unless there was a single overall commander. He made sure that this premise was accepted and acknowledged. He assured Allied forces all issues would be discussed and decisions arrived at on a basis other than national pride. An integrated command—combining the forces of several nations—is considered Eisenhower's greatest accomplishment.

Eisenhower put first things first. In North Africa, he deferred his integration scheme, important though it was, in order to capture Tunis before the bad weather. Roosevelt urged him to send troops into Rome; the city's liberation would glorify his own reputation and that of the United States. Eisenhower refused. He sought more time to prepare for the invasion of France.

Eisenhower originally wanted to commense an invasion of southern France to accompany the Normandy attack. A shortage of landing craft and related factors forced him to scuttle the idea. British Brigadier General Sixsmith, a biographer, holds the view that this decision "was typical of the man," for "he liked to keep his options open."[2]

As a military strategist, Eisenhower made mistakes. He allowed German military divisions in Sicily to escape. He balked at sending an airborne division to capture Rome. He opened up a gap that permitted Hitler to launch the perilous and costly Battle of the Bulge. It took the Allied forces, despite their complete domination of the air and vast superiority on the ground, nearly a year after they crossed the channel to bring Germany to defeat.

Allied values and identity were uppermost in Eisenhower's thinking. The ordering of internal conflicts challenged Ike almost daily. A great storm over the English Channel forced the invasion of Europe to be postponed from June 4 until June 6, 1944. Operation Overlord, as the famous D-Day invasion was named, spoke loudly of values and a distinctive identity. The value was to free Europe from Hitler's slaughterhouse. The identity was to afford as many generals, officers, foot soldiers, and nationalities as possible the opportunity to participate in the overthrow of Nazi Germany.

The Allied landing force included 156,000 men who attacked the Nazis on Normandy's beaches. Some 6,000 ships were joined by thousands of airplanes. Ike was assisted by 16,312 officers and enlisted men. The ordering of internal conflicts underscored the widespread diversity of the mission. The Americans, British, French, Canadians, and others volunteered for the prospect of victory and the chance of injury and death.

Eisenhower's command was crowded with huge military egos—in his theater and among alliance countries. Strong personalities—such as Walter Bedell Smith, Chief of Staff; Omar Bradley; George C. Patton; Montgomery; and Charles de Gaulle, the Free French leader exerted competing interests and claims on Ike's decision-making options. Despite sharing similar values and a distinctive identity, these military leaders argued over the implementation of military strategies. Ike held deep convictions, which he never ceded or compromised at any point he felt was important.

Behavioral Side of Military Forces

Eisenhower understood the behavioral side of military forces. The challenge of leadership is the challenge of humanism. He realized that the likes of Patton and Montgomery had strengths, but also displayed weaknesses of person and command. "Morale," Ike once wrote, "is at one and the same time the strongest and the most delicate of growths. It withstands shocks, even disasters, on the battlefield, but can be destroyed utterly by favoritism, neglect, or injustice."[3]

Cries to bring the European war to a speedy end with a minimum of Allied bloodshed required outstanding managerial and human skills. Eisenhower approached this awesome task with modesty and geniality. He shared his thoughts with his subordinates as if they were his equals. He framed his commands as if they were advice.

According to General Sixsmith, he was a superb delegator of authority—yet he was able "to keep his finger on all that was going on. His subordinates were able to see that they were expected to act, they were told what was in Eisenhower's mind, and they knew he would not shrink from responsibility."[4]

Eisenhower issued a directive early in the campaign that newspaper stories criticizing him should not under any circumstances be censored. At the Normandy beach invasion of France, he prepared a statement for

use in the event that the invasion failed. In it, Eisenhower accepted full blame for its failure. During the actual campaign across Europe that followed, he discounted persistent attempts in the British press to give all the credit for Allied successes to the British generals.

Eisenhower's managerial skills are illustrated by his tenuous treatment of General George C. Patton. He recognized that Patton was in many ways an excellent combat commander, particularly in tank warfare. He further realized that the Germans had a very high opinion of Patton and feared him as they feared no other Allied combat general. Eisenhower was also painfully aware of Patton's weaknesses, such as his egotism, his officiousness, and his reactionary cast of mind.

When Patton set off an uproar in the United States by slapping American soldiers hospitalized with bad nerves or battle fatigue, Eisenhower refused to relieve him of command. Instead, he ordered Patton to make personal apologies to the slapped men, the medical personnel, and all others concerned. Patton complied, as he was desperate to continue in command. During the savage Nazi combat at the Battle of the Bulge, Patton's troops rescued the besieged U.S. forces. Eisenhower's decision to keep Patton was vindicated.

Eisenhower's toleration of Patton's behavior had limits. After the war ended, Patton insisted on employing ex-Nazis in his occupation zone. Eisenhower moved to replace him. Even at this point, he tried to ease Patton's humiliation by asking Patton whom he would prefer as his replacement. When Patton named someone who was acceptable to Eisenhower, the American commander appointed him.

Ike's tact and concern were not only evident in giving orders to theater commanders. He also regularly toured the ranks, talking with soldiers, and looking after their well-being. He sharply reproved any base commander who utilized his best facilities for administrative quarters instead of providing them for the rest and relaxation of the fighting troops.

Finally, Eisenhower demonstrated a capacity for communication. As an aide to General MacArthur in the 1930s, Eisenhower drafted most of McArthur's eloquent speeches. As Commander of the Allied forces in World War II, Ike wrote delicate orders that were considered models of tact and understanding. Ike's verbal abilities served him well.

According to Sixsmith, he was by no means a poor strategist, constantly beset as he was by conflicting pressures. In the north, Montgomery insisted that the full Allied thrust be put into his control. He was supported by feverish public opinion in England, not simply because he was their general but also because they feared the German rockets that were being launched from the area that Montgomery was trying to capture.

Farther south, Patton demanded more gasoline, supplies, and troops. The American public opinion sought a hero, and Patton could not be completely restrained. Meanwhile, the French were clamoring for the liberation of Paris—a move that would not only detract from the route of advance but could hinder further advances. Supplies and trucks to carry them would have to be siphoned off to maintain the city afterward.

Eisenhower adequately orchestrated the strategist role. He superbly managed his administrative and political roles. At Germany's surrender, General Marshall, elusive in his congratulations to Eisenhower, stated: "You have commanded with outstanding success . . . you have met and successfully disposed of every conceivable difficulty . . . you have triumphed over inconceivable logistical problems and military obstacles . . . you have made history, great history for the good of mankind. . . ."[5]

Eisenhower remained in Europe for the duration of World War II. He accepted the unconditional surrender of the German army at Rheims, France, on May 8, 1945.

Maintaining a Mature Objectivity

Eisenhower was committed to maintaining a mature objectivity in his working life. Among his principles were "Remember that belligerence is the hallmark of insecurity," and "Forget yourself and personal fortunes." He was more intelligent than creative, realistic than optimistic—exhibiting good judgment regarding both people and battle scenarios. Whereas Patton and Montgomery might "give into their emotions," Eisenhower—steadfast in the technical expertise of military training—remained decisive but uncharismatic in battle.

As Supreme Commander, Eisenhower was absolutely committed to maintaining harmony among the Allies. He would not tolerate internal bickering or rivalry among commanders. Marshall, FDR, and Churchill supported Eisenhower. Any field commander too far out of line could be relieved of command.

Ike was perceived to be an unassuming but calculated risk-taker. He was a compromiser, yet a stabilizing force. Eisenhower was articulate, charming, confident, tolerant, tactful, and discreet. He ordered internal conflicts quickly and decisively. Eisenhower was a cool property administering a hot item—the most destructive war in the history of the world.

The Eisenhower Case Study describes primarily policy and system politics—or administrative politics. This review tells the story of a leader inside a public institution—the U.S. military. As an administrative leader, Eisenhower implemented the institutional mission and role, embodiment of purpose, institutional integrity, and ordering of internal conflicts.

The war's ultimate challenges—evil, strengths, weaknesses, mayhem, destruction, deaths—were challenges to all humanity. Leaders create their situations, to be sure, but situations also create their leaders. Such was the case with Dwight D. Eisenhower.

Questions and Instructions

1. Can leadership be learned? Explain.
2. The ability to make good decisions is crucial if a leader is to be successful. What does this case study say about President Eisenhower's ability to make decisions?
3. Leaders create their situations, but situations also create their leaders. Which premise seems more applicable to Eisenhower?
4. Why is Eisenhower considered a more effective war administrator than presidential administrator?
5. How did Eisenhower's network of prior associations and preferences contribute to his success as war administrator, yet detract from his record as presidential administrator? Explain.
6. How did the leadership styles of Eisenhower and General Patton differ?
7. What role, if any, did charisma play in Eisenhower's approach to leadership?
8. Why do leaders place more emphasis upon reasoned judgment than creativity? In his roles as war and presidential administrators, did Eisenhower exude creativity, exercise good judgment, or both?
9. To lead successfully, a person must believe that his or her leadership will make a difference. In his roles as war and presidential administrators, did Eisenhower make a difference? Explain.

Insights-Issues/The Supreme Allied Commander

Clearly and briefly describe and illustrate the following concepts and issues. Interpret the word *role* as meaning impacts, applications, importance, effects, and/or illustrations of certain facts, concerns, or issues from the case study.

1. Eisenhower's roles as leader and manager. What circumstances afforded Ike opportunities, as Supreme Allied Commander, to emerge as a leader, and when did he act as a manager? Explain.
2. What roles did the political situation play in Eisenhower's leadership as a Supreme Allied Commander and as President? Explain.

3. How did Eisenhower define the institutional mission and roles as Supreme Allied Commander? Explain.
4. How did Eisenhower order the internal conflicts as Supreme Allied Commander? Explain.
5. Leadership qualities include optimism, energy, enterprise, intelligence, verbal ability, creativity, and judgment. In what ways did Eisenhower demonstrate some or all of these characteristics? Explain.

Case Endnotes

1. The principal source of material for this case study is E. K. G. Sixsmith, *Eisenhower as Military Commander* (New York: Stein & Day, 1973). Another source is Ladislas Fargo, *Patton: Ordeal and Triumph* (New York: Dell Publishing, 1970).

2. Sixsmith, *Eisenhower.*
3. *Ibid.*
4. *Ibid.*
5. *Ibid.*

Case Sources

Steven Ambrose, "Character Above All: Dwight D. Eisenhower Essay," http://www.pbs.org/newshour/character/essays/eisenhower.html; "Dwight D. Eisenhower: Biography," *Encyclopedia Americana,* http://www.grolier.com/presidents/ea/bios/34peise.html; "Dwight Eisenhower: 34th President (1953–1961); http://www.americanpresident.org/kotrain/courses/DE/DE_In_Brief.htm; "Eisenhower, Dwight David (1890–1969)," German Corner Website,

German-American Mall; http://www.germanheritage.com/biographies/atol/eisenhower.html; Michael Maccoby, "Making Sense of the Leadership Literature," *Research Technology Management,* Vol. 44, No. 5 (September–October 2001): 58–60, http://www.maccoby.com/Articles/LeaderLit.html; John M. Shalikashvili, "The Three Pillars of Leadership," *Defense Issues,* Vol. 10, No. 42, http://www.defenselink.mil/speeches/1995/s19950412-shali.html.

Chapter Endnotes

1. Douglas McGregor, *Leadership and Motivation* (Cambridge, MA: MIT Press, 1966), p. 73.
2. William J. Reddin, *Managerial Effectiveness* (New York: McGraw-Hill, 1970), p. 35.
3. Karlene Kerfoot, "Leadership: When Success Leads to Failure," *Nursing Economics* 15, no. 5 (September–October, 1997): 275–277.
4. Arthur M. Schlesinger, Jr., *A Thousand Days* (New York: Fawcett World Library, 1967), p. 403.

5. Harlan Cleveland, "A Philosophy for the Public Executive," in *Perspectives on Public Management,* ed. Robert T. Golembiewski (Itasca, Ill.: F. E. Peacock, 1968).
6. "Good Leaders Must First Be Good People," *Black Issues in Higher Education* 13, no. 9 (June 27, 1996): 64.
7. David Halberstam, *The Best and the Brightest* (New York: Random House, 1969), pp. 318–319.

8. Daniel Katz and Robert L. Kahn, *The Social Psychology of Organizations* (New York: John Wiley, 1966), pp. 293–294.

9. Burleigh Gardner, "Successful and Unsuccessful Executives," *Advanced Management* (September 1948).

10. Katz and Kahn, *The Social Psychology,* p. 115.

11. David E. Lilienthal, *Management: A Humanist Art* (New York: Columbia University Press, 1967), p. 17.

12. Townsend Hoopes, *The Limits of Intervention* (New York: David McKay, 1969), pp. 79–80.

13. C. P. Snow, *Science and Government* (New York: New American Library, 1962), p. 73.

14. Anyone who believes that dynamic dictators are immune to such a tendency may find the following quotation from Adolph Hitler of interest: "Unless I have the incorruptible conviction: This is the Solution, I do nothing—not even if the whole party tried to drive me to action. I will not act. I will wait no matter what happens." Quoted in Walter C. Lanager, *The Mind of Adolf Hitler* (New York: Basic Books, 1972), p. 81.

15. Katz and Kahn, *The Social Psychology,* pp. 545–546.

16. Daniel Katz, "Patterns of Leadership," *Handbook of Political Psychology* (San Francisco: Jossey-Bass Publishers, 1973), pp. 216–217.

17. A. M. Henderson and Talcott Parsons, eds., *Max Weber: The Theory of Social and Economic Organization* (New York: Oxford University Press, 1947), p. 328.

18. Rom. 12, New English Bible with Apocrypha.

19. Michael Hill, *A Sociology of Religion* (London: Heinmann Educational Books, 1973), p. 147.

20. 1 Cor. 12:4, New English Bible with Apocrypha.

21. John M. Pfiffner and Frank P. Sherwood, *Administrative Organization* (Englewood Cliffs, N.J.: Prentice-Hall, 1960), pp. 55–56.

22. Robert J. House, "A 1976 Theory of Charismatic Leadership," in *Leadership: The Cutting Edge,* eds. James G. Hunt and Lars L. Larson (Carbondale, Ill.: Southern Illinois University Press, 1977), pp. 193–204.

23. *Ibid.,* p. 204.

24. Reinhard Bendix, *Max Weber: An Intellectual Portrait* (Garden City, N.Y.: Doubleday, 1947), p. 245.

25. Robert C. Tucker, "The Theory of Charismatic Leaderhip," *Daedalus* 97, no. 3 (Summer 1968): 745.

26. Rajnandini Pillai, "Crisis and the Emergence of Charismatic Leadership in Groups: An Experimental Investigation," *Journal of Applied Social Psychology* 26, no. 6, (March 16, 1996): 543–563.

27. Lyn Ragsdale and John J. Thesis, III, "The Institutionalization of the American Presidency, 1924–92," *American Journal of Political Science* 41, no. 4 (October 1997): 1280–1318.

28. *Ibid.,* p. 1282.

29. Charles Frankel, *High on Foggy Bottom* (New York: Harper and Row, 1968), p. 56.

30. Rosemary Stewart, *The Reality of Organizations* (New York: Anchor Books, 1972), p. 48.

31. For an interesting and informative view of some of the Tsar's leadership problems, see the earlier chapters of Robert K. Massie, *Nicholas and Alexandra* (New York: Atheneum, 1969).

32. David E. Lilienthal, *Management: A Humanist Art* (New York: Columbia University Press, 1967), pp. 16–17.

33. Peter F. Drucker, *The Practice of Management* (New York: Harper & Row, 1954), p. 122.

C H A P T E R   **8**

Communication

Chapter Highlights

Communication and Public Administration

Formal and Informal Communication

The Advantages of the Paper Trail

The Disadvantages of the Paper Trail

The Information Highway

E-Government and Communications

The Other Organization

Upward, Downward, and Across Communications

Summary

Student Government Association at Steady State University: Communications

Purposes

The Student Government Association (SGA) at Steady State University (SSU), College Corner, State of Commonwealth, has six major purposes:

- To represent the interest of the student body in student, university, and governmental affairs.
- To provide services that improve the quality of life of SSU students.
- To keep the student body informed of relevant issues.
- To coordinate and regulate student activities and funds in the interests of the student body.
- To maintain an interactive relationship between the student body and the local community.
- To serve as the chief representative body of students at SSU. This mission, as well as our operating procedures, can be found in the SGA Constitution, Bylaws, and Guidelines.

Steady State University (SSU)

Steady State University is a comprehensive, state-funded institution of higher education. Its mission is to provide excellent education. It is located in College Corner, 69 miles from Big Burb, the state capital. Students enrolled at SSU are subsidized by the State of Commonwealth. All SSU graduates are expected to be able to analyze information, think critically, solve problems, communicate effectively, demonstrate competency with computers, and converse in at least one foreign language.

Meetings and Membership

SGA meetings are held every other Tuesday at 6.30 P.M. at 2468 Steady State Alumni Hall, unless otherwise specified. All students are welcome to attend. Any accredited student enrolled at SSU can become a member of the SGA. If you are interested, fill out a membership form at http://www.ssu.edu/sga.

Committees

Within SGA are nine committees, each dedicated to fulfilling a certain part of our mission. These committees are:

- *SSU Campus Improvements.* The purpose of the Campus Improvements Committee is to receive and respond to student concerns and suggestions that focus on physical changes to campus. Past projects include an addition to the Student Center and a twenty-four-hour study area. The committee also works to improve campus safety.
- *Web Administration.* The Web Administration Committee is responsible for maintaining the SGA website and providing web-related assistance to student organizations. Due to the work-intensive nature of the committee, Web Administration members are not required to serve project hours.
- *External Funding.* The External Funding Committee reviews applications for the Club Appropriations Fund, the Nonvarsity Sports Fund, and the Professional Projects Fund. Recommendations for the appropriations of these funds are then presented to the SGA.
- *Intercultural Relations.* Intercultural Relations assists SSU-recognized organizations in promoting intercultural events on campus. The committee helps international and minority groups with programming and publicity for campuswide events, such as campuswide diversity workshops. The committee offers proposals and provides insights to the SGA and the University regarding cultural issues. Specifically, this committee coordinates Diversity Week activities.
- *Issues Committee.* Got a problem? Have you and your friends been discussing things that are missing on campus—services, policies, programs, or people? Are you perturbed by a recent incident on campus? The Issues Committee coordinates investigative panels to examine campus issues brought forward by members of the SSU student body. This committee recommends likely solutions to the SSU administration.
- *Parent-Alumni Relations.* The Parent-Alumni Relations Committee serves as a liaison to the Parents Association and the Alumni Board and makes recommendations to these two groups on projects that would benefit the student body as a whole. The committee keeps track of SSU SGA alumni and coordinates an SGA reunion reception during Homecoming as well as a student-alumni mentoring program. In addition, this committee seeks new sources of funds for SGA.
- *Student Services and Activities.* The Student Services Committee improves current SSU services and provides new services to help students at SSU. This committee organizes a student-run book sale every semester. This committee also facilitates interorganization activities, organizes four yearly blood drives on campus, and coordinates the SGA Student Leadership Recognition Banquet.
- *Student Activity Fee Board.* The Student Activity Fee Board serves as exchequer for the student body and the independent organization. It provides financial guidance and assistance to the organizations it influences and makes certain all monies are used for their intended purpose. The Student Activity Fee Board provides recommendations and information to the SGA membership free of favoritism or discrimination.
- *University Relations.* The purpose of the University Relations Committee is to act as a direct liaison between students and the University. This committee receives and responds to student complaints that involve University policy and directs those complaints to the proper channels for resolution. Some projects include improvements to the current advising and registration systems.

Inquiries SSU Student Council

Inquiries may be sent by e-mail or snail-mail to:

> Student Council President
> Steady State University
> 2468 Steady State Alumni Hall
> College Corner, Commonwealth 69069
> Phone: (069) 690-6906 or FAX: (069) 690-0696
> http://www.ssu.edu/sga

Dedicated to serving the Students of Steady State University.

The SSU Student Government Association is the legislative body of the Student Government Association (SGA). Each SGA member represents a department, college, institute, or special unit of SSU. Some departments, colleges, institutes, and units have more than one SGA representative. There are 65 members of SGA.

The departments, colleges, institutes, and units include accounting, anthropology, applied sciences and technology, architecture, art, biology, business, chemistry, computer science, continuing education, counseling psychology, criminal justice, economics, educational psychology, elementary education, English, finance, geography, geology, gerontology, graduate school, history, humanities, lab school, industry and technology, international programs, journalism, management, marketing, mathematical sciences, military science, modern languages, music, natural resources, nursing, parking services, philosophy, planning, religious studies, physics, physiology and health science, political science, psychology, social work, sociology, special education, speech pathology and audiology, telecommunications, theatre and dance, urban planning, and wellness.

The SSU SGA meets once each week. Students do not have to be SGA members to come to SSU SGA sessions. All meetings are open to everyone. Students are welcome to come and participate in SGA discussions. A special time is reserved every week to hear concerns from any member of the SSU community. This time is called Student Open Forum, and it begins at 7:15 P.M. Students do not have to call anyone or be on the SGA agenda. Just raise your hand, stand up, and say what's on your mind.

The Lowdown on SSU and SGA

SSU is a formal, government-funded and -regulated organization. It is chartered by the State of Commonwealth and operates according to the laws of Commonwealth and the United States. Communications that occur at SSU do so within the culture of governments and laws. SSU is an opportunity institution.

Formal communications are written. The SGA constitution, bylaws, and guidelines are formal communications. Informal communications are oral. SGA discussions are informal exchanges among council members. (The SGA secretary takes notes on the proposals and conversations, and the notes formalize SGA member comments.) Inflections, gestures, and even body language are part of the informality of SGA debates.

SGA students come from public administration class. They think they have experienced a base case of communication overload: too many acronyms, agencies, programs, policies, and problems. SGA members not only decide public policy controversies, they attempt to make common sense of why SSU vice presidents do what they do. SGA members try to find rationality within a university community of ethnic and racial diversity.

The organizational size of the Steady State University contributes to SGA's challenges. SSU has 18,000 graduate and undergraduate students. The larger the government organization, the more likely it is to rely on formal communications. The public character of SSU does not go without notice. Government agencies get their missions from laws, rules, regulations, and money.

SSU did not escape the ravages of the paper revolution. Records are carefully maintained. Every student creates a "paper trail" at SSU with grade sheets. SSU enrollment is the beginning of a process of meeting the requirements of a certain number of courses in a particular academic major. Professors have task specializations. The exponential growth of communications technologies—computers, cell phones, answering machines, photostat machines, and used cars—affords students all kinds of possibilities and some problems.

The small-group dynamic is evident in SGA deliberations. SGA members from the humanities, sciences, and media majors more easily form coalitions to pass legislation than do members from the business and architecture colleges. Primary peer contacts between members take precedence over secondary relationships.

Who makes the rules? SSU SGA students make the rules. A prelaw student usually assumes the task of SGA parliamentarian. Students are primarily interested in keeping tuition fees low and state legislator-taxpayer funding high. Tuition hikes and state subsidies pique the interests of SSU students. SGA leaders have state government funding at the top of their legislative agenda. SSU administrators and professors have little interest in SGA activities.

Lateral communication is prevalent within SGA. All SGA members are students at SSU, and students form a peer group. SGA members furnish emotional and social support to one another as they act on matters that affect the entire student body. Psychological forces cause communication among peers. People in the same boat share the same problems.

Upward communication is not particularly important. In decades past, freshmen paid some attention to the experience and views of seniors. Freshmen often think they have a better grasp of SSU welfare-state politics than senior SGA lead-

ers. The egalitarian nature of being a SSU student makes downward communication problematic. Everybody is an expert, yet nobody knows a lot about anything. Effective downward communication is rare because SGA leaders often lack skills and knowledge of the issues.

The grapevine flourishes at SSU. The "other" organization within SGA is manned by fraternity members who sit in the back row and poke fun at SGA leaders. SGA formal communication restrains arbitrariness, capriciousness, favoritism, and communication. SGA members tend to obey only those rules in which they believe.

The SSU SGA tries to build rationality from a diversity of issues and student interests. The formal SGA organization cannot exist without its informal counterpart. SSU is a state-funded university. As a unit subject to the laws and budgets of the State of Commonwealth, SGA leaders and members must adhere to all laws—respecting due process, or fairness, in all actions.

Will SGA members make a difference within the SSU, College Corner, or State of Commonwealth communities? Perhaps they will—if they create ideas they can market among other publics, including administrators, professors, alumni, state legislators, and entrepreneurs.

Communication and Public Administration

Communication and public administration, or organizational structure, are crucial factors for achieving the integration and coordination of agency goals, rules, and human resources. Structures, processes, and cultures of government bureaus must be defined and communicated. Organizational structure sways communication direction and substance. Formal communication and the formal authority structure merge. Vertical communication is transmitted between government executives and agency employees. Horizontal communication probes the roles of tasks, work units, and divisions.

Human communication is ongoing and interactive. Communication is dynamic, ongoing, ever-changing, and continuous. The message is sent. The receiver perceives and accepts the message. Communication models find their origins in Greek antiquity. Aristotle recognized the speaker, speech, and audience as communication components. Five hundred years before Christ, the Greek philosopher Heraclitus, observed that "a man (or woman) can never step into the river twice. The man (or woman) is different and so is the river."[1] Change and continuity are interwined—as

The Politics of Greeting

Male primates have elaborate greeting rituals that include touching one another's genitals. Human males greet one another and interact in a far more ca-sual manner than do women. Women put a great deal of effort into putting others at ease.

Source: Michael Segell, "The Politics of Greeting," *Esquire* 128, no. 1 (July 1997): 84–86.

men or women step into the river—in a process of actions which flow through the ages. Communication is a process and flows like a stream through time.

Communication presents as many problems as any other aspect of administration, if not more. There are, first, the *technical* problems. Communication problems arise not only from information that is too slow, incomplete, or distorted, but also from information that is overabundant. This is the problem of *communication overload.* Occasionally, this communication problem arises by intent. For example, school superintendents sometimes purposely flood their school board members with reports and other documents, which, although completely accurate, are so voluminous it is impossible for the board members to know what is happening. As the board members struggle in vain to keep abreast of the swelling tide of information, the superintendent calmly proceeds to do pretty much whatever he or she wants to do.

Most overload problems, however, arise from sheer force of circumstance, and the circumstances that make for too much communication are increasing all the time. The growing complexity, specialization, and interdependence of today's organizational world are adding to the rising flood of information—a process being aided and abetted by the exponential growth of *communications technology.* An organization may take great care and achieve great success in developing excellent lines and flows of communication, only to sink under the profusion of information that may develop as a result.

Formal and Informal Communication

Communication falls into two basic and easily defined categories, formal and informal. *Formal communication is written communication; informal is oral.* Of course, not all informal communication is verbal. Attitudes and even ideas can be transmitted by means of inflection, gesture, and body language, but although nonverbal communication has a place in organizational life, its role is usually not great and, in any case, it is hard to analyze and define. Consequently, our discussion of informal communication will be directed toward verbal communication. What factors govern the use of one form of communication over the other? Under what conditions does formal communication take precedence over informal, and vice versa?

Usually, two factors foster the use of formal communication. One of these is *organizational size.* As organizations grow, they tend to make increasing use of formal communication and, correspondingly, diminishing use of informal. The other factor is *public character.* Public organizations tend to rely more heavily on formal communication than do private ones. A brief examination of the merits of formal communication will show why this is true.

Bureaucratic establishments are inclined to depend on written official documents that keep, process, and update images of reality. Organizations harbor and manage distrust so they rely on these papers, or the written word. Images must be shared and binding, and the way they are updated must be regulated. Organizations make and maintain what is called "papereality," a world of symbols or written representations that take precedence over the things and events they portray.[2]

The Advantages of the Paper Trail

Formal communication fosters *accountability*. This makes it indispensable for governmental affairs, particularly in a democracy. Unless the public and those who serve its information needs, such as the press and legislators, can find out what orders were given and who gave them, they cannot make the judgments needed to ensure a truly democratic government.

By facilitating accountability, formal communication places natural restraints on arbitrariness, capriciousness, favoritism, and discrimination. By proceeding on formal instructions and keeping records of their transactions, public officials find it much more difficult, although certainly not impossible, to depart from acceptable standards of impartiality and fairness. Of course, the rules and standards may be unfair, but if so, this is at least a matter of public record and can be easily determined. An administrator with integrity will welcome the opportunity to document his or her actions.

Formal communication in this way curbs the disparities and discrepancies that can occur even without express design. With all the good will in the world, distortions can and will creep in when formal communication is absent. Written communication allows everyone concerned to receive the same message and to check back if anyone is at any time uncertain as to what it says.

This brings us to still another asset of formal communication: It saves time. In any large organization, it would be difficult to issue all instructions orally. Not only would distortions occur as the message was relayed from person to person or group, but time would be needlessly consumed. Written communication allows an almost infinite number of people to receive the same message at the same time, and if these people forget any portions of it, they do not have to check back with the sender of the message, for they have it in front of them.

Finally, written communication not only helps to inform the recipient but may also do the same for the sender. By accumulating data in writing, the administrator encounters items that may have been overlooked. Expressing ideas in written form usually helps the person doing the writing to ferret out details previously disregarded and to see relationships and implications previously missed.

There are many good reasons the written word looms so large in the operations of government. We should bear them in mind when we discuss some of the less attractive aspects of written communication.

Proponents argue formal communication is:

- official and more binding and is more likely to be obeyed;
- written and more precise and less likely to be misunderstood;

Miscommunication about Incorrect Assumptions

Many government services are underused because the paperwork is complex and was designed without the appropriate audience in mind. Moreover, most people do not adequately read instructions. Government form compilers make incorrect assumptions concerning respondents' attitudes, ability, and knowledge. Compilers expect that respondents will read the whole form at a higher reading level than most possess, as well as assume an unavailable background knowledge. To make government programs more effective, reductions in the forms' complexity are necessary as well as changing the respondents attitudes toward reading instructions.

Source: Carel Jansen and Michael Steelhouder, *Journal of Technical Writing and Communication* 22, no. 2 (Spring 1992): 179–195.

- inscribed, so that it may be traced at any time and preserved for numerous distributions;
- official, and establishes responsibility of the sender and receiver beyond any doubt;
- routinized, saving time and efforts otherwise consumed in informal talks, discussions, and even arguments; and
- more definite, avoiding the embarrassment of the face-to-face contact between persons if the communication is sensitive or painful.[3]

The Disadvantages of the Paper Trail

Shortly after he was appointed Secretary of Housing and Urban Development, George Romney held a press conference and displayed a stack of paper that stood two-and-a-half feet high and weighed fifty-six pounds. This, he said, represented the paper generated by an application for a single urban renewal project.[4]

Although the problem, as Romney explained it, was caused more by faulty organization than by a sheer obsession with formal documents, it does illustrate that one of the ways in which organizational pathologies work is by generating a profusion of paper. The use of the written word tends to encourage its further use, and many a governmental and private organization have found themselves swamped in a *sea of documentation.*

Romney's display is only one of many incidents that have shed light on this startling problem. In a desperate effort to stem the ever-swelling flow, Congress enacted the Paperwork Reduction Act of 1980. This legislation gives the Office of Management and Budget near absolute authority to approve activities, such as requests for information, that would generate more paper. Sponsors of the Act claimed that a mere 1 percent reduction in bureaucratic paperwork would save the nation a billion dollars. The act also established the Federal Information Locator System to provide an index to information sources within the federal government. Such a system would, it was hoped, encourage federal agencies to share information and keep them from collecting data other agencies had already compiled.[5]

The main goal of the 1980 paperwork legislation was to reduce the public's paperwork burden by 25 percent. For example, paperwork for federal employment guidelines, defense procurement contracts, and even individual income tax forms was to be reduced. The result of the legislation, however, has been to enhance the

FIGURE 8.1 The Paper Trail.

Source: From "Congress or the White House: Who Controls the Agencies?" by Kitty Dumas, *Congressional Quarterly Weekly Report.* Copyright © 2002 by Congressional Quarterly Inc. Reproduced with permission of Congressional Quarterly Inc. in the format Textbook via Copyright Clearance Center.

power of the White House, especially the Office of Management and Budget (OMB), at the expense of the Congress. In the struggle for control of the regulatory process, the executive branch won this battle over the form and content of regulations issued by federal departments and agencies.

Members of Congress argue that they are empowered to oversee departments and agencies. Congressional committees use appropriations power to control decisions of executive agencies. OMB insists that the responsibility to determine if regulations are an unnecessary burden on the public belongs to the president. However, more than fifty years ago, Congress ceded statutory authority to the executive branch on what and how information was collected by the federal departments and agencies. The struggle between the two branches of government over the content and process of the regulatory paperwork continues. The formal communication process in this balance-of-powers debate creates a massive paper trail, as outlined in figure 8.1.

The states, too, have been moving ahead to abridge the rising tide of paperwork. Praiseworthy and productive as such steps may be, one must not forget that the growing crush of paper is in many respects a symptom of other organizational problems, not just a problem in itself. One frequent cause of excess paperwork is an insufficiency of delegation.

Some of the advantages of written communication lead to its abuse. If it promotes accountability, then it also fosters self-protection. People may put something in writing so that they cannot be accused of having done something improperly or so that they can point to the record later on and show where they were right.

Whatever the causes of paper profusion, its cost can be immense. Formal communication, by virtue of being formal, is less humane. It may have a dispiriting and even deadening effect on human relations.

Detractors argue that formal communication is

- too rigidly defined; it limits information within the department to that sanctioned by the chief executive or supervisor;
- codified by language; it may obscure the real meaning of communication, permit more than one interpretation, or be penned in cautious phraseology—sometimes recognized as "bureaucratic jargon";
- substantively superficial; it fails to identify the reasons for the message—causing the recipient consternation and frustration;
- costly in terms of secretarial efforts, reproduction costs, and delivery time;
- top-down; it reflects authoritarianism as the formal arrangement is based on the descent of executive information—not on the ascent of employee concerns;
- impersonal and final—failing to motivate employees;
- elementary and trivial; it devalues the intelligence of recipients; and
- divisive; it separates personnel into "recipients" and "nonrecipients."[6]

The Information Highway

Technology impacts modes of communication, formal and informal. In an era of faxes, computers, and photostat machines, communication challenges will emerge that are even more complex, demanding, and technical. Cell phones, e-mail, and telephone answering machines contribute to the narrowing of the gulf between formal and informal communication distinctions.

Technology is crucial in the development of the information highway that would link every home to a fiber-optic network over which voice, data, television, and other services would be transmitted. The internet's architecture is determined by an informal group of U.S.-based software and computer engineers. The internet's global scope and electronic commerce's growth make its management an international policy issue. Analysts and government believe a hands-off approach is best.[7]

People and organizations determine the course of the future, not computers. As a form of communication, the internet can be used by individuals, private corporations, and government agencies for good or bad, but it cannot influence the direction our society chooses to take. The internet only reflects the society that created it. The development and use of the telegraph and telephone provide a definitive pattern for how the newest form of networked communication, the internet, will be used in the future.[8]

The lack of accountability and civility have increased as the anonymity in U.S. society has increased, states newspaper columnist Ellen Goodman. She cites the anonymous zones of talk radio and cyberspace among the fox holes for people who want to say anything and everything with impunity.[9]

Despite the downside of the information highway, internet access has made communication between local government and citizens much easier nationwide. Public records access, personnel postings, permit applications, and legislative updates are available online in dozens of cities and counties.[10]

The technology of the internet may afford the masses access to much more information and many more options. Internet technology is neither evil nor good. "Thanks to the internet and satellite TV, the world is being wired together technologically, but not socially, politically, or culturally," concludes *New York Times* columnist Thomas L. Friedman. "We are now seeing and hearing one another faster and better, but with no corresponding improvement in our ability to learn from, or understand, one another. So integration, at this stage, is producing more anger than anything else."[11]

The internet educates people faster than any previous technology the world has known. However, the internet can just as easily infiltrate the minds of millions with lies, half-truths, and hatreds. "The internet," says Friedman, "at its ugliest, is just an open sewer: an electronic conduit for untreated, unfiltered information." The internet and satellite TV may inflame emotions and cultural biases, resulting in less understanding and tolerance. Government programs are built on political consensus. Legislation is enacted for the long term. Compromises are based on education, exchanges, diplomacy, and human interaction.

Advances in the use of information technology (IT) and the internet continue to change the way that federal agencies communicate, use, and disseminate information, deliver services, and do business. Electronic government (e-government) refers to the use of technology, particularly web-based internet applications.

The World Wide Web—the Internet—as Community?

Is the internet public or private? The World Wide Web is not the domain of any government or group of governments. The internet functions informally, as a worldwide community of communicators. Is that communication formal or informal? Employ the delete button, and poof—your copy disappears into cyberspace. But if you print your copy, the informality of the internet becomes formalized by paper and ink.

The internet was originally formed in 1969 as a military network at the Department of Defense (DOD). The early cyberspace version was called the Advanced Research Projects Agency network (ARPAnet). Nonmilitary users were given access to the network in the 1970s. Universities and companies doing defense-related research came on board first. The WWW began to flourish as most universities and many businesses around the world came online. In 1989, Tim Berners-Lee proposed the World Wide Web project. This endeavor is credited with bringing the internet to the masses. In 1991, commercial providers began selling internet connections to individuals, and WWW usage exploded. A new era of computer communications began.

Founded in 1985 as Quantum Computer Services, American Online officially became AOL in 1989. By 1993, AOL had 500,000 members; by 1997, 9 million; by 2001, 21 million. The history of internet servers encompasses more than merely connections between computers; the purpose is to connect people. In this perspective, AOL is a very large unincorporated world community.

Source: See American Online, http://www.aol.com/nethelp/misc/history.html.

Employers and E-Mail

Most people are introduced to e-mail and internet access in the workplace. It's in the workplace that they discover, too often, a lesser-known aspect of this exceptionally fluid and informal form of communication: *It has no guarantee of privacy.* For reasons that have occasioned much armchair psychological speculation, most of those new to e-mail seem to act as if they had a high expectation of privacy—indeed, as if they are talking to intimate friends. E-mailers also frequently blurt out things electronically that would never be said face-to-face.

Source: "Employers and E-mail," *The Washington Post,* April 18, 1998, p. 18A.

Informal Communication

Oral communication offers a solution to many of the problems encountered in written communication. It does not flood the office worker's desk or clog the files. It can evoke immediate feedback, which, in turn, can lead to a resolution of issues or clarification of misunderstood points. In the process, the one communicating can be assured that his or her information has been received. Speaking and listening permit shading, emphasis, and gesture. Conversation is also significantly more human and often more humane. People are dealing together directly.

Efforts have long been underway to substitute oral for written communication. President Johnson's task force on cutting red tape, for example, urged federal officials to make more extensive use of the telephone and less use of "time-consuming written communications."[12] It is possible that the use of oral communication will grow apace in governmental agencies, although it will most likely never replace formal communication. For reasons noted earlier, the written word and the printed document will probably continue to serve as the mainstay of the communications process in any developed democracy.

Grapevines

Any agency that has an informal organization will also have an informal communications system, often referred to as the "grapevine." Informal organizations are found in almost all organizations; therefore, grapevines are ubiquitous.

The "grapevine," or informal communication network in government organizations, can have negative effects such as resentment, embarrassment for upper-level administrators, distorted messages, rumor diffusion, and subversion of administrative decision making. Grapevines develop when employees share common hobbies, lunch schedules, families ties, common hometowns, and social relationships. These informal networks operate quickly, often accurately, and with resilience. It is suggested that management should use the network for its own purposes to complement formal networks. Administrators should also be candid about information if possible.[13]

Grapevines can also be terribly efficient. "With the rapidity of a burning powder train," says Keith Davis, a professor of management who has studied grapevines for years, "information flows out of the woodwork, past the manager's door and the janitor's mop closet, through steel walls or construction-glass partitions."[14] What is more, Davis claims, over three-fourths of this information is accurate.

Even when it is not accurate, says Davis, the grapevine may convey a psychological truth, for many rumors that run rampant through an organization are "symbolic expressions of feelings." If the rumor is that a certain employee is planning to quit, it may reflect the wish on the part of fellow employees that he or she would quit. Or it may reflect the employee's own desire to leave.

Proponents argue that informal communication is:

- less official, less intimidating, and that it enhances the new flow of ideas and solicits plans without fear or punishment;
- personal, and that it embraces enthusiasm, reflects the zeal of the participants, and plays down the relevance of dry, bureaucratic logic;
- usually verbal, and that it allows informal communication, permits exploration of hidden dimensions of government organization, and facilitates two-way communications;
- revealing of underlying motives and pressures, and that it promotes an atmosphere of free, yet discreet, discussions, and explains to employees why the department works the way it does;
- better at refuting rumors and putting an end to office gossip filtering through the formal environment, complete with unanswered questions;
- reflective of a spirit of comraderie which unites workers by the discovery of shared concerns and interests; and
- able to sustain a harmonious relationship between officers and their superiors—promoting cooperation based on mutual understanding and concern.

Detractors argue that informal communication is:

- difficult to define or apply in systematic ways;
- inaccurate, and that it spreads half-truths and may result in second-and-third-source information being represented as original, factual, and trustworthy;
- indiscriminate and may disclose classified information;
- emotional, and that it distorts or changes meaning and fits the personal sentiments of the bearer;
- verbal and difficult to trace, and that it makes further inquiry problematic; and
- of questionable social advantage, as it is only as constructive as participants deem it to be.[15]

Formal communication—certainly historic and more traditional—functions as a means of controlling agency activities. Authoritative policies and procedures circulate among personnel. Formal specifications state what is to be done when, where, how, and by whom. Formal communication allows the organization to "track" issues through organization "channels."

Organizations are groupings of social beings, however. A certain amount of informal and personal communication occurs within the ranks. Participants seek the "right" mixtures of informal and formal communications. No magic formula exists for arriving at this mixture. A proper blend of formal and informal communications depends upon participants and organization leaders.

The organization's environment and the needs of personnel—along with the maturity and intelligence of leaders—determine the appropriateness of a given mixture of informal and formal communications. Informal communications—in a trustworthy language—may supplement the formal structure. In this fashion, workers are reassured, improve their attitudes, and deepen their commitments to the department.[16]

E-Government and Communications

E-government seeks to improve relationships between the private citizen and public sector services. This mostly informal, sometimes formal, application of government includes every technology from fax machines to wireless Palm Pilots. E-government is not exclusively an internet-driven activity. Cost-effective and efficient, e-government enhances citizens access to government information, services, and expertise. Five guiding principles ensure citizen participation in—and satisfaction with—the governing process:

- Building services around citizens' choices
- Making government and its services more accessible
- Promoting inclusive social relations
- Providing information in responsible fashion
- Using human resources effectively and efficiently[17]

E-government, then, is not "just putting government online. It is changing the way agencies interact with citizens, businesses and federal employees as they perform the government's business."[18] The demands for more effective government services increase as the days pass. E-government initiatives keep pace as government leaders and employees search for innovations to meet the demands.

Effective communications are vital to the well-being of American democracy and bureaucracy. Commitments to government-online systems lead to:

1. *Connected governments,* or improved communications and information management between federal, state, and local governments—and nongovernmental organizations.
2. *Connected communities,* or online integrated services readily available and conveniently accessed twenty-four hours a day, seven days a week, delivered to homes, businesses, and other locations by the internet and media.
3. *Connected people,* or effective and efficient electronic communication used by elected leaders, government officials, agencies, and the community at large.[19]

What do citizens say they want from electronic government services? Peter D. Hart and Robert M. Teeter surveyed 1,003 citizens; 150 government officials in federal, state, and local governments; and 155 institutional customers of government in the business and nonprofit sectors about the potential uses of e-government services, the benefits of e-government, how quickly e-government develops, and what concerns them about the digital divide. Issues of mobility, voting, and recreation were at the top of their lists, including:

- Driver's license renewal
- Voter registration

- State park information and reservations
- Internet voting
- Access to one-stop shopping (one portal for all government services)
- Birth, death, and marriage certificate retrieval
- State tax filing
- Hunting and fishing licenses
- Accessing medical information from the National Institute of Health[20]

The Other Organization

Organizational charts and manuals of procedure rarely provide us with an accurate picture of an organization. What is not official or even readily visible may often be the most important. Even the most formal organizations, which pride themselves on going strictly "by the book," rarely do so. An informal system of authority, which supersedes, at least to some extent, the formal one, may arise. In the army, for example, the lieutenant clearly outranks the sergeant. But when the sergeant has had twenty years of army service and the lieutenant is fresh from a college Reserve Officers Training Program (ROTC), the sergeant, rather than the lieutenant, may end up running the platoon.

Communication also frequently flows through informal channels. The office grapevine is usually faster and more complete than the office memo. Aboard a ship, for example, the real communications center is often not the captain's office, but the kitchen or galley, and navy cooks are usually better sources of news than commanding officers. This is how the term "scuttlebutt" came to have its current meaning. The informal organization may spawn a network of relationships for which the organization chart and the manual of procedure provide few clues.

One of the most extreme examples of how the informal organization can overwhelm the formal organization is the U.S. prison system. Ostensibly, prisons are run by wardens and correction officers according to prescribed rules and regulations. In practice, this has rarely been the case. Sociologists and criminologists who have studied prisons have found out that most prisons have traditionally been run by the prisoners.[21]

In most cases, the informal organization does not loom so large on the administrative scene, and its role should not be overstressed. It usually colors the formal organization but does not radically alter it. No matter how expert and experienced a sergeant may be, and no matter how naive and nervous the lieutenant may be, it is the lieutenant and not the sergeant who bears the final responsibility for the platoon. There is a limit as to how much authority the sergeant can acquire and how much the lieutenant can abdicate. Nevertheless, informal elements influence the operation of nearly all organizations, and the administrator must be alert as to what these elements are and what they do.

There are two aspects of informal organization that merit special attention. One concerns the role of *informal rules;* the other concerns the role of *small groups.*

Whose Rules?

Employees of organizations, like citizens of nations, tend to obey only those rules they believe in. Workers will accept a rule only if they regard it as legitimate in terms of their values. They will not accept it just because those who issued it had a legal right to do so.

Employees have also become adept at evading rules or bending them to suit their needs and desires, and the more rules the organization tends to set down, the more dexterity its members may show. The informal organization not only achieves frequent and sometimes spectacular success in sabotaging the formal organization's rules, but it also manages to establish and enforce rules of its own. Many of these rules concern work output. Those who exceed the informal quota may be branded as "ratebusters," while those who fail to carry their fair share of the load may earn the title of "slacker" or "chiseler." Seniority is another rule that governs many procedures of many informal organizations. Those with job seniority get the better assignments and more congenial conditions. The most junior members may not only get the less desirable assignments, but may also experience various petty harassments, like being sent to fetch the "left-handed monkey wrench." Sometimes the harassment is not so petty. College fraternities' hazing rituals have resulted in injuries and occasional deaths.

Probably no informal rule is more widespread than the ban on "squealing." This prohibition is instilled in most Americans during their school years and tends to stay with them the rest of their lives. The taboo against "tattling" is so widely and deeply ingrained that even those who would stand to benefit from it tend to dislike it. The "informer" or "spotter," no matter how useful he or she may be, rarely wins esteem in the eyes of management, and though the informer may increase his or her earnings, "squealing" seldom enhances one's chances for promotion.

While the formal organization often encounters difficulty in enforcing its rules, the informal organization usually succeeds in securing support and adherence to its own codes of behavior. Sanctions against offenders can take many forms, not excluding violence.

Many informal rules are benign. While the *golden rule* remains an unattainable goal, it has become a nearly universal governing principle and, as such, governs a good deal of organizational behavior. If people do not naturally love their neighbors as themselves, they do tend to help others who have helped them, or at least try to refrain from injuring them.

The Small Group

The basic unit for the formal organization may be the division, the department, the section, or all three, plus others. The primary basis for the informal organization is usually the small group. Although many informal norms and rules apply organizationwide, many others are promulgated and enforced by small work groups. The small group consists of no set number of individuals. Rather, it designates any group whose members are in continual, face-to-face contact with each other. Such groups often follow the structural lines of the formal organization. The small group in the army infantry is typically the squad. In the university, it is usually the department. Whether it conforms to any formally recognized structure, forces from within customarily dictate a good deal of its behavior.

The importance of the small group springs chiefly from the importance of primary relationships over secondary relationships in human behavior. Those people we work with every day invariably become more important to us than those whom we see infrequently or with whom we conduct relations at a distance. Out of such primary relationships come norms, codes, procedures, and the means for their enforcement. The famed "silent treatment" is most powerfully exercised on those with whom we are in daily contact.

Such are the workings of small groups and informal organizations.

The Informal Balance Sheet

The informal organization and the small groups that make it up can do a great deal of damage. They may, and often do, subvert the purposes of the organization, because they show a persistent tendency to do what is most congenial to their members and reject organizational endeavors that may conflict with their own basic goals.

The informal organization can not only make things difficult for the formal organization, but it can also make things difficult for its members. Not only are the ratebusters or the chiselers usually punished, but sanctions may also be invoked against the member who dresses differently, who espouses radical views, or who in any way speaks or acts in a manner that marks him or her as different.

Sometimes the informal organization acts in an entirely opposite way, but this can prove even more counterproductive to organizational goals. It may cover up for one or more of its members who fail to do what is expected. Such practices harm not only the organization but also the individual, because they permit the person to avoid confronting his or her problem and trying to resolve it. The sense of team loyalty that the informal organization fosters can generate a variety of evils.

The informal organization also has a positive role to play, and organizational theorists are coming to accept and avow this:[22]

> The incompleteness of the formal plan provides a vacuum which, like other vacuums, proves abhorrent to nature. (Simon, Smithburg, and Thompson)

> No organization chart and no book of policies and procedures can specify every act and prescribe for every contingency encountered in a complex organization. To attempt such specification merely produces an array of instructions so ponderous that they are ignored for the sake of transacting the business of the organization. Moreover, even if such specifications could be provided, they would soon be out of date. . . . (Katz and Kahn)

> It would not, in any sense, be an exaggeration to assert that any large organization would come to a grinding halt within a month if all its members began behaving strictly in accordance with the structure of responsibility and authority defined by the formal organization chart, the position description, and formal controls. (McGregor)

> Reduced to its formal power, to the theoretical pact which constitutes it, every organization, every human enterprise is incapable of adapting itself to its environment. (Crozier)

What these writers are saying is: *The formal organization cannot exist without its informal counterpart.* All organizational design is inevitably incomplete and imperfect, for there is too much complexity and variability in the interaction of human beings ever to be compressed into a formal system.

As employees come and go, as new technologies develop and new problems arise, the formal plans and procedures, no matter how well designed, become increasingly outmoded. Periodic revamping can help, but it can never hope to keep pace with the rate and sweep of the changes that affect organizational operations. Consequently, the facts of organizational life frequently become the unofficial rules and procedures.

If the seasoned sergeant does exercise more authority than the neophyte lieutenant, then undoubtedly many a soldier's life has been saved because of it. Young ROTC lieutenants used to be told, "Be good to your sergeant lest he carry out every order you give." If small groups tend to call the shots as they see them, at least they often see them much better than does top management.

This brings us to the question of how the informal organization affects organizational productivity. You have read several ways in which it can sabotage and subvert organizational goals. However, it can also do the reverse. Informal work-group norms can affect productivity in a positive way. The correlation between informal group norms and productivity is likely to go in the way the organization would like it to go.[23]

The small group has an important role in the informal organization. Research indicates that the larger the work unit, the greater the absenteeism and accidents. Small groups meet social and emotional needs, and such needs remain important for organizational purposes.

The ultimate aim is to make the formal and the informal organization merge. Can this be achieved? According to Chris Argyris, informal organization results from the desires of organization members to satisfy needs that the formal organization neglects or even thwarts.[24]

Upward, Downward, and Across Communications

Information in government agencies moves in three basic directions:

- upward from subordinate to superior,
- downward from superior to subordinate, and
- horizontally from one organizational unit to another.

No matter which way it flows, however, it runs into problems.

Communicating Upward

According to Katz and Kahn, communication up the line may occur in many forms, but such information may be reduced to what the person says

1. about himself, his performance, and his problems;
2. about others and their problems;
3. about organizational practices and policies; and
4. about what needs to be done and how it can be done.[25]

The basic problem of upward communication is the nature of the hierarchical administrative structure because the first role requirement of executives and supervisors is to direct, coordinate, and control the activities of persons below them. Therefore, employees fear that information passed along the hierarchical chain of command may be used for control purposes. The employees are unlikely to pass along information that may affect them adversely. This concern makes the upward route the most difficult.

Upward communication networks are an important way for government employees to relay information to line officials. A functioning network can

- facilitate quick and efficient upper-level administrative feedback;
- use government employee skills, knowledge, and expertise;
- communicate unique, yet valuable, information;
- improve public sector employee morale.

Employees may have personal reasons for withholding or manipulating information. They may fear that the action such information would produce would prove disadvantageous to their interests. Or, if others stand a chance of being adversely affected, they may be fearful of being cast in the role of the informer. This particular problem in upward communication reflects problems inherent in hierarchy. Information received from a low-status person, notes Chester Barnard, will often receive scant attention, while information received from a high-status person may set off a reaction well beyond what was intended.[26]

A superior is supposed to give orders and a subordinate is supposed to receive them. Upward communication goes against the organizational grain, for the subordinate is not used to telling things to the superior, and the superior is not used to listening to things from the subordinate.[27]

Unplugging the Upward Flow

Perhaps the most important step an administrator can take in resolving or at least reducing these impediments to the upward passage of information lies in his or her own conduct. If he or she acts on the belief that information should move swiftly and surely upward, then the information is much more likely to do so. If he or she shows subordinates that the bad news should be passed along with the good, and in as fresh and pure a form as possible, subordinates will not only be more inclined to do so, but will also be more likely to deal with their own subordinates in the same way.

In an organization of any size and complexity, however, this will not be enough. Fortunately, there are other ways and means of seeing to it that those above are kept adequately informed by those below.

Other means for improving the upward information flow include formal devices for hearing complaints. These may include grievance committees, appeals boards, and various clientele service units. Investigatory units can also prove helpful in this regard.

An executive can also disregard the chain of command on occasion and call someone several levels below for some direct conversation. An executive may also stipulate a period each week or month when the office door will be open to anyone within the organization who has a matter to discuss. Surveys and polls of the organization's members and of its clients may also provide valuable information in addition to indications as to how the upward communications process is working.

There are, in short, many means available to ensure an upward flow of communication. Any public manager who wants an undistorted picture of what is going on in the organization should experience no trouble in obtaining it.

Communicating Downward

According to Katz and Kahn, there are five varieties of communications down the line, from superior to subordinate:

1. Specific task directives: job instructions
2. Information designed to produce understanding of the task and its relationship to other organizational tasks: job rationale
3. Information about organizational procedures and practices
4. Feedback to the subordinate about his or her performance.
5. Information of an ideological character to inculcate a sense of mission: indoctrination of goals.[28]

While downward communication is less problematic than upward, communication down the line nevertheless encounters numerous obstacles and impediments. When it is oral, downward communication is subject to almost all the alterations that can creep in when communication moves upward.

When downward communication is written, difficulties may develop. The message may not be complete, or the recipient may not be willing to accept it. The biggest problem, however, is probably the inability or the refusal of the recipient to absorb the information that seems to be cascading downward. Memoranda senders encounter persistent problems in this respect.

Organizations have tried to surmount this difficulty in many ways. People will often read material on bulletin boards that they might ignore if it is placed in their agency mail slots. This is particularly true if the bulletin board also carries other information besides that which emanates from the front office. Consequently, a notice placed on a bulletin board can score a greater impact than if it were sent individually to each organization member.

Another useful device is the organization publication or house organ. Such publications usually depend for their appeal on the reporting of a wide range of personal items within the organization.

Whatever the means used, the astute public administrator will develop techniques for making sure that the information he or she has sent has gotten through to those for whom it is intended, and the manager will check for feedback from employees. Not infrequently, the way in which a decision has been communicated will have a greater effect on agency operations than the substance of the decision.

Cross-Communication

According to Katz and Kahn, communication among peers, in addition to providing task coordination, also furnishes emotional and social support to the individual. The mutual understanding of colleagues is one reason for the power of the peer group. Psychological forces always push people toward communication with peers; people in the same boat share the same problems.

On the other hand, if there are no problems of task coordination left to a group of peers, the content of their communication can take forms irrelevant or destructive to the organization's functioning.[29] The communication channels become dysfunctional if line officials in the organizational hierarchy are charged with initiating all communications. The agency softball team or annual picnic, for examples, should be informal arrangements where someone other than the line officials communicate directions.

Staff meetings can be particularly helpful in stimulating cross-communication. This assumes of course, that they are genuine interchanges of ideas and data, and not just monologues by the person who presides. Within a broader context, interdepartmental committees may also aid the lateral communications process. And house organs, bulletin boards, and many of the other devices already cited can, and usually do, aid in spreading information from one section of the organization to another.

Physical arrangements can also play an important role in either helping or hampering cross-communication. Organizational practices designed to resolve other problems may foster cross-communication as well. In-service training, for example, may bring people from various parts of the organization together and result in a good deal of cross-communication. Organization-wide activities, such as bowling teams or hobby clubs, and an organizationally run cafeteria or dining room will also bring employees together and may lead to an interchange of information.

Rotation of employees is also useful in improving cross-communication. The rotated employee can give new coworkers a better understanding of how things operate "over there." More importantly, these new relationships can be used to maintain some communication flow with the employee's former work unit. In any case, the rotated employee is likely to meet ex-colleagues from time to time and fill them in on what is happening at the new assignment.

Summary

- Administrators and administrative theorists place increasing emphasis on communication.
- Communication problems arise not only from information that is too slow, incomplete, or distorted, but also from information that is too abundant. This is a problem of communication overload.
- Communication falls into two basic categories— formal and informal. Formal communication is written. Informal communication is oral. Formal communication fosters accountability, while informal communication does not produce mounds of paperwork.
- Formal communication restrains arbitrariness, capriciousness, favoritism, and discrimination.
- Organizational size and public character are factors affecting the use of formal communication.
- Among the symptoms of organizational pathology is the generation of a profusion of paper—a set of documents.
- The paper trail includes the regulatory department or agency, the office of Management and Budget (OMB), public notice and comment, and codification of the rule in first the *Federal Register* and finally the *Code of Federal Regulations.*
- The informal communications system is often referred to as the "grapevine."
- Organizations are groupings of social beings. A certain amount of informal and personal communication occurs within the ranks. Participants seek the "right" mixture of informal and formal communications.

- The internet educates people faster than any previous technology that the world has known. The internet is neither evil nor good.
- The internet was originally formed in 1969 as a military network at the Department of Defense (DOD). The early cyberspace version was called the Advanced Research Projects Agency Network (ARPAnet).
- Upward communication focuses on the employee, his or her performance, and problems; others and their problems; organizational practices and policies; and what needs to be done and how it can be done.
- Information moves in three basic directions: upward from subordinate to superior, downward from superior to subordinate, and horizontally from one organizational unit to another.
- Downward communication includes job instructions, job rationale, information about organizational procedures and practices, feedback to the subordinate about his or her performance, and indoctrination of goals.
- The growth of specialization and interdependency is making it increasingly vital for information to flow through the organization as well as to move up and down its ranks.
- Informal organization is more important in determining worker cooperation than formal organization. In this "other organization," the output is set by social norms, not individual abilities, and the group greatly influences the behavior of individual workers.
- Employees of organizations, like citizens of nations, tend to obey those rules they believe in.
- The importance of the small group is based upon the centrality of primary relationships over secondary relationships in human behavior.

Case Study

Communicator par Excellence

If any single leader—experienced in partisan, policy, and system politics—in the history of the modern era knew the importance of formal and informal communications, that person had to be Winston Churchill. Churchill, British war-time Prime Minister, was a communicator par excellence.

> I say to the House [of Commons] as I said to ministers who have joined this government, I have nothing to offer but blood, toil, tears, and sweat.
>
> *—Winston Churchill*
> *Prime Minister of Great Britain, May 13, 1940*

The bombs were falling on London day and night. The Luftwaffe, the air force of Nazi Germany, kept returning. The Battle of Britain was in high gear, and the British people lived in mortal fear: The German invasion of the British Isles appeared imminent. The Nazis planned to occupy Britain. At this point, the British had no allies—France had fallen and was occupied by the Nazis—and Britain stood alone. The United States had not yet entered the war. The British organized an effective air defense against the Luftwaffe planes.

Winston Churchill, British Prime Minister, refused to agree to Adolf Hitler's offers of "peace." Churchill and the British military forces opened a second front against the Nazi alliance—striking against Italy's Mussolini. The second-front idea was that of a military genius—one of the boldest strategic decisions in history. Hitler was both humiliated and infuriated. Churchill's military, political, and rhetorical skills, plus his grasp of history, led some British citizens to call him "the greatest living Englishman."[1]

Churchill was a man of wealth, privilege, and connections who came to identify with democracy— while hating tyranny and dictators during a most fascinating life of ninety years. His father was English, his mother American; he was a soldier, a gifted man, energetic, charming, egotistical, overbearing; a husband, father, writer, artist, and politician; a passionate world leader; an articulate champion of democracy; a fighter against evil, a risk-taker, and a communicator par excellence.[2]

Churchill was born in 1874 and died in 1965. He witnessed many events that occurred in between. He took a leading part in serving in the Indian army in the 1897 Malakand expedition, reporting on the 1899 South African War; he became a member of Parliament in 1901 for Oldham (Lancashire) as a Conservative, laying the foundations for the British welfare state and preparing the Royal Navy for World War I. He was involved in settling the political boundaries in the Middle East after the first war, eventually emerging as British Prime Minister on May 10, 1940. As Prime Minister, Churchill defended the British Isles against invasion from Hitler and Nazi Germany, building an alliance with the United States and losing his job in July 1945 as the Labour Party won a large majority in Parliament. He later warned the West against the Soviet Union's aims and the aggrandizement of communism.

Formal and Informal Communications

If any single leader—experienced in partisan, policy, and system politics—in the history of the modern era knew the importance of formal and informal communications, that person had to be Winston Churchill. He spoke and wrote for a living. He was profoundly historically minded, had prophetic foresight, received the Nobel Prize in literature, and was the ultimate master of oratory.

By November 12, 1940, prospects for a Nazi invasion were receding. Churchill wrote a memo that carried the prestige of 10 Downing Street. He shunned the use of first names. The Prime Minister noticed that Private Secretaries often addressed each other by their Christian names when writing about matters of an official character. These informal habits were increasing, or so he perceived, and he thought they ought to be stopped. First names should only be used in brief notes, Churchill reasoned, or in personal and private communications.

But Churchill could not control what had become part of the administrative culture. During the war, King George VI often wrote to the British Prime Minister, affectionately addressing him as "My dear Winston." Churchill's objection to informality among officials found practical application. "It is hard enough to follow people by their surnames," he concluded. By the end of his ninety years on Planet Earth, informality had become even more common in government settings. It was no longer realistic to expect to be addressed by last names—with or without a Mister. The use of first names was common.[3]

In any event, Churchill placed great importance on communication—especially in time of war. During World War II, Prime Minister Churchill wrote a memo to the First Lord of the Admiralty that stated: "Pray state this day—on one side of a sheet of paper—how the Royal Navy is being adapted to meet the conditions of modern warfare." The request asked for brevity—on a single-sided page. By indicating he wanted the reply on one side of the page, Churchill was insisting on a clear, concise, to-the-point reply.

Formal communication, such as personal memoranda, permitted Churchill to personally direct much of Britain's governmental activity. He employed his well-known verbal communication skills to inspire the British people during their darkest hours. His attempts at formal communication included *The World Crisis* (four volumes, 1923–1929), *The Second World War* (six volumes, 1948–1953), and *A History of the English-Speaking Peoples* (four volumes, 1956–1958).

Churchill nourished communications with persons in the lower ranks, he did not spend time talking to higher-ups; he kept downward communication lines continually open. As Robin Maugham writes, "Throughout the war, Churchill was more interested in talking to junior officers than to the top brass—partly from pure kindness, partly from his knowledge that it was from the men in the field that he could discover what was really going on."[4]

Maugham was a tank corps lieutenant during the war. He recalls how Churchill asked him after the fall of France if he and his fellows were ready to repel a German invasion. When Maugham replied that many tanks could not move for want of a spring in their trackpins, Churchill exploded in anger—and immediately set the whole British government into action. By nightfall, the springs had been delivered and were in place.

Words always came easily to Winston Churchill. As a young man, he engaged in many daring exploits while serving as a lieutenant with British forces in India and later in South Africa. It was not so much the tours, however, but his skill in writing about them that gained him the prominence that was to win him a seat in Parliament and commence his political career.

Churchill emphasized the written word. "Let it be very clearly understood," he informed his war cabinet, "that all directions emanating from me are made in writing, or should be immediately afterwards confirmed in writing, and that I do not accept any responsibility for matters relating to national defense on which I am alleged to have given decisions unless they are recorded in writing."[5]

War Bureaucracy = Crisis Management Administration

A war bureaucracy is a crisis-management administration and can lead to considerable confusion. Orders given in a hurry and quickly passed down can easily be misunderstood—with dire results. Orders that are vital may go unheeded or become lost in the far-flung and fast-moving governmental machinery. Churchill wanted none of that. He had no problem with the written word. He used this mode to keep intermediaries at a minimum and to stay in direct touch with vast numbers of people.

Written communication—and the discipline it imposed—prevented Churchill from getting carried away by whims. He made a point never to give orders that were not confirmed in writing.

The profuse stream of memoranda issued from his office signified his distinct personal style. He usually opened with the phrase, "Pray tell me . . ." These phrases were by no means literary extravaganzas. He could be remarkably concise, as when he once ordered the mass production of a controversial new weapon. His memo read, "Sticky bombs—make one million—WSC." As he once noted, "It is sheer laziness not compressing information in a reasonable space."[6]

Churchill bitterly denounced Britain's appeasement towards Hitler and the Nazis during the 1930s. "These are the years when the locust has eaten," he said as he described these awful times. As Prime Minister during the war, he warmed the hearts and rallied the spirits of his fellow Britons. He delivered stirring speeches in what he called "England's darkest hour."[7]

Through formal communication, Churchill personally directed much of Britain's governmental activity. He retained for himself the Cabinet post of Minister of Defense. Wearing two hats in the Cabinet did not cause Churchill to impede Britain's efforts. Most accounts of Britain's history indicate that the country survived quite well with the Prime Minister acting in a dual capacity.

Personal memoranda, all of which carried the imprint of Churchill's personal style with his signature or initials, had an invigorating impact on the entire government. An official several ranks below might find a message from the Prime Minister. In the words of Cabinet Secretary Lord Normanbrook, these messages often had a "startling effect."

Churchill insisted that subordinates follow the same policy in reporting to him. He spent little time interviewing people. Instead, they were to address him in writing. All such correspondence was put in a box. He reviewed the paperwork at the start or end of the day, or at moments through the day. When a crisis erupted, he rarely canceled his personal appointments.

Rules of Brevity

Churchill demanded that those addressing him adhere to the rules of brevity—as he did himself. He was particularly aware of needless banalities and truisms. On one occasion, he replied to an official's memo by pointing out that this chap employed every cliché in the English language except the British men's room admonition, "Please adjust your dress before leaving."

Churchill did not disdain the spoken word. He reserved verbal communications for times when they could be used effectively. He encouraged spirited discussions in meetings, at least at the start of his governance. He urged anyone having a dissenting viewpoint to "Fight your corner." When one attendee once remarked, "I have tried to present my case fairly," Churchill replied, "That's a very dangerous thing to do."[8]

Despite his personal ways, Churchill did not neglect that traditional British device—the committee. He frequently created one group to provide information and then established a second group to supply advice on what action to take with the information.

In informal communication modes, Churchill often gave dinner parties or after-dinner gatherings with some of the best minds both within and without the government for stimulating, if rambling, conversations. These gatherings became known as "Midnight Follies." Churchill's guests often stayed into the early hours of the morning. These informal gatherings originated many ideas that filtered through his administration.

Dysfunctions of Style?

Churchill had dysfunctions in his communication style. He frequently attempted to take on too much; consequently, he neglected many things. Matters that were of no or little interest cluttered his in-box. His personality too easily dominated any meeting at which he presided. Toward the end of the war, he was less receptive to ideas from others in the coalition Cabinet. The Labour Party ministers protested that his Cabinet meetings were becoming monologues.

Churchill remained open to scientific and technical advice. However, war weariness set in. He became infatuated with his own way of doing things. He listened too exclusively to his own science adviser—and failed to consult other scientists. He ordered, on the basis of false data, the rather fruitless and possibly even counterproductive saturation-bombing raids on Germany.

In Britain's war bureaucracy, Churchill dealt with communication overload, communication technologies, personal accountability, "seas" of documentation, grapevines, channels, rules, small groups, languages, and downward-lateral-upward communications in his extensive public service career. Government employees encounter similar obstacles in the twenty-first century.

Did Churchill's communication style match the circumstances of his times? His communication policy reflected his leadership policy. Both reflected Churchill's persona. From Churchill's wartime leadership, Britain and its government found a new spirit, resolve, and will. Formal communication cannot exist without its informal counterpart.

Questions and Instructions

1. How are communication modes reflective of a leader's personal style? What did Prime Minister Winston Churchill's communication style say about his approach to communicating effectively? Explain.
2. Why did Churchill place so much emphasis upon formal communications?
3. How and when did Churchill employ informal communications as Minister of Defense?
4. How did Churchill avoid communication overload?
5. Were Churchill's communications mostly downward, across, or upward? Explain.
6. How did Churchill evaluate downward communication?
7. Why did Churchill shy away from most modes of informal communication during his war administration?
8. Was Churchill a less humane person because of his penchant for formal, written communications? Explain.
9. Churchill was truly a "romantic," but also truly a "democrat." Explain this dichotomy.

Insights-Issues/Communicator par Excellence

Clearly and briefly describe and illustrate these concepts and issues. Interpret the word *role* as meaning impacts, applications, importance, effects, and/or illustrations of certain facts, concerns, or issues from the case study.

1. Role of formal communication for enhancing administrative effectiveness.
2. Role of informal communication for enhancing administrative effectiveness.
3. Role of persona, personality, and/or personal style in developing communication approaches.
4. Role of communication overload and/or "sea of documentation" in effecting communication.
5. Role of two aspects of Churchill's character: a literary bent and an interest in public affairs.

Case Endnotes

1. John Keegan, "Time 100: Leaders and Revolutionaries: Winston Churchill," http://www.time.com/time/time100/leaders/profile/churchill.html.
2. "Winston Churchill," http://gi.grolier.com/wwii/wwii_churchill.html.
3. George Watson, "Call Me Mister," *The Wilson Quarterly,* http://wwics.si.edu/OUTREACH/WQ/WQSELECT/WATSON.HTM.
4. Robert Maugham, *Escape from the Shadows* (New York: McGraw-Hill, 1973), pp. 108–109.
5. Sir John Wheeler-Bennett, ed., *Action This Day: Working with Churchill; Memoirs of Lord Normanbrook and Others* (New York: St. Martin's Press, 1969).
6. *Ibid.*
7. *Ibid.*
8. *Ibid.*

Case Sources

"The Freshman Experience: Sir Winston Churchill (1874–1965),"
http://www2.gasou.edu/facstaff/drhrw/leader-bio-w-churchill.html; Walter
Russell Mead, "The Liberal Lion," *Foreign Affairs,* May/June, 2002;

http://www.foreignaffairs.org/20020501faessay8065/ walter-russell-mead/the-
liberal-lion.html.

Chapter Endnotes

1. David K. Berlo, *The Process of Communication: An Introduction to Theory and Practice* (New York: Holt, Rinehart, & Winston, 1960), pp. 23–24; Harold F. Gortner, Julianne Mahler, and Jeanne Bell Nicholson, *Organization Theory: A Public Perspective,* 2nd ed. (Fort Worth, Tex.: Harcourt Brace, 1997), pp. 135–141.

2. David Dery, " 'Paperreality' and Learning in Bureaucratic Organizations," *Administration & Society* 29, no. 6 (January 1998): 677–690.

3. See http://www.ualr.edu/dllaufferswei/cj3306/formalcomm.html.

4. Frederick V. Malek, "Executive in Washington," *Harvard Business Review* (September–October 1972): 63–68.

5. *Public Administration Times,* January 15, 1981.

6. See http://www.ualr.edu/dllanferswei/cj3306/formalcomm.html.

7. Kenneth Cukier, "Who Runs the Internet?" *World Press Review* 45, no. 5 (May 1998): 39–41.

8. David E. Nye, "Shaping Communication Networks: Telegraph, Telephone, Computer," *Social Research* 64, no. 3 (fall 1997): 1067–1092.

9. Ellen Goodman, "Anonymity Breeds Incivility," *Boston Globe,* September 5, 1996, p. 17A.

10. Brandi Bowser, "Opening the Window to Online Democracy: www.localgovernment.com," *American City & County* 113, no. 1 (January 1998): 36–38.

11. Thomas L. Friedman, "Global Village Idiocy," *The New York Times,* May 12, 2002.

12. *The Detroit Free Press,* September 28, 1967.

13. Alan Zaremba, "Working with the Organizational Grapevine," *Personnel Journal* 67, no. 7 (July 1988): 38–41.

14. *Time,* June 18, 1973, p. 67.

15. See http://www.ualr.edu/dllaufferswei/cj3306/formalcomm.html.

16. *Ibid.*

17. UNPAN, "Global Survey of E-Government; What Is E-Government?" See http://upan.org/egovernment2.asp.

18. "Tech Watch: Give Federal Employees Tools to Exploit E-Government," *Federal Times,* December 17, 2001.

19. See http://www.jerseyisc.org/e-government/e-government-introduction. html.

20. Meghan E. Cook, "What Citizens Want from E-Government," Center for Technology in Government, State University of New York, Albany. See http://www.ctg.albany.edu/egov/what_want.html.

21. Vincent O'Leary and David Duffy, "Managerial Behavior and Correctional Policy," *Public Administration Review* (November–December 1971).

22. Herbert A. Simon, Donald W. Smithburg, and Victor A. Thompson, *Public Administration* (New York: Alfred A. Knopf, 1950); Katz and Kahn, *The Social Psychology of Organizations.* Douglas McGregor's statement is from his posthumously published book, *The Professional Manager* (New York: McGraw-Hill, 1967). The quote from Crozier is from *La Societé Bloque* (Paris: Editions du Seuil, 1970).

23. Daniel Katz and Robert L. Kahn, *The Social Psychology of Organizations* (New York: John Wiley, 1966), p. 379.
24. Chris Argyris, *Personality and Organization* (New York: Harper & Row, 1957).
25. Katz and Kahn, *The Social Psychology of Organizations,* p. 245.
26. Chester I. Barnard, *Organization and Management* (Cambridge, Mass.: Harvard University Press, 1948); see Chapter 9, especially footnote on p. 231.
27. Katz and Kahn, *The Social Psychology of Organizations,* pp. 245–246.
28. *Ibid.*
29. *Ibid.*

C H A P T E R 9

Taxing, Budgeting, and Spending

Chapter Highlights

Local Budgets and Ecology

All economic decision making has environmental consequences—just as all environmental decision making has economic consequences. A budget entails outlays of how a community spends citizens' hard-earned dollars for the common good.

Water, air, and land—natural resources—are among the earth's greatest assets. Protecting them means protecting human health, but that protection has costs. Federal and state legislatures set fees for public water supply systems and storm-water permits. The residents of Fountain Inn, State of Commonwealth, found that they had an emerging water crisis after last year's spring floods.

Fountain Inn is located in the scenic rolling hills of the State of Commonwealth, one hour by interstate to Commonwealth's state capital, Big Burb. The town is a progressive, growing community. Despite population increases, Fountain Inn offers the friendliness and closeness of a small town.

In 1970, the town had a population of 3,308, and by 1990, it had jumped to 11,708, a 254 percent increase. The 2000 population was 14,488, in-creased by 23.74 percent since 1990. Sixty-one percent of the population is under the age of 35, 31 percent under the age of 18, and 24 percent between the ages of 35 and 54.

The town economic base is a combination of small business and heavy industry that moved out of the city center of Big Burb. Many residents commute to Big Burb for their jobs. High-tech industry is beginning to consider Fountain Inn as a location for development opportunities. Stay-at-home moms are utilizing their liberal arts degrees to start entrepreneurial computer-based jobs. Fathers long ago found out that their family responsibilies are more than merely "bringing home the bacon."

Street sweepers and pet-poop patrols could become commonplace in Fountain Inn, located along Commonwealth's primary interstate route, as local communities begin the task of meeting new clean water standards that are applied to storm-water runoff. Elected officials are pressured to raise taxes as they devote more of their cities' budgets to meeting the new water-quality standards required by the federal Environmental Protection Agency (EPA).[1]

Government-imposed regulations constrain or encourage many sorts of activities in order to meet the goals of modern societies. Many existing and emerging town policies have a fundamental flaw: their design and implementation does not adequately consider environmental or ecological impacts.[2]

Towns like Fountain Inn are responsible for local economic and social development, environment and the quality of life, and planning.[3] Specific local government responsibilities include:

- Roads, parks, and cemetaries
- Markets, street traders, and shop licenses
- Local police and fire services
- Street lighting
- Electricity distribution
- Water, sewerage, and rubbish disposal
- Public transport
- Preschool education and primary schools
- Adult education
- Libraries and museums
- Sports stadia and facilities
- Lowest-level health facilities
- Low-cost housing

Storm-water runoff is excess water that drains off streets, lawns, and parking lots into creeks, rivers, and lakes—many of which are sources of drinking water. The runoff carries with it elements of oil, grease, chemicals, fertilizers, pesticides, fecal material from animals, and other pollutants. Measures for improving the quality of runoff water include sweeping streets to keep excess dirt out of the water, implementing erosion controls at development sites, enforcing animal control ordinances to prevent animal manure from washing down storm drains, and monitoring the use of fertilizer and pesticide applications.

The Commonwealth state Department of Health and Environmental Control (CDHEC) wrote regulations to meet the new storm-water standards. The goal of the new regulations is to control the quality of storm water prior to its release. This ecological ordinance by Fountain Inn means that its city council has no choice but to prepare future budgets to deal with an issue confronting the entire community.

What Commonwealth Citizens Get for Their Tax Money

Commonwealth citizens' taxes pay for several environmental protection programs and services:

- CDHEC emergency responders from the Office of Land Quality deal with about 2,000 oil and hazardous material spills a year.
- The Office of Water Quality upholds standards for 4,500 public water supply systems and over 2,000 wastewater treatment facilities.

The state's Environmental Permit Programs also:

- Process and issue operating permits to all facilities
- Process and issue permits for new facilities and modifications
- Conduct compliance inspections of all facilities
- Review compliance information generated by all facilities
- Educate the public and facilities on aspects of rule and permit requirements
- Pursue enforcement where warranted
- Provide legal support to permit programs as needed.

The implementation of new water runoff standards cannot be financed by state or federal monies; instead, the costs for meeting new runoff standards are met by raising local taxes. "I think there's going to be no other recourse than the necessity to raise taxes," said Tommy Tickedoff, a Fountain Inn councilman.[4]

A budget plan explains how elected government officials would pay for citizen interests and activities. The 2004–2005 proposed city budget sets aside $25,000 to comply with storm-water regulations. But councilman Tickedoff predicts the costs will be substantially higher. Buying a street sweeper may cost the taxpayers between $80,000 and $120,000. The purchase would be funded through the city's general fund on a lease-purchase arrangement over five or six years.

Councilman Tickedoff laments that the new water standard illustrates how the State of Commonwealth dumps unfunded mandates on towns and cities. "There's only so much that local property owners can continue carrying on their backs," he said. "I think the quality of our water is something everyone ought to be concerned about. But some of these regulations seem a little excessive. I don't know how we would be able to have dog-poop police."[5]

Commonwealth state law requires Fountain Inn to implement a Storm-Water Management Plan, which has to incorporate

- surface drainage and flood protection;
- the preservation or rehabilitation of natural systems;
- protection of aquatic habitat and life;
- reduction of storm-water pollutants;
- erosion and sediment controls;
- enhanced aesthetics and recreational opportunities;
- reuse of storm-water as a valuable resource;
- a comprehensive community education program (awareness raising and action);
- adequate funding; and
- commitment from the Storm-Water Manager.[6]

The operation and maintenance of the sanitary sewer system was funded through the Wastewater Revolving Fund. The Fountain Inn city council endorsed the concept of self-sufficiency and agreed to an annual 16.3 percent increase in the fee. The Storm-Water Management Fee supports operating and capital budgets for the Drainage Cost Centers. Revenues are generally consistent, because the fee is based on total impervious area not affected by water. The maintenance program and its components are mandated by the State of Commonwealth Pollution Discharge Elimination System (CPDES) permit.

The Fountain Inn city council established the position of Public Works Manager to operate the Storm-Water Division. He or she will oversee the planning, directing, and implementation of goals, strategies, and programs. Qualifications include a Master's degree in Public Administration and a Bachelor of Science degree in Civil Engineering or a related field.

Local government officials demand more authority—and power—over matters that directly affect them. As local governments gain power and experience, they take over more responsibilities. Next they must consider the matter of costs, raising taxes, and implementing budgets effectively. At this juncture in Fountain Inn politics, the possibility of increasing property taxes merits further notice.

The State of Commonwealth does not permit local governments to incur budget deficits. Raising taxes and cutting spending in order to balance budgets creates a "between a-rock-and-a-hard-place" scenario for Fountain Inn officials—both elected and appointed. Property owners balk at paying higher taxes. Business district entrepreneurs from Fountain Inn's city center offer similar views.

"Public and private are not categories of nature," Dwight Waldo cautioned. "They are categories of history and culture, of law and custom. They are contextual and subject to change and redefinition."[7] Waldo's maxim is causing residents of Fountain Inn to reconsider personal and collective priorities. Government policy of Fountain Inn, as acted upon by its city council, impacts numerous individual and community economic activities.

Civic decisions on the environment have economic consequences. They entail deliberations about the Wastewater Revolving Fund, Storm-Water Management Fees, and services of the Public Works Manager in Fountain Inn's Storm-Water Division. Almost everyone in Fountain Inn agrees economic decisions—by individuals, private businesses, and local government agencies—have consequences for the ecology of their community. The effects are long-term.

Budget making requires compromises as everyone gets taxed, but some residents are assessed more than others. If budgets are instruments of coordination, control, and planning, and if administrative politics is deciding who gets what amount of money, are levying property taxes a matter of "whose ox is being gored" or whose basement is being flooded for the third time this spring?

Endnotes

[1]L. C. Leach III, "Storm Water Rules Could Run Off with City Budgets," *Tribune-Times.* http://tribunetimes.com/stories/2002/04/09/200204092728.htm

[2]"Government Budgets: Green Budget Reform," http://iisdl.iisd.ca/greenbud/default.htm.

[3]"The News in Brief . . . Budget Crunch May Harm Environmental Protection," *The Financial Times of Indiana,* February 11, 2002.

[4]Leach, *op.cit.*

[5]Leach, *op.cit.*

[6]Peter J. Morison and Geoffrey J. Hunter, "Implementation of Storm-Water Management Plans—It Costs a Lot to Build Bad Products." In Conference proceedings "Thinking Outside the Square—Stormwater Management Strategies in the Hawkesbury—Nepean Catchment," Stormwater Industry Association: Hawkesbury-Nepean Stormwater Management Workshop, Windsor, Sydney, March 6, 2001, pp. 2.1–2.15. http://www.ipwea.au/papers/download/Peter%20Morison.doc

[7]Dwight Waldo, *The Enterprise of Public Administration* (Novato, Calif.: Chandler & Sharp, 1980), p. 164.

If politics is sometimes defined as the process of deciding who gets what, administrative politics often becomes the process of deciding *who gets what amount of money.* Consequently, whether one department or individual is favored over another or whether one program or policy is supported over another usually translates into a budgetary decision. In this sense, budgets are political documents.

It is not enough, however, to call attention to the political aspects of budgeting to define what budgeting is. Budgets are also instruments of *coordination, control,* and *planning.* They govern nearly all aspects of administration and confer a great deal of power on those who prepare them.

Who Gets What Amount of Money?

Budgeting practices in the United States are the result of American ideology, federalism, and decision-making models. The political environment of budgeting is defined by our democratic ideology, which involves varying concepts of representative government. Democratic ideology is, in turn, defined by the idea of capitalism, a system that assumes that a growth-directed economy supports government's ability to appropriate sufficient funds for public services.

Public sector monies are raised from taxes on *individuals* and *businesses.* It's tough to maintain viable public services if revenues supporting such activities are low or nonexistent. Whether citizen taxpayers are providing education, unemployment compensation, or national defense, they need a growth economy to finance these citizen benefits. From a capitalistic economy we are, therefore, able to afford programs that benefit all citizens. The appropriate mix of capitalism and socialism affects the size and scope of government and budgeting policies.

Deciding which level of government should provide a certain service is a matter of *federalism,* with its ever-changing division of power. The American system of federalism helps determine the scope, size, and nature of national, state, and local budget priorities. If state law conflicts with federal law, state law gives way.

If local legislation conflicts with state or federal provisions, local ordinances are overruled. State boundaries, overlapping jurisdictions, the economic decline of certain states and cities, and suburban growth patterns contribute to the dilemmas of budgeting in a federal system.

Cycles in Congressional Budgeting

A historical review of five distinct congressional budget cycles (table 9.1) affords readers opportunities to comprehend current budgetary conflicts. The ebb and flow of power between the president and Congress, between the House and Senate, between committees, and even between subcommittees explains how the president and Congress experienced these cycles of interactions.

Cycle 1: Dominance of the Appropriations and Tax Committees until 1965

The appropriations and tax committees dominated congressional budgeting from the 1920s until the mid-1960s. The appropriations committees embodied the congressional power of the purse. Due in part to the constitutional requirement that tax and appropriation bills originate in the House, the House appropriations committee overshadowed its counterpart in the Senate. The roles of the committees evolved. The House committee became the guardian of the purse, saving money by cutting budgets. The Senate appropriations committee became the committee for appeals, frequently restoring funds for programs and projects deleted by the House committee.[1]

Members of the appropriations committee focused on the president's budget. Strong committee chairs and ranking minority members dominated deliberations. Thirteen subcommittees monitored thirteen appropriation bills covering the programs of departments and agencies. Members became the most knowledgeable legislators in Congress on the details of the executive budget. Basically conservative, members of the appropriations committees valued economy and efficiency in an arena of spenders. They focused on weak spots in departmental requests for funds. They were not especially program-oriented; agencies had to justify any increases. Budget cutting built member reputations and earned respect. The tax committees rarely agreed with the appropriations committees on expenditure and revenue analyses. Happenstance, not explicit planning, produced fiscal policy.

Cycle 2: The Budget Wars of 1965 to 1974

During these years, the authorizing committees took power from the fiscal committees, the president from Congress. Great Society programs, the Vietnam War, inflation, and recurring recessions contributed to these changes. Selection of priorities, allocation of funds, and methods of financing the budget were hammered out in the budget process. The power of the relatively conservative fiscal committees declined. The influence of more liberal program advocates in the authorizing committees grew. The insulation of entitlement expenditures from the appropriations process gained leverage. Congress increasingly intervened in budget implementation, once an executive prerogative. Legislative staffs expanded and became more professional.

TABLE 9.1

Receipts, Outlays, and U.S. Government Deficit History
(dollars in millions)

Year	Receipts	Outlays	Deficit
2000**	1,882,992	1,765,687	**117,305**
1999**	1,806,334	1,727,071	**79,263**
1998	1,721,798	1,652,552	**69,246**
1997	1,579,292	1,601,235	−21,943
1996	1,453,062	1,560,512	−107,450
1995	1,351,830	1,515,729	−163,899
1994	1,265,000	1,467,000	−202,000
1993	1,153,535	1,408,205	−254,670
1992	1,090,453	1,380,856	−290,403
1991	1,054,272	1,323,793	−269,521
1990	1,031,308	1,251,703	−220,395
1989	990,691	1,144,069	−153,378
1988	908,954	1,064,051	−155,097
1987	854,143	1,003,830	−149,687
1986	769,091	990,258	−221,167
1985	734,057	946,316	−212,259
1984	666,457	851,781	−185,324
1983	600,562	808,327	−207,765
1982	617,766	745,706	−127,940
1981	599,272	678,209	−78,937
1980	517,112	590,920	−73,808
1979	463,302	503,464	−40,162
1978	399,561	458,729	−59,168
1977	355,559	409,203	−53,644
1976	298,060	371,779	−73,719
1975	279,090	332,332	−53,242
1974	263,224	269,359	−6,135
1973	230,799	245,707	−14,908
1972	207,309	230,681	−23,372
1971	187,139	210,172	−23,033
1970	192,807	195,649	−2,842
1969	186,882	183,640	**3,242**
1968	152,973	178,134	−25,161
1967	148,822	157,464	−8,642
1966	130,835	134,532	−3,697
1965	116,817	118,228	−1,411
1964	112,613	118,528	−5,915
1963	106,560	111,316	−4,756
1962	99,676	106,821	−7,145
1961	94,388	97,723	−3,335
1960	92,492	92,191	**301**

**Estimate from Historical Tables, 2000 President's Budget, published by the White House.

Source: Historical Tables, 2000 President's Budget. *Institute for Better Education Through Resource Technology (IBERT),* http://ibert.org/deficit.html.

What Is the Budget?

The federal budget is:

- *a plan for how the government spends your money.*
  What activities are funded? How much does it spend for defense, national parks, the FBI, Medicare, and meat and fish inspection?
- *a plan for how the government pays for its activities.*
  How much revenue does it raise through different kinds of taxes—income taxes, excise taxes, and social insurance payroll taxes?
- *a plan for government borrowing or repayment of borrowing.*
  If revenues are greater than spending, the government runs a surplus. When there is a

surplus, the government can reduce the national debt.
- *a plan that affects the nation's economy.*
  Some types of spending—such as improvements in education and support for science and technology—increase productivity and raise incomes in the future. Taxes, on the other hand, reduce incomes, leaving people with less money to spend.
- *a plan that is affected by the nation's economy.*
  When the economy is doing well, people earn more and unemployment drops. In this atmosphere, revenues increase and the deficit shrinks.
- *a historical record.*
  The budget reports on how the government has spent money in the past and how that spending was financed.

How Does the Federal Government Spend Citizen Dollars?
(cents on the dollar)

	2003 (projected)	1993	1983	1973	1963
National Defense	18	21	26	31	48
Social Security	22	22	21	20	14
Health and Medical	22	16	10	7	1
Income Security	15	15	15	12	8
Energy and Environment	2	2	3	2	3
Commerce and Transportation	4	2	4	6	5
Education and Social Services	4	3	3	5	1
Veterans	3	3	3	5	5
Net Interest	9	14	11	7	7
Other	3	3	3	5	8

*Some budgets total more or less than 100 cents due to rounding.

Total Outlays

1963 fiscal year: $ 111.32 billion.
1973 fiscal year: $ 245.71 billion.
1983 fiscal year: $ 808.33 billion.
1993 fiscal year: $1,408.21 billion.
2003 fiscal year: $2,128.23 billion.

In the fiscal year 2003 federal budget, discretionary spending on defense, education, and transportation, accounts for about 30 cents on a dollar—and plays a comparatively minor role. Mandatory spending and net interest now account for 68 cents. In contrast, during fiscal year 1963, discretionary spending averaged about 68 cents of every federal tax dollar. Entitlements and net interest payments garnered about 32 cents of a dollar.

The most significant changes in the last four decades have been expenditures on health-related programs and on national defense. In fiscal year 1963, 1 cent of every tax dollar was earmarked for health. After Medicare and Medicaid were enacted in 1965, the cost of health rose to 7 cents on the dollar in 1973 and 16 cents in 1983. In fiscal year 2003, 59 cents of every dollar are appropriated for Social Security, health and medical, and income security. These ex-

penditures are mandated. The federal government automatically spends a legally determined amount of money for these commitments.

"Income security" includes General Retirement and Disability, Federal Employee Retirement and Disability, Unemployment Compensation, Food and Nutrition Assistance, Supplemental Security Income, Family and Other Support Assistance, Earned Income Tax Credit, Offsetting Receipts, Housing Assistance, and other programs. The "Other" category in the table includes International Affairs, General Science, Space and Technology, Agriculture, Administration of Justice, General government Allowances, and Undistributed Offsetting Receipts.

Source: Tax Foundation, "How Does Uncle Sam Plan to Spend Your Federal Tax Dollar in FY 2003," http://www.taxfoundation.org/taxdollar.html, 2002.

The enlargement and liberalization of the House Appropriations Committee occurred in the early 1970s. The seniority system broke down. Advocates of program expansion and greater expenditures now controlled appropriation committees in both houses. The appropriations committees became spenders, like the authorizing committees. These changes resulted in the increase rather than decrease of the President's budget. In the 1960s, the Congressional appropriations were usually lower than the president's budget requests. By the early 1970s, the reverse secenario was true.

The appropriations committees and revenue committees no longer controlled spending over Social Security, income maintenance programs, and health delivery systems financed by the federal government (Medicare). The authorizing committees now controlled expenditures. Congressional budgeting was distributed among the appropriations, tax, and authorizing committees. The legislative process was more fragmented. The President orchestrated his priorities through the Office of Management and Budget. Congress had no congressional budget to consider the budget as a whole. No comprehensive development of program priorities occurred. No coordination of fiscal and economic policies emerged. Congressional actions took place gradually. Decisions appeared isolated and sometimes unrelated, and consensus on fiscal policy between the President and Congress became increasingly difficult. Uncontrollable expenditures soared. Deficits grew larger. Inflation worsened. President Nixon impounded $18 billion of water pollution control, transportation, housing, education, rural development, and other domestic programs. In 1973 the impoundments were unprecedented in size, scope, and severity. The confrontational Nixon sought to dismantle the Great Society of the 1960s with an ideological fervor. In 1974, Congress, on a bipartisan basis, approved the Budget and Impoundment Control Act. Nixon acquiesced.

Cycle 3: The Congressional Budget Act of 1974

The Congressional Budget Act of 1974 rivals the Budget and Accounting Act of 1921—in significance, scope, and potential impact (see table 9.2). The 1921 legislation created the executive budget system in the federal government. The 1974 legislation provided a broad framework for

- simultaneously considering expenditures, revenue, deficits, and debt;
- formulating fiscal and economic policy;
- controlling expenditures;
- developing independent sources of information to evaluate the President's budget; and
- controlling the President's implementation of the budget.

Two new standing committees, the budget committees, played a central role in the reorganization. The four fiscal committees, appropriations and revenue, remained. The budget committees recommended overall fiscal policy and broad national priorities. They would guide other committees in their spending and tax decisions.

The framework for congressional budgeting rested in the first and second concurrent resolutions. No later than April 15, or approximately two and one-half months after submission of the executive budget, the budget committees were required to include in the first concurrent resolution recommendations for the following:

- Total budget authority (appropriations) in the aggregate and for each of the twenty functions
- Total budget outlays (expenditures based on new and old budget authority) in the aggregate and for each of the twenty functions
- The level of revenue, with recommended increases or decreases
- The proposed budget surplus or deficit based on the difference between outlays and revenues
- The level of debt, with recommended increases or decreases
- The level of loan obligations and loan guarantees (added in 1985 and 1990 to control the credit activities of the federal government)

The budget committees relied heavily on analyses and estimates by the Congressional Budget Office (CBO) and other standing committees. Action by both houses on the first resolution was to occur by May 15.

Congress was required to adopt a second concurrent resolution by September 15. The first resolution was tentative. However, the second resolution was to be firm and binding. Once Congress had adopted the second resolution, no bills raising expenditures or lowering revenues could be approved without special congressional action. The second concurrent resolution was intended to synthesize Congress's final decisions on fiscal policy and program priorities.

The Budget and Impoundment Control Act of 1974 did not usher in a revolution in congressional budgeting. It did focus attention on major problems. It forced legislators to examine problems closely. It spelled out the consequences of alternative actions. It provided vastly improved and authoritative data for debate and decision making. The CBO provided independent economic analysis, policy analysis, and program evaluation. The act expanded the dialogue on fiscal issues between legislators and their constituents.

TABLE 9.2

Milestones in Federal Budgeting, 1979–2002

Year	Event	Significance
1789	Constitution	Gives Congress the power to levy taxes and requires appropriations by Congress before funds are distributed.
1802–1867	Committee structure	House Ways and Means Committee established as standing committee in 1802. House Appropriations Committee established in 1865. Senate Finance established in 1816. Senate Appropriations Committee established in 1867.
1837, 1850	House and Senate Rules	House and Senate bar unauthorized appropriations.
1870, 1905–1906	Antideficiency Act	Requires apportionment of funds to prevent overexposure.
1921	Budget and Accounting Act	Provides for an executive budget. Establishes the Bureau of the Budget and the General Accounting Office.
1939	Reorganization Plan No. 1	Transfers Bureau of the Budget to the new Executive Office of the President and expands the Bureau's role.
1967	President's Commission on Budget Concepts	Adoption of the unified budget, including trust funds.
1974	Congressional Budget and Impoundment Control Act	Establishes the congressional budget process, House and Senate budget committees, and the Congressional Budget Office. Also establishes procedures for legislative review of impoundments.
1980	Reconciliation process	Reconciliation used for the first time at start of congressional budget process.
1985, 1987	Gramm-Rudman-Hollings Act	Sets deficit-reduction targets and sequestration procedures.
1990	Budget Enforcement Act	Shifts from fixed to adjustable deficit targets, caps discretionary spending, establishes pay-as-you-go rules for revenues and direct spending, and directs and establishes new budgeting rules for direct and guaranteed loans.
1990	Chief Financial Officers Act	Provides for a chief financial officer in major agencies to oversee financial management and integrate accounting and budgeting.
1993	Omnibus Budget-Reconciliation Act	Establishes a new deficit-reduction target of $514 billion over a five-year period, maintains discretionary spending caps at or below fiscal year 1993 levels for five years, and sets in motion the largest tax increase in peacetime.
1997	Balanced Budget Act	Bipartisan efforts create deficit-reduction legislation with political advantages without offering substantive reform. Compromise promises a balanced budget by 2002, but no provisions to reduce government size, cut corporate subsidies, or restructure Medicare.
2002	Deficits and Debt	Interest paid on the national debt is second in the federal budget only to wealth distribution. In 2001, $360 billion of taxpayer money was spent on interest payments.

Sources: Allen Schick, *The Federal Budget: Politics, Policy, Process* (Washington, D.C.: The Brookings Institution, 1994), p. 36; Donald Axelrod, *Budgeting for Modern Government* (New York: St. Martin's Press, 1994), p. 205; Jonathan Rauch and Eliza Newlin Carney, "The Easy Way Out," *National Journal* 29, no. 19 (May 10, 1997): 928–931; National Debt Awareness Center, http://www.federalbudget.com/.

The new timetable and fiscal ceilings proved useful. The control of impound-ments materialized. The reconciliation process indirectly helped control entitle-ments. However, no budget process can convince members of Congress to over-come ideological, partisan, and economic differences. Building a coalition on fiscal policy and national priorities requires political will. A brilliantly contrived budget process is no substitute for political consensus.

Cycle 4: The Balanced Budget and Emergency Deficit Control Act of 1985

The 1974 budget legislation did not reduce deficits. The act's timetable was not ad-hered to. Committee squabbles became common. The act could not overcome a gov-ernment controlled by two parties and a divided and paralyzed Congress. The Presi-dent and Congress could not ignore uncontrollable deficits and debt. With no political consensus on priorities and policies, the legislators could only focus on process. The Balanced Budget and Emergency Deficit Control Act, better known as Gramm-Rudman-Hollings (GRH), became law late in 1985. GRH set a maximum deficit amount for federal spending for each of the fiscal years 1986 through 1991. By the latter date, the deficit would be progressively reduced to zero. The 1985 budget legis-lation called for across-the-board cuts in federal spending to reach the targeted deficit level if the budget deficit exceeded the prescribed maxiumum by a specified sum in any given fiscal year. This last provision was written as if the complicated, political decision-making needed for balancing federal budgets of $1.7 trillion could be put on autopilot. Like the 1974 act, the 1985 act turned out to be a paper tiger. Deficits con-tinued to grow. No autopilot system would get this budget plane safely back on the the ground. A system of automatic cuts pleased no one. GRH needed a good boost. But no party or political faction could muster the strength to give it one.

Cycle 5: The Budget Enforcement Act of 1990 (BEA)

The first President Bush and Democratic congressional leaders could not meet the GRH target of $64 billion for fiscal year 1991. The deficit was more than $100 billion greater than that figure. If the GRH targets were to be followed, deep across-the-board cuts, known as sequestrations, in domestic and defense programs would be forthcoming. Bush and legislative leaders held a summit meeting. They decided to abandon the GRH deficit-reduction targets. They substituted expenditure limits on discretionary programs (excluding Social Security and deposit insurance) over five years. But there were no annual deficit targets. No priorities were changed. Political priorities were frozen. Entitlements, representing 60 percent of the expenditures, were protected. Budgeting control emphasized only on discretionary programs—about 40 percent of federal spending. Many argued that the BEA was the first serious attempt to slice expenditures. Deficits were smaller than they otherwise would have been.

The Democratic Party, at least in numbers, controlled both houses of Con-gress and the executive in 1993. Despite these majorities, political consensus on ex-penditures, taxes, deficits, and debt remained fleeting. The 1993 Omnibus Budget-Reconciliation Act was passed by a bare majority in both chambers and without a single Republican vote. The bill provided $504.8 billion in deficit reduction according to the White House, but only $433 billion according to the Congressional Budget Office. Tax increases primarily affected the wealthy and defense cuts were the majority of spending reductions.[2]

The perception that he was raising taxes resulted in political defeats for President Bush after he supported the BEA. The more traditional economic thinkers in the Republican Party skewered Bush in the 1992 presidential primaries, mocking his promise that he would not raise taxes. A similar perception of raising taxes occurred again in 1993—this time with the Democratic Party majorities in Congress. Although the 1993 economic package proved to be the beginning of economic recovery that included a balanced budget in 1997, the Republicans used the issue to skewer the Democrats in the 1994 off-year elections.

Voters appear to demand political reform, observes Jonathan Rauch, but government is unlikely to change except in political composition. The unwieldly size and contradictory complexity developed due to the cumulative inertia of entrenched lobbyists and special interest groups. Reforms will continue, Rauch emphasizes, but they will be gradual. Substantive change can come from the presidency and the electorate, but not unless citizens make personal sacrifices for widespread social welfare.[3]

Prospects for balanced budget agreements obscure the urgent need for entitlement reforms. According to Rauch, deficits—less than 2 percent of the nation's gross domestic product in 1996—are a minor concern. Entitlements, growing by more than 10 percent a year after 2030, constitute the federal government's biggest long-term financial problems,[4] Republicans and Democrats, claim Rauch and Eliza Newlin Carney, created deficit-reduction legislation in 1997 that had political advantages without offering substantive reform. The compromise appears to promise a balanced budget by 2002, but there are no provisions to reduce government size, cut corporate subsidies, or restructure Medicare.[5] (See figures 9.1 to 9.4.)

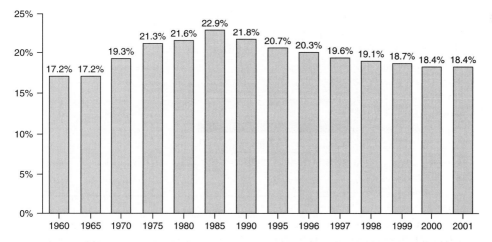

FIGURE 9.1 Federal spending as a percentage of the economy.

Total federal outlays as a percentage of the gross domestic product, 1960–2001.

Source: From www.publicagenda.org. © Public Agenda 2002. No reproduction/distribution without permission. www.publicagenda.org. Reprinted by permission.

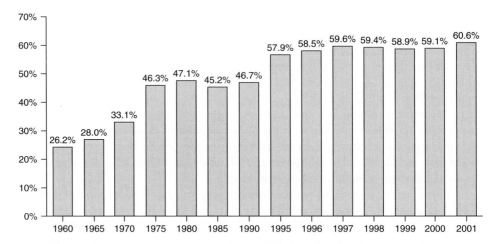

FIGURE 9.2 Most of the budget is spent on individual benefits.

Payments to individuals as a percentage of total federal outlays, 1960–2001.

Source: From www.publicagenda.org. © Public Agenda 2002. No reproduction/distribution without permission. www.publicagenda.org. Reprinted by permission.

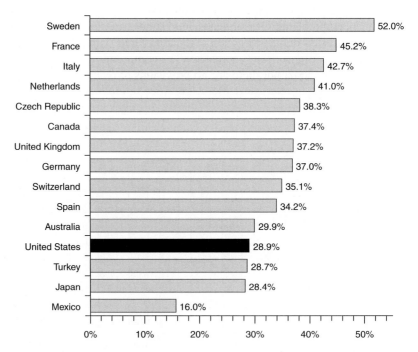

FIGURE 9.3 International tax burdens.

Total taxes as a percentage of the Gross Domestic Product, 1998.

Note: Data includes selected OECD countries.

Source: From www.publicagenda.org. © Public Agenda 2002. No reproduction/distribution without permission. www.publicagenda.org. Reprinted by permission.

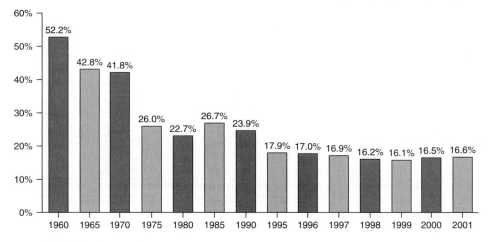

FIGURE 9.4 Defense spending.

Spending on national defense as a percentage of total federal outlays, 1960–2001.

Source: From www.publicagenda.org. © Public Agenda 2002. No reproduction/distribution without permission. www.publicagenda.org. Reprinted by permission.

Phases of the Budget Cycle

Federal budgeting can be understood in four phases: executive preparation, legislative consideration, implementation and control of the enacted budget, and audit and evaluation. According to Douglas Lee, a "budget, after all, is only an accounting of the financial cost of many political and social decisions.[6] The term *budget* originates from the Middle English word for pouch or purse.[7] Federal budgeting is a continuous and overlapping process, with stages of the budget cycle linked. The findings of audit/evaluation are important data for preparation of future budgets. The federal fiscal year begins in October. Many local governments start their fiscal years in January. Excepting Alabama, Michigan, New York, and Texas, state governments begin their fiscal years in July. The fiscal year in Alabama and Michigan begins in October. New York starts in April, and Texas begins in September. Fiscal years are named after the year in which they end; the federal fiscal year that began on October 1, 2002, was the 2003 fiscal year.

Executive preparation. The president (or governor, mayor, or chief executive on the state and local levels) transmits general directions for department and agency request preparation. The department or agency reviews current operations, program objectives, issues, and future plans as they relate to the upcoming annual budget. Cabinet secretaries and agency heads submit projections for requirements reflecting current operations and future plans. Supporting memoranda and related analytic studies identify major issues, alternatives for resolving issues, and comparisons of costs and effectiveness.

The Office of Management and Budget (OMB) develops economic assumptions, obtains forecasts of international and domestic situations, and prepares fiscal projections. The OMB compiles total outlay estimates for comparison with revenue

The Congressional Budget Timetable

The Congressional budget process begins nine months prior to the beginning of the budget year, which begins on October 1.

Five days prior to the transmittal of the President's budget to Congress: The Congressional Budget Office (CBO) issues its sequestration preview report for the year beginning October 1 (the budget year).

On or after the first Monday in January, but no later than the first Monday in February: The President's budget is transmitted to Congress.

On or before February 15: The CBO issues its *Budget and Economic Outlook* for the budget year.

February 25: Deadline for Congressional committees to submit their budget estimate to Budget Committees.

April 15: Congress completes action on budget resolution.

June 15: Congress completes action on reconciliation bills.

June 30: House completes action on appropriation bills.

July 15: The OMB (Office of Management and Budget) midsession budget estimate report is due.

August 15: The CBO issues its updated sequestration report.

August 20: The OMB issues its updated sequestration report.

October 1: The new fiscal year begins.

Ten days after the end of the congressional session: The CBO issues its final sequestration report for the year that began on October 1.

Fifteen days after the end of the congressional session: The OMB issues its final sequestration report.

Forty-five days after the end of the congressional session: GAO (General Accounting Office) issues its sequestration compliance report.

Source: http://members.bellatlantic.net/~vze25f7j/budget/timetable.htm.

---

estimates. It develops recommendations for the President on fiscal policy, program issues, and budget levels.

As appropriate, the President discusses budgetary outlook and policies with the director of the OMB and with Cabinet secretaries and agency heads. He reviews budget recommendations and decides on department and agency budget estimates, grounding his decisions on overall budget assumptions and policies. He may often revise his budget message. He transmits recommended budget estimates to Congress within fifteen days after Congress convenes.[8]

Legislative consideration. The predominant legislative power in the Western world is the power of the purse.[9] Congress acts on requests for budget authority and does not vote directly on outlays of taxpayer dollars. Instead, Congress grants budget authority to departments and agencies. Budget authority permits the agencies to incur obligations and to spend federal monies. This is accomplished through passage of appropriation bills.

The budget committees hold hearings as they prepare for the drafting of the first concurrent resolution on the budget. The appropriations committees hold special hearings on the budget overview with the director of the OMB, Secretary of the Treasury, and Chair of the Council of Economic Advisors. Subcommittees of the appropriation committees also hold hearings and review justifications from each department and agency. The House appropriations subcommittees draft appropriation bills and reports. The budget committees receive the views and budget estimates of all committees and draft the first concurrent resolution.

Congress receives the President's budget within fifteen days after Congress convenes. It adopts the first concurrent resolution on the budget by April 15. The House of Representatives debates and passes appropriation bills, with or without amendments. The Senate receives the House-passed versions of appropriation bills and refers them to the Senate Appropriations Committee. The Senate debates and passes appropriation bills with or without amendments. If Senate bills differ from House versions, bills are sent to conference. Conference committees consider items of disagreement between the two Houses and make recommendations for resolving differences in conference reports. These reports are submitted to each body for action. Congress adopts the second concurrent resolution of the budget on August 15.

Authorizing legislation is substantive legislation enacted by Congress that sets up or continues the legal operation of a federal program or agency either indefinitely or for a specific period or sanctions a particular type of obligation or expenditure within a program. Authorizing legislation is usually a prerequisite for appropriations. An appropriation act is a statute, under the jurisdiction of the House and Senate Committees on Appropriations, that provides authorization for federal agencies to incur obligations and to make payments out of the treasury for specified purposes. There are thirteen regular appropriation acts enacted annually.

Implementation and control of the enacted budget. Spending of federal taxpayer dollars must proceed in a manner consistent with appropriation laws. Once the appropriation bill is approved, the Treasury Department draws an appropriation warrant, countersigned by the General Accounting Office (GAO) and forwarded to the department or agency. The departments and agencies revise operating budgets in view of approved appropriations and program developments. The director of the OMB distributes budget authority to each department and agency by time periods, usually every three months, or by activities over the duration of the appropriation. The departments and agencies allot apportioned funds to various programs or activities. The budgetary term for allotments is *apportionment.* Central budget-office discretion to curtail allotments is often limited. The term for the President's withholding of federal appropriations is *impounding.* Since 1974, Presidents have been able to continue to impound funds. Congress, however, can veto these impoundments.

Audit and evaluation. An audit is an "examination of records, facilities, systems, and other evidence to discover or verify desired information. Internal audits are those performed by professionals employed by the entity being audited; external audits are performed by outside professionals who are independent of the entity."[10] Different forms of audits include

- financial audit, or a review of financial records to determine whether the funds were spent legally, if receipts were properly recorded and controlled, and if financial records and statements are complete and reliable;
- management or operations audit, or a focus on the efficiency of operations, on waste of government resources, and on use and control of resources;
- program audit, or an examination of the extent to which desired results are being achieved, on objectives of the program being met, and whether there might be lower-cost alternatives to reach the desired results; and
- performance audit, apart of sunset legislation, which establishes "a set schedule for legislative review of programs and agencies unless affirmative legislative action is taken to reauthorize them. Thus, the 'sun sets' on agencies and programs,"[11] causing an assessment of the total operations of a department or agency, including compliance, management, and program audits.

To illustrate the focus of each audit, consider a state highway department appropriation to purchase road salt for snow and ice removal. A financial audit considers whether the department purchased the salt, if the salt was actually delivered, if competitive practices were used in selecting a supplier, and if the department spent the correct amount on salt. A management audit considers whether the salt inventory is adequately protected from the environment, if the inventory is adequate or excessive, and if other methods of selecting a supplier would result in lower costs. A program audit considers whether the prevailing level of winter highway clearing is an appropriate use of community resources and if alternatives to deployment of salt would be less costly to the community. Finally, a performance audit examines all operations of the highway department.[12]

The GAO conducts an independent audit of financial records, transactions, and financial management and makes reports to Congress. The departments and agencies review compliance with established policies, procedures, and requirements. They evaluate the accomplishments of program plans and the effectiveness of management and operations. The OMB reviews department and agency operations and evaluates programs and performance. The OMB conducts and guides departments and agencies in organization and management studies and assists the President in improving management and organization of the executive branch.

The Budget and Accounting Act of 1921 set the start of the fiscal year at July 1. It created the Bureau of the Budget (changed in 1970 to the Office of Management and Budget) and the General Accounting Office. This legislation authorizes the President's budget message to Congress. The Congressional Budget and Impoundment Control Act of 1974 set the start of the fiscal year at October 1. It created the Congressional Budget Office and House and Senate Budget Committees. It requires the current services budget and congressional budget resolutions.

The Incrementalism Budgeting Perspective

The incrementalism perspective of budgeting states that budgeting is primarily, if not exclusively, a process of political strategy.[13] Budgeting, is incremental, says Aaron Wildavsky. "The largest determining factor of the size and content of this year's budget is last year's budget. Most of the budget is a product of previous decisions. . . . The budget may be conceived of as an iceberg with by far the largest part below the surface, outside the control of anyone. Many items in the budget are standard and are simply reenacted every year unless there is a special reason to challenge them."[14]

Incremental budgeting demands little inquiry because the increment, not the base, is considered. Incremental decision making entails routine, requires negotiations and accommodation grounded upon mutual respect, is delegated to specialists, and is almost invisible. It is distributive, historical, annual, repetitive, predictable, and automatic. It is rewarding and can create stable coalitions.

Incremental budgeting distributes only the increment, but takes nothing away from anyone; decremental budgeting, meanwhile, redistributes resources from people who absorb cuts in appropriations. Incremental budgeting rewards increments to everyone, as credit for such enhancement is to be shared; decremental budgeting engenders blame for the pain of losing accustomed funding.

The incremental model minimizes the intellectual task of creating a new budget every year, facilitates the political task of adopting a budget, and appears ethical. Such a model, accepting the base as a given, eliminates the necessity for rethinking the entire budget. The political task of building a coalition to support this year's new budget allows a majority of political interests with economic stakes to form and take hold. No one appears hurt; everyone gains a little in incremental budgeting.

Decremental budgeting is chaotic and conflict-laden. It may result in coercion, involve confrontation, and generate mistrust. It is clearly redistributive, breaks precedents, is multiyear, erratic, unpredictable, painful, can foster unstable coalitions, and requires active leadership for overcoming such obstacles.

Decrementalism suggests a centralized political system dominated by top-down budgeting. Incrementalism treats budgeting as a bottom-up process. What's the difference? The budgeting process includes the countervailing forces of centralization and decentralization, autonomy and interdependence, micropolitics and macropolitics. The president and his key advisors dominate the top-down process. A limited number of people are involved in such an approach; the developments are less visible to the public. Top-down strategy confronts the mixture of defense and domestic components of the budget, the budget's size, the impact of the budget upon fiscal policies, and the executive's policy initiatives to force cutbacks. As suggested in our discussion of decrementalism, routine is not a common feature of the top-down process.

There have been top-down characteristics of the budgetary process since the passage of the Budget and Accounting Act of 1921. Top-down elements are more difficult to document as the process is less routine, involves fewer people, and receives less publicity, and as such have garnered less attention than the bottom-up developments. Researchers find it difficult to observe, conceptualize, and explain the top-down process. According to budget theorists Barry Bozeman and Jeffrey D. Straussman, such features are often ignored or relegated to historical "disturbances."[15]

Incrementalism reflects the bottom-up budgeting process. The late budget theorist Aaron Wildavsky reported that incrementalism focuses on the significance of adjusting the margins from last year's budgetary base with little, if any, examination of the assumed baseline.

Why the emphasis upon the bottom-up process? First, incrementalism is explainable. Budget variations may be explained by using simple projections. Second, incrementalism gives an adequate account of the bottom-up process. Third, incrementalism is emphasized extensively in the administration and budgeting literature. Finally, incrementalism dominates policymakers' perceptions of how budgeting actually occurs and portrays the actual experience of policymakers themselves.

Top-down and bottom-up processes are operative in every budget cycle. As the demands of the budget cycle change with developments in fiscal policy, presidential leadership, economic growth, foreign conflict, congressional assertiveness, and other factors, the use of the respective processes changes. Although the top-down process of federal budgeting grew more important in the Ford and Carter administrations, the Reagan administration implemented perhaps the most important shift in budget policy, determining that the "controllable" portion of the budget includes entitlements offering social services to the middle class.

Budget Components and Reform Techniques

- **The Capital Budget.** A budget that deals with large expenditures for capital items normally financed by borrowing. Capital projects calls for long-range returns and life spans, are relatively expensive, have physical presence, and involve investments in community facilities. Examples include buildings, roads, and sewage systems.[1]
- **The Operating or Expense Budget.** This is an annual projection of revenues and expenditures for regular and recurring operations of governments which serves as a primary instrument of planning and financial control. Examples of expenditures include wages, salaries, personnel costs, supplies, materials, and travel costs.
- **Performance Budgets.** Performance budgets focus upon departmental objectives and accomplishments. They do not emphasize the purchase of resources utilized by the department. This technique accounts for the cost of performing measured accomplishments during the fiscal year. A performance budget includes sections on demand, workload, productivity, and effectiveness.[2]
- **Program Budgets.** In a program budget, the focus is on output. The concept rests not on

what governments purchase, nor on the tasks in which government is involved, but upon the outputs of government, as nearly as they may be defined. This technique delineates the goals of a department and categorizes tasks contributing to each goal. The focus is on product, not input. Planning Programming Budgeting Systems, or PPBS, focuses on accountability.[3]

- **Zero-Based Budgets (ZBB).** ZBB requires its practitioners to adopt two basic terms and three procedures for implementation. The ZBB terms are *decision units* and *decision packages:* The ZBB steps are *identification, formation,* and *ranking.*[4]

1. Rauch, "A Capital Idea for the Budget," *National Journal* 18, no. 49 (6 December 1986): 2948–2949.
2. Mikesell, *Fiscal Administration,* 135–155.
3. Samuel M. Greenhouse, "The Planning-Programming-Budgeting System: Rationale, Language, and Idea-Relationships," *Public Administration Review* 26, no. 6 (December 1966): 271–277.
4. See Peter A. Pyhrr, "The Zero-Base Approach to Government Budgeting," *Public Administration Review* 37, no. 1 (January–February 1977): 1–8; see also Allen Schick, "The Road from ZBB," *Public Administration Review* 38, no. 2 (March–April 1978): 177–180.

The baseline federal outlay projections for entitlements consist of social insurance programs such as Social Security, Medicare, unemployment insurance, and railroad retirement; means-tested programs such as Medicaid, food stamps, assistance payments, supplemental security income, veterans' pensions, guaranteed student loans, and child nutrition; civilian and military employee retirement and disability; and programs offering veterans' benefits, farm price supports, general revenue sharing, and other social services.[16]

The desire to curb the development of middle-class entitlement spending, promote economic changes, and alter public perception of economic issues and economic thinking encouraged Reagan administration policymakers to adopt top-down strategies. Bozeman and Straussman state that conventional budgeting wisdom did not keep pace with events. Concluding that budget theory should be reformulated, these theorists argue that the political and economic environments changed and led to a perceived demand for reductions in the rate and level of spending. Such cutback management, they argue, may be achieved only through coordinated fiscal management with top-down strategies. Under such conditions, incrementalism becomes a less satisfactory explanation of federal budgeting.[17]

More federal spending was added to the national debt during Reagan's presidential tenure than was added during all previous administrations combined. Perhaps Reagan's chief contribution to budgetary politics, on the other hand, was calling attention to excessive middle-class entitlements and moving from incremental budgeting to decremental estimates. From domestic to defense spending, the representatives of the American people have yet to find the line-items that allow for equal sacrifice in implementing federal budgetary policies.

Budgets are grounded in percentage increments to the historic budget base according to some notion of fairness for continuing the funding of each department and agency. The annual focus is on determining percentage monetary adjustments to existing programs.

Operating departments and agencies are units of government bureaucracies that spend taxpayer monies for the delivery of services. They focus on the clientele they serve. Their purpose is to expand service opportunities.

The office of the chief executive (President, governor, mayor) employs budget specialists to argue on behalf of government departments and agencies and their programs. At the federal level, the budget specialists are located in the OMB. In the states, various titles designate the units of executive office budget specialists. For example, in Mississippi, it's the Budget Office. In Arizona, it's the Finance Division. In Iowa, it's the State Controller's Office. In Kentucky, it's the Office of Policy and Management. In Washington state, it's the Office of Planning and Fiscal Management.

Budget analysts are guided by the priorities of the chief executive. The chief executive must balance the priorities and interests of the population. Departments and agencies have a clientele orientation. Not all programs have equal weight. Those with the strongest support in the legislature will do better in the budgeting process than others.

Elected members of the national, state, and municipal *legislatures* champion the priorities of their constituencies. They advocate programs and projects that benefit the people who elect them.

But legislators often cannot compete with the expertise of chief executives, departments, and agencies. Most state legislators are part-time legislators. The role and institutional history of the national legislatuture are more developed than those at the state, local government, and special district levels.

Executives, department and agency heads, legislators, and numerous clientele use budgetary strategies for maintaining or increasing the amount of monies available to them.[18] These strategies emphasize *cultivating clientele* and *developing confidence.*

Departments and agencies cultivate active clientele for lobbying the legislature and chief executive. Most departments and agencies experience little difficulty in locating clientele. Interest groups find ways to petition government decision making and spend funds. Departments and agencies accessing and servicing large and strategically placed clientele are less likely to have their budgets reduced. They not only concentrate on individual constituencies, but seek to expand their clientele. They proactively secure feedback on their programs and their effectiveness. They want constituents to offer suggestions for improving services.

The development of confidence, or deploying actions of personnel and programs to fit in with the expectations of others playing the power game, is a vital part of group strategies. Budget officials are guardians of the department or agency treasury. Presentations are geared to that end. As guardians, budgeteers espouse the effectiveness of programs and promise efficiency in spending taxpayer dollars.

Budget Terms

Authorizations: Involves the determination of maximum spending levels for each program approved by the legislative branch; the responsibility of standing committees of the U.S. House of Representatives and U.S. Senate.

Appropriations: One of the most crucial to budget making; entails the power to spend or to incur financial obligations; "spending" committees in the U.S. House of Representatives and U.S. Senate exercise major roles in this stage of the budgetary process.

Authorizing Legislation: Legislation enacted by Congress to permit the establishment or continuation of a federal program or agency. Authorizing legislation is normally required before the enactment of budget authority, and such authority is usually provided in separate legislation.

Budget Authority (BA): Authority provided by law to enter into obligations that will result in immediate or future outlays. It may be classified by the period of availability, by the timing of congressional action, or by the manner of determining the amount available.

Budget: The President's request to Congress for new programs, allocation of resources to serve national objectives, embodiment of fiscal policy for programs, and information about the national economy essential for the private sector.

Budget Cycle: Executive formulation and transmittal, legislative authorization and appropriation, budget execution and control, review and audit.

Continuing Resolution: Legislation that provides budget authority for specific ongoing activities when a regular appropriation for those activities has not been enacted by the beginning of the fiscal year. Some continuing resolutions provide interim funding for part of the fiscal year until the regular appropriations bill is enacted. Others provide funding for the full fiscal year.

Fiscal Year: The federal government's yearly accounting period, which begins on October 1 and ends on the following September 30.

Outlays: Government spending. Outlays are payments, normally in the form of checks issued, cash disbursed, and electronic fund transfers, net of refunds, reimbursements, and offsetting collections. Outlays include interest accrued on public issues of the public debt.

Receipts: Government income. All income collected from the public by the federal government in its sovereign capacity, primarily through the exercise of its power to tax.

Sequestration: Reduction of new budget authority or other budgetary resources, as defined in the Balanced Budget and Emergency Deficit Control Act of 1985, as amended.

Preparation is important as administrative leaders develop and maintain confidence. Public hearings afford officials opportunities to exude confidence in their department or agency missions and programs. Requests for information must be met promptly and in appropriate details.

Contingent strategies depend on budget circumstances. In defending its base for budget cuts, officials might suggest that a politically popular program be eliminated. In Indiana, for example, where the political culture nurtures high school basketball programs, budget officials call for reduction of athletic budgets when school districts confront fiscal problems. Officials argue that the community's high school basketball program faces an all-or-nothing choice. Any budgetary reduction would make the program impossible. It might as well be eliminated. In the Hoosier state, high school basketball has a jurisdictional, or statewide, clientele base. Strong clientele may prevent across-the-board reductions. Therefore, Indiana school districts and their elected school boards may decide to cut art, music, or history programs, rather than basketball appropriations.

Departments and agencies prepare their budgets incrementally. The most rational guide for next year's budget is based on the development, implementation, and evaluation of this year's appropriations. Departments and agencies must not

Administrative Audiences

Thomas J. Anton points out that an administrator must try to appease three audiences:

1. The administrator's own *employees,* who look to the administrator to preserve and, if possible, enhance their working conditions and status. Such considerations can be met by increasing the organization's appropriation.
2. The agency's *clientele group.* The people from this group also desire increased funds for the agency, because they are usually the most direct beneficiaries of the agency's expenditures. These

first two pressures for budgeting increases would probably exist under any form of budgeting.

3. Finally, there are the *review officials,* including superiors, budget bureau officials, and legislators. All of these, but particularly the latter, have an interest in being able to cut the budget. In making cuts, they achieve a sense of fulfillment and importance.

Source: Thomas J. Anton, "Roles and Symbols in the Determination of State Expenditures," *Midwest Journal of Political Science* 11, no. 1 (February 1967): 29.

strive to be "too successful," for they may "win" their "program war," making next year's budget unnecessary.[19]

Roots of the Deficit Problem

The budget deficit was not of major concern to policymakers from the end of World War II through the mid-1970s. From 1947 until 1974, deficits averaged less than 1 percent of the gross domestic product (GDP). As a result of World War II and the Great Depression, the public debt reached 114 percent of the GDP in 1946. But the budget situation became significantly worse after the mid-1970s. Deficits averaged 2.9 percent of GDP during the last half of the 1970s, 4.0 percent during the 1980s, and during the first three years of the 1990s, 4.4 percent. The public debt increased faster than the economy. The ratio of public debt to GDP more than doubled. In 1992, the federal government had revenues of $1.076 trillion and outlays of $1.475 trillion. The budget deficit equaled 37 percent of revenues.

The deterioration of the country's fiscal circumstances was caused by the interaction of several factors. There were systemic policy mistakes. Unanticipated and unpredictable changes occurred in the fiscal environment. The policymakers had little or no direct control over these changes.

First, an unexpected economic slowdown began in the mid-1970s. The slowdown baffled economists. The rate of economic growth slowed by approximately 1 percent after 1973. From the late 1940s through 1973, real per capita GDP expanded at an average annual rate of 2.5 percent, and real output per hour of labor expanded at an average rate of 2.1 percent. From 1973 through 1995, real per capita GDP expanded at only 1.5 percent a year, and output per hour of labor expanded at only 0.8 percent a year. Federal revenues expand as the economy increases. This economic slowdown had a significant impact on federal budgets.[20]

Second, the domestic entitlements the federal government committed to during the 1962–1972 period contributed significantly to growing deficits. Congress and three Presidents enacted laws establishing Medicare, Medicaid, food stamps, guaranteed student loans, Title XX social services, and supplemental security income programs. The slowdown in the economy resulted in a decline in income growth. Increasing numbers of people became eligible for means-tested domestic programs. Unexpected demographic developments made more persons eligible for domestic entitlements: The divorce rate doubled. The fraction of births to unwed mothers more than tripled. The poverty rate declined from 22.4 percent in 1959 to 11.1 percent in 1973. The poverty rate increased an average of over 14 percent from 1980 through 1995. Healthcare costs, new entitlement commitments, were unexpectedly expensive. With the enactment of Medicare and Medicaid in 1965, the federal government assumed more responsibility for the country's healthcare provisions.

Third, the Reagan administration began the 1980s with large increases in defense spending. The Republican President made an ambitious effort to increase defense capabilities. Defense outlays increased from 4.9 percent of GDP in 1980 to 6.3 percent in 1986. Reagan called for cutbacks on the domestic side of government. Wage increases had elevated many Americans into higher tax brackets. Reagan promoted reductions in tax burdens, an effort that made the deficit problems worse. The nondefense domestic discretionary budget declined from 5.2 percent of GDP in 1980 to 3.8 percent in 1986. However, the Reagan administration could not convince the Democratic Congress to significantly slow the increase in domestic entitlement spending programs.

Finally, the weak cyclical performance of the economy after 1974 contributed to growing deficits. Between fiscal years 1955 and 1974, the economy operated at or above its capacity in twelve of the twenty fiscal years. Between fiscal years 1964 and 1974, the economy operated at or above its capacity in nine of eleven fiscal years. Between fiscal years 1975 and 1996, the economy operated at or above capacity in only four fiscal years. The 1964–1974 period economic indicators were misleading.

The economic practice of sustaining increasing domestic entitlements without corresponding tax increases was sliding into deficit spending. Rising interest rates contributed to economic downturns. The growing size of the structural deficit caused federal expenditures on net interest to rise. Between 1951 and 1977, federal expenditures on net interest amounted to no more than 1.5 percent of GDP. After 1984, they expanded to 3 percent or more. Profound changes occurred in the composition of federal spending and taxes. Entitlements, other mandatory expenditures, and interest payments had lawmakers thinking benefit levels and eligibility criteria.[21]

Fiscal and Monetary Policies

Fiscal policy encompasses federal government policy with respect to taxes, spending, and debt management, and is intended to promote the nation's macroeconomic goals, particularly with respect to employment, gross domestic product, price level stability, and equilibrium in balance of payments. The budget process is a major vehicle for determining and implementing federal fiscal policy.

The other major component of federal macroeconomic policy is monetary policy. Monetary policy entails policies that affect the money supply, interest rates, and credit availability, and is intended to promote national macroeconomic goals, particularly with respect to employment, gross domestic product, price level stability, and equilibrium in balance of payments. Monetary policy is directed primarily by the Board of Governors of the Federal Reserve System and the Federal Open Market Committee. Monetary policy works by influencing the cost and availability of bank reserves.

Source: A Glossary of Terms Used in the Federal Budget Process (Washington, D.C.: General Accounting Office, March, 1981), pp. 59, 97.

In summary, factors contributing to growing federal deficits over the last thirty years were:

- the unexpected economic slowdown of the mid-1970s;
- domestic entitlement commitments the federal government enacted between 1962 and 1972;
- Reagan administration policies for increasing national defense capabilities and appropriations, decreasing nondefense discretionary budget spending, and reducing tax burdens; and
- a weak cyclical performance of the economy since 1974.

According to John Steele Gordon, five trends have increasingly affected government fiscal policies over the last sixty years.

> First, a powerful but fundamentally flawed concept in the discipline of economics has completely changed the way both economists and politicians view the national economy and their responsibilities toward it.
>
> Second, the responsibilities of government in general and the federal government in particular, as viewed by the public, have greatly increased.
>
> Third, a shift in power from the Executive to Congress has balkanized the budget process by sharply limiting the influence of the one politician in Washington whose constituency is national in scope, the President.
>
> Fourth, the decay of party discipline and the seniority system within Congress itself has further balkanized the budget process, dividing it among innumerable committees and subcommittees. This has made logrolling (you vote for my program and I'll vote for yours) the order of the day on Capitol Hill.
>
> Finally, the political-action-committee system of financing congressional elections has given greatly increased influence to spending constituencies (often called special interests, especially when they are funding someone else's campaign) while sharply reducing that of the electorate as a whole, which picks up the tab.[22]

Economic Growth, Taxes, and Savings

Economic growth, central to many of the country's concerns as a society, requires investment, which, over the longer term, depends on savings. The nation's savings consist of the private saving of households and businesses and the savings or lack of savings of all levels of government. In general, government budget deficits represent the opposite of savings; they subtract national savings that could be used for investment. Conversely, government surpluses add to savings.

American hostilities toward taxes are well-documented. However, the per capita tax level in the United States is not considered high; the people of the United States are not overtaxed. Taxation as a percentage of national income is lower in the United States than in any other major industrialized country. The opposition to taxes clearly cannot be traced to a heavy tax burden. Citizens rebel against higher taxes because they believe that governments are inefficient—even wasteful—in spending assessed revenues for their various operations.[23]

Since the 1970s, private saving has declined while federal budget deficits have consumed a large share of these increasingly scarce savings. The result has been to decrease the amount of national saving potentially available for investment.

The depressing effect of deficits on growth might have been mitigated had they financed higher levels of public investment. However, as a share of gross domestic product (GDP), federal investment spending has declined over the past two decades. Therefore, private saving remains low. Federal budget deficits declined significantly from the levels of the 1980s and early 1990s, making available some additional funds for investment.

Nevertheless, total national saving and investment remain significantly below the levels of the 1960s and 1970s. Economists note that these low levels of saving and investment raise concerns for the nation's future productive capacity and future generations' standard of living. The most certain way to increase the resources available for investment is to increase national saving, and the most direct way for the federal government to increase national saving is to achieve and maintain a balanced federal budget. Budget surpluses increase saving and allow the government to reduce the level of federal debt held by the public.

Growing deficits and the resulting lower savings lead to dwindling investment, slower growth, and finally a decline in real gross domestic product. Living standards, in turn, stagnate and fall. Therefore actions on the deficit might be postponed, but they cannot be avoided. Since 1995, robust economic growth and policy action combined to sharply reduce the deficit. Major progress was made on deficit reduction, culminating in the passage of the Balanced Budget Act of 1997.

Policy action accounted for about 25 percent of the late-1990s improvement in the CBO's budget estimates. The remainder of the improvement was due primarily to economic factors.[24] At the close of the century, the decline in the deficit significantly slowed growth in the federal debt held by the public.

The economic benefits of a sustainable budget policy include increased saving and investment levels and faster economic growth, which results in higher living standards. The future implications of current policy decisions are usually not captured in the budget process. The budget is a short-term, cash-based spending plan focusing on the short- to medium-term cash implications of government obligations and fiscal decisions. While the sustainability of the government's fiscal policy is driven primarily by future spending for Social Security and healthcare commitments, the federal government's commitments and responsibilities extend far beyond these programs.

The main influence of budget policy on long-term economic performance is through the effect of the federal deficit on national savings. Conversely, the rate of economic growth helps determine the overall deficit or surplus through its effect on revenues and spending. Federal deficits reduce national savings, while federal surpluses increase national savings. The level of savings affects investment and, in turn, GDP growth.[25]

Tax policymaking combines elements of partisan, policy, and system politics. The citizenry welcomes lower taxes. But do legislators deliver on corresponding government spending cuts? Oftentimes not. Local, state, and federal tax policies determine the range of programs and services government offers.

The purpose of tax policy is to spur economic growth. Expanding economic growth means more revenues for government coffers and more profits and wage increases. Tax policy also includes prospects for balancing budgets, lowering the national debt, and recession spending.

The conventional wisdom is that the Republican Party favors lower taxes and the Democratic Party campaigns for higher taxes. This assertion is partly true, but it is misleading and incomplete. The economy cannot cope with excessively high taxes, but basic government services cannot be provided if taxes are excessively low. The crux of tax policy is to find some happy medium between too few and too many revenues—or between what the state owes the citizenry and what the citizenry owes the government or state.

Democrats favor tax cuts targeting certain segments of the population. Democrats usually do not favor tax cuts for the wealthiest Americans. Republicans promote tax breaks that favor people in all taxing categories. These tax cuts tend to be larger, but require more reductions in government services in order to cover costs.[26]

Terms such as *federal deficit, federal debt,* and *debt service* require explanation. The *federal deficit* is the annual shortfall between the government's revenues, or what it takes in, and outlays, or the amount it spends every year on goods, services, transfer payments, and net interest. *Federal debt* is the outstanding debt that the federal government accumulates over time, and *debt service* is the interest on the federal debt. Debt service has been about 15 percent of the total federal budget. The federal deficit does not consider the value of state and local surpluses, capital investments, the impact of inflation on federal government accounts, and the business cycle.[27]

In August 2002, the Congressional Budget Office (CBO) projected the federal budget for the 2003–2012 period. The CBO forecast that the federal government would run a combined surplus of $1 trillion over this time frame. But as tax revenues declined, the budget numbers decreased once again. The economy was obviously slowing. President George W. Bush ushered in a tax cut, which Democrats argued would worsen the deficits. The latest data indicate a $157 billion deficit for 2002 fiscal year and steadily declining deficits through 2006. These tabulations do not consider a war in Iraq or the costs of a prescription drug benefit program for retirees. With partisanship expected to rise, political consensus on any matter except the basics will be difficult to achieve.[28]

The 1990s reflected exceptional economic vigor. Output increased nearly 40 percent, investments more than doubled, and consumption grew just over 40 percent. A spending spree reduced personal savings to almost zero. Spending grew faster than the country's earnings. A trade deficit got worse. By the close of 2000, income expenditure excesses climbed to about 4 percent of the United States GDP.

Borrowing and selling assets are ways out of debt for citizens and countries. In the case of nations, creditors and buyers of assets are foreigners. Why be concerned about this development? If the debt is small and remains under control, the creditors are not worried. But if the debt is out of control and the debtor becomes less credible, the creditors may decide not to finance a country's growing debt. This scenario could bring very unpleasant consequences for Americans. Depreciation of the dollar would make imports very expensive and exports very cheap. The trade deficit might be eliminated.[29]

America's persistent and growing trade deficit is rapidly deteriorating. A nation accumulating deeper debts is more and more dependent on its creditors, who are private investors and governments from Europe and Asia. The creditors have no advantage in disrupting their unfettered access to the largest consumer market in the world—producing trade surpluses and greater market shares for their countries. Creditor nations will eventually ask the United States to pay its debts. Creditors want their money. "You can't sustain an empire from a debtor's weakening position—sooner or later, the creditors pull the plug," emphasizes William Greider. Deficits at $400 billion a year will grow the trade debt to alarming levels.[30]

With the President and Congress divided on so many domestic and foreign issues, reaching political consensus for taxing, spending, and budgeting might prove a challenge larger than any one person, personality, or party. If consensus is not reached, policymaking returns to the *status quo ante,* or the previous state of affairs.

Federal Spending in the States

Some states assume much larger federal tax burdens than others. The federal tax burdens on states can be compared with the most recent data from the United States Bureau of the Census (2000). Tax Foundation senior economist Scott Moody ranks the states that got the best returns in 2000 from American tax and spending policies.

New Mexico taxes $2.03 for every dollar they invest in the federal government. No other state realizes a 2-1 ratio. The federal government spent $1.8 for every tax dollar in North Dakota, $1.78 in Mississippi, and $1.75 in West Virginia, respectively. Although obviously not a state, the District of Columbia benefited the most—receiving $6.49 in federal outlays for every dollar DC taxpayers sent to the United States Treasury.

Several factors influence this shifting of federal dollars, including the locations of people who receive Social Security, Medicare, and other federal entitlements; the locations of federal employees; federal procurement decisions; and grants to state and local governments. Connecticut receives only 62 cents in federal spending for every dollar its taxpayers send to Washington. New Jersey (66 cents), Nevada (69 cents), New Hampshire (71 cents), and Illinois (74 cents) maintained low federal spending-to-tax ratios in fiscal year 2000.

In the 1990s, federal spending rose from $1.20 to $1.68 in Alaska. Hawaii, West Virginia, North Dakota, Oklahoma, and Vermont ranged from 21 to 43 cents more per dollar of tax. Colorado, Utah, Massachusetts, and Connecticut fared none too well as locations for federal spending. In fiscal year 2001, the federal government collected $2.099 trillion in tax revenue—a 5.9 percent increase over fiscal year 2000.

Table 9.3 shows federal spending by state per tax dollar sent to Washington for fiscal years 1990 and 2000.

The federal government provided $1.8 trillion to the fifty states in 2001. California benefited more than any state, receiving $189 billion, followed by New York at $116 billion, Texas at $113 billion, Florida at $100 billion, and Pennsylvania at $79 billion. Altogether, Social Security, Medicare, and Medicaid accounted for $854 billion, or 48 percent of the U.S. government's domestic spending in 2001.

The top five states in Defense Department spending in 2001 were California ($31.3 billion), Virginia ($30 billion), Texas ($18.1 billion), Florida ($13.7 billion), and Georgia ($11 billion). The top five counties or county-equivalent areas that received federal defense funds were Los Angeles County ($8.3 billion), San Diego County ($7.7 billion), Newport News City, Virginia ($6.4 billion), Fairfax County, Virginia ($5.6 billion), and Cobb County, Georgia ($4.9 billion).[31]

TABLE 9.3

Federal Spending by State per Tax Dollar Sent to Washington
(Fiscal Years 1990 and 2000)

	Expenditures per Dollar of Taxes		Ranking	
	FY 1990	**FY 2000**	**FY 1990**	**FY 2000**
Total	1.00	1.00	—	—
Alabama	1.43	1.54	6	8
Alaska	1.20	1.68	20	5
Arizona	1.25	1.18	16	22
Arkansas	1.31	1.38	12	14
California	.89	.86	38	40
Colorado	1.16	.85	21	41
Connecticut	.78	.62	45	50
Delaware	.75	.84	48	42
Florida	.96	1.00	34	31
Georgia	.94	.99	36	32
Hawaii	1.13	1.56	23	7
Idaho	1.28	1.30	14	17
Illinois	.75	.74	47	46
Indiana	.88	.92	39	36
Iowa	1.08	1.04	26	29
Kansas	1.06	1.02	29	30
Kentucky	1.27	1.41	15	12
Louisiana	1.30	1.39	13	13
Maine	1.22	1.32	19	15
Maryland	1.23	1.32	18	16
Massachusetts	1.08	.86	25	38
Michigan	.82	.81	44	44
Minnesota	.86	.76	41	45
Mississippi	1.66	1.78	2	3
Missouri	1.36	1.26	8	19
Montana	1.44	1.59	5	6
Nebraska	1.12	1.09	24	24
Nevada	.77	.69	46	48
New Hampshire	.74	.71	49	47
New Jersey	.68	.66	50	49
New Mexico	2.05	2.03	1	1
New York	.83	.86	43	39
North Carolina	.93	1.06	37	28
North Dakota	1.52	1.86	3	2
Ohio	.99	.97	30	33
Oklahoma	1.24	1.46	17	11

continued

TABLE 9.3

Federal Spending by State per Tax Dollar Sent to Washington, *continued*
(Fiscal Years 1990 and 2000)

	Expenditures per Dollar of Taxes		Ranking	
	FY 1990	**FY 2000**	**FY 1990**	**FY 2000**
Oregon	.95	.93	35	35
Pennsylvania	.96	1.06	33	26
Rhode Island	1.06	1.18	28	21
South Carolina	1.32	1.27	11	18
South Dakota	1.35	1.46	9	10
Tennessee	1.14	1.20	22	20
Texas	.97	.96	31	34
Utah	1.34	1.06	10	27
Vermont	.87	1.08	40	25
Virginia	1.44	1.48	4	9
Washington	.96	.87	32	37
West Virginia	1.39	1.75	7	4
Wisconsin	.86	.83	42	43
Wyoming	1.07	1.09	27	23
District of Columbia	$ 5.59	$ 6.49	—	—

Source: From Tax Foundation website. www.taxfoundation.org. Reprinted by permission.

State Tax Burdens

The 1990s were good times for state and local governments, a period of exceptionally strong growth in most sectors of the economy. The 1990s saw abundant tax revenues in state governments throughout the United States. Income and sales taxes during the 1990s added to the boom for expanding state and local government operations. Income-tax-dependent states witnessed rapid growth in citizens' personal incomes. Strong consumer spending promoted state and local government operations dependent on the sales tax.

However, the boom times of the 1990s appear to be over. For fiscal year 2002, state government increased taxes by an estimated $303.8 million. Personal income taxes decreased by $671.2 million. Sales taxes increased by $186.1 million, corporate income taxes by $381.6 million, and cigarette, tobacco, and alcohol taxes by $98.7 million. Other taxes and fees increased by $308.6 million.

As the 1990s came to an end, state tax and fee collections grew 8 percent. This growth in overall tax collections was substantial when adjusted for inflation—5.7 percent. Inflation rates reflect a decade-long trend. Property taxes rose at an annual growth rate of 7.8 percent. Individual income taxes rose at an average growth rate of 7.3 percent. The overall distribution of taxes indicates that states derive the majority of their tax collections from general sales taxes (32.3 percent) and the individual income tax (36 percent).

Some states rely disproportionately on one or the other. States that rely on the sales tax for over 50 percent of their tax collections are: Washington (61.6 percent), Florida (60.5 percent), Tennessee (57.4 percent), South Dakota (52.6 percent), Nevada (52.2 percent), and Texas (51.1 percent). States who rely on the individual income tax for over 50 percent of their tax collections are: Oregon (68.9 percent), Massachusetts (56 percent), New York (55.6 percent), Virginia (54 percent), and Colorado (51.4 percent). Table 9.4 lists state tax collections and distributions by type of tax for fiscal year 2000.

During the 1990s, state governments' tax collections grew faster than taxpayers' personal income. In fiscal year 2000, state tax collections grew 1.82 percent faster than personal incomes. The growth rate of state tax collections relative to that of personal income varies substantially from state to state. Table 9.5 compares state tax growth to personal income (PI) growth for fiscal year 1990 and 2000.

States with the highest per capita tax collections include Connecticut, Hawaii, and Minnesota. States with the lowest tax collections include South Dakota, Texas, and New Hampshire. States with the highest levels of tax collections per $1,000 of personal income include Hawaii, New Mexico, and Vermont. States with the lowest levels of tax collections per $41,000 of personal income were Texas, South Dakota, and New Hampshire. See table 9.6 for state tax collections per capita and per $1,000 of personal income with the corresponding ranks of the states.

Various measurements of state tax collections differ substantially. The disparity may be explained by differences in income per capita in example states Mississippi and New Jersey. Income per capita in Mississippi is approximately 57 percent of that in New Jersey. As a result, Mississippi is ranked 37th in tax collections per capita. But in terms of tax collections per $1,000 of personal income, it ranks 11th highest. New Jersey ranks 16th in tax collections per capita, but only 40th in tax collections per $1,000 of personal income.

The fiscal year 2000 state tax collections are based on Bureau of the Census data. The census data record tax collections from various taxes levied at the state level. The data are limited by their applications to the computation of individual tax burdens by state. Tax incidence analysis best determines tax burdens and which taxpayers ultimately bear the real burden of taxes. Income taxes paid by corporations to one state may not be fully borne by the residents of that state. Some portions of the real tax burdens are borne by residents of other states—as customers, out-of-state employees, or shareholders.

State governments spent $1.1 trillion in fiscal year 2000. Fiscal year 2000 ended in June in all states except Alabama, Michigan, New York, and Texas. The 2000 Annual Survey of State Government Finances indicates that spending on education continues to be the largest states' expenditure—$347 billion, or 32 percent. Other major categories of state spending were public welfare (22 percent), highways, health and hospitals (7 percent each), and police and corrections (4 percent).[32]

Tax collections constituted the largest share of state revenues—$539 billion, or 43 percent. Intergovernmental revenues totaled $274 billion, or 22 percent, most of which came from the federal government. Current operations ($523 billion) accounted for most state government spending. Local governments spend about 30 percent ($328 billion). States appropriated $76 billion on capital projects, $105 billion on insurance benefits, and more than $30 billion on debt interest.

TABLE 9.4

State Tax Collections and Distribution by Type of Tax
(Fiscal Year 2000)

	Total ($Thousands)	Distribution					
		General Sales and Use	Individual Income	Corporate Income	Motor Fuels	Licenses	All Other
All States[1]	539,640,411	32.3%	36.0%	6.0%	5.6%	6.1%	14.0%
Alabama	6,438,438	26.4%	32.2%	3.8%	7.8%	8.4%	21.4%
Alaska	1,423,287	0.0%	0.0%	30.8%	3.0%	6.4%	59.8%
Arizona	8,100,737	44.8%	28.3%	6.5%	7.3%	3.2%	9.9%
Arkansas	4,870,561	35.0%	30.2%	4.9%	8.0%	5.3%	16.6%
California	83,807,959	28.0%	47.2%	7.9%	3.6%	4.4%	8.8%
Colorado	7,075,047	26.1%	51.4%	4.7%	7.7%	4.2%	5.8%
Connecticut	10,171,242	33.6%	39.1%	4.2%	5.3%	3.6%	14.2%
Delaware	2,132,131	0.0%	34.4%	11.3%	4.9%	36.4%	13.0%
Florida	24,817,263	60.5%	0.0%	4.8%	6.5%	6.1%	22.2%
Georgia	13,511,275	34.3%	47.1%	5.3%	4.7%	3.5%	5.2%
Hawaii	3,334,743	46.1%	31.9%	2.3%	2.2%	3.3%	14.2%
Idaho	2,377,251	31.4%	40.6%	5.3%	8.8%	9.1%	4.8%
Illinois	22,788,799	28.1%	33.5%	9.9%	6.0%	6.9%	15.7%
Indiana	10,104,353	35.4%	37.1%	9.2%	6.9%	2.4%	8.9%
Iowa	5,185,394	33.2%	36.5%	4.1%	6.7%	9.5%	10.0%
Kansas	4,865,305	35.8%	38.3%	5.6%	7.3%	4.9%	8.1%
Kentucky	7,694,610	28.2%	35.1%	4.0%	5.7%	7.0%	20.0%
Louisiana	6,512,382	31.6%	24.3%	3.4%	8.4%	7.5%	24.7%
Maine	2,661,080	31.8%	40.5%	5.6%	6.8%	5.0%	10.2%
Maryland	10,354,447	24.1%	44.6%	4.2%	6.3%	3.7%	17.2%
Massachusetts	16,152,874	22.1%	56.0%	8.1%	4.0%	2.8%	7.0%
Michigan	22,756,403	33.7%	31.6%	10.5%	4.7%	5.3%	14.2%
Minnesota	13,338,532	27.9%	41.6%	6.0%	4.6%	7.3%	12.6%
Mississippi	4,711,594	49.5%	21.4%	4.8%	8.9%	5.9%	9.5%
Missouri	8,571,548	32.5%	41.4%	3.1%	8.1%	6.7%	8.1%
Montana	1,410,760	0.0%	36.6%	7.1%	13.4%	8.7%	34.3%
Nebraska	2,981,047	34.5%	39.4%	4.7%	9.4%	6.4%	5.7%

continued

TABLE 9.4

State Tax Collections and Distribution by Type of Tax, *continued*
(Fiscal Year 2000)

	Total ($Thousands)	Distribution					
		General Sales and Use	Individual Income	Corporate Income	Motor Fuels	Licenses	All Other
Nevada	3,717,255	52.2%	0.0%	0.0%	7.0%	9.8%	31.0%
New Hampshire	1,696,085	0.0%	3.9%	18.4%	6.9%	8.4%	62.4%
New Jersey	18,147,604	30.4%	39.7%	7.4%	2.8%	4.4%	15.4%
New Mexico	3,743,178	40.1%	23.5%	4.3%	6.2%	5.5%	20.3%
New York	41,735,841	20.5%	55.6%	6.6%	1.2%	2.3%	13.7%
North Carolina	15,216,066	22.1%	46.6%	6.5%	8.0%	6.0%	10.8%
North Dakota	1,172,373	28.2%	16.9%	6.7%	9.4%	7.4%	31.3%
Ohio	19,676,365	31.8%	41.9%	3.2%	7.1%	7.9%	8.0%
Oklahoma	5,851,814	24.6%	36.5%	3.3%	6.9%	14.4%	14.3%
Oregon	5,945,675	0.0%	68.9%	6.8%	8.0%	10.2%	6.1%
Pennsylvania	22,466,906	31.4%	30.1%	7.6%	3.4%	10.1%	17.4%
Rhode Island	2,034,909	30.5%	40.7%	3.7%	6.4%	4.5%	14.2%
South Carolina	6,381,391	38.5%	38.3%	3.6%	5.8%	5.9%	7.9%
South Dakota	927,245	52.6%	0.0%	4.9%	13.5%	12.8%	16.3%
Tennessee	7,739,590	57.4%	2.3%	7.9%	10.2%	11.6%	10.5%
Texas	27,424,142	51.1%	0.0%	0.0%	9.8%	13.9%	25.2%
Utah	3,978,697	35.8%	41.5%	4.4%	8.3%	3.5%	6.6%
Vermont	1,470,828	14.6%	29.4%	3.0%	4.1%	4.6%	44.2%
Virginia	12,648,071	19.5%	54.0%	4.5%	6.4%	4.1%	11.5%
Washington	12,567,383	61.6%	0.0%	0.0%	6.2%	4.8%	27.4%
West Virginia	3,343,266	27.4%	28.9%	6.5%	7.2%	5.2%	24.8%
Wisconsin	12,643,015	27.7%	47.1%	4.6%	7.2%	5.4%	7.9%
Wyoming	963,650	38.3%	0.0%	0.0%	8.4%	9.3%	44.0%
District of Columbia[2]	3,197,087	18.2%	34.5%	5.4%	1.0%	1.4%	39.4%

[1]Does not include the District of Columbia.

[2]Based on quarterly data.

Source: From Tax Foundation website www.taxfoundation.org. Reprinted by permission.

TABLE 9.5

State Tax Growth Compared to Personal Income (PI) Growth
(Fiscal Years 1990–2000)

	Avg. Annual Tax Growth FY 1990–2000 (Real 2000$)	Avg. Annual PI Growth FY 1990–2000 (Real 2000$)[1]	Avg. Annual Growth of Taxes Relative to PI FY 1990–2000 (Real 2000$)[2]	Tax Growth Rank FY 1990–2000	Growth of Taxes Relative to PI FY 1999–2000 (Current $)[2]	Tax Growth Rank FY 1999–2000
All States[3]	3.83%	2.95%	0.89%	—	1.82%	—
Alabama	3.18	2.64	0.54	37	2.46	15
Alaska	−2.88	1.60	−4.48	50	53.28	1
Arizona	4.15	4.80	−0.65	24	0.28	31
Arkansas	5.74	3.21	2.52	6	1.23	26
California	4.58	2.58	2.00	15	6.74	5
Colorado	6.46	5.27	1.18	3	−1.17	44
Connecticut	4.59	2.15	2.44	14	−0.07	34
Delaware	4.35	2.93	1.42	19	−1.15	43
Florida	4.24	3.12	1.12	20	−1.26	45
Georgia	4.47	4.49	−0.02	18	1.35	23
Hawaii	1.48	0.78	0.70	49	2.26	18
Idaho	5.41	4.13	1.28	8	2.79	14
Illinois	3.67	2.82	0.85	28	2.82	13
Indiana	2.99	2.82	0.17	39	−1.14	42
Iowa	2.41	2.38	0.03	46	2.20	19
Kansas	3.99	2.69	1.30	26	1.26	24
Kentucky	3.89	3.00	0.89	27	−0.86	39
Louisiana	2.60	2.51	0.09	44	−2.53	47
Maine	3.29	1.77	1.53	34	−0.38	37
Maryland	2.67	2.43	0.24	43	2.85	12
Massachusetts	3.41	2.91	0.50	32	1.49	22
Michigan	4.99	2.64	2.35	9	−0.74	38
Minnesota	4.72	3.47	1.25	12	0.45	30
Mississippi	4.78	3.39	1.39	11	−0.99	40
Missouri	3.48	2.83	0.65	30	−4.83	50
Montana	2.92	2.67	0.26	41	0.45	29
Nebraska	4.80	2.75	2.05	10	6.93	4
Nevada	6.65	6.42	0.23	2	1.25	25

continued

TABLE 9.5

State Tax Growth Compared to Personal Income (PI) Growth, *continued*
(Fiscal Years 1990–2000)

	Avg. Annual Tax Growth FY 1990–2000 (Real 2000$)	Avg. Annual PI Growth FY 1990–2000 (Real 2000$)[1]	Avg. Annual Growth of Taxes Relative to PI FY 1990–2000 (Real 2000$)[2]	Tax Growth Rank FY 1990–2000	Growth of Taxes Relative to PI FY 1999–2000 (Current $)[2]	Tax Growth Rank FY 1999–2000
New Hampshire	8.74	3.26	5.47	1	50.71	2
New Jersey	3.50	2.43	1.07	29	0.87	28
New Mexico	4.19	3.35	0.83	22	3.94	8
New York	1.69	2.08	−0.39	48	2.06	21
North Carolina	4.61	3.85	0.76	13	−0.13	35
North Dakota	3.45	2.09	1.37	31	1.03	27
Ohio	3.39	2.15	1.23	33	4.45	7
Oklahoma	3.16	2.34	0.82	38	3.14	10
Oregon	5.64	3.68	1.96	7	5.65	6
Pennsylvania	3.26	1.96	1.30	35	−1.03	41
Rhode Island	2.96	1.78	1.17	40	2.15	20
South Carolina	2.78	3.10	−0.32	42	−1.97	46
South Dakota	4.16	3.14	1.02	23	0.13	32
Tennessee	3.99	3.57	0.42	25	2.32	17
Texas	4.22	4.31	−0.09	21	−0.15	36
Utah	6.20	4.78	1.42	4	3.00	11
Vermont	6.01	2.37	3.63	5	−0.01	33
Virginia	4.51	3.06	1.45	17	2.35	16
Washington	3.22	4.03	−0.81	36	−4.61	49
West Virginia	1.97	1.83	0.15	47	−2.55	48
Wisconsin	4.57	2.99	1.58	16	3.74	9
Wyoming	2.48	2.69	−0.21	45	12.11	3
District of Columbia	1.46	1.10	0.36	—	1.46	—

[1]Personal income figures adjusted into fiscal years.

[2]If tax growth exceeds income growth, the relationship will be positive. If income growth exceeds tax growth, the relationship will be negative.

[3]Does not include the District of Columbia.

Source: From Tax Foundation website www.taxfoundation.org. Reprinted by permission.

TABLE 9.6

Effective State and Local Tax Burdens by State and Rank
(Calendar Year 2002)

	State and Local			Total		
	Tax Burden	Rank		Tax Burden	Rank	Change in Ranking
Total	10.2%			32.1%		
Maine	12.8%	1	Maine	32.7%	11	−10
New York	12.3%	2	New York	34.7%	3	−1
Wisconsin	12.0%	3	Wisconsin	33.2%	6	−3
Hawaii	11.6%	4	Hawaii	30.9%	30	−26
Minnesota	11.3%	5	Minnesota	32.9%	7	−2
Rhode Island	11.3%	6	Rhode Island	32.5%	13	−7
Arkansas	11.3%	7	Arkansas	31.2%	26	−19
Utah	11.2%	8	Utah	31.2%	27	−19
Ohio	11.2%	9	Ohio	31.6%	20	−11
Vermont	11.0%	10	Vermont	32.1%	16	−6
Connecticut	10.9%	11	Connecticut	36.7%	1	10
New Mexico	10.9%	12	New Mexico	30.4%	34	−22
Nebraska	10.8%	13	Nebraska	31.6%	19	−6
Michigan	10.7%	14	Michigan	32.8%	8	6
Mississippi	10.7%	15	Mississippi	29.8%	43	−28
Louisiana	10.5%	16	Louisiana	30.1%	41	−25
Idaho	10.5%	17	Idaho	30.3%	37	−20
Kentucky	10.5%	18	Kentucky	30.2%	39	−21
West Virginia	10.5%	19	West Virginia	29.1%	48	−29
Washington	10.5%	20	Washington	35.6%	2	18
Kansas	10.4%	21	Kansas	31.4%	23	−2
Iowa	10.4%	22	Iowa	30.6%	32	−10
New Jersey	10.3%	23	New Jersey	34.3%	4	19
California	10.3%	24	California	32.7%	10	14
Georgia	10.2%	25	Georgia	31.4%	22	3
North Dakota	10.2%	26	North Dakota	29.5%	45	−19

continued

TABLE 9.6

Effective State and Local Tax Burdens by State and Rank, *continued*
(Calendar Year 2002)

	State and Local			Total		
	Tax Burden	**Rank**		**Tax Burden**	**Rank**	**Change in Ranking**
Delaware	10.2%	27	Delaware	31.7%	17	10
Arizona	10.1%	28	Arizona	31.7%	18	10
North Carolina	10.1%	29	North Carolina	30.4%	35	−6
South Carolina	10.0%	30	South Carolina	30.2%	40	−10
Illinois	10.0%	31	Illinois	32.8%	9	22
Montana	10.0%	32	Montana	29.8%	42	−10
Oklahoma	9.9%	33	Oklahoma	29.0%	49	−16
Indiana	9.9%	34	Indiana	30.9%	31	3
Pennsylvania	9.9%	35	Pennsylvania	31.1%	28	7
Wyoming	9.8%	36	Wyoming	34.1%	5	31
Maryland	9.7%	37	Maryland	31.1%	29	8
Missouri	9.7%	38	Missouri	30.2%	38	0
Massachusetts	9.5%	39	Massachusetts	32.6%	12	27
Virginia	9.4%	40	Virginia	31.3%	25	15
Oregon	9.4%	41	Oregon	30.5%	33	8
Florida	9.3%	42	Florida	32.2%	15	27
Nevada	9.2%	43	Nevada	32.3%	14	29
South Dakota	9.1%	44	South Dakota	29.7%	44	0
Colorado	9.1%	45	Colorado	31.3%	24	21
Alabama	9.1%	46	Alabama	29.1%	47	−1
Texas	9.0%	47	Texas	30.4%	36	11
New Hampshire	8.6%	48	New Hampshire	31.6%	21	27
Tennessee	8.4%	49	Tennessee	29.2%	46	3
Alaska	6.3%	50	Alaska	27.0%	50	0
District of Columbia	13.9%	—		37.6%		

Source: From Tax Foundation website http://www.taxfoundation.org/ Reprinted by permission.

Summary

- The Federal budget is a plan for how the government spends your money, how the government pays for its activities, and for government borrowing or repayment of borrowing. It is also something that affects the nation's economy, something that is affected by the nation's economy, and a historical record.

- If politics is sometimes defined as the process of deciding who gets what, administrative politics often becomes the process of deciding *who gets what amount of money*. If budgets are essentially political documents, the politics involved are often veiled.

- It is not enough to call attention to the political aspects of budgeting to define budgeting. Budgets are also instruments of *coordination, control,* and *planning.* They govern nearly all aspects of administration and confer a great deal of power on those who prepare them.

- Public sector budgets are raised from taxes on individuals and businesses. It's tough to maintain effective public services if revenues supporting such activities are low or nonexistent. Whether we are providing national defense or unemployment compensation, we need a *growth economy* to finance government benefits.

- Deciding which level of government should provide a certain service is a matter of federalism, with its ever-changing division of power.

- Budgeting occurs in the realm of certain *myths* about American policymaking. Myths concern living standards, the middle class, isolationism, free market expectations, power of elected executives, corruption, and effectiveness of local governments.

- *Functions of budgeting* include allocating resources to achieve governmental priorities, goals, and policies; raising funds through taxes and loans to finance the budget; stabilizing the economy through fiscal and monetary policies; holding operating agencies accountable for the use of budgeted resources; controlling expenditures; tranferring funds from one level of government to another; achieving planned social and economic development; and improving management in operating departments and agencies.

- *Budget cycles* feature the dominance of the appropriations and tax committees; the rise of power of the authorizing committees; the enactment of the Budget and Impoundment Control Act of 1974 and introduction of the budget committees; the paper tiger effect of the Balanced Budget and Emergency Deficit Control Act of 1985; and the Budget Enforcement Act of 1990, followed by the Budget Acts of 1993 and 1997.

- *Stages of the budget cycle* are executive preparation, legislative consideration, implementation and control of the enacted budget, and audit and evaluation.

- Operating departments and agencies, chief executives, and legislatures play roles in the budget process and offer *strategies* for *cultivating clientele* and *developing confidence* in their ideas, priorities, and programs.

- Growing deficits and the resulting lower savings lead to dwindling investments, slower economic growth, and finally decline in real gross domestic product. Living standards, in turn, stagnate and fall.

- Major progress was made on deficit reduction in the past several years, culminating in the passage of the *Balanced Budget Act of 1997.* Policy action accounted for about 25 percent of the improvement in the Congressional Budget Office's budget estimates. The remainder of the improvement was due primarily to economic factors.

- The roots of federal deficits are grounded in the unexpected economic slowdown in the mid-1970s, the domestic entitlements the federal government committed to during the 1962–1972 period, the Reagan administration's commitment to increased defense spending in the 1980s, and the weak cyclical performance of the American economy after 1974.

- America's persistent and growing trade deficit is rapidly deteriorating.
- *Fiscal policy* entails federal government policies with respect to taxes, spending, and debt management, and is intended to promote the nation's macroeconomic goals, particularly employment, gross domestic product, price level stability, and equilibrium in balance of payments.
- *Monetary policy* entails policies that affect the money supply, interest rates, and credit availability, and is intended to promote national macroeconomic goals—particularly employment, gross domestic product, price level stability, and equilibrium in balance of payments.
- Incremental budgeting demands little inquiry because the increment, not the base, is considered.
- Decremental budgeting is chaotic and conflict-laden. It may result in coercion, involve confrontation, and generate mistrust.
- Some states assume much larger federal tax burdens than do others.
- The 1990s were boom times for state and local governments.

- The key to the economic development of any state is the money it can bring into its economy from out-of-state. The per capita distribution of total federal spending varies from a high of $2.03 per dollar of tax revenue from New Mexico to 66 cents per dollar from New Jersey. In fiscal year 2001, total federal spending in the states amounted to $1.8 trillion.
- Most of America's governments divide their budgets into two sections, one for *capital* projects, the other for *expenses.*
- *Line-item budgets* usually include categories for personnel, equipment, and maintenance, among others.
- Performance budgets, program budgets, and zero-based budgets constitute *budgetary reforms.*
- The *per capita tax level* in the United States is not high with respect to America's economic competitors. The people of the United States are not overtaxed. Taxation as a percentage of national income is lower in the United States than in any other major industrialized country.
- The American philosophy of taxation is: "Don't tax me. Don't tax thee. Tax the fellow behind the tree."

Case Study
Budgeting Homeland Security

In order to coordinate intelligence about terror and make more secure domestic defenses, the Department of Homeland Security represents the most ambitious reorganization of the government's national security structure in more than a half-century. Not only are lines of authority changed. Budget responsibilities must be integrated into operations of the new federal department. The challenges are more complex than merely merging computer systems from 22 federal agencies. Security budgeting probes an interesting mixture of partisan, policy, and system politics.

"You can't have this sort of profound change in the agencies without profound changes in the Congress as well," stated an aide to J. Dennis Hassert (R-Illinois)

Speaker, U.S. House of Representatives, June 7, 2002

"The President's most important job," states the White House proposal for the Department of Homeland Security, "is to protect and defend the American people."[1] Prior to September 11, 2001, no one single government agency had homeland security as its primary mission. Responsibilities for homeland security were dispersed among more than one hundred different government organizations.

President George W. Bush argues that the United States needs a single, unified homeland security administrative structure. This administrative reorganization is massive. The President used his maximum legal authority to establish the White House Office of Homeland Security and Homeland Security Council. Bush asked Homeland Security Advisor Tom Ridge to examine components of the federal government to determine appropriate policy options. The new department would replace a confusing patchwork of government activities into a single department.

The central task of the megabureaucracy is to "analyze intelligence and act on it to protect against and prevent terrorist attacks on U.S. soil."[2] The challenges are almost endless. They range from merging different technology and communications systems to designing uniforms for border patrol personnel. A new department headquarters will house more than 7,000 employees throughout the Washington area.

President Bush's DHS budget for 2003—the federal government's first post-September 11 budget—almost doubles spending to secure the homeland. The $37.45 billion fiscal year 2003 homeland security budget enhances first responder programs. First responders are America's front-line soldiers: police officers, fire fighters, and emergency medical teams. First responders have the greatest potential to save lives and limit casualties.

First responder activities include support for state and local governments in developing comprehensive plans; for purchasing equipment; for fire fighters, police officers, and emergency medical technicians to respond and operate in a chemical or biological environment; and for improving response capabilities. First responders include one million firefighters, 556,000 full-time police officers, 180,000 sworn sheriffs, and over 155,000 registered emergency medical technicians.[3]

Besides the first responder emphasis, the Department of Homeland Security (DHS) focuses on securing America's borders, combatting bioterrorism, strengthening intelligence sharing, and improving transportation security. The $37.45 billion fiscal year 2003 budget represents an increase from $19.5 billion during fiscal year 2002.

According to President Bush, a single federal department makes Americans safer because one government bureaucracy would

- have a primary mission to protect the American homeland;

- be responsible for securing our borders, our transportation sector, our ports, and our critical infrastructure;
- synthesize and analyze homeland security intelligence from multiple sources;
- coordinate communications with state and local governments, private industry, and the American people about threats and preparedness;
- coordinate efforts to protect the American people against bioterrorism and other weapons of mass destruction;
- train and equip first responders;
- manage federal emergency response activities;
- station more security officers in the field working to stop terrorists;
- reduce duplicative and redundant activities that drain critical homeland security resources.[4]

The organization of the Department of Homeland Security, according to the White House proposal, calls for a clear and efficient organization structure with four divisions:

- *The Border and Transportation Security* division takes over the Immigration and Naturalization Service (INS) from the Department of Justice, the Customs Service from the Treasury Department, and the Coast Guard from the Department of Transportation. The portion of the Animal Plant and Health Inspection Service that governs agricultural quarantine inspections at points of entry will be housed in this division, as will the Transportation Security Administration.
- *The Emergency Preparedness and Response* division assumes tasks and personnel from the Federal Emergency Management Agency (FEMA).
- *The Chemical, Biological, Radiological and Nuclear Countermeasures* division takes over the Lawrence Livermore National Lab in California.
- *The Information Analysis and Infrastructure Protection* division draws personnel from the Federal Bureau of Investigation (FBI) and Central Intelligence Agency (CIA).[5]

In addition, the Secret Service moves from the Treasury Department to DHS.

Terrorism begins and ends with deteriorating human relations—in the Middle East and elsewhere. Pumping huge sums of taxpayer dollars into new administrative structures, routinizing employee functions in order to capture perpetrators of terror, and draining

(contiunued on page 298)

The Core of the Bush Fiscal Year 2003 Program

- **$5.9 billion to fight bioterrorism.** The budget plan calls bioterrorism "a new American vulnerability laid bare" by the anthrax attacks. A big infusion of cash would pay for research and development, state and local health systems, federal stockpiles for treating victims, and improved communications.

  1. Almost $1.7 billion would go to the National Institutes of Health for research on developing vaccines, tests, therapies, and other work to fight anthrax and other biological agents. The Defense Department would get $420 million to study bioterrorists and ways to fight biological weapons.
  2. Some $851 million would be set aside to help the government respond to a bioattack, including stockpiling antibiotics to treat 20 million people, improving the nation's supply of smallpox vaccine, and improving food safety.

- **$3.5 billion to help first responders such as fire fighters, police, and rescue squads.** The money would go for personal protective equipment, emergency medical gear, and detection equipment for biological and chemical agents, communications, and other items. It also could be used to conduct more frequent terrorism drills, improve emergency communication systems, and set up a new Homeland Security Corps.

- **$10.6 billion for protecting borders, "targeting illegal traffic while welcoming legitimate travelers."** The budget would more than double the number of Border Patrol agents and inspectors across the northern border, which "has become an attractive route for potential terrorists," Bush's budget proposals avers. The budget includes $380 million to set up a reliable way to track the entry and exit of immigrants, especially those seen as security threats.

- **$722 million to improve communication among federal agencies, states, and other jurisdictions.** To illustrate the need, the budget plan says that Sheik Omar Abdel Rahman, involved in the 1993 World Trade Center bombing, entered the United States legally and was granted permanent resident alien status despite a terrorist past. "Improved information sharing could make a repeat of such tragic mistakes unlikely."

- **$4.8 billion for aviation security through the new Transportation Security Agency.**
- **$12.2 billion scattered elsewhere throughout the government.**

Government Changes in the Twentieth Century

1906: Department of Agriculture and Bureau of Immigration and Naturalization created.

1908: Bureau of Investigation formed. Becomes FBI in 1935.

1913: Departments of Commerce and Labor created.

1914: Trade Commission created.

1920: Power Commission created.

1930: Veterans Administration made independent agency.

1934: Federal Communications Commission and National Labor Relations Board created.

1939: Executive Office of the President created. Three agencies moved to new Federal Security Agency.

1942: Office of Strategic Services (forerunner of CIA) created.

1948: Atomic Energy Commission created.

1947: National Security Act merges military and creates CIA and National Security Council.

1949: Defense Department created. General Services Administration consolidates six agencies.

1963: Health, Education and Welfare Department created.

1965: Housing and Urban Development Department created.

1966: Transportation Department, combining six agencies, is created.

1970: Environmental Protection Agency and Occupational Safety and Health Administration created.

1977: Energy Department, combining five agencies, is created.

1979: Health, Education and Welfare split into two departments: Education, and Health and Human Services.

Source: Curt Anderson, "Homeland Security: Not Likely Soon," *The Detroit News,* August 15, 2002, http://www.detnews.com/2002/politics/0208/ 18/a08-562491.htm. Reprinted with permission of The Associated Press.

resources from federal, state, and local budgets—and ultimately, the American people—may become a dysfunctional process.

This combination of policy and system politics may also prove unpopular as it becomes more expensive. "You can have all the reorganization in the world, but if you don't have more resources, you're going to end up with empty boxes," stated Wisconsin representative David Obey. "The transition costs are going to be enormous, and as far as I can tell, they haven't given any thought to it."[6]

The President is granted flexibility to bypass civil service rules in hiring, firing, and promoting the 170,000 workers from 22 agencies in the new department. The chief executive may waive collective bargaining rights if he deems national security to be at stake. Government unions may adjudicate disputes over work rules. They may respond to proposed work rule changes within 30 days. If agreement is not reached, the department may send a letter to Congress explaining the dispute. Members of Congress may protest. Another 30 days are allocated for mediation. Conditions of employment are central in the establishment of this department. Employee salaries and benefits are an expensive budgetary item in the government campaign against terror.[7]

"Don't let Homeland Security become homeland pork," write Stephen Moore and Phil Kerpen, President and Research Assistant, respectively, for the Club for Growth. Moore and Kerpen conclude: "Republicans are in danger of trying so hard to appease every special interest group in Washington that they will alienate the one forgotten group that got them elected to office in the first place: taxpayers." These authors ask if the war on terror will defeat the war on big government.[8]

The procurement budget could place DHS in a league with NASA (National Aeronautics and Space Administration), the Department of Energy, and the Department of Defense. In fiscal year 2000, the Energy department awarded nearly $17 billion in prime contracts. Approximately one hundred acquisition employees and more than $500 million in procurement dollars will find their way to DHS with Customs Service and Secret Service private sector contracts. DHS would become a very big spender; its procurement budget would climb to more than $5 billion annually. Will DHS acquisition operations be decentralized? How will DHS write and award multibillion-dollar homeland security contracts?[9]

Congressional lawmakers control Cabinet department budgets. They seek authority over the DHS budget. "The war on terrorism has been expanded to include the war on turf," points out Jane Harman, California representative. DHS has taken budgets, skills, knowledge, and expertise from other departments and agencies. Yet, the "mindsets" of those units are still in play. "My concern would be that a junior Cabinet agency is not going to be able to order Treasury and Justice and Defense around," said U.S. Senator Jeff Sessions of Alabama. "I worked with all those agencies as an U.S. attorney, and they're like foreign nations."[10]

The first location of DHS headquarters was not very impressive. DHS headquarters, located on Nebraska Avenue in a predominantly residential neighborhood, was approximately five miles from the White House. The material culture of the Department's borrowed physical structure did not match the symbolism of the new megabureaucracy. Tom Ridge, the DHS leader, occupies a very weak power position among senior Bush administration bureaucrats. Ridge must organize DHS and lobby for DHS programs on Capitol Hill.[11]

Transferring dozens of federal agencies—and large budgets—from one box in agency flowcharts to another box in a projected Homeland Security flowchart is a daunting endeavor. Federal bureaucrats are often entrenched. Elected representatives focus on the the daily grind back in their districts.

Jeffrey H. Birnbaum points out that just because agencies are housed under the same roof does not mean that they work well together. Various DHS units are scattered throughout Washington and the country. Birnbaum asks: Why make these changes? Will DHS really improve our security at home and abroad? According to Birnbaum, "Sadly, the answer may be no. Or more probably, not much."[12]

Two intervening variables might delay or even waylay the Department of Homeland Security. The first is money—costs or budgets. According to the White House, the public and private sectors are already spending $100 billion per year on homeland security. Questions are being raised about the effects of more government spending on the expanding budget deficit, especially as difficult economic times are causing the states and local governments budgeting difficulties.[13]

A second intervening variable is citizen trust in government. Overall trust in government fell from the very high levels reported after the September 11 terrorist attacks. Despite this decline in trust, citizens still favor a new Cabinet-level Department of Homeland Security to prevent future attacks. In a CNN/Gallup/*USA Today* poll conducted Labor Day 2002, 60 percent of respondents said Congress should enact laws to create the new department. Only 29 percent opposed the idea.[14]

It appears that citizens expect satisfactory (not optional) levels of agency programming and express satisfactory (not optional) amounts of confidence in the federal government to protect them from terror attacks. Citizens wonder how the country can pay for the President's homeland security strategy.

Paul C. Light, Vice President and Director of Governmental Studies at the Brookings Institution, asks four basic questions regarding the DHS reorganization: (1) Should there be a reorganization at all? (2) Does this reorganization go too far? (3) Can the proposed department be effectively managed? (4) Does the proposal leave anything out?[15]

In this drama, the last question should come first. Why were so many Americans at the World Trade Center and Pentagon victims to international terror? What did Americans do, if anything, to contribute to their victim status? No structural-functional administrative arrangement, no inflated budgets, no coherence of line-and-staff positions, no rigid laws of commerce, and no flag waving will serve the taxpayers well until those inquiries are debated and resolved.

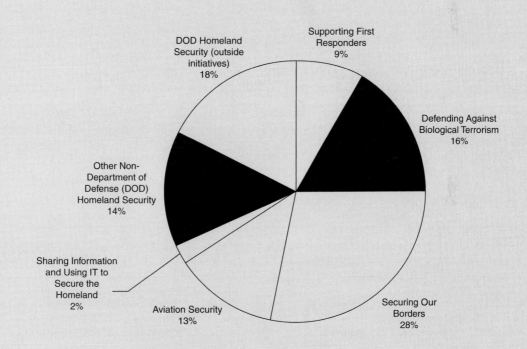

$37.7 Billion

Fiscal Year 2003 Homeland Security distribution by purpose.

Source: "FY 2003 Homeland Security Distribution by Purpose" as appeared on the website, www.input.com. Copyright © INPUT 2002. All rights reserved. Reprinted with permission.

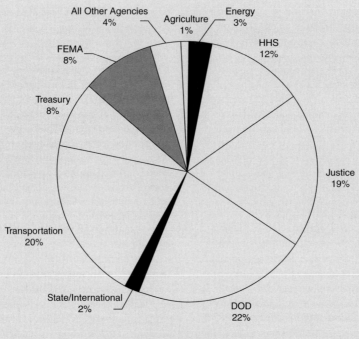

$37.7 Billion

Fiscal Year 2003 Homeland Security distribution by agency.

Source: "FY 2003 Homeland Security Distribution by Agency" as appeared on the website, www.input.com. Copyright © INPUT 2002. All rights reserved. Reprinted with permission.

Questions and Instructions

1. Why is a unified homeland security administrative structure preferred over the multidepartmental approach? Explain.
2. In what ways are the challenges of homeland security almost endless? Explain and illustrate.
3. "Terrorism begins and ends with deteriorating human relations." How so? Explain and illustrate.
4. Why do some express concerns about homeland security becoming homeland pork? Explain and illustrate.
5. The Department of Homeland Security takes budgets, skills, knowledge, and expertise from other departments and agencies. Yet the mindsets of those units are still in play. Why is this so? Explain and illustrate.

6. Why is the material culture of the Department of Homeland Security symbolic? Explain.
7. Do sophisticated technologies really improve our chances of being more secure? Explain.
8. If the costs of creating the Department of Homeland Security are prohibitive, will Americans choose lower budget deficits and less formalized security measures? If so, why? Explain and illustrate.
9. What did Americans do, if anything, to contribute to their status as victims of terror? Explain and illustrate.

Insights-Issues/Budgeting Homeland Security

Clearly and briefly describe and illustrate the following concepts and issues. Interpret the word *role* as meaning impacts, applications, importance, effects, and/or illustrations of certain facts, concerns, or issues from the case study.

1. Role of higher federal budgets (more dollars) in fighting terrorism.
2. Role of procurement budgeting (contracting out to private entrepreneurs) in fighting terrorism.

3. Role of first responders (government employees)—and federal budgets—in fighting terrorism.
4. Role of taking budgets, skills, knowledge, and expertise from former staff-line portfolios to the Department of Homeland Security.
5. Role of patriotism and flag waving in raising budgets and fighting terrorism.

Case Endnotes

1. "Full Text of White House Proposals for Homeland Security Department," *Government Executive Magazine,* June 6, 2002, http://www.govexec.com/news/index.cfm?mode=report&articleid=23108&printerfriendlyVers=1.
2. Curt Anderson, "Homeland Security: Not Likely Soon," *The Detroit News,* August 15, 2002, http://www.detnews.com/2002/politics/0208/18/a08-562491.htm.3. See also Office of International Information Programs, U.S. Department of State, Washington File, "Fact Sheet: White House Increased Funding for Homeland Security," January 24, 2002; http://usinfo.state.gov/topical/pol/terror/02012415.htm.
4. "Full Text" *op.cit.*
5. Ron Fournier, "Bush Seeks Homeland Security Department," *Amarillo Globe-News,* June 6, 2002, http://www.amarillonet.com/stories/060602/usn_bushseeks.shtml.
6. William M. Welsch, "Skeptics: Bush Underestimates Costs of New Cabinet," *USA Today,* June 18, 2002, http://www.usatoday.com/news/washdc/2002/06/18/homeland-security.htm.
7. Helen Dewar, "Homeland Bill Gets Boost," *The Washington Post,* November 12, 2002, http://www.washingtonpost.com/wp-dyn/articles/A45457-2002Nov12.html.
8. Stephen Moore and Phil Kerpen, "Don't Let Homeland Security Become Homeland Pork," *Human Events Online,* February 18, 2002, http://www/humaneventsonline.com/articles/02-18-02/moorekerpen.htm.
9. George Cahlink and Shane Harris, "Big Homeland Security Department Would Spend Big Dollars,"

GovExec.com, June 20, 2002, http://www.govexec.com/news/index.cfm?mode=report.cfm?mode=report&articleid=23130&printerfriendlyVers=1.
10. Mark Benjamin and Nicholas M. Horrock, "Bush's Homeland Security Flounders," *The Washington Times,* May 7, 2002, http://asp.washtimes.com/printarticle.asp?action=print&ArticleID=07052002-084036-3663r.
11. Judy Keen and Richard Benedetto, "Bush Proposes Homeland Department," *USA Today,* June 6, 2002, http://www.usatoday.com/news/attack/2002/06/06/attacks-bush.htm.
12. Jeffrey H. Birnbaum, "Do We Need a Homeland Security Department?" *Fortune.com,* June 13, 2002, http://www.fortune.com/indext.jhtml?channel=print_article.jhtml@doc_id=208415.
13. Bill Miller, "Homeland Security Cost Weighed," *The Washington Post,* July 17, 2002; p. A08, http://www.washingtonpost.com/ac2/ wp-dyn/A15821-2002Jul16?language=printer.
14. Tom Shoop, "Americans Favor Homeland Agency Even as Trust in Government Drops," *GovExec.com,* September 9, 2002, http://www.govexec.com/news/index.cfm?mode=report&articleid=23825&printerfriendlyVers=1.
15. Paul C. Light, "Assessing the Department of Homeland Security," Brookings Institution, June 25, 2002, http://www.brookings.edu/printme.wns?page=/pagedefs/a6bd8ec4adcff3b7fffa1090a141465.xml.

Note: The author expresses appreciation to Eric E. Richardson, graduate assistant, Ball State University, for his commentary on this case study and security issues.

Chapter Endnotes

1. Donald Axelrod, *Budgeting for Modern Government* (New York: St. Martin's Press, 1995).

2. "1993 Budget-Reconciliation Act," *Congressional Quarterly Weekly Report* 51, no. 37 (September 18, 1993): 2482–2498.

3. Jonathan Rauch, "The End of Government," *National Journal* 28, no. 36 (September 7, 1996): 1890–1896.

4. Jonathan Rauch, "Ducking the Challenge," *National Journal* 29, no. 6 (February 8, 1997): 260–265.

5. Jonathan Rauch and Eliza Newlin Carney, "The Easy Way Out," *National Journal* 29, no. 19 (May 10, 1997): 928–931.

6. L. Douglas Lee, "How Congress Handles the Budget," *The Wharton Magazine* 4 (Winter 1980): 29.

7. Marshall E. Dimock, Gladys Ogden Dimock, and Douglas M. Fox, *Public Administration* (New York: Holt, Rinehart and Winston, 1983), p. 359.

8. John L. Mikesell, *Fiscal Administration: Analysis and Applications for the Public Sector,* 2nd ed. (Chicago: Dorsey Press, 1986), pp. 75–85.

9. Dimock, Dimock, and Fox, *Public Administration,* p. 367.

10. Peter F. Rousmaniere, *Local Governments Auditing—A Manual for Public Officials* (New York: Council on Muncipal Performance, 1980), p. 83.

11. Advisory Commission on Intergovernmental Relations, "Sunset Legislation and Zero-Based Budgeting," *Information Bulletin* 76, no. 5 (December 1976): 1.

12. Mikesell, *Fiscal Administration,* p. 48.

13. Mikesell, *Fiscal Administration,* pp. 56–60.

14. Aaron Wildavsky, *The Politics of the Budgetary Process* (Boston: Little, Brown and Co., 1984), pp. 63–126.

15. Barry Bozeman and Jeffrey D. Straussman, "Shrinking Budgets and the Shrinkage of Budget Theory," *Public Administration Review* 42, no. 6 (November–December 1982): 509–515. Lance T. LeLoup, *Budgetary Politics* (Brunswick, OH: King's Court Communications, 1986), pp. 16–21; Greenhouse, "The Planning-Programming-Budgeting System," see also Robert D. Behn, "Cutback Budgeting," pp. 155–177.

16. Murray L. Weidenbaum, "Budget Dilemma and Its Solution," in *Control of Federal Spending,* ed. C. Lowell Harris (New York: The Academy of Political Science, 1985), pp. 47–58.

17. Bozeman and Straussman, "Shrinking Budgets," pp. 511.

18. Mikesell, *Fiscal Administration,* pp. 56–60.

19. Mikesell, *Fiscal Administration,* pp. 56–60.

20. Robert D. Reischauer, "The Budget: Crucible for the Policy Agenda," in *Setting National Priorities: Budget Choices for the Next Century,* ed. Robert D. Reischauer (Washington, D.C.: The Brookings Institution Press, 1997), pp. 4–11.

21. Reischauer, "The Budget," pp. 4–11.

22. John Steele Gordon, "The Federal Debt," *American Heritage* 47, no. 7 (November 1995): 82–92.

23. For more detailed explanations of the comparatively low U.S. tax burden, see Louis Ferleger and Jay R. Mantle, "America's Hostility Toward Taxes," *Challenge* 14, no. 4 (July–August 1991): 54; "No Pain, No Gain: Taxes, Productivity, and Economic Growth," *Challenge* 36, no. 3 (May–June 1993): 11–20; and *A New Mandate: Democratic Choices for a Prosperous Economy* (Columbia, Mo: University of Missouri Press, 1994).

24. See *Federal Debt and Interest Costs* (Congressional Budget Office, May 1993), and *Federal Debt: Answers to Frequently Asked Questions* (November 27, 1996).

25. *Budget Issues: Analysis of Long-Term Fiscal Outlook* (Congressional Budget Office, October 1997; GAO/AIMD/OCE-98-19).

26. "Tax & Economic Policy," http://www.onlytheissues.com/politics.cgi?issue=4.
27. "The Basics: Balancing the Budget: An Anatomy of the Deficit," http://www.tcf.org/Publications/Basics/Balanced_Budget/Anatomy_of_the_Deficit.html.
28. "Policy News: Budget Forecast Worsens Sharply," *Almanac of Policy Issues,* August 27, 2002, http://www.policyalmanac.org/economic/news/budget-2002-08-10.shtml.
29. Franco Modigliani and Robert M. Solow, "America Is Borrowing Trouble," *The New York Times,* April 9, 2001.
30. William Greider, "The End of Empire," *The Nation,* Vol. 275, No. 9 (September 23, 2002), pp. 13–15.
31. The Tax Foundation, "Tax and Spending Policies Benefit Some States, Leave Others Footing the Bill," http://www.taxfoundation.org/pr-fedtaxspendingratio.html; Patricia Buscher, "Federal Domestic Spending Up 9 Percent in 2001, Census Bureau Reports, *Census Bureau News,* April 23, 2002.
32. "State Finance Data: Overall Tax Burdens by State, State Finance Report," Tax Foundation's State Finance Section, http://www.taxfoundation.org/statefinance.html; Public Information Office, "State Government Spending Tops $1 Trillion, Census Bureau Reports," May 31, 2002; see also: "State Revenue Report," Fiscal Studies Program: The Nelson A. Rockefeller Institute of Government, December 2001, No. 46; "The Fiscal Survey of States," The National Governors Association and the National Association of State Budget Officers, December 2001.

The Productivity Challenge: Working Smarter While Doing More with Less

Chapter Highlights

What Is Excellence?

Efficiency and Effectiveness

Privatization of the Public Sector

Evaluating Government Programs

Citizen-Driven Government Performance

People Crisis and/or Opportunity?

The Highway Performance Monitoring System (HPMS)

Summary

SETs, Program Evaluation, and College Professors

Student power at Steady State University is known throughout higher education. For example, a non-tenured professor was removed as the instructor of an introductory chemistry course when a student petition with signatures from 100 of his 200 students claimed he demonstrated an "inability to teach new information" and a "willful academic demoralization of students."

Three perspectives emerged. Some students said he was a victim of "whiny" students—that he was simply a tough teacher. Many students feared that a low grade in a difficult subject would keep them from admission to graduate school. Others said he ignored student questions—and made tests more difficult than they needed to be.[1]

In a world of "corporate responsibility" and "human error," validity is not easy to access. SETs, or student evaluations of teaching, provide historical trends for rating the production of college professors. The "convergent validity" of student ratings correlates with other measures of teaching effectiveness.[2] Grading practices, SETs ratings, student motivations, and the skills, knowledge, and expertise of professors contribute to program evaluations of higher-education productivity.

How do colleges and universities, especially those that are taxpayer-funded, evaluate teaching effectiveness? Validity, bias, and utility measures are critical. Teaching effectiveness is multidimensional. SETs attempt to measure a composite of delivering instruction, facilitating interactions, and ascertaining student learning. SETs, then, are positively correlated with expected course grades. Pedagogy at SSU focuses on processing as much as content. The SSU administration, after all, pays professor salaries. Student enrollees pay ever-higher tuition fees. The culture for academic disciplines is not well-established at SSU.

Like other state universities, SSU employs SETs for tenure and promotion purposes. Professors initially used SETs for feedback so that they might know student needs. Now the primary purpose is to make personnel decisions—that is, to make decisions for retention, promotion, tenure, and salary increases.

Despite this trend, SSU refuses to confront the problems of defining teaching effectiveness. SSU promotes politically correct or popular standards and perceptions in the classroom. Low student academic preparation is not taken into account. The SSU Teachers' College is known for fostering a grading system where "students pay their fees—and get their Bs."

"Teachers have no duty to teach using a particular style, only to teach successfully," argues Michael Scriven.[3] Elements of success, achievement, excellence, effectiveness, and efficiency are based on teaching and learning cultures. Teaching styles, therefore, constitute but one aspect of a complex evaluative theory of teaching productivity.

Scriven identifies the duties of college professors in the following framework:[4]

1. *Knowledge of subject matter* (curriculum demands)
2. *Instructional competence* (communication, course construction skills)
3. *Assessment competence* (test construction and grading criteria)
4. *Professionalism* (ethics and attitudes)
5. *Nonstandard but contractual duties* (community service)

SETs and program evaluations at Steady State University are *context-dependent:* They take into account constituents' needs, wants, and expectations. Pertinent societal values, customs, and mores are recognized. Relevant laws and statutes, economic dynamics, political forces, media interests, and protocols cannot be ignored by evaluators. The organizational mission, goals, and priorities of Steady State University are driving forces in how professors produce in the classroom. The organizational governance and management of SSU indicate how employees feel and react to policies. SSU's history and current challenges make SETs context-dependent.

The SSU Student Government Association (SGA) contributes to the program evaluation of Steady State professors. The SGA consists of volunteer students, elected by the student body, working for all students at SSU. SGA is composed of legislative, executive, and judicial branches. Getting involved in SGA is simple; students apply for positions and committee memberships, and attend SGA meetings.

The SSU/SGA constitution spells out that SGA:

- provides a forum for the expression of student views and interests;
- focuses on academic freedoms, academic responsibilities, and student rights;
- seeks to facilitate improvements in student cultural, social, and physical welfare;
- acknowledges that the achievement of skills, knowledge, and expertise is the primary reason for attending SSU;
- promotes the development of more effective instruction standards, classroom facilities, and teaching and learning methods;
- emphasizes student knowledge of history, politics, economics, languages, and cultures;
- recognizes the rights and responsibilities of students in regard to the mission, goals, and priorities of SSU, the community of College Corner, the state of Commonwealth, and humanity.[5]

At SSU, taxpayer resources flow to students and student programs. Proactive initiatives are commended and rewarded. Because students learn at different rates, SSU learning is individualized. Students, professors, and administrators recognize that classroom production differs from other kinds of production. Outcomes from SETs are not considered standards. However, SSU professors long ago dismissed SETs as helpful feedback for improving teaching methods.

Market values drive program functions, organization structures, academic standards, and emerging technologies at SSU. Inductive thinking is piecemeal, at best. Senior administrative staff are committed to centralized budgeting methods—or determining who gets what amount of money.

Program evaluation is constant—reflecting the mission, goals, and priorities of SSU. SETs—as SSU program evaluation techniques—are utilized to promote, penalize, or otherwise discipline professors. Yet, SSU administrative leaders insist that professors enjoy academic freedom as they probe the depths of young minds.

Raising agendas and making a difference is what program evaluation—for professors, administrators, and student productivity—is all about at Steady State University. This taxpayer-funded, state-financed university is an "opportunity institution"—a marketplace of student rights, decremental budgeting, fleeting accountability, and routinized program responsibilities.

Endnotes

[1]Robert E. Haskell, "Academic Freedom, Tenure, and Student Evaluation of Faculty: Galloping Polls in the 21st Century," *Education Policy Analysis Archives,* Vol. 5, No. 6 (February 12, 1997).

[2]"Student Ratings of Professors: A Series of Articles in *The American Psychologist,* November 1997," http://www.luc.edu/faculty/eposava/amerpsyc.htm.

[3]Michael Scriven, "Duties of the Teacher," *Journal of Personnel Evaluation in Education,* Vol. 8, No. 2 (1994), pp. 151–184.

[4]*Ibid.*

[5]"Buttons Will Go Here!" SGA@OSU. https://you.okstate.edu/sga/.

Sources

Ernest R. House and Kenneth R. Howe, "Deliberative Democratic Evaluation Checklist," October, 2000; http://www.wmich.edu/evalctr/checklists/dd_checklist.htm Benjamin Levin, "Students and Educational Productivity," *Educational Policy Analysis Archives,* Vol. 1, No. 5 (May 4, 1993), http://epaa.asu.edu/epaa/v1n5.html; Daniel L. Stufflebeam, "Evaluation Values and Criteria Checklist," March 2001; Evaluation Checklists Project, www.wmich.edu/evalctr/checklists. "Institutionalizing Evaluation Checklist," July 15, 2002; http://www.wmich.edu/evalctr/checklists/values_criteria.pdf. Phillip N. Venditti, "Defining the Productivity of Community College Administrators," *Leadership Abstracts,* Vol. 8, No. 4 (April 1995).

What Is Excellence?

Productivity in the public sector refers to excellence in individual and collective performance—especially in times when public employees are expected to do more with less. The employees could be public school teachers, occupational safety inspectors, highway patrol officers, fire fighters, air traffic controllers, maintenance crews removing snow from the streets, or sanitation workers removing waste and technological excess from communities.

Among these areas of worker expertise, there are widely divergent views as to what excellence is. *Excellence,* in its various forms, is based on the cultural context of a particular function. Therefore, measuring excellence and employee productivity in government-funded organizations is a problematic assignment. The public sector usually deals in services, which, because they are intangible and often widely variable, almost always present problems in productivity measurement. Many government experts concede that some public sector functions are not measurable with the mechanisms currently available.

Despite these difficulties, an organization should adapt excellence as its main component. The system should enable an organization to achieve high-performance levels from their employees. Outstanding performance not only benefits the organization but also improves the delivery of services to the citizens.[1] Most citizens care about the performance of their public institutions. Parents worry about the quality of their children's schools. City dwellers anxiously scan the latest crime statistics.

Drivers pray for better roads, transit riders for dependable buses and subways, air travelers for effective air traffic control.[2]

Posing particular difficulties for analyses are numerous staff operations, such as personnel work and social casework. One has only to think of the complexities involved in trying to measure the productivity of a caseworker in a public welfare office to realize some of the difficulty. Should the caseworker be rated on how many cases he or she clears from the welfare rolls, or on how many people he or she adds? Using either standard can produce distortions.

Efficiency and Effectiveness

Related to these problems is the central task of distinguishing between efficiency and effectiveness. Efficiency means *doing things well,* while effectiveness means *doing the right things well. Efficiency,* essentially, is the input of labor, capital, and other resources into an effort matched against the output of product, regardless of the mechanism selected to gauge output. *Effectiveness,* meanwhile, calls for a preestablished standard of comparison; a focus upon a certain quality of production; an ability to mobilize, organize, and direct resources for specified purposes, taken within a certain cultural context.

Government Performance Perceptions

Mark Abramson explains citizen dissatisfaction with government performance with four points of emphasis:

Democracy is "messy." Democratic governments are designed to promote equity and fairness. Pluralism is central to the way American society is organized. The inherent nature of our government admits to inefficiency and ineffectiveness. Citizens expect only satisfactory—not optimum—performance from government units. Democracy is not cost-effective.

Government takes a "bum rap." The media, politicians, academics, and government oversight agencies accentuate what's wrong with government bureaucracies. U.S. public bureaucracies are not actually the stereotyped discriminators and bunglers they are made out to be. They are not homogeneous, antipoor, and antiminority. Markets are perfect; societies fail because governments fail.

Government must "shape up." Disincentives must be overcome. Government support systems should encourage and reward public administrators rather than penalize them for taking risks. No public philosophy exists for judging the effectiveness of government programs. Partisan consensus for maintaining the government welfare state prevents some government agencies from being downsized. Innovations threaten the status quo.

The country must "shape up." Productivity problems are not unique to government operations. The performance of the nation as a whole, not only the public sector, is important for a national common purpose. Federal deficits are traced to a society grounded in short-term consumer decision making with little, if any, long-term commitments to values that promote savings and investments for the future.

War and terror threats are priority. Political dissentions prevent the nation from "shaping up." Attacks against the World Trade Center and Pentagon have delayed an emerging consensus for policymaking. The citizenry is divided on many issues. Partisan politics takes priority over policy and system politics. Fragmentation is a catalyst for enhanced economic disparities.

Sources: Mark A. Abramson, "The Public Manager and Excellence," *The Bureaucrat,* Vol. 14, No. 3 (Fall 1985): 9–13; see also Charles T. Goodsell, *The Case for Bureaucracy: A Public Administration Polemic* (Chatham, N.J.: Chatham House Publishers, 1983), pp. 55–60.

Government, Morality, and Family

The government has a role to play in restoring morality to public life, argues William R. Marty. Marty says that government should not reflect the views held by religious fanatics or libertarian lunatics, but strive to guarantee that government institutions that support moral growth remain strong. This gov-

ernment role involves support for the traditional family structure, guarantees some degree of moral education in the schools, and gives parents flexible choices in the education of their children.

Source: William R. Marty, "Government, Morality, and the Family," *Journal of Interdisciplinary Studies* 7, nos. 1–2 (Annual 1995): 1–25.

As one commentator noted, a man might be efficient in driving nails into a table. Effectiveness enters the picture when we question whether he should be driving nails into a table at all. Questions regarding quality make the public productivity measurer's task still more of a hazard and a hassle. A fiddler isn't necessarily producing more by fiddling faster. Nor can a pianist be hailed as especially productive for playing Chopin's Minute Waltz in fifty seconds. On a more mundane and realistic level, a narcotics squad that makes a lot of arrest quotas for their narcotic divisions had to change them when they realized that such productivity measures were not producing "quality" arrests—in other words, arrests of major dealers.[3]

Privatization of the Public Sector

Privatization means that a service previously produced by a government agency is now produced by a nongovernmental organization. The government may sell to private buyers, or a private concern may sell to government. *Contracting out,* as it is often called, is thought to be more efficient because:

- It harnesses competitive forces and brings the pressure of the marketplace to bear on inefficient workers.
- It permits better management, free of most of the distractions characteristic of overtly political organizations.
- It places the costs and benefits of managerial decisions more directly on the decision maker, whose own rewards are directly at stake.[4]

As government at all levels has come under attack, the conclusion that the private sector performs and produces more effectively has received considerable credibility. If privatization is the answer in general, however, no one seems to agree on the particulars, such as what products will be produced privately or what provisions for private entrepreneurship will follow.

Conflicting definitions of privatization center around provisions, or providing, and production, or producing.[5] Executives, legislators, and judges make and interpret policies that provide services. Government functions as buyer and seller. A good example of services that are privatized to varying degrees are security services. One can lay out a four-part scheme of possible overlap of sectors, government and nongovernment, providing and producing security services. Of the four possibilities, there are two admixtures of responsibility and two possibilities where one sector or the other takes full responsibility for the provision and production of security.

- *Case 1.* Government does both—The legislature writes the law and provides the money; the Department of Corrections runs the prison. Neither function is private.
- *Case 2.* Production is private—The City of Bloomington decides to provide security when the high school hockey teams play at the city arena. The city contracts with Pinkertons for the guards.
- *Case 3.* Provision is private—Government sells to private buyers. The North Stars hockey team wants security at Metropolitan Sports Center, and it contracts with the Bloomington city police.
- *Case 4.* Both activities are private—A department store decides that it wants uniformed security and employs (or contracts privately for) its own guards. Government performs neither activity.[6]

The policy decision in Case 1, the pure-case public sector, shows government as a public bureau producing the service. Case 2 entails the controversial system of a government contracting out. Case 3 illustrates government selling services to a private buyer. Case 4 portrays a pure case of a private agency selling to a private buyer. Of the two words, *provision* is the more complicated to explain. The word *providing* can be confusing. For example, society (or government) provides medical care to the elderly; however, medical doctors are the providers. To provide in this context means to make policy, to decide, to buy, to regulate, to franchise, to finance, to subsidize.

A publicly provided service is described in this manner:

1. The decision whether to have the service (and the decisions about who shall have it and how much of it) is a political decision.
2. Government arranges for the recipients not to have to pay directly for the service themselves.
3. Government selects the producer that will serve them.

A privately provided service is described in this way:

1. Individuals and nongovernmental organizations make their own decisions whether or not to have the service.
2. If they choose to have it, they pay for it in full out of their own resources, whatever these may be.
3. They select the producer themselves.[7]

There are mixed cases of public and private provisions as well. Government may provide a service and allow citizens to decide whether to use it. The financing of such provisions may be divided between public and private sectors as users finance part and the government pays part of the costs. Some citizens (the wealthy) may pay the full cost of provisions, while government picks up the complete tab for others (the poor). Government may finance the complete cost but permit the user to choose the vendor. The provision of schools is financed, publicly, via taxes.

Nontax devices, such as regulations and franchising, are used as well. Government regulations require restaurant owners to clean the premises themselves at their own expense; in franchising provisions of water, gas, or electricity, government allows a monopoly to develop, which, in turn, permits an average price, overcharging some customers while subsidizing still others. In privatizing the provision of services, government withdraws or reduces its role as buyer, regulator, standard setter, or decision maker.

Now let us examine the concept of *production* as it applies to activities of government. Government officials decide to produce the services they determine should be provided. In other words, government operates, delivers, runs, performs, sells, and administers services. As emphasized, service production is less complicated than service provision. Production may be divided into line services, and support or staff services; production may be divided into labor-intensive functions, equipment and facilities; production may focus upon the substance of the work itself, or on the management or administration of work. For example, a municipality may divide refuse collection among several garbage collection companies or the management of worker pension funds among several financial institutions.

In privatizing public sector production, the question of competition is an important one. If the shift is merely from a public sector provider to a single private sector one, a monopoly supplier still exists. The deregulation of railroads, aviation, trucking, banking, healthcare, and telecommunications has taken place in the private sphere to encourage competition. Despite such efforts, questions concerning competitiveness remain.

The neat distinctions between government's primary policy decision providing a service and the secondary decision producing a service are not, in reality, easily discerned. The Federal Aviation Administration administers air safety for public and private good. The Department of Defense contracts with private providers for base support and maintenance. Pinkerton and Wells Fargo, private security firms, have a long history of public service. Public day-care centers allow young mothers economic opportunities in the private sphere.

Privatization of some government services, notably Social Security and the Postal Service, is being considered to decrease costs and increase efficiency. Proponents think that the competition created by contracting out will improve federal government programs. So far, many state and local governments are experimenting with privatization, but the federal government resists. Unions oppose the practice because they fear the adverse effects on employee salaries and benefits.[8]

The George W. Bush administration did not need approval of Congress to place nearly half the federal civilian workforce, approximately 850,000 government jobs, in the private contractor competitive marketplace. The Bush privatization plan is a major expansion of trends taking place in government at all levels for the past two decades. According to OMB, 60 percent of the privatized jobs make their way to small businesses and companies owned by women and minorities.

Bush's goal is to "create a market-based government unafraid of competition, innovation and choice." Savings from privatization plans are targeted to be 20 to 30 percent. However, after taking over government jobs, contractors may perform poorly or encounter legal or financial trouble. Bobby L. Harnage, Sr., president of American Federation of Government Employees, a government union representing 600,000 federal workers, protested that Bush had "declared all-out war on federal

Public versus Private Postal Productivity

Perhaps the most maligned public agency is the U.S. Postal Service (USPS). The cost of a first-class stamp has risen in the past and will certainly rise steadily in the future. Statutes prohibit private firms from competition with the U.S. Postal Service for first-class service. It is possible that private entrepreneurs could find cheaper, more effective ways to deliver a huge volume of first-class mail, but the U.S. Postal Service is more than a national post office. USPS is a conduit, a catalyst for undergirding capitalism by facilitating consumer advertising through the mail, for bolstering the free press, disseminating information through newspapers and magazines, and for promoting commerce in general.

By comparison, United Parcel Service (UPS) delivers twice the number of parcels as the U.S. Postal Service, with lower rates, faster deliveries, and an 80 percent lower damage rate, and still makes a profit. But will UPS deliver your favorite fashion catalog, news magazine, or church bulletin for mere pennies? The U.S. Postal Service subsidizes at a reasonable cost many and varied cultural, economic, and even political activities in the United States.

employees." Harnage insisted that federal employees almost always offer more expertise and experience than outside contractors.[9]

Contract compliance programs help companies comply with numerous laws governing contracts and subcontracts with the federal government, avoid criminal prosecution, and reduce violation fines. Contract compliance programs include

- codes of ethics to be adhered to by private sector employees;
- strategies for effective delegation of responsibilities;
- procedures for reporting violations, corrective measures for noncompliance, and constant evaluation of the compliance program; and
- a records management system for keeping records for the contract duration as specified by law.[9a]

Privatization, therefore, is an effective way of providing necessary services, usually provided by the government, and overcoming the problem of shrinking federal, state, and local government budgets and ailing infrastructure. The government plays the role of prudent purchaser and manager of services offered by private sector contractors. Privatization aims at creating a market-driven partnership for the betterment of taxpayers, but it faces resistance from citizens as they fear elimination of services.[10] Privatizing government functions, then, is seen as a way of increasing efficiency and producing significant savings.

Empirical evidence *usually* shows private enterprises to be more efficient than public enterprises. Public sector productivity is lower than private sector productivity, labor costs are higher in the public sector than in the private sphere, and public utilities are less cost-effective than private utilities.[11] On the other hand, no one promised that democratic government was cost-effective, at least when measuring efficiency. *Fairness* is a more accurate standard for ascertaining the effectiveness of government services.

Employee Motivation Indicators and Peformance Guidelines

Gordon Maner, Carl Vinson Institute of Government, suggests certain indicators of lack of employee motivation. They are:

- *Little interest in achieving established goals.* Poorly motivated employees do not envision work unit goals as important. They will not work to reach goals. They may reject supervisor efforts to motivate them for personal or other reasons.
- *Unsatisfactory output and quality.* Poorly motivated employees are not careful workers. They often will not complete tasks adequately.
- *Absenteeism or tardiness.* Poorly motivated employees tend to arrive late or be absent from work. Absenteeism is considered a crucial indicator for detecting employee dissatisfaction.
- *Time killing/clock-watching activities.* Poorly motivated employees show signs of boredom with assigned tasks and responsibilities. However, they make no efforts to change employment.
- *Frequent request for help in solving minor problems.* Poorly motivated employees lack initiative in completing challenging tasks.
- *No desire to improve job knowledge.* Poorly motivated employees need attitude adjustments: "Why should I learn more?—I will still be doing the same old job." Improvements could lead to different opportunities for promotion, transfer, or the expansion of current tasks.

Maner recommends guidelines for correcting and improving employee performance. He emphasizes that constructive confrontation is a basic duty of any supervisor. The challenge, notes Maner, is to get employees to accept corrections without resentment. The guidelines are:

- *Know the attitudes and personality traits* of the employee you confront. Watch for indicators of frustration.
- *Be sure your own attitude is one of genuine helpfulness.* Exercising one's authority for authority's sake is not productive. The employee should not be confronted in anger; allow yourself to calm down. Think rationally before approaching an employee regarding improvement in his or her performance.
- *Get all the facts first.* Looking the role and doing the job are two separate things. Job performance may not reflect employee appearance, credentials, or communication skills.

Source: Software Techniques, 13105 Booker T. Washington Highway, Hardy, Va., 24101. See http://www.softwaretech.com/hrad/articles/.

Evaluating Government Programs

The taxing, budgeting, and government spending priorities place program evaluation *at the center, not at the periphery,* of policymaking in the public sector. To improve the effectiveness of program evaluation, such priorities need to assume their rightful place at the center of the policymaking and budget-making processes. Program evaluation needs consideration alongside financial and political lines. When Planning Programming Budgeting Systems (PPBS) began to diminish in the federal bureaucracy, many found a replacement in another analytical device—program evaluation. Some state and municipal governments have warmly welcomed this technique and have set up offices to evaluate their program performance.

According to Ralph C. Chandler and Jack C. Plano, program evaluation is:

> . . . an assessment of the effectiveness of a program through the application of a research design aimed at obtaining valid and verifiable information on the structure, processes, outputs, and impacts of the program. Program evaluation is an effort to help decision makers determine whether to maintain, modify, or discontinue a specified program. Program evaluation is concerned with whether program

activities have been successful in resolving the public problem identified, and the extent to which other factors may have contributed to the problem's resolution."[12]

There are three phases in program evaluation:

1. Selection and identification of goals and objectives of the program
2. Execution of the evaluation according to scientific guidelines
3. Feedback on results and recommendations

The overall goals of program evaluation, or PE as it is sometimes called, can be simply stated. PE increases our understanding of government activities, leads to governmental improvements, and produces financial savings. The tools it uses seem familiar—for the most part, they greatly resemble the types of analytical devices developed for PPBS, Zero-Based Budgets (ZBB), and Management by Objectives (MBO).

Legislative backing and buttressing have played a major role in the flourishing of program evaluation at all government levels.

The productivity challenge in the public sector is hampered by structural and environmental barriers; therefore, the need for evaluation of productivity is always present. In the private sphere, technology becomes an intervening factor between monetary rewards and corporate failures. However, productivity indices in the public sector are grounded in politics, with merit principles sometimes receiving less emphasis. As citizens, elected officials, and administrators consider the effectiveness of the bottom-line delivery of public services, there will be enhanced interest in proactive, rather than reactive, program evaluations and employee performance evaluations.

Citizens and policymakers seek evidence regarding program results from taxpayer-supported programs. Program evaluation efforts may identify problems and demonstrate results. Findings may impact state policies. In California, program evaluation of welfare reforms, smoking prevention efforts, and state prison drug treatment programs resulted in definitive policy impacts.

The California legislature recognizes high-priority program evaluation projects need adequate planning, time, and resources. Guidelines, in the form of questions, are posted as the legislature drafts legislative language calling for the evaluation of state-sponsored programs. Policymakers utilize guidelines with pertinent questions for the strategic investment of limited evaluation resources.

The guideline inquiries are:

1. Is evaluation of this program an important investment of state resources?
2. What questions does the legislature need to have answered about this program?
3. What will it take to answer the legislature's questions—and can adequate resources be provided?
4. What will it take to ensure credible evaluation findings?
5. Who should be involved in this evaluation—from inception to results?
6. When should evaluation findings be expected from this program?
7. What is the role of state agencies in this evaluation?
8. What information needs to be available for statewide evaluation?

Problems with program evaluation results may arise. Policymakers, legislative staff, and state government evaluation specialists reveal that evaluation reports sometimes do not focus on key policy questions. Legislators seek analytical reports when reviews merely describe clients and activities. Certain key stakeholders may be omitted. Findings may be misunderstood and not utilized. The request for program evaluation may come too soon in the life of the government program. Earmarked funding may prove inadequate for the rigorous work demanded. If the evaluator is not independent from the program, evaluation findings may lack credibility. Local government programs may not be required to collect standardized data.[13]

The United States Department of Education shifted in 2002 to a new approach to program evaluation—the Performance-Based Data Management Initiative. This centralized, consolidated, electronic system replaces the department's myriad data collections. The reform dramatically reduces reporting burdens on elementary and secondary schools. The focus is to gather much better data about program effectiveness.[14]

The Centers for Disease Control (CDC) Office on Smoking and Health (OSH) assists state tobacco control program managers and staff in the planning, design, implementation, and use of comprehensive evaluations of tobacco control efforts. Tobacco use is the leading preventable cause of death and disease in the United States—contributing to more than 430,000 deaths annually.

Tobacco control programs are designed to reduce disease, disability, and death related to tobacco use. To determine the effectiveness of prevention and control programs, evaluators document and measure program implementation and effects.

Program evaluation examines implementation protocols and operations, effectiveness, and accountability. CDC goals call for preventing the initiation of tobacco use among young people, promoting quitting among young people and adults, eliminating nonsmokers' exposure to environmental tobacco smoke (ETS), and identifying and eliminating disparities related to tobacco use and its effects among different population groups.

Measuring Government Operations

Harry P. Hatry and Diana R. Dunn offer ways of measuring the effectiveness of a government-operated recreation facility.

Accessibility. The number of people who reside within so many miles or so many minutes of the facility, proximity to public transportation, and other data on convenience of location determine its accessibility.

Usage. Likewise, the number of persons using the facility, how often they use it, and for how long are indicators of unit productivity. How often do citizens come to the facility, what services do they use, and how long do they stay?

Safety. What is the rate of injury at the facility? What about crime? Is the facility dangerous? The lack of recreation outlets may be linked to increased crime.

Attractiveness. Does the facility contribute to the neighborhood's physical design? Does it upgrade the neighborhood? What are its impacts on property values? How is commerce effected?

Overall satisfaction. This focus combines accessibility, use, safety, attractiveness, and culture impacts. How does the facility affect egalitarian values, mores, and citizen behavior? Is recreation afforded all citizens, or merely segments of the state and community?

Are community-state recreation opportunities excellent, good, fair, or poor?

Source: Harry P. Hatry and Diana R. Dunn, *Measuring the Effectiveness of Local Government Services: Recreation* (Washington, D.C.: Urban Institute, 1971).

Accountability includes assessing and documenting the effectiveness of programs, measuring program outcomes, documenting implementation and cost effectiveness, and increasing the impact of programs. Strategies stress community mobilization, policy and regulatory action, and the strategic use of media. Program evaluation examines the effectiveness of these strategies for meeting program goals.[15]

Performance-Based Management

Transportation services—more so than other government-produced programs—are likely to be routinized into performance measurement within a strategic planning framework. The Pennsylvania Department of Transportation (PENNDOT) creates a new agency agenda every four years. PENNDOT is committed to managing change.

A scorecard of measures clearly link performance metrics with agency goals and objectives. PENNDOT defines effective scorecard measures as those which make a difference to customers and stakeholders, drive behavior throughout the organization, and can be utilized for evaluation and decision making. PENNDOT, a public sector agency with 12,000 employees, commenced a four-year improvement program designed to condition measurable targets of organization performance with rigorous strategic planning practices. Findings focused on effectively setting directions, achieving market-based results, and sustaining cultural changes.

The tasks of PENNDOT'S strategic management system transcend partisan politics with an emphasis on policy and system transportation politics. The tasks are divided into four phases: determine the approach, develop the agenda, align market-based plans, and manage with measures.

Phase 1: Determine the approach (1998): Proposed agency goals and objectives are reviewed according to leadership direction, client expectations, client service capabilities, priority tasks and strategies, and plans and performance targets. Continuous feedback and performance measurement promote objectives and measures which assess performance from both process and product perspectives—taking into account internal and external factors.

Phase 2: Develop the agenda (1999). PENNDOT gathers data from clients, stakeholders, partners, and employees. Despite this empirical emphasis, replacing opinions with facts remains a challenge. Extensive surveys and interviews supplement existing data—suggesting value-added strategies. Strengths, weaknesses, opportunities, and threats (SWOT) are probed from reviewing internal and external data. Goals and objectives are not divorced from performance measurement targets. According to David Margolis, "front-end feedback data" identify "meaningful back-end performance measures."[16]

Phase 3: Align market-based plans (2002). Agency agenda offer perspectives for initiating the alignment phase. Decision makers adopt thirteen high-level goals and twenty-one strategic objectives from eight strategic focus areas. A scorecard of measures helps determine whether agency goals and objectives are supported. Indicators suggest measures for short- and long-term targets. SWOT and agency agenda commence the process, and PENNDOT units develop objectives and scorecards. Workshops permit employees—and managers—to consider top-down directives in the context of bottom-up priorities. Market plans and budget outlines focus on strategies and performance targets. A higher degree of program alignment is confirmed.

Motivation and Empowerment

The promotions are gone. A raise is out of the question. Budget cuts prevent managers from providing public sector employees any material incentives. How do managers motivate or empower government employees? People view themselves as outstanding rather than ordinary. If managers encourage employees, they must empower them, too.

Three secrets of empowerment are:

- Managers must share information with employees. Employees want to be partners in the operation. They want to know about the budget.
- Managers must project a vision. A clear vision often means a clear purpose. Employees want to understand what managers are trying to

accomplish. Being empowered is knowing what to do.

- Managers, part of the supervisor hierarchy, will be replaced by teams. Empowered teams may say "no" to the status quo. Teams may create a vision and determine goals, and they are less expensive to the taxpayer.

Empowerment, says Ken Blanchard, begins with vision—meaning purpose, values, image, and goals. People would rather be outstanding than ordinary. Employees must be partners with management, not adversaries.

Source: Ken Blanchard, "Motivation Q&A with Ken Blanchard," http://www.smartbiz.com/sbs/arts/pos6.htm.

Phase 4: Manage with measures (2001). Workshops give employees opportunities to create dashboard measures for suplementing market-based scorecards. Leading indicators and interim outcome measures are added. Dashboards monitor progress toward scorecard metrics and fundamental core market-based targets. Dashboards permit tactical and resource decisions at monthly reviews. Decision makers emphasize proactive problem solving—not reactive thinking. Continuous improvement is a constant theme.

Lessons learned from PENNDOT's strategic planning and performance measurement improvement efforts include:

- Senior PENNDOT leaders were engaged throughout the process.
- Widespread participation took place throughout PENNDOT with ongoing feedback.
- An "adapt, don't adopt" philosophy developed as a mechanism for evaluating the best practices and policies.

Before performance-based management at PENNDOT, decisions occurred within the partisan and ideological parameters of Pennsylvania state government. PENNDOT's focus on strategic planning and performance measurement favors policy and systemwide decision making as evolving, policy-neutral tools. Partisan politics is secondary; policy and system politics are primary. Agency missions, meaningful data, and market results dominate performance-based management at the Pennsylvania Department of Transportation (PENNDOT).

Citizen-Driven Government Performance

Over the last decade, a market has developed for citizen-driven, results-oriented government performance. The emphasis is on assessing and improving how local governments serve their communities. Involvement of community stakeholders in assessing performance is a priority; citizen-driven influence is paramount. Elected leaders and government services respond to community needs and priorities—as stakeholders get involved, participate, and contribute.

How do citizens think impartial experts rate agency performance? What grades do these experts give your city bureaucracies—A, B, C, D, or worse? Is performance improving or deteriorating? How city services should be measured draws little political consensus. However, democratic institutions—cities, towns, counties, states, and even the country—function effectively only with satisfactory levels of trust in government and the long-term health of legally formalized communities.[17]

Improvements in the performance of governments—all 87,525 in the United States—is a widespread expectation for democratic capitalism. The principal idea of the Government Performance and Results Act of 1993 is that federal agencies will produce strategic policymaking plans for revitalizing government units.

The Pew Charitable Trust, in a private sector project called "Grading Governments," generously funded researchers at the Maxwell School of Citizenship and Public Affairs at Syracuse University to study forty federal agencies, all fifty state governments, and forty major units of local government. At the federal level, financial management, human resource management, deployment of information technology, executive leadership capacity, and managing for results—or measuring unit performance—are management categories studied by the Syracuse researchers.

No universally accepted term exists for measuring an organization's performance. Productivity, work measurement, and effectiveness describe similar challenges dictated by the concept of "performance measurement." According to Paul D. Epstein, performance measurement is government's mechanism for providing a quality product at a reasonable cost. Based on the Civil Service Reform Act of 1978, performance measurement, as defined by the GAO in 1980, includes measures of productivity, effectiveness, quality, and timeliness. Different performance measures supplement each other—and should not be perceived as divergent or contradictory.

Experts developed criteria for assessing the skills governments use to confront issues of financial management, human resources, information technology, capital management, and managing-for-results. These criteria were refined and improved over time. City grades, as outlined in table 10.1, therefore do have rationale. The thirty-five cities in the table were selected based not on population, but on total revenues. Researchers from the Maxwell School at Syracuse University analyzed, coded, computerized, and reflected on the data. In the spirit of the craft of public administration, the research methodology included applications from both art and science.[18]

Though in some cases some might argue the researchers were comparing apples and oranges, apples and oranges are, nevertheless, still relevant. New York City spends an amount equal to Buffalo's *annual* budget *twice per week.* However, New York operates its own schools. Many other cities do not. Every city has an information technology system. The vast majority of city officials completed the entire Maxwell School survey. Richmond is included and Miami is not because Miami's expenditures do not reach the level of the top thirty-five cities.

The Government Performance Project (GPP) researchers surveyed government management capacities for forty of the country's largest county governments, releasing data in 2002. Counties provide an array of services to citizens. However, county officials do not have the power to address, appropriately, all countrywide

TABLE 10.1

City Grades at a Glance

	Average Grade	Financial Management	Human Resources	Information Technology	Capital Management	Managing for Results
Anchorage	C	C+	C	C	B–	C–
Atlanta	C+	B–	B–	D+	C	B–
Austin	A–	A	A–	B	A–	A–
Baltimore	B–	B+	C+	C	B	B
Boston	B–	B–	C–	B	B+	C+
Buffalo	C–	C	D	C	C–	D+
Chicago	B–	B	C–	B–	B+	C+
Cleveland	C	B–	C–	C–	B–	C
Columbus	C	B–	C–	D+	B–	D
Dallas	C+	B+	C	D+	B–	B
Denver	B–	B+	B–	C+	B–	B–
Detroit	B–	B–	B–	B–	C	B–
Honolulu	B	B–	C	B+	A–	B
Houston	C+	B+	C	C–	B–	B–
Indianapolis	B+	B	A–	B	B+	A–
Jacksonville	B–	B	C+	C	B	B
Kansas City	B–	B+	B	C	B+	B–
Long Beach	B	A–	C	B	B	B–
Long Angeles	C	B–	C–	C–	C+	C–
Memphis	C+	B	D	C	B	B–
Milwaukee	B	B+	C+	B–	B+	A–
Minneapolis	B+	A–	B	A–	B+	B–
Nashville	C+	B	B	D+	C+	C–
New Orleans	C–	C–	F	B–	B–	D+
New York City	B	B	B–	B	B+	B
Philadelphia	B	B–	B–	B+	B–	B
Phoenix	A	A	A	A–	A	A
Richmond	C+	B	C	C	C–	C+
San Antonio	B	B+	B+	B–	B	B+
San Diego	B	B+	C	C	B+	A–
San Francisco	C+	B	C	C+	C+	C
San Jose	B–	B+	C	C	A–	C+
Seattle	B	B+	B	B	B+	B
Virginia Beach	B+	A–	B	B	A–	B
Washington	C+	B–	B–	C+	C	C+

Source: From "The Government Performance Project 2000," as appeared on website, www.governing.com, 2000. Reprinted with permission, Governing, copyright © 2000.

problems. The county average grade is C plus. Leading counties in the GPP evaluation are Maricopa, Arizona, and Fairfax, Virginia. Both received grades of A minus.[19]

Counties do an excellent job with financial reporting. However, the absence of a unified county personnel system hampers the development of human resources. Tight job markets force many counties to revise recruitment and merit pay policies. Decentralized county cultures prevent integrated information technology systems, making efficient technology implementation difficult.

Standards from the Governmental Accounting Standards Board require counties to maintain more complete data regarding assets and capital management needs. Only 25 percent of GPP counties formalize countrywide strategic plans. (Managing for results is more common at the unit or department level.) Plans often lack common formats. Budgets are the primary vehicles for communicating county goals and results.

Performance Measurement in Local Governments

Performance management contributes to better decision making, performance appraisal, accountability, service delivery, public participation, and civic discourse.[20] Performance measurements, as shown in table 10.2, include input, outputs or workload, outcome or effectiveness, cost-effectiveness, and productivity indicators. Explanatory information probes indicators for service efforts and accomplishments.

TABLE 10.2

Types of Performance Measurement Indicators: An Example

Municipal Function	Input Measures	Output/ Workload Measures	Efficiency Measures	Effectiveness measures	Productivity Measures	Explanatory Information
Sanitation	The amount of labor-hours of the Sanitation Department, the budget of the Sanitation Department; number of vehicles	Tons of refuse collected; miles of road cleaned; number of customers served	Employee-hours per ton of refuse collected; dollars spent for one mile of snow removal	Percentage of clean streets (e.g., measured by periodical visual inspection; citizen surveys)	Cost per mile of a clean street (i.e., total cost of all road cleaning divided by the total miles of clean streets)	Composition of solid waste; climatic conditions; terrain; crew size of vehicles; type of vehicles

Source: From "Citizen-Driven Government Performance" on website www.newark.rutgers.edu. Reprinted by permission of Professor Marc Holzer.

Designing and implementing a performance measurement system requires a thorough understanding of what the program is attempting to accomplish and who the clientele are, as well as a knowledge of the public services currently provided by the government unit. Steps in the process include:

Step 1: Identification of a program. Government activities are identified by distinct programs. Street resurfacing, patching, seal coating, and repairing are part of street maintenance. Animal control, the clerk's office, code enforcement, corrections, courts, fire prevention, fire suppression, housing code enforcement, landfill operations, library, parks maintenance, police patrol, recreation services, senior services, waste collection, street cleaning, utility billing, wastewater collection, and water distribution are popular local government programs. These programs are included in the city's operating budget.

Step 2: Statement of purpose. Preparation of a well-articulated statement of purpose for a program reflects a clearly understood mission. Programs are not self-serving. They provide services to the citizens of a certain government jurisdiction.

Step 3: Identification of program inputs, outputs, efficiency, and productivity indicators. Operating budget, number of labor-hours, and full-time-equivalent employees are delineated. Outputs reflect workload measures—or the quantity of service delivered to users. Unit of output spells out the quantity of each service. Efficiency and productivity measures address how the service is provided, and efficiency measures focus on costs (dollars and/or employee hours).

Step 4: Setting targets for accomplishment. Service effectiveness and quality measures are established. How do government officials determine if objectives are met? Goals, quantities, dates, and targets are closely adhered to. The goals of a program are set according to a specified period of time. Quantities include percentages for recognizing achievements; dates focus on a timer frame. Targets include input and output factors.

Step 5: Monitoring. Continuous monitoring of targets is a given. Monitoring is a way of keeping tabs on program operations. Monitoring gauges whether the target has been reached or not. Is everything going as a planned? Are there seasonal or cyclical patterns to clientele satisfaction? Data gathering should be reasonable—and not overwhelm the unit's fiscal and human capacities. Monitoring varies according to the service and the target.

Step 6: Performance reporting. Indicators are summarized. Results are compared to set targets. Reports include comparisons with previous time frames, similar jurisdictions, technically developed standards or norms, geographic areas of clientele within the same jurisdiction, and public sector/private sector costs and results. Performance reporting includes the program name, unit jurisdiction, purpose statement, workloads/outputs, inputs, productivity and/or efficiency ratios, and synopses of explanatory information.

Step 7: Analysis and action. Well-developed performance measurement systems permit clientele to recognize weaknesses, strengths, threats, and opportunities. Relevant actions may be taken. Unit growth capabilities may be diagnosed.[21]

Success: Measures of Careers Well-Lived?

What is success? By what yardstick does one measure it? What are the means (career, job, lifestyle) by which success (productivity, achievement) is measured?

"Defining one's own success," says Linda Gast, "means ascribing to a personal set of values and beliefs. It means that we must know what our values are and commit ourselves to living and accomplishing in accordance with those values. . . . When we choose to define our success by our own values, our decisions have a firmer foundation."

An employee's acceptance of or change in jobs based on the degree to which those jobs embrace, express, or fit his or her personal values puts compensation packages, job responsibilities, and advancement options in perspective.

How do we want our successes—and achievements—to be judged? By whose standards are our efforts to be evaluated? Are we judged by our own values, or the values of others? How do we live out our values in our everyday lives?

"Success," writes Bill Galston, former deputy assistant to President Clinton, "is intimately connected with integrity. By integrity I mean not honest and honorable deeds, but, more broadly, living in accordance with one's deepest convictions about what gives life purpose and meaning." Personal convictions of integrity vary widely from person to person. Integrity is often met at the junction of personal honesty and professional productivity.

"Integrity may seem straightforward," suggests Galston, "but the appearance is deceptive. . . . there is no guarantee that our understanding of life's meaning and purpose will correspond to our natural talents." We may produce at a high level of performance in a field we consider of secondary importance. Or we may perform in mediocre fashion in a field that we think is fundamental. A measure of dissatisfaction—and even unhappiness—often results.

Does success bring happiness? Not necessarily, says Galston. Integrity is not always sufficient for happiness. The mismatch between our convictions (values) and talents (personal skills) affects how we perceive factors both internal and external to us.

"Success," concludes Galston, "is the skillful exercise of integrity in those choices and acts that are within our power. . . . there is no guarantee that each person's beliefs about what really matters will fit together into a harmonious whole." Or to reverse the predicament, as Galston states, "*Failure* means a high level of moral discomfort with the choices that have defined one's life."

Definitions of success—and achievement—emphasize the personal and ethical measures of careers well-lived.

Source: Linda Gast and William A. Galston, "Viewpoint: Success: What Is Your Yardstick?" *The University of Maryland Magazine,* Spring, 2000. pp. 6–7.

People Crisis and/or Opportunity?

People are the federal government's most valuable asset. Studies of private and public sector organizations show that high-performing organizations value and invest in their employees—their human capital—and align their "people policies" to support organizational performance goals. In the federal government, however, strategic human capital management is a pervasive challenge.[22]

The General Accounting Office (GAO) includes human capital on its high-risk list. Critical skill shortages in federal departments and agencies cause difficulties in the implementation of the programs and agendas of the President and Congress.[23]

Several reforms are in process.

First, an emphasis on workforce planning and restructuring requires federal agencies to flatten their organizational hierarchy and improve their work processes. To optimize the services provided to citizens, federal employees must understand the link between their daily work and the results their government employer seeks to achieve.

Second, administrative reforms must recast job descriptions. Job responsibilities need restructuring to make work more interesting and promote greater employee teamwork. The very way in which agencies design work for their employees needs rethinking. Narrow job descriptions are not attractive to employees who are likely to strive to make contributions in the public arena.

Third, performance management measures are ineffective. The Government Performance and Results Act (GPRA) requires agencies to be performance-driven. But agencies must restructure their performance appraisal systems to measure individual performance against target outcomes.

Finally, recruitment for hard-to-fill positions needs reevaluation.

Agencies evaluated in this study include the Federal Aviation Administration, the Office of Personnel Management, the Veterans Benefits Administration, the Internal Revenue Service, and the Federal Emergency Management Agency. By studying the efforts of these five agencies, the GAO found that directly involving employees in performance planning and important agency decisions empowered the workforce. The provision of regular training to employees, proactive communication with unions on personnel changes, and serious efforts to make human resources a visibly high priority resulted in positive employee impacts.

For the initiatives GAO reviewed, agencies had to overcome organizational and cultural barriers—including lack of trust, resistance to change, lack of buy-in from front-line employees and managers, and workload demands. The agencies developed open communication with employees and reevaluated their systems for reassigning and hiring personnel.[24]

According to the GAO, granting employees decision-making authority not only improved morale, but also streamlined government processes. Once managers and employees perceived the benefits of improved communication and new personnel practices, they adapted to agency changes.

The Highway Performance Monitoring System (HPMS)

The Federal Highway Administration (FHWA) and states implement a continuous data collection system—the Highway Performance Monitoring System (HPMS). HPMS contains over 110,000 highway sample segments and is the most comprehensive nationwide data system cataloging the physical condition and usage of the nation's highway infrastructure.

HPMS policymaking models are used by state governments, metropolitan planning organizations (MPOs), and local government agencies to assess the physical condition, safety, service, and operating efficiency of their respective highway systems. HPMS helps governments to

- assess base-year conditions and performance;
- forecast highway system needs;

- simulate highway system conditions;
- analyze investment strategies; and
- estimate user costs.

FHWA modified the HPMS policymaking models for use by the states. Non-federal government agencies utilize HPMS policymaking models to evaluate highway designs and operations. State performance model applications include:

- *Highway adequacy ratings.* For states, local government agencies, and MPOs, highway adequacy ratings focus on four indices: condition, safety, service, and a composite of the three. Kentucky was the first state to use adequacy ratings for highway planning purposes.
- *Highway needs (investment requirements).* Estimates of investment requirements are benchmarks for the development and evaluation of transportation policy and program options. Idaho studied multijurisdiction highway needs and finance prospects—addressing state, county, highway district, and city road systems. This performance plan cited deficiencies and estimated investment requirements for improved roadways.
- *Investment performance relationships.* This performance program assesses the highway improvements and highway system conditions expected under various funding scenarios—providing an understanding of what kind of performance is expected when funding is inadequate. North Carolina utilized this assessment procedure—projecting future performance and condition effects resulting from alternative policy and funding scenarios.
- *Corridor planning.* This model assesses the sufficiency for satisfying a specific requirement or standard. Oregon officials adopted this concept in planning improvements to major corridors. Some sixteen corridors were designated to be of statewide significance. Congestion levels, travel speeds, and geometric deficiencies determine two potential scenarios: No Build and Total Build (full needs).
- *State transportation plans.* This strategic and systems highway planning defines the current status and existing backlog of highway deficiencies, identifies future conditions of the highway system, estimates investment requirements, and assesses the condition and performance of the highway system under alternative funding scenarios. South Carolina employed this HPMS policymaking model.
- *Strategic planning.* As one of FHWA's major strategic planning tools, the HPMS is designed to measure and monitor the condition, performance, usage, and operating characteristics of the nation's highways for use by policy decision makers and Congress in developing and evaluating federal-aid highway programs and funding levels. Texas transportation officials utilize the principal characteristics of HPMS to comply with state legislative highway mandates.
- *Performance monitoring.* Periodic updates on the HPMS database provide excellent opportunities for state benchmarking/performance monitoring. California employs this policymaking model to compile mileage and travel by weighted design speed, volume-service flow ratio, pavement condition, lane width, horizontal alignment adequacy, and vertical alignment adequacy.

- *VMT (vehicle miles of travel) tracking.* HPMS provides a standard, recognized database for the entire United States. The Environmental Protection Agency (EPA) relies upon HPMS to estimate vehicle miles of travel (VMT) in order to conform with air quality standards pursuant to the 1990 Clean Air Act Amendments. Illinois invests in similar estimation processes for its roadways.
- *System classification.* Kansas used federal functional classification criteria for its highway planning processes. State officials reclassified federal specifications with categories defined as Classes A through E. They reconfigured the road-user costs of program funding allocations and standards based on the reclassified system.
- *Highway user cost analysis.* These HPMS models gauge travel speeds, accidents, emissions, fuel consumption, and operating costs. North Carolina officials studied need estimates, investment-system performance relationships, and user cost effects. Investments were calculated for zero funding, maintenance conditions, and total funding levels.
- *Roadway inventory database.* This HPMS database is the primary source of information for the federal government on the nation's highway infrastructure. Database information is gathered on pavement condition, roadway features, traffic characteristics, and system performance. North Dakota relies heavily on this highway database to support its planning functions.
- *State informational booklet.* This media effort is a joint federal and state undertaking. States supply the HPMS database with facts, figures, and developments. Washington State developed a booklet, *Washington State Roadways: Selected Data and Analysis from the Highway Performance Monitoring System (HPMS)* to describe its highway system, characteristics, performance ratings, and roadway improvement needs.

HPMS focuses on program utility, effectiveness, and efficiency at all levels of transportation policymaking, develops efficient, state-of-the-art software systems, and provides analytical studies for promoting transportation partnerships with regions, states, and local citizen groups. HPMS model policymaking criteria may be adjusted to reflect state or local circumstances, practices, and funding constraints.[25]

Summary

- Most citizens care about the *performance* of their public institutions.
- Excellence is based on the cultural context of a particular function.
- Productivity in the public sector refers to *excellence in individual and collective performance.* There are widely divergent views as to what excellence is.
- Government organizations should strive for *excellence.*

- *Efficiency* means doing things well, while effectiveness means doing the right things well. Efficiency is essentially the input or contribution of labor, capital, and other resources into an effort measured against the output produced, regardless of the mechanism selected to gauge output.
- *Effectiveness* calls for a preestablished standard of comparison; a focus upon a certain quality of production; and an ability to mobilize, organize,

and direct resources for specified purposes, all taken within a certain cultural context.

- The reasons there are citizen complaints with government performance are: *Democracy is messy. Government takes a bum rap. Government must shape up. The country must shape up.*
- Privatization of public responsibilities center around *provisions,* or providing, and *production,* or producing, of goods and services. *Privatization,* often called contracting out, means that a service previously produced by a government agency is now produced by a nongovernmental organization.
- Accessibility, use, safety, attractiveness, and overall satisfaction constitute preset *ways of measuring the effectiveness of public services.*
- Political autonomy is essential for bureaucratic effectiveness. Public managers should be encouraged to act not only as *"administrative entrepreneurs,"* but also as *"political entrepreneurs."*
- Barriers to productivity measurement are numerous. The *budget process* is a significant structural barrier to federal productivity improvement. *Personnel systems* may restrict, delay, or prevent the hiring of qualified personnel and the discharge of nonproductive personnel. *Structural barriers* may cause

problems with centralized decision making. Regional and field offices may duplicate and fragment lines of authority. *Lack of accountability* is an obstacle to productivity improvement, as are low morale, inadequate pay structure, managerial inexperience, senior administrator turnover, and misplaced priorities for policy making and direction.

- Measuring productivity may also provide a basis for *deemphasizing rules, regulations,* and *supervision.*
- The purposes of program evaluation are to bring rigorous analytical perspective to influence agency budget requests, assess agency effectiveness for meeting program objectives established by elected leaders, and develop program performance measures for agency implementation.
- Transportation services—more so than other government produced programs—are likely to be routinized into performance measurement within a strategic planning network.
- Empowering employees begins with vision—meaning purpose, values, image, and goals.
- Performance measurement in local governments contributes to better decision making, performance appraisal, accountability, service delivery, participation, and civic discourse.
- People are government's most valuable asset.

 # Case Study

"Going Postal" Injures Performance, Kills Motivation

The United States Postal Service (USPS)—a government corporation—is a conduit for freedom and capitalism. "Going postal" became part of the American vocabulary of workplace violence. USPS had an employee crisis. Services and the economy were endangered. In the case study that follows, grievance reforms emerged as a by-product of workplace violence.

Workplace violence isn't a remote risk. And the hurt can cut deeply into the bottom line.

—*John P. Mello, Jr.*
Woonsocket, Rhode Island

Thomas McIlvane had been fired from his job at the United States Postal Service (USPS), Royal Oak Post Office, Royal Oak, Michigan, for alleged time-card fraud. Less than one week after his dismissal was upheld by an arbitrator, McIlvane went on a killing spree that wounded five and murdered four USPS employees. Then McIlvane turned the gun on himself.[1]

The post office killer had previously been dishonorably discharged from the U.S. Marines. (Allegedly, he had run a car over with a tank.) The rifle he used at Royal Oak was illegal. His dishonorable discharge prohibited McIlvane from owning firearms. No background check was required.

Patrick Sherrill, a full-time substitute letter carrier and ex-Marine sharpshooter, murdered fourteen USPS employees in Edmond, Oklahoma. He, too, committed suicide. The morning before the murders, Sherrill met with Richard Esser, who later was among the dead, and Bill Bland to discuss his work performance. Police sources said that Bland threatened to terminate Sherrill; the USPS claimed they made no efforts to terminate the murderer.[2]

Was Sherrill's killing rampage—the third worst mass murder in American history—an act of revenge? The details were not clear. Coworkers viewed Sherrill as often angry and frequently depressed. But no real evidence came forth that his work performance had ever been seriously questioned. However, it was said that Sherrill preferred keeping his own company to the usual workplace socialization. At best enigmatic, he was not well-understood by those who knew him. His workplace mayhem was seemingly without purpose.

The USPS has gotten a "bad rap" for public sector workplace violence, as is illustrated by the deaths in Royal Oak and Edmond. "Going postal" has become part of the American vocabulary of violence. The USPS had an employee crisis. Incidents of murder and mayhem were isolated. Could anything come out of events that were so evil? Performance and motivation at the USPS, a conduit to American capitalism, were in serious jeopardy.[3]

Employers are increasingly aware that employee motivation and unit productivity are linked. Partisan, policy, and system politics support the government's public services improvement agenda. New technologies impact the ways we live and work. High-performing employers excel at instilling employee motivation. Workforce strategies link motivation, individual performance, and unit performance.

USPS, a public sector corporation, was forced to resolve citizen concerns regarding employee tensions, safety, and security in its workplaces. "Going postal" threatened not only USPS employees, it endangered services, and therefore, the economy. Like air traffic control and the interstate highway system, the USPS functions to promote personal exchanges and economic developments—namely, freedom and capitalism.

USPS as Conduit for Freedom and Capitalism

Each week the USPS delivers billions of pieces of mail—including letters, bills, advertisements, and packages. It employs about 860,000 persons. Qualification is based on an examination. The number of qualified applicants continues to encourage keen competition as applicant numbers are expected to exceed the number of job openings.

The nationwide private mailing industry generates $155 billion yearly, excluding postage, and employs 6.2 million people. USPS employees carry more mail to more people over a larger geographic area than postal employees in any other country. Three of the postal service's six product lines—correspondence and transactions, business advertising, and expedited delivery—would qualify as Fortune 500 companies.[4]

USPS serves 7 million customers daily through 38,000 retail outlets. Mail is collected from more than 312,000 street mail collection boxes. Every two weeks, USPS pays out $1.6 billion in employee salaries and benefits. The average carrier delivers about 2,500 pieces of mail a day to 500 addresses. Many postage stamps raise awareness of social issues.[5]

Postal clerks, typically classified by job duties, perform a variety of functions. They may work as window or counter clerks; sell stamps, money orders, postal stationary, envelopes, and boxes; weigh packages to determine postage; and check packages for satisfactory mailing conditions. Distribution clerks sort local mail for delivery to individual customers. Mail processors operate optical character readers (OCRs) and barcode sorters for scanning, coding, and sorting mail. Carriers cover routes by foot and/or vehicle.

Working conditions vary. Window clerks usally work in clean, well-ventilated, and well-lit buildings. They rarely work at night. They may, however, deal with upset customers, stand for long periods, and be held accountable for the assigned stock of stamps and funds. Despite the use of automated equipment, postal clerks may have to do physically demanding work. Most carriers begin work in the morning. Overtime hours are frequently required during peak delivery times. Employment of postal service workers is expected to decline slightly through 2010.[6]

Approximately 40,000 postal workers are hired each year. Retirements, transfers, departures, and deaths open the way for new hires. USPS advertises internally. The Office of Personnel Management (OPM) has no jurisdiction. In 1971, the politicized Post Office Department became the United States Postal Service—an independent, public corporation.

The Postal Pay Act determines pay scales, which are not part of the General Pay Schedule. The Postal Service pays extra compensation, overtime, and night shift differentials. Special pay scales are used for rural letter carriers. A cost-of-living adjustment (COLA) acrues to the employee salary base at the rate of 1 cent per hour for each .4-point increase in the Consumer Price Index. Benefits include vacation and sick leave, health and life insurance, and retirement considerations.

Classification requirements must be met for carrier, clerk, machine distribution clerk, flat-sorting machine opeator, mail handler, mail processor, and automated mark-up clerk positions. You must be eighteen or older to apply. Applicants do not have to be U.S. citizens. Physical requirements are determined by the job. Carriers must be able to lift a 70-pound mail sack. All applicants must be able to efficiently perform their assigned duties. USPS maintains a comprehensive program to insure a drug-free workplace. Employees are scheduled for drug screening tests. Veterans receive five- or ten-point hiring preference.[7]

Postal Service Violence in a Larger Context

Death, we might argue, is a very personal matter. At some juncture, every living thing—plant, animal, human, even government bureaucracy—is going to die. The workplace violence in Royal Oak and Edmond remains a personal matter for those postal workers who met untimely deaths and for their families and loved ones. But violence in postal offices occurs in a comparative context of nationwide employment.

The mass murders affected the employment, training, performance, motivation, and psyches of USPS employees and their citizen clients. In 1998, postal officials asked Joseph A. Califano, Jr., chairman of the United States Postal Service Commission on A Safe and Secure Workplace and president of The National Center on Addiction and Substance Abuse (CASA) at Columbia University, to investigate.

The Commission's staff included sixty professionals—including sixteen with doctorates and fifteen

with masters in business, communications, computer engineering, criminology, economics, education, government, history, journalism, linguistics, medicine, psychiatry, psychology, public health, public policy, social work, sociology, and statistics—one medical doctor, and three attorneys. CASA conducted demonstration programs at thirty-eight sites in twenty-five cities in sixteen states.

CASA prepared a 249-page report. The commission examined twenty-nine incidents of workplace homicide involving postal workers as either victims or perpetrators from 1986 to 1999. According to the two-year report, postal workers are no more likely to commit or be victims of violence, and only a third as likely as those in the general national workforce, to be homicide victims (0.26 vs. 0.77 per 100,000 workers each year between 1992 and 1998).

Fifteen postal-employee perpetrators killed thirty-four postal employees. Nineteen nonpostal workers killed fourteen postal employees. Fourteen out of fifteen postal perpetrators had troubled histories of violence, mental illness, substance abuse, and/or criminal convictions. Male veterans were no more likely than other male postal employees to commit homicides. Guns were used in all the homicides committed by postal employee perpetrators and by 90 percent of the homicides committed by nonpostal perpetrators. Motives included robbery, problems in intimate relationships, and employment termination.

" 'Going postal' is a myth, a bad rap," concluded Califano, "causing unnecessary apprehension and fear among 900,000 postal workers. This report should shatter the myth that postal workers are more violent than other workers and discourage the pejorative use of that expression."[8]

The dynamics of "going postal" did affect the USPS employment environment. The commission survey found postal employees to be less angry, aggressive, hostile, depressed, and stressed than those in the national workforce and better suited to cope. However, USPS management and workers expressed more negative attitudes about work.

Postal workers project that they are

• nearly six times more likely than those in the national workforce to be victims of violence by coworkers (17 versus 3 percent). In reality, the probability is almost identical (4 percent versus 3 percent).

- less confident in management's fairness and honesty (37 percent versus 60 percent); and
- less likely to agree that their employer—USPS—takes action to protect them (52 percent versus 70 percent).[9]

USPS Grievance Reforms as a By-Product of Violence

In the early 1990s, USPS encountered an employee crisis. The shootings received media attention, but these incidents were isolated. In some respects, the internal battles of USPS local units mirrored the depressing, deadly chaos that USPS's government—and very corporate—image portrayed to the country. Charges of racial discrimination, sexual harassment, and similar management abuses and informal complaints resulted in 30,000 grievance filings per year.

Some complaints escalated into costly litigation. In 1994, as part of a settlement of a class-action lawsuit, lawyers at USPS created REDRESS™ to settle disputes using neutral outside mediators. The program was tested in certain cities before going national in 1997.

The results proved spectacular. The first twenty-two months of full operation of REDRESS saw 17,645 informal disputes mediated. Eighty percent of those were resolved. Formal complaints, which peaked at 14,000 by 1997, declined by 30 percent. Prior to REDRESS, USPS employee-management disputes lasted for years. The REDRESS program offered disgruntled workers mediation.

Attempts to short-circuit controversies can prompt justice. An employee who filed an informal complaint would agree to employ REDRESS. A meeting would be set up, and a mediator would hear both sides of the dispute. In most instances, the mediator would propose a solution within a day. REDRESS made mediation available at any stage of the grievance process—not just the beginning.

REDRESS emerged as a very productive tool for USPS. Corporate America took notice. High-profile racial discrimination and sexual-harassment class-action lawsuits against industry giants like Texaco and Coca-Cola point out that government agencies are not the only jurisdictions in which professional conflicts and controversies occur.[10]

Cynthia J. Hallberlin, former chief legal council at USPS, placed issues of employment productivity and motivation at USPS in perspective: "You're never going to get rid of conflict," Hallberlin said, "you just want to handle it better."[11]

Questions and Instructions

1. For whom, if anyone, are USPS production services efficient, effective, and/or excellent? Explain and illustrate.
2. How do USPS dynamics afford commentary on adages such as "democracy is messy," "government takes a bum rap," "government must shape up," and "the country must shape up"? Illustrate.
3. What are the limitations for further privatization of postal service tasks and functions? Explain.
4. How is the USPS a conduit for freedom and capitalism? Explain and illustrate.
5. Did any good come out of the evils of the Royal Oak and Edmond mass murders? What insights were gleaned about conflicts and fairness? Explain.
6. How do effective USPS job classifications promote a more effective postal workforce? Explain.
7. People work for one of three basic reasons: money, people, and job. Place in rank order the reasons why USPS employees are likely to toil as postal workers. Explain your rankings.
8. Was the report of the United States Postal Service Commission on A Safe and Secure Workplace inductive thinking, deductive thinking, or a combination of the two? Why?
9. Assuming issues of labor, management, technology, volume, and nationwide consumer demand for personal economy will continue, can the USPS be "reinvented" to promote both egalitarian access and efficiency?

Insights-Issues/"Going Postal" Injures Performance, Kills Motivation

Clearly and briefly describe and illustrate the following concepts and issues. Interpret the word *role* as meaning impacts, applications, importance, effects, and/or illustrations of certain facts, concerns, or issues from the case study.

1. Role of USPS production services—as efficient, effective, and/or excellent for whom?
2. Role of USPS as a conduit for freedom and capitalism.

3. Role of mass murders in raising the agenda for evaluating morale factors in 38,000 labor-intensive USPS units.
4. Role of USPS Commission on A Safe and Secure Workplace as an inductive or deductive (or combination) contributor to solutions.
5. Roles of money, people, and jobs as reasons why employees work.

Case Endnotes

1. Violence Policy Center, "Where'd They Get Their Guns? An Analysis of the Firearms Used in High-Profile Shootings, 1963 to 2001," November 14, 1991; http://www.vpc.org/studies/wgun911114.htm.
2. "A Public Awakening—The Edmond Post Office Massacre," http://www. svn.net/mikekell/v5.html.
3. National Center on Addiction and Substance Abuse at Columbia University, *Postal Commission Releases Groundbreaking Report on Workplace Violence,* August 31, 2000, http://www. casacolumbia.org/newsletter1457/newsletter_show.htm?doc_id=34000.
4. Stephen Barr, "Struggling Postal Service Makes Case for Transformation," *The Washington Post,* May 14, 2002, p. B02.
5. United States Postal Service, "Postal Facts," http://www.usps. com/history/pfact00.htm.

6. Jonathan W. Kelinson, *1998–99 Occupational Outlook Handbook,* Bureau of Labor Statistics, "Postal Clerks and Mail Carriers," http://www. umsl.edu/services/govdocs/ooh9899/135.htm.
7. Dennis V. Damp, *Post Office Jobs: How to Get a Job with the U.S. Postal Service,* 2nd ed. La Crosse, WI: (Brookhaven Press, 2000), http://federaljobs.net/uspscont.htm.
8. " 'Going Postal' Is a Myth, Report Says," *CNEWSFeatures,* August 31, 2000, http://www. fan590.com/CNEWSFeatures0008/31_postal.html.
9. National Center on Addiction and Substance Abuse at Columbia University, *op. cit.*
10. Mickey Meese, "Companies Adopting Postal Service Process," *The New York Times,* September 6, 2000, http://www.spea.indiana.edu/icri/nytsepa.htm.
11. *Ibid.*

Case Sources

American Management Association, "Motivating for Results: Bringing Out the Best in People," http://www.amanet.org/seminars/cmd2/2275.htm; Kathy Bunch, "When Employees Turn Deadly at Work," February 26, 2001, http://my.webmd.com/printing/article/1685.51170; Bureau of Labor Statistics, Occupational Outlook Handbook, 2002–03 edition, http://stats.bls.gov/oco/ocos141.htm; "Case Studies: Research & Ideas," http://www.theworkfoundation.com/casestudies/casestudy05.jsp; Debbie DeVoe and Loretta W. Prencipe,

"Mastering motivation," *InforWorld,* November 16, 2001, http://staging.infoworld.com/articles/pe/xml/01/11/19/011119pemotivate.xml?Template=/storypa. Colin Johnson, "Federal Employees—'Give us a Chance to Do Our Jobs,' " http://www.brook.edu/dybdocroot/comm/news/1030publicservice.htm; John P. Mello, Jr., "Hell in Your Hallways," http://www.cfo.com/printarticle/0, 5317, 1477!,00.html; "Productivity Bonus Program," http://www.tipc.state.tx.us/overview/pbp/pbp.htm.

Chapter Endnotes

1. G. Chris Hartung, "Institutionalized Excellence: Not Just More Pop Government Jargon?" *Public Management* 78, no. 7 (July 1996): 25–29.
2. David Osborne, "Grading Governments, *The Washington Post,* April 13, 1997, p. A8.
3. *The New York Times,* April 20, 1971.
4. E. S. Savas, *Privatizing the Public Sector* (Chatham, N.J.: Chatham House, 1982), p. 89.
5. Ted Kolderie, "The Two Different Concepts of Privatization," *Public Administration Review* 46, no. 4 (July–August 1986): 285–291.
6. Kolderie, "The Two Different Concepts," p. 285.
7. Kolderie, "The Two Different Concepts," p. 286.
8. Richard L. Worsnop, "Privatizing Government Services: Can For-Profit Businesses Do a Better Job?" *CO Researcher* 6, no. 30 (August 9, 1996): 699–717.
9. Richard W. Stevenson, "Government Plan May Make Private Up to 850,000 Jobs," *The New York Times,* November 15, 2002, http://www.nytimes.com/2002/11/15/politics/15PRIV.html?pagewanted=print=top.
9a. Richard D. Lieberman, "The 'Criminalization' of Government Procurement," *Civil Engineering* 63, no. 3 (March 1993); 68–70.
10. Charles R. Rendall, "Privatization: A Cure for Our Ailing Infrastructure?" *Civil Engineering* 66, no. 12 (December 1996): 6.
11. Steve H. Hanke, "Privatization: Theory, Evidence, and Implementation," in *Control of Spending,* ed. C. Lowell Harris, *Proceedings of the Academy of Political Science* 35, no. 4 (New York: 1985), 101–113.
12. Ralph C. Chandler and Jack C. Plano, *The Public Administration Dictionary* (New York: John Wiley & Sons, 1982), p. 91.
13. David A. Dowell, "Guidelines for Legislative Language for State Program Evaluation," Long Beach, Calif.: California State University, 1998, http://www.csulb.edu/~ddowell/guidelines.htm.
14. David Thomas, "Department of Education Announces New Approach to Program Evaluation," http://www.ed.gov/PressReleases/04-2002/04052002a.html.
15. "Introduction to Program Evaluation for Comprehensive Tobacco Control Programs," Centers for Disease Control and Prevention, February 6, 2002, http://www.cdc.gov/tobacco/evaluation_manual/executive_summary.html.
16. David Margolis, "Performance-Based Management in PENNDOT," *PA Times,* Vol. 25, No. 6 (July 2002), p. 3.
17. "Editor's Notebook," *Government Executive Magazine,* January 1, 1997; http://www.govexec.com/news/index/cfm.
18. Katherine Barrett and Richard Greene, "The Government Performance Project: Grading the Cities—A Management Report Card," *Governing,* (February 2000); see http://64.67.181.148/gpp/gp0intro.htm.
19. Government Performance Project, "Management Matters and Performance Counts," January 29, 2002, http://www.maxwell.syr.edu/gpp.County's_2002/county_main_page.htm.
20. David Osborne and Peter Plasrik, "Grading Governments," http://www.psgrp.com/resources/Publications/op4-13.html.
21. The National Center for Public Productivity, "A Brief Guide for Performance Measurement in Local Government," http://newark.rutgers/~ncpp/Manual.htm.
22. Gail C. Christopher and Robert J. O'Neill, Jr., "The Federal Government's People Crisis," *Federal Times,* December 2000.
23. General Accounting Office, *Human Capital: Practices that Empowered and Involved Employees,* GAO-01-1070, September 14, 2000.
24. Kellie Lunney, "Managers Should Involve Employees in Decision Making," *Government Executive Magazine,* October 10, 2001, http://www.govexec.com
25. The Highway Performance Monitoring System (HPMS), Nonfederal Applications of the Highway Performance Monitoring System (HPMS), http://www.fhwa.dot.gov/ohim/nahpms.html.

Administrative Law and Control

Chapter Highlights

The Impact of Administrative Growth on Democratic
Ideals and Administrative Law

Traditional and Contemporary Cornerstones
of American Administrative Law

What Is Administrative Law?

Administrative Discretion and Its Limits

Opening Up the Government

Administrative Law Judges and Federal Regulations

Internal and External Administrative Controls

The Whistle-Blower as Tell-All

Law and Control: How Much Is Enough?

Summary

Sexual Harassment at Steady State U?

Whether it is racial or sexual harassment, stalking, or bullying at work, harassment is an important legal and social subject. Harassment may be difficult for the victim to prove. Scant physical evidence may be available. Malicious accusations are likewise unfair to the wrongly accused.[1]

Tom Mills, professor of political literature at Steady State University for twenty-five years, was fired from his meritorious, position-classified state government job based on the findings of the State of Commonwealth administrative law judge who heard the case.

Matthew Petersen, administrative law judge, State of Commonwealth, presided over seven days of hearings and testimony from more than two dozen witnesses. Judge Petersen ruled that Steady State University proved by "a preponderance of the evidence" that Professor Mills harassed at least two female graduate students. The judge found that the professor engaged in *quid pro quo* sexual harassment, created a hostile academic and work en-

vironment, engaged in a pattern of sexual harassment, and sexually abused a student.[2]

Broadly speaking, administrative law governs how power is transferred from the State of Commonwealth General Assembly (legislature) to administrative agencies, how Steady State University (an administrative agency) uses power, and how the policies, procedures, and actions of Steady State University are viewed by the courts. More specifically, administrative laws catalog legal developments enhancing the powers and scope of the administrative agencies.

According to the judge's ruling, one of the women accused Professor Mills of, among other things, "*quid pro quo* harassment." She testified that Professor Mills suggested that she engage in a sexual threesome with him and another female graduate student with whom Professor Mills said he was having a sexual relationship. The woman testified that Professor Mills stated that he could give her financial help to continue with her studies.

Professor Mills contends that the events the women described as sexual harassment never took place. He stated that his lawyer would challenge Judge Petersen's ruling. Mills asserted that "there is no requirement that there be witnesses to acts of sexual harassment, other than the accuser and the accused, in order for the accuser to be believed." Professor Mills insists that he is the victim of a "witch-hunt."[3]

Professor Mills is appealing his dismissal from Steady State University to the Board of Trustees.

Sexual Harassment Policy— Steady State University

A. *Policy:* Sexual harassment and related retaliation is prohibited by Steady State University.

   1. For the purposes of this Policy, sexual harassment means unwelcome sexual advances, requests for sexual favors, and other verbal or physical contact of a sexual nature when: (1) submission to such conduct is made either explicitly or implicitly a term or condition of an individual's employment, living conditions and/or educational evaluation; (2) submission to or rejection of such conduct by an individual is used as the basis for tangible employment or educational decisions affecting such individuals; or (3) such conduct has the purpose or effect of unreasonably interfering with an individual's work or academic performance or creating an intimidating, hostile, or offensive working or educational environment.

     Hostile-environment sexual harassment, just described in subpart (3), is unwelcome sexual conduct that is sufficiently severe or pervasive that it alters the conditions of education or employment and creates an environment that a reasonable person would find intimidating, hostile, or offensive. The determination of whether an environment is "hostile" must be based on all of the circumstances. These circumstances could include the frequency of the conduct, its severity, and whether it is threatening or humilating.

   2. Making false complaints or providing false information regarding a complaint is prohibited.

   3. Individuals who violate this Policy will be disciplined or subjected to corrective action, up to and including termination or expulsion from Steady State University.

B. *Procedures.* All reports or complaints shall be made as promptly as feasible after the occurrence. If an investigation is conducted, the alleged victim and the respondent shall have the right to: (1) at the commencement of the investigation, receive written notice of the report or complaint, including a statement of the allegations; (2) present relevant information to the investigators; and (3) receive, at the conclusion of the investigation, a copy of the investigator's report, to the extent permitted by law. All records of sexual harassment reports and investigations shall be considered confidential and shall not be disclosed publicly except to the extent required by law.

C. *Legal Groundings.* In 1980, the Equal Employment Opportunities Commission (EEOC) issued government regulations defining sexual harassment and stating that it was a form of sex discrimination prohibited by the Civil Rights Act of 1964. In 1986, the U.S. Supreme Court held that sexual harassment was a form of job discrimination and that it is illegal.

Under State of Commonwealth law, sexual harassment may include verbal conduct, including epithets, derogatory comments, or slurs; or physical conduct, including assault, impeding or blocking movements, or physical interference with normal work or movements; or sexual favors, including unwanted sexual advances where sexual favors are asked for in exchange for an employment benefit. Commonwealth law provides for monetary damages for victims and reimbursement of attorney fees.[4]

Endnotes

[1]Idaho Human Rights Commission, "Sexual Harassment on the Job," http://www2.state.id.us/ihrc/sex.htm; "Sexual harassment takes many forms, such as: pinching, grabbing, patting, repeated requests for dates, embarrassing stories or "jokes," comments or questions about your body or sexual activities, displays of pornographic materials, indecent exposure, assault, or even rape."

[2]Courtney Leatherman, "Iowa State University Fires Professor for Sexual Abuse and Harassment," *The Chronicle of Higher Education,* 1998. See http://www.public.iastate.edu/~aaup.sexh/chronicle.htm.

[3]*Ibid.*

[4]University of Colorado, Administrative Policy Statements, University Policy on Sexual Harassment, July 1, 1999, http://www.cu.edu/~policies/Personnel/sexharass.html.

Source

See also 9 to 5, National Association of Working Women, "Sexual Harassment FAQ," http://www.nolo.com/lawcenter/ency/article.cfm.

During the first one hundred years of U.S. history, several factors conspired to keep the administrative sector of our many governments comparatively small and weak. Fragmentation and personalism, for example, deterred the growth of large and formalized bureaucracies like those starting to emerge in Europe. The antigovernmental attitudes of the American people probably acted as an even greater deterrent. In the end, our legalistic approach to governmental problems may have served as the greatest deterrent. The ways in which U.S. legalism imposed limits on, and even substituted for, administrative power were noticed by Lord James Bryce, the perceptive British observer who began visiting our shores late in the nineteenth century. In his 1888 book, *The American Commonwealth,* Bryce wrote:

> It is a great merit of American government that it relies very little on officials [administrators] and arms them with little power of arbitrary interference. . . . [The government] has taken the direction of acting through the law rather than through the officials. That is to say, when it prescribes to the citizen a particular course of action it has relied upon the ordinary legal sanctions, instead of investing the administrative officers with inquisitional duties or powers that might prove oppressive.[1]

As the quotation suggests, Bryce wholly approved of this approach. Had he been more legalistically trained or oriented himself, he might have pointed to a particular legalistic feature of our system that served as the main roadblock to a greater assumption of power and responsibility by U.S. administrators. This feature is our constitutionally enshrined principle of separation of powers.

The Constitution stipulates that the legislative branch enact the laws and the executive branch execute and enforce them. Through the first century of our existence, the courts—the judicial branch—took a particularly rigorous attitude toward this demarcation of authority. They ruled that Congress could not give away its power, even if it voted in such a manner. Consequently, efforts to bestow substantial discretion on any administrator or administrative agency drew the Supreme Court's prompt disapproval. Congress, said the Court, could not delegate its fundamental powers. Rules and regulations that would have the force of law would have to be passed by the body charged with passing laws.

As Bryce was writing his 1888 book, however, the Court was readying to alter the course of U.S. administrative history. Congress, confronted with the pressing need to regulate the country's expanding railroad industry, realized that it could not possibly devote the continuous time and effort that such a task demanded and passed the Interstate Commerce Act of 1887. This act set up a new agency, the Interstate Commerce Commission (ICC), to carry out this regulatory function. In a landmark decision, the Supreme Court ruled the Interstate Commerce Act, along with the agency it established, to be constitutional.

The newly created Surface Transportation Board was scarcely given carte blanche discretion. Congress set down specific standards regarding its jurisdiction and prescribed rather detailed criteria for use of its discretionary power in policing the railroads. Congress even spelled out the various forms of misbehavior that the Surface Transportation Board was to police, such as rebating, rate discrimination, and pooling. The new regulatory commission was, in the words of Theodore Lowi, "relatively well shackled by clear standards of public policy, as stated in the statute and as understood in common law."[2]

From this time on, Congress, along with most state legislatures, began delegating more and more legislative power to administrative agencies, and the Supreme Court became increasingly cooperative in permitting them to do so. When Congress amplified the ICC's powers, for instance, by passing the Transportation Act of 1920, the Court let the Act stand, even though the increased powers were accompanied by far fewer specific criteria to guide and control their application.

Although the court modified its once hard-line stand on delegation, it was still not ready to capitulate completely. The Court, for example, invalidated order after order of the Federal Trade Commission on grounds that its "unfair method of competition" standard was too vague. In the regulatory agency's first two decades, or from 1915 until the mid-1930s, the Court judged that the FTC's congressionally imposed standard gave the agency too much discretionary power.[3]

The New Deal brought the issue to a head when President Roosevelt, trying to wield broad executive power to pull the country out of the Depression, found himself on a collision course with the nation's highest tribunal, leading to a series of hostile Court decisions which culminated in the famous Schechter case of 1934.[4] In this case, a majority of the justices struck down the National Recovery Act and with it the elaborate planning machinery and the wide blanket of administrative power that the Act had promulgated. The Reagan administration approached things differently. According to Harold Seidman and Robert Gilmour, Roosevelt's "New Deal" marked the birth of the positive state, and the "Reagan Revolution" was geared to end it.[5] "The evolution from the positive to the regulatory state commenced in the 1960s, but President Reagan was the first to redefine the federal government's role as limited, wherever possible, to providing services without producing them."[6] Reagan worked to privatize government services in an effort to minimize the negative aspects of big government.

During the last fifty years of the twentieth century, the administrative sector surged forward, spurred on by what might be called the permissive attitude the Court took toward the delegation issue. Administrative agencies acquired increasing functions along with more powers to carry them out. They may prescribe rules

Defining Administrative Law

Administrative law is an amorphous body of law. . . . Administrative law is created or affected by the activities of government agencies. The term *administrative law* is akin to many other conceptual terms and is hard to define.

—*Joseph J. Simeone*

Administrative law controls a system: a system which, in the simplest terms, has only one goal: to deliver government services to its citizens.

—*Charles Koch, Jr.*

1. That branch of law concerned with the procedures by which administrative agencies make rules and adjudicate cases; the conditions under which these actions can be reviewed by courts. 2. The legislation that creates administrative agencies. 3. The rules and regulations promulgated by administrative agencies. 4. The law governing judicial review of administrative actions.

—*Jay M. Shafritz*

Broadly speaking, administrative law deals with (1) the ways in which power is transferred from legislative bodies to administrative agencies; (2) how administrative agencies use power; and (3) how the actions taken by administrative agencies are reviewed by the courts. More specifically, administrative law is concerned with the legal developments which have so dramatically increased the powers and scope of the administrative branch.

—*Kenneth F. Warren*

Sources: Joseph J. Simeone, "The Function, Flexibility, and Future of United States Judges of the Executive Branch," *Administrative Law Review* 44, no. 1 (Winter 1992): 159–161; Charles Koch Jr., *Administrative Law and Practice* (New York: West Publishing Co., 1985); Jay M. Shafritz, *The Dorsey Dictionary of American Government and Politics* (Chicago: The Dorsey Press, 1988); Kenneth F. Warren, *Administrative Law in the Political System*, 3d ed. (Upper Saddle River, N.J.: Prentice Hall, 1997), p. 23.

and issue orders that have the force of law and may impose penalties on those who disobey. Some agencies have even acquired the subpoena power and/or the contempt power. What were once the closely guarded prerogatives of elected officials increasingly have been placed into the hands of nonelected functionaries.

The Congress, state legislatures, and city councils bear the responsibility for administering and enforcing legislation. The president, state governors, and mayors—and their executive branches—bear the responsibility for administering and enforcing legislation. However, "upon reflection the Congress is institutionally incapable of providing in legislation itself a detailed answer for every issue that may arise under it. The same is true for state legislatures."[7] Therefore, the United States, a country espousing democratic capitalism, exists in the *era of the administrative state.*

The Impact of Administrative Growth on Democratic Ideals and Administrative Law

The administrative presidency, with corresponding implications for state governors, county executives, and municipal mayors, finds philosophical origins in George Washington's first cabinet. Thomas Jefferson, the original "outsider" advocating state's rights and decentralization of power, called for the pluralist model of presidential leadership. Alexander Hamilton—called our first accountant of the nation's purse—called for a strong chief administrator with direct, accountable lines of program authority.

Jefferson represented values of equality of uniform participation, or democratic ideals, while Hamilton called for efficient administration, articulated in hierarchy and bureaucracy. How has the emergence of the modern administrative state redefined the basic democratic principles of our 1787 U.S. Constitution? Tenets of administrative law are grounded in constitutionalism, shared governmental powers, popular government, individualism, and political equality.[8]

Constitutionalism. A constitutional governmental system regards the people, not the government, as sovereign. Rule of law emphasizes supremacy of the law and the notion of limited government. A constitutional government is politically legitimate if it rests securely upon popular consent.

Many Americans believe that the growth of administrative expertise challenges the primacy of democratic constitutionalism. According to this argument, administrative discretion permits public administrators to "govern" the United States, and governmental regulations are threats to democratic constitutionalism. The undemocratic character of administrative experts compromises constitutional democracy. The new cadre of governmental experts forms an administrative elite that evolves into a democratically irresponsible oligarchy.

Shared Powers. The division of powers among the chief executive, administrative, legislative, and judicial branches and among different levels of government permits each political entity a limited check over the powers of other authorities in the governmental system. Decision-making powers in this system are not monopolized by a single governmental branch. Presidents, legislators, and judges tend to delegate more of their prescribed powers to government bureaucrats as the weight of increasing governmental regulation increases.

The expansion of administrative policymaking powers is enhanced as other branches of government become increasingly bogged down with peripheral concerns. Public administrators, for example, absorb more power as constitutionally elected politicians agonize over the role of government in the resolution of moral dilemmas. Many citizens perceive the public administration system as a closed political system that circumvents the open decision-making structure authored by the constitutional framers. Political bureaucracy emerges with a less than well-defined philosophy of the public interest.

Popular Government. Democratic government implies that the ultimate determination of public policy resides with the people. Stressing majority will, individual rights, and liberty, popular government is the opposite of absolutism. The shift of power from political institutions to administrative agencies raises questions about the democratic functioning of popular government.[9]

If public policy making is "farmed out" to government bureaucrats, how "popular" can government be? The administrative state, grounded in structures, functions, and rationality, may not be suited to the flexibility required to meet the public's demands. A system based on knowledge, skills, and expertise conflicts with a system based on partisan politics and spoils. All government officials, elected and appointed, are servants of the people and should be held accountable for their performance in the public's interest. It can be difficult to ensure that a nonelected official can be that accountable.

Individualism. Freedom, personal well-being, and capabilities of individuals may conflict with the regulation of society by public bureaucracies. According to

Why Administrative Law Matters

1. The growth of government by public administrators is the most important political innovation in modern times.
2. In the present day, the effects of administrative government influence us literally every moment of our lives.
3. Bureaucratic government has provided no utopian cure for the shortcomings of free enterprise.

4. Administrative law seeks to reduce the tendencies toward arbitrariness and unfairness in bureaucratic government.
5. Administrative law, a relatively new and open-ended field of law, has not yet succeeded in playing its assigned role effectively.

Source: Lief H. Carter, *Administrative Law and Politics: Cases and Comments* (Boston: Little, Brown, 1983), p. 4.

some, bureaucracy stymies the will of citizens, expressing the powers of the system and not the individual.

The tug of war between societal rights and individual rights challenges the political consensus of democratic governments. Regulatory agencies prescribe rules that may destroy the freedom of individuals, with new structures of apolitical power over individuals emerging in their place.

In balancing societal and individual rights, government regulators are called upon to implement guidelines of federal, state, and local laws in a "fair" manner. Issues of administrative law ultimately involve questions of due process of law. The question is: Due process or fair treatment for whom? Liberty is sacrificed and our way of life is altered when an administrative agency or a court makes a decision that benefits a larger group at the expense of the individual. The rights of the individual—bolstered by the Fourth Amendment to the U.S. Constitution, which monitors unreasonable searches and seizures, and the Fifth Amendment, which guards against self-incrimination—can be undermined by the exercise of excessive regulatory control.

Political Equality. Grounded in democratic philosophies of equality under the law and equal opportunity for all persons, government is to treat and represent all persons equally. Laws forbid arbitrary treatment of citizens by government officials, but in practice U.S. administrative agencies do not afford complete equality to all persons or groups. The reality of U.S. political bureaucracy is that preferential treatment is given to special interests.

Sexual and racial discrimination are well-known and publicized aspects of our society. Since the Great Society of the 1960s, citizen groups have been organized to represent the interests of women and minorities. Affirmative action programs call for special compensatory measures from government to rectify past discriminatory practices by society. In theory, at least, the rule-of-law principle demands that government bureaucrats treat all individuals equally. Public bureaucracy, as prescribed by Max Weber's "ideal-type," rests upon knowledge, skills, and expertise, and not upon equality or political influence.

Constitutionalism, shared powers, popular government, individualism, and political equality are the political philosophies upon which administrative laws find implementation in modern American society. The individual needs the assurance of protection in law from the potential misuse of regulatory power. The

TABLE 11.1

James Q. Wilson's Four Periods of Bureaucratic Growth

Period	Focus	Key Acts Passed
1887–1890	Control monopolies and rates	Interstate Commerce Act
		Sherman Act
1906–1915	Regulate product quality	Pure Food and Drug Act
		Meat Inspection Act
		Federal Trade Commission
		Clayton Act
1930–1940	Extend regulation to cover various socioeconomic areas, especially new technologies	Food, Drug, and Cosmetic
		Public Utility Holding Company Act
		National Labor Relations Act
		Securities and Exchange Act
		Natural Gas Act
1960–1979	Expand regulation to make America a cleaner, healthier, safer, and fairer place to live and work	Economic Opportunity Act
		Civil Rights Acts of 1960, 1964, and 1968
		National Environmental Policy Act
		Clean Air Act
		Occupational Safety and Health Act
1978–1993	Deregulation movement as a reaction to bureaucratic overexpansion	Paperwork Reduction Act
		Air Deregulation Act
		Radio and TV deregulation
		Banking deregulation

Sources: James Q. Wilson, "The Rise of the Bureaucratic State," *Policy Making,* ed. Francis E. Rourke, 4th ed. (Boston: Little, Brown, 1986), pp. 125–148; and Kenneth F. Warren, *Administrative Law in the Political System,* 3d ed. (Upper Saddle River, N.J.: Prentice-Hall, 1997), p. 45.

conflicts between individual citizens and their governments and the resolution of these conflicts by the law allow understanding of how these philosophies are played out in American life.

Prospects for federal government growth post September 11, 2001, is juxtaposed for comparison and contrast to the four periods of previous bureaucratic growth as categorized, then described by James Q. Wilson, and later supplemented by Kenneth F. Warren (table 11.1).

Traditional and Contemporary Cornerstones of American Administrative Law

The traditional cornerstones of administrative law are the independent regulatory agency, a uniform administrative procedure law (Administrative Procedure Act, 1946, as amended), substantial evidence judicial review, and notice and comment ruling.[10]

The **independent regulatory agency,** as a descriptive concept, is a misnomer. All agencies are directly dependent in unique ways upon the executive and legislative branches of government and indirectly upon the judicial branch. The independent agencies, as they are called, emerged from the American constitutional provision of separation of powers.

There are three types of regulation. The best known is the old-style economic regulation. The second type, the new social regulation, is a product of the 1970s. A third type of regulation is subsidiary regulation.[11] Economic regulation emerged from the social and economic challenges of the 1930s. From the devastating consequences of the Depression, the New Deal created the Federal Deposit Insurance Corporation (FDIC), Tennessee Valley Authority (TVA), Federal Communications Commission (FCC), Securities and Exchange Commission (SEC), National Labor Relations Board (NLRB), and Civil Aeronautics Board (CAB). These regulatory bodies were established from 1933 through 1938.

After World War II, other agencies were created to monitor and confront emerging national problems. The Atomic Energy Commission (AEC), Selective Service System (SSS), National Aeronautics and Space Administration (NASA), Federal Maritime Commission (FMC), Equal Employment Opportunity Commission (EEOC), Environmental Protection Agency (EPA), Occupational Safety and Health Administration (OSHA), and Consumer Product Safety Commission (CPSC) were created to administer and regulate, respectively, programs concerning atomic energy, military conscription, space exploration, shipping, employment discrimination, environmental protection, occupational safety, and consumer product safety. In addition, there is a need to regulate the activities of agencies implementing Social Security, medical care, welfare, food stamps, veterans' benefits, and internal revenue programs.

The development and enactment of a **uniform administrative procedure law** is the *second* traditional cornerstone of administrative law. The Administrative Procedure Act, enacted in 1946, brings a degree of standardization to administrative practices and procedures and public access to those procedures. Before the enactment of APA, administrative practice and procedure questions were decided on a constitutional basis. The APA brought order from chaos. Unless they can find justifiable exception, agencies must follow the fundamental outlines of APA's broad and general statute. Such legislation was an advance of immeasurable proportions in administrative law and the protection of citizen rights.

Judicial review is the *third* traditional cornerstone of administrative law. Substantial evidence review is a dominant feature of administrative practice and procedure. The courts may rule on the merits of agency action if things go askew. Derived from statutory and nonstatutory sources, judicial review permits judges to scrutinize allegedly illegal administrative actions. Judicial review, as a basic right, rests on the congressional grant of general jurisdiction under Article 3 of the U.S. Constitution.

The **rule-making procedure** (notice and comment ruling) constitutes the *fourth* and final traditional cornerstone of administrative law. Rule making guides the subsequent application of policy, and, it is argued, clear rules promote fairness. Rule making is also a forceful, efficient, yet democratic way for agencies to implement their mandates. Prior to the advent of rule making, agencies resorted to policy interpretation on a case by case, *ad hoc* basis. Rule making is a more rational means of policymaking than adjudication, because adjudication is reactive and potentially disjointed. Rule making is more comprehensive, facilitating planning and coordination.

Contemporary pressing demands call attention to new cornerstones of administrative law. These are public participation in the administrative process, administrative process in informal and discretionary governmental activity, and the evolving definition of the mission of administrative agencies and development of effective oversight of their activities.[12]

The courts have held that **public participation** is pertinent to sound and equitable decision making in administrative processes. Until the mid-1960s, the prevailing perspective was that the agency was representative of the public interest. The courts insisted upon citizen rights to participate in the administrative process; Congress and the agencies soon recognized the validity of public participation as well.

The **administrative process in formal and discretionary governmental activity** is a *second* contemporary cornerstone. The development of procedural law to cover persons in public institutions, aliens, and the governance of educational institutions emphasizes the broadening development for protecting the rights of citizens in previously neglected areas. Aspects of administration once thought purely discretionary are subject to regulation as well.

A *third,* and final, contemporary cornerstone of administrative law is the **continuing definition of the mission of administrative agencies and development of effective oversight of their activities.** Each new administration advocates regulatory reform, but each administration fails to redefine the mission with sweeping regulatory reform. Congress may strengthen its oversight functions by demanding better analyses of the potential effects of proposed legislation, stronger program evaluation requirements in legislation, greater oversight of program design and development of regulations, and more use of program evaluation information. The final cornerstone, then, is the continuing development and fulfillment of mission and likewise improvement in oversight.

What Is Administrative Law?

There is no commonly agreed upon subject matter of administrative law. There are, however, certain parameters wherein the application of administrative law is appropriate.

Bernard Schwartz argues that administrative law does not relate to public administration in the same manner that commercial law relates to commerce and land law relates to land. Rather, the definition of administrative law centers around powers and remedies to answer the following inquiries: (1) What powers may be vested in administrative agencies? (2) What are the limits of those powers? (3) What are the ways in which agencies are kept within these limits?[13]

All law may be generally categorized as either procedural or substantive. For example, the Environmental Protection Agency establishes New Source Performance Standards that prohibit emissions from industrial, stoker-fired boilers in excess of 0.10 pounds of fly ash per million BTU of heat input. The Administrative Procedure Act specifies that such a rule be published in *The Federal Register* so that interested persons may comment before the ruling becomes final. The requirement for publishing the rule in *The Federal Register* is procedural; the rule for limiting emissions from stoker-fired boilers is substantive.[14]

Administrative law originates primarily from interpretations of legal statements that describe procedures agencies follow. Such judicial interpretations emanate primarily but not exclusively from due process clauses as detailed in constitutions, from applicable administrative procedure statutes, and sometimes from clauses within statutes establishing an agency and also prescribing a procedure to follow.

Administrative law is not regulatory law. The differences between regulatory and administrative law are the subject of the next chapter. Numerous government agencies and departments, cooperating with legislatures, create regulatory laws that affect even the most trivial of activities. Several of the more recognizable regulatory agencies include the Federal Communications Commission (FCC), which regulates broadcasting and interstate telephone rates; the Occupational Safety and Health Administration (OSHA), which regulates the safety of the workplace; and the Food and Drug Administration (FDA), which tests drugs for marketing and monitors the contents of the food we eat. The laws, consent decrees, rules, and regulations made and enforced by these agencies are not administrative law. Instead, "regulatory law governs the citizenry; administrative law governs the government. We might say that administrative law governs the bureaucracy as other constitutional provisions govern the judicial, legislative, and presidential powers in government."[15]

Administrative law applies legal principles originating from statutes, common law, constitutions, and regulatory laws to the government agencies affected.

Administrative Discretion and Its Limits

The exercise of discretion occurs in the context of the informal administrative process. The difficulty lies in ascertaining ways to restrict discretion without unduly limiting the flexibility of the administrator. Administrators need some discretion for implementing their functions in a reasonable and efficient manner; excessive discretion may result, however, in the violation of the rights of private citizens. To find the proper balance, author Kenneth Culp Davis suggests that greater use of administrative rule making curbs unreasonable discretion. The tremendous rise in rule making has helped make this dilemma less of a problem.

Although administrators find themselves blessed with powers their predecessors little dreamed of possessing, they also find themselves subjected to numerous restraints as well. The legislative and judicial branches of government have not been content to stand aside and let administrators run the country, subject only to broad policy prescriptions and rather vague standards regarding the public interest. These two branches have acted to limit administrative discretion by, among other things, imposing increasingly strict standards on how administrators may use their new prerogatives.

Congress first took action in 1946 through the passage of the Administrative Procedure Act (APA). This detailed piece of legislation set down specific rules on the ways in which administrative agencies are to proceed. The courts have since taken up the task, and, based on broadened interpretations of the "due process" clauses in the Fifth and Fourteenth Amendments to the Constitution and the Administrative Procedure Act itself, they have subjected administrative actions to progressively stricter review.

Judicial review since the Schechter case has focused not so much on matters of substance as on matters of procedure. In other words, the courts have concerned themselves less with what the administrative sector is doing and more with how it is doing it. The judges have, in effect, admitted that they do not have the expertise to determine whether a drug is safe, a welfare payment is adequate, or a highway route is well designed. As long as the administrative agency can show that its decisions in such matters are not arbitrary but are based on some legitimate rationale, the judges will not be inclined to interfere. They have become increasingly disposed to speak out, however, when they find that the agency is proceeding in a manner contrary to administrative due process.

"Administrative due process," writes Lewis Mainzer, "is that procedure which will normally be accepted by the courts as reasonable under the circumstances, whether or not the judge thinks the substantive decision was correct."[16] Davis puts it this way: "The dominant tendency in both state courts and federal courts is toward the middle position known as the substantial-evidence rule . . . the court decides questions of law but limits itself to the test of reasonableness in reviewing findings of fact."[17]

Due process, however, is not fully encapsulated by the criterion of "reasonableness" alone. It also implies what the Supreme Court has referred to as the criterion of "fundamental fairness." In attempting to set up standards for administrative due process, the courts, basing their findings on the federal government's Administrative Procedure Act and similar state acts and on their new interpretations of the Constitution, have worked out a fairly strict set of rules that administrators must follow to meet due process requirements. The following set of rules has developed as case law on administrative due process accumulates.

1. **Adequate Notice.** Before administrators or agencies can take any action that would directly affect one or more persons or institutions, they must usually give such affected parties adequate notice. How much notice is adequate? This depends on the circumstances and often becomes a matter of litigation before the courts. Rarely is a period of less than thirty days deemed to be adequate, and frequently a much longer interval is required.

    The adequacy of the notice, the timeliness of the information, and the proper distribution of the notice are of particular importance. Concerning adequacy, the APA states that: "Persons entitled to notice of an agency shall be timely informed of—(1) the time, place, and nature of the hearing; (2) the legal authority and jurisdiction under which the hearing is to be held; and (3) the matters of fact and law asserted."[18]

    However, in some situations, administrative agencies are empowered to act with scarcely any notice. If a building inspector finds a structure so unsafe it is in danger of collapse at any moment, for example, or a health inspector finds a restaurant serving contaminated food, they can usually order the situation remedied immediately. Unless it can be shown that the public safety demands precipitate action, however, the rule of adequate notice must govern.

2. **Disclosure of Reasons.** In addition to giving adequate notice, administrative agencies are usually required to state their reasons for taking their intended action. In most instances, the affected party may demand that the agency put

these reasons in writing. This tends to deter agencies from acting in an arbitrary and capricious manner and at least gives the affected party written evidence to use in seeking subsequent redress in the courts.

3. **The Right to a Hearing.** Beginning in the late 1960s, the courts began to broaden dramatically the right of aggrieved parties to have a hearing. Motorists deprived of their licenses, welfare clients deprived of their benefits, public-housing tenants faced with eviction, and prisoners sentenced to solitary confinement sued for the right to be heard with favorable results in the courts.[19] Even the private sector found itself affected by the dictum in certain cases as students faced with expulsion were also granted the right to be heard.

   The expansion that has taken place in requiring hearings also affects rule making. Agencies that seek to promulgate new rules must usually schedule hearings and allow those who think differently to state their case. Even those who may not be directly affected by the new rule can have their voices heard.[20]

4. **The Right to Further Appeal.** If, after a hearing, the protesting party is still not satisfied, he or she may appeal to a higher echelon within the agency and, as a last step, to the courts. Available figures suggest that increasing numbers of citizens are taking this final step.

The aggrieved party may seek judicial redress on the grounds that he or she was not given adequate notice, that the agency's procedures are not clear, that the agency is not abiding by administrative due process or its own procedures, that it has behaved in an arbitrary or discriminatory manner, or that the agency lacks jurisdiction in doing what it did or plans to do. As Mainzer points out, "Despite the Administrative Procedure Act and mountains of court opinion, the standards of administrative due process are extraordinarily indefinite."[21] Thus, numerous possibilities exist for carrying administrative issues into the courtroom.

There are, at the same time, numerous limitations on using the courts to reverse or mitigate administrative actions. First, the courts will not entertain the case until the petitioner has exhausted all recourse within the administrative agency. The courts will likewise not intervene in cases where there is no remedy. Finally, as previously noted, the courts balk at deciding questions of fact or weighing the validity of one expert opinion against another. They prefer to confine themselves to questions of law and procedure.

Opening Up the Government

Citizen access and participation in the administrative process gained support during the late 1960s and 1970s. The presumption is in favor of public access whenever possible. There are circumstances where information and participation are denied under the law, but in general, the department or agency searches for an appropriate balance between citizen interests and governmental needs for secrecy. The federal Freedom of Information Act (1966), the Privacy Act (1974), the "government in sunshine" laws, and provisions for increased citizen participation in governmental policymaking and decision-making processes have made important contributions to opening the government.

The Freedom of Information Act, or FOIA, is part of the Administrative Procedure Act (1946). Prior to its adoption, governmental information and records could be revealed only to "persons properly and directly concerned." Such records could be subject to secrecy if a policy was "in the public interest" or if said data pertained "solely to the internal management of an agency." The FOIA reversed such practices, guaranteeing openness to "any person" (see table 11.2). If information is withheld, the burden of proof for the necessity of secrecy is placed upon the agency. The agency has ten days to respond; if the decision goes against the petitioner, he or she may appeal to a higher level in the agency. Certain items such as "trade secrets and commercial or financial information

TABLE 11.2
How to Make an FOIA Request

General information regarding the FOIA (Freedom of Information Act) law can be found at the U.S. Department of Justice (DOJ) website (www.usdoj.gov). This site includes most of the Office of Information and Privacy documents related to policies regulating the government-wide FOIA programs.

Federal Aviation Administration (FAA) publications and much regulatory information and data are publicly available, and an FOIA request may not be necessary to obtain it. If you have questions about the need for an FOIA request, please contact the headquarters FOIA office. An FOIA request must be written and must be for FAA records; it is not appropriate to ask questions under the FOIA law. You may make a request by indicating that you are seeking records under the Freedom of Information Act.

Each request should describe the particular record to the fullest extent. The request should describe the subject matter of the record, and, if known, indicate the date of the record, the place where it originated, and the name of the originating person or office.

A processing fee may be assessed for search, review, and duplication activities associated with an FOIA request. Fees are assessed depending on the category of the requester. The four categories of requesters are: commercial; educational or noncommerical scientific institutions; news media; and all other requesters. More information on FOIA fees may be found in the DOJ Freedom of Information Act Guide, pages 413–415; or Department of Transportation 49 *Code of Federal Regulations,* Part 7, "Public Availability of Information" (7.43).

Requesters should indicate their willingness to pay applicable fees in their FOIA requests. The envelope in which the request is sent should be marked "FOIA" and mailed to:

> Freedom of Information Act Program, AAD-40
> Headquarters Office
> Federal Aviation Administration
> 800 Independence Avenue, SW
> Washington, DC 20591
> Main Number (202) 267-9165
> Email: 9.ahr.foia@faa.dot.gov

Source: Federal Aviation Administration, website, www.faa.gov.

obtained from a person," deemed "privileged and confidential," and "personal and medical files or similar files the disclosure of which would constitute a clearly un-warranted invasion of personal privacy" are not subject to disclosure.

Agencies with significant numbers of requests from businesses brought in the largest fees. Fee leaders included DOD, HHS, EPA, Treasury, Transportation, Agriculture, and Labor. Almost 75 percent of the FOIA requests originate from business and law firms. An estimated 91 percent of requests are honored. A research assistant at a college in California and a newspaper reporter in Oregon asked the Department of Energy for details on the Nuclear Emergency Search Team (NEST). A consulting firm in Maryland asked the Department of the Navy for copies of procurement contracts. An inmate at a prison in the midwest asked the Department of the Army for instructions on how to make a bomb and where to detonate the mechanism in Denver. A hospital in Massachusetts asked for a Quality Assurance Profile from the FDA.[22]

The Privacy Act is a part of the Administrative Procedure Act and addresses what information is collected on citizens and how that information is used, requiring agencies to publicly report the existence of systems of records maintained on individuals; requiring that the information contained in these record systems be accurate, complete, relevant, and up-to-date; providing procedures whereby individuals can inspect and correct inaccuracies in almost all federal files about themselves; specifying that information about an individual gathered for one purpose not be used for another without the individual's consent; and requiring agencies to keep an accurate accounting of the disclosure of records and, with certain exceptions, making these disclosures available to the subject of the record. The potential conflict with the FOIA is avoided with the disclaimer dictating disclosure as required under Section 552, or the FOIA section of the Administrative Procedure Act. The common-law right of access to information is an important source for legal development in the states. Nearly all states include statutory counterparts of the FOIA and Privacy Act.

Like the FOIA and the Privacy Act, the Federal Sunshine Act, passed by Congress in 1976, is also part of the Administrative Procedure Act. Enhancing access to government operations is the purpose of sunshine laws. The degree of openness varies from statute to statute. Most statutes permit exceptions to guarantees of openness, most notably, in labor negotiations and personnel matters. In some states, and on the federal level, a governmental body may enter executive session, and then, by majority vote, close the meeting to the public. In other states, even informal meetings are subject to sunshine statutes.

Citizen participation also opens government to the public. Citizen-initiated activities, or the citizen action movement, and government-initiated activities, or the citizen involvement movement, illustrate attempts to involve citizens. The second approach is relevant to the practice of administrative law. Hundreds of provisions require or permit some form of citizen participation in administrative policymaking or decision making because of congressional mandates. Such legislatively induced participation ranges from the creation of citizen advisory committees to requirements that public hearings be conducted prior to the adoption of a policy.

Open the Doors: Family Planning Dispute

A controversy over distribution of federal family planning funds has the potential for disrupting traditional programs and closing some clinics in areas of East Central Indiana.

If so, that could make it difficult for patients and others who have come to depend on the services. Whether it would border on tragedy might depend on whether alternative services of similar quality become available. Full understanding of that point has been hard to come by, and that is part of the controversy.

Planned Parenthood of East Central Indiana (PPECI) is at the center of the funding debate. It stands to lose significantly when final approval is given to federal funding proposals.

Currently, the organization's annual subsidy under the federal Title 10 family planning program is $743,484. That would drop to $271,218 next year, according to a proposal from the Indiana Family Health Council, a state agency that funnels federal dollars to local organizations.

Planned Parenthood has said some of its clinics could simply disappear—Winchester being one of the examples. And services at its main Muncie clinic, 424 West Main Street, could be affected. Presumably, some of those services would be transferred to Open Door BMH Health Center, which was encouraged to apply for family planning dollars by the state health council. Open Door is slated to receive $200,000 in 1998 for services at its clinic on South Walnut Street. Family planning grants fund a number of reproductive health services, including testing and treatment of sexually transmitted diseases, pregnancy testing and counseling, and several informational and educational programs aimed at lower-income populations.

It could be possible that Planned Parenthood, for years a nationally militant organization on the issue of abortion freedom for women, is now paying a price for that advocacy. If so, the cost is reflected in its inability to tap conventional funding sources as easily as in the past.

Locally, the organization has been critical of the health council's decision to award funds to Open Door, which it says is a family-practice clinic not solely focused on reproductive health care. Whether that would prevent Open Door from doing an equally good job in the family planning area is debatable. Competition between agency programs could be healthy.

Also, some who are more attuned to philosophical differences on the abortion issue would welcome Open Door's announced intention of providing no abortion procedures, counseling or referrals. That could be considered as a needed counter-point to Planned Parenthood's traditional policy on abortion counseling.

Nevertheless, there is a troublesome aspect to the switch of some funds from Planned Parenthood to Open Door. That is the Family Health Council's totally inadequate job of explaining the change. The council apparently handled the competitive bidding process behind closed doors. This has resulted in the state Planned Parenthood organization filing an Open Door lawsuit claiming the council violated public access laws by closing its meetings. Since its funding decision, the council's staff has declined to give specifics that might explain the basis for its decisions to award money to some agencies but not to others.

These are public monies involved, and the council would appear to have no legal right to prevent the public from observing its decision-making process.

If the council won't open its meetings, how can the public inform itself on whether the new funding decisions are in its best interests? How does the public know that the new providers, here and elsewhere in Indiana, will be able to offer the same level of service as Planned Parenthood? And how does the council rationalize the much higher cost-per-patient aspect of the Open Door grant compared to the Planned Parenthood grant?

There might be reasonable answers to these questions, but they won't be forthcoming unless the Indiana Family Health Council lifts its veil of secrecy.

Source: "Family Planning Dispute: Open the Doors," in *The Muncie Star Press,* November 13, 1997. Reprinted with permission.

Administrative Law Judges and Federal Regulations

The Administrative Procedure Act of 1946 ruled out any evidence that would be "irrelevant, immaterial or unduly repetitious," but did not go so far as to outlaw hearsay evidence as such. In 1971, the Supreme Court held that uncorroborated hearsay evidence can constitute "substantial evidence," sufficient to support an administrative ruling.[23] This did not mean that all such evidence was to be indiscriminately accepted. It would have to be relevant and reliable and support the point for which it was being used. Material "without a basis in evidence having rationality and probative force" would not meet the Court's standard.

Such a ruling does not close the door on the issue but only opens it wider. Hotly contested disputes can erupt at any time on whether a particular piece of hearsay evidence meets the criteria for relevance and probative value. Many, meanwhile, still question whether any hearsay evidence should be allowed to influence administrative action. The consequences of administrative decision making can frequently exceed those of a court trial, therefore it is only right and proper, so the argument goes, that those who would have to bear these consequences should benefit from the safeguards enjoyed by those subject to a court trial. Others contend, however, that there is nothing inherently evil about hearsay evidence. Such evidence is admissible in even criminal trials in most countries in the world, including most democratic countries. To bar it from the hearing room, they contend, would only hinder administrative tribunals from making informed and judicious decisions.

The dilemma of hearsay evidence is not the only controversy confronting administrative law judges. The prospect that the administrative law judges prosecute and adjudicate cases brought before him or her is a very serious concern. When an agency discharges or demotes an employee or deprives an individual or a group of some benefit or right, the agency first brings the charges and then, during the hearing, sits in judgment on these charges. In effect, it seems to be sitting in judgment on itself. To many lawyers, this is inherently unfair and contrary to both the spirit and intent of due process. They claim the affected party should possess the right to have the charges decided by a completely external body.

While most administrative agencies adjudicate their own charges and complaints, they usually use special employees to do so. These officials are customarily called hearing examiners in most local and some state bureaucracies, but in a few states as well as at the federal level they bear the more prestigious title of administrative law judges. Formerly referred to as "Washington's hybrids," "the hidden judiciary," "trial examiner," or a "hearing officer," they adjudicate cases for federal agencies.[24]

The administrative law judge exercises his or her prerogatives when a corporation or a private citizen disputes the decision of a federal department or agency. For example, if your grandfather is denied a disability pension from the Social Security Administration or if a state university is charged with unfair labor practices by the faculty union, the administrative law judge decides the case. Until 1978, the 1,100 administrative law judges were called "hearing officers." They, according to the United States Supreme Court, are "functionally comparable" to federal court judges. The Office of Personnel Management certifies the administrative law judge and maintains a central registry from which agencies select judges. The position is a lifetime job in which pay ranges from $86,500 to $130,000 per year.

Administrative Law Judges

Introduction

The position of Administrative Law Judge (ALJ), originally called hearing examiner, was created by the Administrative Procedure Act of 1946, Public Law 79-404. The Act insured fairness and due process in federal agency rule making and adjudication proceedings. It provided those parties, whose affairs are controlled or regulated by agencies of the federal government, an opportunity for a *formal* hearing on the record before an impartial hearing officer. It also provided for a merit selection system administered by the U.S. office of Personnel Management and statutory protection of the judge's decisional independence from undue agency influence.

Examination Suspended

On October 20, 2000, the United States Merit Systems Protection Board affirmed, in part, and modified its earlier initial decision in the class-action suit captioned *Ann S. Azdell and Donald B. Fishman v. Office of Personnel Management,* dated April 22, 1999. On November 24, 2000, OPM petitioned the Board to reconsider its earlier decision. On July 13, 2001, the Board denied OPM's petition. On September 17, 2001, OPM appealed the case to the U.S. Court of Appeals for the Federal Circuit. OPM is complying

with the Board's remedy, as ordered in its October 20, 2000 opinion.

On March 9, 2001, OPM notified all candidates on the register of their final ratings. Candidates entitled to priority consideration were also notified. OPM informed appellants and their counsel of the individual class members entitled to priority consideration. The examination remains suspended until further notice, and OPM is taking steps to create a new ALJ examination. ALJ applications will not be accepted during the examination suspension Additional information will be posted as it becomes available on the USAJOBS web site at: http:\\www.usajobs.opm.gov.

Qualifications Requirements

Applicants must be attorneys and have a minimum of seven (7) years administrative law and/or trial experience involving formal administrative hearing proceedings before local, state, or federal administrative agencies, courts, or other administrative bodies. In addition, applicants must demonstrate that they have had two years of qualifying experience at a level of difficulty and responsibility characteristic of at least senior level GS-13, or one year characteristic of at least GS-14 or GS-15 federal government attorneys actively involved in administrative law and/or litigation work.

Administrative law judges interpret federal regulations enforced by a particular department or agency to which they are assigned. "There's a perception that people are not getting a fair shake from us because we're Department of Labor ALJs," said Nahum Litt, the Labor Department's chief administrative law judge. Some administrative law judges are former staff attorneys for particular agencies and are, on occasion, perceived as officials for those federal bureaucracies instead of independent judges.

More than 800 administrative law judges are employed by the Social Security Administration, eighty in the Department of Labor, and eighty-four in the National Labor Relations Board. The remaining number are divided among twenty-six other departments and agencies around the country. Administrative law judges in the Social Security Administration alone hear 300,000 appeals a year.[25]

Although federal ALJs are employees of the agency whose cases they adjudicate, their qualifications and civil service status have given them virtual immunity from normal agency pressures. They frequently counteract and contradict the policies of their agencies. When the Social Security Administration attempted to use the Reagan administration's stricter guidelines to pare nearly a quarter million peo-

Duties and Responsibilities

ALJs prepared for and preside at formal hearings which federal agencies are required by statute to hold under, or in substantial accord with, provisions of the Administrative Procedure Act, Sections 553–559 of Title 5, United States Code. ALJs function as independent, impartial triers of fact in formal hearings in a manner similar to that of trial judge conducting civil trials without a jury.

Rating Criteria and Procedures

All applicants who meet the minimum qualification and filing requirements will be eligible to participate in subsequent stages of the examination: supplemental qualifications statement; written demonstration; panel interview; and personal reference inquiries.

Opportunities for Employment

There are approximately 1,400 incumbent ALJs in 29 federal government agencies at various locations across the continental United States, Hawaii, and Puerto Rico. Competition for the relatively few positions which may become vacant from year to year is keen. Only very highly qualified applicants whose qualifications substantially exceed the minimum examination requirements should include such a position in their career plans.

Pay

Public Law 101-509 established a new ALJ pay system for former GS-15, 16, 17, and 18 ALJ positions established under Section 3105 of Title 5, United States Code. The minimum rate for ALJ positions is set at 65 percent of level IV of the Executive Schedule and the maximum rate is set at 100 percent of level IV of the Executive Schedule.

The current ALJ pay ranges, exclusive of locality differentials, are as follows:

AL-3/A	$ 86,500
AL-3/B	93,100
AL-3/C	99,800
AL-3/D	106,500
AL-3/E	113,100
AL-3/F	119,700
AL-2	126,500
AL-1	130,000

As of 1/2002

Source: United States Office of Personnel Management, Employment Service, Federal Employment Information Factsheet, February 7, 2002.

ple from the rolls of its recipients, it found itself on a collision course with its ALJs. The ALJs, using the more liberal standards of the Supreme Court, reinstated approximately three-fifths of those who appealed their loss of benefits. Their actions infuriated the heads of Social Security, who overruled many of the reinstatements. This, in turn, riled the ALJs, who felt they had acted as they should, in other words, as independent judicial officers and not as "mere bureaucrats."

Administrative agencies adjudicate individual claims or cases. The procedures are diverse. Administrative hearings focus on disputed questions of fact. They determine policy in a specific factual setting. The ALJ orders compliance with laws and regulations. Adjudicative hearings deal with a variety of subjects, including individual claims for workers' compensation, welfare, or Social Security benefits.

Hearings may also be held to settle multimillion-dollar disputes about business mergers and antitrust rulings. An administrative order is the final disposition of hearings, adjudications, or adjudicatory proceedings. An administrative hearing has no jury. The administrative law judge, or hearing examiner, is usually an expert in the field. The judge is likely to be more concerned with overall policies. The particular merits of one party's case have less consequence. Agencies accomplish most work with informal procedures. They may exercise discretion granted to them by statute. The courts, according to the APA, may not second-guess agencies when the agencies are exercising discretion.

Judicial review of agency action posts controls over administrative behavior. For the person who is harmed by a particular agency decision, judicial review operates to provide relief. Over a period of years, judicial review evolved into a complex system of statutory, constitutional, and judicial doctrines. These doctrines define the proper boundaries of the oversight system. The trend of judicial decisions and the APA make judicial review more widely and easily available.[26]

Despite the independence and integrity that ALJs have usually shown, some observers continue to express doubts as to whether an agency employee should preside over a case in which the agency itself is a party of interest.

Suggestions have been made to divorce ALJs completely from any particular agency, setting up, in effect, a new administrative unit in the federal bureaucracy that would assign them to different agencies as cases arose. This would give them more independence, but would reduce their expertise in the matters under dispute, for they would no longer be specialized in the work of one agency.

Critical examination of the formal agency adjudicative process and the role of the ALJ reveals two trends. First, there is growing dissatisfaction with formal trial procedures for resolving licensing, merger, and related economic regulation policy issues. Second, the number of benefits and enforcement cases have increased dramatically. Social Security Administration (SSA) ALJs decide 300,000 cases annually; Department of Labor ALJs resolve thousands of cases concerning black-lung benefits claims and longshoremen's compensation. Enforcement is another growth area. ALJs discipline license holders, revoke licenses, issue cease-and-desist orders, and issue civil money penalties.

ALJs license and route certification of transportation by air, rail, motor vehicle, or ship; regulate radio and television broadcasting; establish rates for gas, electrical, communication, and transportation services; monitor compliance with federal standards relating to interstate trade, labor-management relations, advertising, communications, consumer products, food and drugs, corporate mergers, and antitrust; regulate health and safety in mining, transportation, and industry; regulate trading in securities, commodities, and futures; and adjudicate claims relating to Social Security benefits, workers' compensation, international trade, and mining. The brief history of ALJs reflects tension between the need for fact-finder independence and the need for policy and management control.

Internal and External Administrative Controls

In the fifty-first of their famous *Federalist Papers,* James Madison and Alexander Hamilton pointed out,

> If men were angels, no government would be necessary. If angels were to govern men, neither external nor internal controls on government would be necessary. In framing a government which is to be administered by men over men, the great difficulty lies in this: you must first enable the government to control the governed; and in the next place oblige it to control itself. A dependence on the

people is, no doubt, the primary control of the government; but experience has taught mankind the necessity of auxiliary precaution.[27]

As the writers of *The Federalist Papers* perceptively noted, there are two aspects of administrative control.

Internal Controls: One is the control that agencies must exercise over their own constituent elements, be they subunits or individuals. Staff units and their personnel frequently perform a controlling function even when they have no authority or mandate to do so. This is what frequently makes them suspect to line employees. Staff services provide internal control, even when they are not expressly designed to do so. Many staff services are, however, expressly designed with a control function in mind.

Internal control mechanisms include the *personnel department.* If it enjoys appropriate authority, the personnel department influences how line departments and line officials confront personnel problems. The *budget office* of any agency or any government obviously exercises a high degree of control, for it may decide who gets what amount of money for what purpose. Another staff department that exercises financial control is the *purchasing office.* Perhaps the most important financial control unit is the *auditing branch. Field inspections* support internal controls.

External Controls: The instrumentality that is most expressly charged with controlling administration is the *legislative branch of government.* Legislatures *control expenditures* and *confirm appointments.* The most well-known power legislative bodies exercise over administrative ones is the *power to investigate and expose.* The authority of the "independent" prosecutor in the Watergate and Monica Lewinsky controversies originated with legislative prerogatives to investigate the professional—and personal—activities of the President. The General Accounting Office is the investigative arm of Congress and is charged with examining all matters relating to the receipt and disbursement of public funds.

The Whistle-Blower as Tell-All

A form of government employee control at times controversial, yet often effective, is that of *whistle-blower.* The term *whistle-blower* was originated by Ralph Nader to categorize those public employees who, in effect, blow the whistle on acts by their own agencies when they deem such acts to be improper.[28] Some of the more famous whistle-blowers during the early 1970s were Gordon Rule, the Navy's director of procurement, who challenged extravagant cost overruns and claims for extra compensation by Navy suppliers; A. Ernest Fitzgerald, the Pentagon cost analyst who called attention to similar cost overruns in conjunction with the Air Force's C-5A transport jet; Frank Serpico, the New York City patrolman whose reports on corruption in his department touched off a wide-ranging investigation that culminated in numerous indictments and shake-ups in the city's constabulary; and Linda Tripp, secretary in the Clinton White House who secretly recorded telephone conversations with Monica Lewinsky, the intern with whom President Clinton had "inappropriate intimate contact."

A typical whistle-blower is about fifty years old, never demonstrated in the 1960s, has been at the same job for many years, and is conservative in personal style and political outlook.[29] Despite the Whistleblower Protection Act, many government employees are afraid to expose corruption for fear of reprisals. The Office of Special Counsel (OSC), charged with protecting whistle-blowers, has never won a case restoring a whistle-blower's job.[30] Wrongdoing in government and business has increasingly been exposed by persons who "blow the whistle" on illegal or improper practices. Sometimes whistle-blowers are regarded as heroes, but they are often given poor performance reviews, dismissed, and regarded as traitors.[31]

Tripp learned about the political power of knowledge in her secretarial jobs while employed at the White House.[32] Many theories exist regarding why Tripp, age forty-eight, secretly recorded the "girl talk" of Lewinsky, age twenty-four, and the latter's sexual proclivities with the President. The upbringing and background of Tripp, plus her distaste for the Clinton White House, motivated Tripp to become a whistle-blower.[33]

Tripp, a White House secretary during George Bush's presidency and subsequently that of President Bill Clinton, gave the term *whistle-blower* new parameters. Her determination to record the President's sexual malfeasance resulted in the impeachment of Clinton. The secret Lewinsky-Tripp he-said/she-said telephone recordings were on tape—and to the chagrin of Clinton and his backers, the President's transgressions were against the law.

At the urging of her friend, Lucianne Goldberg, Tripp recorded secret tapes of coworker Monica Lewinsky's allegations of a sexual relationship with Clinton. On January 12, 1998, Tripp gave the tapes to Independent Counsel Kenneth Starr. The following day Starr had FBI agents wire Lewinsky with a hidden microphone to record a conversation between Clinton and Lewinsky.[36]

Tripp portrayed herself as an "average American" without political motive. She was accused of betraying a friend's trust. She claimed that she had been "vilified for taking the path of truth."[37] Tripp felt contempt for Clinton. She had ties to conservative activists who waged war against Clinton. "The Linda Tripp I knew was old school, someone with old-fashioned values," said Tony Snow, a conservative commentator who worked closely with Tripp in the George Bush White House.[38]

Tripp was a divorced middle-aged mother of two. She was a chain-smoking government employee who kept her political opinions to herself. She lacked strong political views. She registered as a political independent in Howard County, Maryland. She tended dutifully to her administrative tasks. She was not described as a deeply embittered worker. She stirred no controversy. She had few enemies.

As a whistle-blower, Tripp evolved in her motivation to:

- spend twenty hours secretly taping her distraught young colleague Monica Lewinsky as she discussed an alleged sexual affair with President Clinton;
- take the information she had gathered from Lewinsky to independent counsel Starr, who was investigating Clinton; and
- serve as the catalyst in a government sting to document Lewinsky's allegations.[39]

Her misgivings about Clinton grew. But Tripp kept working and kept quiet. She earned a promotion to be an assistant to White House Counsel Bernard Nussbaum. She was a trusted employee who toiled in the White House inner circle. Once she was asked to photocopy all of the Clinton's tax records. However, Tripp tended to speak bluntly. She could not conceal her contempt for Clinton.

Checks and Balances?

A system of checks and balances enables each branch of government to have some influence on the operations of the others. The separation-of-powers principle restrains one branch from usurping the powers of others. Since the Office of Independent Counsel was enacted in 1978, twenty independent counsels have investigated high-level officials.

On January 16, 1998, Kenneth Starr, Independent Counsel from the Office of Independent Counsel (OIC), expanded the OIC's jurisdiction to permit investigation of "whether Monica Lewinsky or others suborned perjury, obstructed justice, intimidated witnesses, or otherwise violated federal law . . . in dealing with witnesses, potential witnesses, attorneys, or others concerning the civil case of *Jones v. Clinton.*"[40] Starr's expansion of OIC jurisdiction to include the Paula Jones case was no legal coincidence.

"A prosecutor has no business getting into that case [Paula Jones] unless there's something terrible happening," former Independent Counsel Lawrence Walsh told the *Chicago Tribune.* "I question Starr's judgment in going into it so hard."[41] The sequence of events suggests that Starr deliberately delayed the request for jurisdiction expansion. The OIC had only the taped evidence illegally—created by Tripp.

In his January 17, 1998, deposition for the Jones case, Clinton denied having a sexual relationship with Lewinsky. Starr accused the President of "illegal attempts" to keep his relationship with Lewinsky secret. Jones's team of lawyers was bankrolled by the Rutherford Institute—a conservative advocacy group. Rutherford lawyers introduced testimony about illicit sexual encounters allegedly involving Clinton.[42]

By the time Starr had completed his investigation of the Clintons, the cost of investigating top administration officials during the Clinton era reached $76 million. Starr's investigation of the former President and his wife, Hillary Rodham Clinton, now a U.S. Senator from New York, is the most expensive independent counsel inquiry ever. By comparison, the probe of the Reagan administration regarding arms and money deals with Iran and the secret war against the Communist-led government of Nicaragua totaled $48.5 million. Elizabeth Ray, a spokeswomen for the OIC, said: The monumental effort required to conduct the investigation of Monica Lewinsky and others required unusual commitments of resources."[43]

Many factors account for the growing prominence of whistle-blowers as agents of administrative control. One of them is the development of *administrative law* and the safeguards it extends to public employees. When the Nixon administration attempted to discharge Fitzgerald, for example, by eliminating his job, he fought back through the courts and won.[34] A midwestern high school teacher fired after he sent a letter to a local newspaper criticizing his school board won similar reinstatement. In general, the courts have become increasingly protective of whistle-blowing employees.

Ethics: Public Administration's Challenge of the Twenty-First Century

Honesty, fairness, and productivity are characteristics of American patriotism and must be practiced consistently by every government employee. Even from the point of view of effectiveness it is smart for public administrators to be moral in carrying out government functions. The credibility of government is at stake. Laws, rules, and regulations of government should be grounded in ethics, integrity, and organization commitments.

Government employee performance and policy leadership should reflect emphasis on the following themes:

- Make ethics a part of employee orientation and training programs.
- Include ethics in the performance evaluations and regular feedback provided to employees.

- Publicize ethical dilemmas and the organization's perception of them.
- Review management practices in different parts of the organization to help identify existing or potential ethics problems.
- Develop a code of ethics.
- The actions of top government officials must be consistent with their expectations for employee conduct. Leadership by example is an effective tool to establish an ethical perspective among members of the federal, state, or local government organization.

Source: Stephan J. Bonczek, "Ethics: Challenge of the 1990s: A Local Government Perspective," *Public Management* 72, no. 8 (July 1990): 17–19.

A second factor that has encouraged whistle-blowing has been the development of the *news media.* In this connection, the press has long played an active and aggressive role in controlling administrative actions. "I fear three newspapers more than I fear three thousand bayonets," Napoleon once remarked, while an English contemporary, philosopher Jeremy Bentham, observed that "Without publicity, all checks are inefficient; in comparison to publicity, all checks are of small account."[35]

The development of broadcast journalism, particularly television news, and the growth of public awareness and interest in government have made the news media a form of control that rivals, if it does not exceed, that exerted by legislative bodies. This is particularly true in the United States, which does not have a government-owned television and radio network and has a long muckraking tradition. The media is not only important for what it does on its own but for the help it provides other forms of control. It has encouraged and strengthened whistle-blowing by providing considerable publicity to the whistle-blowers. It also has stimulated legislative control by providing headlines and coverage for legislative exposés. Furthermore, many newspapers and radio and TV stations act as ombudspersons, soliciting citizen complaints against the bureaucracy and then checking them out.

A third instrument of control over an administrative agency is its *clientele.* For reasons that will be more fully discussed in the next chapter, administrators, particularly in the United States, need considerable cooperation from their clientele, and the clientele often seize upon this to exercise some countervailing influence over administrators. Sometimes this takes dramatic and violent forms, such as the client takeovers of welfare offices, the student rebellions of the 1960s, and the prison riots of the early 1970s. More often, however, clients exercise control by refusing to comply with policies they do not like.

Finally, a form of control that often receives little attention but that plays an important role in constraining many administrative agencies is the control exercised by *competing agencies.* Agencies are frequently locked in combat over jurisdiction, funding, and so on. In their continual jousting for power and position, agencies tend to control each other. James Madison saw this as one of the most effective forms of control. In a well-known passage in *The Federalist* he noted, "Ambition must be made to counteract ambition . . . the constant aim is to divide and arrange the several offices in such a manner that each may be a check on the other—that the private interest of every individual may be a sentinel over the public rights."[44]

Law and Control: How Much Is Enough?

Democratic government rests on such principles as accountability and responsibility. We have seen that the realization of such principles requires a comprehensive system of administrative control. The public has a right to demand and administrators have a need to accept a widespread network of restraints and restrictions on administrative activity. *Democratic government is controlled government.*

Of course, administrators often find such controls irksome and irritating. They are, by nature, active men and women who wish to "get on with the job." It would be strange if they did not frequently chafe at curbs placed upon their actions. In the long run, however, they, too, benefit from a suitable system of control. Control, or at least extensive control, can be counterproductive. Carried too far, it can render government ineffectual and even inert, leaving the way clear for less savory and less responsible forces to operate. As we saw in our examination of administrative law, the judicialization of the administrative process has proved to be a bonanza to various business interests that use the safeguards imposed on administrative agents to perpetuate or prolong questionable activities.

Too much control also breeds a climate of conflict and distrust that can result in a great deal of dysfunctional behavior. If it refuses to resign itself to relative immobility, an agency straitjacketed with a strict system of controls may dissipate so much of its energy trying to overcome obstacles to action that it may have little energy left to serve the public. Furthermore, it may respond to the distrust that extensive control suggests by meriting such distrust.

American statesman Henry L. Stimson, who served in many high government positions before and during World War II, once observed that one way to make a man trustworthy is to trust him.[45] The reverse may also be true. Certainly, the distrust that pervasive control fosters does little to encourage candor and cooperation. Control, whether exercised through legalistic or other means, has its limits if the ends of democratic society are to be served.

Fortunately, some of the changes now buffeting administration may help alleviate some of the problems it poses. Programmed budgeting, productivity measures, management by objectives, and other techniques may increase responsibility and accountability while replacing or reducing the role of negative control, that is, control for its own sake. Some systems of control will continue to be needed and the problems they present will doubtless persist, but the increasing professionalism also starting to characterize public administration may make extensive and elaborate control systems somewhat less necessary.

Summary

- The principles of *administrative law* are grounded in constitutionalism, shared powers, popular government, individualism, and political equality.
- Independent regulatory agencies, uniform administrative procedure law, judicial review, and rule making are *traditional cornerstones* of administrative law. Public participation in the administrative process, the administrative process in formal and informal governmental activity, and the evolving definition of the mission of administrative agencies and development of oversight of their activities are *contemporary cornerstones* of U.S. administrative law.
- Honesty, fairness, and productivity are characteristics of American patriotism and must be practiced by every government employee. Even from the standpoint of effectiveness, it is smart for public administrators to be *moral* in carrying out government functions. The credibility of government is at stake. Laws, rules, and government regulations should be grounded in ethics, integrity, and organizational commitments.
- The United States has entered the era of the *administrative state.* During the past fifty years, the administrative sector has surged forward, spurred on by what might be called the permissive attitude that the courts have taken on the delegation-of-power issue. Administrative agencies have acquired increasing functions, along with more power to carry them out.
- Franklin Roosevelt's "New Deal" gave birth to the idea of the *positive,* or welfare, state, whereby government provided a "safety net" of programs to enhance the "quality of life." Ronald Reagan's "revolution," redefining the federal government's role as limited, or privatizing government services whenever possible, responded to the regulatory, or *negative,* aspects of big government.
- Administrative law and regulatory law act in *tandem,* but they are not the same. Agencies and departments, cooperating with legislatures, create regulatory law. *Regulatory law* governs the private activities of citizens; *administrative law* governs the regulators, applying principles originating from statutes, common law, constitutions, and regulatory laws. The provisions of adequate notice, disclosure of reasons, the right to a hearing, and right to further appeal entail a set of rules that administrators must follow to meet due process requirements.
- After a century of intense litigation and adjudication, the field of administrative law is still alive with issues. *Hearsay evidence* and the *double role* of judge and prosecutor are key controversies of administrative law, affecting public administrators and clientele. The majority of administrative law judges function as hearing examiners in the Social Security Administration.
- The major aspects of the *administrative process* include delegation of power, judicial review, the investigatory power, the rule-making process, the right to be heard and adjudicatory policymaking, informal activity and the exercise of discretion, remedies against improper administrative acts, and opening up the government. The Freedom of Information Act (1967) and Privacy Act (1974) are amendments to the Administrative Procedure Act (1946), all of which concern due process guarantees.
- Administrative agencies adjudicate individual claims or cases. The procedures are diverse. Administrative hearings focus on disputed questions of fact.
- An administrative hearing has no jury. The administrative law judge, or hearing examiner, is likely to be concerned about overall policies. The particular merits of one party's case have less consequence.
- Agencies accomplish most work with informal procedures. They exercise discretion granted to them by statute.
- Judicial review of agency action posts controls over administrative behavior. For the person

who is harmed by a particular agency decision, judicial review operates to provide relief.
- The question of administrative control has two distinct aspects—*internal* and *external* controls.
- By the time Independent Counsel Kenneth Starr completed his investigation of Bill and Hillary Clinton, the cost of investigating top administration officials during the Clinton era reached $76 million. The probe of the Reagan administration regarding arms and money deals with Iran and the secret war against the

Communist-led government of Nicaragua totaled $48.5 million.
- Democratic government rests on principles such as *accountability* and *responsibility;* the realization of such principles requires a comprehensive system of administrative control. The public has a right to demand, and administrators have a need to accept, a widespread network of restraints and restrictions on administrative activity. Democratic government is *controlled* government.

Case Study

Whistle-Blowing at the FBI

Administrative laws outline the prospects and limits of whistle-blowers. The FBI and CIA reflect developments of policy and system politics, but impact partisan politics. Whistle-blowers emerge as agents of administrative control. Breaking through the FBI culture to fight terrorism makes the job of FBI whistle-blower ever more challenging. The case study which follows illustrates that point.

If she sees something she believes is wrong, she is not going to sweep it under the carpet.

—*A former coworker of FBI Agent Coleen Rowley,*
May 25, 2002

As whistle-blower, FBI Agent Coleen Rowley insisted that the public interest was more important than that of her employer. She blew the whistle on the nation's premier law enforcement agency. She ignited a storm of criticism of the bureau's management practices.

The FBI, she said, discouraged innovation. Investigators felt overcome with paperwork. Agents who sought to cut through many layers of risk-adverse superiors in Washington were punished. Rowley operated from a field office. Seven to nine levels of officials at headquarters often second-guess the decisions of agents in the field.[1] Rowley has been praised for her courage in criticizing senior FBI officials over the September 11 massacre.

Rowley, General Counsel with the FBI's Minneapolis field office, wrote to Director Robert Mueller on May 21, 2002: "I have deep concerns that a delicate and subtle shading/skewing of facts by you and others at the highest levels of FBI management has occurred and is occurring. I feel certain facts have been omitted, downplayed, glossed over and/or mischaracterized in an effort to avoid or minimize personal and/or institutional embarrassment on the part of the FBI and/or perhaps even for improper political reasons."[2]

What Is a Whistle-Blower?

A whistle-blower is a person who takes a concern about fraud or mistreatment outside of the organization in which the abuse or suspected abuse is occurring and with which the whistle-blower is affiliated. Not all whistle-blowing is adversarial to the affected organization. That the organization cannot correct its own problems, nevertheless, is an embarrassment.

Rowley emerged as "an American hero," wrote John Carlson, newspaper columnist for *The Des Moines Register*. The mother of four, Rowley exuded the values of integrity, honesty, courage, and patriotism. As a kid, the bespectacled Rowley was "gutsy," observed Carlson. As a forty-seven-year-old whistle-blower, armed with a law degree, she carried out a "full-bore butt-kicking of her (FBI) bosses."[3] Rowley was the Iowa kid who knew—in the fifth grade—that she wanted to be an FBI agent. Well-schooled to be a whistle-blower, Rowley was said to be straightforward, intelligent, thoughtful, outspoken, but not out of control. FBI coworkers back home described the career official as a model agent.

FBI headquarters officials refused permission for Minneapolis agents to obtain warrants to search suspected terrorist Zacarias Moussaoui's computer and other properties. Rowley reported that her superiors at headquarters prevented field agents from pursuing their suspicions of Moussaoui, the so-called twentieth highjacker, and part of a larger conspiracy involving flight training and airplanes. After September 11, they found that Moussaoui had ties to several hijackers. The Minneapolis FBI agent was determined to bring the truth to power—focusing on the FBI's "willful refusal to investigate and a deliberate suppression of information."[4]

Rowley hand-delivered her thirteen-page memo to FBI Director Mueller and the staff of the U.S. Senate Intelligence Committee. Democrat Diane Feinstein of California and Republican Richard Shelby of Alabama, ranking members on the committee, also received copies. Whistle-blower Rowley provided specifics of persons within the FBI hierarchy who blocked the investigation of Zacarias Moussaoui—charged as a coconspirator in the September 11, 2001, suicide hijackings that killed more than three thousand persons.

The FBI claims that Moussaoui, a thirty-four-year-old French-Morroccan, Islamic fundamentalist, paid $8,000 cash for training to fly a Boeing 747 at a Minneapolis-area flight school. However, Moussaoui was only interested in steering a jumbo jet in flight—and not in learning how to take off or land. French intelligence sources reported Osama bin Laden's Al Qaeda organization had recruited Moussaoui.[5]

According to Rowley, Minneapolis FBI agents became so frustrated by inaction at FBI headquarters that they went directly to the CIA for assistance in establishing a case against Moussaoui. They did this without the knowledge of their FBI superiors. Officials at FBI headquarters reprimanded them for breach of Bureau protocol. Rowley, knowing the consequences of speaking truth to power, sought federal whistle-blower protection. FBI Director Mueller asserted that Rowley faced no retaliation or intimidation for writing her letter or talking to the Committee. Rowley's right

to criticize the structure, culture, and mission of the FBI is protected by amendments of the Whistle-blower Protection Act (WPA).

Bill Miller and Dan Eggen, reporters for *The Washington Post,* wrote that Rowley's FBI whistle-blower statement was "a scathing indictment of FBI culture and its impact on the way FBI headquarters handled the case of Zacarias Moussaoui."[6] Daniel Franklin, writing in *The American Prospect,* stated: "As in most bureaucracies, the bureau was more concerned with upholding the chain of command than with increasing its effectiveness."[7]

To his credit, Mueller welcomed Rowley's criticisms of FBI policies and personnel. The FBI's insular culture is called into question.[8]

In July 2001, Kenneth Williams wrote a memo from the FBI's Phoenix office to two task forces at FBI headquarters, including the

- Radical Fundamentalist Unit task force, and the
- Osama bin Laden task force.

The FBI memo addressed the frequency of Middle Eastern men enrolled in flying lessons. On August 15, 2001, Moussaoui came to the attention of FBI agents in Minneapolis. The agents received information about Moussaoui's flight training. The FBI, working with the U.S. Immigration and Naturalization Service, detained Moussaoui on visa violations.[9]

On December 11, 2001, a federal grand jury in Alexandria, Virginia, indicted Moussaoui for six counts of conspiracy—accusing him of plotting with bin Laden and members of Al Qaeda to murder thousands of people at the World Trade Center and the Pentagon. Bin Laden and the nineteen dead hijackers were named as unindicted co-conspirators.[10]

Terrorism and the FBI Culture

Mueller used the opportunity provided by Rowley not to be defensive about the FBI and its culture lag over the events of September 11. The director led the greatest reorganization of the FBI in its history. He appeared to be employing Rowley's thirteen-page memo as his reorganizing principle. Mueller directed that the FBI be decentralized. More control was given to agents in the field. The first priority of the FBI would be the prevention of terrorism.

The FBI suffered a terrorism "rethink." The whistle-blower counterterrorism initiative produced a plan whereby 3,718 agents and other law enforcement officials focus on counterterrorism—up from 2,178. A shift of 480 FBI agents were reassigned from fighting drugs, white collar crime, and violent crime.[11]

Rowley charged that the FBI operates in "a climate of fear which has chilled aggressive . . . law enforcement action."[12] In a police agency where hierarchy and "do it my way or hit the highway" are readily acceptable modes of operation, protecting whistle-blowers' "freedom to warn" tolerates drawbacks. Increasing and centralizing the power of FBI headquarters could reinforce the paralyzing culture of fear. The vulnerabilities of terror might be exacerbated by promoting excessive government secrecy.

The reorganization chart does not address the cultural problems facing the FBI. When Rowley hand-delivered her memo to Mueller, she circumvented eight different layers of leadership. FBI headquarters personnel chastised her for not following bureau protocol. They made direct contact with the CIA's Counterterrorism Center.

The FBI must change not only what it does, but how it thinks, how it perceives itself, and the people and agencies with whom it works. Not everyone agrees on what the "cultural problems" of the Bureau are. "If the Bureau's recent history proves anything," Franklin writes, "it's that it can't fix a problem that its own agents don't perceive."[13]

The FBI is America's national police force. Its jurisdictions are controlled by law. The personnel department, budget office, auditing branch, and field inspections are internal FBI controls. The fallout from September 11 brought the FBI, as a bureaucracy, challenges of great magnitude. New funding included a $1.5 billion budget increase. The investigative latitude for agents was made more liberal. Agents could open preliminary investigations and maintain them for a year without approval from headquarters.

FBI mistakes reflect an inability to digest an over-abundance of resources—not a lack of them. Between 1997 and 2002, the Bureau increased its payroll by 1,000 employees. Virtually all new hires were positioned at headquarters. Almost none were stationed in field offices. Rowley bypassed eight layers of administrative leaders to get her message to Mueller.

Police bureaus are quasimilitary operations. Obeying the chain of command is priority. Administrative law—by promoting whistle-blowers—seeks to reduce arbitrariness and unfairness in government. Rowley, from her perspective, tried to change internal FBI practices.

External controls are found in the legislative branch of government. Legislators control expenditures and confirm appointments. They have the power to investigate and expose. Congress and its committees write laws for agents to obey and implement. Through the General Accounting Office (GAO), representatives seek audits of departments, agencies, and bureaus. Rowley carried her message to the very top of her government bureaucracy—the FBI. But she also contacted prominent members of the U.S. Senate Judiciary Committee.

Administrative laws outline the prospects and limits of whistle-blowers. The FBI reflects policy and system politics—but impacts partisan politics. The consensus of partisan politics is that the activities of the FBI and CIA should enhance, even promote, electoral politics or democracy. The most effective way to fight terrorism is through popular—and elected—governments. Administration of the FBI and CIA depends on shared powers—among democratic institutions and with citizens.

The FBI and CIA are competing agencies. The FBI focuses on internal terrorism. The CIA pursues terror on an international scale. In the culture of the Cold War, these distinctions may have been easier to define. In post-September 11 politics, FBI-CIA activities are often blurred. Clientele responding to the agenda raised by this whistle-blower included the media, FBI employees, the security establishment, Congress, the executive, and the American people.

Government employees must be able to speak truth to power. This employee's predicament reminds citizens of government bureaucracy's need to protect a whistle-blower's "freedom to warn." Civil liberties may be in the balance. A culture of fear and excessive government secrecy promote "risk-adverse careerism" at security agencies.[14]

Mrs. Rowley is a portrait in American individualism. She made a difference.

Questions and Instructions

1. The FBI—and the intelligence community—are cited for not being prepared for major terrorist attacks. How do the developments and facts from this case study enable the FBI, as a public organization, to be better prepared in the future? Explain and illustrate.
2. Coleen Rowley charged that the FBI operated in "a climate of fear" which "chilled" agressive law enforcement. Explain.
3. How does increasing and centralizing the power of institutions (like the FBI) reinforce the paralyzing culture of fear which, in turn, exacerbates the vulnerabilities to terror? Explain and illustrate.
4. How are the Bureau's "cultural problems" of serious consequence to FBI operations? Explain and illustrate.
5. Why did Coleen Rowley seek whistle-blowing status at the FBI? In what ways did Rowley breach Bureau protocols? Explain and illustrate.
6. FBI Director Robert Mueller welcomed criticism from Coleen Rowley—asserting that she would face no retaliations or intimidations for writing her memo or talking to the joint Senate-House Intelligence Committee. Why were these decisions in the best interests of the country and FBI? Explain and illustrate.
7. Prior to September 11, 2001, why were security agencies—including the FBI—preoccupied "above all" with questions of administrative procedure? Explain and illustrate.
8. What actions, if any, did Coleen Rowley take to merit being called "an American hero?" What values did she espouse in this case study? Explain and illustrate.
9. New investigatory powers provided to FBI agents allow them to visit internet sites, libraries, churches, and political organizations as they seek to find and prosecute terrorists. Do these FBI prerogatives infringe on citizens' civil rights and liberties? Explain and illustrate.
10. How are internal and external administrative controls manifest in this case study? Explain and illustrate.

Insights-Issues/Whistle-Blowing at the FBI

Clearly and briefly describe and illustrate the following concepts and issues. Interpret the word *role* as meaning impacts, applications, importance, effects, and/or illustrations of certain facts, concerns, or issues from the case study.

1. Role of whistle-blower Coleen Rowley (individualism) in efforts to refocus (culture) and reorganize (administrative structure) the FBI.
2. Role of the Bureau's "cultural problems" in refocus (priorities) and reorganization (administrative procedures and structures).
3. Role of partisan, policy, and systems politics in the terror debate.
4. Role of the expansion of FBI powers, the culture of fear, and the guarantee of political freedoms.
5. Role of internal and external administrative controls in—and of—the FBI.

Case Endnotes

1. David Johnston and Neil A. Lewis, "Traces of Terror: The Congressional Hearings; Whistle-Blower Recounts Inside the FBI," *The New York Times,* June 7, 2002, p. 1A; Dan Eggen, "FBI Whistle-Blower Assails Bloated Bureaucracy," *The Washington Post,* June 7, 2002, p. A02.
2. "Coleen Rowley's Memo to FBI Director Robert Mueller," *Time,* http://www.time.com/time/nation/printout/0,8816,249997,00.html.
3. John Carlson, "As an Iowa Kid, FBI Memo Writer was Sharp, Gutsy, Neighbor Recalls, "*The Des Moines Register,* May 29, 2002, http://desmoinesregister.com/news/stories/c5917686/18308626.html.

4. Patrick Martin, "New Evidence that U.S. Government Suppressed September 11 Warnings," *Sierra Times,* May 27, 2002, http://www. sierratimes. com/cgi-bin/warroom/printpage/cgi?forum= 15&topic=25.

5. *Ibid.*

6. Bill Miller and Dan Eggen, "FBI Culture Blamed for Missteps on Moussaoui," *The Washington Post,* May 25, 2002, p. A1, http://www. washingtonpost.com/ac2/wp-dyn/A7214-2002May24?language=printer.

7. Daniel Franklin, "Dollars Don't Do It: Throwing Money at the FBI Only Deepens the Problem," *The American Prospect,* Vol. 13, No. 13, http://www.prospect.org/print-friendly/print/V13/13/franklin-d.html.

8. Richard S. Dunham, "Of Zipped Lips and Blown Tips," *BusinessWeek Online,* May 29, 2002,

http://www.businessweek.com:/print/bwdaily/dnflash/may2002/nf20020529_9307.htm.

9. Franklin, *op.cit.*

10. Jerry Seper, "Moussaoui's Notes Say He Is a Terrorist," *The Washington Times,* July 3, 2002, http://asp.washtimes.com/printarticle. asp?action=print@ArticleID=20020703-70254835.

11. "FBI Has a Terrorism Rethink," *News12.com,* May 30, 2002, http://www.news24.com/News24/World/Americas/0,1113,2-10-33_1192314,00.html.

12. Martin Edwin Andersen, "Rowley's Risk," *The Washington Times,* May 30, 2002, http://www.washtimes.com/op-ed/20020530-1343644.htm.

13. Franklin, *op.cit.*

14. Andersen, *op.cit.*

Case Sources

David Corn, "The Loyal Opposition: Playing The 9/11 Blame Game," http://www.tompaine.com/feature.cfm/ID/5714/view/print; Edward Helmore, "Agent Blasts FBI Over September 11, 'Cover-Up,' " *Guardian Unlimited,* http://www.guardian.co.uk/september11/story/0,11209,722428,00.html; "Leadership the Issue, Not Expanded Powers, in FBI Misadventures," *Gainesville Times,* June 1, 2002, http://www.gainesvilletimes.com/news/stories/20020601/opinion/ 426174.html; David Risen and David Johnston, "Traces of Terror: The Intelligence Reports; Agent Complaints Lead FBI Director to Ask for Inquiry," *The New York Times,* May 24, 2002, p. 1A; Laura Rosen, "Seeking a Higher Intelligence: Will Congress Push for Real Reform in the CIA and FBI?" *The American Prospect,* Vol. 13, No. 12, http://www.prospect.org/print-friendly/print/V13/12/ rosen-1.html; Jerry Seper, "Moussaoui's Notes Say He is a Terrorist," *The Washington Times,* http://asp.washtimes.com/printarticle. asp?action-print&ArticleID-20020703-70254835; "Sharp Note from a Whistle-Blower," *The Los Angeles Times,* May 28, 2002, http://www. smh.com.au/articles/2002/05/28/1022243318693.html.

Chapter Endnotes

1. James Bryce, *The American Commonwealth* (1888), from the chapter, "The Strength of American Democracy," quoted in Theodore J. Lowi, *The End of Liberalism* (New York: W.W. Norton, 1979), p. 94.

2. Lowi, *The End of Liberalism,* p. 131.

3. *Ibid.,* p. 132.

4. *A. L. A. Schechter Poultry Corporation v. United States,* 295 US 495 (1935).

5. Harold Seidman and Robert Gilmour, *Politics, Position, and Power: From the Positive to the Regulatory State* (New York: Oxford University Press, 1986), p. 119.

6. *Ibid.,* p. 119.

7. Daniel J. Gifford, *Administrative Law: Cases and Materials* (Cincinnati: Anderson, 1992), p. 1.

8. Jerre S. Williams, "Cornerstone of American Administrative Law," *Administrative Law Review* 28 (1976): v–xii.

9. Florence Heffron and Neil McFeeley, *The Administrative Regulatory Process* (New York: Longman, 1883), pp. 347–371.

10. Williams, "Cornerstone," pp. v–xii.

11. Kenneth F. Warren, *Administrative Law in the American System* (St. Paul, Minn.: West, 1982), pp. 111–122.

12. Dwight Waldo, *The Enterprise of Public Administration: A Summary View* (Novato, Calif.: Chandler & Sharp, 1980). See especially Chapter 6: "Bureaucracy and Democracy: Reconciling the Irreconcilable," pp. 81–98.

13. Bernard Schwartz, *Administrative Law* (Boston: Little, Brown, 1976), p. 2.

14. Stanley A. Reigel and P. John Owen, *Administrative Law: The Law of Government Agencies* (Ann Arbor, Mich.: Ann Arbor Science, The Butterworth Group, 1982), pp. 4–5.

15. Lief H. Carter, *Administrative Law and Politics: Cases and Comments* (Boston: Little, Brown, 1983), p. 60.

16. Lewis C. Mainzer, *Political Bureaucracy* (Glenview, Ill.: Scott, Foresman, 1973), p. 62.

17. Kenneth Culp Davis, *Administrative Law and Government* (St. Paul, Minn.: West, 1960), p. 463, quoted in Mainzer, *Political Bureaucracy,* p. 50.

18. See Administrative Procedure Act, P.L. 404, 60 Stat. 237 (1946), as amended. 5 U.S.C., 554(b), Adjudications.

19. For an interesting, although scarcely disinterested, account of a leading decision regarding prisoners' rights, see editorial, Tom Wicker, "In the Nation: Due Process for Prisoners," *The New York Times,* June 18, 1970, p. 44.

20. For a more readable, but less profound, account of the explanation of this right, see "Toward Greater Fairness for All," *Time,* Vol. 101, No. 9 (February 26, 1973): 95–96.

21. Mainzer, *Political Bureaucracy,* p. 37.

22. For analysis of the history and management of the FOIA, consult Lotte E. Feinberg, "Managing the Freedom of Information Act and Federal Information Policy," *Public Administration Review* 46, no. 6 (November/December, 1986): 615–621. See also Donald D. Barry and Howard R. Whitcomb, *The Legal Foundation of Public Administration* (St. Paul, Minn.: West, 1981), pp. 331–332.

23. *Richardson v. Perales,* 402 US 389 (1971).

24. "The 'Hidden Judiciary' and What It Does," *U.S. News & World Report,* November 1, 1982.

25. Martin Tolchin, "Are Judge and Agency Too Close for Justice?" *The New York Times,* February 5, 1989, p. E3; Joseph J. Simeone, "The Function, Flexibility, and Future of United States Judges of the Executive Department," *Administrative Law Review* 44, no. 1 (Winter 1992): 159–188.

26. "Administrative Law and Procedure—continued," *West Legal Directory,* July 4, 2002; http://www.wld.com/conbus/weal/wadmin2.htm.

27. Alexander Hamilton, John Jay, and James Madison, *The Federalist Papers* (New York: Modern Library, n.d.), p. 337.

28. Ralph Nader, Peter Petkas, and Kate Blackwell, eds., *Whistle-Blowing* (New York: Bantam Books, 1972).

29. Robert A. Rosenblatt, "Whistle-Blowers," *The Los Angeles Times,* October 5, 1997, p. D4.

30. Timothy W. Maier, "Entrapping the Whistle-Blowers," *Insight on the News* 14, no. 4 (February 2, 1998): 8–12.

31. Charles S. Clark, "Whistle-blowers: Are they Heroes or Disloyal Publicity Hounds? *CO Researcher* 7, no. 45 (December 5, 1997): 1059–1074.

32. John Cloud, "Hot Off the Wiretap: Knowledge—Especially If It's on Tape—Can Be Powerful and Scary in Washington. Just ask Linda Tripp," *Time* 151, no. 4 (February 2, 1998): 42–45.

33. Jane Mayer, "Portrait of a Whistle-Blower: The Family History Behind Linda Tripp's Anger," *The New Yorker* 74, no. 5 (March 23, 1998): 34–39.

34. Nader, Petkas, and Blackwell, *Whistle-Blowing,* pp. 39–55.

35. Quoted in George E. Berkley, *The Democratic Policeman* (Boston: Beacon Press, 1969), pp. 159–160.

36. "Key Player: Linda R. Tripp," *The Washington Post,* February 25, 1999,

http://www.washingtonpost.com/wp-srv/
politics/special/clinton/players/tripp.htm.

37. *Ibid.*

38. Rene Sanchez, "In Linda Tripp's Career, Clues to Her Motivation," *The Washington Post,* January 25, 1998, p. A20, http://www.washingtonpost.com/wp-srv/ politics/special/clinton/stories/tripp012598.htm.

39. *Ibid.*

40. "Page 9: VIII. The Lewinsky Expansion of the Whitewater Investigation," *Yahoo News,* 1998, http://www.bbs.ingedigit.com/news/informe/ r009.html.

41. *The Chicago Tribune,* January 25, 1998.

42. "Key Player: Paula Jones," *The Washington Post,* October 2, 1998. http://www. washingtonpost.com/wp-srv/politics/special/ clinton/players/jones.htm.

43. "Starr Costs on Pace To Be Most Expensive Ever," *Amarillo Globe-News,* April 1, 1999, http://www.amarillonet.com/stories/040199/ usn_pace.shtml.

44. Hamilton, Jay, and Madison, *The Federalist Papers,* p. 337.

45. McGeorge Bundy, *The Strength of Government* (Cambridge, Mass.: Harvard University Press, 1968), p. 56.

Government Regulations and Regulatory Behaviors

Chapter Highlights

If Not Taxes, Perhaps Regulations?	The Administrative Procedure Act
Market Failure and Regulations	Regulatory Restraint and Modification
Is the United States a Regulatory State?	The Stages of Rule Making
Economic, Social, and Subsidiary Regulations	What Is the Public Interest?
Administrative Rules and Rule Making	Summary

Sunset Limited Jettisoned into Regulatory History

Amtrak's eastbound Sunset Limited, a passenger train headed for Mobile, Alabama, during the early hours of September 22, 1993, was about to meet its final destiny and the subsequent deaths of 47 of its more than 220 people aboard. The accident not only costs lives, but it resulted in almost $20 million in equipment damage—plus an unknown amount of civil liability.

The Amtrak train, speeding at 72 miles per hour, derailed off the CSX railway bridge built in 1909, as three locomotives and the first four passengers cars were jettisoned into the Big Bayou Canot, a shallow waterway not suitable for commercial barge navigation.

The south Alabama fog settled across the landscape that fateful morning. Willie Odom was working the midnight-to-6 A.M. shift as pilot of the Mauvilla towboat. Captain Odom was navigating his towboat—pushing six 1,500-ton barges aligned side by side in three rows. Each barge was 195 feet long and 35 feet wide. The barge flotilla moved at

three to four knots, or less than five miles per hour. The weight of the towboat accumulated about 9,000 tons of deadly force.[1]

Odom became disoriented by the dense fog. The captain thought his towboat and barges were moving along the Mobile River. The six heavy-laden barges pushed coal, cement, and wood chips from Mobile to Birmingham and Tuscaloosa. The railroad bridge stood about seven feet above the water. Barges could not flow under the structure. The CSX freight railway owned the bridge. A CSX official phoned the United States Coast Guard to report the derailment.

Odom was lost in the fog, but he did not know it until he "heard this noise—whoosh!—and I seen this fire."[2] Odom's barges had nudged out the alignment of the center portion of the three-section railroad bridge. A single railroad track was suddenly out of line—by 28 inches. A heavy girder was directly in the path of the speeding locomotives. A tremendous impact ensued. Lives would be lost—and many more lives would be changed forever.

The railroad safety system had been in use for a century. The circuit track system automatically turns signals red if a bridge collapses. If a rail is broken, the small electrical current passing through it is turned off, and the "fail-safe" signals turn red. The barge collision shifted the CSX track, but it did not break it. Towboats were not intended to float under this trestle.

Accident Aftershocks Effect Regulations

The aftershocks of this horrible accident continue to impact government regulations monitoring inland operators of towing vessels.

The masters, pilots, tankermen, and deckhands laboring in the country's towboat industry had toiled in obscurity—excepting an occasional oil spill or drowning. "The industry as a whole was invisible," noted Captain John Sutton, a towboat pilot from Hahnville, Louisiana, and past president of the American Inland Mariners Association. The phrase *human error* was taking on new meaning. Odom's wrong turn made headlines and history. The towboat industry would change.[3]

The Coast Guard had failed to establish higher standards for the licensing of inland operators of towing vessels. The new rule making affects 13,024 mariners employed by 1,252 towing companies, on 5,400 registered towing vessels.[4] The Preamble of the new rule states: "This rule will place its primary economic burden on the mariner, not on the mariners' employer."[5]

The Coast Guard, as government regulator, sought inputs on new regulations from towboat owners, employees, and clients. The USGC received 787 comment letters in its original Notice of Proposed Rule Making (NPRM) and conducted extensive public hearings before issuing its regulations. The USGC encouraged the public to participate in towboat rule making by submitting comments and related materials.[6]

The USCG, in its discussions of comments and regulatory changes, promulgated standards for the apprentice mate (steersman), assistance towing, grandfathering of licenses, horsepower, profi-

ciency demonstrations, refresher courses and training, examiners and exam centers, responsibility of the master, safety, costs, and whistle-blowers.

The NTSB investigates accidents, identifies human errors and facilitating factors, and recommends changes, corrections, and strategies to government and industry officials who effect changes and enhance safety measures. The NTSB found that Odom, the towboat operator, had no experience in operating barges in fog. Though he had radar on his tug, the captain had no formal training in the use and interpretation of radar technologies. The towboat company was of no assistance to Odom. The tow was not equipped—nor was it required to be equipped—with a compass or charts to assist in correcting human errors. Neither the company nor the USCG required formal radar training.

The NTSB assessed blame on Odom's inexperience with radar, the company's failure to provide Odom with proper radar training, and the USCG's reluctance to establish more strict licensing standards for towboats and captains. Would radar skills have prevented this disaster? Marsh and mud, consistent with the bayou's geography, are cause for very poor reflectors. As long as expectations for tugboat equipment and pilot skills are low, the public may never find out. (The USCG reviewed 12,000 towboat accidents between 1982 and 1991. It determined that only 18 percent were caused by equipment or structural failure. The Coast Guard attributed 62 percent of towboat accidents to human error.)

Interest groups, including the American Waterways Operators Association, the American Inland Mariners Association, and the National Association of Maritime Educators (NAME), became involved in the rule-making debate and provided input to the USCG regulators. NAME insisted that

- the USCG did not possess sufficient first-hand experience working in the commercial towing industry;
- the Coast Guard had not adequately monitored licensing of towing vessels in the past;
- the USCG was overly dependent on information provided by representatives of large towing companies;

- the mariners working in the towing industry are—for the most part—not represented by labor unions; and
- the new rules promulgated by the USCG regulate the mariner while refusing to adequately or effectively regulate the towing vessel.[7]

Change in Industry Culture?

The media coverage of the Amtrak disaster and USCG investigations has brought to the inland mariner-towboat industry what some call a "change in culture." Operators are attending radar classes, having their skills evaluated and licenses restricted, and asking why the death rate in the industry is eight times the national average. Prior to September 22, 1993, few persons outside the industry cared about its trial-by-fire methods or tendency to lose deckhands. The emphasis on merit and skills were irritating to the older masters and pilots. They relied more on intuition than formal training.

"Individual human errors do not occur in a vacuum," stated Jim Hall, then chairman of the National Transportation Safety Board (NTSB). "They take place within a cultural, social, and organizational context. That is, there are underlying causes and conditions that shape, facilitate, or even nurture the behavior and actions of an accident-causing individual. These causes and conditions arise from government, industry, or individual company policies, procedures, and programs that either do not exist or do not properly address the issues at hand."[8]

If a CSX freight train had jettisoned off a century-old railway trestle that September morning, who would have noticed? The deaths would have been minimized. The relationships between the towboat industry, government, and citizens would not have been altered. Regulations would not be an issue. But that scenario is not reality—and it is not regulatory history.

Endnotes

[1]Don Phillips, "Towboat Captain May Have Hit Railroad Bridge in Fog," *The Washington Post,* Vol. 113, No. 44, September 24, 1993, p. 2.

[2]Jim Morris, "New Rules Pushing Towboat Industry: Aftershocks Still Being Felt in Wake of Deadly 1993 Accident," *The Houston Chronicle,* December 15, 1996, p. 1, http://www.chron.com/ content/chronicle/page1/96/12/15/barges.html.

[3]*Ibid.*

[4]Richard A. Block, "Interim Rule for Licensing Towing Vessel Officers," *N.A.M.E. Newsletter,* No. 86 (December 1999), http://www.metbooks.com/name/name86.html.

[5]Gulf Coast Mariners Association, "Rule Making and Regulations: Towing Vessel Licensing," http://gulfcoastmariners. org/gulf/rulemaking_license.htm.

[6]Block, *op.cit.*

[7]Gulf Coast Mariners Association, *op.cit.*

[8]Jim Hall, Remarks before the International Marine Transit Association, Vancouver, Canada, September 23, 1996, http://www.ntsb.gov/speeches/former/hall/jh960923.htm.

Source

U.S. Department of Transportation, Coast Guard, "Licensing and Manning for Officers of Towing Vessels," *The Federal Register,* Vol. 64, No. 223, pp. 63213–63235, http://frwebgate. access.gpo.gov/cgi-bin/getdoc.cgi?

If Not Taxes, Perhaps Regulations?

Government regulations affect all Americans—through the food and beverages we consume, the medications our medical doctors prescribe, the way we invest our savings, how we develop private property, and the procedures by which we operate profit-making businesses. The direct costs of regulation are typically imposed on businesses and governments. These costs, however, are passed along to consumers.

Critics of regulation point out that federal agencies have not developed systems for making rational, well-informed decisions on ways to allocate human re-

Regulatory Agencies

- Office of Information and Regulatory Affairs
- Office of Management and Budget
- Animal and Plant Health Inspection Service
- Antitrust Division
- Bureau of Alcohol, Tobacco and Firearms
- Commodity Futures Trading Commission
- Comptroller of the Currency
- Consumer Product Safety Commission
- Federal Aviation Administration
- Federal Communications Commission
- Federal Election Commission
- Federal Energy Regulatory Commission
- Federal Maritime Commission
- Federal Motor Carrier Safety Administration
- Federal Railroad Administration
- Federal Trade Commission

- Fish & Wildlife Service
- Food and Drug Administration
- Food Safety and Inspection Service
- International Trade Commission
- Mine Safety and Health Administration
- National Highway Traffic Safety Administration
- National Labor Relations Board
- Nuclear Regulatory Commission
- Occupational Safety and Health Administration
- Office of Thrift Supervision
- Securities and Exchange Commission
- Small Business Administration, Office of Advocacy
- Surface Transportation Board

Source: http://www.regulation.org.

sources efficiently—to maximize health, safety, and environmental protection. Would citizens rather have local health boards not inspect restaurants, the Food and Drug Administration not regulate prescription drug policies, the zoning commission not check the use of private property, the Security and Exchange Commission not monitor financial investments, and government safety experts not probe the quality of our automobiles? As imperfect as they are, government regulations are here to stay.

No better illustration exists of what citizens owe the country, and what the country owes them. The conflicts between public and private are never ending. Regulations typically do not require substantial burdens of taxation or government spending. Regulations act as hidden taxes. The indirect costs are passed along to consumers, employees, and employers. Regulatory impacts are more difficult to measure. From this perspective, regulations are politically convenient ways to implement public policies. This appeals especially in times of fiscal budget constraint.[1]

According to W. Mark Crain and Thomas D. Hopkins, the cost of federal regulations reached $843 billion in 2000 and was equal to 8 percent of the national gross domestic product.[2] In fiscal year 2001, the administrative costs to write and enforce federal regulations climbed to an all-time high of $19.8 billion. This figure was a 4.8 percent increase over the estimated figure for fiscal year 2000. As of 2001, in current dollars, 2001 spending was the highest level of spending ever projected for the administrative budgets of the fifty-four regulatory agencies.[3]

Projections for fiscal year 2001 indicated that the regulatory spending proposed by President Clinton would increase by more than 22 percent. Between 2000 and 2001, forty-one regulatory agencies were slated to increase expenditures. Four agencies had less regulatory spending, whereas nine agency budgets remained the same.[4] Federal regulatory spending is budgeted to increase by 16.8 percent in 2002 and decline by 2.1 percent in 2003.

Federal regulatory staffing expanded in the 1970s due to new social and economic demands placed upon government departments and agencies by proactive Democratic-Party Congresses. The 1970s witnessed the addition of nearly 50,000 personnel, or an increase of 71 percent. Social regulatory agencies gained 42,000 new employees. Economic agencies added 8,000 staff members.

The Ronald Reagan era brought on a 12 percent or 15,000-employee decrease in regulatory agency personnel. Most of the reductions came on the social agency side—nearly 13 percent of staff employment. Economic regulatory staff levels declined by 9 percent during the 1980s. At the end of the 1990s, 11,000 new federal regulatory employees were added to the employment rolls. By 2002, another 6,300 staff members joined the federal regulatory forces. If current trends continue, federal regulatory employment will increase by 25 percent by the end of the decade.[5]

Market Failure and Regulations

Regulations take force because the market or markets fail or otherwise do not work effectively. U.S. regulations commenced with the establishment of the Interstate Commerce Commission in 1887. Information is a scarce commodity. Decision makers cannot collect all relevant information. They act in a state of partial ignorance and uncertainty. They use the best source of information available: *what just has happened.* Government oversight and information occur in this perspective. Railroads, motor carriers, and airlines were deregulated. Public choice may be defined as "the economic study of nonmarket decision making, or simply as the application of economics to political science."[6] Public choice assumes that rational individuals pursue their own interests.

Market failure. The normal operations of the marketplace fail to protect the public from actual or potential abuses of power by business firms. Utilities, for example, are widely regulated on the premise that particular services can be effectively provided by a single firm. That firm, by definition, is a monopoly supplier. Governments regulate the suppliers of local telephone, electricity, natural gas, and water services. Regulatory functions protect the public from monopoly power.

The Occupational Safety and Health Act and other statutes regulate working conditions, grounded in the premise that the market does not operate effectively to produce safe working conditions. The Federal Trade Commission regulates methods of competition, helping the markets to operate more effectively. The Clean Air Act and other statutes are necessary because the market would not discourage air and other pollution. In these cases, regulation is justified on a theory of market failure.[7]

Transportation regulation. The Interstate Commerce Act of 1887 established the Interstate Commerce Commisson (ICC). Federal regulation over transportation followed. Federal supervision focused on interstate commerce, while states supervised intrastate commerce. The emergence of the ICC came as many believed the railroads exploited their monopoly positions and discriminated in their rate structures between long- and short-distance shippers. Regulation was imposed to fight the prerogatives of monopolies yet protect competition where it worked.

The Civil Aeronautics Act commenced airline regulation in 1938 to encouraged a fledgling aviation industry. This regulation was enacted to protect the airline industry from excessive or cutthroat competition. A freely operating motor carrier industry would threaten government regulation of railroad rates. The regulation of motor transport commenced in 1935.

Governmental oversight and information. A regulatory agency focuses its attention on a particular industry or upon a narrow area of human behaviors. The agency develops an "expertise" in its area of regulation. However, governmental oversight addresses the boundaries of the expertise function, asking if the function of regulation is the economic well-being of an industry. If this approach is so, government decision making becomes more important than individual business decision making. Public attention is now focused on political elements inherent in governmental decision making. If the U.S. government adopts an industrial policy, or policies, government decision makers select particular industries for special forms of government support. Is the future of economic regulation grounded in subsidizing sunset industries?

Deregulation. By the late 1970s, airline regulation—by the CAB's control of airline rates and routes—was not working well. The removal of regulation, it was argued, would encourage airline competition to fill flights. Airplanes are easily transferable from city to city. Existing carriers would allocate their equipment according to supply and demand. New carriers would enter the market to meet the demands of the market.

Deregulation permits flights to respond to passenger demand, producing ticket prices geared to filling flights and reduced passenger costs. Airline deregulation produces lower per-passenger costs, lower fares, and allocation of flights to routes according to demand. But will airline mergers result in a less responsive industry? Will a more concentrated and oligopolistic airline industry continue producing in the postregulation competitive era?

Under deregulation, profitable routes no longer subsidize the unprofitable routes. No longer is a carrier obligated to serve an unremunerative market. Resources are allocated in a way that produces maximum consumer benefits. However, arguments favoring deregulation of the transportation industries usually do not apply to all regulation. Transportation deregulation has worked because it produces more social benefits than those produced under regulation.

Public choice. In the 1980s, critics argued that elected officials acted not to further the overall social good, but to bolster chances of their reelection to public office. This meant that government decision makers might capitulate to interest group pressures rather than acting for the good of the entire community.

Elected officials try not to offend powerful interest groups. Legislators, seeking compromises, may avoid making difficult policy choices and legislate in generalities. They delegate to administrators the tasks of interpreting intentionally vague or ambiguous statutory terms. Legislators may blame administrators when one interest group of citizens complains about regulatory actions, yet take credit for the same decision if a different constituent interest group approves.[8]

Introduction to Laws and Regulations

Laws and regulations are a major tool in protecting the environment. Congress passes laws that govern the United States. To put those laws into effect, Congress authorizes certain government agencies, including the Environmental Protection Agency (EPA), to create and enforce regulations. The following is a basic description of how laws and regulations come to be, what they are, and where to find them, with an emphasis on environmental laws and regulations.

1. **Creating a Law**
   Step 1: A member of Congress proposes a bill. A bill is a document that, if approved, will become a law.
   Step 2: If both houses of Congress approve a bill, it goes to the President, who has the option to either approve it or veto it. If approved, the new law is called an Act, and the text of the Act is known as a public statute. Some of the better-known laws related to the environment are the Clean Air Act, the Clean Water Act, and the Safe Drinking Water Act.
   Step 3: Once an Act is passed, the House of Representatives standardizes the text of the law and publishes it in the *United States Code.* The *U.S. Code* is the official record of federal laws.
2. **Putting the Law to Work**
   Now that the law is official, how is it put into practice? Laws often do not include all the details. The *U.S. Code* would not tell you, for example, what the speed limit is in front of your house. To make the laws work on a day-to-day level, Congress authorizes certain government agencies, including the EPA, to create regulations. Regulations set specific rules about what is legal and what isn't. For example, a regulation issued by EPA to implement the Clean Air Act might state what levels of a pollutant—such as sulfur dioxide—are considered safe. It would tell industries how much sulfur dioxide they can legally emit into the air and what the penalty will be if they emit too much. Once the regulation is in effect, EPA then works to help Americans comply with and enforce the law.
3. **Creating a Regulation**
   First, an authorized agency, such as the EPA, decides that a regulation may be needed. The agency researches it and, if necessary, proposes a regulation. The proposal is listed in *The Federal Register* so that members of the public can consider it and send their comments to the agency. The agency considers the comments, revises the regulation accordingly, and issues a final rule. At each stage in the process, the agency publishes a notice in *The Federal Register.* These notices include the original proposal, requests for public comment, notices about public meetings where the proposal will be discussed, and the text of the final regulation.

Is the United States a Regulatory State?

In 1789, Congress granted the President the prerogative to select an administrator to "estimate the duties payable on imports." Since then, Congress continues to delegate rule-making power to administrative agencies. The full scope of regulatory power, in addition to the power to formulate rules, includes the authority for interpreting laws and regulations, enforcing rules and regulations, trying cases concerning violations of those rules, holding hearings investigating and adjudicating such circumstances, and imposing sanctions on violators. In a single agency, administrative regulatory power combines legislative, executive, and judicial powers.[9]

Administrative power expands as the power and responsibilities of government in our society expand. An industrialized, urbanized, interdependent society requires a more active role for government. The protection of individual rights, mediation of disputes, provision of benefits, and stabilization of the economy reflect

(*The Federal Register* includes other types of notices, too.)

- *The Federal Register* notices related to the environment are available on the EPA's website (www.epa.gov).
- A complete record of *The Federal Register* notices issued by the entire federal government is available from the Government Printing Office (website: www.gpo.gov).

4. Carrying Out the Law

Among the environmental laws enacted by Congress through which EPA carries out its efforts are the following:

1938 Federal Food, Drug, and Cosmetic Act

1947 Federal Insecticide, Fungicide, and Rodenticide Act

1948 Federal Water Pollution Control Act (also known as the Clean Water Act)

1955 Clean Air Act

1965 Shoreline Erosion Protection Act

1965 Solid Waste Disposal Act

1970 National Environmental Policy Act

1970 Pollution Prevention Packaging Act

1970 Resource Recovery Act

1971 Lead-Based Paint Poisoning Prevention Act

1972 Marine Protection, Research, and Sanctuaries Act

1972 Ocean Dumping Act

1973 Endangered Species Act

1974 Safe Drinking Water Act

1974 Shoreline Erosion Control Demonstration Act

1975 Hazardous Materials Transportation Act

1976 Resource Conservation and Recovery Act

1976 Toxic Substances Control Act

1977 Surface Mining Control and Reclamation Act

1978 Uranium Mill-Tailings Radiation Control Act

1980 Asbestos School Hazard Detection and Control Act

1980 Comprehensive Environmental Response, Compensation, and Liability Act

1982 Nuclear Waste Policy Act

1984 Asbestos School Hazard Abatement Act

1986 Asbestos Hazard Emergency Response Act

1986 Emergency Planning and Community Right to Know Act

1988 Indoor Radon Abatement Act

1988 Lead Contamination Control Act

1988 Medical Waste Tracking Act

1988 Ocean Dumping Ban Act

1988 Shore Protection Act

1990 National Environmental Education Act

Source: Environmental Protection Agency, www.epa.gov. See Carol Browner, "Creating a Healthier Environment: How EPA Works for You," *EPA Journal* 21, no. 1 (Winter 1995): 33–49.

accepted activities of modern U.S. government. As the 1980s began, at least fifty-eight federal agencies exercised rule-making authority and issued approximately seven thousand rules and policy statements each year.[10]

Administrative regulatory powers are vested in state and local government agencies as well. State regulatory powers and responsibilities include licensing of physicians, barbers, lawyers, architects, cosmeticians, liquor dealers, and funeral directors. States regulate commerce within their boundaries and supervise the governance of all public educational institutions. Local government agencies enforce building codes, fire, health, and safety regulations and standards. Agencies of state or local governments may also be charged with implementation of national programs via functional federalism.

Murray Weidenbaum argues that the process of regulation is not widely understood. Regulation is the way in which a national priority or concern is translated into a specific rule. Regulation does not commence when a government department or agency issues a ruling. Regulation has it origins in Congress, when the national legislature passes a law establishing a regulatory agency, providing a mandate to issue rules governing a particular activity. The writing of a particular statute is usually the most important action of an extended rule-making process. The regulatory department or agency cannot cure basic defects in the enabling legislation.

First, Congress perceives a "market failure," or private sector inability to achieve a social goal. Departments or agencies promulgate regulations in response to laws passed by Congress to correct that market failure. Regulatory proceedings are not, Weidenbaum says, mere matters of procedure and conformance. Regulations originate from demands for clean air, safe drinking water, safe workplaces, reliable financial markets, improved medicines, and competitive industries. The regulatory process, Weidenbaum concludes, is fundamentally bureaucratic—with all the powers and defects of government institutions—and at best is a blunt and imperfect mechanism for attempting to create a better society.[11]

As argued in the previous chapter, the *United States is a regulatory state.* The vast majority of direct contacts for most citizens are likely to be with federal, state, or local administrative agencies. We are a society where nearly every activity, whether of organizations or individuals, is included in the scope of administrative regulation and control. The responsibilities and powers of administrative agencies include the following partial listing:

1. The rates that consumers pay for telephone service and electricity are determined by administrative agencies, as are the interest rates that savings and loan institutions may pay depositors.
2. Administrative agencies protect individuals from racial, sexual, and age discrimination in the major aspects of their lives: employment, education, and housing.
3. Administrative agencies determine who does and does not get radio and television licenses.
4. Administrative agencies ensure that the food we eat is pure, wholesome, and free from harmful additives and that the drugs that we purchase are safe and effective.
5. The right to join a labor union and to be protected from unfair labor practices is safeguarded by administrative regulatory power.
6. Administrative agencies are responsible for ensuring the safety of our workplaces; our methods of transportation; and the countless products that we purchase as consumers, from toys to clothing to automobiles.
7. Administrative agencies are responsible for protecting us against monopolies, false advertising, air and water pollution, incompetent healthcare professionals, subminimum wages and working conditions, unfair and misleading credit transactions, and fraud in securities purchases.
8. Administrative agencies determine who is eligible for welfare, food stamps, veterans benefits, Medicaid, Medicare, and Social Security.
9. Administrative agencies determine how much of our income we get to keep and whether a person may be admitted to or remain in this country.[12]

Overhead operations, independent regulatory commissions, cabinet departments, independent agencies, government corporations, the Executive Office of the

President (EOP), and a variety of assorted federal agencies of more and lesser consequence issue administrative regulations daily in *The Federal Register* and annually in the *The Code of Federal Regulations.*

Overhead units carry out functions for the entire federal government. The General Accounting Office (GAO), Government Printing Office (GPO), Congressional Budget Office (CBO), Office of Management and Budget (OMB), General Services Administration (GSA), and Office of Personnel Management (OPM) issue regulations and administer support functions for most of the federal bureaucracy.

Since the creation of the Interstate Commerce Commission more than one hundred years ago, **independent regulatory commissions** have been prominent in the government regulation of business. Such commissions are multiheaded, bipartisan in composition, organizationally separated from other departments and agencies, and not directly in the President's chain of command. They provide nonpartisan flexibility, continuity, and expertise in the regulatory process; assign commissioners with terms longer than the President; protect commissioners from presidential dismissal; and allow lengthy tenure for maximizing commissioner expertise and independence. These characteristics and aspirations may not be realized in each commission on every day of every year; however, these commissions possess widespread responsibilities for regulating specific industries and for protecting consumers and workers.

Examples of prominent, independent regulatory commissions are the Federal Communications Commission (FCC), Surface Transportation Board, Nuclear Regulatory Commission (NRC), Postal Rate Commission, Securities and Exchange Commission (SEC), Federal Maritime Commission (FMC), Federal Reserve System (FED), Consumer Product Safety Commission (CPSC), and Equal Employment Opportunity Commission (EEOC).

Cabinet departments enjoy a scope, type, and impact of regulatory power similar to that of independent regulatory commissions. Major distinctions between the two types of agencies include administrative form and operations within executive departments or agencies. Cabinet agencies are led by a single administrator; cabinet secretaries are directly responsible to the President for programming. For example, the Food and Drug Administration (FDA), within the Department of Health and Human Services (HHS), is responsible for ensuring the purity and safety of food, drugs, and cosmetics; the Internal Revenue Service (IRS), within the Department of Treasury, implements tax laws; the Immigration and Naturalization Service (INS), within the Department of Justice, regulates the entry, residence, and exit of aliens; and the Occupational Safety and Health Administration (OSHA), within the Department of Labor, attempts to ensure that places of work are free from hazards affecting the health and safety of workers.

Independent agencies, such as the Federal Emergency Management Agency (FEMA), Selective Service System, the National Foundation on the Arts and Humanities, and Small Business Administration (SBA), share characteristics in common with independent regulatory commissions and cabinet departments. Independent agencies are accountable to the President for direction and control; they have a single administrative leader, and they are not positioned within a cabinet department.

The **government corporations,** such as AMTRAK, a passenger railroad; Federal Deposit Insurance Corporation (FDIC), an insurance company; Tennessee

TABLE 12.1

Steps of Administrative Regulatory Process

Step 1:	Authorizing Legislation
Step 2:	Agency Interpretation-Enforcement (rule making)
Step 3:	Complaint
Step 4:	Investigation
Step 5:	Informal Proceedings
Step 6:	Prosecution
Step 7:	Formal Hearing (adjudication)
Step 8:	Agency Review
Step 9:	Judicial Review
Step 10:	Agency Enforcement

Source: Florence Heffron with Neil McFeeley, from *The Administrative Regulatory Process,* 1983. Reprinted by permission of Pearson Education, Inc.

Valley Authority (TVA), an electric power generating facility; or the U.S. Postal Service, a post office, issue regulations as well. Such public corporations are multi-headed (with a board of directors), however, the President may dismiss corporation board members.

Distrust and dislike of the chief executive encouraged the establishment of independent regulatory commissions. A powerful clientele group, such as the environmental lobby, called for the promotion and protection of a particular concern or interest within a single-headed independent agency. An agency within a department may seek refuge there from hostile or corrupt influences.

The total administrative regulatory process includes ten procedures, or steps. Most regulatory activities do not touch all ten bases, either because the rule is obeyed without discussion or controversy or the agency does not actively enforce the regulation. The procedures or steps of the administrative regulatory process are identified in table 12.1.

Economic, Social, and Subsidiary Regulations

The regulatory establishment expanded dramatically between 1970 and 1975. Between 1975 and 1980, regulatory expenditures increased 27 percent. From 1980 to 1985, costs decreased by 3 percent. Reagan's attempts to shut down the regulatory establishment came to a halt in 1984. Growth in the regulatory establishment resumed between 1985 and 1990, rising by 18 percent, making up lost time for the previous period.

Priorities for the broad, regulatory categories changed significantly in the 1970–1990 period. Spending for job safety and other working conditions increased by 217 percent between 1970 and 1980 and decreased by 13 percent between 1980 and 1990. Between 1970 and 1980, spending for industry-specific regulation increased by 66 percent but decreased by 23 percent from 1980 until 1990, reflecting Reagan's attempts to halt regulatory activities. Consumer safety and health regulatory expenditures decreased between 1980 and 1990, but less dramatically.

The 1970–1990 period saw a 46 percent increase in the number of regulatory personnel, with all but 3 percent of this rise coming between 1970 and 1975. Between 1970 and 1975, staffing for social regulatory activities jumped 50 percent. As the number of personnel employed by the regulatory bureaucracy grew greatly, so did its intrusion into the everyday decision-making processes of the private sector. Regulatory staffing patterns declined during the 1980–1985 period, however, as there were 15 percent fewer personnel in 1985 than in 1980.[13]

In 2000, 54 federal departments and agencies and 134,000 federal employees spent over $18.7 billion writing and enforcing federal regulations. From fiscal year 1970 to fiscal year 2000, permanent, full-time positions at the 54 federal departments and agencies increased from 69,946 to 131,587. In 1976, the total number of actual pages in the *Federal Register* was 50,505. By 1999, the total rose to 134,932. In 1970, federal expenditures on regulatory activities was $4,807,000 (1996 dollars). By 2001, it had climbed to $18,340,000. Between 1996 and 2001, federal departments and agencies issued 21,653 major and minor rules.

Social regulatory programs deal with health, safety, and environmental issues. Social regulatory agencies are limited to a specific policy area, but they have power to regulate across all industries. Social regulatory agencies include the Environmental Protection Agency (EPA), Drug Enforcement Administration (DEA), Food and Drug Administration (FDA), Occupational Safety and Health Administration (OSHA), National Transportation Safety Board (NTSB), and National Labor Relations Board (NLRB).

The social regulatory functions are divided into (1) consumer safety and health, (2) transportation, (3) job safety and other working conditions, (4) environment, and (5) energy. The largest projected real percentage increase in 2002 occurred in agencies that regulate transportation functions.

Economic regulatory agencies focus on specific industries. Economic controls include the use of price ceilings and service parameters. The Federal Communications Commission (FCC), Federal Deposit Insurance Corporation (FDIC), and Federal Trade Commission (FTC) are economic regulatory agencies. Economic regulatory tasks are divided into (1) finance and banking, (2) industry-specific regulation, and (3) general business.[14]

The costs of compliance with federal requirements have shifted over the decades. Thomas Hopkins identifies three groups of federal regulation compliance requirements:

- **Environmental and risk reduction regulations** attempt to lessen pollution and other societal risks. These include air emission and water pollution, solid waste disposal regulation, handling and labeling of hazardous materials, noise regulations, superfund compliance, and nuclear power safety.
- **Price and entry control regulations** restrict rates on business entry and include government controls on labor markets and on product prices and availability. Components include price and entry control regulations on international trade regulations, wage and hour standards (overtime, minimum wage, Davis-Bacon wages), regulations on pricing and marketing of agricultural products and services, energy rate and conservation regulations, and transporation price and entry restrictions.

- **Paperwork regulations** entail tax compliance procedures and related paperwork requirements, the latter of which do not have a direct social or economic function. Taxpayers spend time complying with the intricacies of the tax code.[15]

Public sector expenditures are a small proportion of the total cost of regulation by society. Regulatory behaviors fall into three categories—economic, social, and subsidiary regulations.

Economic Regulations

What we will call *Regulation I,* or *economic regulation,* focuses upon market aspects of industrial behavior, including rates, quality, and quantity of service, and competitive practices within a specific industry or segment of the economy. Categories of economic regulation include finance and banking, industry-specific regulation, and general business regulation. Regulators for finance and banking activities include the

- Comptroller of the Currency
- Farm Credit Administration
- Federal Deposit Insurance Corporation
- Federal Reserve Banks
- National Credit Union Administration

Agencies that deal with industry-specific regulations include the

- Commodity Futures Trading Commission
- Federal Communications Commission
- Federal Energy Regulatory Commission
- Federal Maritime Commission
- Interstate Commerce Commission

General business regulators that deal with non-industry-specific agencies and agencies not directly related to finance and banking include the

- Patent and Trademark Office in the Department of Commerce
- Antitrust Division in the Department of Justice
- Federal Election Commission
- Federal Trade Commission
- Securities and Exchange Commission

Economic regulation is usually industry-specific and focuses on market structure and firm conduct, regulating the entry, exit, merger, and rates within markets.[16] For example, the ICC regulates railroads and trucking, and the FCC regulates communications. The ICC and FCC each concentrate on a specific industry and each agency has no other responsibilities. Regulation I also concerns enforcement of congressionally mandated antitrust policies. The Justice Department and FTC regulate the frequency of mergers and combinations within particular industries. The goal of antitrust policies is maintaining and restoring competition within the market system. Competition and economic efficiency are objectives of Regulation I.

One of the most criticized forms of economic regulation is the effort of the FTC to demand that businesses tell consumers the truth, the whole truth, and nothing but the truth. The disclosure of full and accurate information by business, however, should prove compatible with desired outcomes of sellers and buyers in the market system. The most active economic regulatory agencies in terms of spending remained relatively stable over the 1970–1990 period.

Economic regulatory agencies account for about 20 percent of the administrative costs for 2002 and 2003. Economic regulatory agency subcategories include:

- *Finance and banking,* which projects budgets of about $2 billion in 2002 and 2003
- *Industry-specific regulation,* with increases at a real rate of 4 percent over the two-year span to $0.9 billion
- *General business,* which was projected to reach $2.2 billion in 2002 and $2.5 billion in 2003—a real increase of over 19 percent.[17]

Social Regulations

Regulation II, or *social regulation,* controls the nature and types of goods and services and production processes.

Social regulations entail consumer safety and health, job safety and working conditions, environment, and energy. Consumer safety and health regulators include the

- Consumer Product Safety Commission
- Department of Agriculture
- Department of Health and Human Services
- Department of Housing and Urban Development
- Department of Justice
- Department of Transportation
- Department of Treasury
- National Transportation Safety Board

Job safety and working conditions regulators include the

- Employment Standards Administration (Department of Labor)
- Occupational Safety and Health Administration (Department of Labor)
- Equal Employment Opportunity Commission
- National Labor Relations Board

Environmental regulators include

- Army Corps of Engineers in the Department of Defense
- Fish and Wildlife Service
- Office of Surface Mining Reclamation and Enforcement (Department of Interior)
- Environmental Protection Agency

Energy regulators include the

- Economic Regulatory Administration (Department of Energy)
- Nuclear Regulatory Commission.[18]

Regulating the Flag?

Flying the American flag is governed by many regulations. After September 11, 2001, mania resulted in the increased proliferation of flying the American flag by commercial businesses and homeowners. Flag flyers appear to be proud Americans. Flags must "be displayed in a respectful manner consistent with Title 36 U.S.C. chapter 10 and any local ordinances."

Section 174 of chapter 10 records that:

It is universal custom to display the flag from sunrise to sunset only on buildings and stationary flagstaffs in the open. However, a flag may be displayed 24 hours a day if property illuminated during the hours of darkness if a patriotic effect is desired.

The flag is to be hoisted briskly and lowered ceremoniously.

The flag should not be displayed in inclement weather unless an all-weather flag is displayed.

The flag should be displayed daily on or near the main administration building of every public institution, in or near every polling place on election days, and during school days in or near every schoolhouse.

The flag should never be used for advertising purposes in any manner whatsoever.

No part of the flag should ever be used as a costume or athletic uniform.

The flag should be displayed in a respectful way. The proper way to retire a United States flag is to either ceremoniously burn or bury it.

Source: Rob Samouce, "Flying the American Flag Is Governed by Many Regulations," *The Naples News,* May 5, 2002, http://cfapps. naplesnews.com/sendlink/printthis.cfm; *United States Code, Title 36,* Chapter 10, Sections 173–178; Executive Order 10834, http:// www.treefort.org//~rgrogan/web/flaglaw.htm.

Social regulation usually cuts across industries, regulating issues such as employment opportunity, environmental protection, and occupational safety.[19] Social regulation assumes control or elimination of socially harmful impacts occurring as by-products of the production process and protection of consumers and the public from unsafe or unhealthy products. If conservatives find Regulation I unpopular, they believe Regulation II an anathema. Regulation II focuses upon the subtle regulation of clean air, occupational safety, poison prevention, boat safety, lead-based paint elimination, product safety, political campaigns, pesticide control, water pollution, noise control, flood disaster, energy, commodity futures trading, hazardous materials transportation, and similar potential abuses.

Regulation II covers more industries and directly affects more consumers than Regulation I. For example, OSHA's regulations govern the activities of every employer whose business affects commerce. In other words, government is involved with detailed, sometimes minute, facets of the production process.

Two concerns are raised by Regulation II. First, the apparatus of the presidency concentrates significant power and influence regulating health, safety, and environmental activities. Second, the accretion of new regulatory powers and controls could undermine citizens' faith in government, a negative reaction to the over-strengthening of government and regulatory excesses of the mid-1970s.

Social regulation may be costly because certain regulatory decisions are grounded in grossly inadequate information. Even if information is forthcoming, regulatory decisions may reflect the most extreme and unrealistic assumptions about the problem's potential social interference. There could be strong resistance to alternative and innovative problem solutions. The ranking of the top ten social regulatory agencies during the 1970s and 1980s illustrates interesting changes in federal regulatory priorities.

Federal Trade Commission

Vision, Mission, & Goals

The Federal Trade Commission (FTC) enforces a variety of federal antitrust and consumer protection laws. The Commission has enforcement and administrative responsibilities under forty-six laws in three categories. They are: (1) statutes relating to both competition and consumer protection missions, (2) statutes relating principally to the competition mission, and (3) statutes relating principally to the consumer protection mission.

The FTC seeks to ensure that the nation's markets function competively—and are vigorous, efficient, and free of undue restrictions. The Commission also works to enhance the smooth operation of the marketplace by eliminating acts or practices that are unfair or deceptive. The FTC's efforts are directed toward stopping actions that threaten consumer opportunities to exercise informed choice. When requested, the Commission undertakes an economic analysis to support its law enforcement efforts and to contribute to the policy deliberations of Congress, the Executive Branch, other independent agencies, and state and local governments.

In 1914, Congress passed the Federal Trade Commission Act (FTCA)—Public Law Number 203, thereby creating the FTC. The protection of business and competition was its original intent; no direct responsibility to protect consumers was included. The FTC found that the interests of business and consumers were not mutually exclusive. Rogue businesses could steal clients from a competitor by deceiving consumers. The FTC is the primary federal agency responsible for preventing citizens from being deceived, or otherwise injured, by advertising and other marketing practices.

The phrase *unfair methods of competition* is not defined in the FTCA. The vagueness is permitted to allow the FTC to adapt to the ever-changing marketplace. The courts support this leverage. The FTC addresses vertical and horizontal restraints. Vertical restraints entail agreements between companies and suppliers that might harm competition. Horizontal restraints occur when direct competitors enter into a competition-limiting agreement. The FTC may intervene when the intent of the parties is to reduce competition—as in mergers and buy-outs.

The FTC files a complaint when it has reason to believe that the law has been or is being violated, and it appears to the Commission that a proceeding is in the public interest. The complaint is not a finding or ruling that the defendants violated the law. Cases are decided by the courts.

The FTC works for the consumer to prevent fraudulent, deceptive, and unfair business practices in the marketplace—providing information to help consumers spot, stop, and avoid them. The FTC enters internet, telemarketing, identify theft, and other fraud-related complaints into Consumer Sentinel, a secure online database available to civil and criminal law enforcement agencies throughout the United States.

Copies of complaints and Stipulated Final Judgments and Orders are available from the FTC's website at http:/www.ftc.gov and also from the FTC's Consumer Response Center, Room 130, 600 Pennsylvania Avenue NW, Washington, DC, 20580. Citizens may file a complaint or get free information on 150 consumer topics by calling 1-877-FTC-HELP (1-877-382-4357) toll-free, or they may use the complaint form at http://ww.ftc.gov.

Sources: Jef Richards, "The Federal Trade Commission," http://www.museum.tv/archieves/etv/F/htmlF/federaltrade/federaltrade.htm. See the FTC's website at http://www.ftc.gov/ftc/mission.htm.

Social regulatory agencies account for about 80 percent of the administrative costs for federal regulation in 2002 and 2003. Social regulatory agency subcategories include (see table 12.2):

- *Consumer safety and health,* which was projected to climb to $4.9 billion in 2002 (a real increase of 11.5 percent) and $5 billion in 2003 (a real increase of 0.7 percent);
- *Transportation,* with an increase of $5.5 billion in 2002 (a real increase of 30.3 percent) and $5.9 billion in 2003 (a real increase of 5.3 percent);

TABLE 12.2

Spending Summary for the Federal Regulatory Agencies, Selected Years

(Fiscal Years, Millions of Dollars in "Obligations")

	1960	1970	1980	1990	2000	2001	2002 (Estimated)	2003 (Estimated)	% Change 2001–02	% Change 2002–03
Current (Nominal) Dollars										
Social Regulation										
Consumer Safety and Health	111	236	1,245	1,908	3,672	4,272	4,861	4,982	13.8%	2.5%
Transportation	86	284	1,037	1,727	3,239	4,137	5,500	5,898	33.0%	7.2%
Job Safety and Workplace	35	128	753	1,002	1,450	1,642	1,712	1,702	4.2%	-0.6%
Environment	21	214	1,651	4,164	5,641	6,049	7,244	5,933	19.7%	-18.1%
Energy	12	64	481	485	610	661	746	723	12.9%	-3.1%
Total Social Regulation	265	926	5,167	9,286	14,612	16,761	20,063	19,237	19.7%	-4.1%
Economic Regulation										
Finance and Banking	30	86	362	1,355	1,850	1,941	2,011	2,012	3.6%	0.0%
Industry-Specific Regulation	102	281	492	497	729	826	869	895	5.3%	3.0%
General Business	47	115	355	743	1,717	2,003	2,215	2,479	10.6%	11.9%
Total Economic Regulation	179	482	1,209	2,595	4,296	4,770	5,095	5,386	6.8%	5.7%
Grand Total	444	1,408	6,376	11,881	18,908	21,531	25,158	24,622	**16.8%**	**-2.1%**
Annualized Percentage Change		12.2%	16.3%	6.4%	4.8%	13.9%	16.8%	-2.1%		
Constant (Real) 1996 Dollars										
Social Regulation										
Consumer Safety and Health	500	812	2,182	2,205	3,430	3,901	4,352	4,382	11.5%	0.7%
Transportation	388	978	1,818	1,996	3,026	3,778	4,924	5,187	30.3%	5.3%
Job Safety and Workplace	157	441	1,320	1,158	1,355	1,500	1,533	1,497	2.2%	-2.4%
Environment	95	737	2,894	4,812	5,270	5,524	6,485	5,218	17.4%	-19.5%
Energy	54	220	843	560	570	604	668	636	10.6%	-4.8%
Total Social Regulation	1,194	3,188	9,057	10,732	13,651	15,307	17,961	16,919	17.3%	-5.8%
Economic Regulation										
Finance and Banking	135	296	635	1,566	1,728	1,773	1,800	1,770	1.6%	-1.7%
Industry-Specific Regulation	460	967	862	574	681	754	778	787	3.2%	1.2%
General Business	212	396	622	859	1,604	1,829	1,983	2,180	8.4%	10.0%
Total Economic Regulation	807	1,659	2,119	2,999	4,013	4,356	4,561	4,737	4.7%	3.8%
Grand Total	2,001	4,847	11,176	13,730	17,664	19,663	22,523	21,656	**14.5%**	**-3.8%**
Annualized Percentage Change		9.3%	8.7%	2.1%	2.6%	11.3%	14.5%	-3.8%		

Note: Numbers may not add to totals due to rounding.

Source: From "Regulatory Response: An Analysis of the Shifting Priorities of the U.S. Budget for Fiscal Years 2002 & 2003" by Susan Dudley and Melinda Warren. Reprinted by permission of Melinda Warren, Weidenbaum Center on the Economy, Government, and Public Policy, Washington University and Mercatus Center, George Mason University.

- *Job safety and other working conditions,* which were projected to be about $1.7 billion (real increases of 2.2 percent in 2002 and –2.4 percent in 2003);
- *The environment,* with projected increases of 17.4 percent in 2002—with a budget of $7.2 billion—and which is expected to decline by 19.5 percent in real terms to $5.9 billion in 2003; and
- *Energy,* projected to increase by 11 percent to reach $0.7 billion in 2002, remaining level in 2003.[20]

Figures 12.1 and 12.2, along with tables 12.2 and 12.3, summarize the increases in administrative costs and staffing related to federal regulation over the past several decades.

Subsidiary Regulations

Regulation III, or *subsidiary regulation,* entails all regulatory activities accompanying Social Security, Medicare, Medicaid, Aid to Families with Dependent Children (AFDC), food stamps, veterans' benefits programs, Internal Revenue Service regulatory concerns, and categorical grant program regulations. Clientele of subsidiary regulations include individuals or state and local governments.

The general public has mixed feelings toward Regulation III. Americans would like to believe that there is no such thing as a free lunch. Freeloaders, welfare cheats, and food stamp chiselers invoke citizen suspicion, mistrust, and hostility. Most Americans do, however, consider Social Security, unemployment compensation, and veterans' benefits as legitimate.

Unless there are clear and specific regulations for such benefit programs, the opportunities for cheating are almost limitless, making the costs and benefits of

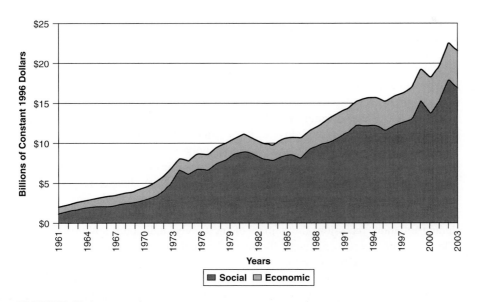

FIGURE 12.1 Administrative costs of federal regulation.

Source: From "Regulatory Response: An Analysis of the Shifting Priorities of the U.S. Budget for Fiscal Years 2002 & 2003" by Susan Dudley and Melinda Warren. Reprinted by permission of Melinda Warren, Weidenbaum Center on the Economy, Government, and Public Policy, Washington University and Mercatus Center, Georgby Mason University.

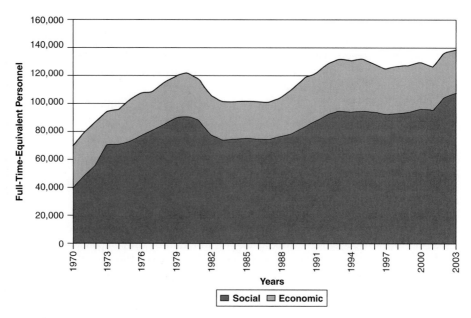

FIGURE 12.2 Staffing of federal regulatory agencies.

Source: From "Regulatory Response: An Analysis of the Shifting Priorities of the U.S. Budget for Fiscal Years 2002 & 2003" by Susan Dudley and Melinda Warren. Reprinted by permission of Melinda Warren, Weidenbaum Center on the Economy, Government, and Public Policy, Washington University and Mercatus Center, George Mason University.

Regulation III difficult to quantify. Programs range from deciding eligibility for benefit programs to providing equal sports opportunities for women in college and equal educational opportunities for the handicapped. Costs are largely intangible; the market value is not readily apparent.

Between 1994 and 1999, welfare rolls declined an amazing 54 percent from their historic high of 5 million families. How much of this decline is due to welfare reform? How much of it is the result of the economy? What are the effects of low-income families? Lower-economic-class welfare is easier for Congress to control and influence: The poor rarely join interest groups to support elected officials. The largesse in middle economic class welfare is more difficult to identify and eliminate. Middle class citizens vote and protect the pork.

Economic, social, and subsidiary regulations are diverse, contradictory, and value laden. The growth of administrative regulatory power changes responsibilities and relationships among branches and levels of government. Regulations control or restrict one's choices and/or behavior, and are blamed for all sorts of societal ills, including inflation, recession, the demise of the family, individual initiative, and the federal system. Despite criticisms, the societal conditions demanding counterbalance to the vast power that private corporations and industry exercise over the lives, health, safety, and happiness of Americans are still evident. In addition, nationwide polls indicate that the American public supports, generally, the concept of regulations.[21]

When the Reagan administration came to power in 1981, one of its goals was to trim down the federal regulatory agencies. Attempts to "rein in the regulatory establishment," however, virtually ceased in fiscal 1983.[22] In the first two years of the

TABLE 12.3

Staffing Summary for the Federal Regulatory Agencies, Selected Years

(Fiscal Years, Full-Time-Equivalent Employment)

	1970	1980	1990	2000	2001	(Estimated) 2002	2003	% Change 2001–02	% Change 2002–03
Social Regulation									
Consumer Safety and Health	13,912	33,242	28,730	31,150	32,141	34,628	36,221	7.7%	4.6%
Transportation	14,678	19,824	18,388	25,724	23,649	29,912	31,304	26.5%	4.7%
Job Safety and Other Working Conditions	6,486	17,894	13,610	12,141	12,218	12,680	12,367	3.8%	-2.5%
Environment	4,525	16,993	20,057	24,555	24,814	24,747	24,635	-0.3%	-0.5%
Energy	219	3,225	3,293	2,923	2,897	2,956	2,970	2.0%	0.5%
Total Social Regulation	39,820	91,178	84,078	96,493	95,719	104,922	107,498	9.6%	2.5%
Economic Regulation									
Finance and Banking	4,969	9,524	16,299	14,080	10,682	10,775	10,601	0.9%	-1.6%
Industry-Specific Regulation	18,548	11,885	7,977	6,438	6,384	6,527	6,568	2.2%	0.6%
General Business	6,609	9,251	9,611	12,509	12,839	13,747	14,335	7.1%	4.3%
Total Economic Regulation	30,126	30,660	33,887	33,027	29,905	31,048	31,504	3.8%	1.5%
Grand Total	**69,946**	**121,838**	**117,965**	**129,520**	**125,624**	**135,970**	**139,002**	**8.2%**	**2.2%**
Annualized Percentage Change		10.6%	7.0%	7.7%	-3.0%	8.2%	2.2%		

Source: From "Regulatory Response: An Analysis of the Shifting Priorities of the U.S. Budget for Fiscal Years 2002 & 2003" by Susan Dudley and Melinda Warren. Reprinted by permission of Melinda Warren, Weidenbaum Center on the Economy, Government, and Public Policy, Washington University and Mercatus Center, George Mason University.

administration, budgets and staffing were reduced across the board. But in the last six years of the Reagan administration, expenditures for regulatory agencies (especially the Environmental Protection Agency) increased at a pace similar to the growth that took place under the Carter administration. Staffing increased as well.

Administrative Rules and Rule Making

Rule making and adjudication are not the same process. Rule making, in general, focuses on the future and is broad in scope. Adjudication is particular, focusing upon an instance in the present or the past. Prior to the adjudication of a person's rights, the individual is entitled to a hearing under the Due Process Clause of the Fifth Amendment for federal agencies and the Fourteenth Amendment for state agencies. The development of administrative rules follows the commercial development of the American west, tragedies of transportation accidents, development of the federal government as collector of revenues, government as benefit provider, and the populist rebuttal to the exploitation of the farmer by the rail trust.[23]

Regulatory law and administrative law, as stated earlier, work in tandem, but are not the same thing. *Congress does not like controversy.* Congress is a provincial political institution. In other words, members of Congress do not enjoy conflict-laden issues where they are likely to have constituents split over the solutions. Each member of Congress comes from a narrow, provincial political base. Each member of Congress looks out for his or her district's narrow economic interests and not those of the entire nation. Partly because Congress is composed of politicians representing 535 political jurisdictions, they pass laws that do not speak clearly. It is not difficult, therefore, to explain the presence of vague, ambiguous, and general laws that allow wide human discretion.

Administrative agencies serve to interpret the vagueness, ambiguity, and generality of these laws. For example, the FCC, by rule, restricts the number of commercial broadcasting stations a private corporation may operate. The IRS, by rule, determines which groups in society must pay or are exempted from paying taxes. The FCC creates communications law; the IRS makes tax law. Independent regulatory commissions, Cabinet agencies, independent agencies, public corporations, and the EOP have similar functions.

The Administrative Procedure Act

The Administrative Procedure Act, although not a comprehensive code of administrative procedure, provides a general framework of fundamental importance. The APA, in the minds of some authorities, serves as the "Magna Carta of Administrative Law." Regulatory law regulates citizen behaviors; administrative law oversees the administrative discretion of bureaucrats.

Judges interpret legal statements and prescribe the procedures that agencies and their employees follow. Judicial interpretation originates from Constitutions; the primary, but not exclusive, origin for interpretation comes from due process clauses. Judges also interpret administrative procedure statutes, if applicable; some clauses within a statute require agencies to follow certain procedures, including conducting a full hearing of the concern. Administrative law, meanwhile, applies

Types of Agency Rules

There are four types of agency rules.

- Legislative or substantive rules, presuming they are authorized by statute, do not exceed or contradict the statute, and are applied according to correct procedure, having the force and effect of law.
- Interpretative rules advise clientele on what the agency interprets a statute or regulation to mean. Interpretative rules examine the construction of a law that an agency administers.

- Procedural rules regulate an agency's internal practices. All agencies establish rules governing their own procedures.
- General policy statements are philosophical commentary and are not accountable to the rule-making provisions of the APA. Procedural, interpretative, and general policy statements are published in *The Federal Register.*

Source: Stanley A. Reigel and P. John Owen, *Administrative Law: The Law of Government Agencies* (Ann Arbor, Mich.: Ann Arbor Science, The Butterworth Group, 1982), pp. 39–59.

legal principles originating from statutes, common law, constitutions, and regulatory law.[24] Public administrators, as implementors of regulatory law, implement rules. The terms *rule* and *regulation* are nearly synonymous. Unless rules are successfully undermined in a lawsuit as unconstitutional, rules have the force of law. What is a rule? The APA defines a rule as

> . . . the whole or a part of an agency statement of general or particular applicability and future effect designed to implement, interpret, or prescribe law or policy or describing the organization, procedure, or practice requirements of an agency and includes the approval or prescription of the future of rates, wages, corporate or financial structures or reorganizations thereof; prices, facilities, appliances, services, or allowances thereof; or of valuations, costs, or practices bearing on any of the foregoing.[25]

The first of the two types of rule making delineated by the APA is informal or "notice and comment" rule making. The characteristics of this procedure are advance notice and public participation. Notice of proposed rule making gives the time, place, and nature of the rule-making proceeding, refers to the authority, or statute, under which the rule is proposed, and includes the terms or substance of the proposed rule or a description of the subjects and issues therein.

The second type of rule making, "on the record" formal rule making, occurs when a "trial-type" hearing precedes rules. The hearing is an adversarial process entailing production of evidence, testimony by witnesses, cross-examination, and representation by counsel. The more formal requirements apply when a statute determines that rules must be cited "on the record after opportunity for an agency hearing."

The Federal Register and *The Code of Federal Regulations* publish notices of proposed rule making. The Federal Register Act of 1935 established a system of federal rules publication. The Act designated *The Federal Register* as the official publication of federal rules, regulations, orders, and other documents of "general applicability and legal effect." On March 14, 1936, *The Federal Register* began publishing every day, Monday through Friday. In 1936, *The Register* published 2,619 pages of rules, orders, and other actions. In 1980, or more than forty years later, *The Register* totaled more than 87,000 pages.[26]

After each year, the issues of *The Register* are bound and indexed. The regulations published in *The Federal Register* for the preceding year are codified with regulations previously issued and still in effect. *The Code of Federal Regulations,* a collection of paperback books grouped together by agency, is divided into fifty titles, as each title more or less represents a particular agency or a broad subject area.

Regulatory Restraint and Modification

Between 1970 and 1980, as measured in constant dollars, regulatory budgets nearly quadrupled. For example, during the decade of the 1970s, the FTC perceived its legislative mandate as a consumer police officer for the economy. For every six persons employed in federal regulatory activities in 1980, there were five employed in 1984. By 1988, the nation's federal regulatory agency employed 9 percent fewer persons than in 1980. The decline in regulatory staffing between 1980 and 1988 occurred in Consumer Safety and Health, Job Safety and Other Working Conditions, and Industry-Specific Regulation (see table 12.3). With a 14 percent reduction in real terms from 1980 to 1984, regulatory budgets declined in the early 1980s.[27]

In the early 1980s, President Reagan realized cuts in federal regulatory budgets, but these early reductions were more than countered by steady spending increases in the President's second term. In real dollars, the federal government spent 10 percent more on regulation in 1988 than was appropriated in 1980. The EPA, the largest of the regulatory agencies in terms of budgeting and staffing, experienced a 25 percent decline in spending on research and development in the 1981–1984 period, but Reagan was unable to convince members of Congress to keep EPA's regulatory budget at a low ebb. During the Reagan years, real spending for this agency increased by almost $1 billion, an increase of 63 percent. Growth in regulatory spending during the Reagan era increased by 62 percent in Finance and Banking, 34 percent in General Business, and 30 percent in Environment and Energy.

The Federal Register and *The Code of Federal Regulations*

- *The Federal Register,* published daily, Monday through Friday, provides a uniform system for making available to the public regulations and legal notices issued by federal departments and agencies. These include presidential proclamations and Executive Orders and federal agency documents having general applicability and legal effect, documents required to be published by act of Congress, and other federal agency documents of public interest.
- *The Code of Federal Regulations* is a codification of the general and permanent rules published in *The Federal Register* by the executive departments and agencies of the federal government. The *Code* is divided into fifty titles which represent broad areas subject to federal regulation. Each title is subdivided into chapters which usually bear the name of the issuing agency. Each chapter is further subdivided into parts covering specific regulatory areas.
- *The Federal Register* and *The Code of Federal Regulations* must be used together to determine the latest version of any given rule. Each volume of the *Code* contains amendments published in *The Federal Register* since the last revision of that volume of the *Code.* Source citations for the regulations are referred to by volume number and page number of *The Federal Register* and date of publication.

Therefore, the 1980s constitute an era of regulatory contradictions, restraint, and expansion in the financing of regulations and the workforce committed to such activities. For example, in General Business, the Antitrust Division of the Department of Justice and the FTC had a real spending cut of more than 25 percent since 1980, whereas the International Trade Administration and the International Trade Commission had a boost in real spending by 139 percent since 1980. Reagan administration efforts to reduce the size and costs of the regulatory establishment placed additional emphasis upon improving the substantive aspects of the statutes themselves that empower agencies to make regulations. In other words, the quality of regulations is as important as the quantity.[28]

The Stages of Rule Making

Rule making is easier understood by perceiving developments as a sequence of activities. All but the first of the eleven stages are affected by the stages preceding it.[29]

Stage 1: Origin of Rule Making Activity. Congress is the true origin of rule making. No rule is valid unless it is authorized by a law prescribed by Congress. The rule exists to promote a statutory purpose. The degree of agency discretion, procedural requirements, and volume and frequency of rules to be produced are matters dealt with in Stage 1.

Stage 2: Origin of Individual Rule Making. Deadlines and hammers are prominent in this stage. Hammers provide that statutes will take effect on a certain date if the agency fails to issue an alternative regulation. Hammers are used to convince agencies to expedite the rule-making process. Internal and external sources are available when rules are not explicitly mandated. Internal sources of ideas are political leadership, senior career service personnel, advisory committees, program office staff, office of the general counsel, field staff, and enforcement officials. External sources are not confined to the public sector. However, the White House, Congress, agencies, and citizen action are primary sources of ideas for writing better rules. The APA permits anyone to petition an agency to make a rule.

Administrative Responsibility

Administrative responsibility incorporates accountability, competence, fairness, and responsiveness.

- *Accountability* is answerability—answering, in particular, to someone or something outside the organization. Accountability also refers to direction and control, for if things go wrong, someone is held liable.
- *Competence* implies expertise, prudence, and care for consequences rather than negligence. Recognizable objective standards guide the formulation and implementation of public policy.

- *Fairness* combines the individual concern for due process with the notion of justice and is designed to protect the individual from arbitrary and capricious decisions.
- *Responsiveness* acknowledges an organization's yielding to citizen demands for policy change and entails the initiation of proposed solutions for problems.

Source: Paul N. Tramontozzi with Kenneth W. Chilton, *U.S. Regulatory Agencies Under Reagan, 1980–1988* (St. Louis, Mo.: Center for the Study of Business, 1987), pp. 11–14.

Stage 3: Authorization to Proceed with Rule Making. This stage includes a priority-setting system and agency approval process. By establishing priorities throughout its jurisdiction, an agency controls the types of rules and sequencing of rules. Priority setting enables the agency to determine how it will respond to external demands and how the agency's resources devoted to rule-making will be allocated. Mechanisms to authorize rule making vary dramatically. Some are highly structured and rigid. Others are permissive.

Stage 4: Planning the Rule Making. Who in the agency is responsible for developing the rule, what the objective of the rule being written is, and how the public will be involved are pursuits of this stage. The content may not be determined at this stage. But the quality of work accomplished in this stage influences the ease and speed with which rule making is carried out. Goals of the rule, legal requirements, technical and political information requirements, and participation plans occur at this stage. The securing of necessary resources and assignment of staff also take place at this juncture along the rule-making pathway.

Stage 5: Developing the Draft Rule. Collection of information, analysis of information, impact studies, internal consultations, informal external consultations, draft language of preamble and rule, and implementation plan dominate the activities of this stage. Impact studies include the following inquiries: Will the rule have an effect on the physical environment? Will it have a disproportionate impact on small businesses and other entities? Does it curtail in any way the normal legal prerogatives of state and local governments? Will it necessitate the collection and reporting of additional information?

Stage 6: Internal Review of the Draft Rule. Internal reviews occur horizontally and vertically. The horizontal review takes place across the agency. Various offices determine if the proposed rule has any effect on the areas under their jurisdiction. The influence of particular offices depends on the relative power that particular office enjoys in the bureaucratic pecking order. Vertical reviews involve supervisors and senior officials. Rules are developed at a relatively low level of the agency. This review allows supervisors and senior officials to monitor the consistency of agency programs.

Stage 7: External Review of the Draft Rule. The Office of Management and Budget, Congress, interest groups, and agencies participate at this stage of rule making. OMB affects the substance and process of rules. If other agencies are affected by the contents of a new rule, they may be asked to examine the proposed new rule. Congress and interest groups will be consulted on the contents of the draft rule.

Stage 8: Revision and Publication of a Draft Rule. The guidelines of *The Federal Register* must be met. The specifications of *The Register* may require agencies to resubmit draft rules, thereby meeting the stringent guidelines of *The Register*. This stage is routine in rule making but should not be underestimated.

Stage 9: Public Participation. This stage includes the receipt of written comment, conduct of public hearings, review and analysis of public input, and draft responses to public input. The choice between written comment and the conduction of public hearings is more a matter of politics and public relations than the quality of input expected. In this stage, the agency must manage the receipt of comments, ensure that those submitted are retained, and then make them available in a location accessible to citizens.

Stage 10: Action on the Draft Rule. This stage is crucial. All essential technical and political information have been collected, and all internal and external constituencies have been heard from. For still-unfinished rule making, several alternative paths may be taken:

1. When no changes are needed, the agency has succeeded in producing a draft that can stand as is. All that remains is the preparation of the appropriate notice for *The Federal Register* and final clearance by the OMB.
2. When only minor revisions are needed, those drafting the rule may circulate it for another round of internal and external reviews. If the revisions are minor, they will be made as a matter of form. Review of the final rule by the OMB is required, however.
3. Another round of participation is pursued only when comments by the public are unclear and raise issues that cannot be resolved internally. Usually, the notice issued will ask the public to respond to a specific set of questions.
4. When major revisions are needed, the agency will, in effect, reproduce the process starting with Stage 5, because the changes constitute a new proposed rule.
5. Abandoning the rule making and starting over is a more extreme version of option 4. Here the agency is convinced that its work was for naught and begins anew.
6. A rule making is abandoned altogether if the agency is convinced that its decision to write a rule was wrong. It will notify the public that no rule will be issued through a notice in *The Federal Register.*[30]

Stage 11: Post-Rule-Making Activities. If rule making works to everyone's expectations, this stage is not active. If rule making is flawed, lawsuits are probable. Most rule-making alternatives are less dramatic, however. Staff may be called on to reinterpret vague or unclear provisions of a rule. Parties affected by the new rule may file petitions for reconsideration. Frequently agencies issue technical corrections or amendments of flawed rules. Rule making is not a process that has a definite start and finish. Aspects of rules may be challenged and altered at any time in this process.

What Is the Public Interest?

In casting about for answers to the question of responsibility, we are at the outset likely to come across the phrase, *the public interest.* Many see the entire solution to the question neatly encapsulated in this phrase, as though an administrator need only resolve to serve the public interest, and his or her problems concerning responsibility will vanish.

This solution, like so many other easy solutions to difficult problems, raises more questions than it answers. The most basic is this: *What is the public interest?* Walter Lippman once claimed that "The public interest may be what men would choose if they saw clearly, thought rationally, and acted disinterestedly

---

Types of Accountability

There are four types of accountability:

- *Bureaucratic accountability* entails an organized and legitimate superior/subordinate relationship with close supervision or a surrogate system of standard operating procedures or clearly stated rules and regulations.
- *Legal accountability,* similar to bureaucratic accountability, is grounded upon relationships between a controlling party outside the agency, typically lawmakers, and members of the organization. Bureaucratic accountability portrays a hierarchical relationship, grounded upon the ability of supervisors to reward or punish subordinates, while legal accountability presents a relationship of two relatively autonomous parties, involving a formal or

implied trustee agreement between the public agency and its legal monitor.

- *Professional accountability* relies upon skilled and expert employees for providing appropriate solutions. Deference to expertise within the agency is the key to professional accountability.
- *Political accountability* asks: Whom does the public administrator represent? The general public, elected officials, agency heads, agency clientele, special interest groups, and future generations constitute potential constituencies. The key relationship is between the public administrator and his or her constituents.

Source: Barbara S. Romzek and Melvin J. Dubnick, "Accountability in the Public Sector: Lessons from the Challenger Tragedy," *Public Administration Review* 47, no. 3 (May/June 1987): 227–238.

---

and benevolently.[31] This leaves us with the task of defining "clear" vision and "rational" thought, concepts that, in practice, seem susceptible to varying interpretations. Even deciding what course of action is "benevolent" and "disinterested" may produce more controversy than it settles. "It may be somewhat difficult for some readers to accept the conclusion that there is no public interest theory worthy of the name," concluded political scientist Glendon Shubert.[32]

Another maxim that often presents itself is "following one's conscience." This, too, fails to furnish a usable guideline. The enforcers of the Inquisition who burned thousands of heretics at the stake felt they were following the most lofty appeals to conscience. The same can be said for many other appalling actions that people have perpetrated on others. As Carl Friedrich noted, "Autocratic and arbitrary abuse of power has characterized the officialdom of a government service bound only by the dictates of conscience."[33]

While Friedrich rules out the use of conscience as a means of ensuring responsibility, he does have some positive ideas to offer in its place. "We have a right to call such a policy irresponsible if it can be shown that it was adopted without proper regard to the existing sum of human knowledge concerning the technical issues involved; we have also a right to call it irresponsible if it can be shown that it was adopted without proper regard for existing preference in the community and more particularly its prevailing majority."[34]

In keeping with this admonition, Friedrich sees the solution to the question of administrative responsibility lying in two areas: *professionalism* and *participation.* Professionals usually have been conditioned to uphold certain standards, and they usually subscribe to a code of ethics that governs the practice of their profession. As Friedrich sees it, professionalism constitutes something of an "inner check" on administrative irresponsibility. Participation, meanwhile, means that administrators must consult more interests and listen to more points of view. Allowing divergent parties to share in decision making should make that process less arbitrary and subjective and more responsive and responsible.

To Friedrich's twin safeguards of professionalism and participation can be added a third protective device: *publicity.* Directing the public spotlight onto administrative decision making should make such decision making more responsible. Secrecy has rarely led to improved administrative decisions or better administrative behavior.

Professionalism, participation, and publicity do not in themselves guarantee responsible administration. Professionals can act irresponsibly, and shared decision making can produce irresponsible decisions. Publicity can, on occasion, distort an administrator's perspective, because what is immediate "good press" is not always most beneficial to the public. These caveats notwithstanding, these three "Ps"—professionalism, participation, and publicity—provide a basis for better public management. As they become more a part of bureaucratic behavior, such behavior may move closer toward meeting the desires and demands of the American people.

Summary

- The fragmentation and personalism of our political system makes the typical administrative agency an isolated entity, continually developing and maintaining sources of support. Administrators assume an activist role in developing that support. *Size, dispersion, degree of organization,* and *degree of passion, enthusiasm,* and *zeal* contribute to the effectiveness of an agency's clientele.

- Regulations take force because the market or markets fail or otherwise do not work effectively. U.S. regulatory activities began with the establishment of the Interstate Commerce Commission in 1887. Information is a scarce commodity. Decision makers cannot collect all relevant information. They act in a state of partial ignorance and uncertainty. They use the best source of information available: *what just has happened.* Government oversight and information occur in this perspective. Railroads, motor carriers, and airlines were deregulated. Public choice assumes that rational individuals pursue their own interests.

- *Advisory committees,* complaint handling, and public hearings play roles in developing strategies for support by clientele. *Advisory committees* serve as a two-way transmission system for communication, bringing clients' concerns to the agency and bringing the agency's problems to the clients.

- Two developments increase clientele effectiveness and influence in U.S. public bureaucracies. The *orientation* and *structure* of public agencies based on interest groups, or clientele, and the *administrative decentralization* of program functions enhance the power of clientele.

- The full scope of *regulatory power*—in addition to the power to formulate rules—includes the authority for interpreting laws and regulations, enforcing rules and regulations, trying cases concerning violations of those rules, holding hearings for investigating and adjudicating such circumstances, and imposing sanctions on violators. Administrative regulatory power combines legislative, executive, and judicial powers.

- The United States is a *regulatory state* where nearly all activities of organizations and individuals are part of administrative regulations and controls. There are three types of regulatory behaviors: *economic, social,* and *subsidiary.*
- *Operational costs* for the federal regulatory establishment for fiscal year 1999 were $17.9 billion. Spending and staffing at the sixty-one regulatory departments and agencies are divided into two categories: *economic* and *social regulations.* Total staffing for economic regulation in 1999 was 29,836, a 1.3 percent increase over 1998. Total staffing at social regulatory agencies was 98,091, a 0.9 percent increase over 1998.
- *Economic regulation* is the more traditional, industry-specific form of regulation. These regulators employ economic controls such as price ceilings and service parameters. These departments and agencies regulate a broad base of activities in particular industries. Examples of economic regulatory agencies are the Federal Communications Commission (FCC), the Federal Deposit Insurance Corporation (FDIC), and the Federal Trade Commission (FTC).
- *Social regulation* focuses on achieving cleaner air, equal employment opportunity, safer work environments, and consumer safety. Social regulatory departments and agencies are limited to a specific issue, but their prerogatives include regulatory powers that penetrate and spread through industry boundaries. Illustrations are the Environmental Protection Agency (EPA), the Drug Enforcement Agency (DEA), and National Labor Relations Board (NLRB).
- The cost of federal regulations reached $843 billion in 2000 and is equal to 8 percent of the gross domestic product.
- If current trends continue, federal regulatory employment will increase by 25 percent by the end of the decade.
- Social regulatory agencies accounted or will account for about 80 percent of the administrative costs for federal regulation in 2002 and 2003.
- *The Federal Register* provides a uniform system for making available to the public regulations and legal notices issued by federal departments and agencies. *The Register* includes presidential proclamations and Executive Orders and federal agency documents having general applicability and legal effect.
- *The Code of Federal Regulations* is a codification of the general and permanent rules published in *The Federal Register* by the executive departments and agencies of the federal government. *The Federal Register* and *The Code of Federal Regulations* are used in tandem to determine the latest version of any rule or regulation.
- Administrative power expands as the power and responsibilities of government expand. An industrialized, urbanized, interdependent society requires a more active role for government.
- Rule making and adjudication are not the same. *Rule making* is general and focuses upon the future. *Adjudication* is particular, focusing upon the present or the past. Administrative agencies interpret vagueness, ambiguity, and generality of laws; public administrators, as implementors of regulatory law, interpret rules. The terms *rules* and *regulations* are synonymous. There are four *types of agency rules:* legislative, or substantive, rules; interpretative rules; procedural rules; and general policy statements.
- *Administrative responsibility* entails the ideas of accountability, competence, fairness, and responsiveness. Executive control, pluralism, professionalism, and representative bureaucracy are especially important for achieving administrative responsibility. There are four types of *accountability:* bureaucratic, legal, professional, and political.
- *Professionalism, participation,* and *publicity* contribute significantly to administrative responsibility and provide a sound basis for better public management.

Case Study

Smoking Rights versus Health and Safety

Cigarettes are as much a part of American culture and history as baseball or the automobile. However, adults who choose to smoke make a personal decision that carries with it certain responsibilities and rights. The Steady State University Board of Trustees delegates implementation of its smoking regulations to the Substance Abuse Review Board (SARB). Voluntary compliance with provisions of this policy is expected by all members of the university community.

> Smoking takes away a smoker's free choice. . . . Smoking destroys good health.
>
> —*Wendy Schwartz*
> *ERIC Clearinghouse on Urban Education*

Smoking has been a subject of controversy and social commentary for 400 years. About 400,000 Americans die each year from smoking-related diseases. That figure is more than from AIDS, alcohol, car accidents, fires, illegal drugs, murders, and suicides combined. Cigarettes are as much a part of American culture and history as baseball or the automobile.[1]

Originally cigarettes were used as a medicinal product to relieve pain and heal infections. In the early 1600s, an emerging middle-class desired to emulate the habits of the rich and famous. Smoking tobacco was part of this identity, although almost all smokers were men. It was mainly used in the forms of pipe tobacco, chewing tobacco, and snuff.

In 1919, the first recorded cases of lung cancer began slowly to appear. Chesterfield broke the gender gap with a 1926 ad campaign aimed primarily at women. Throughout the 1980s and 1990s, legislatures enacted restrictions on where and near whom smokers could smoke. In the 1990s, government buildings, including individual offices, became nonsmoker facilities. In 1995, smoking was banned in all restaurants in California. Bars followed suit by 1998. State universities banned smoking in classrooms, residence halls, restaurants, bookstores, arenas, auditoriums, and administrative offices. These regulatory measures were taken in order to protect the health and safety of citizens.

Adults who choose to smoke make a personal decision that carries with it certain responsibilities and rights. Among other things, smokers have a responsibility to be respectful and courteous in the manner and places where they smoke, especially when children are present. Smokers also have a responsibility to properly dispose of cigarette butts and empty cigarette packages. Legislative and regulatory edicts are forever in play.[2]

Forty years ago, smoking was readily accepted in society. Smoking was a status symbol for youth and the upwardly mobile. The movies and television portrayed images of heroes and heroines drawing puffs from cigarettes. In 1964, the Surgeon General first reported that smoking is harmful to health. Links between lung cancer and smoking are now firmly established. Laws forced cigarette companies to label cigarette packages with warnings to consumers of smoking health hazards.[3]

Many Americans who have difficulties coping with stress use cigarette smoking as a coping strategy. A survey of 1,805 adults from across the nation found that Americans employ negative stress management by drinking alcohol, smoking cigarettes, and eating too much. "Men and women are not coping well," stated Dr. Pamela Peeke of the University of Maryland School of Medicine. "The majority of Americans are really doing things that are more self-destructive."[4]

College Students Puff, Puff Those Cigarettes

The Board of Trustees, Steady State University, prohibits smoking in all enclosed places of employment; classrooms; motion picture, stage production, or similar performance theaters; and indoor sports events. Smoking is a violation of Labor Code section 6403 rules, as enacted by the legislature of the State of Commonwealth.[5]

Smoking of any form of tobacco is a health hazard, states the SSU regulation. It may be a cause of material annoyance, inconvenience, and discomfort to SSU faculty, students, and campus guests. The SSU Board of Trustees delegates implementation of its smoking regulations to the Substance Abuse Review Board (SARB). Members of the SARB include Steady State's University President, Faculty Senate President, Vice President for Student Affairs, four professors representing colleges within SSU, and two students.

Smoking at SSU is viewed as a health and safety issue rather than one of individual choice or individual rights. Smoking in enclosed public places is of vital concern to the citizenry's health, safety, and welfare. SSU smoking regulations, grounded in state law, state:

> Voluntary compliance with the provisions of this policy is expected of all members of the university community. Smoking in a prohibited area may subject the violator to a civil penalty under the law. Persons who refuse to extinguish said smoking material upon request will be reported to the SSU security office immediately. A report of the violation will be filed. The outcome of this action could mean SSU will take disciplinary action in addition to any civil penalty that may be levied under law.[6]

Youth underestimate the addictive nature of tobacco. The first national study to report on cigarette and noncigarette tobacco use by college students found that nearly one-half of college students (46 percent) report having used tobacco products in the previous year.[7] A representative sample of 14,138 college students included respondents from 119 colleges in 39 states.[8]

About 28 percent of male and female students were cigarette smokers, but total tobacco use was much higher among males. A key component to discouraging cigarette and cigar use is making all college buildings, including dormitories and living quarters, smoke-free. Smoke-free dormitories discourage students from taking up smoking.

As appropriate, SARB regulates—and adjudicates violations in regard to—the smoking of tobacco, plant, or processed substance in SSU administrative offices, classroom buildings, residence halls, and enclosed spaces. Smoking includes carrying or holding a lighted pipe, cigar, or cigarette of any kind, or any other lit smoking equipment, or lighting or emitting or exhaling the smoke of a pipe, cigar, or cigarette of any kind.

SSU students who knowingly violate rules pertaining to smoking are subject to student disciplinary regulations. "College students are playing with fire, putting themselves at risk of a lifelong addiction to nicotine," says Nancy Herman, lead author and director of Tobacco Research and Treatment at Commonwealth State Hospital. "Smoke-free dormitories . . . make it easier for current smokers to stop and even reduce fire hazards."[9]

SARB expelled one student and suspended three students for two years for allegedly setting their couch on fire in Alumni Hall. They face legal charges of criminal mischief. The three suspended students must stand for a jury trial for the criminal charges. Smith Reagan, Moses Clinton, Matthew Carter, and Rector Ford—all former residents of Alumni Hall—now reside in a dingy apartment on Railroad Street. All are appealing to SARB to reconsider their penalties.

Witnesses said Rector Ford, an SSU junior majoring in prelaw, ignited the late-night fire while drunk, playing with his cigarette lighter and smoking a cigarette. Ford paid a fine for his offense and performed community service as partial fulfillment of his criminal sentence.

Smoking Leading Cause of Fires

Smoking-caused fires cost $31 billion each year. Research data indicate that smoking is a leading cause of fires. Every year, careless smoking starts about 35,000 fires which result in more than 1,200 deaths. They lead to hundreds of millions of dollars in property losses. Cigarettes may smolder under cushions of chairs and sofas for many hours before igniting. Matches and lighters must be treated as dangerous weapons.[10]

SARB expelled Ford from SSU. He was charged by College Corner police for "reckless burning." The Vice President for Student Affairs, Doug McCormmack, and College Corner Chief of Police, Wilma Malone, would not comment on the case. Eyewitnesses to charges of "reckless burning" stated: Ford returned from the Locker Room, a College Corner sports bar, around

1 A.M. on October 3. Once he returned to his taxpayer-purchased dormitory room, Ford ignited tattered pieces of the common room couch. He then urged others to take pictures of the flames before putting them out.

College Corner Police Chief Malone confiscated pictures taken by Reagan, one of Ford's three roommates. SARB members used the photographs to provide evidence in its expulsion hearing. SSU police and fire authorities determined that the Alumni Hall couch fire was caused by Ford's dropped cigarette. "The fire and SARB administrative procedures," said Carter, "have put our lives on hold."[11]

Local lawyer Missy Franklin, however, came to the students' rescue, orchestrating their twelve-page appeal to SARB. Friends of Ford, Reagan, Clinton, and Carter insisted that SSU's punishment was too harsh. "What is gained from expulsion is nothing," opined fellow student Morgan Bush. "In general, especially at school, people deserve a second chance. I think they never got that second chance."[12] Student opinions at SSU were mixed. Some said circumstances of the fire should have been taken more fully into account. Others said they felt SSU acted appropriately, assuming the potential danger to hundreds of residents.

SARB is awaiting the appointment of new chair and student representatives before it considers the appeals of the suspended students. According to SSU Undergraduate Regulations, SARB declines action on appeals cases if SARB ignored pertinent evidence or long-standing precedents, committed procedural errors, or failed to consider "certain key principles of Steady State University."[13]

Two months after the incident, SARB met to reconsider Ford's expulsion and suspension reductions for Reagan, Clinton, and Carter for couch burning in Alumni Hall. The SSU suspensions were cut back by one full academic year. Ford's expulsion was revoked, but he was not permitted to reenter SSU for two years. The four students declined to comment on either the case facts or the SARB decision.

Former SARB secretary, Sally Friedman, said she does not know of another SARB decision where the committee revoked an expulsion. SARB chair Perry Sargent, a political science profesor, says that "Expulsions are very rare at SSU . . . and as a result, there are not a large number of appeals. My guess is that there haven't been any [revocations of expulsions] until very recently."[14]

SARB members say they rehear cases on appeal if relevant precedents are not clear. New SARB members argued that precedents used by the former committee were obscure enough to warrent reexamination. Sargent stated that the criteria of the couch-burning incident lacked clarity and hence merited a second hearing.

SARB's reconsiderations applied only to SSU regulations for Alumni Hall fire safety measures. The charges by College Corner police chief Malone, that of "reckless burning," was not debated. Malone refused to offer comments on any new testimony he may have made before SARB. The chief insisted that the "incident was clear-cut in our minds."[15] Malone did not speculate on measures the county prosecutor might pursue. SSU smoking regulations and arson laws are located in the State of Commonwealth legislative code, but at different places.

Market Failure, Rule Making, and Adjudication

The normal operations of the marketplace fail to protect the public from actual or potential abuses of power by business firms. In this case, the cigarette industry poses dangers to the health of citizens. A fire resulted. The state legislature delegated rule making to SSU. SARB does not make rules; it adjudicates rules. Adjudication is particular, as in the case of Rector Ford. It focuses upon an instance in the present or past. Bureaucrats, as in SSU administrative officers, make regulatory laws—regulating citizen behaviors as in adjudicating civil penalties for Ford. Administrative law oversees the administrative discretion of bureaucrats, such as SARB members.

The State of Commonwealth legislature is the source of rule making. No state rule applied to SSU is valid unless it is authorized by the state legislatures. Responsibility, professionalism, and participation probe what is the public interest in the charge of "reckless burning." The SARB members, the College Corner police chief, and SSU administrative personnel are challenged to be responsible decision makers. Students are encouraged to participate in the policy outcome. Professionalism is pertinent if the decision is to be respected—and accepted—by all parties.

Questions and Instructions

1. What responsibilities and rights do smokers owe citizens? Explain. Illustrate.
2. What are the functions of the Substance Abuse Review Board (SARB)? Explain and illustrate.
3. Argue the case for making smoking a health and safety issue. Illustrate.
4. Argue the case for making smoking an individual rights issue. Illustrate.
5. Of the parties commissioned to carry out civil and criminal aspects of the Rector Ford case, who did what, and why did they do it? Explain.
6. How and why did market forces fail to function effectively in this scenario? Explain.
7. Which persons and units made rules? Which persons and units adjudicated the rules? Explain.
8. Why is the legislature the true source of rule making? Explain.
9. How do responsibility, professionalism, and participation effect the policy outcomes of Rector Ford's fate? Explain.

Insights-Issues/Smoking Rights versus Health and Safety

Clearly and briefly describe and illustrate the following concepts and issues. Interpret the word *role* as meaning impacts, applications, importance, effects, and/or illustrations of certain facts, concerns, or issues from the case study.

1. Role of rights and community (health and safety) in the adjudication of this case.
2. Role of the Substance Abuse Review Board(SARB) in policymaking in this case.
3. Role of criminal and civil jurisdictions for disposing of these charges.
4. Role of market failure of the cigarette industry.
5. Role of rule making and adjudication for determining the outcome of these case study facts.
6. Role of responsibility, professionalism, and participation for deciding this case.

Case Endnotes

1. David Haeg, "America's Vice?" http://www.drake.edu/journalism/CenturysEnd/smoking.html.
2. R. J. Reynolds Tobacco Company, "Tobacco Issues: Smokers' Rights," http://www.rjrt.com/TI2/Pages/TISmokersRightsPage.asp.
3. "To Smoke, or Not to Smoke?" East Coast Economic Studies, http://occawlonline.pearsoned.com/bookbind/pubbooks/miller2001_awl/medialib/download/east/.
4. "Americans Turn to Smoking to Cope with Stress," July 5, 2002, http://www.jointogether.org/sa/news/summaries/print/0,1856,552384,00.html.
5. See Los Angeles Community Colleges, Office of the Chancellor, Administrative Regulations, Smoking Regulations, http://marlin.laccd.edu/district/admin_regs/BRegs/B6_Reg.htm.
6. Salem State College Alcohol & Drug Regulations, http://www.salem.mass.edu/counseling/Alcohol_Drug_and_Hazing_Policy_flyer.htm.
7. Harvard School of Public Health, "Nearly Half of College Students Used Tobacco in One-Year Period, According to JAMA Study," August 8, 2000, http://www.hsph.harvard.edu/press/releases/press0808200.html.
8. *Ibid.*
9. *Ibid.*
10. "KIDDE: Home Safety Education Center," http://www.kiddesafety.com/kiddesafety/pages/cigarett.htm.
11. Jake Sullivan, "Ex Comm Reverses JE Arson Expulsion," *Yale Daily News,* November 17, 1995; http://www.yaledailynews.com/articlefunctions/Printerfriendly.asp?AID=9147.
12. Judy Hirschfeld, "Suspended Students Ask Yale to Reconsider," *Yale Daily News,* September 11, 1995, http://www.yaledailynews.com/articlefunctions/Printerfriendly.asp?AID=6504.
13. *Ibid.*
14. Sullivan, *op.cit.*
15. *Ibid.*

Case Sources

Laura Mansnerus, "Smokers Gasp, Not Just from Cigarettes," *The New York Times*, June 25, 2002, p. 5b; Wendy Schwartz, "ERIC Clearinghouse on Urban Education," http://www.parentsassociation.com/health/smoking_strategies.html; Randy

Wilson, "Tobacco Regulations Clouded," http://my.webmd.com/questions_and_answer/1691.50119.

Chapter Endnotes

1. "Why Regulation Matters," The Regulation Home Page, regulation.org, http://www.regulation.org/whyregs.html.

2. W. Mark Crain and Thomas D. Hopkins, "The Impact of Regulatory Cost on Small Firms," Office of Advocacy, Small Business Administration, Washington, D.C., April 2, 2002, http://www.sba.gov./advo/research/rs207tot.pdf.

3. Melinda Warren, "Federal Regulatory Spending Reaches a New Height: An Analysis of the Budget of the U.S. Government for the Year 2001" (St. Louis: Center for the Study of American Business, 2000), p. 6, http://wc.wustl.edu/csab/CSAB%20pubs-pdf%20files/RBR/RBR%2023.pdf; April 2, 2002.

4. *Ibid.*

5. Susan Dudley & Melinda Warren, "Regulatory Response: An Analysis of the Shifting Priorities of the U.S. Budget for Fiscal Years 2002 and 2003," Mercatus Center, Arlington, Va., and the Murray Weidenbaum Center on the Economy, Government, and Public Policy, St. Louis, Mo., 2002, www.mercatus.org & www.wc.wust.edu.

6. Daniel J. Gifford, *Administrative Law: Cases and Materials* (Cincinnati: Anderson, 1992), pp. 1–9.

7. Dennis L. Mueller, "Public Choice: A Survey," *Journal of Economic Literature* 14, no. 2 (1976):395.

8. Lief H. Carter, *Administrative Law and Politics: Cases and Comments* (Boston: Little, Brown, 1983), pp. 14–39.

9. Florence Heffron with Neil McFeeley, *The Administrative Regulatory Process* (New York: Longmans, 1983), pp. 1–23.

10. Douglas Costle, "In Defense of the Public Service," *Public Administration Times* (May 1, 1980): 3.

11. Murray Weidenbaum, *A New Approach to Regulatory Reform* (St. Louis, Mo.: Center for the Study of American Business, 1998), pp. 2–3. See also Thomas D. Hopkins, *Regulatory Costs in Profile* (St. Louis, Mo.: Center for the Study of American Business, 1996).

12. Heffron with McFeeley, *The Administrative Regulatory Process,* p. 6.

13. Melinda Warren and Kenneth Chilton, *The Regulatory Legacy of the Reagan Revolution: An Analysis of 1990 Federal Regulatory Budgets and Staffing* (St. Louis, Mo.: Center for the Study of Business, 1989), pp. 9–12. See Melinda Warren and Barry Jones, *Reinventing the Regulatory System: No Downsizing in Administration Plan* (St. Louis, Mo.: Center for the Study of Business, 1995), pp. 8–20.

14. Dudley and Warren, *op. cit.*

15. Thomas D. Hopkins, *Regulatory Costs in Profile* (St. Louis: Center for the Study of American Business, Policy Study Paper Number 132, August, 1996), pp. 3–12; Murray Weidenbaum, *A New Approach to Regulatory Reform* (St. Louis: Center for the Study of American Business, Policy Study Paper Number 147, August, 1998), pp. 2–8.

16. Douglas R. Wholey and Susan M. Sanchez, "The Effects of Regulatory Tools on Organizational Populations," *Academy of Management Review* 16, no. 4 (October 1991): 743–767.

17. Dudley and Warren, *op. cit.*

18. Melinda Warren and James Lis, *Regulatory Standstill: Analysis of the 1993 Federal*

Regulatory Budget (St. Louis, Mo.: Center for the Study of American Business, 1992), pp. 1–2, 5, 7–9. See Warren and Barry Jones, *Reinventing the Regulatory System,* pp. 8–20.

19. Wholey and Sanchez, "The Effects of Regulatory Tools," pp. 743–767.
20. Dudley and Warren, *op. cit.*
21. Heffron with McFeeley, *The Administrative Regulatory Process,* pp. 347–371.
22. Warren and Chilton, *1989 Federal Regulatory Budget and Staffing: Effects of the Reagan Presidency* (St. Louis, Mo.: Center for the Study of Business, 1988), p. 4. See Warren and Jones, *Reinventing the Regulatory System,* pp. 8–20.
23. James T. O'Reilly, *Administrative Rule Making: Structuring, Opposing, and Defending Federal Agency Regulations* (New York: McGraw-Hill), pp. 4–6.
24. Lief H. Carter, *Administrative Law and Politics: Cases and Comments* (Boston: Little, Brown, 1983), pp. 14–39.
25. Administrative Procedure Act, P.L. 404, 60 Stat. 237(1946), 5 U.S.C.A. 551.
26. William F. West, *Administrative Rule-making: Politics and Processes* (Westport, Conn: Greenwood Press, 1985), p. 17.
27. Murray L. Weidenbaum and Ronald J. Penoyer, *The Next Step in Regulatory Reform: Updating the Statutes* (St. Louis, Mo.: Center for the Study of Business, 1983), pp. 24–32.
28. Paul N. Tramontozzi with Kenneth W. Chilton, *U.S. Regulatory Agencies Under Reagan, 1980–1988* (St. Louis, Mo.: Center for the Study of Business, 1987), pp. 11–14.
29. Cornelius M. Kerwin, *Rulemaking* (Washington, D.C.: CQ Press, 1994). See O'Reilly, *Administrative Rulemaking,* pp. 90, 131.
30. Kerwin, *Rulemaking,* p. 84.
31. Walter Lippman, *The Public Philosophy* (Boston: Little, Brown, 1955), p. 42.
32. Glendon A. Shubert, Jr., *The Public Interest* (New York: Free Press, 1952), p. 223.
33. Carl Friedrich, "Public Policy and the Nature of Administrative Responsibility" in *The Politics of the Federal Bureaucracy,* ed. Alan A. Altshuler (New York: Dodd, Mead, 1968), p. 417.
34. Friedrich, "Public Policy," p. 417.

Seven Ways to Land a Great Internship*

Summary

| Internships Can Provide the Experience Needed to Land a Job | Explore the Many Different Avenues Toward Internship Opportunities |

It's one of the most common and frustrating career dilemmas college students face: "To get a good job after graduation, I need experience. But how do I get experience without having a job in the first place?" One common, and wise, solution—an internship, paid or unpaid, part-time or full-time.

Easy enough. But how do you get one? Well, one or more of the following strategies is likely to do the trick.

Work with a Career Counselor at Your School

Career counselors know where other students from your school are interning now or have interned before. They also work closely with on-campus recruiters from organizations in the area and even nationally. Thus, career counselors can be a prime source of internship leads for you.

Talk to Your Professors

Like career counselors, your professors will also know where at least some students are interning now or have interned before. Additionally, many professors have consulting, research, and other ties to various companies and organizations outside of academia; thus, they may be aware of internship programs hosted by these organizations.

Network with Your Fellow Students

If a student you know has an internship that intrigues you, ask him or her for advice on landing a similar internship yourself, either with the same organization or elsewhere. Chances are that students who have internships now have a better sense of the many internship opportunities that exist, in both their own organizations and in others. So be sure to tap into their collective knowledge, especially as it relates to people you should contact.

Use Your School's Alumni Network

Most campuses, usually through their career services or alumni offices, work hard to establish and maintain contacts with alumni working in various organizations and industries. Consider contacting some alumni from your school to check into internships in their places of employment. You'd be surprised by how strong the fellow alum tie can be.

*"Seven Ways to Land a Great Internship" by Peter Vogt on website monster.com. Copyright 2002—TMP Interactive Inc. All Rights Reserved. You may not copy, reproduce or distribute this article without the prior written permission of TMP Interactive. This article first appeared on Monster, the leading online global network for careers. To see other career-related articles visit http://content.monster.com.

Tap into the Resources of Your Own Family, Friends, and Acquaintances

Does your mother's company have an internship program? Does your sister's friend's nonprofit organization offer any internship possibilities? Many college students don't think to ask their family members, friends, and acquaintances to help them with career-related tasks like internship hunting. Be sure you don't fall into this trap.

Page Through an Internship Directory

If you stop by your school's career services or campus library, or spend some time browsing in your campus or local bookstore, you'll undoubtedly find one or more internship directory listing internship programs at organizations around the U.S. Several companies publish these guides, including Peterson's Internships 2001 and The Internship Bible 2001. These books are typically well indexed so you can search for internships by organization, field of interest, and geographic location.

Check out Internship Sites on the Web

Search for internship opportunities on the Web. If you're willing to go almost anywhere for your internship, you'll be able to find many opportunities across the country on Monster.com.

Once you've developed a list of internships to apply for, you can work with a career counselor to ready yourself for the important tasks to follow. Including developing and writing a resume and cover letter, learning how to follow up with prospective internship providers to keep yourself in the front of their minds, and preparing for internship interviews.

With time and diligence, your efforts will pay off—in an internship that gives you the experience you need to land the future job you want.

Selected Policy/Public Administration Websites

American Society for Public Administration (ASPA) Internship Programs Page
http://www.aspanet.org/careers/internship.html

National Association of Schools of Public Affairs and Administration (NASPAA) Careers and Internship Page
http://www.naspaa.org/students/careers/careers.asp

Presidential Management Intern Program
http://www.pmi.opm.gov

StudentJobs.gov
http://www.studentjobs.gov

Federal Government/USA Jobs
www.usajobs.opm.gov

Polling Report/Job Bank/Internships/ Survey Research
PollingReport.com

Jobs in Higher Education
www.academic360.com

National Council of State Legislatures
www.ncsl.org/public/joblegis.htm

National Governor's Association
www.nga.org/employment.htm

National League of Cities
www.nlc.org/jobs.htm

The Concord Coalition
http://www.concordcoalition.org

The Concord Coalition/Youth Outreach Campaign
http://www.concordcoalition.org/youth_outreach/

The Dirksen Congressional Center/ Civic Engagement
www.pekin.net/dirksen/

Humphrey Institute/Center for Democracy and Citizenship
www.hhh.umn.edu/centers/cdc

Civic Learning & Engagement/
University of Maryland
http://www.civicyouth.org

The Craft of Public Administration/John Rouse
jrouse@bsu.edu

Studying in Washington: A Guide to Academic Internships in the Nation's Capital
http://www.apsanet.org/pubs

Service Learning in Political Science
http://www.apsanet.org/teach/service/

StudentJobs.gov
http://www.studentjobs.gov/aboutus.htm

Index